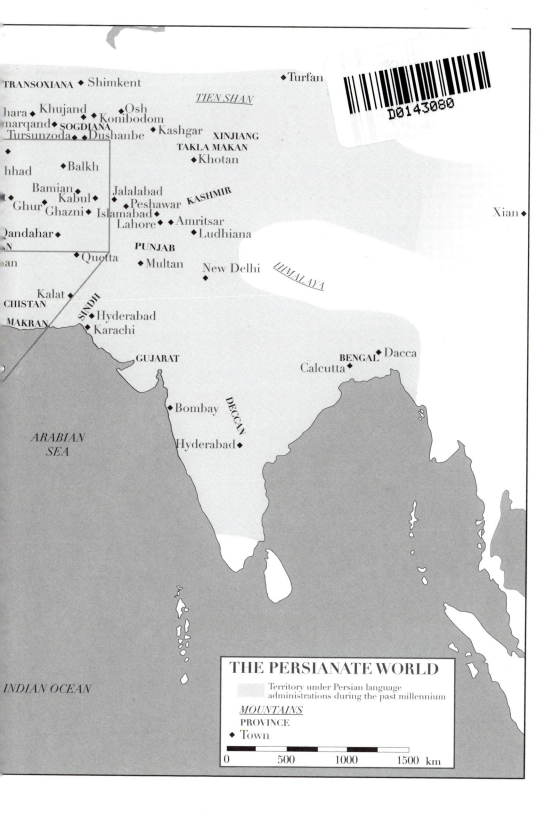

TRANSOXIANA ◆ Shimkent
◆ Turfan
TIEN SHAN

hara ◆ Khujand ◆ Osh
marqand ◆ SOGDIANA ◆ Konibodom
Tursunzoda ◆ Dushanbe ◆ Kashgar XINJIANG
TAKLA MAKAN
◆ Khotan

hhad ◆ Balkh

Bamian ◆ Jalalabad
Ghur ◆ Kabul ◆ Peshawar KASHMIR
Ghazni ◆ Islamabad ◆ Amritsar
Lahore ◆ Ludhiana
Qandahar ◆
N ◆ Quetta PUNJAB
an ◆ Multan ◆ New Delhi *HIMALAYA*

Kalat ◆
CHISTAN SINDH ◆ Hyderabad
MAKRAN ◆ Karachi

GUJARAT BENGAL ◆ Dacca
Calcutta ◆

◆ Bombay DECCAN

*ARABIAN
SEA* Hyderabad ◆

Xian ◆

INDIAN OCEAN

THE PERSIANATE WORLD

    Territory under Persian language
    administrations during the past millennium

MOUNTAINS
PROVINCE
◆ Town

0   500   1000   1500 km

LITERACY
in the
PERSIANATE WORLD

Penn Museum International Research Conferences
Holly Pittman, Series Editor, Conference Publications

Volume 4: Proceedings of "Comparative Diplomatics:
Historical and Cultural Implications,"
Philadelphia, October 5–8, 2006

PMIRC volumes

1. *Landscapes of Movement: Trails, Paths, and Roads in
Anthropological Perspective,* edited by James E. Snead,
Clark L. Erickson, and J. Andrew Darling, 2009
2. *Mapping Mongolia: Situating Mongolia in the World from
Geologic Time to the Present,* edited by Paula L.W. Sabloff, 2011
3. *Sustainable Lifeways: Cultural Persistence in an
Ever-changing Environment,* edited by Naomi F. Miller,
Katherine M. Moore, and Kathleen Ryan, 2011

LITERACY
in the
PERSIANATE WORLD
Writing and the Social Order

EDITED BY

Brian Spooner and William L. Hanaway

University of Pennsylvania Museum of Archaeology and Anthropology
Philadelphia

Library of Congress Cataloging-in-Publication Data

Literacy in the Persianate world : writing and the social order / edited by Brian Spooner
and William L. Hanaway.
p. cm.
Includes bibliographical references and index.
ISBN-13: 978-1-934536-45-2 (hardcover : alk. paper)
ISBN-10: 1-934536-45-8 (hardcover : alk. paper)
1. Persian language—History. 2. Persian language—Written Persian—History. 3. Writing—Iran—History. 4. Literacy—Iran—History. 5. Iran—Intellectual life. 6. Iran—
Social life and customs. I. Spooner, Brian. II. Hanaway, William L., 1929–
PK6225.L57 2012
491'.5509—dc23
2011041955

Endpaper illustration by Kimberly Leaman.

Published for the University of Pennsylvania Museum of Archaeology and Anthropology
by the University of Pennsylvania Press.

Printed in the United States of America on acid-free paper.

Contents

Penn Museum International Research Conferences

Foreword

For more than a century, a core mission of the University of Pennsylvania Museum of Archaeology and Anthropology has been to foster research that leads to new understandings about human culture. For much of the 20th century, this research took the form of worldwide expeditions that brought back both raw data and artifacts whose analysis continues to shed light on early complex societies of the New and Old worlds. The civilizations of pharonic Egypt, Mesopotamia, Iran, Greece, Rome, Mexico, Peru, and Native Americans have been represented in galleries that display only the most remarkable of Penn Museum's vast holding of artifacts. These collections have long provided primary evidence of many distinct research programs engaging scholars from around the world.

As we moved into a new century, indeed a new millennium, Penn Museum sought to reinvigorate its commitment to research focused on questions of human societies. In 2005, working with then Williams Director Richard M. Leventhal, Michael J. Kowalski, Chairman of the Board of Overseers of Penn Museum, gave a generous gift to the Museum to seed a new program of high level conferences designed to engage themes central to the museum's core research mission. According to Leventhal's vision, generating new knowledge and frameworks for understanding requires more than raw data and collections. More than ever, it depends on collaboration among communities of scholars investigating problems using distinct lines of evidence and different modes of analysis. Recognizing the importance of collaborative and multidisciplinary endeavors in the social sciences, Penn Museum used the gift to launch a program of International Research Conferences that each brought together ten to fifteen scholars who had reached a critical point in the consideration of a shared problem.

During the three years until the spring of 2008, it was my privilege to identify, develop, run, and now oversee the publication of eight such conferences. The dozen or so papers for each conference were submitted to all participants one month in advance of the meeting. The fact that the papers were circulated beforehand meant that no time was lost introducing new material to the group. Rather, after each paper was briefly summarized by its author, an intense and extended critique followed that allowed for sustained consideration of the contribution that both the data and the argument made to the larger questions. The discussions of individual papers were followed by a day discussing crosscutting issues and concluded with an overarching synthesis of ideas.

"Comparative Diplomatics: Historical and Cultural Implications" was the second conference in the series, held in the fall of 2006. It is the fourth of the conferences to see publication. As Series Editor, I look forward to four more volumes that will appear will appear over the next few years. The publication of the results of these conferences allows the new knowledge and understanding that they achieved to be shared broadly and to contribute to the uniquely human enterprise of self understanding.

HOLLY PITTMAN
Series Editor
Deputy Director for Academic Programs, Penn Museum, 2005–2008
Curator, Near East Section
Professor, History of Art
Bok Family Professor in the Humanities, University of Pennsylvania

Preface

BRIAN SPOONER AND WILLIAM L. HANAWAY

The revolution that culminated with the departure of the Shāh in 1979 changed the way we think of Iran. During the 1980s a large Iranian diaspora established communities in key cities in America, Europe, and Asia. Some began to question whether modern Iran remains the same country as the Persia we knew from the past. Should we think of it more in terms of the relationship between modern and ancient Greece? The subject matter of Persian Studies was also changing, and appeared less secure in the Western curriculum. It was in this environment that the idea for this book began to develop.

In the 1980s the new Iran redefined its relationship with the past in ways that raised questions about the history of Persian civilization and the historical nature of Iranian identity. A number of Iranian intellectuals as well as Western Iranists began to engage these questions. Are we still on the same historical trajectory that began with the prophet Zoroaster and Cyrus the Great in the middle of the 1st millennium BC? Is there a continuous line of development in civilization and identity from the foundational monotheism of Zoroaster and the administration of the Achaemenian Empire (550–330 BC) through the courts of the Sasanian Shāhs supported by their landed aristocracy and gentry (AD 224–651), their cultural successors under the Caliphate in the Samanid amirates (AD 819–999) and the later sultanates of Central Asia, to the conscious regeneration of an explicitly Iranian Shia identity by the Safavids in the 16th century, which was continued through the Zands, Qajars, and Pahlavis and regenerated by Khomeini? What would be the substance of such an idea of identity? Is it patriotism? Does it inhere in the land, which was represented as *Iran-shahr* by the Sasanians, and later as *Iran-zamin*? Is it cultural, inhering in institutions, unaffected by the fact that early capitals were as much in Mesopotamia (Ctesiphon, in modern Iraq) as what we have learned to call the Iranian Plateau (Persepolis, the ceremonial capital of the Achaemenians, in southern Iran), or off the Plateau to the northeast in the plains of Transoxiana (Zoroaster and the Samanids). Or is it ethnic, even though most rulers of the Iranian world have been Turks since the 11th century. It is difficult to find any Iranian constant that continues from the ancient world through to the present except perhaps in the assumptions adopted in Iran from western philological and historical scholarship in the 19th century.

There is, however, one constant that may suffice to connect Zoroaster and Khomeini: the Persian language. But this continuity is not in the language of speech, which until half a century ago had always been highly differentiated in every part of the vast region of western Asia that is historically associated with Persian civilization. Rather, it is in the language of writing. From the earliest records of over 2500 years ago, written Persian has been identified not only with the region of Persepolis in the south of modern Iran but with every historical situation we associate with Persian civilization from Mesopotamia to Central Asia and beyond in both directions.

This book explores the social history of written Persian. The data and the arguments presented here have relevance for our modern understanding not only of written Persian in relation to Iranian identity, but also of the historical background of modern identities in general and of the significance of written language and of literacy. Persian has been one of the major written languages in world history. Few, if any, other languages have enjoyed a continuous history of two and a half millennia as the primary vehicle of written communication. It is further distinguished from any rivals by its slow rate of change over such a long period and its maintenance of standard vocabulary and syntax over such a vast territory. There is much to be learned about its historical development and social functioning that will inform a larger world-historical perspective. In short, the study of Persian is too important to be left to linguists alone.

There was another motive for a new historical study of Persian. In existing studies there has been an insidious cultural weighting in favor of what has been better known from Western experience. We would like to counter some of the effects of this weighting (which is particularly inherent in the study of languages, and especially of written language and of literacy) by comparing the historical record of written Persian with the other major traditions of writing on either side of it, the Latinate and the Sinitic. By means of this triangulation we aim, at least to some extent, to avoid the "us vs. them" presentation that is typical in the study of other cultural traditions. We also hope to be better able to represent the historical significance of writing in premodern times to a potential readership for whom the ability to write (now that it has become essentially universal) has already lost the social values it carried in the past.

This book is about a language that was anchored in stable forms of writing for perhaps longer than any other in world history, and over a larger area. An important function of this relative stability was the relationship over time between the written and spoken forms of the language. Written texts were not simply a material representation of speech. Rather, the written text embodied the culture, organized the society, and proclaimed the protocols and standards of public behavior. The same may of course also be said of Latin, even though Latin evolved from the Republic to the Empire to the Church, whereas Persian served the administration of a single form of government from the 9th to the 19th century. But as we shall see, written Persian has been embedded in the structure of Persianate society in distinctive ways that are particularly instructive. Those who wrote were an elite few, members of a social class recruited largely but by no means exclusively from the landed aristocracy, and in writing they continued an elite tradition, which because of its social value made them the supreme arbiters of the culture and its social norms. Their authority, and their conservatism in the interests of their class, inhibited change. The pace of change began to accelerate significantly only in the second half of the 20th century, when exogenous forces for change offered new opportunities, making possible the launching of a Literacy Corps that would transform Persian literacy in Iran by universalizing it. Similar forces led to change in the historical relationship between the spoken and written language in other parts of the Persianate world within a short time.

As represented in this volume, these ideas are the product of an international seminar which was held at the University of Pennsylvania, under the auspices of the Penn Museum, October 5–8, 2006. The central focus of the meeting was written Persian, its unity and diversity from the 9th to the

19th centuries, and from the Ottoman Empire to Yuan China and Mughal India. But the significance of the presentations on Persian was contextualized by others on the neighboring traditions of literacy in Chinese, Tamil, Arabic, and Latin, and on the prehistory of these languages in the ancient world. The presentations were written up after the meeting, in the light of the discussions and some further consultation, to provide what may be the first comparative study in the historical sociology of a tradition of literacy. While it could not be exhaustive, and the Tamil and Arabic studies could not included in this volume, we have raised and begun to answer some of the important questions that a comparative perspective generates. It is important to note the difference between the orientation to the study of literacy presented here and that of the literature on literacy that has accumulated since the 1960s. The difference is conscious and is elaborated in a section of the introduction.

The conference was the culmination of a series of seminars we had organized at intervals over the previous decade and a half. To begin with—the first was in 1990, the second in 1993—the meetings were focused on the mechanics of writing and what made the activity of writing in Persian different from writing in other scripts. We wanted to help non-native writers not only in their writing but in their reading of medieval textual sources. This effort led to our publication in 1995 of *Reading Nasta'liq: Persian and Urdu Hands from 1500 to the Present,* which was reprinted in a second revised edition in 2007. Following that publication we focused on various aspects of Persian diplomatics (a term which is discussed in more detail in the Introduction, because we have found it so often misunderstood): the relationship between the form and the content of what was written, and the variation in both over the space of a millennium and more than a single continent. We held four more meetings, in Philadelphia in 1995 (with Robert McChesney, Maria Subtelny, Igor Kopytoff, and Susan Blum); Mt. Lemon, AZ, in 1997 (with A.G. Rawan Farhadi, Senzil Nawid, and John Perry); Lyman, NH, in 1999 (with Gene Garthwaite, A.G. Rawan Farhadi, and Senzil Nawid); and Hyderābād, A.P., India, in 2005 (with Aditya Behl, Nomanul Haq, David Lelyveld, Victor Mair, Anwar Moazzam, Senzil Nawid, Jim Nye, and John Perry). At Penn in October 2006, with Aditya Behl, Joseph Farrell, Michael Fisher, Grant Frame, Victor Mair, Anwar Moazzam, Colin Mitchell, David Morgan, A.H. Morton, Roy Mottahedeh, Senzil Nawid, John Perry, A.G. Rawan Farhadi, Bhavani Raman, and Aslam Syed, our objective was to pull it all together and contextualize it. We are grateful to the Salar Jang Museum for hosting our meeting in Hyderābād in September 2005. We also wish to thank the Council of American Overseas Research Centers for helping with the international arrangements for the Hyderābād meeting, which included participation from the American Institutes of Indian, Iranian, and Pakistan Studies. Additionally, we are grateful to the University of Pennsylvania's Middle East Center for funding all the meetings in Philadelphia 1990–1995, and, finally, the Penn Museum for hosting the 2006 meeting and funding both that and this publication. Apart from the participants in all the meetings, who have already been named, we would like to thank Matthew Stolper for his willingness to answer questions. We are happy to acknowledge all these contributions and the support that accompanied them.

The result—this volume—is based on the hypothesis that written language has had a dynamic that is distinct from that of spoken language—essentially a culture of its own. Although it may always have been related to spoken language, the nature of the relationship has varied over time, and the variation is a function of social factors, factors involved in the organization of increasingly larger and more complex societies. Second, we argue that the history of Persian in particular offers copious data for the exploration of this hypothesis. Our aim, therefore, has been to bring together a variety of investigations from people working in a number of different academic subcommunities: philology, linguistics, textual criticism, history, and anthropology, as they relate to different parts of west, central, and south Asia, where Persian served for many centuries as the language both of administration and of belles lettres, and to situate those investigations in relation to similar interests in Classics and Sinology. We hope that the result, though only a beginning, will be of interest to people working both in narrow specialized fields relating to the production of ancient and medieval texts (palaeography, diplomatics, textual criticism), and in the larger modern fields relating to language and literacy, and not only Islamic history but world history. We have sought to make each chapter readable for a wide audience. Although Persian text is provided in a few of the chapters (in script or transliteration) for readers who will appreciate what it illustrates, knowledge of Persian is not necessary for following the argument of any chapter.

Every investigation leads to further questions. We have tried to clarify our position on some of these questions—those we are aware of—in the Introduction. The most important are in the field of diplomatics, and textual (in our case, oriental) studies, and the modern study of literacy. We hope this book makes some contribution to each of these fields. But we also want to register an effort to raise Persian studies out of the ghetto-like compartmentalization of the old curriculum and give it a place in the world-historical curriculum that is currently developing—lest it fall forever into a similar ghetto-like subcompartment of ethnic studies. Persian studies, in the sense of the study of the textual record of the past millennium, have a place in world history. When pursued with this awareness, this field of study enriches our understanding of the history of the world at large.

When we began this project we sensed that we were at the beginning of a period of major transition. Now we have finished we can see that Persian, written as well as spoken, like all modern languages, has begun to change at an accelerating rate as a result of the rising literacy rates of its speakers, their increasing socio-political awareness, and the cultural effects of overall globalization. Writing is no longer the unique instrument of remote communication and administrative bureaucracy. It shares the field with new technologies which progressively pervade global society more and more thoroughly. But the heritage of the ways writing has functioned in the various script traditions of the past will continue for a while yet to cast a shadow over our continuing trajectory, and affect the organization of society as well as our knowledge of the world for some generations to come.

Contributors

Linda T. Darling
History Dept.
University of Arizona
Tucson, AZ

Joseph Farrell
Dept. of Classical Studies
University of Pennsylvania
Philadelphia, PA

Michael H. Fisher
History Dept.
Oberlin College
Oberlin, OH

William L. Hanaway, emeritus
Dept. of Near Eastern Languages and Civilizations
University of Pennsylvania
Philadelphia, PA

Victor H. Mair
Dept. of East Asian Languages and Civilizations
University of Pennsylvania
Philadelphia, PA

Colin P. Mitchell
History Dept.
Dalhousie University
Halifax, NS, CANADA

Anwar Moazzam
Urdu Documentation Centre
Maulana Azad National Urdu University
Hyderabad, INDIA

David Morgan, emeritus
Dept. of History and Religious Studies
University of Wisconsin
Madison, WI

A.H. Morton
Former Lecturer in Persian
Dept. of the Near and Middle East at the School of Oriental and African
    Studies
University of London
London, UK

Senzil Nawid
Center for Middle Eastern Studies
University of Arizona
Tucson, AZ

John R. Perry
Dept. of Near Eastern Languages and Civilizations
University of Chicago
Chicago, IL

Brian Spooner
Dept. of Anthropology
University of Pennsylvania
Philadelphia, PA

Aslam Syed
Former Professor of History
Quaid-i-Azam University
Islamabad, PAKISTAN

Note on Transliteration
and Referencing

Romanization of the Perso-Arabic script is a perennial problem in scholarly publication. Although standardization has always been a basic aim, each scholarly subcommunity has its own perspective on the problem. In reconciling the differences we have been unable to live up to Bacon's precept that consistency is the foundation of virtue, and have taken refuge rather in Wilde's comment that it is the last refuge of the unimaginative. Since any effort to standardize the Roman representation of usage of the Arabic script from all the areas of the Persianate world covered in this volume, although it would please some readers, would unavoidably alienate others, we have allowed the intrusion of more than one "standard," aiming at consistency so far as possible within chapters but not over the whole volume. With regard to diacritics our policy has been minimalist, and is based on the assumption that for readers who know the languages diacritics are redundant, while for readers who do not know the languages they serve no useful purpose. We have, however, bowed in the direction of one pre-publication reader and distinguished long from short /a/ by the use of macrons where it seemed useful to do so. Otherwise we hope the Glossary will serve to clarify any confusion.

Referencing is a similar problem—one that varies by the disciplinary training of the author rather than by the history of Western study of the particular language. We have dealt with it by means of a similar compromise, striving for consistency within chapters, within a larger relaxed framework for the volume. But in this case minimalism was not an option, and the result has produced some repetition between information included in endnotes, lists of citations, and in-text references. It should, however, be easily intelligible to readers of any background.

Introduction

Persian as Koine: Written Persian in World-historical Perspective

BRIAN SPOONER AND WILLIAM L. HANAWAY

I. THE HISTORICAL COURSE OF WRITTEN PERSIAN

Persian emerged as the common language of court life and administration in the Islamic world east of Baghdad in the 8th and 9th centuries (2nd and 3rd centuries into the Islamic era). The process began in Khurasan, the large historical region of southwest-central Asia, which besides the northeast quadrant of modern Iran included most of modern Turkmenistan, Uzbekistan, and Tajikistan, and northern Afghanistan. Persian radiated out from the pre-Islamic cities that became new power centers, filling the vacuum left by the declining political (as distinct from symbolic) role of the Caliphate in Baghdad. Persian spread to its greatest extent five centuries later, under Mongol and Turkic administrations, when it stretched from the Balkans in the west to southern India in the south and along the trade routes into central China in the east. A century later, it began to give way to the rise of vernacular languages—first in the west, where the use of Ottoman Turkish increased in the 15th century. It finally declined significantly in the east in India in the 19th century, where the British replaced it formally with Urdu and English in 1835. Over the past century and a half Persian has undergone a process of functional transformation, passing into the status of a classical language, as locally people began to write in Pashto, Sindhi, Urdu, and other vernaculars in the peripheral territories of the Islamic world. In the 20th century, at the expense of losing its unitary identity and universally standard form, Persian achieved the modern status of national language in three countries—in Afghanistan, (where it was renamed *dari*), in Iran (as *Fārsi*), and in Tajikistan (where it was renamed *tajiki,* or *tojiki* when transliterated from Cyrillic). It is still spoken widely in Pakistan, Uzbekistan, and the southern littoral of the Persian Gulf, and continues to flourish among post-revolutionary diaspora communities in America, Asia, and Europe.

Persian has always been known by native speakers as Fārsi (the language of Fars, an area in southern Iran, now a modern province), but *dari* (as it was officially named in Afghanistan's 1964 constitution) was also in common use for Persian in the early centuries of the Islamic era in the northeast (Khurasan)—appropriately so, since *dari* signifies the language of the court (*dar*) of the ruler, which was the site of its reemergence in the Arabic script. The name was changed from Fārsi to tojiki in Soviet Tajikistan in 1929, along with another change of script calculated to separate the Soviet language community from their non-Soviet co-linguals in Afghanistan and Iran.[1] The modern Afghan change from Fārsi to *dari* was a consequence of the competing 20th-century nationalisms of Afghanistan and Iran. Differences in written usage in these three countries has become significant only since they were separated by colonial boundaries, and is noticeable primarily in the adoption of Pashto official terms in *dari* and Soviet Russian terms in tajiki, which was also separated from the Persian canon by the change of script.

The advance of Persian in the Arabic script in the 9th century (known in Western literature as New Persian, in distinction from the Middle Persian and Old Persian of the Sasanian-Parthian and Achaemenian periods, respectively) heralded a millennium of Persianate civilization. It expanded quickly to supplant Arabic in a niche that had evolved in the civilizations of western Asia over the previous two and a half millennia. Other languages, and earlier forms of Persian, all of which had been written first in cuneiform and later in various forms of the Aramaic script, had served the needs of the succession of empires from the Assyrian to the Achaemenian in an administrative niche created originally in Mesopotamia with Akkadian, which (as the niche expanded beyond the plain) was joined first by Old Persian and Aramaic. Aramaic has continued in use in western Asia into the modern period. But after less than a century of Greek under Alexander and the Seleucids, Persian returned (as Middle Persian) with the rise of the Parthians in the second half of the 3rd century BC. In AD 224 the Parthians were followed by the Sasanians, who administered their empire in Middle Persian (with some use of Aramaic) until the Arab conquest in 651. In the gradual process of political and administrative re-accommodation that followed the initial half century or so of the Arab-Islamic sweep through western Asia, Persian gradually resumed its administrative role re-outfitted in the Arabic script and incorporating extensive Arabo-Islamic vocabulary.

The newly universalistic social principles of Islam which were embedded in the new Islamic legal order, based on the principles of the *shari`a* (which was derived from the prescriptions of the Qur'an, supplemented by the record of the Prophet's life and sayings), facilitated the expansion of the administrative arena far beyond the extent of the earlier dynasty-based empires. Over the following millennium, and well into the 19th century, Persian provided the vocabulary that served as the medium not only for the continuation of protocols of administration, diplomacy, and public life (derived from Sasanian and possibly earlier practice), but also for important cultural features relating to administration and social norms for the whole society, and over a much larger area. It is worth noting that a similar relationship between language and organization was developing at roughly the same time in the West between Latin and the Christian Church in the newly established Holy Roman Empire, and in Tang China by the initial establishment of the imperial examination system that coincided with the advance of Buddhism. In the ensuing five centuries Persian became the language of one of the world's greatest literatures—in the sense of the extent and duration of its currency, as well as the variety and quality of its genres. Significant examples have been translated into the world's other major literary languages. Persian also served as the language of administration through Islamic Asia east and north of Mesopotamia. No other language has ever maintained such a monopoly of the medium of writing over so large a territory for so long a period.

The type of data needed to explain this phenomenon are hard to come by. But the explanation appears to lie in the uniqueness of the combination of the cultural heritage of Sasanian court life, administrative practice, and the social formation of its writing class on the one hand, and the canon of literature that developed in the sultanates of the medieval period on the other. Although Persian did change over the ensuing centuries and over that vast geographical range, as all languages change, nevertheless the change was such that middle and upper-class Persian-speakers from anywhere in this vast region in the 20th century read, enjoyed, recited from memory, and used in conversation the classical literature written as much as a thousand years earlier. Even poorer illiterate people in rural communities recited and used passages of poetry from the medieval canon. The rather different awareness of Chaucer compared to Shakespeare among members of different social levels of English-speakers in the 20th century provides an illuminating comparison.

The essays in this volume explore various aspects of this historical phenomenon. They include illustrations of types of change that linguists would expect, while at the same time demonstrating the validity of the standard that extended from west to east Asia and from the 9th century to the 20th. It is the maintenance of this standard over such a vast area for so long a period that is interesting, particularly because it goes against the expectations of modern linguists, who assume that language changes at predictable rates irrespective of its social and cultural context. This book is based on the hypothesis that the relationship between spoken and written language differs according to historical context, that the differences are not all usefully explained by the linguistic terminology associated with the phenomenon of diglossia, and therefore the dynamics of change in written language may be different from those of spoken language in some cases. Our investigation of the Persian case is organized around a series of particular hypotheses concerning the relationship between the written form of the Persian language and the civilization that was identified with it. This civilization has been called Persianate (cf. Hodgson 1974, 2:293; see also Arjomand 2008:2–3), and we will follow that usage in order to indicate the culture embedded in the use of Persian over the past millennium throughout an area much larger than any territory we could call Persia or Iran.

A straightforward investigation of this type, focusing on another language and its culture, tends to lead readers to compare it unconsciously with their own general understanding of modern language and culture, particularly of English. In order to avoid this unconscious self-comparison, we have endeavored to set Persian in a premodern comparative context, specifically in relation to the other two most obviously comparable languages of premodern writing, in administration and literature, Chinese and Latin. We can expect that much of what is significant for Persian may also hold for other such widely used languages, but explicit comparison besides bringing out similarities will also alert us to differences that would not appear from the study of any one of them alone. Moreover, we will also be able to show more clearly by this comparison that certain social and historical factors make Persian a special case, from which something new can be learned about the historical significance of writing in the organization of premodern society in general—a significance that still casts a shadow over modern times. These factors derive from the sociology of the recruitment and training of writers, and the understandings that facilitated their control of their professional status and the boundaries of their social class. In part IV of this introductory chapter we shall need to distinguish our conclusions from those of the voluminous discussion of literacy that has developed in English over the past fifty years.

Persian stands out among languages with comparable historical records by virtue of a combination of factors which arise not only from the extraordinary geographical and temporal extent of its currency, but also from the general organization of the society in which it was used in the eastern half of the Islamic world, east and north of Mesopotamia, where it was the medium of administration, trade, and intellectual and artistic activity, and even much religious writing—in fact, any interaction that involved writing—over varying proportions of the past millennium. The history of Persian is a function of the history of its use in society, in social interaction, in both speaking and writing (as distinct from the history of its grammatical and syntactical development), in the choice of literary and other content. It was shaped by the way its speakers understood their identities and social rights and obligations in relation to each other and to the non-literate. The cultural heritage of literacy in the Sasanian empire and the religious value of the text of the Qur'an in Islamic civilization merged to secure the status of the literate class of the Persianate world, most of whom were professional administrators of one type or another.

It is important to remember also that Persian has had a particular historical relationship with the West, different from that of any other non-European language. Renaissance humanism brought it within our horizons through the study of Herodotus. Written Persian has been an object of discussion and direct study in Europe since it was discovered by travelers and merchants in India as early as the 16th century. The idea that it was an Indo-European language, like Latin and Greek, with which it enjoys roughly the same historical depth, was demonstrated in greater and greater detail from the 16th through the 19th centuries. The first English primers for it were published in the 18th century. Since the middle of the 20th century a number of Western scholars have sought to explain its unique historical role: from its re-establishment in Central Asia in the 9th century, to the various landmarks of its remarkable trajectory from then down to the present. In the wake of the development programs financed by the oil boom of 1973, interest in it spread beyond philologists and orientalists to consultants and travelers who brought its native name *Fārsi* into English. Finally, since the Iranian revolution in 1979 and the breakup of the Soviet Union in 1991, our understanding of the relationship between the various Persian-speaking areas of central and western Asia, conditioned by the nationalisms induced by opposition to late colonial administrations, has undergone some re-evaluation.

We have already had several occasions to use two terms—Iran(ian) and Persia(n)—in contexts where they appear to be interchangeable, which to a large extent they are. But since their connotations and associations differ, it is important to distinguish them. Moreover, in modern usage they have acquired additional connotations that we must be careful not to project back into the past. Both terms originated with the Achaemenians in the 6th century BC. Iran comes from Aryan (which English adopted from the Sanskrit), a term which Darius the Great used in identifying himself in the Bisitun inscription (viz. "I am Darius the Great King… son of Hystaspes, an Achaemenian, a Persian, son of a Persian, an Aryan, having Aryan lineage" in Kent 1950:138). Pars was already the name for the region in the southwest of the plateau where the Achaemenians had built their summer capital (which we know from the Greek as Persepolis). Herodotus called the people he was investigating "Persians," the people from Pars, and that remained their only name in Western languages until 1935. (The Greeks seem to have assumed some relationship with their mythic hero, Perseus.) These same people called their language *parsi* (later Arabized as *Fārsi*) because it began as the vernacular of that area. In 1935 Reza Shāh Pahlavi, then reigning Shāh of Iran (1925–1941), introduced the requirement that in all diplomatic correspondence the country be referred to by the name its people used, Iran. His initiative was the earliest of several re-namings inspired by the emerging non-Western nationalism of the time (cf. Burkina Faso, Sri Lanka, Myanmar). Gradually general Western usage began to shift: Persia is now rarely used as the name of the modern country, but remains in common use for its cultural heritage.

This much is common knowledge. In the meantime, however, other initiatives had added significantly to the connotations of each term. As the genetic relationships between languages were worked out in the 19th century, historical linguists divided all those that could be traced back to a supposed proto-Indo-European original into subgroupings. Because it was already known in the West as a language with a long textual tradition, "Iranian" was used to designate one of those subgroupings. Among others, the Iranian subgroup includes such modern languages as Persian, Pashto, Balochi, Kurdish, and Ossetic, as well as others with fewer speakers. As a result of the contemporaneous rise of nationalist thinking, the implication that speakers of other languages in that subgroup outside Afghanistan, Iran, and Tajikistan were also culturally or ethnically Iranian became difficult to avoid. Baloch, Kurds, Ossetes, Pashtuns were the most obvious candidates because their languages had acquired a written form and they were beginning to develop a sense of community identity. Second, at about the same time nationalism began to grow as a political force in western Asia generally. A little later the finer distinctions of ethnicity also began to appear. Consequently, any use of "Iranian" for any historical period tacitly acquired a nationalistic flavor, and implied at least a cultural association with communities that spoke other Iranian languages. "Persian" did not have this association. Instead any use of "Persian" implied an association with the cultural (monumental and literary) heritage of the area, by extension from what we know from Herodotus. The tendency to use Fārsi in English for the Persian language (by people to whom it would not occur to use *Deutsch* for German, or *hanyu* for Chinese) spread among Westerners who had visited Iran in the 1970s on business or tours (Spooner 1993). Throughout this volume we have avoided any phrasing that might appear to impute Iranian nationality or ethnicity to any community either on the basis of language or at a time before the emergence of nationalist thinking, but the modern tendency in this regard is so insidious that we may not have entirely succeeded.

Historically, Persian was not simply a language with an associated technique of writing; it was also a library of inherited textual models that continued not only to serve social needs but to condition social functions. The production and circulation of new text, derived to a large extent from these time-honored models, were in the hands of scribes (known by the Persian term *dabir,* but more commonly by the Arabic term *munshi*), who were a small elite minority distributed throughout the urban centers of the Persianate world. They were among the literati who served as the arbiters of correct usage not only in language, but in all interaction insofar as it was legitimized by textual models. So long as they remained arbiters of correct usage they were also arbiters of the use of writing. This control of models through the control of writing tended to inhibit or retard socio-cultural change, including change in the written language and in forms of speech that continued to be modeled on written usage.

Finally, in order to avoid the impression that the Persianate millennium was somehow timeless, we would draw attention to the fact that its relationship to the rest of the world did change continuously. As Persianate civilization began it was at the vanguard of human achievement, political, legal, scientific, technical, literary, and artistic. The Persian language facilitated its rise by providing the medium for the formation of an unprecedentedly large arena of interaction, with a common market. Early scholars of the period, such as Al-Khwarazmi and Avicenna, have a secure place in world history. A millennium later Persianate civilization had been overtaken by the Latinate West. If Persian facilitated its rise, could Persian also be implicated in its decline? If the spread of the language was a function of the social organization of its use in writing, and the resulting forms stagnated rather than changing with the times, such a connection is possible. We will revisit this question at the end of the volume. Meanwhile, this chapter introduces the issues that arise in this Persian story: issues of continuity and change, of the organizational significance of writing, and of what distinguishes the historical functionality of Persian from other written languages.

II. CONTINUITY AND CHANGE

The era of civilization that began with the Arab conquests under the banner of Islam in the 7th century contained the seeds of a logic of organization that was qualitatively new and different from what preceded it. In central and western Asia it was culturally Persianate while being religiously and legally Islamic. The Persianate features harked back to the empires of the Sasanians and their predecessors. The Islamic features were based on an elaboration, and universalization, of the conception of law that entered our history in association with the name of Hammurabi, and evolved in complexity and religiosity up to its written formulation associated with the name of Moses in the Hebrew Torah. This combination of administrative experience and universalistic conception of society offered unprecedented opportunities. The organization of society, the universal rule of (Islamic) law, the legitimation of authority (though not, unfortunately, of political succession), the freedom of long-distance trade—all were differently conceptualized from what obtained before. But as with even the most categorical revolution, there were continuities. Our habit of classifying history by periods has led us to separate Islam from its heritage and its influences, which have become a separate academic specialization. As a result the continuities from earlier regimes that conditioned much of the substance of life in the following centuries, though not entirely ignored, are too generally passed over.

Writing evolved in a relationship to society. It was adopted for particular uses, developed and elaborated for those uses as the prerogative of the people socially allocated to them. The earliest extant writing is in records of commercial transactions that date from before 3,000 BC. These texts were written in the ancestor of Sumerian cuneiform on clay tablets. Later, in the 3rd millennium, writing was used more generally in administration. By that time it was in Akkadian cuneiform. After 2,000 BC a literary dimension developed. But it is important to note that literary texts were the records of oral literature. The Achaemenians, who took over the Mesopotamian world in the 6th century BC, used Elamite scribes in their court chancelleries (559–330 BC). The Persian term *dabir*, "secretary," may be a borrowing from Elamite (de Blois 1994). But although their own language, which we know as Old Persian—a lineal precursor of New Persian (Persian in the Islamic era)—appears to have played a secondary role, the administrative apparatus of government must have been at least tri-lingual, since at least one administrative text written in Old Persian has come down to us (Stolper and Tavernier 2007).

We do not know under what circumstances Old Persian became a written language or who read it, but it appears to have been associated with the identity of the kings because it was used for royal inscriptions. Aramaic was also beginning to be used (Vallat 1994:274n74). In fact for communication throughout the empire a form of Aramaic known as Imperial or Achaemenid Aramaic soon became the common language. But under later empires of the Parthians and Sasanians, after the disruption of Alexander's invasion and the Seleucid interlude that followed it, a new form of Persian, which we know as Middle Persian, gradually replaced the non-Iranian languages in all formal functions, oral and written (Frye 1974:63–64). Where Old Persian emerged in association with Akkadian cuneiform on clay tablets, Middle Persian was written in a simplified form of the Aramaic alphabet (an alphabet without vowels) on papyrus. The rate of change throughout this period appears to have been steady and continuous.

Writing was similarly important in the administration of the Egyptian empire, where the ability to write was similarly associated with membership of a class that had a particular function and relationship with political authority. Only people from certain backgrounds were allowed to train to become scribes, in the service of temple, pharaonic, and military authorities. Like the cuneiform and Aramaic systems of writing, the hieroglyph system was also difficult to learn—not intellectually, but socially. In later centuries the social boundaries of the class were reinforced as a means of preserving the writers' social status.

Starting in the late 3rd millennium Akkadian had been the first language to serve as a medium for advancing administrative and commercial activity beyond southern Mesopotamia. It was the first common language (cf. Gr. *koine*), and its cuneiform script enjoyed a long steady decline into the 1st millennium (cf. Cooper in Houston, Baines, and Cooper 2003). But long before the demise of its cuneiform script Akkadian was replaced by Aramaic, the use of which overlapped in the Eastern Mediterranean with Greek well into the medieval period. It would appear that rulers who needed things written hired the writers who were available, but the writers began by using the language they were trained to work in, and only later adapted to working in the new language. Achaemenian royal texts were apparently dictated in Old Persian by the king, translated into Elamite, and then retranslated and reformulated in either Old Persian or Akkadian or both. Writers became a professional class early on. But at the end of the 4th century BC, in the wake of Alexander's campaigns and the administrative reorganization that succeeded them, these languages all gave ground to Hellenistic Greek, known at the time as the koine or common language. It is worth noting that Greek writing did not support a professional class; neither did Latin, but Chinese did. Should we seek the reason for this in the nature of the language, the way it was written, or in the way the society was organized?

Although the evidence is sketchy, each written language was probably used over a larger area for a broader set of functions and by a larger number of writers than its predecessor. But we can assume that the proportion of the population in western Asia that created written or textual materials continued to be very small, even though written material was probably being handled by increasing numbers of people, and increasing numbers were learning how to distinguish the significance of different types of documents without being able to read. There appears to have been a steady rise in the cultural value ascribed to anything in writing from the Sumerians to the Romans, and again from the early medieval through to the modern period. But the rise was uneven, and varied inversely according to the proportion of those who could write in a particular language to those who could not. People who could not read understood the significance of writing and ascribed value to written texts because they lived in societies that depended on writing for more and more of their organization, and for the legitimacy of any authority.

In the age of Greek, which at its apogee under the Seleucids extended from the Mediterranean into central and south Asia, the ability to read and write became more widespread—due partly no doubt to the range of textual material from the Athenian past that extended far beyond the functions previously served by writing in Mesopotamia and elsewhere. But it is important to note also that post-Athenian Greek society was structured very differently from the communities of western Asia. It was more egalitarian and more mobile, as well as being more literate. Could there be a relationship between these qualities? People in Athens were more socially mobile, and writing was not associated with any particular class. Everyone with a certain level of social awareness assumed they should be able to write. It may be partly due to this type of social orientation that whatever the final sum of Greek migration to the eastern parts of the Seleucid world was, Greek did not take root in the east because Greek social formations did not percolate into local societies. Neither did Greek entirely supplant Aramaic further west. It was a language that went with a different social structure, a different mode of social interaction. If you spoke Greek you did Greek. If you spoke Aramaic you did Aramaic. Learning a new language was one thing—people do it all the time. Multi-lingual arenas of interaction are not uncommon. Learning a new way to interact, or fitting into a new social niche, is more problematic. Achieving acceptance in a community with different interaction patterns is even more difficult. With the rise of the Parthians in the late 3rd century BC Greek actually receded westwards along with the culture embedded in it and with Seleucid power. In the 2nd century the wars between Rome and Parthia led to the irrevocable association of Greek with the enemy (by the Parthians), first in the form of the alien invader from the West, and later more generally with Christianity in distinction from Islam.

Meanwhile, the use of pre-Islamic forms of written Persian had expanded. After the introduction of Old Persian cuneiform under the Achaemenians, a related form of the same language (a Middle Persian language written in a simplified form of the Aramaic consonantal alphabet) continued as the vehicle of administration under the Parthians. Although we know little of Parthian administrative practice we may assume it provided the basis for the Sasanian administration that followed it in a closely related form of Middle Persian, and in a related script, in the 3rd century AD. The emergence and quick spread of Persian in the Arabic script in the 8th and 9th centuries was simply a continuation of this long trajectory of expanding administrative practice. The larger the empire, the greater the dependence on writing for administration. The displacement of the rulers by new people who brought new ideals and a new plan for organizing society hid the social continuity of the bureaucratic class, who despite their conversion to Islam resumed their customary procedures in ways very similar to what has been documented in the post-Roman kingdoms of 5th and 6th century Europe.[2] In the ensuing Persianate civilization public life was an arena in which people not only spoke and wrote Persian, they did Persian.

It is important to remember, however, that in the pre-Islamic period under the Achaemenians and the Sasanians writing may have been used only for government activities. Religious texts were transmitted breast to breast (*sina ba sina*). No one thought of writing them down until well into the 3rd century AD. The point was to know them by heart (Tafazzoli 2000). This pattern has three significant implications: from the beginning the Persianate written tradition was primarily a court tradition relating to formal behavior. Our current understandings of the crucial importance of the textual tradition in religious and other non-administrative functions may date only from a similar late period everywhere, when the use of sacred texts spread beyond local communities, led by Greek speakers. But did Greek lead in this function because of the unprecedentedly analytical character of its adaptation of the Phoenician alphabet, taking the hint from the use of *matres lectionis* in the earlier consonantal alphabets and introducing vowels on a level with consonants, or because Greek writing was not associated with class or occupation?

In the process of routinization that set in within a hundred years of the Arab-Islamic conquest, the Persian language slipped easily into the niche that was developed in western Asia first by Akkadian, then Aramaic, then Greek, and finally (under the Sasanians, 224–651) by Middle Persian or Pahlavi. The language had acquired the vocabulary and protocols for this role from the usage of earlier administrations, especially the Achaemenian and Sasanian, and since the writers were the same people they simply continued their role doing what they knew how to do. Although the language of supreme value in Islam is Arabic, and Arabic was the dominant language throughout the Islamic world well into the 2nd century of Islamic history, beginning in the 8th century in the core areas of the earlier Sasanian empire Arabic was gradually reduced to a status comparable to that of Latin in later medieval Europe. Why should Persian have supplanted Arabic at all, let alone achieve nothing less than parity with it everywhere outside the formal environment of the *madrasa*? And why should this achievement be geographically limited to the east? West of the Zagros mountains and south of the Fertile Crescent the use of Persian diminished, even though large parts of these western areas had similarly experienced Persian rule and the activity of Persian bureaucrats before Islam. Although no earlier use of Arabic had developed a comparable range of administrative vocabulary and protocol, Persian did not supplant Arabic to any significant extent west of the Plateau, probably because fewer writers with Persian experience were involved in the new administration or court life of those areas. Once again the stage may have been set for this linguistic divide by earlier usage, since there is a correlation between the historical distribution of Aramaic followed by Arabic on the one hand and the failure of Greek to take root and the resumption of the role of Persian on the other. Persian hegemony had already begun to give way to the Eastern Roman Empire, and Aramaic was more deeply rooted. The general populations of greater Syria and Egypt did not become mainly Arabic-speaking until centuries later, well after the emergence of Persian in the east.

From Baghdad to Morocco and the Sahel, Arabic functioned comparably to the way Persian functioned from Hamadan to Kashghar and beyond in the east, and eventually Hyderābād in the south and the Ottoman Balkans in the northwest. Together the two languages constituted the medium of communication, organization, and cultural integration of the entire Islamic world, a larger area and a larger population by far than had been interrelated into a single community, at any level of cultural integration, at any earlier period, or perhaps even since. This Arabo-Persian world was politically fragmented, but there was freedom of movement and trade throughout its length and breadth, facilitated, perhaps even encouraged by the common languages. What is most remarkable is the lack of any central authority to govern usage or establish models of correctness. It is interesting that there was also no central authority to interpret or enforce the *shari`a,* which provided the legal framework for social interaction everywhere. There was, however, a universally recognized structure of procedures for interpreting it. There was similarly no central authority for Arabic usage. But there was a single fundamental text that provided the final authority for all Arabic usage as well as for everything Islamic, the Qur'an. For Persian, on the other hand, there was neither a primary text nor any other type of authority besides the heritage of Sasanian bureaucrats, which was gradually succeeded by the evolving canon of secular Persian literary texts. In this connection it may be worth noting that Islamic civilization in general was characterized by a lesser degree of centralization than other parts of the world, until perhaps the later emergence of what Hodgson (1974) calls the Gunpowder Empires: the Ottomans, Safavids, and Mughals.

Although the relationship has not been static, Arabic and Persian were more intimately intertwined down to the 19th century at least than even Greek and Latin in the Roman Empire, or Latin and English in the 17th– 19th centuries, or English and French in early modern international diplomacy. Not only had Persian adopted its Islamic vocabulary from Arabic, but Persian (in its Middle Persian form) had influenced Arabic before Islam, and both languages had been influenced by Aramaic. (In this connection it is interesting to remember that one of the earliest converts to Islam was Badhan, the Sasanian governor of San`a in Yemen in 621.) Moreover, the written forms of both Arabic and Persian were standardized during the same period in closely related and overlapping communities of writers.

The canon of literary texts that appears to have served as the anchor for Persian writing was the product of the court life of the Sultans who had introduced Persian as their language of administration, beginning with the Samanids in Samarqand in 851, and the ever broadening circle of interaction among them down to the Safavid and Mughal periods in the 16th–18th centuries. Whereas Akkadian had spread from Mesopotamia, Aramaic from Syria, and Greek from the northeast Mediterranean, Persian (in Middle Persian forms) had already been in use throughout western Asia, and (as New Persian) emerged in the eastern part of that area where the earlier written languages had not taken root. It was therefore much better situated to spread eastwards. (Its modern exclusive association with the state of Iran, separate from Afghanistan, along with the current borders between them is a historical irony, dating only from the period of British and Russian interference in the region in the 19th century.) Despite these historical complications, from the 9th to the 19th century, over a vast area of Eurasia, Persian had the status of a common language comparable to the earlier role of the Hellenistic koine. But in the case of each of these languages the extent of their spatial and temporal homogeneity and continuity would not have been possible without writing: usage was anchored in the language as written, by means of constant reference to the written materials that circulated. Authority resided in the text. The supreme authority was in the text of the Qur'an. The social value of Persian writing and the status of those who wrote it was a major feature in the organization of Persianate society, which finally gave way to local languages only as the result of expanding socio-political horizons which broke down class barriers. The first successor language was Ottoman Turkish which emerged as the Ottoman horizons extended beyond the Islamic world into Europe. The replacement of Persian by successor languages in the east took off only in the 19th century when horizons were expanded by Western imperialism.

Until the end of the medieval period, perhaps as late as the 18th century, the rate of change in Persian written usage continued to be held in check by the power of written texts, the use in everyday life of the protocols embedded in them, and the interests of the writing classes. But the rise of social awareness reflected in the spread of printing and the Reformation in 16th–17th century Europe eventually expanded into Asia and broke down the social boundaries of writing everywhere. The cultural value of writing was so well established that it eroded only slowly. But as the skills of reading and writing began finally to spread much faster after the Industrial Revolution, first through each Western society and then later throughout the world, a qualitative change set in. One of the consequences of the emergence of mass writing has been a steady reduction of the social value of being literate. When (almost) all are literate, there is no longer a literate class to create peer pressure for conformity to the codes and confirmation of the canon that were the foundations of the symbolic value of the text.

Today language in general is no longer anchored by any socially established rules. This change is reflected in changing emphases in education and the academic enterprise. For example, philology, which grew out of classics as the study of language through texts, has been replaced in the 20th century by linguistics, which grew out of anthropology and focuses on the dynamics of spoken language. Linguistics has shown us that in the modern situation, now that the written word has lost much of its power to define correct practice and correct speech, there are no longer any built-in constraints on the rate of linguistic change. Not only English, but now Turkish and Hindi, as well as Persian and other languages previously rooted in a written tradition, have changed at unprecedented rates since the middle of the 20th century. If change in general throughout the Persianate world was slower than elsewhere, the social function of writing may have had something to do with it.

III. PERSIANATE LANGUAGE AND CULTURE

The long-term stability of Persianate language and culture over such a vast area was made possible, perhaps uniquely in world history, not by a power center or other political institutions, but—to list the significant factors in the order they emerged—by a combination of bureaucratic heritage, the status of a secretarial class, a universally accepted legal framework (the *shariʿa*), and a literary canon. So long as the *shariʿa* continued to be the overall organizing framework for social life, and its function was not questioned, this universal revealed law ensured stability and standard practice. Linguistic stability goes hand in hand with social stability. All the continuities from the past were reinterpreted within this new expanding framework. The adverse effects of recurrent political instabilities were mitigated by the confidence of faith in the validity of the Islamic legal framework. Islam finds its justification in past historical events, and does not expect change. It is essentially conservative. (The Western world on the other hand is conditioned by Christianity to see nothing ideal in the past. Although it was launched by an historical event, this event was soon understood as promising something better in the future, rather than providing a blueprint for the day-to-day management of society.) Within this Islamic framework the Persian language and Persianate civilization were spread and maintained by ritualistic repetition of institutionalized activities, mostly rooted in or associated with textual models. These models were elaborated in the course of the millennium. Styles evolved. Arrangements became more complex. But the semblance of innovation was deprecated, and nothing needed to be consciously discarded.

At no time was the use of written Persian dominated by a single administration, or an institution, such as the papacy. Neither was it controlled by any pre-eminent group of users either within or outside the secretarial (*munshi*) profession. There was no Roman Curia, no Chinese Imperial examination system, no academy. Social and political organization in the Islamic world in general differed in this way from what we are familiar with in Western history. The only formal organizational framework in any part of the Islamic world that extended beyond the bureaucracy of the particular local ruler was the conceptual-legal framework of Islamic jurisprudence (*fiqh*). The most important duty of the ruler, that alone justified his tenure, was the maintenance of public order under this framework. Everything that happened had to be rationalized in terms of the *shari`a*, and it was taken for granted that the *shari`a* was interpreted by scholars (*ulama*), whose training was certified by their seniors in the *madrasa* where they were trained. Although neither the *shari`a* nor the ulama were related in any formal way to the standards of Persian usage, they represented and legitimized the larger framework of social order within which Persian spread. This social order was in principle egalitarian. Villagers and trade apprentices from the bazaar could enter the *madrasa*. The names in medieval biographical dictionaries show that senior scholars commonly came from rural backgrounds. But it was also conservative in that it protected private property (though it also provided rules for its redistribution in inheritance), and it encouraged trade. Under this framework, despite the enormous sparsely populated distances between cities and the very slow speeds of long-distance travel (cf. Knauer 1998), widely distributed networks of interaction in Persian were sustained by travel and by correspondence. The models for correct Persian usage emerged in the 9th century from the pre-Islamic heritage of the epistolographic practices of the Sasanian Empire (AD 224–651), and were maintained through the interaction within and between chancelleries and the court communities of multiple sultanates that were widely separated geographically, and represented different underlying vernacular traditions. The historical dynamics of change in written Persian were the product of routine interaction over great distances through the medium of writing and travel. Possibly the universalism implicit in the new Islamic orientation to the world may have played a part. But there was no formal or recognized framework to ensure correct usage or inhibit change over time, and no political reinforcement.

The crucial role in these networks was that of the *munshi*. *Munshi*s constituted a professional class with high social status, political involvements, literary talents, and wealth. In her study of the historian Bayhaqi, Waldman has commented interestingly on the professional rigor of *munshi*s in the 10th century. Bayhaqi was himself a *munshi*. He continued to use the pre-Islamic Persian term *dabir* for his profession. What he writes about the role and heritage of the *dabir* evinces a recognizable snobbishness. Being a *dabir* had been a very special way of life since pre-Islamic times. The great empires of the past had depended on their bureaucracies. In Bayhaqi's time the Ghaznavid empire (centered in Ghazni in southeastern Afghanistan, 975–1187), even though it was the first to be established by Turks, was no different. Being a *dabir* was not simply a nine-to-five job; it was social position, a style of thinking and acting, based on years of education, apprenticeship, and cultivation. *Dabir*s spent much of their time at the palace, living there or nearby; their apprenticeship in the secretarial arts was long; all their work was done in a special section of the palace; much of their socializing, during and after hours, was with other palace officials. The office of *dabir* accrued a much higher status than would be associated with a civil servant or bureaucrat in modern states. Any particular *dabir*'s success depended on his facility in Arabic and Persian style, including his conciseness of expression, the niceties of his turns of phrase, and the accuracy of his technical vocabulary. In short, *dabiri* was also an art, and a very important one, in which experience counted more than anything else (Waldman 1980:40–41, cf. Alam 1998:326–27).

Consideration of this professional situation in a comparative perspective raises some interesting questions. Is reading or writing Persian essentially the same sort of skill for those socialized in the tradition as, say, reading or writing English is for people in the English-speaking world? Or are there qualitative differences that might be significant for this inquiry? Are there factors specific to reading and writing Persian in the *nasta'liq* or *shekasta* styles of the Perso-Arabic script that should be taken into account in assessing the history of Persian? It is easy to see how this question would apply to the Chinese character-based tradition, but since *nasta'liq* is closer to our own Roman in being alphabetic in structure (though not fully analytical) we have not asked the question about Persian.

We may begin to develop an answer to these questions by noting that the Arabic script generally works in practice not by letter but by penstroke, in that it has only a cursive form, with no majuscule-minuscule options like medieval Roman. One penstroke might include from one to four or even five connected letters with less change of direction than in cursive Roman. The variation results from the fact that not every letter can be joined to the next. For this reason the relation of penstroke to word is not always one-to-one as it is in a fully cursive Roman hand. This characteristic is somewhat modified in the *nasta'liq* style of writing (which is governed by calligraphic models), more so in the *shekasta* style (which is essentially a shorthand of bureaucrats).

This form of reading and writing, by pen-stroke (as well as by word), offers different possibilities for organizing writing on a page: straight, even lines are less important. The activity of scanning—speed-reading—a document works differently. While writing is not an interactive medium like speech, it was nevertheless practiced in a dialectical relationship with reading. The writer, especially the professional writer, wrote for a particular set of consumers of writing. Learning to read and write can be by rote, by association, by use of mnemonic strategies, or by logical induction. But the experienced reader does not read analytically. However reading might have been taught, mature reading is always in practice not analytic but pictographic. One reads by shape and scans common indicators. These shapes and indicators are learned not consciously, but rather subconsciously, differently in different communities of writing. Examples of indicators in Roman are upper case, ascenders and descenders, period-space, paragraph breaks, and particular common words (which vary to some extent according to the experience of the reader). In Persian such subconscious recognition works differently because it is by pen-stroke rather than by word or letter. Each letter in the pen-stroke can appear differently according to which letter is on either side of it and whether it is at the beginning or end of the stroke. One reads, therefore, by retrieving subconsciously from a repertoire of pen-strokes that is much larger than the number of letters in the alphabet. (It should be noted, however, that reading *bad* handwriting in English may work essentially the same way.) But since the *nasta'liq* style exaggerates the pen-stroke, we must ask which pen-strokes are common enough to function as signposts to enable the eye of the experienced reader to take in the overall shape of an area of writing? Some are obvious: for example, in Per-

sian *ast, ke*; in Urdu *hai, ka*. Urdu works differently from Persian because
it has additional letters, and different frequencies of particular letters, and
allows longer pen-strokes. The fact that the ka structure is so conspicuous
on an Urdu page makes it much easier to see how this might work in Urdu
than in Persian or Ottoman which do not have comparable linguistic features that stand out so prominently in the script (cf. *ra,* some particular
Turkic agglutinations, the ezafe mediated by *ye*).

What it takes to produce the succession of strokes in a configuration
that a reader will scan with ease differs with different scripts. How many
signs fit on a line, on a page, is different. Consequently, how the reader
reads—the relationship between reader and text—not only differs according to script, and again according to the particular language he is reading
in that script, but it is conditioned by the reader's own relationship as a
writer. This is a field for comparative study that has so far received little or
no systematic attention, despite the fact that it is crucial to any program
designed to promote writing in the modern world. Go back a hundred years
or so to the time when, although printed texts were available, handwriting was the primary form of the written word. Look at the styles of handwriting in (a) Roman: English, French, German, (b) Cyrillic: Russian, (c) Greek,
(d) Hebrew, (e) Chinese, Japanese, Korean, (f) Arabic, Ottoman, Persian,
Urdu. In each case, beyond the personal style and other idiosyncrasies of
the particular writer, aesthetic considerations come into play in the models
by which the writer learned to write, that lend a particular style to each
written language. Among these, Persian stands out in the following ways:
each stroke forms one or more letters, where most languages need one or
more strokes for each letter or sign; many letters take up very little if any
space because they are implied in the form of the pen-stroke that encom-
passes several (mostly one to four) letters—certain strokes may be written
one above the other, or diagonally from upper right to lower left. The same
is true to some extent for other languages in the same script, e.g., Arabic
and Urdu, but not to the same degree as for Persian written in the later
shikasta form of the script (cf. Hanaway and Spooner 2007).

The skill of reading also involves the skill of knowing what is written,
and being able to anticipate it. The fast reader starts from considerable earlier experience in reading and being ready to recognize subconsciously most
of what *might* be written. Then, in the same way that body language and
suprasegmentals (pitch, stress, juncture, loudness) supply complementary

information in face-to-face interaction, the organization of the document supplies information beyond the words of the written communication. Court protocol is a formalization of the former, chancellery documents of the latter. We may assume in general that the organization of words on a page, and of whole documents, evolves among users in ways that amplify information and signal intentions (viz. the subject matter of the subfield of diplomatics in European medieval studies). Examples include conventional opening and closing formulae, or phrases such as *va amma* to signal a change of topic. There appear to have been cross-cultural influences in court behavior in relation to writing between (for example) the Safavids, the Ottomans, and the Tudors, and there are organizational parallels between Islamic documents and Western medieval documents. Handwriting was not just putting spoken language on paper. It was the writing of particular words and phrases that were institutionalized for particular purposes. The practice of writing involved awareness of an expansive cultural community. Persian in particular played a role in the cultural awareness of the eastern Islamic world that Arabic could not have played in the same way because Arabic did not have the same historical protocols.

The academic discussion of Persian writing has been complicated by the distinctive cultural value of calligraphy. We have found it very difficult to engage native readers and writers in any objective, value-neutral discussion of writing, outside the value scheme of calligraphic appraisal. In this inquiry, therefore, we must also take account of the significance of this value scheme in the areas we are investigating. The fact that no word for calligraphy was used at the time (*khwosh-nevisi* is a later coinage in response to the Western conceptualization) makes the discussion more difficult. Models of artistic writing were taken for granted. It is likely that much of the recent discussion in Persian of calligraphy is influenced by Western definitions. If we look at medieval sources we find, for example in the *Dastur-e Dabiri*, written in the 12th century and discussed in chapter 3, the statement that a scribe should possess a good hand (*khatt-e niku*), as well as the other technical skills such as spelling, grammar, knowledge of Arabic, etc. There is nothing here to suggest any more than that they were trained to write intelligibly and gracefully. Writing for a public purpose, whether in a decree or letter or an inscription, was done clearly and gracefully according to accumulated models, the power of which was greater than in other traditions because of the peculiar cultural status of the written Qur'an and the avoidance of figurative artistic expression. The boundary we now recognize between calligraphy and simply "good writing" or "a nice hand" is a later modern development resulting from interaction with other non-Persianate and non-Islamic traditions. Any writing that is in a consistent form or style inevitably draws attention to itself. "Good" writing, in the sense of consistently and easily legible writing, is not necessarily the same as "beautiful writing," in the sense of being self-consciously stylized. The actual words of the *Dastur-i dabiri* make this clear:

> Know that the first resource that is necessary for the secretary is good handwriting. There are many conditions and customs to do with handwriting and the pen but those that appertain to this craft are: first, command of a hand in which the letters are proportional to each other, which makes letter-writing appropriately fluent.

> *Bedān ke nakhostin ellati ke dabir-rā bedān hājat ast khatt-e nikust, va sharāyāt va ādāb-e khatt va qalam besyār ast, ammā ānche bedin sanā'at ta'alloq dārad ān ast ke: avvalan dast bar khatti mansub ke tarassol-rā shāyad ravān gardānad...* (p. 2)

Models of good writing were known throughout the Persianate world. They may have added to the ritualistic aspect of written language discussed in the previous section, in that they generated culturally centripetal forces, and played a part in reinforcing Persianate cultural identity.

The various centers of writing in the Persianate world were related both socially (through the relationships formed in the education and organization of the ulama, through the application of the *shari'a,* and through trade) and culturally through the content of their interaction. The centers differed to the extent that the underlying local vernaculars and other local conditions differed (as of course did the experience and historical memory of both the writing class and the community as a whole). They also differed to the extent that the spoken language of the writers' local non-literate community differed from the language they were writing. Towards the end of the period, as fewer writers of Persian in India and other peripheral areas spoke the language they were writing, the written language changed even more slowly, and usage became more conservative than in the core areas such as the territory that became modern Iran, where it continued to be a spoken language among the urban elites (cf. the example of Latin in the medieval West). Persian was influenced less and less by the normal processes of linguistic change of a speech community. The activities of the Literacy Corps in Iran in the 1960s led to an acceleration of linguistic change in the ensuing decades, which has ironically contributed to the fragmentation of Persian as koine and of the Persianate world. The part that writing played in the social identity of the writing class also militated against change, as did the interaction (in writing, but also by travel) with members of the writing class in other centers. However, despite these forces for uniformity, we should not assume absolute uniformity throughout the region. The possibility of uniformity came to an end when Western imperial spheres of interest divided up the Islamic world. Domination by culturally alien powers (whether or not accompanied by colonial administration) disrupted the institution of writing in its administrative function of organizing the society, and accelerated the processes of social and cultural change. Similar effects can be seen in late Mughal India, Qajar Iran, the Ottoman empire during the *tanzimāt*, and late Qing China.

Language is a cultural artifact. Every language conveys cultural concepts, models, and orientations. Being proficient in a language carries with it not only the ability to speak in a particular speech community, but also the unconscious performance of all the dimensions of the culture of that community. This integrity of language and culture has been admirably explicated for Latin by Farrell (2001; cf. chapter 11 of this volume). But the groundwork for a similar cultural characterization of Persian is unfortunately not yet available. Latin has been intensively studied. The social history of Persian and the later consequences of its hegemony in west, central, and south Asia have been very different, but the studies necessary to illustrate this difference are sparse. Its speakers and writers in the east and west of this vast Persianate area were comprehensible to each other because the models they drew on for their interaction came from the common canons of administrative, commercial, and literary usage. The language of texts written in the 9th century was still readable and recognized as standard in the mid-20th because although the canons evolved, the rate of change was slow. Moreover, both the spatial and temporal ranges of mutual intelligibility were a function not simply of lexicon and syntax, but of a broad range of related behavior relating to kinesics and public interaction, from the choice of wording, the arrangement of words on the page, and the style and order of expression, to the choice of writing materials, and the use of the language-as-written in public oral interaction, including body language and the choice of occasion. Very early on, the literate class in the Islamic world began to produce aids to writing such as mono- and bi-lingual dictionaries, grammars, and biographical dictionaries of scholars and the literate class. Later, self-conscious collections of letters appeared. All these activities must have reinforced the hold of the literate class on writing itself, and on society. The corpus of behavioral models that were embedded in the use of Persian are referred to as *adab*.

Adab had obvious pre-Islamic roots, and the memory of the old Sasanian class system promoted the perpetuation of professional classes, with significant consequences for both writing and cultural communication generally. A major factor in this phenomenon was provided by cumulative regularities in the recruitment, training, and the accepted norms of writers' interaction between various parts of the region and the expectations thus generated. The language and the social dynamic became interdependent and mutually reinforcing. The norms of writing were embedded in a larger administrative structure, which in turn was embedded in the norms of a geographically vast, largely non-literate cultural community. This process may be seen in the emergence of letter-writing as one of the cultural norms and ideals of *adab* that extended throughout the society, and helped to structure it. Beginning under the Umayyad Caliphs (661–750), it developed rapidly under the early 'Abbasids, and evolved into a literary genre, especially in the Eastern Caliphate.

Adab covers the larger cultural framework of the historical use of written Persian. We need to investigate the sociology of its emergence, development, and maintenance. Compared to Latin and Greek, the community of Persianate writing was smaller and highly fragmented but much more widely distributed. For over a millennium Persianate high culture was embedded in the texts of written Persian. Written Persian was not only a means of communication—administrative, epistolary, and literary—but also the legitimizer of public behavior in general over this vast culturally diverse area. In order to understand how this worked we need to consider the writers of Persian throughout west, central, and south Asia as a community of subcommunities of writers. We must isolate the subcommunities and investigate how they participated in the historical dynamic of standardization and adaptation over the centuries. Each subcommunity would have been broken down again into *munshi*s and courtiers, poets and other literati, including the professional administrative elite. Complementary to these literate classes were the non-literate majority who knew Persian and listened to it being read out or recited, but did not write it, and whose lives were framed by the texts they did not read, but whose cultural status they recognized and subscribed to. It is these implications that we must investigate in order to understand more fully both the stability and the cultural power of written Persian.

From the Ottoman west to the Uzbek east and the Deccan south public interaction in Persian followed the unwritten rules of *adab*. At its furthest extent "It was customary for young Venetian noblemen to be sent off to spend their teenage years learning both Arabic and Persian, as well as the business of trade, in the Venetian trading settlements in the Levant, and a number of Venetian doges, such as the longest reigning of all, the fox-like Doge Francesco Foscari (r. 1423–1457), were actually born and grew up there. Doge Andrea Gritti (r. 1523–1538) fathered three illegitimate children in his youth in Istanbul, one of whom later became the close friend of Suleyman the Magnificent's grand vizier, Ibrahim Pasha. It was in this way that a remarkable number of Arabic loan words (as well as some from Persian and Turkish) entered Venetian dialect, including the Venetian term for their gold ducats—zecchino—from the Arabic sikka..." (Dalrymple 2007). Both language and culture were rooted in the textual tradition.

Adab is a cultural continuation of pre-Islamic models which were known by Iranian words such as *frahang* (culture) and *ayin* (custom). They are rooted in Sasanian usage. The change from these Persian terms to the Arabic *adab* parallels the change from *dabir* to *munshi*. By the time *adab* gained currency, it must already have been understood to be rooted in literature (*adabiyyāt*). The essence of *adab* is its service in the role of ensuring the security of public interaction. Herein lies the essential difference between Persianate culture and the Western cultural environment of our discussions, which make it very difficult for Westerners to interpret Persian behavior correctly (medieval or modern). Although our society has changed in recent generations, our heritage is that of a society in which everyone knew their place, and most people stayed in more or less the same social position throughout their lives. It was a stratified society, with a structure derived historically from land ownership. The stability of Persianate society rested on different principles, which were egalitarian rather than hierarchical. These principles were enshrined in Islamic law. It was rare for any family to retain high social status for more than three generations. Public life involved continuous competition for status. The forms of behavior that fall under the general heading of *adab* not only provide respectability but disguise the underlying competition. What we refer to today as "the position of women" in Persianate society is a special and perhaps extreme case of this cultural style. Independent of the history of its development and its formal justification today in response to Western objections, *adab* functions (and therefore persists) in Persianate culture to the extent that it removes conflict with and over women from the public arena and sequesters it in the private sphere. All behavior associated with the concept of *adab* ensures the smoothness of public interaction; any behavior that disrupts smooth public interaction is contrary to *adab*.

The particular cultural flavor of *adab* is centered in a form of civility, discernment, good taste, and the golden mean, which above all respects the privacy of the individual and avoids open public friction. The giver should be grateful to the recipient, not vice versa. It is very different from but culturally equivalent to Latinitas, and the foundation of a pre-nationalist historical identity. The relationship between *adab* and literature (*adabiyyāt*) is comparable to the Chinese association of writing (*wen*) with culture (*wenhua*) and civilization (*wenming*) (cf. chapter 12 of this volume). The continuous elaboration of titles in Persianate administration as the medieval period wore on, and the inflation in their usage in recent times, should also be seen in this light (cf. Ashraf 1989).

Understanding historical sources requires a sensitivity to the assumptions and objectives of the writers at the time. The same is true for any historical period, including the modern, and any writing tradition. We began to study writing because however well our students learned to read and speak Persian, however close they might approach to native reading and speaking ability, their ability to write by hand was always behind, barely competent, like the writing of children. We sensed a general attitude towards handwriting that downvalued it as simply a substitute for printing in the unfortunate situations where printing might not be available. But if we are going to understand medieval writing we have to respect it for the essential form of communication it was at the time, embedded in a social context very different from our own. Because of the close (but changing and often misunderstood) relationship between speech and writing, the appreciation of any use of language requires sensitivity to both media in their own right. The written word leaves a visual impression on the mind, in addition to any oral impression. Before the uniformity and commoditization of the printed word, not only the social value of the ability to produce an acceptable text but also the cost of producing a text imbued the text with a richer variety of meaning that most of us have been educated to see. Some of these textual models of the past continue to illuminate formalities that survive in modern life.

IV. THE HISTORICAL SIGNIFICANCE OF WRITING

Linguistics is a relatively recent arrival in the academic curriculum. As the scientific study of language it has defined its subject matter primarily in terms of speech. Some of its roots extend back into anthropology, and the anthropological study of culture has found some of its most productive models in the study of spoken language. But the role of written language in cultural life, or in society, has received relatively little attention either from anthropologists or linguists, or even from their predecessors in the study of textual language, philologists. Our understanding of the history of written language and its relationship to society has been further confused by a failure to ascribe any significance to the difference of medium, and to be alert to possible differences of dynamic between them. However, since our reconstruction of the past depends mainly on textual sources, any differences that derive from linguistic features that may inhere in written rather than spoken language are of particular significance for any historical enquiry.

Writing has been understood to be the central defining feature of civilization. Consequently, in the study of each civilization we have expected the adoption of writing to have roughly the same consequences. But these expectations ignore the obvious historical differences between the various civilizations of the past five thousand years. They assume that the consequences derive from the skill of writing and the differences from the relative efficiency of each writing tradition. This assumption is only partly valid, for it misses the organizational dimension. On the one hand writing facilitated remote communication beyond local face-to-face interaction, enlarging the arena of interaction, both spatially and temporally. On the other hand, however, since writing was a skill that had to be acquired, its acquisition depended on relationships, and relationships could be controlled. In fact, writing provided the tool for controlling, and therefore also for legitimizing, the way society was organized beyond the face-to-face community. It facilitated both the formation of larger communities and (perhaps more significantly) the formal differentiation and discrimination within and between them. Although these consequences were the same for every writing tradition, they worked out differently in different societies, depending on how the relationships were historically configured and managed.

Before (or without) writing, social differentiation was based exclusively on criteria of descent and territoriality. Writing made possible a qualitatively new form of differentiation. It also facilitated all further forms of social differentiation that have evolved from then up to the 20th century. By extending the reach of administrative control, it also generated the need for further formal criteria for social differentiation, which in turn established inequalities. As a vehicle of documentation it also led to the development of a sense of time, of history, which fed into ideas of legitimacy. Writing provides a communicative framework that facilitates and may socially encourage uniformity (though not equality) and build standards. Societies without writing are tribal, in the sense that they lack firm organizational criteria beyond sex, age, descent, and marriage. They are organized in lineages and descent groups and think of relationships in genealogical terms. Societies with writing, on the other hand, are complex in that they can organize bureaucratically, on a larger scale, providing for routine interaction among unrelated strangers. Descent becomes pedigree and status is legitimized by title to property.

The adoption of writing was therefore a historical landmark no less significant in the historical development of social complexity than the domestication of plants and animals. It generated a revolution in the organization of human life no less significant than the Neolithic. But just as domestication did not spread quickly and evenly to every population throughout the world, and did not finish spreading until the 20th century, so writing did not come to provide the basis for the organization of every society until roughly the same time. The convergence of these two processes was due to the approaching culmination of a larger process—resulting from increasing population size and densities and expanding social awareness—that we have recently come to refer to as globalization. Meanwhile, the implications of literacy have played out very differently in different cultural traditions. Such differences as are recognized are generally assumed to derive from differences in the relationship of the written form of the language to speech:

the extent to which it is phonetically analytical. But this seems not to fit the Persian case. We shall return to this point below, but first we need to look at some other factors.

It is particularly important to note the way writing facilitated the extension of administration beyond local communities, and the building of larger and larger empires. Starting from the beginnings of writing in Mesopotamia and Egypt five millennia ago, each empire was larger than the last as the bureaucratic potential of writing was gradually realized. This expansion occurred not only through the elaboration of bureaucracy, but also through trade (which Morgan pursues in chapter 4 in relation to the eastward expansion of Persian). The process continued through the ancient and medieval periods of history down to the 20th century, when the functions of writing finally began to be enhanced by new technologies that increased the speed of remote communication beyond what had been possible by means of the simple physical movement of written material.

In comparing how the function of writing played out in different civilizations we shall ignore the question of the origins of the various major scripts. For the questions we are investigating the fact that the Greek alphabet was derived from Phoenician is not relevant. The fact that Phoenician may underlie some stage of the development of many, perhaps most, of the surviving writing systems will not affect the current discussion. It will be more useful to classify writing systems in terms of historical script-families, groups of languages that have shared a common script historically, such as Arabic and Persian. Three major script-families have played particularly important roles in world history: Arabic, Latin, and Sinic. (Some may wish to add Brahmi or Sanskritic, which we have not been able to include here.) Many languages have been and continue to be written in each. Languages written in the same script are historically related, whether or not they are also genetically related. They may therefore share features of areal convergence. The world's major empires, and the most significant political and cultural players in world history, have depended on recording, communication, and expression in scripts from one or the other of these three families. But very little academic attention has been given to the comparative study of languages written in different scripts. Although comparative linguistics began with the definition of Indo-European on the basis of observed similarities between written languages, it barely progressed beyond classical languages before the modern expansion of the field into the study of non-written languages, and it paid no attention to the study of writing per se, except with regard to origins and the historical development of alphabets.

As we shall attempt to demonstrate below, languages belonging to different script-families are likely to exhibit greater differences between their textual traditions than languages that use the same script. What we may learn from the study of reading and writing in one language may not be valid for the study of others, especially where the script is different. Because of the Persian preference for *nasta`liq* and *shekasta* styles of the Perso-Arabic script, with their distinctive combination of diacritics and multi-letter pen-strokes, we will argue that even differences in the style of script can be significant. Our study of medieval, early modern, and modern writing in Persian led us further into an appreciation of the significance of different genres and registers of writing and how the writer writes and the reader reads in different situations. Genres may differ culturally, but they are socially constructed. Just as what people understand in oral interaction depends to a large part on non-linguistic factors, such as the body language of the interlocutor, choice of situation, order of presentation, and the relation between what is said and what is left unsaid, so in reading much of what is assimilated derives as much from the medium, the organization, and the style and quality of the writing, as well as the genre, as from the sense of the individual words themselves. But beyond this appreciation of the similarity between speech and writing as media of communication, we became impressed more and more by what we perceived to be differences between writing and speech as media. The more we considered the specifics of writing, the more we saw that our understanding of it (and therefore also of our historical sources) had suffered from lack of attention to its distinctive medium. We noted how little it had been investigated beyond the textual issues that were dealt with by philologists. Over the past fifty years the study of written language has been neglected, while the study of language generally has forged ahead with a focus on language, and languages, as spoken.

Writing has been studied in two ways: the best known has been the connoisseurship of calligraphy, and this interest has tended both to distract attention from the study of everyday writing and to prejudice our evaluation of it. What goes into the physical production of texts, on the other hand, has been studied under the heading of diplomatics, which is a late 17th century formulation for an important subfield in European medieval studies devoted to the systematic study of documents (because early documents were *diplomas,* i.e., folded pieces of paper). However, diplomatics has so far spawned only a very few and somewhat timid excursions into other writing traditions. Historians would be well served by a cross-cultural extension of diplomatics—which would help them to understand in what ways doing things correctly as an acceptable writer is very different from the kinesics of doing things acceptably as a culturally recognizable speaker. In what follows we aim to establish a cross-cultural framework for investigating the historical role of Persian writing as the vehicle for administration and cultural production, for bureaucratic and literary communication. In this sense writing is not simply a skill, or a means of expanding memory and awareness. In addition to these important features it is an institution, in the sense of being a component of a larger organizational system, and it is one of the key institutions of society as we know it, from the Ancient World to the present. Since the later 19th century, following the rise of numeracy in the West, we have grown so accustomed to focusing on statistics, what proportion of a given society (especially in terms of labor) can be directly managed through the written word, that we have lost sight of the significance of the enormous value of writing in societies where only a small proportion of the population can actually read and write. In these premodern situations, where the written word manages the society but is in the control of a privileged minority, knowing how to write alone is insufficient. To be accepted socially as a writer it is essential to write correctly according to established models that must be learned and certified through socialization and apprenticeship with the right people. As our modern writing becomes further removed from the social conditions in which our historical sources were produced, we stand in greater and greater need of a comparative diplomatics that would allow us to go beyond the translation of the words in the text of a document and understand the information that is embedded in the organization of the words on the page and the sociology of its production. Interaction between scholars working in different but parallel traditions would generate cross-cultural questioning and accelerate the research process.

The comparative study of textual traditions has so far barely begun. Initial attempts to pursue this type of enquiry in Islamic history first appeared only in the middle of the last century. Progress since then has been slow and uneven, and mostly in Ottoman studies, despite the potential value to other disciplinary fields of research (cf. bibliography in chapter 5). Writing is necessarily more conscious and less spontaneous than speech. Although writing and speaking can now occur anywhere along a range from barely conscious to fully consciously articulate and considered, in the past, and certainly in the premodern world, we can assume that writing was always fully deliberate. Speech on the other hand can be, and often is, entirely spontaneous. In each case language is only one ingredient of the resulting communication. The parole of speech is not just conditioned, but clothed and provided with fundamental meaning by the kinesic dimension of the communication. Diplomatics is the key to similarly illuminating the meaning of the written text. Both have to do with the immediate mechanics of language in interaction and communication. Beyond this role that the performance of language plays in individual acts of delivery is the much more crucial function of these acts in the social and cultural processes that create history. Since premodern writing was never typically spontaneous, we need to understand better how it was culturally organized if we are to reconstruct historical processes correctly.

Written and spoken language have for the most part been seen simply as different expressions of a single cultural artifact: the particular language of study. In any given case it is assumed (depending on the date and discipline of the speaker) either that the spoken is an imperfect and ephemeral instance of the written, or that the written is a dead, fossilized version of living spoken language. The former opinion prevailed in the 19th century; the latter appeared a hundred years ago and has predominated since the middle of the 20th century. But written language has a different dynamic from spoken language. Its relationship to situation, and therefore also to the society that uses it, is different. It therefore changes according to a different set of factors. The relationship between the two media (speech and writing) has also changed historically, in accordance with the way the functions of writing have changed, and the ratio of writers to non-writers. (The function of speech has not changed, except to the extent that its function is affected by its share of the field: where the question was once about the relationship between what was said and what was left to be conveyed by occasion, social context, and body language, now not only is the arena of communication enlarged to contain potentially the global community, but the list of alternatives to direct speech, besides writing, is growing.) Since the mid-20th century the written word has begun to lose its precedence over the spoken. One important result is that only in the past half century, with rates of literacy approaching 100 percent in many parts of the world and few areas left below 50 percent, the ability to read and write has begun to lose its social value, so that where we used to expect people to speak the way they wrote (and make sure they wrote correctly), it is now becoming normal to write the way one speaks. We are going through a period of re-accommodation between writing and speaking. In the Western world this transitional period began with the spread of public education in the mid-19th century. The transitional period will be far shorter outside the Western world, because the rate of social change generally over the past fifty years has been faster, especially in post-colonial territories. Now, with the rise of digital media everywhere, the relationship between speech and writing may currently be in the process of total transformation.

It would therefore be surprising if spoken and written language did not differ in dynamics. Each has no doubt always been affected by the other, but without being determined by it. However, the functional relationship between them and the way they affect each other has changed. The acceleration of social change and the increased demand for reading materials that facilitated the spread of printing set this relationship in the West on a new trajectory some five to four hundred years ago. In the Islamic world on the other hand, and possibly elsewhere, it appears to have been specifically the culture of writing that inhibited the adoption of printing (which barely began before the 19th century even in territories under colonial administration). As a result, now that printing is fully adopted the earlier relationship between spoken and written in the Persianate world, and the Islamic world generally, is more difficult to understand.

The study of language began as philology, which was the study of language as it was preserved in texts, and paid little attention to the social function of writing or the possible effects of writing on language. In the 19th century philology prepared the way for historical linguistics, which continued to focus on textual data. In the early 20th century the publications of Saussure launched modern linguistics and shifted the focus to speech and languages in general rather than languages with textual traditions. Before Saussure linguistic research focused on the grammar of written language, taking classical languages as models and specializing in the critical analysis and reconstruction of textual sources and of long-term change. The study of language since the 1940s, in new departments of linguistics, has focused more and more on the dynamics of spoken language. The study of written language has lost interest, and "philology" is rarely heard. As with all change, there are losses and gains. But for the medievalist who depends on the analysis and interpretation of textual materials, of written usages and their implications and reflections in public life, it is important to take stock of the situation and to work out what types of work may be suffering from neglect. The same is true for the modernist who feels the need to understand how much of the present is a product of the past and needs to be seen in those terms if it is to be usefully understood. Most documents are produced in order to be read by people who know in advance most of what is written in them, and know how to elicit from them the part that is new information. They are therefore written in a conventional style that has developed for the purpose of conveying information in a form that can be quickly grasped. We tend to look for content. We should be looking just as intently for what we can learn from the conventions of style.

The focus on spoken language led rapidly to the collection of vast libraries of data, and changes of orientation towards language study in general. New ways of measuring linguistic change evolved, typified in lexico-statistics and glottochronology. All language was "stated to change its lexicon at an approximately constant rate of speed when investigated by use of a test list of basic words selected for universality of incidence and minimal cultural notation and connotation" (Zengel 1962:132). Although this has been a very useful research tool, it must be remembered that it does not take account of the way textual models may influence, and perhaps inhibit, change in written languages. However, Zengel did also suggest that written language might have a different dynamic:

> A casual sampling of modern languages suggests that a leaning toward conservatism correlates to some degree with a literate tradition. This correlation may be inferred from observations of the various effects of a literary language on its co-existing spoken counterpart.
>
> Affected facets of speech include grammatical forms, pronunciation, and vocabulary. The conservatism of orthography is too obvious to require comment; yet in this connection, there would seem to be an additional correlation between the quantum of literate tradition among a given people at a given time and the degree of flexibility permitted in spelling. If it is true, as these things would indicate, that writing is attended by a linguistic conservatism, then the dynamics of vocabulary change among a wholly literate people should reflect his fact. (1962:132)

The first step is to recognize that while written language may be influenced by speech, its history has not been determined solely by its relationship to a spoken form so much as by the way the activity of writing is socially organized. The reason for this is that until recently in any of the major script traditions written language has been considered more authoritative than speech. There have been exceptions. Socrates' argument in Plato's Phaedrus is well known: that live dialectical enquiry is more valuable than the fossilized record of it in a written text. (We are lucky, however, that Plato left us the written record!) The Islamic "science of biography" (*'ilmu'l-rijāl*) which was developed to substantiate the written record of the oral tradition of the Prophet's utterances provides a further example. The interpretation of the Book par excellence, the Bible, along with its parallels in other religions that claim justification through revealed texts, has similarly depended on oral tradition controlled by the Church, at least down to the Reformation. Today, despite the idiosyncrasies of Anglo-Saxon law with regard to oral evidence, writing is still generally recognized as being more authoritative than speech (not only because of the importance of signatures in identification of responsibility), but not exclusively so. The interpretation of the text may change even though the text may not. Every text needs an interpreter, whether it be the Church for the Bible, your choice of *mujtahid* (qualified scholar) for the Qur'an, or a modern lawyer for the U.S. Constitution.

One of the major distinctions between writing and speech in premodern times was that writing followed models, while in speech there was always the possibility of spontaneity and innovation. In this way writing is comparable to ritual: innovation endangers its efficacy, but interpretation of what has been written, as of what is acted out in ritual, may change with time. Since the earliest and smallest human communities for which we have information have practices that fit our definition of ritual, it would appear that ritual is a normal organizational feature of human cultural life. Any action that is repeated to the point where it becomes by nature repetitive takes on the quality of ritual. In fact repetitive action may be a good minimal definition of ritual (cf. Wallace 1966:233). Such repeated action, including the recognized repetition of what Bohannan (1995) usefully calls particular "action chains," organizes and channels associations and generates meaning for the participants, and in the process introduces order into their understanding of day-to-day life. It also organizes and programs interaction. It thus provides the necessary centripetal complement to the highly productive but uncontrollable process of random association, which dominates our mental processes. Any process of ordering (in the sense of reducing to order) is necessarily selective: order is achieved only by some degree of simplification; some data fit the patterning of the order and are canonized, some do not fit and are left aside. Ritual in this sense functions to organize memory, knowledge, and identity, as well as to channel action. At the level of each individual's cultural-psychological take on the world, for which the terms habitus and propriospect have been used, this organization is in the form of habit. If it becomes obsessive, it is addiction. At the cultural level obsessive organization becomes national, ethnic, or religious fanaticism. Premodern writing always involved the repetition of established formulas. This repetition had a ritual aspect.

Where all interaction is face-to-face, ritual is similarly face-to-face. As some communities became larger and more complex, they began to develop technological means of remote communication. Their ritual practice proliferated and diversified. Writing, from the time of its earliest invention through the period of its gradual assimilation into the culture of administration, historical record, and creative expression, gradually came to subsume many of the functions of ritual, and to serve as the legitimizing basis of others. Now, in complex society, when writing becomes an established organizational tool (starting not with the earliest writing, but by sometime in the 2nd millennium BC) for administration in government, and for memory and meaning in literature, writing begins to legitimize and even to supersede ritual. For some 2000 years now in most of the world's civilizations almost all ritual has been rooted in writing, in sacred or legal texts. Writing provides the dynamic for the heritage and the identity of a community. This force was particularly powerful at a certain stage of the spread of writing skills, which underlay the age of nationalism (cf. Anderson 1991). Writing was associated with identity before the age of nationalism, but the nature of the identity was different when only a small proportion of any community could write. The spread of nationalisms required the spread of writing skills. Now that the relationship between writing and speech is going through another qualitative change, and the authority of written language is declining, we may be within sight of the end of nationalism.

The relationship between writing and ritual is historical. Consideration of how this relationship has evolved will help to clarify some of the distinctive characteristics of writing as a social function. The Axial Age (as Karl Jaspers, 1949, called the period from 800 to 200 BC which saw the emergence of the concepts that provided the core of all the major religions in world history since then) was the period when particular ideas about human life and how the world worked first began to move beyond the boundaries of local communities. This movement began with the circulation of people, which probably resulted from rising densities of population in the eastern Mediterranean, western Asia, northern India, and central China, and the consequent rise in social awareness. The concepts associated with Gautama, Confucius, Socrates, and Zoroaster, which gradually spread to every part of the world in the guise of Buddhism and Christianity, and later Islam, all date from this period and have served as the basis of all subsequent religious and moral thinking. Only later were these ideas understood to have been written (e.g., the Laws of Moses), committed to writing (the Avesta and the Bible), and finally, although revealed in speech, actually conceived as an eternal book (the Qur'an). Important ideas everywhere eventually became associated with writing as soon as they were adopted by the ruling class. Following this period speech continued to serve as the primary medium of communication, but significant utterances were always recorded in writing. Those who could not read (i.e., the majority) relied on those who could— not just to read, but to say what the text really meant, to interpret it. For the written text lacked the kinesics that frames the meaning of the spoken word. The interpretation of the written record was in the hands of the socially recognized writers. With the large-scale adoption of writing as a social value and a political vehicle, not at the individual level but at the level of the organization of communities, we had entered the age of religious communities, which lasted until the 18th century when it was superseded by the age of nationalism. But as is always the case with such social configurations, they cast a shadow over succeeding centuries, down to the present. The Church (which also subsumed the Socratic-Platonist heritage in its Neo-Platonist form) interpreted the written truth in the West, the `ulama in the Islamic south, and the Buddhist monks and Confucian literati in east and southeast Asia. It is interesting that India, despite its contribution of Buddhism to the eastern half of Asia, remained apart from this development, except insofar as it was later included within the Islamic orbit. One possible explanation of this may lie in the distinctive *jati*-based organization of community life (understood in the West as caste) which inhibited the large-scale demographic circulation that developed in other areas.

In all premodern societies with a socially established writing class important rituals have generally been rooted in written texts. Medieval religion was legitimized by texts. Modern religion continues to depend on them. In fact writing itself became a form of ritual: it was repetitive; the same words and phrases were repeated again and again, in the same combinations, with the same spatial configurations on the page. Just as innovation in religious ritual would endanger its efficacy, its authority, so with writing. Essentially, before the modern period writing was socially a very different type of activity from today, in that its primary function was to record for reference.

The study of the historical dynamics of spoken and written language has been hampered by pervasive assumptions about their interdependence. These assumptions need to be made explicit, so that they can be questioned. For most of the past four thousand years or so since writing became routinely involved in a variety of public functions, its development has been closely interrelated with speech, as well as parallel to it. But a brief discussion will illuminate the necessary differences between the dynamic of each—at least until the spread of writing skills in the 20th century which has finally exposed written language to the same variety of social pressures as speech.

The use of spoken language is one of the definitions of the human condition. It is commonly used as the primary criterion for distinguishing us from our primate cousins. It is the essential means of communication that facilitates the social interaction and group learning that makes us human. It is enjoyed by every full member of every human community, even in cases as unusual as that of Helen Keller. Written language, on the other hand, even in the modern world, has more restricted functions that extend beyond but do not fully overlap with speech.

The functions of writing have been different because rather than being acquired without conscious intervention in the process of socialization, writing was a skill that had to be acquired and its acquisition was socially managed. That management remained essentially the same until not much more than one hundred years ago. But since then it has changed, and the relationship of writing and the written language to other forms of communication and organization has transformed its function. The change was launched by the introduction of printing in the 15th century, but it took off with the spread of mass education in the 19th century. About forty years ago, with the spread not only of the written word but of new media, some of which have encroached on the functions of writing, writing began to lose the cultural status that went with this social management. Even elite speech is no longer securely anchored by the written language. Shaw illustrates this in Pygmalion, which takes place not so long ago when there was truly an elite speech and a "correct" style of writing English. Shaw showed how elite speech could be manipulated to subvert the social hierarchy. In little more than half a century this relationship has been transformed, though it is not entirely forgotten. The standards of written language, and its relationship to elite speech, have been subverted by modern social change. The quality of writing as a medium now retains little of its ritual, and has changed and diversified in function.

In the course of ancient and medieval history, despite frequent setbacks, societies overall expanded and became more complex. Consequently, the literate class grew progressively larger and more differentiated. But the overall proportion of literate people in the population of the ancient world, and perhaps more so in the early medieval world, remained small. It is not surprising, therefore, that writing conformed more strictly than ever to established genres and ever more intricate codes, which acquired unique cultural, even symbolic, value. The combination of socially established codes and symbolic value reinforced the cultural status of written texts and inhibited change in the written language, irrespective of change in vernacular spoken language. Since the texts had come to legitimate administrative and other practices, they anchored the formalities of public behavior. Writing had taken on the function of a social stabilizer. In this connection, however, it is interesting to note that while the written language continued to supply models for the organization of behavior in formal public situations, local vernaculars gave way to one or another lingua franca, such as Turki in parts of the Iranian Plateau, and Hindavi in northern India. The continued growth and increasing density and intermingling of populations was presumably a contributing factor.

With the demise of the Western Roman Empire, the Sasanian Empire in western Asia, and the Sui Dynasty in China, within a period of less than 200 years, the quality of writing everywhere (different as it was in each of these three major divisions of the ancient world) changed and was reborn with similar differentiation in the medieval world of the Holy Roman Empire, the Caliphate, and Tang China. These were three distinctly different, but historically related, textual communities. They were textual communities in the sense that being a part of them involved acknowledging an administrative framework that depended on writing. The new situation has been well described by Stock (1984:18): "What was essential for a textual community, whether large or small, was simply a text, an interpreter, and a public."

The populations of each of these three geographical divisions of the medieval world attributed a particular value to its texts. Stock continues:

> The text did not have to be written: oral record, memory and re-performance sufficed. Nor did the public have to be fully lettered. Often, in fact, only the interpres has a direct contact with the literate culture, and, like the twelfth-century heretic Valdes, memorized and communicated his gospel by word of mouth. Yet whatever the original the effects were always roughly comparable. Through the text, or, more accurately, through the interpretation of it, individuals who previously have little else in common were united around common goals.
>
> Similar social origins comprised a sufficient but not necessary condition of participation. The essential bond was forged by means of belief; its cement was faith in the reality of belonging. And these in turn were by-products of a general agreement on the meaning of a text.
>
> From textual communities it was a short step to new rituals of everyday life...It is one of the persistent scholarly myths concerning medieval civilization, fostered by an oversimplified evolutionism, that as writing and education increased, ritual declined. Certainly a number of rites were on the wane: physical symbolism was replaced by property law; elaborate gift transfers gave way to the market economy; and the sacral element in kingship was balanced by a sense of administrative responsibility. But while such rituals deteriorated, another sort of ritual was brought into being and given a social context by groups articulating their self-consciousness for the first time. Heretics, reformers, pilgrims, crusaders, proponents of communes, and even university intellectuals began to define the norms of their behavior, to seek meaning and values over time, and to attempt to locate individual experience within larger schemata. Ritual as a consequence did not die; it flourished in a different mode. The rites of a putatively oral society...began to be looked upon as survivals of an archaic age, while those more closely oriented around a textual presence gained legitimacy and increasingly determined the direction of group action (1984:18).

Once writing had come to enshrine the truth about the human condition, what was written was recited and the recitation was ritually repeated. We are used to it in the context of religious observance, but have already extended its use figuratively for repetitive activity that has more to do with self-expression, identity, or display than anything functional. In the medieval period all formal ritual was legitimated by written texts. The ritual use of texts in predictably repetitive events acts as a social magnet, and as participation in them expands they generate cultural meaning that inhibits change. Writing not only becomes ritual, but gradually subsumes all ritual. Then as traditional ritual becomes devalued, as orientations towards religion begin to change under humanism, some forms of repetitive ritual behavior that take its place are transformed into what we now understand simply as formality. Similarly, all public behavior that was considered significant was recorded in writing, with the result that writing became associated with formality. Writing in fact became the source of both ritual and formality. Writing worked as ritual so long as writing had high cultural value, and written language was different from and more highly valued than spoken language, so long as it was important to write correctly. Over the past century as writing everywhere has increased and spread more evenly through most societies, this role has diminished, but it still casts a shadow over current life and our understanding of the world, although the stratification on the basis of writing that has ruled social history for five millennia is fading. If we do not reconstruct the history of writing now, these important qualitative details will recede beyond our field of historical vision.

It is generally assumed that the number of people reading and writing in a particular society is a function of the intellectual difficulty of acquiring the skill. This assumption derives from another: that reading and writing becomes easier as modes of writing become closer to straightforward phonetic analysis of speech. But this argument ignores the statistical evidence of the past century (which shows high rates of literacy in, for example, Japan and Kerala), as well as any comparison between the spelling of English and French[3] which do not spell phonetically on the one hand and (for example) Italian or Turkish on the other, which do. It also ignores the historical example of Attic Greek. By the 8th century BC Greek had become the first language ever to be written in a fully analytical alphabet representing all phonemically significant components of speech with a one-to-one consonant and vowel relationship to various local standards of speech. The alphabet was adapted directly from the Phoenician consonantal script. The development from consonant only to full consonant-vowel analysis may have been facilitated by the difficulty of adapting the Semitic values to Greek phonemes (cf. Havelock 1982:12). We do not know how long it took. But by the 5th century this alphabet had not only become standard but was being used throughout the Greek-speaking world of the Mediterranean, Asia Minor, and the Black Sea. Over the succeeding centuries, as its usage spread much further following Alexander's conquests, the pronunciation changed radically, in ways that completely changed the sound-sign relationship by reducing the number of vowel sounds. But little or no change was introduced to spelling or orthography. The orthography of modern Greek continues the spellings of ancient Greek with a different (scarcely recognizable) pronunciation.

The minor reform of English spelling by Webster in the early 19th century provides a similar, though less sensational illustration. It is obviously more important to English speakers in different parts of the world that they should be able to share written material than that they should write the way they speak. When a language becomes a medium of written communication its usage expands into a larger arena. The language of a speech community (insofar as it is unrelated to writing) is subject to no controls besides the desire for mutual intelligibility, and changes according to the spontaneity of speech. A written language, on the other hand, depends on the interest in holding together multiple speech communities in a single universe of communication. The close relationship between spoken and written Italian, or Turkish, is due to the recent date of the establishment of their orthography as national languages (compared to French and English), in addition to (in the case of Turkish, or Tojiki) an explicit interest in breaking certain continuities from the past. Even so, in neither case do their written forms represent country-wide vernacular pronunciation or speech. Writing has been a crucial factor in the history of large-scale organization. But the social organization of the uses of reading and writing and of recruitment or induction into classes of readers and writers has been a much more important factor historically than the nature of the relationship between written and spoken language. It is unlikely that the technical nature of the script, and the degree to which it was analytical, could have been a factor in the recruitment of writers, or any other aspect, positive or negative, of the historical spread of written Persian. Alphabets are anyway rarely 100 percent analytical (cf. the various applications of Roman to modern European languages), and although they may inhibit change in vocabulary and syntax they will always eventually be left behind in the representation not only of phonetic, but also phonemic distinction. Written forms of language, even when launched as the best representation of a spoken vernacular (cf. Tojiki), are never changed in step with change in the spoken language.

Nevertheless, the functionality of writing was not static from 3000 BC to modern times. It evolved, slowly but steadily. It began as a way to record, and later to represent and to legitimate. The type of material it was used to record expanded in stages down to modern times. Its earliest uses were in trade (Schmandt-Besserat 1996), which soon expanded to administration, and only later to literature. Intellectual inquiry came much later. The numbers of writers increased but remained small. They wrote for interaction with each other, and their interaction was exclusive. By virtue of this exclusiveness writers became a new privileged class. If writing is useful and only few people can write to each other, they acquire social status in inverse proportion to their numbers. If, however, their numbers expand significantly, so that they cease to be a minority, and writing becomes a general skill expected of everyone, the value of writing changes. Hence our modern difficulty in understanding medieval society in general and other medieval societies, such as Persianate civilization, in particular. Since written texts represented powerful persons, writing took on power of its own, and soon became an important symbol of power. Its expansion then into the field of ritual and divine power was straightforward. But still its function was to record, whether data, instruction, or narrative. Since it always required a professional to interpret its meaning, the nature of its relationship to speech (phonetic and analytical, or analogical) was irrelevant. The use of writing as an independent medium not only of direct communication but of intellectual exploration, research, and innovation is relatively new, beginning probably in the late medieval period, but it did not become common until the rise of the diary and the novel (in English) in the 17th and 18th centuries. This change in function suggested the need for a direct relationship to speech, and (for the first time) to innovative expression. Martin Amis' *War against Cliché* (2001) could not have been written much more than a hundred years ago (cf. *OED Supplement,* "cliché").

A similar change of values associated with the advance of modernity lies in the rise of numeracy (cf. Porter 1995). Only since the 18th century did it gradually become important to use numbers for the demonstration of significance. If the ability to write were important, we began to need statistics to demonstrate it. The term "literacy" therefore became most commonly associated with the statistical distribution of levels of reading and writing skills in various populations. Data of this type would of course be invaluable for the larger understanding of what we now call "civil society" in premodern times, but unfortunately for the period before the rise of numeracy it is not available.

The requirements and consequences of being able to read and write began to attract academic interest at about the time when it appeared to be within universal reach, in the middle of the last century. A number of studies of the relationship between writing and speech in ancient Greece in the first half of the century were followed in the 1950s by inquiries into what purported to be the significance of literacy in general. Anthropologists became major players in response to a paper by Goody and Watt (1963). Goody alone authored five books on the subject in the following twenty years. This work contrasted literacy with orality, especially literate modern societies with the non-literate societies of the ethnographic literature. It has certainly succeeded in greatly expanding our understanding of the ways in which the ability to record in writing and retrieve from written material, not only data and opinion, but all forms of research and literary work, has changed the quality of human life, in particular the orientation towards time, truth, and logical argument. However, it is surprisingly occidentocentric: it pays little serious attention to the question of whether writing might have functioned differently under different writing technologies, or indeed other differences in social or cultural context. Although it contains references to historical societies that employed non-Western scripts, there is scarcely any contribution from scholars who were socialized in the use of these other scripts, or trained in the academic study of them. Were the consequences of literacy different according to the ratio of writers to non-writers in a given society? What were the differences in the ways people became writers? Are these differences correlated with civilizations, or particular languages, or with what we have called script-families? (These questions are after all obvious anthropological, as well as historical, questions.) Instead the interest throughout, whether the discussion is of ancient, medieval, or modern society, is in the intellectual consequences of the use of writing. Perhaps Margaret Thatcher's famous dictum (talking to *Women's Own* magazine, October 31, 1987) that "there is no such thing as society" represents modern Western cultural orientations to the extent that even anthropologists have been swept up in it. However, our own experience in the study of Persian has convinced us that irrespective of differences in spoken language, there are differences not only in the way people write but also in the way they read—comprehensive differences in the function of literacy that depend on the mechanics of script and even script style (since Persian is written in a distinctive style of the Arabic script, different from other Arabic-script languages except Urdu and some Ottoman). This situation began to change with the introduction of printing, but the conditions of the past continue to cast a shadow over the present and have conditioned the way things worked out later. Since printing spread through the rest of the world unevenly, the shadow of the past is darker in some parts of the world than others—especially in Afghanistan, Iran, and Pakistan where the historical sociology of the writing class before printing still remained an important factor—until the recent introduction of the cell phone.

It is time to look more carefully at the discussion of literacy that has evolved over the past half century. It is worth noting to begin with that the concept "literacy" was coined only recently: the *Oxford English Dictionary* lists the first usage in 1883—as a back-formation (ironically) from "illiteracy" that is cited over two hundred years earlier, in 1660, shortly after the initial acceleration in the spread of writing skills in the wake of the post-Reformation bible-printing boom. In both cases, illiteracy and literacy, it is important to note that the implications were of social status. In the 17th century "illiteracy" was used to exclude the *hoi polloi* from the elite by indicating lack of general education and suitability for citizenship. By the end of the 19th century on the other hand, it was useful to have a word like "literacy" for the inclusion of an increasing proportion of the working class into the fast-evolving modern economy which with the approach of Taylorist systems of production depended more and more on the written word in bureaucratic organization. Obviously these terms carry a historical burden which still colors our understanding and use of them.

Over the past forty years or so the term "literacy" has acquired an iconic quality as one of the major goals and indices of international development. Studies of literacy since the 1960s have been generally lacking in historical and cross-cultural perspective, and have been motivated by a different range of questions from those addressed in this volume. Rather than attempt to exorcise the spirit of this literature, we have considered it preferable to eschew the use of the term literacy as far as possible in our own arguments, except where it is necessary in the discussion of published work. The questions we address deal simply with the medieval sociology of writing and written language. The connotations of our modern terms literacy and illiteracy would be confusing for the arguments we wish to make about the past, as of course any suggestion of a need for statistics would be. However, since we realize that these connotations may suggest themselves to readers anyway, we have thought it necessary in addition to review the products of this literature so that we can distinguish our objectives from it more explicitly.

By the late 1960s the ideas developed by Goody, Watt, and Havelock had come to be known as "the literacy thesis." The arguments seemed to culminate in a number of synthetic publications in the 1980s (see especially the items by Graff) and then disintegrate under criticism in the 1990s (Halverson 1991, 1992, Collins 1995). The general argument was that writing is a technology that transforms human thinking with regard in particular to its relationship to language, to tradition, and to the past in general. This argument projects the functionality of literacy in the 20th century back into the past before the term was coined, and into other writing traditions in which writing has different histories. Little attention was given to the fact that in the ancient world before writing transformed thinking, it transformed and extended the organization of society, and that to a large extent it was its transformation of organization that facilitated the transformation of thought. Despite plentiful references to earlier times and other civilizations by well-known anthropologists as well as other social scientists, it is quite ethnocentrically based on assumptions that have to do with full participation in modern society as we know it in the West, and the difference such participation makes to the quality of life in terms of intellectual awareness. It does not make any serious effort to question or investigate current implicit assumptions such as (a) literacy is good, (b) phonetic alphabetization makes it easier to acquire (to the extent that it is optimally analytical), and (c) other ways of writing (*sc.* all non-Western scripts) are a barrier to progress, because they are considered (sometimes erroneously) to be in varying degrees less analytical. Examples of societies with high rates of participation in text-based communities, using scripts which are less analytical (such as Japanese, Malayalam) are ignored.

The actual thesis begins with the claim that the spread of writing facilitated a fundamental transformation in the nature of knowledge and the quality of culture, including the way people think. In particular, arguments have been made about changes in (a) the understanding of history in relation to myth, (b) understanding of truth (based on logic or systematic critical enquiry) in relation to opinion, and (c) the criteria for skepticism about received tradition. This way of thinking is in tune with the general Western intellectual climate of the time. For example, Derrida (cf. Collins 1995:81) argued for a different purpose that the way thoughts are recorded in writing strongly affects the nature of knowledge. Overall the results are understood to lead in the direction of analysis, logic, individuation, and of changes in attitudes towards authority, favoring democratic tendencies in all social and political situations (Collins 1995:77). Halverson (1992:301) puts it succinctly: "the principal claim of the literacy thesis is that the development of logical thought (syllogistic reasoning, formal operations, higher psychological processes) is dependent on writing, both in theory and in historical fact." The importance of alphabetic writing in this process is also emphasized (Olson 1994).

Goody's work emphasized differences in the quality of thought. This led to a continuous series of publications with similar emphases over the following three decades. Even where Goody addresses the organization of society in relation to writing (1986) he subordinates it even in the title to "the logic of writing." But it did not take long for criticism to begin to appear. Halverson (1992) has very usefully summarized the obvious objections. What remains is no longer a difference in the quality of thought (which would have put us back with Lévy-Bruhl's 1925 characterization of the difference between civilized and primitive thought), but factors that have to do with organization. It is clear that writing adds a new quality to our ability to communicate. It extends both space and time. Speech leaves no record; writing is a record. Moreover, although speech can be formal, even as formal as writing, written communication can never be as spontaneous as speech. Usage in written communication changes according to a different dynamic because the medium is different. Writing also releases the literate, and potentially their whole society, from the sociolinguistic monopoly of oral communication and allows the development of a completely different sociolinguistics, of written communication (see discussion of diplomatics, above). Communication by writing is different because (a) it works in a different quality of relationship, and (b) it facilitates communication beyond the boundaries of group membership. As a result, whereas oral communication is conditioned by the relationship of the interlocutors (authority and other personal factors and needs), communication through writing is conditioned by the symbolism of the way the semantic content of the text is materially presented, and may appear differently in different texts. The term "restricted literacy" has been introduced for the discussion of situations where only a minority can read and write, but without distinguishing between modern situations where writing is encouraged or expected and medieval situations where it was not. The possible association with a difference in the quality of thought remains in the background but the case against it is supported by the argument that if we were able to test IQ cross-culturally (we know we cannot) we assume we would find ranges of IQ in small technologically simple societies without writing similar to those in large modern technologically advanced societies. This argument is supported ingeniously by Wallace (1961).

In the final analysis writing is a different form of communication from talking. Speaking is not only relatively spontaneous and (before electronic recording and stenography) not possible to store or recreate. Of equal importance is the fact that it can be adapted in interaction with the interlocutor while in progress. Writing is relatively planned and subject to more conscious structuring and is available for re-reading, study, commentary, and interpretation, and for use as evidence. It is not interactive. The meaning of speech (before the telephone, cf. Ronell 1989) is incomplete without its accompanying body language, on which it largely depends. Although interlocutors commonly misunderstand or talk past each other, they are always to some degree interacting directly. The meaning of the written text can carry with it only part of the context needed for its interpretation, and that context can be carefully prepared and managed.

We may add that writing also facilitates analysis, both of text and of language itself. (If the 4th century BC Sanskrit grammarian Panini really was unlettered, his work is for that reason unique among studies of grammar.) Since it is in the nature of written languages to be written for communication beyond the immediate spatial and temporal situations of their texts, they expand cultural universes and standardize the expression of all intellectual activity within that expanded cultural framework. Writing in this sense became an integral conditioning feature in our cultural common sense. For this reason it is very difficult for us to reconstruct preliterate cultural processes and the effects on them of what we call the institutionalization of writing. The situation is made much more difficult by the fact that the great majority of people interested in the subject are modernists and Westerners, and do not have personal experience of non-Western forms of writing, or empathy with premodern situations where writing was valued very differently from today.

It is surprising to find that most of the ideas advanced in the discussion of literacy initiated by Goody, Watt, Havelock, and others, in the 1960s, as well as the criticisms summarized later by Halverson, may be found juxtaposed in a publication of the much more widely known author Lévi-Strauss from a decade earlier. Interestingly Lévi-Strauss starts with the social arguments and casts them negatively:

> Writing is a strange thing...[It] might be regarded as a form of artificial memory, whose development should be accompanied by a deeper knowledge of the past and, therefore, by a greater ability to organize the present and the future...The one phenomenon which has invariably accompanied it is the formation of cities and empires: the integration into a political system, that is to say, of a considerable number of individuals, and the distribution of those individuals into a hierarchy of castes and classes. Such is, at any rate, the type of development which we find, from Egypt right across to China, at the moment when writing makes its debuts; it seems to favor rather the exploitation than the enlightenment of mankind. This exploitation made it possible to assemble workpeople by the thousand and set them tasks that taxed them to the limits of their strength: to this, surely, we must attribute the beginnings of architecture as we know it. If my hypothesis is correct, the primary function of writing, as a means of communication, is to facilitate the enslavement of other human beings. The use of writing for disinterested ends, and with a view to satisfactions of the mind in the fields either of science or the arts, is a secondary result of its invention—and may even be no more than a way of reinforcing, justifying, or dissimulating its primary function.
>
> Yet nothing of what we know of writing, or of its role in evolution, can be said to justify this conception... (1961:291–92)

There is in fact a serious flaw in all the arguments that make any claim of causality for writing. If writing were really the cause of something, how will we explain how writing appeared and evolved as it did, differently in particular locations, before becoming more generally distributed? In order to resolve this problem it is necessary to suggest that the phenomena Havelock, Goody, and Olson ascribe to writing are in fact together with writing the consequences of something else that may be evident in the historical record. Jaspers' formulation of the Axial Age—a period during which writing spread significantly—is a useful indication. What was unprecedented about the function of writing in 5th century Athens was its social context, not the fact that it was alphabetic! Writing became more important in China, India, and the Greco-Roman world of the Mediterranean and western Asia in the second half of the 1st millennium BC because of the expanding horizons, rising socio-political awareness, now referred to as imaginaries, that underlay the Axial Age. Earlier stages of the historical development of writing similarly coincided with stages in the historical development of civilizations. We should also remember that when we talk about the beginning of writing at the end of the 4th millennium, we are talking about the earliest writing on materials durable enough to have come down to us. Presumably less permanent records were being made on whatever materials came to hand for current purposes long in advance of this date, in association with other unrecorded stages in the rise of social awareness, which began with the steady increase in the size of communities after the Neolithic transition.

We can now continue with our discussion of the development of writing as an organizational tool, the changing relationship between writers and non-writers in particular medieval societies, and the historical consequences, both formally in government and administration, and informally in trade and other social relations. Writing in this rather different sense—social and societal, rather than individual and cultural (though it is a question more of emphasis than analytical distinction)—replaced genealogical rationalization (which was still an important factor in 5th-century Athens) with bureaucratic administration, and direct and indirect exchange with financial liquidity. It facilitated the separation of social role from family or clan relationship, position from personality, the first step in the development of the idea of the corporation sole, and later the corporation in general, which is the hallmark of modern society. Writing seen in this light was a technological innovation associated with the human ability to organize. Without the will to organize larger and larger numbers of people, writing would have remained no more than an interesting historical curiosity. Who could write and how many could write was a less important question than whether and how writing could be used to organize the society. The illiterate Mongols used writing to organize and administer their (only partly literate) subjects (Brose 2000:397). Even Akbar, the Mughal Emperor, may not have been literate himself. All these sophisticated uses of writing were facilitated by the expansion of social horizons that came with increasing population densities and increasing rates of change accelerated by the disruptions caused by recurrent warfare.

The significance of the idea of writing as an institution in a premodern society is that in any given population, irrespective of the distribution of functional writing, the norms of interaction through writing provide the institutional base of expectations not only for administration but also for formal cultural conceptualization, and even the norms of public behavior. Since the written word, along with the physical document that conveys it, embodies administrative authority, it structures social interaction. Further, through its capacity to formulate and enshrine complex concepts, and to order them hierarchically, written language also structures culture at the level of the civilization in which it is the common form of communication and formal interaction, the koine. In this function writing plays a role in premodern society which is comparable to what in the modern world we might recognize as a national culture. Colonialism disrupted the functions of the institution of writing because it changed the field of awareness by disrupting and expanding it beyond the civilization it was historically associated with it. Disruption always causes change. The institution of writing progressively extended not only the temporal but the geographical awareness of civilized life. It provided organizational time-depth as well as geographic expansion to civilized society. It stabilized administrative practice and standardized the idioms of expressive culture throughout the population that supported the sense of identity. It is an irony of history that the writing of vernacular languages (Ottoman Turkish, Pashto, Sindhi, Urdu, etc.) at the end of the medieval period, which was also a product of rising awareness, actually created boundaries to the field of awareness and facilitated the emergence of nationalism and the division and conflicts associated with it in the modern world.

Besides the literacy debate of recent decades, there is one other modern debate from which we wish to distinguish the objectives of this volume, the idea of diglossia. In the sense in which the term diglossia has been developed by linguists to categorize languages that share a social arena with one or more other languages, Persian is not a diglossic language (see Perry, chapter 1, this volume). The term diglossia was introduced from the French *diglossie* by the linguist C.A. Ferguson (1959) to facilitate discussion of the relationship between two languages used in the same speech community, one for formal or public situations, the other informal or non-public use. This term, which has proved useful for general discussion of many language situations in different parts of the world, especially India, is also extended by some writers to cover the status of written Persian in relation to various other spoken languages in Persianate society. But the use of the term diglossia brings with it all the other assumptions of linguists which because they assume writing to be secondary to speech are unhelpful in the study of the historical role of written Persian. It not only hides the importance of writing as a distinct medium, but suggests a framework for its discussion that is incompatible with the idea that written language may have a distinct dynamic of its own. The point is subtle. Diglossia is typically understood to signify relative social status of language use, but not because of the social function of writing. What is different about the Persian case is the special form of the written language, in that it remained intelligible for so long over such a vast area, and that its relationship to the spoken language varied from place to place and from time to time from something close to a one-to-one relationship to almost no relationship at all. We are concerned with different dynamics of change between written and spoken language. The diglossia discourse is insensitive to this issue and distracts attention from it.

Until the end of the medieval period the rate of change in written Persian continued to be held in check by the cultural value of the canon of written texts and their codes of usage. For this reason now that the Persianate world is fragmented into nation-states, many of the literary figures of the high medieval period are claimed as natives of two, three, or even four modern states. The rise of social awareness reflected in the spread of printing after the Reformation in 16th–17th century Europe eventually broke down the social boundaries of writing. The cultural value of writing was so deeply rooted that it eroded only slowly. As the skills of reading and writing began finally to spread faster after the Industrial Revolution, first through each Western society and then throughout the world, a qualitative change set in. When (almost) all are literate, there is no longer a literate class to insist on conformity to the codes that were the foundation of the symbolic value of the text. Language in general is no longer anchored by any socially established rules. This change is reflected in changing emphases in education and the academic enterprise. The spoken language has carried the written language with it—a process that never happened in situations where writing was still linked to the status of a special class.

The historical relationship between written and spoken language has passed through a number of changes since the emergence of writing five thousand years ago. The nature of the koine changed and developed in relation to other types of change: the language of the civilization was sometimes (but not always) a lingua franca (a second language for oral communication between speakers of different local languages); more recently it has become the national language in the new national-state arenas of Iran, Afghanistan, and Tajikistan. In Afghanistan Persian shares its national status with Pashto, the written language of the Pashtuns who created the polity in the 18th century. Urdu has taken over from Persian in both these roles in Pakistan. The distinction between them is not always clear, because it depends to some extent on the degree to which the written form of the language continues to drive the spoken, which is a function of the rate of modern social change. It is in the nature of a koine (as the common language of a historical civilization) to work largely without the unrecorded element of body language, though the unwritten always lurks to some extent behind the written. A significant property of the koine—especially significant in the case of Persian because of the geographical and temporal extent of its currency—is that its users can and do draw on vast lexical resources and ranges of associations and connotations.

The differences between the organization of writing in Christendom and Islamdom are particularly interesting. Latin writing centered on the Church. Its practice was socially limited in various ways. Hellenistic writing had been built on the heritage of classical Greek. The central features in Islam on the other hand were the Qur'an and the *madrasa*. To these were added first a secular bureaucracy, which in Syria, Mesopotamia, and Iran was adapted from the personnel as well as the norms of the pre-existing imperial administrations, especially the Sasanian. The second significant development (particularly in the Persianate world) was that it spread from the rulers' courts, not from any central institution or even the *madrasa*. The political structure of the Islamic world was distinctively different from anything that preceded it. Beginning in the 9th century the rulers' courts, drawing on the Sasanian heritage but conditioned by the new Islamic ethos, generated new organizational forms, new ways of organizing ideas and nar-

rative or process, not only in protocol but in the various genres of belles
lettres. In all these dimensions of writing there was continuity from pre-
existing usage, stretching back in some measure to the Achaemenians and
their Elamite and earlier Mesopotamian scribes. The overall distinguishing
features of Islamic writing, in our sense, therefore, features that distinguish
it from writing in the West and elsewhere, are (a) cultural orientation to
the Qur'an as a written text, to be read and learned by all, (b) the scribal
tradition, established in a social class in pre-Islamic Sasanian society, and (c)
the combination of Arabic/Islamic and Persian/imperial concepts and the
ordering of the result with New Persian syntax and word-building.

The central features in the West were the Church, the monasteries,
and later the universities. In the Western medieval tradition, writing was
grounded in and stabilized by the study of Latin and Greek, which continued as the primary source of new vocabulary. What the non-literate part
of the population spoke is not always clear. Only later, when some of the
vernacular languages began to displace Latin, was the basis of writing wid-
ened and the spoken language began to show through the new written languages. The Islamic tradition focused on the Qur'an. The latter produced
the *madrasa* system of instruction in writing. As the first four or so centuries
of the Islamic period wore on, the Iranian current supplied the administrative skills and organization to run the government, and especially the
chancelleries. The professional secretaries were educated both within and
outside the *madrasa* tradition, and maintained their class identity, the heritage of Sasanian social organization (cf. Dumezil in Littleton 1982), in the
great scribal families who kept a grip on the profession. In the Islamic world
the basis of writing was the study of the Qur'an and a tradition of memo-
rizing a sacred text, all in a language that most people, to some degree or
other, recognized visually but understood only imperfectly. The emergence
of a social category of professional memorizers of the Qur'an reinforced
the status of written language in a way that was peculiar to the larger Islamic civilization. As a result of these differences in organization, the process of vernacularization that would be comparable to the late medieval
emergence of Italian and French did not emerge in the Islamic world until
later, and it began on the peripheries with Ottoman Turkish, Pashto, Sindhi,
and Urdu where Islamic governments ruled over non-Muslim populations.

In conclusion let us summarize the major points of our argument. We
began the project which led to this volume because we wanted to work

out a way to teach our students, who were socialized to write in Roman, to write Persian in ways that would not immediately give them away as foreigners. We sought to understand the native learning process both as it is taught in today's schools and as the system has developed historically. As we learned more, we found ourselves questioning many of the assumptions we had internalized from reading work on literacy published over the past fifty years, both work on literacy rates in the modern world and how to improve them and work on the significance of literacy in world history. What we learned about Persian writing that challenged these assumptions included:

- the relatively low level of participation in any Persianate reading-writing community (beyond the ability to recite from a text of the Qur'an) down to the beginning of the changes induced by a closer relationship with the more widely literate societies of the West that began in the 19th century, and the relatively slow rate of increase from then until social change began to accelerate in most places in the 1960s.
- the impressive success of the Literacy Corps in Iran following the social change induced by Land Reform in 1963, compared for example with Pakistan which despite the disruptions of war with India in 1965 and 1971 did not experience a major acceleration of social change until later in the 1970s.
- the acceleration in the rate of change since 1963, and especially since 1979, in the relationship between spoken and written Persian in Iran.
- the neglect of Urdu script and the increasing use of Roman in Pakistan (and India), where since the 1980s Urdu is still associated with the social class structure of the past and Roman is the medium of new broader networks of interaction offered by the effects of globalization.

We therefore began to explore the historical relationship between Persianate literacy and its social context. Based on what we learned about the historical record of literacy in Persian, which is illustrated in the following chapters, we have sought in this introduction to shift the emphasis in the study of literacy in general away from an exclusive attention to its (cultural and psychological) role in the facilitation of systematic thinking and the expansion of knowledge to its (social) role in the facilitation of the growth of larger and more complex systems of community organization, imperial administrations, and modern nationalist movements (cf. Anderson 1991).

We would now argue that the latter, the social role, is foundational and serves as a prerequisite for the former, its role in the advancement of knowledge and analytical thought. In this connection it is useful to consider writing in the context of the history of technology and compare the relationship between its invention and adoption with that of other technologies. In a discussion of very different types of technology at roughly the same time the literacy debate was getting underway, the Danish economist Ester Boserup (1964; cf. Spooner 1972) developed the argument that the emergence of new ideas is not predictably related to their adoption. Moreover, it is their adoption rather than their invention that is historically significant, and adoption depends on the relationship to existing social process. In her historical analyses Boserup emphasized demographic process, especially population growth. Demographic change (whether growth, migration, or decline) underlies most social change. Change in the numbers and densities and age-sex pyramids of populations modifies or disrupts relationships and opens up opportunities for spreading new technologies, which in turn facilitate further change. Stable relationships on the other hand inhibit change. As population grew in the ancient world, writing took off first in relation to expanding trade (five thousand years ago), then to expanding needs for administration (2nd millennium BC), more recently to the industrial revolution (19th century), and more recently still to the globalizing processes induced by the new densities of a world population approaching seven billion.

In the case of each of the major languages of historical writing we have touched on besides Persian, especially Latin, Greek, and Chinese, the relationship between the written and spoken has evolved differently. Efforts to explain this difference have always tended to favor arguments from the analytical power of the script. We are challenging such arguments by suggesting first that insofar as writing is learned analytically, it is not in terms of the analysis of the spoken word, but of the components of the writing process; that experienced readers scan pictographically, not analytically; and that a comparison of modern literacy rates does not support it. Secondly, we would argue that the ultimate determinant of literacy rates anywhere has been the way the society has been structured to restrict or encourage reading and writing.

Two further examples may help to clarify as well as support this argument. First, before the 1960s young people in Iran who were taught in maktabs (traditional schools) to read the Qur'an did not in general continue on to read and write Persian. Second, some of the Baloch Spooner worked with in Makran in the 1960s could read and write either Persian or Urdu, but when confronted with a page of text in their own language, Balochi, were unable to read it and uninterested in learning. (Publication in Balochi, for which writing was introduced by missionaries a century ago, was at the time being promoted by the Baloch Academy in Quetta, and a number of publications were becoming available for the first time in Balochi written in the Urdu version of the Arabic script.)

At any given point in the history of any of these traditions the significance of literacy was a function of the relationship between the literate and the non-literate, and the relative numbers of each. As we know from Chomsky, there are essentially no constraints on the rate of change in spoken language, except perhaps in highly formal situations, which are only a very small proportion of all linguistic events. Although spoken language may be composed largely of customary expressions that continually recur in interaction, it can on any particular occasion include wording or phraseology that has never been used before, which in turn may or may not catch on. Other types of change—demographic or environmental—alter the context in which people speak to each other and induce linguistic change. But written language works differently. Before writing began to spread throughout whole populations, only a century and a half ago, not only was the number of writers small, but it differed from one script tradition to another, and to some extent within script families. The reason for this is that medieval societies generally were much more structured. People were born into social slots; each person knew their place. While some manipulated the structure and moved up the ladder, and some slid down, most lived their lives in the social station they were born into. People did not expect change. Progress in the sense we understand it today is a modern concept. Although writing was within the intellectual reach of all, it attached to only certain positions in the society; if you did not occupy one of those positions, being able to write was not only of no use to you, it was of no interest.

The smaller the writing class, the more jealously it guarded admission to its status. To a large degree it was able to control admission to its ranks, and so to govern the use of writing, because it could choose whom to recruit and whom to teach, and it was the arbiter of the established codes of the written language. Strict frameworks of rules were maintained for the use of language in writing. It was essential to be able to write things as they had already been written, both in terms of the choice and ordering of words and in terms of their arrangement in the document. New wording,

phraseology, or arrangement of words was evidence of lack of social quali-
fication and lack of authority. Society did change in the course of the medieval period, but relatively slowly and unevenly. As populations grew urban
communities became larger and denser, and social relations became more
complex, with the result that gradually more people found a use in writing
and became interested in doing it. Growth began to accelerate significantly
only with the spread of printing, but the spread of printing was similarly a
function of socio-economic growth and change. Throughout this period of
change the status of the writing classes in various traditions relative to other
classes of the population varied, but was universally high, because people
who could read and write were not only closer to political and religious
authority, but through the written word their awareness was opened up to
broader horizons beyond the awareness of the non-literate majority, so that
they could both think and do things others could not. By the middle of the
20th century the social structure that privileged correct writing was weakening in America and England and this weakening was spreading through
Europe and (unevenly) into other parts of the world. The Literacy Corps of
the Shāh's White Revolution of 1963 ironically hastened the rise of socio-
political awareness throughout Iran which led to his ouster in 1979, and
continues to facilitate democratic process in the Islamic Republic.

   We do not argue that writing causes social change, but that the ability to read and write spreads hand-in-hand with the type of social change
that expands social horizons. The countries with the lowest rates of literacy
in the modern world, such as Afghanistan and Pakistan, are those where
social change was latest to accelerate. What we recognize as the mark of
modern society in most parts of the world today, irrespective of cultural
flavor, is an unprecedented fluidity in social relations and interaction. In
these social conditions there are no longer any barriers to the spread of
writing, whether visible or invisible. In Pakistan the rate of social change
has accelerated so fast over the past decade, as a result of its strategic location at the crossroads of negative as well as positive forces of globalization,
that ordinary people who barely saw the need to write Urdu now comfortably do text-messaging on their cell phones in Roman. They are using a
combination of new technologies not because they have become smarter
or received better education, or because these technologies have only now
become available, but because they make it possible for them to do things
they now want to do. A decade earlier would have been too soon. For simi-

lar reasons the Apple Newton (in the U.S.) was a flop in 1993, but five years later the Palm Pilot offering the same applications was a major success. The uses of writing, which survived the social and cultural change and recurrent disruptions from the 2nd millennium BC till the middle of the 20th century essentially unchanged, appear now to be moving into a completely new phase that could barely be foreseen as little as a decade ago. We shall return to this topic in the Afterword at the end of the volume.

V. INTRODUCTION TO THE FOLLOWING CHAPTERS

The subject matter of the following chapters is diverse. Although each of the first ten chapters focuses on one or more aspects of the Persian language as it has been written over the past millennium, the discussion ranges not only from the ancient world to the present, but from Europe to China, dealing with the relationship of spoken to written language and the development of genres. The final chapters compare Persian with the Latinate and Sinic traditions to the west and east of it, which though contemporary and parallel are significantly different in ways that illuminate the trajectory and the historical significance of the Persianate case.

As the participants prepared for the meeting on which this volume is based we asked them to give special attention to the following questions:
• What factors underlay the stability and standardization of the Persian koine for so long over such a vast area? What factors might have affected the rate of change?
• How were writers recruited and how was the written language controlled?
• How were readers and other users of documents influenced by the writers and their texts, and vice versa?
• Does the formality of written usage throw light on the procedures of political and other cultural practice?

The discussion returned to these questions regularly throughout the three days of the meeting. Each contributor and discussant addressed them from a different angle, drawing on different research backgrounds. We looked first at the early period when New Persian became established, and then moved on chronologically through its spread east and west, and finally its recent fragmentation, all the time questioning the stability and homogeneity of written Persian in relation to other languages.

We have therefore divided the body of the book into four parts. Part One, Foundations, begins with a detailed account by John Perry of what can be known about how Middle Persian evolved over a space of a century and a half (beginning with the Arab conquest of the mid-7th century) into its function as the core feature of Persianate civilization, and (a millennium later) of Persian ethnic and national identity. Perry's chapter is a detailed inquiry into the issues surrounding the re-emergence of Persian as the primary written language in an Arabic-dominated Islamic world. He describes the relationship of the language that became the koine with the other dialects that were current at the time. In dealing with the challenge of explaining why Persian came to dominate, given the high status of Arabic as the language of the Qur'an and its monopoly of public life for well over a century, he gives special attention to issues such as diglossia which have become standard in the general linguistic literature but may be misleading in the Persian case, and offers other ideas about how Persian could have become so inclusive, so quickly.

The second chapter, by William Hanaway, deals with the writing class, especially the profession of *munshi*. Hanaway discusses the formation and professional activities of the writing class and its social configuration. The third chapter, by A.H. Morton, adds the dimension of the textual tradition, responding to questions about the relationship between different versions of the works that came to form the canon. He helps us understand the processes of continuity and change in the canon by reconstructing the processes of textual transmission over time, and comparing them to the classical record. He shows that we should not assume that once something is written it is unchanging. The cultural value of writing in the medieval period preserved the status of the literate, but paradoxically not the authenticity of what was written. Perhaps partly for that reason, down to the 16th century at least the authority to interpret the text was crucial, and the oral record continued to be important.

In Part Two, which we have called Spread, chapter 4 by David Morgan follows the expansion of the Persianate medium to its limits to the east in Yuan China. Morgan begins with an account of the spread of Persian deep into China in the 13th and 14th centuries—which became known only recently. He demonstrates that Persian was the language of commerce as well as administration not only in Central Asia but even beyond. Next, in chapter 5, Linda Darling takes us to the western limits of the Persianate world in the Ottoman Empire, under which Persian spread to the Balkans. She explains the emergence of the first successor language, Ottoman Turkish, and makes an interesting distinction between the role of Ottoman scribes and their colleagues to the east: "Over the years the Ottomans employed scribes who wrote in Latin, Greek, Italian, Uighur, Persian, Arabic, Serbian, Hungarian, and other languages." Within a century of the arrival of Persian in central China under the Mongols, the Ottomans in the West had begun to outgrow it, perhaps because of the variety of other bureaucratic traditions it encountered in the eastern Roman Empire. In the last chapter of this section, chapter 6, we return to the center of the Persianate world, where Colin Mitchell investigates the sophistication of the main prose genre of *insha,* and the elaboration of other prose models under the Safavids in the 16th and 17th centuries, when Persianate identity was beginning to evolve into Persian ethnic and eventually national identity. Mitchell explains with copious detail how the *munshi's* social function evolved to become the ultimate vehicle for not only administration but the expression of Persianate high culture, *adab,* and provides a window on later stages of development.

Part Three, Vernacularization and Nationalism, takes us into the transitional period of the rise of peripheral vernaculars to general acceptance as vehicles of literacy. The process may have been accelerated by the intrusion of outside (Western) interests, which led to the emergence of nationalism. Four chapters illustrate different stages of the decline and breakup of the Persianate ecumene. The first, chapter 7 by Senzil Nawid, compares the writing of two historians spanning the late 18th to the mid 19th centuries. The second, by Aslam Syed, deals with the competition between Persian and Urdu in northern India in the same period, taking us further into the processes of vernacularization that took place during the British period. The third, by Anwar Moazzam, deals with the final official shift to Urdu in Hyderābād several decades later than northern India. Finally, in chapter 10 Michael Fisher takes us into the early teaching of Persian as a foreign language outside the Persianate world, perhaps the earliest appearance of the modern profession of foreign-language teaching before the emergence of the Levantine dragoman.

Finally, in Part Four, The Larger Context, Joseph Farrell and Victor Mair set the Persian record in a larger world-historical context by comparing it to Latin and Chinese respectively—both traditions of writing which were parallel to the Persian from the ancient world to the present, but which differ in significant ways in both the mechanics and the sociology of writing. The importance of Farrell's contribution lies additionally in the comparability of Latinitas with *adab*. Mair's chapter concludes the argument of the volume by using the Chinese record to make a strong case for the separate study of speech and writing, explaining how the Chinese bureaucracy provided stability, over two millennia, even though many dynasties were non-Sinic (just as most Persianate ruling lines, besides the Mongols, were in fact Turkic). Stability depended on established forms of writing which were important for the illiterate masses as well as for the literate elite.

The relationship between Persian and Persianate civilization is perhaps too large a field for a single volume. What we hope to have achieved is the formulation of some important but neglected problems, with sufficient new analysis to whet some appetites for further exploration. The primary focus of our own work is the dynamic that underlay the particular record of Persian as a medieval koine whose use extended from the Mediterranean to China, and from the Central Asian steppe to India as a stable standard of administrative, literary, and commercial communication, and an explanation of what might be learned from the study of it that would illuminate historical processes more widely, especially insofar as they relate to the history of identities, cultural standards, modes of interaction, and rates of cultural change.

Our initial motivation arose from the sense of a need to explain the geographical and historical extent of a single cultural universe. To achieve its purpose such explanation requires a comparative context. What is it different from and why? We have emphasized the slowness of the pace of change, which allowed mutual intelligibility and a continued sense of common identity over such a vast area despite the exceedingly slow means of transportation, and over a whole millennium or more. However, Persianate civilization was an episode of world history. Despite the continuities of intelligibility and identity, the reader will find plenty of reference to change in the individual articles. All history is the story of change, but at different rates and of different qualities. What these chapters show is that change in the Persianate millennium was both quantitatively and qualitatively different from other regions and other periods of world history, and that the reasons for this difference of pace may illuminate other differences that have tended to be taken for granted. Following the final chapter the Afterword emphasizes the importance of seeing the whole episode as a process of change, but change at very different rates. During the Persianate era change was relatively slow, allowing the continuation of a standard medium of communication over a vast area. The Persianate era ends with the rate of change picking up and becoming differentiated from one part of the area to another.

NOTES

1. Changing the name of a language in order to distinguish it from the same language (as spoken) in a neighboring country suggests comparison with several other cases: e.g., Hindi and Urdu; Serbian and Croatian. In both these cases script is the significant factor in language identity, and the legislated change of script has facilitated divergence in usage between parts of a larger language community divided by non-linguistic factors.
2. Cf. "...Romulus Augustulus' [the last Roman Emperor in the West] removal did nothing to interrupt bureaucratic habits. All the kingdoms that emerged on the Continent during the fifth century relied directly on these inherited techniques of ruling. By appropriating traditional mechanisms of government for their own use, fifth- and sixth-century warrior kings asserted legitimacy, collected revenue, made law, and proclaimed their power" (Smith 2005:29).
3. "In French we write the same vowel four different ways in terrain, plein, matin, chien. Now when this vowel is written ain, I see it in pale yellow like an incompletely baked brick; when it is written ein, it strikes me as a network of purplish veins; when it is written in, I no longer know at all what colour sensation it evokes in my mind, and am inclined to believe that it evokes none" (quoted from Saussure by John E. Joseph in *Times Literary Supplement,* Nov. 14, 2007, p. 15).

REFERENCES

Alam, Muzaffar. 1998. The Pursuit of Persian: Language in Mughal Politics. *Modern Asian Studies* 32(2): 317–49.

—— 2003. The Culture and Politics of Persian in Precolonial Hindustan. In *Literary Cultures in History: Reconstructions from South Asia,* ed. Sheldon Pollock. Berkeley: University of California Press.

Alam, Muzaffar, Françoise 'Nalini' Delvoye, and Marc Gaborieau, eds. 2000. *The Making of Indo-Persian Culture: Indian and French Studies.* New Delhi: Manohar.

Anderson, Benedict. 1991. *Imagined Communities: Reflections on the Origin and Spread of Nationalism.* 2nd ed. London: Verso.

Arjomand, Said Amir. 2008. Defining Persianate Studies. *Journal of Persianate Studies* 1:1–4.

Ashraf, Ahmad. 1989. Alqab va `anavin. *Encyclopaedia Iranica.* Vol. 1, Fasc. 9, pp. 898–906. London: Routledge & Kegan Paul.

Balmukund, Mehta. 1972. *Letters of a King-Maker of the Eighteenth Century (Balmukund Nama),* trans. Satish Chandra, pp. 15–16. Aligarh: Aligarh Muslim University; Asia Publishing House.

Birney, William. 1905. Did the Monks Preserve the Latin Classics? *The Monist* 15:87–108.

Bloch, Maurice. 1998. *How We Think They Think: Anthropological Approaches to Cognition, Memory, and Literacy.* Boulder, CO: Westview Press.

Bohannan, Paul. 1995. *How Culture Works.* New York: Free Press.

Boserup, Ester. 1964. *The Conditions of Agricultural Growth.* Chicago: Aldine.

Bosworth, Clifford E. 1968. Development of Persian Culture under the Early Ghaznavids. *IRAN: Journal of the British Institute of Persian Studies* 6:33–44.

——— 1969. AbdAllāh al-Khwarazm on the Technical Terms of the Secretary's Art: A Contribution to the Administrative History of Medieval Islam. *Journal of the Economic and Social History of the Orient* 12(2): 113–64.

Brose, Michael C. 2000. Strategies of Survival, Uyghur Elites in Yuan and Early-Ming China. Ph.D. diss. in Asian and Middle East Studies, University of Pennsylvania.

Browne, E.G. 1928. *A Literary History of Persia.* 4 vols. Cambridge: Cambridge University Press. See vol. 1, new introduction by J.T.P. de Bruijn (Bethesda, MD: Iranbooks, 1997), p. 109.

Burke, Peter, and Roy Porter, eds. 1987. *The Social History of Language.* Cambridge: Cambridge University Press.

Chafe, Wallace, and Deborah Tannen. 1987. The Relation between Written and Spoken Language. *Annual Review of Anthropology* 16:383–407.

Cicourel, A. 1985. Text and Discourse. *Annual Review of Anthropology* 14:159–85.

Clanchy, Michael T. 1983. Looking Back from the Invention of Printing. In *Literacy in Historical Perspective,* ed. Daniel Resnick, pp. 16–19. Washington, DC: Library of Congress.

——— 2002. Does Writing Construct the State? *Journal of Historical Sociology* 15:68–70.

Collins, James. 1995. Literacy and Literacies. *Annual Review of Anthropology* 24:75–93.

Dalrymple, William. 2007. The Venetian Treasure Hunt. *New York Review of Books* 54(12), July 19.

Daniels, Peter T. 1996. The Study of Writing Systems. In *The World's Writing Systems,* ed. Peter T. Daniels, and William Bright, pp. 1–17. New York: Oxford University Press.

de Blois, L. 1994. Sueto, Aug. 46 und die Manipulation des mittleren Militaerkaders als politisches Instrument. *Historia* 43:324–45.

Derrida, Jacques. 1967. *De la grammatologie.* Paris: Editions de la Minuit.

Eisenstein, Elizabeth L. 1979. *The Printing Press as an Agent of Change.* Cambridge: Cambridge University Press.

Everett, Nicholas. 2003. *Literacy in Lombard, Italy, c. 568–774.* Cambridge: Cambridge University Press.

Farrell, Joseph. 2001. *Latin Language and Latin Culture from Ancient to Modern Times.* Cambridge: Cambridge University Press.

Ferguson, C.A. 1959. Diglossia. *Word* 15:325.

Fleischer, Cornell. 1994. Between the Lines: Realities of Scribal Life in the

Sixteenth Century. In *Studies in Ottoman History in Honour of Professor V.L. Ménage*, ed. Colin Heywood and Colin Imber, pp. 45–61. Istanbul: Isis Press.

Gelb, Ignace. 1952. *A Study of Writing*. Chicago: University of Chicago Press.

Gladwin, Francis. 1781. *The Persian Moonshee*. Calcutta. Reprint 1801 (London: Wilson & Co.).

Goody, Jack, ed. 1968. *Literacy in Traditional Societies*. Cambridge: Cambridge University Press.

—— 1977. The *Domestication of the Savage Mind*. Cambridge: Cambridge University Press.

—— 1986. *The Logic of Writing and the Organization of Society*. Studies in Literacy, the Family, Culture, and the State. Cambridge: Cambridge University Press.

—— 1987. *The Interface between the Written and the Oral*. Studies in Literacy, the Family, Culture, and the State. Cambridge: Cambridge University Press.

—— 2000. *The Power of the Written Tradition*. Washington, DC: Smithsonian Institution Press.

Goody, Jack, and I.P. Watt. 1963. The Consequences of Literacy. *Comparative Studies in Society and History* 5:304–45.

Graff, Harvey J. 1981. *Literacy in History: An Interdisciplinary Research Bibliography*. Garland Reference Library of the Humanities, vol. 254. New York.

—— 1987. *The Legacies of Literacy*. Bloomington: Indiana University Press.

—— 1995. *The Labyrinths of Literacy. Reflections of Literacy Past and Present*. Rev. and exp. Pittsburgh: University of Pittsburgh Press.

Greene, W. 1951. The Spoken and Written Word. *Harvard Studies in Classical Philology* 60:23–59.

Halverson, John. 1991. Olson on Literacy. *Language in Society* 20:619–40.

—— 1992. Goody and the Implosion of the Literacy Thesis. *Man* 27:301–17.

Hanaway, William L., and Brian Spooner. 2007. *Reading Nasta'liq: Persian and Urdu Hands from 1500 to the Present*. 2nd rev. ed. Costa Mesa, CA: Mazda Publications.

Harris, W.V. 1989. *Ancient Literacy*. Cambridge, MA: Harvard University Press.

Havelock, Eric A. 1963. *Preface to Plato*. Cambridge, MA: Harvard University Press.

—— 1982. *The Literate Revolution in Greece and Its Cultural Consequences*. Princeton: Princeton University Press.

—— 1986. *The Muse Learns to Write: Reflections on Orality and Literacy from Antiquity to the Present*. New Haven, CT: Yale University Press.

Heath, S.B. 1984. Oral and Literate Traditions. *International Social Science Journal* 36:41–57.

Heinrichs, Wolfhart. 1990. Introduction. In *Studies in Neo-Aramaic*, ed. Wolfhart Heinrichs, pp. ix–xvii. Atlanta: Scholars Press.

Helms, Mary W. 1988. *Ulysses' Sail: An Ethnographic Odyssey of Power, Knowledge, and Geographical Distance*. Princeton: Princeton University Press.

—— 1993. *Craft and the Kingly Ideal: Art, Trade and Power.* Austin: University of Texas Press.

Hodgson, Marshall. 1974. *The Venture of Islam.* Chicago: University of Chicago Press.

Houston, Stephen, John Baines, and Jerrold Cooper. 2003. Last Writing: Script Obsolescence in Egypt, Mesopotamia, and Mesoamerica. *Comparative Studies in Society and History* 45(3): 430–79.

Ibn Khaldun. 2005. *The Muqaddimah: An Introduction to History,* trans. Franz Rosenthal, abr. and ed. N.J. Dawood, with new intro. by Bruce B. Lawrence. Princeton: Princeton University Press.

Jaspers, Karl. 1949. *Vom Ursprung und Ziel der Geschichte.* München: Piper Verlag.

Kent, Roland G. 1950. *Old Persian; Grammar, Texts, Lexicon.* American Oriental Series, 33. New Haven, CT: American Oriental Society.

Khaleghi-Motlagh, Djalal. 1983. Adab. *Encyclopaedia Iranica,* Vol. 1, Fasc. 4, pp. 432–39. Boston: Routledge.

Knauer, Elfriede Regina. 1998. *The Camel's Load in Life and Death.* Zürich: Akanthus.

Kosto, Adam J. 2001. *Making Agreements in Medieval Catalonia: Power, Order, and the Written Word, 1000–1200.* Cambridge: Cambridge University Press.

Lazard, Gilbert. 1971. Pahlavi, parsi, dari: les langues de l'Iran d'après Ibn al-Muqaffa`. In *Iran and Islam: In Memory of the Late Vladimir Minorsky,* ed. Clifford E. Bosworth, pp. 361–91. Edinburgh: Edinburgh University Press.

Lévy-Bruhl, Lucien. 1925. *How Natives Think* (Les fonctions mentales dans les sociétés inférieures), authorized trans. Lilian A. Clare. New York: Knopf.

Lévi-Strauss, Claude. 1961. *A World on the Wane,* trans. John Russell. New York: Criterion.

Littleton, C.S. 1982. *The New Comparative Mythology.* 3rd ed. Berkeley: University of California Press.

Martin, Henri-Jean. 1994. *The History and Power of Writing,* trans. Lydia G. Cochrane. Chicago: University of Chicago Press.

Milroy, James. 1985. *Authority in Language: Investigating Language Prescription and Standardisation.* Boston: Routledge & Kegan Paul.

Minorsky, Vladimir, trans. and ed. 1943. *Tadhkirat al-mulūk, a Manual of Safavid Administration (circa 1137/1725), Persian Text in Facsimile (B.M. Or. 9496).* Gibb Memorial Series, 16. London: Luzac & Co.

Mottahedeh, Roy P. 1980. *Leadership and Loyalty.* Princeton: Princeton University Press.

Muhiuddin, Momin. 1971. *The Chancellery and Persian Epistolography, under the Mughals, from Babur to Shāh Jahan (1526–1658).* Calcutta: Iran Society.

Olson, David R. 1977. From Utterance to Text: The Bias of Language in Speech and Writing. *Harvard Educational Review* 47:257–81.

—— 1988. Mind and Media: The Epistemic Functions of Literacy. *Journal of Communication* 38(3): 27–36.

—— 1994. *The World on Paper: The Conceptual and Cognitive Implications of Writ-

ing and Reading. Cambridge: Cambridge University Press.

Ong, Walter J. 1982 [1988]. *Orality and Literacy: The Technologizing of the Word.* London: Methuen.

Pei, Mario. 1949 [1960]. *The Story of Language.* New York: Mentor Books.

Pollock, Sheldon, ed. 2003. *Literary Cultures in History: Reconstructions from South Asia.* Berkeley: University of California Press.

Porter, Theodore M. 1995. *Trust in Numbers. The Pursuit of Objectivity in Science and Public Life.* Princeton: Princeton University Press.

Resnick, Daniel P., ed. 1983. *Literacy in Historical Perspective.* Washington, DC: Library of Congress.

Ronell, Avital. 1989. *The Telephone Book: Technology–Schizophrenia–Electric Speech.* Lincoln, NE: University of Nebraska Press.

Schams, Christine. 1998. *Jewish Scribes in the Second-Temple Period.* Sheffield: Sheffield Academic Press.

Schmandt-Besserat, Denise. 1996. *How Writing Came About.* Austin: University of Texas Press.

Scribner, Sylvia, and Michael Cole. 1981. *The Psychology of Literacy.* Cambridge: Harvard University Press.

Al Akbar Shahabi. 1997. Āmuzesh va parvaresh dar makāteb va madāres-e qadim. *Farhang-e Irānzamin* 42(1375): 11–62.

Smirnov, S.D., and N.S. Kamenskiy. 1948. *Sbornik Obraztsov Persidskikh Skoropisnykh Dokumentov i Obraztsov Epistolyarnogo Stilya (dlya starshikh kursov).* Voyennyi Institut Inostrannykh Yazykov, Kafedra persidskogo, arabskogo i afganskogo yazykov. Moscow.

Smith, Julia M.H. 2005. *Europe after Rome, A New Cultural History 500–1000.* Oxford: Oxford University Press.

Spooner, Brian, ed. 1972. *Population Growth: Anthropological Implications.* Cambridge, MA: MIT Press.

—— 1993. Are We Teaching Persian? or Fārsi? or Dari? or Tojiki? In *Persian Studies in America,* ed. Mehdi Marashi, pp. 175–90. Salt Lake City: University of Utah Press.

Spooner, Brian, and William L. Hanaway. 2009. Siyaq: Persianate Numerical Notation and Numeracy. In *Oxford Handbook of the History of Mathematics,* ed. Eleanor Robson and Jacqueline Stedall, pp. 429–47. Oxford: Oxford University Press.

Stock, Brian. 1983. *The Implications of Literacy, Written Language and Models of Interpretation in the Eleventh and Twelfth Centuries.* Princeton: Princeton University Press.

—— 1984. Medieval Literacy, Linguistic Theory, and Social Organization. *New Literary History* 16(1): 13–29.

Stolper, Matthew W. 2004. Elamite. In *The Cambridge Encyclopedia of the World's Ancient Languages,* ed. Roger D. Woodard, pp. 60–94. Cambridge: Cambridge University Press.

Stolper, Matthew W., and Jan Tavernier. 2007. An Old Persian Administrative Tablet from the Persepolis Fortification. Persepolis Fortification Archive Project, 1. *Achaemenid Research on Texts and Archaeology* (ARTA 2007.001). Electronic resource; see http://www.achemenet.com/document/2007.001-Stolper-Tavernier.pdf.

Strauss, G. 1984. Lutheranism and Literacy: A Reassessment. In *Religion and Society in Early Modern Europe,* ed. K. von Greyerz, pp. 109–23. London: Allen and Unwin.

Street, Brian V. 1984. *Literacy in Theory and Practice.* Cambridge Studies in Oral and Literate Culture. Cambridge: Cambridge University Press.

Tafazzoli, Ahmad. 1377/1998. *Tārikh-e adabiyāt-e iran pish az eslām,* pp. 294–95. Tehrān: Intishārāt-i Sukhan.

—— 2000. *Sasanian Society.* New York: Bibliotheca Persica.

Tannen, D., ed. 1982. *Spoken and Written Language: Exploring Orality and Literacy.* Norwood, NJ: Ablex.

Vallat, François. 1994. Succession royale en Īlam au IIème millénaire. In *Cinquante-deux réflexions sur le Proche-Orient ancien offertes en hommage à Léon De Meyer,* ed. H. Gasche, M. Tanret, C. Janssen, and A. Degraeve, pp. 1–14. Mesopotamian History and Environment Occasional Publications 2. Leuven: Peters.

Vygotsky, L.S. 1962. *Thought and Language.* Cambridge, MA: MIT Press.

Waldman, Marilyn Robinson. 1980. *Toward a Theory of Historical Narrative: A Case Study in Perso-Islamicate Historiography.* Columbus: Ohio State University Press.

Wallace, Anthony F.C. 1961. On Being Just Complicated Enough. *Proceedings of the National Academy of Sciences of the United States of America* 47(4): 458–64.

—— 1966. *Religion: An Anthropological View.* New York: Random House.

Windfuhr, Gernot, ed. 2009. *The Iranian Languages.* London: Curzon.

Woodard, Roger D. 2004. *The Cambridge Encyclopedia of the World's Ancient Languages.* Cambridge: Cambridge University Press.

Yates, Francis. 1979. Print Culture. *Encounter* 52(4): 59–64.

Zaehner, R.C. 1937–1939. Nāmak-nipesishnih. *Bulletin of the School of Oriental and African Studies* 9:93–109.

Zengel, Marjorie S. 1962. Literacy as a Factor in Language Change. *American Anthropologist* 64:132–39.

Zilli, Ishtiyāq Ahmad. 2000. Development of Inshā Literature to the End of Akbar's Reign. In *The Making of Indo-Persian Culture: Indian and French Studies,* ed. Muzaffar Alam, Françoise Nalini Delvoye, and Marc Gaborieau, pp. 309–49. New Delhi: Manohar.

Part One: Foundations

1

New Persian: Expansion, Standardization, and Inclusivity

JOHN R. PERRY

S tarting in the 9th century of our era, Persian came to be a major contact vernacular and an international literary language over an area spanning, at its maximal extent, the Iranian plateau from the south Caucasus to the Indus, Central Asia from Khiva to Kashghar, and the northern three-quarters of the Indian subcontinent. As a language of imperial administration and epistolography, and in terms of elite readership of the Persian literary classics and lexical and stylistic influence on other languages, its influence extended to more distant centers such as Konya and Istanbul, Cairo and Mombasa, Saray and Kazan. Its active range was reduced to Iran, Afghanistan, and Tajikistan only during the early decades of the 20th century, as a result of the success of newer imperial languages (chiefly English and Russian) and the emergence of local and national languages on the territories of the old empires.

How did this millennium of cultural hegemony evolve, without (for the most part) political dominion by Persians, and what factors underpinned it? As in most historical developments, part of the explanation lies in a subtle balance between aspects of continuity and innovation. The geopolitical history and philological background is fairly clear and has been outlined in specific cases, if never adequately explained or even fully summarized. Here I shall attempt to look beneath the established strata of sociocultural generalities and individual etymologies, and identify some specific linguistic mechanisms and sociolinguistic processes that arguably facilitated the transition of spoken Middle Persian to literary New Persian and its subsequent cultural ascent.

This nuts-and-bolts approach is not intended to replace the interpretation of sociocultural factors, but to motivate and document it. Ultimately I shall emphasize two such intangibles, which I think best explain the success of Persian as a supranational literary language. The first is its homoglossia, i.e., the essential identity of written and spoken Persian as it expanded its written and spoken domains throughout the pertinent period, as distinct from the more commonly occurring feature of diglossia (a systematic distinction in grammar and lexicon between "high" and "low" stylistic registers) in languages such as Greek and Arabic. Related to this is the inclusivity of Persian, which attracted into its cultural and linguistic realm communities that might have been, or felt, excluded as being ethnically or socially alien from the locus of Persian literature and history. I begin with a fresh look at the given of "Islam" as the matrix for the diachronic dynamism of Persian language and its associated literature and world-view.

PERSIAN AND RELIGION

Persian is rightly regarded as the second language of Islam. Paradoxically, an important but hitherto neglected point is that the direct ancestor of New Persian, i.e., spoken Middle Persian (which Ibn al-Muqaffa` called *Dari*) at the time of the Arab Muslim conquest, was a secular language. In stark contrast with Arabic and with some of the adjacent non-Iranian languages ultimately replaced by Arabic (such as Aramaic and Coptic), it was devoid of immediate religious associations and connotations.

Several living Iranian languages were being written in the 7th century AD, in scripts derived from imperial Aramaic or Syriac Aramaic by priests and missionaries of existing religions. These writing systems included Estrangelo or "Manichaean" script, a Nestorian Christian script, a Buddhist script, Pahlavi script (for the written Middle Persian of the Zoroastrian priesthood), and the Avestan alphabet, derived from Pahlavi. Most of these systems, apart from formal character variations, used features of historical and archaizing spelling which distanced them from the vernacular even of the community they represented, and further served to dissociate them and their readers from members of the broader speech community (e.g., Sogdians or Persians as a whole) who used another script variety for a different purpose (religious or secular), or who did not use writing at all. Thus *Dari* (Middle and Early New Persian, known later, when it began to be written in

Arabic script, as *Pārsi*), the spoken tongue of much of the Iranian plateau during the 7th to the 9th centuries (1st to 3rd Islamic centuries), was not the same as *Pārsik*, Zoroastrian Middle Persian as written in Pahlavi script, and hence often popularly called Pahlavi.

In other words, spoken Persian of the time (for which *Dari* was one name) served as the vernacular for Zoroastrians, Jews, Manichaeans, Christians, and Muslim converts in Iran (for some Jews, additionally in a written form using Hebrew script). It did not, however, serve as an original or regular vehicle for any scripture or liturgy, and was not identified with a particular religion. *Dari* and Pahlavi stood in much the same relationship (from a linguistic and a socio-religious perspective) as Early Romance to Late Latin in Europe of the same period. The other major Iranian language of the region, Sogdian, both spoken and written, was one of several languages of the Silk Road in which Christian, Manichaean, and Buddhist works had been written, but was not identified exclusively with any one religion. It was known to the Arabs in a secular context as a language of diplomacy in which were written some of the letters they received from Devāshtich, the last lord of Samarqand.

These and other Iranian vernaculars (such as Khwarazmian, east of the Caspian sea, and Azeri, to the west of it) evidently posed no ideological threat to Arabic, the scriptural and liturgical language of the victorious Muslims. Incidents are reported of new converts who had difficulties with Arabic being permitted to recite the Koran in Persian or Sogdian translation (Sādeqi 1978:63–64, Narshakhi 1954:48 and n184). It is hard to imagine Aramaic-speaking Jewish, or Syriac- or Coptic-speaking Christian, converts being granted the same leniency, since their vernaculars were also to varying extents scriptural and liturgical languages of the supplanted religions. This factor may well be one of the elusive reasons for the survival and efflorescence of Persian, whereas Aramaic, Syriac, and Coptic had their domains severely reduced in the aftermath of the Islamic conquests of Iraq, Syria, and Egypt.

Almost all the basic concepts of Islam, such as god, prophet, angel, devil, heaven, hell, purgatory, prayer, fasting, and sin, translated smoothly into Persian without the need for loanwords. Most of the Persian terms were already in use by Zoroastrians, Christians, Jews, and Manichaeans and needed, at the most, some specification: thus *namāz* 'prayer' might still be polyvalent, but *namāz-e jom'a* 'Friday prayer' was unambiguously Islamic. Popular Muslim and Zoroastrian superstitions merged: thus in Central Asia the Koranic term *sirāt* 'road' (< Latin *strata* 'paved [highway],' as used in the opening surah (verse) of the Koran in the phrase *al-sirāt al-mustaqim* 'the straight [i.e., righteous] path') now designates the legendary bridge called by Zoroastrians Chinvāt, which mankind must cross on the Day of Judgment (the righteous will reach the other side, while sinners will tumble into the abyss). Here a popular Zoroastrian belief has crossed without fanfare into popular Islam, taking an Arabic name with similar connotations of moral choice and divine judgment.

During the 3rd to 5th centuries of the Hijra (9th–11th c. AD) Persian not only replaced Sogdian as the vernacular of Transoxiana, but having adopted the writing system and much of the vocabulary of Arabic, under the active patronage of local dynasties (notably the Samanids), smoothly eased into a partnership with the invaders' tongue as a complementary literary language of administration, the secular sciences, and the humanities in the lands of the Eastern Caliphate. In subsequent centuries its domain expanded, particularly in the frontier areas of Islamdom such as Anatolia, the Caucasus, Central Asia, and India, and in poetical genres, to embrace even purely religious education and devotion.

Paradoxically, Persian's geographical expansion was initially due to the rapid advance of the Arab armies eastward, where they and their converted Persian auxiliaries from Pārs and western central Iran settled in Khorasan and Transoxiana, forming an economic, military, and political bloc to be reckoned with by the later Umayyads and early Abbasids. The language's further expansion from Anatolia to India was due in large part to the conquests of Turkish and Mongol dynasts, who patronized Persian as a mercantile contact vernacular and a literary language, and promoted the institution of the Persian bureaucrat. Finally, its apotheosis as the primary language of Islam in the East was undoubtedly a consequence of the destruction of the Abbasid caliphate by the Mongols in 1258 and the demise of Arabic as a living language east of Iraq and the Gulf. Nevertheless, the evolution of spoken Persian as a language of both secular and religious literature resulted ultimately from its neutral, non-religious beginnings.

FERDOWSI'S *SHĀHNĀMA*

Likewise related to Persian's secular status is the single most important factor in, and symbol of, the peculiar and unchanging identity of Persia and Persian. The most notable triumph of continuity from Middle to New

Persian literature and ideology belonged to the *dehqāns*, the traditional and conservative landed nobility of the Sasanian realm: this was the recovery of the Iranian national legend and its royal traditions. The Zoroastrian religion was not totally expunged in Iran; having secured the status of protected scriptuaries—"People of the Book"—its adherents were not subject to any greater persecution than Iranian Christians or Jews. However, as a result of conversion and emigration, and the demotion of the priests from political power, the remnants of the faithful in Iran receded to the periphery, where their scholars continued for some time to produce works on a discarded law and theology in an archaic language and a superseded script. Zoroastrianism was never again to be an integral part of Iranian society, and the persona of the Magian priest, the *mogh* or *mobad,* was relegated in later lyric verse to a nostalgic metaphor, the *pir-e moghān* or mentor of Sufi neophytes. (In the Persian dictionary *Me῾yār-e Jamāli,* composed at Shiraz by a contemporary of Hāfez in 1344, *mobad* was defined as 'a learned man; one from whom they listen to stories' (Baevskii 2007:195). The legends of kings and heroes, on the other hand, proved to be more enduring. As secular tales of martial valor and courtly magnificence, they were no ideological threat to Islam; they not only circulated freely in the *Dari* vernacular, but persisted in written accounts in Pahlavi, and both were selectively translated into Arabic by new Muslims who remained old Persians at heart.

The urge to collect all of this national patrimony was clearly manifested in the Samanid realms several generations before Ferdowsi realized it in ca. 1010. Several *shāhnāma*s (no longer extant) were reportedly composed during the course of the 10th century, including at least one in prose, and the beginning of a versified one by Daqiqi, commissioned by the Samanid amir, was incorporated by Ferdowsi in his own *Shāhnāma* after Daqiqi's untimely death in about 979. Nor did this industry cease with Ferdowsi; Asadi of Tus—significantly, one of the first lexicographers of Persian—also produced a historical verse epic, the *Garshāsp-nāma,* in 1066. With the canonization of the Persian royal history and the rapid integration of its ethos into Turco-Iranian regnal practice in the East, this fundamentally secular corpus became a force for the standardization and resistance to change of Persian, but also one of its sources of innovation and expansion, as will be argued under the next two headings.

This definitive literary version of the national legend was in verse (ostensibly in a meter derived from Arabic, but actually a Persian innovation), in an epic form and diction that set a new standard. The work was eagerly learned and recited, and widely imitated throughout the Persianate world. Persian and foreign scholars have of course hailed the *Shāhnāma* as an ideological vector, the prime vehicle of ancient Iranian civilization and essential Persian culture. As Ferdowsi himself claimed, `ajam zenda kardam ba-d-in Pārsi*, "I have resurrected Persia with this Persian of mine." I will argue more specifically that the *Shāhnāma* was a major determiner of the role of written Persian as an Eastern parallel to, and successor of, the language of its old rivals and former conquerors, namely, Greek. This analogy is nowhere explicitly made, since the Persians were ignorant of the literary epics of the Greeks—though not, it seems, of Hellenistic romances (see Davis 2002). Let us however consider the sociolinguistic parallels set forth below.

THE IMPULSE TO A NEW WRITING SYSTEM

The Greek alphabet was brilliantly adapted from the Semitic consonantal system in its Phoenician form, probably about 800 BC, and became not only the vehicle of a uniquely influential philosophical and poetical literature, but the model for all subsequent fully alphabetical writing systems up to the present day. It has been argued that this script was devised by a single individual for the express purpose of writing down Homer's epic poems, the *Iliad* and *Odyssey* (Powell 1991). Though this extreme view is not widely accepted, it seems certain at least that the introduction of an efficient and widely disseminated writing system would challenge poets to re-work the formative literary legends of their particular cultures, hitherto preserved by oral tradition. This is not to say that a definitive written version immediately superseded the oral; in the case of both Homer and Ferdowsi, written versions of the epics remained for long (in the latter case, up until the last century) aides-mémoire for professional reciters.

At first sight, the differences from the case of Ferdowsi and the *Shāhnāma* are more striking than the similarities. Perso-Arabic script was an adaptation of degree, rather than kind, from an existing Semitic consonantal script, and had already been in use to write Persian poetry and prose for several generations when Ferdowsi took up the pen. Moreover, it was Ferdowsi the poet himself who committed his verses to writing, using mostly existing conventions. However, the need to write the Iranian national legend in epic form was no less urgent for the Persians of the 10th century AD than for the

Greeks of the 9th century BC. A self-consciously epic work craves immor-
tality in "authentic" written form as well as in the diverse voices and vacil-
lating memories of its performers, whether rhapsodes or *rāwis* (whether in
the Greek or Muslim tradition). Henceforth, the form of this Persian classic
was to dictate innovations in the new writing system, and the standardization of existing features, that endured in Persian and were transmitted to
derivative systems in Turkic and Indic literary languages.

The Persians' prompt adoption and adaptation of Arabic script was
almost the reverse of the process by which their forebears had adopted
Aramaic script for Middle Persian (MP)—a long and unintentional change,
completed about six centuries previously, which may be characterized
briefly as follows. The Aramaic language, with its established literary tradition, was adopted as the language of imperial administration throughout
the far-flung Achaemenian empire, written on clay tablets and parchment
initially by an Aramaean secretariat. (Old Persian in its cuneiform syllabary
was used only for ceremonial epigraphic inscriptions in Iran.) As Persians
and other Iranians themselves came to use written Aramaic, the text would
be routinely translated orally into Persian (or Parthian) for officials or audiences who did not know Aramaic, until this written-to-spoken translation
register (and the reverse process) became in effect an indirect way of reading and writing (Middle) Persian.

As users became less competent in the grammar and lexis of Aramaic
(which, after the fall of the Achaemenids to Alexander, lost its native-Aramaic
secretariat and its status as an official imperial language), they took to writing Persian words phonetically in Aramaic characters, producing a mixed language in which an Aramaic grammatical skeleton was progressively relexified
by Persian—a literary creole, with no spoken counterpart. Soon enough the
tail was wagging the dog, as forms of this writing (notably literary Middle Persian, or Book Pahlavi) became overwhelmingly Persian in content. The still
considerable Aramaic residue (known as *uzvārishn* in MP) was to be seen in
such as function words (prepositions, e.g., MN 'from, of '), and nouns such as
MLK' standing for *shāh*. Oddly enough, far from eliminating these Aramaeograms, later scribes introduced even more redundant and corrupt ones—perhaps out of professional snobbery (Skalmowski 2004:295–96). These words
were never loanwords, but sigla on the order of "&" or "viz." in English.

Under the Arab Muslim empire, the Persians, like other conquered
peoples, initially used Arabic as the common administrative language (and,

notably in the west of Iran, under the Iranian but arabizing Buwayhid dynasts, as a literary language for court-patronized poetry). The process by which bilingual Persian intellectuals came to write Persian in Arabic characters was not through an accidental loss of rigor by a still-elitist nativized secretariat, but on the contrary a conscious striving for literary parity and comprehensibility on the part of secretaries. scholars, and poets. Arabic was rapidly and selectively adapted to the needs of Persian by appropriation of the writing system and selected vocabulary. As in Luther's Germany, the drive by the literati to promote the vernacular to literary status was actively patronized by ambitious independent princes, such as the Saffarids and Samanids in the east of Iran.

The two languages were not mixed by accident, but kept separate by design. Whereas Middle Persian had relexified a debased form of written Aramaic by default, literary Arabic was used purposefully, but selectively, to relexify New Persian. The swiftly growing body of Arabic vocabulary was assimilated phonologically to spoken Persian, but retained its original orthography in the written language, including the distinctive Arabic letters representing sounds alien to Persian. This lent the loanwords a high profile—recognizability, status, and a degree of semantic and lexical stability—not only in Persian but also in Turkish, Urdu, and other languages into which they were incorporated through the mediation of Persian. Many components of this topmost stratum of Arabic vocabulary nevertheless trickled down into vernacular usage. A few early and common Arabic loanwords, such as *mosalmān* 'Muslim' and *mir* 'emir', show by their orthographic alteration from the Arabic etymon that they were initially incorporated via the spoken language (see below, under Homoglossia).

The conscious reservation of the two languages, Arabic and Persian, for separate and appropriate functions is seen in the attitude of early Muslim Iranian scholars. Biruni (d. after 1050) held that Arabic was the proper language of science and that Persian, being less clear and precise, should stick to epic verse and storytelling. The astronomer Shāhmardān b. Abi'l-Khayr endorsed this position, observing that the would-be popularizers of science in the vernacular "have recourse to words of pure Persian [*dari-ye vizha-ye motlaq*] which are more difficult than Arabic" (Lazard 1975:631–32). The targets of their criticism were colleagues such as Ibn Sinā (d. 1037) and Ghazāli (d. 1111), who sought to equip Persian as a language of philosophy for non-Arabic speakers by excerpting their Arabic *opera magna* in Persian epitomes such as the *Dāneshnāma-ye ʿAlāʾi* and *Kimiyā-ye saʿādat,* for which they coined native technical neologisms. Scribes, poets, and dilettantes argued about the proportions of Arabic and Persian vocabulary appropriate for various functions and stylistic registers of Persian: thus the Ziyārid prince Kay Kāʾus, that consummate Muslim *dehqān,* counsels his son, if he would be a lyric poet, to "avoid heavy and unfamiliar Arabisms (*tāzi-hā*)"; but should he become a secretary, he is advised: "If the letter is in Persian, do not write pure Persian [*pārsi-ye motlaq*], for it is unpleasant" (Kai Kaʾus 1951:109 and 119 respectively).

As in Greek, the use of the Semitic matres lectionis as vowels was expanded to make verse more readable: *w* and *y* each stood for two "long" vowels of Persian, *alef* for a third, and any optional, metrically conditioned vowel shortening (*bud ~ bod, digar ~ degar, shāh ~ shah,* etc.) was systematically indicated by their absence in written verse. The expanded use of matres lectionis was previously a feature of the adaptation of Aramaic and Hebrew scripts to Persian. The optional alternation with zero vowel graphs—apart from a limited application in derivational morphology (e.g., *rah-namāʾi* 'guidance' in preference to *rāh-namāi*)—has remained proper to poetry; similar variations in early prose manuscripts have since been regularized.

Perhaps even more important, the early adaptation of the Arabic prosodic system (ʿaruz) to Persian verse—in combination with the consistent orthography for long and short vowels—provided a stable matrix for the efflorescence of poetry beyond the simple *motaqāreb* meter of the *Shāhnāma.* The system accommodated dialect differences and vowel shifts and still works perfectly today, through a conventional contrast of short and long vowels (and, in combination with consonant clusters, of short, long, and overlong syllables). *ʿAruz* was adapted, with appropriate variations, to Turkic and Indic poetics. With the invention of the *masnavi* form (rhyming couplets), found first in the *motaqāreb* meter of the *Shāhnāma,* Persian poetry evaded the restriction of length imposed by the monorhyme of Arabic and became capable of supporting indefinitely long epic, lyrical, or mystical poems.

Ferdowsi's younger contemporaries among early 11th-century court poets, notably Farrokhi, ʿOnsori, and Manuchehri, distinguished themselves as court encomiasts in the genre of the *qasida,* an ode in monorhyme modeled on Arabic antecedents. They too contributed to the richness of the New Persian lexicon and idiom, but—by virtue mainly of the difference in subject matter—more in terms of Arabic loanwords than Ferdowsi. Whereas the *Shāhnāma* contains about 8.8 percent of Arabic in its vocabulary and a frequency of occurrence of some 2.4 percent (Moinfar 1970:61, 66), `Onsori's verses yield ca. 32 percent and 17 percent respectively (Elwell-Sutton 1987:234).

For its earliest purposes—the preservation and propagation of a national (i.e., supradialectal) poetry—the Perso-Arabic consonant system was superior to the Greek alphabet (in its Homeric context), which—being a narrower transcription—was constrained to record instances of dialect variation. The advantages of a basically underdetermined writing system for a national, supradialectal verse are obvious when contrasted with the overdetermined, phonographic Latin system devised for the Tajiks (Persians of Central Asia) in the late 1920s. One unintended (and unpublicized) result of the switch from Arabic script was that classical Persian verse could no longer be appreciated, or composed, by anyone educated solely in the new alphabet (or its even worse successor, Cyrillic), since this was based on a dialect that allegedly did not distinguish the traditional "long" and "short" vowels (Perry 1997:8). Elsewhere, the "defective" Perso-Arabic system with its overt long and covert short vowels has preserved, promoted, and exported classical Persian verse, which is the heart of the literature.

Three other instances of orthographic innovation had permanent and important consequences for the lexical evolution of New Persian.

First was the Persian spelling of the dichotomous pronunciation of the Arabic feminine ending (in Arabic, a device to distinguish syntactic structures, but written as a unitary graph, the *tā' marbuta*) as two distinct graphic and lexical endings, *-at* and *-a* (the latter pronounced /e/ in modern Persian). This opened a series of doors to semantic sorting and lexical innovation in some 1500 items of the Arabic loan vocabulary (Perry 1991). For example, most of about forty doublets (Arabic feminine-ending loanwords lexicalized in Persian with both variants) show semantic, lexical, or stylistic distinctions in the use of the two forms. Thus *qovvat* 'strength, power,' the original form and meaning, remains a mass noun of quality in modern Persian, whereas *qovva*, a lexical doublet recorded from about 1150, was soon specialized in medical and philosophical literature as a term for 'faculty, capability,' as in *qovva-ye erāda* 'will power'; as a count noun of single instance, it could now pluralize (using either Persian or Arabic forms), and in the 20th century it further acquired the senses of '(industrial) energy' and '(military) force': *qovva-ye barq* 'electric power, electrical energy', *qovā-ye havā'i* 'air forces' (Perry 1991:108–9; 1995:136–37).

The second change was in essence simply a phonographic re-spelling of Persian words that were now simpler in form than their Pahlavi ancestors. It involves two important form classes which had undergone related sound changes shortly before the Arab invasion. Most MP relative adjectives in *-ig* lost the final velar (*pahlavig > pahlavi,* etc.), as also did substantives ending in *-ag* (*dānag > dāna* 'grain', *khoftag > khofta* 'sleeping', etc.). These new forms were written respectively with terminal {y} and {h} (the latter device was probably extended from its application in Arabic loans in the feminine ending that were likewise realized in *-a*: see above). The immediate and massive result was that these large form classes each became indistinguishable from, and in effect merged with, two equally large and important Arabic form classes, members of which were being incorporated rapidly into Persian vocabulary. These were the *nisba* adjective, formed with the suffix *-iyy^{un}* (> New Persian *-i,* as in the borrowing *'arabi* 'Arabic'), and all substantives in the Arabic feminine ending *-a[t]* (whether suffixal or integral to the word) that were incorporated in Persian as *-a* (not *-at*), such as *madrasa* 'school' and *tohfa* 'gift.'

The absolute convergence of the adjectival forms in *-iyy^{un}* and *-i* is apparent from homonyms such as *dudi* 'smoky,' from Persian *dud* 'smoke' + the Persian suffix *-i* (< *-ig*), and *dudi* 'peristaltic, worm-like' (from Arabic *dūd* 'worm' + the Arabic *nisba* suffix), and putative blends such as *fārsi*: is this simply an Arabicized variant of *pārsi* (cf. Persian *pil ~ fil* 'elephant'), or an incorporation of Arabic *fārisiyy^{un}*? The Persian and Arabic word classes in terminal *-a* are semantically less homogeneous than those in *-i*. Nevertheless, the extent of their assimilation into a single broad lexical class is shown by the (early, and usually continued) application of Persian morphophonological rules to these Arabic loans; e.g., *nazzāragān* 'spectators', *khebragān* 'experts' (cf. Pers. *bandagān* 'slaves'), *khebragi* 'expertise' (cf. Pers. *khastagi* 'fatigue').

Today, substantives of both Arabic and Persian origin ending in a (nouns and adjectives; Tehran pronunciation /e/) number at least 9,000, and there are at least 6,000 Persian adjectives of both origins ending in *-i*. There is also, of course, an approximately equally large class of purely Persian nouns ending in *-i* (at least 4,000); these are the abstract nouns of quality or activity formed mainly from adjectives and agentives, such as *bozorgi* 'size, greatness' and *qāli-bāfi* 'carpet weaving.' This formal surface identity, resulting from a similar Arabic respelling of the unrelated formative -*i* (written in Pahlavi script as -*ih*), occasions very little ambiguity, since the function of each ending is exclusive of the other. What these form classes in -*i* do have in common (other than form) is that they are open classes: their identical suffixes are the most productive formatives in Persian. Virtually any toponym, for example, incorporated into Persian, would automatically acquire a plausible relative adjective in -*i* (e.g., *ādamābād-i,* pertaining to a putative place called *ādamābād*), and almost any adjective, agentive, or type noun could derive, as needed, a noun of quality or occupation in -*i* (e.g., *sagbān-i* 'the office of Master of Hounds').

The high-profile stratum of Arabic vocabulary that Persian incorporated was made available for all readers and writers, not only of Persian wherever it spread, but of its adoptive literary offspring Chaghatay, Ottoman, Urdu, etc. Together with this inventory went the rules and examples for continuing lexical incorporation and expansion, principally the semantic and stylistic dichotomy of -*at* and -*a* and the use of auxiliaries (esp. the dummy *kardan*) to "verbalize" many of the borrowed substantives. Above all, the new literary language, following the example of Arabic as the vehicle of a scripture for all believers, was to remain accessible to its speakers. *Pārsik* (Middle Persian, written non-phonographically in an Aramaic-derived script, the purview of a small trained elite) gave way to New Persian (*Pārsi*), the speech and writing of kings, poets, and peasants—in part lexically integrated with Arabic, but functionally separate. A brilliant marriage of the subtly underdetermined Semitic consonant repertory with the morphological simplicity of New Persian had produced just the right balance between phonographic precision and supradialectal universality.

HOMOGLOSSIA

Although the emergence of New Persian, via partial relexification of *Dari* by Arabic, was essentially a literary process in which Arabic vocabulary was initially used in the writings of bilingual scholars and poets from the 9th century on, there was evidently some earlier input from both spoken Arabic and spoken Dari. Common Persian onomastic elements such as *bu* and *bā* (< Ar. *abu, abā* 'father', as in Bu Ja'farak or Bāyazid) and *mir* (< Ar. *amir* 'commander') correspond phonologically to the aphesis characteristic of vernacular Dari, as distinct from Pahlavi (cf. the pairs Anāhid/ Nāhid, Anushiravān/ Nushiravān, and the poetical variants *ayār/yār* 'friend', *abā/bā* 'with', *abar/ bar* 'upon', of which the former is Middle Persian and the latter is New Persian in form). It may also be pointed out that *bu* is a colloquial form in some Arabic dialects, and there is at least one sociolinguistically significant instance where a historical personage has both a formal Arabicate name and a colloquial Persianate variant: "Abu `Ali ebn-e Sinā" is the philosopher-physician Avicenna, while "Bu `Ali" is his vernacular alter ego, the folktale magician.

In course of time, the fusion of Pahlavi and Arabic learned vocabulary with *Dari* phonology and syntax and *Dari* and Arabic vernacular words resulted in a Persian vernacular-cum-literary language with minimal stylistic differences. Any resulting linguistic dichotomy was in the form of bilingualism between Persian and Arabic, or Persian and another Iranian (or, later, a Turkic) language. Some of these languages—Parthian, Sogdian Khwarazmian, (pre-Turkish) Āzari—were overwhelmed by Persian and ceased to be written as their speakers took advantage of Persian, the language of high culture and interregional communication. Their descendants and successors among speakers of current Iranian dialects and minority languages—such as Lori, Semnāni, Yaghnobi, Qashqā'i Turkish—likewise use the written and spoken Persian of their host country in dealing with affairs outside their community, while their mother tongues tend to absorb more Persian elements and shrink in geographical and social domains.

In an earlier paper (Perry 2003) I demonstrated statistically that modern Persian, in comparison with modern Egyptian Arabic, does not represent a case of diglossia (in which a lexically and grammatically distinct form of the language is taught and used for high literature, formal speech, etc., while the current and local vernacular serves for everyday writing and speech). I argued that there are sound historical and linguistic reasons for Persian's escaping the diglossic polarity of Katharevousa and dhimotiki Greek, or *fushā* and *`āmmiyya* Arabic—or indeed *Pārsik* and *Dari* Middle Persian.

Whereas the High form of the language ('H') in modern Egypt or German-speaking Switzerland, earlier modern Greece, Sasanian Iran, etc., is a distinct dialect, evolved in a temporally and/or spatially distant milieu from the vernacular ('L') and superimposed upon it, modern written Persian is (like written English) a minimally varied form evolved from, and evolving with, the vernacular. Islamic New Persian also evolved in symbiosis and competition with Arabic content for the first three or four centuries to resign to Arabic the status of 'H' (the high language of scripture, liturgy, and scholarship), written and spoken Persian thus continued to develop side by side as mutually comprehensible versions of the same language. While written Persian progressively claimed the domains proper to Arabic literature as its own, expanding its lexicon with loanwords, loan compounds, and calques, spoken Persian preserved the common syntactic and lexical basis and incorporated what was borrowed from Arabic as it trickled down from scholarly usage. The principal common bond was Persian poetry, the repository of the national legend, communal and moral values, and spiritual aspirations—which both the literate and the illiterate knew and transmitted orally. Sociolinguistic dichotomy there was, but by way of bilingualism with Arabic, not diglossia within Persian. Most Iranian scientists and philosophers of the pre-Mongol period wrote their scholarly output in Arabic while speaking in Persian (and, like ʿOmar Khayyām and al-Ghazāli, writing popular essays and poetry in Persian).

This state of hierarchical bilingualism was reversed after the Mongol invasions: Arabic throughout the eastern Islamic world suffered a reduction in its intellectual domain, while Persian expanded into philosophy and the religious and secular sciences, written not only by Iranians but also by Turks, Indians, and others who came to be included in the Persianate sphere. Conversely and contemporaneously, spoken Persian was challenged for hegemony as the lingua franca of the same region by other vernaculars, the most important of which were several varieties of Turkish. Once again, Persian was in a hierarchical bilingual (not diglossic) partnership, this time as 'H' to the 'L' of Turkish—a situation that lasted in many parts of the Iranian world up until modern times.

Obviously, bilingualism with Arabic and/or a Turkic or Indic vernacular is a fairly polarized sociolinguistic and cultural state; pressures for linguistic change within such a Kulturbund would likely push toward uniformity rather than diversity. When native speakers of Turkish or, say, Kurdish needed to reach a wider audience, they would use written or spoken Persian; and their style, insofar as they were educated, would tend toward the universal, or more formal, rather than less formal, standard. When a Persophone elite wished to express their identity vis-à-vis the Turks or Arabs in their midst, they would use a Persian comprehensible to, and valued by, their colinguals of whatever socioeconomic station. As the conventions of a valued common tradition of Persian verse proliferated, native and non-native users of the literary koine would (and did) tend toward a poetical standard; consumers and producers—some of whom were technically illiterate, reciting from memory and composing orally—thus tended to keep the "literary" language largely homoglossic with the vernacular. The pressures for a fissure of this language of solidarity along diglossic lines were simply not there.

THE RISE OF PERSIAN LEXICOGRAPHY

If the most obvious triumph of Persian literary survival from pre-Islamic times is that of the hero-tales of the *dehqān* class, a less obtrusive but no less important continuity is seen in the traditions of the third estate of Sasanian society, the *dabir*s or government secretaries. Their primary functions as epistolographers, secretaries, and belletrists are obviously pertinent to the theme of this symposium; but I will here stress a lesser-known achievement of this class which is relevant to a neglected field of Persian language studies—that of historical lexicography.

By way of preparation, let us remember that the Pahlavi language and its writing system were not factors in this continuity, except in the most tenuous way. New Persian, the written embodiment of *Dari,* was newly clothed in Arabic script, which shared with Aramaic-based Pahlavi little more than a right-to-left directionality. The purposes of Middle Persian and New Persian dictionaries were likewise different. The Middle Persian *Frahang-i Pahlavig* (ostensibly a glossary of Aramaeograms) was organized thematically in 30–31 chapters (*dar* 'gate; topic, chapter'). The topics follow in a descending universal taxonomy from the sublime and cosmographic, through flora and fauna, to human types and activities. These last include farming, hunting, horse breeding, royalty, the army, crime and punishment, and (in two chapters) the art of the scribe and chancellery usage. Though the content and arrangement vary in different recensions, the work appears to have been a manual not only of uzvārishn, but of traditional lore and practice for Middle Persian scribes. The topics treated clearly represented a traditional Persian cyclopaedia and were recapitulated to a great extent in New Persian genres of *andarz* (sage counsel) and *adab* (etiquette, established usage) as represented in the 11th century *Qābus-nāma* and *Chahār Maqāla.* Significantly, the word *farhang* (elusively polysemous even in modern Persian) is explained by `Abd al-Rashid Tatavi, the learned Indian lexicographer of Shāhjahān's era, in the introduction to his *Farhang-e Rashidi,* as originally a synonym of the Arabic *adab* 'etiquette, culture' (Dabirsiyaqi 1989:152).

In terms of scribal and lexicographical usage, the *Frahang-i Pahlavig* gave to New Persian *farhangs* (defining dictionaries, which reportedly began to appear before AD 900) not only its designation, but also the name and use of its structural unit, the dār 'topic, category, section, chapter.' The Persian word inspired a calque, Perso-Arabic (and hence Arabic) *bāb* 'chapter,' etc., adding to the Arabic sense of 'gate, door' the abstract metaphor from its Persian synonym. This rubric was applied not only to thematic but also to alphabetical divisions of Persian dictionaries up until the late 19th century (by which time the practice of strict alphabetization had long made it redundant).

The initial and continuing purpose of the New Persian *farhangs*, as the lexicographers themselves tell us, was to explain and help to preserve and promulgate New Persian poetry. Initially they were also designed as active *vade-mecums* for poets, being arranged as reverse, or rhyming, dictionaries. The earliest extant Persian dictionary, the *Loghat-e Fors* of Asadi Tusi, was produced about 1050 explicitly to introduce the prestigious poetical vocabulary of Khorasan to readers in western Iran. Paper, imported from China to Samarqand under Sogdian rule and subsequently manufactured locally, materially aided in this linguistic reconquest. Moreover, in 1055 the Seljuk Turks ousted the Buwayhid rulers (Iranians who nevertheless patronized Arab poets at court) from Baghdad and western Iran. Persia was politically and culturally united, so that poets (and scholars) of all regions found patrons for works in Persian. After about 1300, the most numerous, innovative, and successful Persian dictionaries were produced in India under both Turkish and Indian rulers.

If the concept and, in part, the layout of the dictionary were transmitted by the pre-Islamic scribes, the content was inspired primarily by Ferdowsi's epic. From the time of the earliest Indo-Persian dictionaries, a frequent convention employed in the *dibācha* (author's preface) to explain his motivation was a personal anecdote, as follows: "Once the compiler was reading the *Shāhnāma*, 'the best of all books,' with a group of friends, who were often frustrated by unfamiliar vocabulary. He yielded to their entreaties to compile a glossary" (so the *Farhang-e [Fakhr-e] Qavvās*, ca. 1300, and the *Dastur al-afāzel*, 1340). Some lexicographers add Nezāmi's *Eskandarnāma*, praised as "the companion of kings," as a text in question (e.g., the *Dāneshnāma-yi Qadar Khān* of ca. 1400, fol. 46). All Persian dictionaries compiled in India during the 14th and 15th centuries cite vocabulary from the *Shāhnāma*, whether they include a version of this etiological myth or not (Baevskii 2007:73, 114, 128–29, 132). *Farhangs* thus paralleled the basic poetical corpus itself in establishing norms of interpretation, orthography, and orthoepy for Persian; and in overtly paying homage to their source of inspiration, they contributed a meta-legend that enhanced the aura of the Book of Kings.

THE SPREAD OF AN IDEOLOGY

Ferdowsi's *Shāhnāma* faithfully represented the royal and heroic tradition of the national legend, as distinct from the priestly and mythical. Thus, for instance, his version of the legend of Alexander (who, as the destroyer of the sacred books, was anathema to the Zoroastrian priesthood) legitimizes the Macedonian conqueror as an Iranian king by grafting him onto the Achaemenid lineage. It was this politico-cultural and desacralized history of Iran—beginning with the myths of the pre-Zoroastrian culture heroes of the Aryans, analogues of the Vedic gods, and incorporating Transoxianan Iranian and other steppe peoples, Afghans, Indians, and Macedonians (*Rum*, 'Greeks') into the fabric of the Iranian empire and world-view—that the *Shāhnāma* sold to successive Turkic conquerors and neighbors of Persia, from the Ghaznavids to the Mughals. Even an enemy of Samanid (and Ghaznavid) Persia, the Qarakhanid, or Ilek-khanid, dynasty of Qarluq Turks at Kashghar, was happy to buy into the convention and adopt the dynastic name Al-e Afrāsyāb, alluding to the traditional (and respected) Turanian rival of Iran's kings and heroes: better the villain of the piece than an outsider.

The work was also widely imitated, not only in Iran and Central Asia, but also in India, to flatter royal patrons and portray their conquests as analogous with those of the ancient Shāhs and heroes of Iran (cf. Fragner 1999:60). There is even a 19th-century *Jārj-nāma,* penned by Mullā Feroz, a loyal Parsi subject of the British Raj, extolling the exploits of Clive and Cornwallis in the service of George III. (It was printed in 1837, ironically a few years after the East India Company discontinued Persian as the official language of administration.)

Like Beowulf, much of the *Shāhnāma* is a saga from pagan times retold in the context of the new monotheism. Not overtly anti-Islamic (though the clerical leaders of the Islamic Republic banned it from the curriculum), this secular celebration of *Irānigari,* 'Persianness,' is nevertheless obviously pagan in inspiration and, despite superficial islamization, even in expression. Its acknowledgment of the advent of Zoroaster is perfunctory; the destinies of men are determined by blind fate, not by a merciful God; invocations to the deity are usually to *izad* or *yazdān*—barely singularized denizens (the *yazatas*) of the pre-Zoroastrian pantheon. Despite the carefully even-handed treatment of the Arab Muslims in the final chapter, the work is a semi-conscious reaction to Iran's defeat and conversion; it must be read in the spirit of the old paganism, or more likely a new agnosticism.

This is where the parallel with Greek language, verse, and culture seems most apt. Hellenistic civilization was able to pervade much of the known world not so much through military conquest as by ideological conversion and infection, by incorporating territories as varied as Macedon, Anatolia, Egypt, and Rome, and embracing aspects of Babylonian, Iranian, Indian, Judaic, and its own "pagan" philosophies, on a foundation of Homer and the alphabet. After Alexander's conquest of the East, the Greek language and its alphabet were adopted to varying degrees by Iranian peoples such as the Bactrians and Parthians, together with much of Greek art and philosophy in the realms of music, medicine, military and civic organization—as is attested by the Greek-derived vocabulary in the early *farhangs*. Persianate civilization, retaining much of its Hellenistic experience and catalyzed by the Islamic conquest, infused a large part (territorial and intellectual) of the Islamic East with a neo-pagan sensibility, building on the *Shāhnāma* and a restructured language exemplified in, and evolving from, the epic.

INCLUSIVITY

In the post-Mongol period poetry joined forces with music, and built on the legacy of mystical and lyrical poets who gained an international following in their lifetimes: Rumi, who wrote outside Iran in a non-courtly environment where Greek, Armenian, and Turkish were spoken, and was later claimed for Turkish as much as Iranian culture; Sa`di, a world traveler (or posing as such), who added new words and memorable quotations to Persian, as Shakespeare did to English; Hāfez, invited to India, but too devoted to an idealized Shiraz to leave home.

The inclusiveness of Persian is first of all evident in the many ways in which it incorporated Arabic vocabulary and Islamic lore, processing and manipulating them to its own purposes and those of the Turks, Indians, and other peoples whom it embraced as partners in the complex Persianate venture. It is well known that many Indians (not only Muslims, but Hindus and those of other faiths) joined willingly in the Persianate venture: fusing the fissures between Sunni and Shi'i, *shari`a* and Sufism, Believer and Infidel, and compiling Persian treaties and treatises, dictionaries, grammars, histories, and above all, Persian poetry.

Like Hellenistic civilization, Persianate culture proved to be adaptive and inclusive, which made it popular with a variety of elites in the conquered territories. The underlying reasons for this adaptivity were not necessarily the same. Probably the salient feature of Hellenistic inclusivity was its religious tolerance, whereby local deities and their cults were let be, or (notably in Egypt and Mesopotamia) patronized and assimilated to the Greek pantheon and practices. This was a widespread attribute of polytheistic societies, practiced just as magnanimously (and shrewdly) by the Achaemenians and the Roman republic. As a monotheistic culture, Persianate Islam could not be expected to practice such a degree of tolerance. How, then, could a Persianate culture formally invested in Islam manifest inclusivity for, in particular, Indian polytheists?

It seems unreasonable to expect much cultural accommodation between a society of mainly vegetarian polytheists, venerating the cow and honoring their gods with fruits and garlands of flowers, and an army of carnivorous monotheists whose principal annual holiday culminates in the mass butchery of assorted livestock. Predictably, the first Arab invaders of India set about looting temples and destroying the idols (which were popularly identified with Hubal and other anathematized idols of pre-Islamic Arabia). The Turkish dynast Mahmud of Ghazna renewed this custom some three centuries later, albeit more for the temple treasure than from outraged monotheism. Biruni, the Persian scientist who accompanied his annual campaigns, interviewed pandits and learned to read the Sanskrit scriptures. He has left us a coolly objective ethnography of northern India and a penetrating, sympathetic analysis of the philosophy of Hinduism and the monotheism that underlies its proliferation of divinities. This, and studies like it, no doubt contributed to a theoretical basis for the subsequent treatment of Hindus and Buddhists as People of the Book; though it was in practice the fact that the polytheists were vastly in the majority, and that dead men pay no taxes, that chiefly restrained later Muslim rulers from righteous massacre. Nevertheless, Buddha statues were occasionally defaced (literally, de-faced) by Muslim iconoclasts, and in the case of the colossi in Bamian, Afghanistan, finally destroyed.

After the time of Biruni it was Persian *ulama* and Sufis, and Persianized Turkish rulers and soldiers, who undertook the Islamization and Persianization of India—and who in turn were usually Indianized to a degree. This process was a long and complex affair, not always benign and predictable, and impossible to summarize here. However, I will suggest at the outset that not just the *Shāhnāma* and its congeners, but the bulk of Persian poetry of the classical period carries at least the germ of that same new agnosticism which, in the East, flavored the plain cup of Islam. This attitude is not exclusive to Persian, being seen plainly even in the cynical Arabic wine songs of the half-Persian Abu Nowās and the skeptical verses of Arab poets such as Abu'l-ʿAtāhiya and Abu'l ʿAlā' al-Maʿarri. But it is most overtly manifested in the *robā'is* of ʿOmar Khayyām, which directly challenge the competence and ethics of the conventional deity. Even the less aggressively antinomian *ghazal,* with its mystical "metaphors" of idolatry, drunkenness, and debauchery, seems often to be an elaboration of Khayyām's carpe diem.

At some point in this transaction, a tipping point was reached: the recipient cultures were bringing more to their portion of Persianate civilization than they were receiving. Persian verse in forms such as the *robā'i,* the *moʿammā* (literary riddle), the chronogram, and especially the *ghazal,* as practiced in an Indian and not even necessarily Muslim milieu, was no longer mainly a vehicle for the national legend and sociopolitical ethos of Iran, nor for the pristine message of Islam. Persian poetry and elegant prose mediated between the spiritual and the worldly, particularly in India where its offspring, Urdu, inherited and refined its tradition in a unique regional culture.

This "regional" Indo-Persian culture proved also to be vertically inclusive to a remarkable degree. Given sufficient education, markers such as religion, sect, caste, and ethnicity were no bar to the enjoyment or production of Persian or Urdu verse, their ancillary language sciences, and their aura of *ādāb,* of literary taste and cultural refinement. Not generally appreciated is the extent to which resident foreigners, Farangis, also indulged in the mild intoxicant known as Persian poetry—especially the *ghazal.* During the 18th and 19th centuries, more than sixty Europeans and Indo-Europeans (including six Britons, thirteen Frenchmen, and eight women) dabbled in composing Persian and Urdu poetry, some of them accumulating considerable *divāns* (Saksena 1941).

Several reasons might be adduced for this addiction, such as the genial multicultural milieu of Indian courts, and the exceptional gene pools from which many of these accomplished foreign adventurers (and, in the case of the second generation, their native spouses) sprang. But heading the list, surely, was the unique attraction of the *ghazal*, the sonnet of the East, for those adept at languages. According to one scholar who has spent many years wrestling with theories of the *ghazal,* it is "a comical brain-teaser based on a semantic stunt" (Skalmowski 2004:127). Without endorsing so extreme a position, we must admit that it is an enjoyable and challenging exercise for writer and reader alike (a trait it shares with the *robā'i* and, to an extent, the *masnavi*); and for educated Europeans who already delighted in trying out epigrams in Greek or Latin, to play with another intuitively cohesive set of poetical conventions in a classical language was irresistible—all the more to do so in a living vernacular, Urdu, and bask in the applause of indulgent native speakers.

Whether in Iran, Anatolia, or India, two basic characteristics of the most popular "classical" Persian poetry assured it of an interactive relation with the reader, of whatever cultural origin or class. These are its humor (most commonly manifested as wit—through linguistic techniques such as the pun—but also in drollery, bawdry, and other forms); and its comfortably homoglossic register between styles ranging from the pedantic and archaizing to the colloquial, drawing on dialect and vulgarity. Rumi is the past master of this "high colloquial," both in the *Masnavi* and his *ghazals* (cf. Skalmowski 2004:163–74); but Sa`di and Hāfez follow closely in his footsteps. Persian prose styles have varied much more widely in accordance with the topic, readership, and other imperatives; but since the basic lexicon was established on the poetic corpus, and classical Persian evolved as a vehicle for less specialized literature than Arabic (and for the *haute vulgarisation* of Arabic originals), the homoglossic principle was preserved.

Even more telling is the prestige of the *ghazal* as an absolute intellectual accomplishment. So completely have the challenges of its conventional form eclipsed the relevance of its content that even for someone without a sense of humor, and seemingly opposed to all that the *ghazal* expresses, composing a few typical Persian *ghazals* is a rite of passage. Ayatollah Khomeini (d. 1989), who banned music in Iran, declared in a radio broadcast in 1979: "Allāh did not create man so that he could have fun. The aim of creation was for mankind to be put to the test through hardship and prayer... There are no jokes in Islam. There is no humor in Islam. There is no fun in Islam. There can be no fun and joy in whatever is serious" (Taheri 1986:259). Yet, as a pious seminarian at Qom in the 1930s, under the pseudonym Hendi "the Indian," he penned several *ghazals* in which he ostensibly craves wine and love, bewails his infatuation, frustration, and hypocrisy, and prays for annihilation in the throes of a drunken tryst (Thiesen 1991:211–19). Fifty years later, as ruler of Iran, he wrote—and published—a further collection of *ghazals* and other verse; these also include celebrations of love, wine, and, yes, music ("Close up the shop of abstinence, for... the song of the lute has come again"). Whether these lays of vicarious fun are the secret dreams of an uptight theology student, or metaphors of divine ecstasy or political engagement, the surface form is that of the typical mystical-lyrical *ghazal* (if somewhat over-stuffed with the conventional imagery). So highly regarded is the *ghazal* that even the favorite butt of its barbs, the supposedly hypocritical puritan, must pay it homage; and so strict are the rules of this "comical brain-teaser" that the amateur must always be a lover.

CONCLUSION

Persian began as an Iranian vernacular (*Dari*), related to but distinct from conservative written Middle Persian (Pahlavi), the vehicle of Zoroastrian literature and Sasanian administration. When Islam replaced Zoroastrianism and Arabic hence replaced Pahlavi as the language of scripture, liturgy, and (for some time) administration, *Dari*—being free of specific religious associations—gradually occupied the domain of secular literature in Iran. It presumably already had a foothold in the field of (orally transmitted) poetry, since this was the first genre to be recorded when *Dari* began to be written in Arabic characters, and was often the medium of antinomian or agnostic sentiments.

As the language of the Samanid court in 10th-century Bukhara (used in poetry and local administration under bilingual secretary-litterateurs), Persian orthography became standardized, translations were made from Arabic prose classics, and a controlled flood of Arabic loanwords entered the language (by this time called Pārsi, soon arabicized as Fārsi). The Arabic element in Persian was adapted systematically to Persian, evolving rules for the formation of nominal and verbal compounds and derivatives that were later transmitted to other Iranian, Turkic, and Indic languages as these entered the literary sphere of Islam. In Persian, the rapid trickle-down of learned Arabic borrowings in a milieu that encouraged literary competition, and the spread of *madrasa* education, ensured that the literary language and the vernacular did not split diglossically. Despite (or more likely because of) historical bilingualism with Arabic and Turkish, Persian has remained essentially homoglossic to the present day.

The production of a poetical version of the national legend under the patronage of independent Persianate dynasties established Persian's prestige and viability throughout Iran and Transoxiana. The volume and importance of the *Shāhnāma,* and the large number of unfamiliar words that it preserved from spoken and literary Middle Iranian languages, made it the primary and model corpus, and indeed the impetus, for the earliest Persian dictionaries. On the basis of Ferdowsi's epic and the rising corpus of other Persian verse, early lexicographers in Iran and India set the standards of Persian orthography, orthoepy, and poetics.

Poetry expanded its formal, thematic, and geographical range, spreading not only the ethos of the Iranian national legend but also a code of civil ethics and a message of spiritual enlightenment, each of which hewed ostensibly to Islamic norms but actually owed much to Iranian, Hellenistic, and Indian antecedents. A sense of humor and a propensity for games of wit rendered this verse more interactive and inclusive. The broad acceptability of its non-sectarian content (or, in other words, its adaptability to the subtle expression of different philosophical or religious beliefs), and—thanks to homoglossia—the formal ease of access to this verse by even technically illiterate Persian-speakers and speakers of Persian as a second language, ensured its popularity from Azerbaijan to Bengal, and among readers and amateur poets from the ruling, clerical (in both senses), commercial, and artisan classes. Particularly in India, Persian became the agora in which different peoples, classes, and faiths—Iranian, Turk, and Indian; Muslim, Hindu, and Parsi; ruler, trader, and scholar—could meet and mingle on equal terms. *Pari passu* with the geocultural triumph of Persian poetry, of course, marched the more utilitarian advance of the language in prose genres such as history and belles-lettres, and for purposes as varied as tax-collection, political intrigue, international diplomacy, and business.

The geographical range of Persian at its premodern zenith appears to have exceeded that of Hellenistic Greek east of the Mediterranean. Greek was sprinkled more sparsely over the area, confined in its full usage to the Alexandrias and other major cities; yet the Hellenistic legacy in philosophy and the arts was surprisingly pervasive, as is testified in the numerous Greek loanwords in Persian, the similarities between Greek and Persian romances, and the homage to Hellenistic usages in *adab* literature. After the fall of the Seleucids, none of the successor languages (Parthian, Pahlavi, Aramaic, or even Arabic) adequately filled this interregional geocultural vacuum until its inundation by New Persian. Thanks chiefly to the long-distance trade networks frequented by (in many cases, established by) Persian-speaking merchants, Persian's hegemony as an auxiliary contact vernacular and written language was continued well outside the Iranian plateau during the period of Mongol, and subsequently Turkish, dominance in Asia. From the early 13th century into the late 14th it was arguably the official foreign language in China (see David Morgan in chapter 4). Until well into the 16th century on the upper Volga the term "Tajik" was a synonym for merchant: on the occasion of the Russian conquest of Kazan in 1552, the city was surrounded by a "ditch of the Tajiks" (*tezichkii/teshichkii rov*; Barthold 1934:598b); and as late as the 19th century, as we have seen, Persian was the primary literary vehicle over most of the South Asian subcontinent.

REFERENCES

Alam, Muzaffar. 2004. *The Languages of Political Islam: India 1200–1800.* Reprint. Chicago: University of Chicago Press.

Baevskii, Solomon I. 2007. *Early Persian Lexicography: Farhangs of the 11th to the 15th Centuries,* trans. N. Killian, rev. John R. Perry. London: Global Oriental.

Barthold, V.V. 1934. Tadjık. In *Encyclopedia of Islam,* Vol. 4. Leiden: E.J. Brill.

Dabir Siyāqi, Mohammad. 1368/1989. *Farhanghā-ye Fārsī va farhang-gunahā* (Persian dictionaries and vocabularies). Tehran: Isparak.

Davis, Dick. 2002. *Panthea's Children. Hellenistic Novels and Medieval Persian Romances.* New York: Bibliotheca Persica.

Elwell-Sutton, L.P. 1987. Arabic iii: Arabic Influences in Persian Literature. In *Encyclopædia Iranica,* Vol. 2, ed. E. Yarshater, pp. 233–37. Boston: Routledge and Kegan Paul.

Fragner, Bert G. 1999. *Die "Persophonie": Regionalität, Identität und Sprachkontakt in der Geschichte Asiens.* ANOR No. 5. Berlin: Das Arabische Buch.

Hovannisian, Richard G., and Georges Sabagh, eds. 1998. *The Persian Presence in the Islamic World.* Cambridge: Cambridge University Press.

Kai Kā'ūs b. Iskandar b. Qābūs b. Washmgir. 1951. *Nasīhat-nāma Known as Qābûs-nāma,* ed. and trans. Reuben Levy. E.J.W. Gibb Memorial Series, n.s. 18. London: Luzac.

Keshāni, Khosraw. 1993. *Farhang-e fārsi-ye zānsu* (Reverse Dictionary of Persian). Tehran: Markaz-e Našr-e Dānešgāhi.

Khomeini, Ruhollah. 1997. *Five Mystical Ghazals,* trans. W. Hanaway. *Iranian*

Studies 30(3-4): 273–76.

Lazard, Gilbert. 1975. The Rise of the New Persian Language. In *Cambridge History of Iran,* vol. 4, ed. R.N. Frye, pp. 595–632. Cambridge: Cambridge University Press.

MacKenzie, D.N. 2001. Frahang i Pahlawig. In *Encyclopædia Iranica,* vol. 10, ed. E. Yarshater, pp. 123–25. Boston: Routledge and Kegan Paul.

J[alal] M[atini]. 1984. Ketābhā-ye darsi dar Jomhuri-ye Eslāmi (The Textbooks of the Islamic Republic). *Irān Nāmeh* 3.1 (Autumn 1363): 1–25 (English summary, pp. 1–3).

Moïnfar, Mohammad Dj. 1970. *Le vocabulaire arabe dans le Livre des Rois de Firdausi.* Wiesbaden: Harrassowitz.

Narshakhi, Abu Bakr b. Mohammad. 1954. *The History of Bukhara,* trans. and ed. Richard N. Frye. Cambridge, MA: Medieval Academy of America.

`Oryān, Sa`id, ed. 1998. *Vāzha-nāma-ye Pahlavi–Pāzand.* Tehran.

Perry, John R. 1991. *Form and Meaning in Persian Vocabulary: The Arabic Feminine Ending.* Costa Mesa, CA: Bibliotheca Persica and Mazda Publishers.

—— 1995. Lexical Doublets as a Derivational Device in Persian: The Arabic Feminine Ending. In *Acta Orient. Hung.* (Telegdi festschrift) 48:127–53.

—— 1997. Script and Scripture: The Three Alphabets of Tajik Persian, 1927–1997. *Journal of Central Asian Studies* 2(1): 2–18.

—— 2003. Persian as a Homoglossic Language. In *Iran, questions et connaissances.* Vol. 3, *Cultures et sociétés contemporaines,* ed. B. Hourcade, pp. 11–28. Studia Iranica, Cahier 27. Actes du 4ᵉ Congrès européen d'études iraniennes organisé par la Societas Iranologica Europea, Paris, 6–10 septembre 1999. Paris: Peeters.

Powell, Barry B. 1991. *Homer and the Origin of the Greek Alphabet.* Cambridge: University Press.

Sādeqi, `Ali-Ashraf. 1978. *Takvin-e zabān-e fārsi.* Tehran.

Saksena, Ram Babu. 1941. *European and Indo-European Poets of Urdu and Persian.* Lucknow: Newul Kishore Press.

Skalmowski, Woiciech. 2004. *Studies in Iranian Linguistics and Philology.* Cracow: Wydawnictwo Uniwersytetu Jagiellońskiego.

Skjaervø, Prods Oktor. 2006. Iranian Languages and Scripts. In *Encyclopædia Iranica,* vol. 13, ed. E. Yarshater, pp. 344–77. Boston: Routledge and Kegan Paul.

Taheri, Amir. 1986. *The Spirit of Allāh: Khomeini and the Iranian Revolution.* Bethesda, MD: Celer & Celer.

Thiesen, Finn. 1991. A Draught of Love. In *Corolla Iranica,* ed. R.E. Emmerick and D. Weber, pp. 211–19. Frankfurt am Main: P. Lang.

2

Secretaries, Poets, and the Literary Language

WILLIAM L. HANAWAY

INTRODUCTION: THE LITERATI AND THE WRITTEN LANGUAGE

I will try to show in this chapter that the formal, written, courtly language of the Persian-using courts, at least up to the 13th or early 14th century, was created and developed as result of the dynamic interaction of the work of the secretaries and the poets, with an increasingly important contribution from the lexicographers. Poets and secretaries interacted with each other in their work and in their social life, and with other *adibs* in the intellectual and artistic circles of the courts. Many secretaries wrote divans of poetry in Persian and Arabic in addition to their official prose, and at least one, Rashid al-Din Vatvāt, became better known as a poet than as the secretary that he was. Poets, on the other hand, knew the epistolary terminology and style and wrote letters in verse, even saying that they were letters. In their ease with, and mastery of, the written language, poets and secretaries borrowed devices of language and meaning freely from each other or from the common pool. They also shared a literary form, the tripartite structure of many *qasidas*. The early Persian courts provided the setting or the matrix from which emerged a written language that became standard throughout the Persianate world, which later included the Ottoman court, many Central Asian courts, and the Mughal courts of the Indian subcontinent.

Many aspects of formal written Persian and its history need to be isolated and examined before we can begin to see more clearly the reasons and implications of its stability and seeming resistance to change over a millennium. John Perry discusses in this volume the evidence necessary to describe the transition of the language from the written Middle Persian of the late Sasanian period to the early New Persian of the Islamic period. The main source of written Persian from the 7th to the early 10th century AD, the period from which the earliest written texts survive, was the courts of sovereigns and provincial officials where the work of governing was carried out, and particularly the chancelleries of these courts, where there was the greatest concentration of educated, literate men and the greatest need for a standard written language. Much additional research will be necessary before we can describe the development of written Persian in any significant detail. Broadly speaking, the courts remained the main source of written Persian at least until the end of the Seljuq period (1038–1194), when Sufi establishments and the schools called *nizāmiyyas* (see below) began to play a more significant role in the production and standardization of written Persian. This chapter focuses on two problems: first, the role of the literati in the creation and development of the formal written language of the courts in the Persianate world from the 10th through the 15th century; second, possible reasons for the relative stability of this written language over so many centuries and across a wide geographical area.

The courts of the Persianate world, from the Sasanian period onward, were the milieux of the *ahl-i qalam* (men of the pen), or the literati. The literati comprised all those who used written, formal Persian in the course of their professional work and, in many cases, in their leisure-time activities as well. They would have been the viziers, other administrators and bureaucrats, secretaries and scribes, poets, accountants, historians and chroniclers, jurisprudents, lexicographers, other scholars and *adibs* (cultivated men of letters). The core of the literati were the secretaries—the *munshis, dabirs*, or *kātibs*—for it was they who were most instrumental in the transition in the use of Pahlavi in the pre-Islamic courts to the use of Arabic and then New Persian in the Islamic courts.[1] They were also the transmitters of the bureaucratic and administrative skills and traditions from the Zoroastrian regime of the Sasanians to the regimes of the Muslim rulers. *Munshi* retained its basic meaning of "secretary" throughout the Persianate world until at least the 18th century, occasionally being used to mean "author," as it was by the Il-Khanid-period ruler Muhammad Zangi Bukhārī.[2] In Persian-using South Asia, the meaning of *munshi* began to evolve during the 18th century and gradually assumed the sense of "translator" or "language teacher" in addition to its more traditional sense of "secretary." In Ottoman lands, the function of translator came to be filled not by the *munshi* but by the dragoman (ultimately from Ar. *turjumān,* "translator").

From among the literati, the two groups at court most involved with the written language were the secretaries and the poets. *Munshis* (the word derives from an Arabic root meaning "to create, to produce, to compose something in writing") were professional producers of *inshā* (prose composition). I.A. Zilli, in discussing *inshā* as a literary form or genre, says that from its dictionary meaning of "creation, construction," it came to mean prose compositions, letters, documents, and state papers. Later it became a synonym for *munsha'āt* "documents composed in accordance with certain norms prescribed for such compositions that would distinguish their form, style and diction from ordinary prose. Gradually...[it] came to be used to represent a distinct genre in Arabic and later in Persian literature as well. It became defined as a branch of learning that discerned the merits and defects of the prose composition of letters and documents...as distinct from regular treatises and books" (2000:309–49). The whole genre of inshā became very ramified according to the relative status of the writer and recipient, and the content of the document.[3] In the present context *inshā* is assumed to be prose, although strictly speaking the term allows for poetry too.

H.R. Roemer may be the first Western scholar to write about inshā as a literary genre.[4] A word about "literature" would be in order here. Today we think of literature as belles lettres, something written for its own sake or as an end in itself rather than to be informative; hence, by and large, we think of literature as poetry and prose fiction, and possibly essays. We must not, however, project this understanding of literature onto the past, particularly a past that is not part of our own tradition. In medieval Islam, *adabiyāt* (literature) was written by individuals who considered themselves *adibs*, or littérateurs. The scope of "prose literature" was considerably wider than it is today. Therefore the sort of prose writing that I will refer to here—history, collections of letters (*inshā*), manuals of prosody, mirrors for princes, books of ethics and similar works—are all firmly within the boundaries of *adabiyāt*.

Persians, in differentiating poetry from prose, followed the Arabic practice from before Islam. Generic distinctions are more numerous and clearly defined in Persian poetry than they are in prose. Prose genres lack some of the prominent defining features of poetry, and tend to be thought of in terms of their content alone rather than their content and their form together.

Inshā has not received as much scholarly attention as have other prose genres, although there is a significant amount of it available in manuscript and print.

Genres always change, and change to some degree with every new example that appears. Nevertheless, Persian genres changed very slowly; they remained fairly stable over a long time because genre boundaries were considered important. If, for example, a poet should disregard any of the formal requirements for the sort of poem he wanted to write, it would have been rejected and not been considered poetry. The question of genre stability, steadiness within the larger processes of change, is central to our discussion of the written language of government administration.

The secretaries did the work of the chancellery, the *divān* (department) of the medieval Persian courts where official government documents and records were created and kept. This department was called the *divān-i risālat, divān-i rasā'il, divān-i kitābat,* or *divān-i inshā,* and the chief of this *divān* ranked high in the court and in several cases (more below) was promoted to the position of vizier or chief minister. It is important to note that while the rulers had their chief secretary and a *divān-i risālat* or chancellery, other officials too had secretaries. For example, Bayhaqi mentions a Bu Saʿid, secretary and *kadkhudā* (chief of staff) to Hājib Amir ʿAli Qarib, a powerful figure in the early days on the reign of Sultan Masʿud (r. 388–421 / 1030–41).[5] Poets were employed specifically to create poetry, much of it occasional, that would flatter the ruler or patron and enhance his reputation. Throughout the Seljuq period, court poets were the leading poets of their time. This situation changed with the foundation of the *nizāmiyyas* in the 12th century and the rise of Sufism, when Sufi centers became new sources of poetry and prose and some Sufi leaders entered the ranks of the literati. The courts, however, were for a long time almost the only source of employment or patronage for poets. A notable exception to this was the poet Firdawsi, author of the *Shāhnāma,* whose patron was a local *dihqān* (landowner). There were, no doubt, others like this, but compared with court patronage, rather few. The changes that came about during the Seljuq period did much to give the court poets the status of professional practitioners of their art.

While at first glance, secretaries and poets appear to be quite separate and distinct from each other in purpose and practice, both groups were professional writers, each pursuing a function that was different from, but complementary to, the other. The secretaries wrote prose letters and documents and, incidentally, some poetry, while the poets wrote poetry and, incidentally, some prose. Each was necessary to the ruler personally and to the proper operation of the government. Looked at from the inside by Nizāmi ʿAruzi of Samarqand, a 12th-century *adib* and theorist of court organization, a wise king and a smoothly functioning court required the presence of four professional practitioners: the secretary, the poet, the physician, and the astrologer. The first of these was concerned with the successful functioning of the court as an administrative unit, while the second was concerned with the fame and reputation of the ruler. The third looked after the health of the king and the courtiers, and the fourth aided the ruler in making decisions. Nizāmi ʿAruzi does not overtly suggest a ranking in importance or priority of these four but maybe the order in which he presented them served that purpose.

How can we account for the production of the special sort of Persian prose that emanated from the courts? One might argue that the secretaries were a close-knit, inward-looking, hereditary professional group that was very conscious of its role in developing prose style to meet the diplomatic and administrative needs of the court. Their written style must bring credit to their ruler from other rulers, and to themselves as skilled professional secretaries. This would require them to use their talents and skills to bring about innovations in prose style and to be constantly in the forefront of prose composition. Their professional work was quite different from what the poets were doing, in that the work of the secretaries was visible on paper. They had to write in a good hand in correct and elegant style and observe all the refinements of address and reference, line length and spacing, white space on the page, and proper folding of the document. The poets, for their part, had to compose within a more restrictive framework of both form and language. Persian poetic style, like the style of prose, evolved constantly but slowly throughout its history. Innovation came through improving upon received tradition but not departing from it. In innovating in this manner the poets displayed their real talent by working in the narrow space between convention and invention. Almost all of the poetry was composed to be recited, sung, or declaimed rather than to be read silently and, as a result, the impression they made was aural rather than visual. In this regard, the work of the secretaries and the poets sometimes converged. As far as we know, when a letter was presented to a king or high official in open court, it was generally read out loud by the chief secretary or vizier, and the aural impression that it made must have been carefully calculated by the secretary who composed it. Only a small (but very important) proportion of the work of a secretary, however, was writing letters that would have been read aloud.

While this line of argument may sound plausible, it has a major weakness. By viewing the secretaries and the poets as separate, self-concerned groups it ignores the existence of a powerful stratum of Persian society that we have called the literati, and the shared literary culture of the court within which each group functioned. The ideals of *adab* culture (educated and refined taste and behavior) prevailed among the literati and it is entirely natural that there be dynamic interaction between the poets and secretaries as literary creators. Poets and secretaries could no more have operated independently of each other than could scholars and divines. Therefore, I will argue that courtly, literary, written Persian, i.e., the Persian language written with a standard but evolving grammar, syntax, and register of vocabulary, developed and evolved at least until the end of the Seljuq period as a result of the interests of the literati and especially the dynamic interaction of the secretaries and the poets. This was the written language of the literati, the educated, aristocratic, courtly class who in the early part of this period were essentially the only class that could read and write. There were others who were literate, of course, but not many. Classical poetry and prose were highly refined forms, written for a purpose and not for their own sake. Later this too was to change as the courtly language of prose became more self-conscious and *masnu'i* (artificial), but for the early period poetry and prose were linked in the minds of the writers and poets by the shared theory of *adab* and the shared ideology of the class that produced and used it.[6]

Poets and secretaries were present in the courts and linked in the minds of courtiers and the literati from at least the time of the Samanids and the Saffarids (early 9th to early 11th centuries; more below). By the 12th and 13th centuries other contexts for the production of written Persian had gained in importance, although the courts still remained the primary source.

The chancellery, or secretarial, practice of the Persian courts of the Islamic period was a direct continuation of the practices of the Sasanian courts and possibly even earlier ones. In spite of the major change in ideology in the transition from Zoroastrianism to Islam and the adoption of a new script, Sasanian epistolary practices and the forms of documents produced by court secretaries were clearly the forerunners of what the secretaries wrote in the early Islamic courts in eastern Persia.[7] A Sasanian manual for the writing of letters has survived and much of what it says sounds similar to what we read in later manuals.[8] Not much remains of Sasanian epistolography, but a study of early Arabic histories and other sorts of works can give us a fair idea of Sasanian chancellery practice and the sorts of letters and documents that were written in those times.[9] Quite a bit of Pahlavi *tarassul* (epistolography) was translated into Arabic and was used by Arabic historians in writing the history of the Sasanians. For example, a number of letters from Shāpur I (r. D. 220–72) to the Byzantine Emperor and to the king of Armenia, likewise letters from Ardashir I (r. 225–40), were translated into Arabic by Ibn al-Muqaffa' (d. ca. 757) and were cited by Islamic historians such as Ibn Qutayba, Ibn Muskaway, Jahshyari, Mas'udi, Tabari, and others. These letters preserved, even in translation, the prose style and format of the Pahlavi originals and had a noticeable effect on both Arabic prose style of the early Islamic period and on the style of letter writing in the early Islamic chancelleries.

Most of the basic types of letters written in the Islamic chancelleries had also been written in the Sasanian period and possibly earlier. In addition to *sultāniyyāt* (royal decrees and orders), *ikhvāniyyāt* (letters among friends), the Sasanian chancelleries produced *fath nāmas* (announcements of victory), *'ahd nāmas* (agreements), *sawgand nāmas* (sworn statements), *tasliyyat nāmas* (letters of condolence), and others. The pre-Islamic forms of these letters show close parallels with their Islamic counterparts. Opening and closing formulae were similar in their content and phraseology. Titles, laudatory epithets, and closing prayers were also similar. In the late Sasanian period, the Persians hired Arabs to write the court correspondence from Ctesiphon. These scribes formed a semi-hereditary profession, an example being 'Abdi b. Zayd of Hira (d. ca. 590) who was also a sort of under-secretary for Arab affairs. He had succeeded his father in the position as an Arabic-writing scribe, and was subsequently succeeded by two of his own sons. Danner speculates that Persian scribes probably taught their skills to their own children as artisans passed on their expertise and techniques. In the early days of Islam, and probably later too, the scribes did not pursue the usual routes of Muslim learning, partly because many of them were Zoroastrians.[10] The high status enjoyed by the Sasanian scribes was also transmitted to their successors in the Islamic period and the reputation of the pre-Islamic Persian chancellery scribes was still strong centuries later. Muhammad Nakhjavāni, called Shams al-munshi (The Secretary's Sun), a

14th-century secretary and author of *Dastur al-kātib* (see below) says, "in the old days the kings of [pre-Islamic] Persia did not give permission to work as a scribe to any whose fathers and grandfathers had not also been scribes," and "They say that when the kings of Persia entered the *divān[-i risālat]*, the scribes of the *divān* did not stand up for them but rather did not neglect what they were engaged in for one moment."[11] The truth of falsity of these statements is less important than the fact that they show what later secretaries believed about their professional forebears, and the respect that they bore them.

Qābus b. Vashmgir (late 10th to early 11th century), in this book of advice to his son known as *Qābus Nāma*, devotes a chapter to "The Etiquette and Practice of Secretaryship and the Requirements for Being a Scribe." He says that the individual needs a complete mastery of usage, a good hand, and a lot of practice. He should embellish his letters with metaphors and verses from the Qur'an and the Hadith. He must not write in pure Persian because that is not good, and *Dari* is not known well and should never be written under any circumstances, for [in this regard] the unsaid is better than what is said…In Arabic letters, it is well known when to use rhetorical adornments, and *saj'* (rhymed prose) is a virtue and is welcome, but in Persian letters it is unpleasant and is better not used. Anything that he writes should be elevated, metaphorical and concise.

> The secretary should always be present in court and know the background of every matter, have quick understanding and a good memory, have an inquiring mind and keep notes on what he is asked to do and not to do. He should be aware of the business of everyone in the ministry, and look into things. He should keep all secrets carefully and not inquire openly into the affairs of the vizier, but keep them secret. The greatest art of the scribe is holding his tongue and not revealing the secrets of his master. It is a great asset if he is familiar with all styles of script and can write them, but he should keep this skill very secret from others lest he be known as a forger, because that would make his master lose confidence in him, and if someone else forges something and nobody knows who did it, they will blame him. [If he is going to forge something] he should not forge anything trivial because when he really needs to do it, it will have great benefits. Then, nobody will suspect him, for because of forged documents wise viziers have executed many expert and reputable scribes.[12]

و شرط کاتبی آنست که مادام مجاور حضرت باشی و سابق کار یاد داری و تیزفهم و نا
فراموش کار باشی متفحص باشی و از همه کارها تذکره همی داری از آنچه ترا فرمایند و از
آنچه ترا نه فرمایند. بر حال همه اهل دیوان واقف باشی و از معاملات همه اعمالها آگاه باش
و تجسس کن و از همه گونه تعریف اعمالها همی کن اگر چه در وقت بکارت نیاید، باشد که
وقتی دیگرت بکار آید ولکن آن سر با کس مگوی مگر وقتی که ناگزیر بود و بظاهر کدن
تفحص شغل وزیر منمای و لکن در باطن از همه چیز آگاه باش. و بر حساب قادر باش و یک
ساعت از تعرف کدخدایی و ناسهای معاملان نبشتن خالی مباش که این همه در کاتبان
هنرست. و بزرگترین هنری که کاتب را زبان نگاه داشتن است و سر ولی نعمت پیدا نا کردن
و خداوند خویش را از هر شغلی آگاه کردن و فضولی نابودن. اما اگر چنانچه خطاطی و قادر
باشی و از هر گونه خطی که بینی بدانی نبشت، این دانش سخت نیکست ولکن بر کسی پیدا
مکن تا بمزور کردن معروف نشوی که آنگاه اعتماد ولی نعمت تو از تو بر خیزد، و اگر کسی
دیگر مزوری کند چون ندانند که کردست بر تو بندند. و بهر محقری مزوری مکن تا اگر
وقتی بکار آید چون منافعی بزرگ خواهد بود، آنگه اگر بکنی کس بر تو گمان نبرد، که بسیار
کاتبان فاضل و محتشم را وزیران عالم هلاک کردند بسبب خطهای مزرور ایشان....

Another important early source that speaks in general terms about the
basic requirements for a secretary is Nizāmi 'Aruzi's *Chahār Maqāla*, written
around 550/1155. Nizāmi 'Aruzi was not a secretary but rather an *adib* and
poet, a court litterateur, who wrote his treatise to advise his patron Abu
al-Hasan Husām al-Din 'Ali, a Ghurid prince. He is, naturally, much closer
to home when he talks about the requirements for being a poet than he is
when discussing the qualifications of a physician or an astrologer. In the
case of the secretary (or *munshi*), we feel that he does express an educated
opinion and even a personal interest, since the domains of the secretary and
the poet in some ways were fairly close or even overlapping. This is what
Nizāmi 'Aruzi says about the secretary (*dabir*):

ON THE NATURE OF SECRETARYSHIP AND THE QUALITIES OF
THE ACCOMPLISHED SECRETARY, AND WHAT APPERTAINS TO THIS

*Secretaryship is a profession that comprises a mode of discourse that
is persuasive and eloquent, that is useful in communication among people in
the way of common conversation, consultation or altercation, in praise or
blame, in deception or kindness or instigation, in inflating subjects and de-
flating topics, in making various excuses or reproaches, in strengthening firm
bonds and recalling precedents, and in setting out the order and arrangement
of words on every occasion so that they are expressed in the fittest and worthi-
est manner.*

Thus the secretary must be liberal in nature, noble of soul, accurate in observation, profound of thought and penetrating of vision. He should be blessed with a broad sense of culture and its fruits, and not be distant from, or a stranger to, logical reasoning. He should recognize the degrees of rank of men of his time and take the measure of his contemporaries. He should not concern himself with the things of this world and their deceptions, nor should he pay any regard to the praise or blame of special interests and connivers. In the content of his official correspondence he should preserve the honor of his employer from any occasion of harm or sign of disrespect. During the course of his writing and carrying on correspondence he should not anger those deserving of respect and honor, and even though there be animosity between his master and his correspondent, he should control his pen and not damage his [i.e., the correspondent's] honor, except in the case of someone who has exceeded the proper limits and has placed the footstep of respect outside the circle of decency...[13]

در ماهيت دبيرى و كيفيت دبير كامل و آنچه تعلق بدين دارد

دبيرى صناعتى است مشتمل بر قياساتِ خطابى و بلاغى ، منتفع در مخاطباتى كه در ميان مردم است بر سبيل محاورت و مشاورت و مخاصمت ، در مدح و ذمّ و حيلت و استعطاف و اغراء و بزرگ گردانيدنِ اعمال و خُرد گردانيدنِ اشغال و ساختنِ وجوه عذر و عتاب و اكام وثائق و اذكار سوابق ، ظاهر گردانيدن ترتيب و نظام سخن در هر واقعه تا بر وجه اولى و احرى ادا كرده آيد. پس دبير بايد كه كريم الاصل شريف العرض دقيق النظر عميق الفكر ثاقب الرّأى باشد، و از ادب و ثمرات آن قسم اكبر و حظّ اوفر نصيب او رسيده باشد، و از قياسات منطقى بعيد و بيگانه نباشد، و مراتب ابناء زمانه شناسدو مقادير اهل روزگار داند، و بحطام دنياوى و مزخرفات آن مشغول نباشد، و به تحسين و تقبيح اصحاب اغراض و ارباب اغماض التفات نكند و غرّه نشود، و عرض مخدوم را در مقامات ترسّل از مواضع نازل و مراسم خامل محفوظ دارد ؛ و در اثناء كتابت و مساق ترسّل بر ارباب حرمت و اصحاب حشمت نستيزد، و اگر چه ميان مخدوم و مخاطب او مخاصمت باشد، او قلم نگاه دارد و در عرض او وقيعت نكند الا بدان كس كه تجاوزِ حدّ كرده باشد، و قدم حُرمت از دايره حشمت بيرون نهاده...[13]

Nizāmi ʿAruzi's words, at least as they pertain to secretaries, were respected by others of the profession. Muhammad Nakhjavāni, for example, writing two centuries later during the reign of Sultan Uvays the Jalāyirid (r. 1356–74), praised Nizāmi ʿAruzi highly and included all ten anecdotes about secretaries from *Chahār Maqāla* in his *Dastur al-kātib,* with only minor differences in wording.[14]

PROMINENT SECRETARIES

To give an idea of what the secretaries did professionally and what their contribution was to the formation and development of the literary language, it will be helpful to mention some of the most prominent of the early secretaries and describe what they wrote in addition to their letters and documents.

Secretaries and poets have been associated with each other in Persian courts from the earliest times. Tradition holds that Muhammad b. Vasif (fl. 865–909), secretary (*dabir*) of Ya'qub b. Layth the Saffarid (r. 867–79), was the first one to write poetry in Persian. The anonymous author of *Tārikh-i Sistān*, writing between 1277 and 1281, says:

> When this poem was read out [in Arabic], he [i.e., Ya'qub] was not learned and did not understand it. Muhammad b. Vasif was present and he was the secretary for correspondence and was very cultivated. In those days letters were not written in Persian. Ya'qub said, 'Why is it necessary to say something that I do not understand?' Muhammad b. Vasif then began to write poetry in Persian. The first Persian poetry in Persia was written by him, and before him nobody had written it.[15]

چون این شعر بر خواندند او عالم نبود در نیافت، محمد بن وصیف حاضر بود و دبیر رسایل او بود و ادب نیکو دانست و بدان روزگار نامه پارسی نبود، پس یعقوب گفت : چیزی که من اندر نیایم چرا باید گفت؟ محمد وصیف وخپس شعر پارسی گفتن گرفت. و اول شعر پارسی اندر عجم او گفت، و پیش از و کسی نگفته بود...[15]

At this time there was still a fair amount of prose and poetry being written in Arabic by secretaries in Persian courts. One example is Abu 'Abd-Allāh Muhammad b. Yusuf al-Kātib, of Khwārizm. Little is known about him except that he wrote, in Arabic, *Mafātih al-'ulum*, a compendium of the sciences, in 366–67 / 976. This work contained a chapter on *kitābat* (writing) in which the author discusses the prose style of the secretary and gives many of the technical terms used in the chancellery and other government departments.[16] In the early period there was considerable mutual influence between the chancelleries of the Umayyads and early Abbasids.[17] This was also the time when the secretaries in the Persian courts were beginning to write more and more of their correspondence in Persian, and this trend continued, with one short interruption in the Ghaznavid period.

An important early secretary is Abu al-Fazl Bayhaqi. After studying in Nishapur, Bayhaqi entered the *divān-i rasā'il* (chancellery) of Sultan Mahmud, which was then under the directorship of Abu Nasr Mushkān (d. 1039–40). Abu Nasr had become chief of the chancellery when Abu al-Hasan Maymandi was promoted from that position to vizier. Bayhaqi himself became chief of the chancellery in ca. 1048–49, but was later accused of an (unspecified) offense by rivals and jailed. After he was released he retired from office, and died in about 1077–78. In addition to his famous *Tārikh-i Mas'udi* (History of the Reign of Mas'ud), he is said to have written *Zinat al-Kuttāb,* a treatise on the art of letter writing. Little needs be said here about his *Tārikh-i Mas'udi* except that it is considered to be both a great classic of Persian history and a landmark of Persian prose style.

All the sources emphasize that the secretary should have an excellent command of Persian and Arabic. At any time, for example, a secretary could be called upon to produce an instant translation from one language to the other. Bayhaqi gives an interesting example of this when he describes the arrival at the Ghaznavid court in the year 423/1033 of an envoy from Baghdad bringing a letter announcing the death of the caliph al-Qādir and the accession of the new caliph, al-Qā'im. The envoy, wearing black, was taken to the Amir:

> *The chief minister, Ahmad-i Hasan [Maymandi] responded [to his greeting]…and spoke for a while in excellent Arabic, and during that time motioned to the envoy to deliver the letter. The envoy…carried the letter, which was enclosed in a black silk sheath, to the throne, presented it to the Amir….The Amir called Khwāja Bu Nasr [Mushkān, chief of the divān-i risālat]. He went to the throne, opened the sheath and read the letter. When he had finished, the Amir said, "Read a translation of it so that it will be clear to everyone." He [i.e., Bu Nasr] read it out in Persian in such a way that the listeners declared that nobody [else] had such ability.*[18]

خواجه بزرگ فصلی سخن بگفت بتازی سخت نیکو درین معنی و اشارت کرد در آن فصل سوی رسول تا نامه را برساند. رسول... بر خاست و نامه در خریطه دیبای سیاه پیش تخت برد و بدست امیر داد... امیر خواجه بو نصر را آواز داد، پیش تخت شد... و خریطه بگشاد و نامه بخواند، چون بپایان آمد امیر گفت ترجمه اش بخوان تا همگام را مقرّر گردد. بخواند بپارسی چنانکه اقرار دادند شنوندگان که کسی را این کفایت نیست.[18]

In the chancellery around the same time as Bayhaqi or slightly earlier was Abu al-Fath Busti, whom `Awfi calls "chief of the worthies and scribes" and says that he left divans of both Arabic and Persian poetry. Bayhaqi praises his Arabic poetry and twice quotes some of it.[19] Another secretary in the Ghaznavid chancellery at this time is Abu Nasr Muhammad b. `Abd al-Jabbār `Utbi (AD 961–1035). He became chief of the postal service in Nishapur in the late 10th century. As Samanid power declined, `Utbi became secretary successively to Abu `Alā' Simjuri, Qābus b. Vashmgir and Amir Sebüktigin. While he was secretary to Sebüktigin, Abu al-Fath Busti entered the chancellery service. `Utbi is famous for writing, in Arabic, *Tārikh-i Yamini* (History of the Reign of Sultan Mahmud, who was called Yamin al-Dawla) which Abu al-Sharaf Nāsih b. Zafar Munshi Jurfādaqāni (Gulpāyagāni), a secretary in the courts of the Atābegs of Azerbaijan, translated into Persian in 1206–7.[20] Jurfādaqāni wrote other prose works in Arabic and left a quantity of poetry in Persian and Arabic.

One of the most famous statesmen of the late Seljuq period was the powerful vizier Abu `Ali Hasan Nizām al-Mulk (1018 or 1019–1092), who had been secretary to Abu `Ali b. Shādhān in Balkh and to Alp Arslān before he became the vizier of Malik Shāh, for whom he wrote his *Siyar al-muluk* or *Siyāsat Nāma*, a book of advice for kings. In the Arab courts of the time, as in the Persian courts, there was a close relationship between the chief secretary and the vizier.[21] It was not uncommon for the chief of the chancellery to be promoted to vizier; the case of Maymandi has already been mentioned.[22]

In the late 12th and early 13th centuries Nur al-Din Muhammad `Awfi, author of *Lubāb al-albāb,* the earliest *tazkira* (anthology) to survive in Persian, and of the collection of stories called *Javāma` al-hikāyāt,* was in charge of the chancellery (*divān-i inshā'*) of the Qarākhānid ruler Kılıj Arslān Khāqān Nusrat al-Din Uthmān b. Ibrāhim (r. 1204–12).[23]

Muhammad Nakhjavāni, 14th century author of *Dastur al-kātib,* provides a different example of the linguistic prowess possessed by the greatest secretaries. Nakhjavāni's mastery of Persian was such that his book, like Bayhaqi's, is a classic of Persian prose of his period. His Arabic was said to be equal to his Persian, and neither language was his mother tongue.[24] Indeed, Nakhjavāni was quite aware of his abilities in the two languages, and says:

> *If the Sultan...issues the command that cannot be disobeyed...and if life*
> *and time lend their aid, this feeble one will prepare and write another book [like*

this one] about letter writing in Arabic so that students of Arabic epistolography also will be able to reach their object in the easiest possible way... And may it be known and confirmed to the royal mind that just as this feeble and weak one rides kingly steeds on the fields of the Persian language, he is [also] able to be the companion of wing-footed Arabic mounts in the deserts of Arabic competence and can obtain any object that he desires mounted on Arabic coursers.[25]

و اگر صوایب آرای حضرت سلطان...حکم يرليغ مطاع و فرمان واجب الاتباع ارزانی فرمايد...و اين ضعيف را وقت و عمر مساعدت و مسامحت کند بر همين نمط کتابی ديگر در منشئات عربی مصنف و مرتب گرداند تا طالبان انشاء عربی نيز بر ايسر وجوه بمطالب خود را رسند...و راس همايون را معلوم و محقق شود که اين ضعيف نحيف همچنانک در ميدان فارسی زبانی که بر مراکب خسروانی سواری می کند رد بيداء عربيت نيز با باديايان تازی انبازی می تواند نمود و بر تکاوران عربی بهر مقصد که می خواهد می تواند روانيد...[25]

MANUALS FOR SECRETARIES

An examination of some of the manuals for secretaries will show in some detail what the secretary had to know in order to do his job properly. The earliest manual for secretaries that we have is *Dastur-i dabiri,* by Muhammad b. ʿAbd al-Khāliq al-Mayhani. Written in the Seljuq period, it appears to be a manual for rank beginners, possibly for young men just entering service in the chancellery. It is, typically, divided into two major sections: the first describes the technical details of the profession such as maintaining the pen, organizing the information of a document on the page, folding documents, the various forms of address and reference, and, interestingly, provides some basic Arabic grammar and a glossary of Arabic equivalents of some common Persian epistolary terms. This suggests that the knowledge of Arabic was not universal among young men who had not received a *madrasa* education.

The second part of the book is devoted to sample letters according to the relative rank of the sender and the recipient (superior to inferior, equal to equal, inferior to superior) according to the categories of *sultāniyyāt* and *ikhvāniyyāt,* and according to the subjects of possible letters. It makes the points that all such manuals make, namely, that the secretary must write in a good hand, that he have an easy command of the correct titles and forms of address for all ranks of society that would receive correspondence from the chancellery, and that he know Persian and Arabic well. In this connection, C. Fleisher's description of the youths who were recruited into the Ottoman secretarial bureaucracy in the 16th century is interesting. He points out that many of the young entrants into the scribal ranks were rather poorly educated but could write in a good calligraphic hand. This was often sufficient to secure them a job, but they ran into difficulties when they had to write documents containing many Persian and Arabic words. The petition of one scribe, Kasım, who had an educated father, is "filled with egregious spelling errors that show, if nothing else, that his acquaintance with Arabic and Persian must have been rudimentary at best.... While Kasım's calligraphy may have been impressive...he was clearly at a loss when required to compose a document without a written model before him... Mahmud's [another young scribe] orthography is somewhat better than Kasım's (though by no means perfect) but his style is as unpolished as that of his colleague."[26]

Another such manual, written in 690/1291 is Hasan b. `Abd al-Mu'min al-Khu'i's *Ghunyat al-kātib va munyat al-tālib* and its accompanying *Rusum al-rasā'il va nujum al-fazā'il*. The author says that he wrote this for his son in a brief and condensed manner so that when he became ready for the *dabiristān* (secondary school) he would know the basics of secretarial practice and therefore remember his father favorably.[27] The author understood well that a secretarial career was a very desirable one for his son, "because it is not hidden from the minds of the wise that the *fann-i kitābat* (art of secretaryship) is the noblest of practices and that a knowledge of eloquence is the most useful stock-in-trade, and that by virtue of this skill [a young man] becomes worthy of being close to the presence of the great men of the government and of sharing in the important secrets of the state and nation..."[28]

که بر رای خردمندان پوشیده نیست که فنّ کتابت اشرف صناعاتست و تحصیلِ علمِ
بلاغت انفعِ بضاعات و بوسیلتِ این فضلیت شایسته قربتِ حضرتِ اکابرِ دولت و
مساهمِ اسرارِ اعاظمِ ملک و ملّت توان شد....[28]

The first volume contains "the preliminaries of secretaryship," which divides those individuals who are worthy of having letters addressed to them into two groups: "pillars of the state," and "grandees of the religion." These groups are then minutely subdivided and all the forms of address and reference that the beginner would need to know are listed. The second volume opens with the conventional claim that a group of generous and well-meaning friends urged him to write another brief treatise (before writing a fully detailed one), because a longer one would have been concerned with the art of letter writing and would have contained rare verses, many unusual words, and some of "sections of the essentials of the principles of the science of explanation,"[29] the details of which the beginner would not be able to grapple with. A briefer book would greatly benefit the learner. It is divided into four detailed sections: the preliminaries to the art of letter writing; letters to friends; the conferring of administrative appointments; and the conferring of religious appointments. Sample letters are provided, including a *mahzar* (letter of complaint) and an *āzād nāma* (letter of manumission), plus opening and closing greetings and prayers.

This is the most laconic of the three manuals with which I am familiar. The forms of address are given in a bare, almost tabular form and there is no discussion of the need to write in a good hand or to know Persian and Arabic very well. There is an interesting glossary at the end of the first book, where the different sorts of written communications are defined. It seems to be a product of the Chupanid court (ca. 1227–ca. 1309) in Anatolia.

The third, and most interesting, of the secretarial manuals is *Dastur al-kātib fi ta'yin al-marātib* by Hindushāh Nakhjavāni (mid-14th century). Nakhjavāni devised an extremely detailed and ramified scheme for presenting his material, which he does in far greater detail than does any other author of such a manual.[30] After the usual opening discussion of the tools of the secretary (pen, ink pot, etc.) and how to use them, there follows a section devoted to what poets and writers of the past have said (in Arabic and Persian) about the tools of writing, where he begins with: *dar sifat-i ālāt va adavāt-i kitābat nazman va nathran* (Description of the tools and implements of writing in poetry and in prose).[31] He provides letters with examples of the forms of address, greetings, and closing prayers that should be used in correspondence between men, women, and children of equal or unequal status, and when mentioning rulers and high officials he never fails to indicate how to address their consorts (i.e., the *khavātin-i khavāqin*). Then come royal letters of appointment and their administrative counterparts, and, finally, much wise advice and counsel to secretaries: for example, that the etiquette of correspondence between rulers demands that the secretary writing the letter not express desire or enthusiasm for a meeting because meetings between rulers are fraught with innumerable dangers, or the appropriate amount of white space to leave between the lines of different sorts of letters, or that the secretary should not write too quickly because in doing so he cannot control the two most important qualities of his writing: beauty of script and of expression.[32] His letters have the ring of authenticity and they appear to be copies of letters that Nakhjavāni actually wrote.

COLLECTIONS OF LETTERS

Muntajab al-Din Badi` Atābik al-Juvayni, a secretary and member of a great secretarial family, was a contemporary of Rashid al-Din Vatvāt (d. 1177–78) and of the poet Anvari (d. ca. 1187). His dates of birth and death are unknown, but he says in his introduction to `Atabat al-kataba, one of the first collections of a secretary's own letters that has come down to us, that from his youth he had wanted to study Arabic, especially since an ancestor of his had been secretary to Shams al-Ma`āli Kay Qābus b. Vashmgir and that several pieces of his official correspondence had come down to him. The desire to master Arabic inspired him in 516/1122 as a young man to go to Marv, then the *dār al-mulk* (capital), to learn the skills of secretaryship. Soon after this he traveled to Ghazni and was able to secure a post in the *divān-i istifā* ("auditing department"). Because of the quality of his prose and poetry he was transferred to the *divān-i inshā* ("chancellery"), where his career flourished.[33] He later became secretary to Sultan Sanjar and then was promoted to vizier. He compiled the book `Atabat al-kataba probably between 528/1133 and 548/1153.[34] It is difficult to determine whether these letters are all actual letters written by Muntajab al-Din and sent from the chancellery, or sample letters typical of the kind that he would have written for various purposes. In any case, they are marvels of the epistolary style of the time. Muhammad `Awfi mentions him among the viziers who were also poets,[35] and Bahār says of him, "This excellent writer and secretary, like most of the famous secretaries of that era, also composed poetry."[36] Another famous and influential collection of correspondence is *al-Tavassul ilā al-tarassul* by Bahā al-Din al-Bāghdādi, who was the chief secretary of `Alā al-Din Khwārazmshāh (r. 1172–99). In the introduction to his collection he characterizes the prose of his predecessors in chancellery writing as falling into two categories: it is either complicated, or pleasant. Within these large classes secretaries followed many different paths according to their own inclinations in writing Arabic or Persian documents, and he recommends that the beginner in this pursuit memorize a number of documents that are in a style to his liking. Thus he will become skilled and polished in this art. The contents of the volume are divided conventionally into: state papers, documents and letters; letters from the ruler to other rulers and nobles of his court; and private letters and miscellaneous writings of the author.

It appears that many secretaries were proud of their skills at writing formal prose, and many such collections from later periods have survived, some deliberately produced as models for aspiring secretaries, and others simply as monuments of excellent prose per se. After the Mongol period, collections of letters became one of the most popular genres of prose writing, and catalogs of Persian manuscripts in European and South Asian libraries contain dozens of examples. I will mention two further examples here. The first, entitled by the editor simply *Inshā'-i Māhru*, is by `Ayn al-Din `Ayn al-Mulk `Abd-Allāh b. Māhru (fl. 1300–60). During the Khalji and Tughluqid periods of the Delhi Sultanate (1290–1414), Māhru was a secretary, provincial governor, military leader, and, finally, governor of Multan. He was another example of a person being both *ahl-i shamshir* and *ahl-i qalam* (a man of the sword and a man of the pen): a master of Persian and a great stylist, often using special vocabulary and imagery appropriate to the subject matter of the letter he was writing, skill that we will encounter later in connection with Zayn al-Din Vāsifi. For example, in a letter to Shams al-Din al-Mutavakkili he uses the word *`ayn* twenty-four times, each time [he claims] with a different meaning.[37]

The last example of collections of letters is the *Sharaf nāma* of `Abd-Allāh Marvārid.[38] Marvārid (d. 922/1516) was an educated and talented courtier who held several high positions in the court of Sultan Husayn Bayqara, including that of *sadr* (religious dignitary), *amir* (commander), and keeper of the royal seal. In addition to the *Sharaf Nāma*, he left, among other writings, a divan of poetry, a *masnavi* (an extended narrative poem in rhyming couplets) of Khusraw and Shirin, and an unfinished prose history of Shāh Ismā`il I. Marvārid is a good example of the literary versatility of the courtier. Compiled in about 1506, the *Sharaf Nāma* consists of letters of appointment and other royal documents, state correspondence, and private letters, and is a good example of late Timurid inshā.

MANUALS OF PROSODY

Because of the technical nature of these manuals, it is important to describe them and indicate what they can tell us about the development of the literary language. Manuals of prosody typically discuss the rules for forming rhymes, the meters used in Persian poetry, and the various rhetorical devices of word and meaning employed by poets and prose writers in Persian (and sometimes Arabic). Secretaries and/or poets wrote them and they codified existing literary practice, thus being useful mirrors of the technical side of the literary art. The earliest such manual that we have in Persian is *Tarjumān al-balāgha* by Muhammad ʿUmar al-Rāduyāni, possibly a secretary, written sometime between 1088 and 1114.[39] What seems to have escaped the notice of critics is that in his book, Rāduyāni talks not only about poetry but establishes (or continues) the practice of carefully emphasizing the devices of rhetoric appropriate to prose. For example, about the verbal device called *tarsiʿ*, he says "the secretary and poet [writing] in verse and prose..."

Rashid al-Din Vatvāt was chief of the *divān-i inshā* of Ātsız the Khwārazmshāh (r. 1127–56) at the court in Balkh, and while holding that position he wrote one of the most influential manuals of prosody of the medieval period. Tradition has it that Ātsız was looking at Rāduyāni's book one day and suggested to his chief secretary Rashid al-Din that he bring it up to date. Rashid al-Din was a well-trained and talented secretary who wrote Arabic and Persian poetry and prose, of which we still have a good quantity. He found *Tarjumān al-balāgha* deficient and out of date, and his updating of it, entitled *Hadā'iq al-sihr fi daqā'iq al-shiʿr,* set the pattern of providing both Persian and Arabic examples for each of the rhetorical devices, many of these examples written by Rashid al-Din himself.[40] He, too, carefully pointed out more than twenty devices that were used by prose writers as well as by poets. For example, again for the device tarsiʿ he says (following Rāduyāni), "this device is such that the secretary or poet...," or regarding *tajnisāt* he says "in speaking or writing, in prose or verse..."

Rashid al-Din's manual was widely acclaimed and imitated. One such imitation is *Haqā'iq al-hadā'iq* by Sharaf al-Din Rāmi, author of the better-known *Anis al-ʿushshāq.* Written between 1356 and 1374, this too points out devices used by prose writers as well as poets. Also from the 14th century, this time from Asia Minor, is *Daqā'iq al-shiʿr* by ʿAli b. Muhammad, called Tāj al-Halāvi, who had Rashid al-Din very much in mind when he wrote his manual. He says about *sajʿ i mutavāzi,* "Rashid al-Din has specified this device for prose," and about *musahhaf: "musahhaf* is what the poet and secretary [use] in prose and verse." There are many more such manuals but probably the most famous of all is *al-Muʿjam fi maʿāyir ashʿār al-ʿajam* by Shams-i Qays of Rayy. Written around 1232–33, it too takes account of both poetry and prose, although the stress is on poetry. The title of an important chapter in *al-Muʿjam* is: "Concerning the beauties of poetry and a sampling of elegant rhetorical devices that are employed in poetry and prose." He says, for example, "Although in this matter those poets who work hard at poetry have gone on at great length and have studied this matter, in this book we will confine ourselves to what is attested to and current among modern persons of talent, and to what the stallions among poets and expert writers have esteemed."[41]

DECLINE IN THE KNOWLEDGE OF ARABIC

Beginning in 352/963 with the Persian translation from Arabic and adaptation by Abu ʿAli Muhammad Balʿami of the section of Abu Jaʿfar Muhammad b. Jarir al-Tabari's Tārikh al-rusul va al-muluk that dealt with Iran, and also of Tabari's commentary on the Qur'an, there are scraps of evidence that the secretaries and the literati sensed a decline in the knowledge of Arabic among the young men entering the profession and among littérateurs in general, which they deplored. Actually this decline should not be surprising, since the Samanids encouraged the writing of Persian poetry and prose, and the language of the chancellery was changed from Arabic to Persian except for briefly in the early Ghaznavid period. In such an atmosphere, the dominance of Arabic in the Persian courts was bound to decline as time went on; for example, after the Samanid period we find relatively few examples of bilingual secretaries or *adib*s, although there certainly remained a body of educated literati who could handle Arabic with skill and ease. This decline, as perceived by secretaries and other literati, raises interesting questions about stability and change in formal written Persian. Before the Seljuq period there is reason to believe that many young men training to become secretaries did not pass through the conventional course of *madrasa* education but rather were educated in the skills of secretaryship, including Arabic, by their families at home. Secretaryship lies on the borderline between craft and art, for it requires the mastery of a body of technical knowledge and techniques, and it also requires creative imagination and subtle judgment in the exercise of these. Many traditional crafts were passed down from father to son, and many of the secretaries seem to have done this with the technical side of their profession.

Writing around the turn of the 12th century, Muhammad b. Rāduyāni, probably a secretary, composed *Tarjumān al-balāgha,* the earliest manual of prosody that has survived in Persian. He says in his introduction that he examined a great many such manuals in Arabic and found only two in Persian. He also found many people in his own time claiming a knowledge of prosody but their pretensions were great and devoid of content. Since he felt that to follow their guidance would lead to no good outcome, he decided to write a manual of his own, translating various aspects of eloquence from Arabic into Persian.[42]

The *nizāmiyyas* were *madrasas* founded by Nizām al-Mulk in Baghdad, Iraq, and Khorasan in around 1067 for several purposes, including educating a loyal cadre of secretaries and bureaucrats to run the Seljuq Empire. They stressed traditional Arabic learning in their curricula and also the study of Persian language and literature. These *madrasas* attracted talented pupils who were given a thorough education, broader and more rigorous than they would have received in a traditional *madrasa.* While these schools did provide a good Islamic education, they did not seem able to stem the decline in the knowledge of Arabic. Rashid al-Din Vatvāt, for example, attended the *nizāmiyya* in Balkh and was well-enough schooled in Arabic to leave a divan of Arabic poetry and many Arabic prose writings, in addition to poetry and prose in Persian. In his *Latā'if al-amthāl va tarā'if al-aqvāl,* written late in his life, he says that the ruler (Qutb al-Din Muhammad Khwārazmshāh) possessed an interest in knowing more Arabic proverbs and expressions to make his speech more eloquent and asked Vatvāt to write a book that would help him. It is a collection of proverbs and expressions in Arabic, taken from other collections, on which Vatvāt commented and explained their meaning in Persian, "so that the benefits of it would become more general and its advantages be more widespread."[43]

Around the same time Nasr-Allāh Munshi (d. between 555/1160 and 573/1177) made his famous translation of a collection of Indian tales from the Panchatantra, which he called *Kalila va Dimna.* In his introduction, where he translates many of the Arabic sentences that he quotes, he says regarding his book that when the kingdom of Khorasan fell to Nasr b. Ahmad the Samanid (d. 331/942–43), "he requested Rudaki the poet (d. 369/979–80) to versify it because the desire of the creative temperament is for versified words (*sukhan-i manzum*)." And later,

Others translated this book after [the prose version of] Ibn al-Muqaffa` [which contained no poetry at all] and Rudaki's versified version, and each person stepped onto the field of expression to the extent of his own ability, but it appears that their goals were to write stories and set down tales, not to teach wisdom and admonition, for they expressed themselves very briefly and confined themselves to telling stories.

In short, since people's desire to study Arabic books has waned and those bits of wisdom and admonition have been forsaken, nay even obliterated, it seemed to me that it should be translated and the discourse expanded and the allusions revealed in a satisfying manner, and that it should be strengthened with verses from the Qur'an, and Hadiths, and poetry and proverbs so that this book, which is the cream of several thousand years, be revived and people not be denied its usefulness and its benefits.[44]

و این کتاب را پس از ترجمه ابن المقفّع و نظم رودکی ترجمها کرده اند و هر کس در میدانِ بیان بر اندازه خود قدمی گزارده اند ؛ لکن می نماید که مراد ایشان تقریرِ سَمَر و تحریر حکایت بوده است نه تفحیمِ حکمت و موعظت ، چه سخن نیک مبتر رانده اند و بر ایرادِ قصّه اختصار نموده.

و در جمله ، چون رغبتِ مردمان از مطالعتِ کتبِ تازی قاصر گشته است ، و آن حِکَم و مواعظ مهجور مانده بود بلکه مدروس شده ، بر خاطر گذشت که آن را ترجمه کرده آید و در بسطِ سخن و کشفِ اشارات آن اشباعی رود و آن را بآیات و اخبار و ابیات و امثالِ مؤکّد گردانیده شود ، تا اینْ کتاب را که زبده چند هزار ساله است احیائی باشد و مردمان از فواید و منافع آن محروم نمانند.

Note the allusions by Rashid al-Din Vatvāt and Nasr-Allāh Munshi, two well-known secretaries and littérateurs, to a decline in the knowledge of Arabic and how Nasr-Allāh felt the need to translate many Arabic sentences in his introduction and to render the book into the current style of language, as Rudaki and others before him had done.

Shams-i Qays of Rayy wrote *al-Muʿjam*, the most detailed and analytical manual of prosody in Persian, in about 1232. After describing the loss of his original Arabic manuscript during the Mongol invasion, he notes that he finally succumbed to the insistence of his friends and the principal literati of Shiraz and wrote it out again, employing the conventional literary motif for why one writes a technical book. He recalls that Rashid al-Din Vatvāt wrote his *Hadā'iq al-sihr* (here Shams-i Qays' memory failed him: it was actually Vatvāt's *Latā'f al-amthāl*) in Persian and echoes him when he justifies writing his own book in Persian rather than in Arabic:

He [Rashid al-Din] knew that its benefits would be more general and that the desire of most people to study it [in Persian] would be greater because every would-be Arabist has the ability to understand the Persian language but not every Persian-writing poet would have the basic expertise in Arabic.[45]

جی دانست که فائده آن عامتر باشذ و رغبت اکثر مردم بمطاله آن بیشتر

بوذ از بهر آنکه هر مستعرب را قوّت ادراک لغت پارسی باشد و هر شاعر

پارسی کوی را بایه مهارت در لغت عرب نبوذ[45]

About sixty years later Ahmad b. Ahmad Dumānisi compiled his *Mujmal al-aqvāl fi al-hikam va al-amthāl.* Written in 693/1293–94, probably in Sivas, Anatolia, the book was in Arabic with some parts of it translated into Persian. It contained Qur'anic verses, proverbs, moral and ethical aphorisms, and poetry. The author says in his introduction (fol. 4r) that he compiled this book for the courtiers of his patron to study, and on fol. 5r he says:

This book about the artful use of proverbs and expressions that are accepted by educated people and sought after by the literati was realized, so that in expressing every meaning by way of relating and approximating [words], secretaries and prose stylists would be helped by an appropriate Qur'anic verse or some proverbs or even some lines of [Arabic] poetry to insert into their discourse.[46]

این کتاب اصلی گشت در فن امثال و محاضرات که مقبول ارباب فضل و مطلوب اهل

هنرست...چه در هر معنی که اهل انشا و بلاغت و ارباب براعت و فصاحت را چون

بطریق تناسب و تقارب آیتی و امائلی و اما مثلی و اما شعری موافق دست دهد و در

کلام درج کنند نظام آن داده باشد

He clearly intends it to be a reference book for secretaries and other employees of the chancellery who need a source of material of this nature with which to adorn their prose. More interesting, however, is that he also says that he plans to translate this book from beginning to end into Persian in order to extend its usefulness to more people:

و چون میخواست که فایده عامتر و جمله اصناف مردم را از ا و بهره و نصیب

بود التزام نمود که تمامت کتاب من اوله الی آجره از آیت و اخبار و امثال و اشعار

جمله بپارسی مترجم باشد (fol. 5v)[46]

This suggests that the knowledge of Arabic, at least at smaller or provincial courts, was not strong. Barthold notes that in a discussion of al-Narshakhi's (d. 959) history of Bukhara (written in Arabic), Abu Nasr Ahmad b. Muhammad al-Qubavi, who translated the book into Persian, says that in the 13th century, when people "for the greater part nourished no inclination towards the study of Arabic books," he gave in to the request of his friends and translated al-Narshakhi's work into Persian.[47]

We have seen expressions of concern about the decline of knowledge of Arabic from Khorasan, Anatolia, and Transoxiana, and at almost the same time a similar hint sounds from India. `Ayn al-Din b. Māhru (see above), in a letter to his son `Imād al-Din, reproving him for neglecting his education and pointing out the advantages of being educated, as are the sons of his peers, says:

Because at the time of life at which my son is, it is appropriate for the sons of educated people to have passed on from the beginnings and introductory stages of learning and have achieved higher levels and be prepared in the science of meaning and expression and its roots and its branches, and rational thinking, and have the pen of composition, invention, transformation, creation and innovation in hand, and be capable of connecting exact meanings...and not have to read written Persian only with great effort, and not get stuck when an arabicised (or, half-vocalized?) letter arrives...[48]

زیرا که ابنای جنس اهل فضل را درین سن که آن فرزند است شاید که از
مبادی و مقدمات تعلم گذشته و حاوی مقامات و مفصل شده و مستعد علم
المعانی و البیان و فروع و اصول و معقول گشته و قلم انشاء و اختراع و
تصرف و تسنیف و ابداع بر دست باشد ، و بر تلفیق معانی دقیق قادر...نه آن
که مکتوب فارسی صرف بحیل بسیار بخواند و اگر مکترب نیم معرب برسد در
ماند...[48]

Here is another example of the concern that a professional secretary (and here, also a concerned father) showed about the state of education of young men, especially when languages other than Persian were involved.

Sharaf al-Din Rāmi (see above), poet and prosodist, about a half century later in the introduction to his *Haqā'iq al-hadā'iq,* which he wrote in response to Vatvāt's *Hadā'iq al-sihr,* says: "Since the text of *Hadā'iq* was summary and abbreviated, perforce I analyzed and perfected it, and in place of the Arabic examples in Vatvāt's book I selected examples of verse in current Persian and added these." Again, we notice that his *Risāla-yi badāya‛ al-sanāya‛*, a very short and little-known work on rhetorical devices, has no Arabic examples whatever.[49] Until these works were written, I am not aware of any books on prosody to eschew examples in Arabic.

Two examples do not always make a trend, but we have another case parallel to that of Sharaf al-Din Rāmi in Kamāl al-Din Husayn Vā‛iz Kāshifi's (d. 910/1504–5) *Badāya‛ al-afkār fi sanāya‛ al-ash‛ār*. Written before 1498, this is a very thorough manual of rhetorical devices containing no Arabic examples at all.[50]

Kāshifi again alludes to problems with Arabic in a book written at an earlier time. In his introduction to his recasting of *Kalila va Dimna* as *Anvār-i Suhayli* he begins by characterizing Nasr-Allāh's version:

> In truth it is a work like the sweet soul in delicacy and like colorful coral in freshness; its heart-deceiving words are like the wink of an exciting, sugar-lipped [beauty], and its life-enhancing meanings cling to the heart like the ring-lets of a newly-bearded youth...
>
> But through its use of rare and strange words and its exaggeration in ex-pressing the virtues of Arabic rhetoric, and hyperbole in its various metaphors and similes, and wordiness and prolixity of difficult words and phrases, the listener's mind is prevented from savoring the object of the book and from per-ceiving the point of its chapters, and the reader's skill fails in relating the begin-ning of a story to its ending and in connecting the opening of a discourse to its conclusion, and this problem will certainly be the cause of fatigue in the reader and listener, especially in this time of elegance of sensibility when the talents of its individuals have achieved such a level of fineness that they desire to sense a meaning without the words being put on show like a bride on her throne. Indeed, for some words it is necessary to consult a dictionary and have recourse to a glos-sary and because of this, a book of this elegance is close to being abandoned and forsaken and the people of the world deprived of and denied its benefits...
>
> With an eye toward making its usefulness more general to people and in-creasing its benefits for high and low, a royal order was issued that I...attempt to array the book in question in new clothes, and the beauty of the articulation of its meanings, which veils of difficult words and curtains of obscure expressions have hidden and concealed, be shown in clear displays of phrases and elegant exhibitions of metaphor in such a manner that the eye of anyone who can see can share in the beauty of those flirts in the bridal chamber of explanation with-

out looking deeply or having any depth of vision, and the heart of every learned
person be enabled to partake of union with those alluring creatures of their own
private chambers without vexing their imagination or imagining vexation.[51]

With this he makes clear what he thought the problems were with the earlier version, and they all involved difficulties with Arabic. It must not be supposed, however, that Kāshifi's aim was merely to simplify the text of *Kalila va Dimna*. C. van Ruymbeke argues that because of their didactic nature such texts were meant to be read slowly and thoughtfully and that Kāshifi brought the text into line with the taste of the times but did not simplify it.[52]

SHARED LITERARY CULTURE

The reasons for mentioning these manuals of prosody have been to empha-size, first, that these manuals were often written by men who were secretar-ies rather than "professional poets" and, second, that the manuals were all intended for prose writers as well as for poets. Clearly those secretaries who compiled and systematized the most technical aspects of literary poetry and prose in the rhetorical manuals made no difference between poetry and prose, at least as far as devices of rhetoric were concerned. These devices were as useful to the secretary as to the poet, and the two genres of the written language shared a good measure of the pool of technical resources available. Naturally, not all the poetic devices would be appropriate for use in prose, but as time went on and prose style became increasingly compli-cated, verbose, and more interlarded with poetry, we find a greater variety of rhetorical devices employed. A final example will broaden the perspec-tive on how language was used by poets and secretaries.

Nizāmi ʿAruzi associates the secretary and the poet in an abstract and theoretical way. He says,

> *The secretary, the poet, the astrologer and the physician are special and*
> *close to the ruler, and he cannot do without them. The support of the kingdom*
> *is with the secretary; the eternal persistence of [the king's] name is with the*
> *poet; the ordering of affairs is with the astrologer, and the health of [the king's]*
> *body is with the physician, and these difficult callings and noble sciences are*
> *among the branches of the science of knowledge: secretaryship and being poet*
> *are branches of the science of logic.*[53]

اما دبیر و شاعر و منجّم و طبیب از خواص پادشاهند و از ایشان چاره ای
نیست . قوام ملک بدبیر است ، و بقاء اسم جاودانی بشاعر ، و نظام امور
بمنجم ، و صحّت بدن بطبیب ، و این چهار عمل شاق و علم شریف از فروع
علم حکمت است . دبیری و شاعری از فروع علم منطق است[53]

In fact, the line between secretary and court poet, in the senses of "prose
writer" and "writer of poetry," was not always sharply drawn, as in the cases
of Muhammad b. Vasif, Abu al-Fath al-Busti, Muntajab al-Din Badi` Atābik Ju-
vayni, and Sa`d al-Din Varāvini (about each of whom Bahar says: "This accom-
plished writer and secretary, like most well-known secretaries of that age, also
wrote poetry."[54] This applies as well to Abu al-Sharaf Nāsih Jurfādaqāni, Rashid
al-Din Vatvāt, `Abd al-Rahmān Jāmi, and, no doubt, to many others. Each did
what he was employed to do, but both were brought together as members of
the literati in the development, use, and spread of the formal written language
under the general umbrella of *adab,* and only the inexperienced or untalented
would fail to venture into other realms of literary creation. Mujtabā Minovi, in
the introduction to his edition of *Kalila va Dimna,* says:

> We do not know whether Bahrām Shāh, like his ancestors, spoke Turkish
> or whether he had become a Persian speaker, and if he had, whether he knew
> it well enough to savor the subtleties of Nasr-Allāh's prose and was able to
> distinguish between his prose and that of another secretary of that period...
> Writers and poets...of the courts of Sultan Mahmud and Sultan Mas`ud and
> other Ghaznavid and Seljuq rulers...wrote poetry for each other and books for
> the cultivated, learned and critically-minded [literati].[55]

نمی دانیم که بهرامشاه هم مثل اجداد خود بترکی تکلّم می کرد یا فارسی
زبان شده بود ، و اگر فارسی زبان شده بوده است آیا در ادراک دقایق و
لطایف و ریزه کاریهای زبان آن قدر وارد بوده است که بین انشای نصر الله
منشی و انشای منشی قدر دیگری در آن عصر فرق بگذارد.... نویسنده یا
شاعر...در دربار سلطان محمود و سلطان مسعود و سلاطین دیگری غزنوی
و سلجوقی...شعر از برای یکدیگر می سرودند ، و کتاب از برای فارسی
زبانان فهیم و فارسی دانان و معانی شناسان فاضل می نوشتند.[55]

The idea of a shared literary culture among secretaries and poets as they
exploited the resources of the language highlights the essentially self-conscious

nature of how they used language. The great prose stylists and poets were the innovators who propelled the evolution of style; in today's terms they were at the forefront of stylistic creativity. Writing for each other, for fellow *adibs*, for the literati in general, and for their patrons, they consciously pushed forward the borders of their shared medium, courtly written Persian, developing the lexicon and actually sharing forms. ʿAyn al-Din Māhru makes very clear the shared literary culture in the courtly milieu. In a letter to Shams al-Din Yaḥyā, a high official, Māhru praises Shams al-Din's prose style and says:

In this day and age, in inventing expressions and composing rhetorically, the masters of eloquence and the most highly skilled [writers] cannot approach him.[56]

در این عصر و زمان در اختراع بدایع و انشاءِ صنایع ، ارباب بلاغت و اصحاب براعت را بدان جناب نسبتی نیست[56]

It would be a mistake, however, to think that the surface of this quiet pool of literary creation was never ruffled. Muntajab al-Din Badiʿ, author of *ʿAtabat al-Kataba,* has no hesitation in asserting that prose is superior to verse. In the introduction to his collection of letters he says this:

The traces and signs of the blessing of discourse are most obvious of all, and the majesty of its virtue is to such a degree that in the Glorious Qur'an the youth of it (i.e., discourse) goes back to the statement 'Unto Moses God spoke directly' (4:162). Books were revealed to the prophets and to the Messenger as testimonies and proofs of this standing and good fortune, and prose has the preference and precedence over poetry due to its similarity to the word of God. This resemblance and likeness is the greatest of its excellent qualities and sources of pride; and the versification of speech and its ordering in the necklace of rhyme were invented to make it more attractive and make recording it easier and so that it would be more fluent on people's tongues.[57]

و آثار و امارات دولت سخن از همه ظاهر تر و شرف منقبت آن بدرجه است که در قرآن مجید ذکر تشبیب آن بحضرت عزت ربانی می آید و علم الله موسی تکلیما ، کتب منزل بر انبیا و رسل...از شواهد و براهین آن رتبت و دولت است ، و سخن منثور را بر منظوم فضیلت تقدم و مزیت شرف تشبیهست بکلام ایزد...و این تشابه و تجانس بزرگترین فضایل و مفاخرت و نظم سخن و تلفیق آن در عقد قوافی از جهت آن ابداع کرده اند تا آراسته تر نماید و ضبط آن آسان تر باشد و بر زبان خلق سایر تر . [57]

THE LEXICOGRAPHERS

Up to this point we have focused largely on the work of the secretaries and poets in creating and developing the formal written language. The court literati, however, included others who were professionally concerned with the written language, and the most prominent of these may have been the lexicographers. The first monolingual Persian dictionary, no longer extant, was written in the 7th century. Following the translation into Persian of part of Tabari's History and his commentary on the Qur'an, the first Arabic-Persian bilingual dictionaries appeared in Iran, which may suggest the beginnings of the decline in the knowledge of Arabic among the Persian literati.[58] In about 1066 Asadi Tusi compiled the earliest surviving Persian monolingual defining dictionary, *Lughat-i Furs,* although four pre-Asadi dictionaries are attested in early sources beginning in the late 9th century.[59] From then, with a gap in the 10th century which may mean simply that nothing from that century has survived, a stream of Persian-Persian dictionaries began to appear. The question of how the entries should be arranged reveals one strong impetus for writing these dictionaries. Beginning with Asadi's dictionary and probably the now-lost dictionaries that preceded Asadi, the entry words were arranged according to the last letter of the word instead of the first, as our dictionaries are arranged today. Arranging the entries by the final letter met the primary need that these dictionaries filled, namely to be an aid or a manual for reading poetry.[60] Accordingly, the size of these early dictionaries was small and they did not aspire to encompass all the words in the language. The great need was to define archaic and dialect words, not to define common words that everyone knew. Since Firdawsi's *Shāhnāma* was a fundamental cultural monument and everyone read and knew it thoroughly, older words that had dropped out of usage and the names of persons and places became more challenging for readers as time passed.

An additional problem for readers of poetry was the regional or dialect words that they were bound to encounter when reading poetry written by poets from different, and often widely separated, parts of Iran such as Shiraz and Bukhara. Listing such words began, as far as we know, with Asadi. He was from Tus in Khorasan and he noted a number of words in his dictionary as being from Transoxiana or Bukhara.[61] Nāsir Khusraw (394/1004–456 or 470/1072 or 1077) cites another example of this problem in his *Safar nāma:*

*In Tabriz I saw a poet named Qatrān; he wrote good poetry but he did
not know Persian well. He came to me and brought the divans of Manjik and
Daqiqi and read them to [or, with] me. He asked me about every meaning that
he found difficult. I explained these to him and he wrote out the explanation,
and he read [or, recited] his own poetry to me.*[62]

در تبریز قطران نام شاعری را دیدم ، شعری نیکو می گفت ،
اما زبان فارسی نیکو نمی دانست . پیشِ من آمد . دیوانِ منجیک و
دیوانِ   دقیقی بیاورد و پیشِ من بخواند . و هر معنی که اورا
مشکلَ بود از من بپرسید . با او بگفتم و شرح آن بنوشت و اشعار
خود بر من بخواند.[62]

Nāsir Khusraw was from Qubādiān in northeastern Khorasan, while
Manjik was from Tirmiz and Daqiqi was from Samarqand, Bukhara, Balkh,
or Tus. All of these cities were closer to each other than any of them was
to Tabriz, the birthplace of Qatrān, so it is not surprising that Nāsir had no
trouble understanding the local words in the poetry of Manjik and Daqiqi
and was able to explain them to Qatrān.

Returning to the discussion of early dictionaries, I think that it is fair
to interpret the work of the lexicographers as an additional element in
the dynamic interaction among members of the literati that has been thus
far attributed to poets and secretaries. The dictionaries helped to make
understandable the poetry from other courts at a time when long-distance
communication was slow and difficult. The dictionary writers reacted to
a need within their own local literary circle, and by doing so they helped
tie together the literati from various courts by removing obstacles to the
understanding of others' poetry. This must have done a lot to prevent local
language peculiarities from isolating centers of literacy from one another
and at the same time helped to keep the language stable. It must be recalled that the local language of poetry was limited in the range and register of its vocabulary and, therefore, its images and metaphors, and was
not yet ready to accept words and expressions from the colloquial spoken
language. The tangible work of the lexicographers went hand in hand with
the cultural and literary norms operating on poetry and (as seen above) indirectly on prose, greatly assisting in maintaining the stability of the written language.

SHARED ASPECTS OF FORMAL ORGANIZATION

It is a commonplace that when languages are in contact and borrowing occurs from one to the other, the borrowing tends to be largely lexical and to a lesser extent syntactic and morphological, although over time they tend to undergo parallel syntactic and morphological development so that "areal" features emerge. There is a certain parallel in the case of the closely knit literary society of the Persian courts, where secretaries and poets were the dominant users of the written language. In a literary culture where almost all poetry and prose were written with a rhetorical purpose and devices of rhetoric and meaning were shared, even a literary form could be shared. A brief discussion of this sharing of form will clarify what I mean.

The formal make-up of the classical panegyric *qasida* is familiar to all students of Persian poetry. This sort of poem was the court poet's stock-in-trade during the period in which the *qasida* was still the dominant poetic form and the divans always contain a large number of these panegyric poems. Many but not all of these *qasida*s, the proportion varying over time, comprised three major sections with transitional passages separating them. The first section, the *nasib* or *tashbib*, was usually a description of nature or of the beloved. This is followed by a transitional passage, the *guriz-gāh*, that leads directly to the second section. This section, often called the *madih*, contains the purpose or point (*qasd*) of the poem, usually praises of the patron, and was followed by another *guriz-gāh* that leads to the third and concluding section, the *du'ā*. This latter was a prayer for the well-being of the patron and the eternal endurance of his reign and kingdom. These three sections were not always of uniform length and one of them, usually the last, might be quite short. With this form in mind, we can now turn back to the secretary.

The secretary's principal duty was composing letters and documents for the ruler. If we read *Dastur-i dabiri*, the 12th-century manual for secretaries mentioned above, we find detailed instructions for organizing the contents of official letters. Each sort of letter (superior to inferior, etc.) had its specific forms of address at the beginning and its own register of language and closing formulas, but the overall form or organization of the letter was very much the same in all cases. There was always an opening section, *matla'* or *tashbib*, that included an invocation, a superscription containing the names and titles of the addressee, and greetings. This was followed by a transitional section that led to the main subject of body of the letter. Then followed another transition and a closing section, *maqta*`, that included the blessing or prayer for the recipient and other expressions depending on his or her rank and status. It is clear that the form of an official letter and of a panegyric *qasida* can be the same: a tripartite arrangement with transitional passages between the three major sections. What are the implications of this for Persian courtly writing? Before answering this question, it should be noted that tripartite arrangements in literary texts are found in many literary cultures and are not unique to Persian writing.

Since many courtly *qasida*s have the same form or organization that an official letter has, is it possible that the *qasida* could be used as a letter? The place to seek an answer to this would be in *qasida*s in which the poet was asking for something from the patron. A famous example is the great *qasida* by Anvari (d. ca. 1187) conventionally called in English "The Tears of Khorāsān."[63] It was written around 1157 (the same time as the composition of *Chahār maqāla*) after the Ghuzz had captured Sultan Sanjar and plundered the greater part of Khorasan. Here Anvari, or the voice speaking the *qasida,* pleads on behalf of the people of Khorasan to the Khāqān of Samarqand, asking him to send an army and free them from the depredations of the Ghuzz. Here are the first four lines:

> *O Morning Breeze, if you pass by Samarqand / Take this letter (nāma) from the people of Khorasan to the Khāqān.*
>
> *It is a letter the opening (matla') of which is pain of the body and distress of the soul / A letter the ending (maqta') of which is sadness of heart and pain of mind.*
>
> *It is a letter in the lines (raqam) of which the sighs of friends are apparent / A letter in the folds (shikan) of which is the blood of martyrs.*
>
> *Its writing (naqsh-i tahrir) is dry from the [burning] breasts of victims / Its opening line (`unvān) is damp from the tears of the desolate.*

نامه اهل خراسان ببر خاقان بر	بسمرقند اگر بگذری ای باد سحر
نامه ای مقطع آن درد دل و سوز جگر	نامه ای مطلع آن رنج تن و آفت جان
نامه ای در شکنش خون شهیدان مضمر	نامه ای بر رقمش آه عزیزان پیدا
سطر عنوانش از دیده محرومان تر	نقش تحریرش از سینه مظلومان خشک

There are a few more lines in this opening section before the transition to the main point of the letter. Some sixty lines later there is another transitional line and then the final prayer for the Khāqān. Here is a *qasida* cast as a letter: a letter that tells the listener (or reader) that it is, in fact, a letter and which uses six technical terms of letter-writing to make that clear, and which is organized just as a letter should be.

This is not the only example of a *qasida* being used as a letter. Mas`ud-i Sa`d-i Salmān (ca. 1046 or 1048–1121) was born in Lahore and was employed in the later Ghaznavid courts. For political reasons he spent some eighteen years of his life in various prisons. While in prison he composed many *qasidas*, some of which are his greatest poems. In these prison poems he complains about his condition and pleads with the ruler to let him out. Prison poems are part of a larger category that could be called *shikāyat-i ruzgār* (complaint poems), in which two *topoi* are often found: the message and the messenger. The messenger carries the message (as the morning breeze does in the *qasida* by Anvari above), which can then be a letter.[64] The prison *qasidas* of Mas`ud-i Sa`d are, in fact, letters to the ruler, letters in verse that were probably more convincing than any prose letter he might have written.

Another example comes in a *qasida* that begins:

I know very well how the world is / How can I say it without bringing on trouble.

اوساف جهان سخت نیک دانم \ از بیم بلا گفت کی توانم

Line 39 says:

I cannot create adornments while in prison / My clever tongue/language is stuck in my letter.

در حبس آرایش نجیزد از من \ بر نامه به ماندست تر زبانم

And line 50:

You know how much I suffer / To send poetry and prose to you.[65]

دانی تو که چه مایه رنج بینم \ تا نظمی و نثری به تو رسانم

Mas`ud-i Sa`d says plainly that this is a letter. In it he stresses his fidelity and loyalty, and trusts in that of the king. He reports that his morale is so low in prison that he cannot even adorn his speech, but he struggles and suffers to send prose and verse to his patron.

Again, in the *qasida* beginning:

> *The usefulness of one's efforts is curtailed / by the imprisonment and bonds of this suffering and feeble body.*

مقصور شد مصالح کار جهانیان \ بر حبس و بند این تن رنجور ناتوان

Line 82 says:

> *Heed my petition and then grant generously / Grant me forgiveness, I who am unfortunate and lost to sight.* [*Qissa is used here in its technical sense of "petition."*]

بنیوش قصّهٔ من و آنگاه کریموار \ بخشایش آر بر من بد بخت گم نشان

Line 87:

> *O Spring Breeze and O Perfumed Breeze / Take this praise (i.e., qasida) of mine and deliver it to that court.*[66]

ای باد نو بهاری وای مشک بوی باد \ این مدح من بگیر و بدان پیشگاه رسان

The poet is presenting this poem as a petition to be delivered to the patron's court. We find again the messenger, and the message called a *qissa* (petition). There are more such *qasidas* in the divan of Mas`ud-i Sa`d, but these samples should be sufficient to show that this poet is perfectly at ease using his *qasidas* as letters.

`Abd al-Rahmān Jāmi (d. 1492) wrote a *qasida* in reply to a letter written in prose interlarded with poetry that he had received from the *malik al-tujjār* (Chief Merchant). Jāmi praises the language and the use of rhetorical devices in it:

> *If you open its folds you will find its inventive poetry and prose / Filled*

with rhetorical devices from beginning to end...

To see its poetry and prose you would think that the secretary of the heavens / Had placed the necklace of the Pleiades on the daughters of The Bear.

Or that treasures of jewels had fallen to earth / Some connected, some separate.

Paragraphs of its prose are nurture for ten generations of art / Its poetic turns brighten the rays of the sun.

پر ز صنعت یابی اش از ابتدا تا انتها...   لفّ اورا گر کنی نثر از بدیع نظم و نثر

عقد پروین را در اثنای بنات النعش جا   نظم و نثرش بین که پنداری دبیر چرخ کرد

بر بساط عرض بعضی متّصل بعضی جدا   یا خود افتاده است مخزونات گنج پر گوهر

نکته های نظم او و روشنگر تیغ ذکا   فقره های نثر او قوت ده پشت هنر

He hastens to compose a reply:

In order to compose a reply, my secretary of wisdom said / "Do not raise the veil of chastity from the face of thought...

This thought is necessary, so take the path of poetry / The poet is allowed to do things that are inappropriate for the non-poet."

When my secretary of wisdom had given me this considered advice...[67]

بر مدار از چهره ای اندیشه جلبت حیا...   تا جواب آن کنم انشاء دبیر عقل گفت

ناروای غیر شاعر هست شاعر را روا   در ضرورت باشد این معنی طریق شعر گیر

  چون دبیر عقل زد بهر من از این سنجیده رای ...

In this exchange Jāmi is playing the role of the *adib* to the limit. He praises his correspondent's prose and poetry for such a degree of elegance and technical skill that he is inspired by his *dabir-i ʿaql* (i.e., his muse), who advises him what tone to assume in order to reply in kind. He, being a poet, is allowed to do things from which a non-poet such as the *malik al-tujjār* is barred. Jāmi, alluding to the central role of the secretary (*dabir*) in the world of the literati by couching his thoughts in the words of his *dabir-i ʿaql* for the sake of modesty, makes it clear how superior his language is to that of his correspondent, reaffirming the excellence of his poetry and, indeed, of all poetry, over prose:

When the straight cypress raises its head in the gardens of excellence / it is inappropriate for the violet to show itself off with its bent back.

در رياض فضل چون بالا كشد سرو سهى \ از بنفشه نيست لايق جلوه با پشت دو تا

Here is the consummate literatus, at home in both poetry and prose, rec-ognizing the merits of each and confirming the generic hierarchy that had ruled classical Persian since the coming of Islam. There are many other examples of this in pre-Safavid divans.

One result of this borrowing between the secretaries and the poets was the tripartite prose preface to Muhammad ʿAwfi's *Lubāb al-albāb*. Written in 1220–21, this is the earliest *tazkira* (anthology) that we have in Persian. The preface, dedicated to ʿAyn al-Mulk Husayn b. Sharaf al-Mulk al-Ashʿari, the vizier of Nāsir al-Din Qabācha, begins with an extended passage describing nature, followed by a transition to the main dedication. Then comes a long transition and, finally, a prayer for the patron: precisely the form seen in so many panegyric *qasidas*.

Another variation on the theme of the interchange of prose and poetry is the *qasida* in prose. This sounds like a contradiction in terms since, tech-nically, *"qasida"* is defined as a verse form with certain specific functions and, in this case, a certain formal arrangement. In Rāvandi's *Rāhat al-sudur,* for example, there is a prose *qasida* (with some verses added) addressed to the Seljuq Sultan Abu al-Fath Kaykhusraw b. Qılıj Arslān (r. 1192–97, 1205–11).[68] This prose *qasida* contains all the conventional sections that the normal poetic *qasida* has and the imagery in it is entirely that of panegyric poetry. Khatibi quotes two other examples of prose *qasidas*, and there are undoubtedly more to be found.[69]

From the mid-11th century on, the descriptive language of poetry began to infiltrate prose writing. Beginning with simple descriptions of nature, followed by descriptions of less tangible things such as darkness or cold, the use of poetry language and ways of expression began to appear in prose in a full-scale manner. The prose *qasida* shows the extent to which the descrip-tive language of poetry had permeated prose writing. This change in the formal written language coincided with the increasing influence of Arabic in the education of Persians that resulted from the rise of the *nizāmiyyas* as important educational institutions. We know, for example, that Rashid al-Din Vatvāt had studied in the *nizāmiyya* of Balkh, and there can be no doubt that many other secretaries were now entering chancelleries with this sort of education.

In addition, at around this time courtly Persian prose style began again to show its ability to influence Arabic style. Ibn Khaldun (1332–1406) speaks of this trend with disfavor (emphasis added):

> *Recent authors employ the methods of poetry in writing prose. Their writing contains a great deal of rhymed prose and obligatory rhymes. When one examines such prose, (one gets the impression that) it has actually become a kind of poetry...In recent times, secretaries took this up and employed it in government correspondence...They avoided straight prose and affected to forget it,* especially the people of the East...*From the point of view of good style, it is not correct, since in good style one looks for conformity between what is said and the requirements of the given situations in which the speaker and the person addressed find themselves. It is necessary that government correspondence be kept free from this (type of prose)...Government correspondence done...in a method proper to poetry deserves censure. The only reason our contemporaries do it is the fact that* non-Arab (speech habits) exercise a firm hold over their tongues...Present-day poets and secretaries in the East use this method most and apply it in an exaggerated manner to all kinds of speech. *They go so far as to tamper with vowel endings and inflections of words (to achieve this end). (Ibn Khaldun 1967:7442–43)*[70]

References to people and practices "of the East" must refer to the Persians. In fact, Abu Hilāl al-`Askari (d. after 1010) discusses the political uses of the straightforward style (preferred by Ibn Khaldun) and the opaque style coming into use in his time. He asserts that "the cardinal rule of composition is an awareness of the social status and linguistic ability of the addressee."[71]

STABILITY OF LANGUAGE

It has been mentioned that written courtly Persian remained quite uniform and relatively stable over many centuries and across a very broad area of the Middle East, Central, and South Asia. By uniform I mean that without having a strong political or administrative center to set the example for formal prose style, the grammar, lexicon, and style of this kind of Persian varied, synchronically, hardly at all across the Persian-using world. The prose written in the courts of Central Asia showed no marked features that could identify its origin when compared with prose of the same period written in Khorasan or the subcontinent. Persian *inshā* did change over time, as would be expected, but it changed slowly and this is what is meant by stability. Without a central court whose chancellery could establish a style that would be imitated by provincial courts, what were the forces that held back change and promoted stability?

One strong force was the prestige of classical Persian poetry. Persian poetry began to be written down in the Samanid courts of Bukhara, or possible earlier. By the Seljuq period, when Arabic had long ceased to be the language of the chancellery, there was a considerable body of this poetry available. Of all the poets writing at this time, the greatest were patronized by the Samanid, Ghaznavid, and Seljuq rulers. These poets, and poetry itself, developed and maintained its prestige through the authority of language.

Soon after the year 1000 the poets of the Ghaznavid court had codified a use language that maintained its authority until the 20th century. Poets moved from court to court and their work provided a background of rhetorical and lexical usage that was known to the whole body of literati. The efforts of the poets were supported by the work of the lexicographers. We have seen how prose and poetry, secretaries and poets, interacted within courtly society. The authority that language gave to poetry, or that poets claimed for themselves, must have been internalized by the writers of prose. Many of the latter, as we have seen, were also poets. This poetry was self-consciously conservative in style. Nizāmi ʿAruzi tells us that the way to become a poet is to read and learn thousands of lines of the verse of your predecessors and contemporaries. Rules for meter and rhyme were to be strictly adhered to and the inventory of images and the lexicon in general was very restricted. The weight of the poetic tradition must have borne heavily on the writers of prose.

Another, less obvious force that inhibited change was the influence of classical Arabic and the language of the Qurʾan. By Seljuq times, while relatively little of the routine work of the chancellery was done in Arabic, all educated persons knew the Qurʾan and the Hadith well and, in general, were able to quote easily from both. Any competent secretary would have been able to compose a document in Arabic should that become necessary. If a secretary had acquired his education in a *nizāmiyya*, he would have a very sound knowledge of Arabic and in particular the language of the Qurʾan and the Hadith. The language of the Qurʾan was an inimitable ideal toward which educated users of Arabic strove in their own use of language, and this effort to approximate the unreachable register of Qur'anic Arabic had a powerful effect in Arabic circles on the stability of the classical language. In the case of the Persians, I suggest, this attitude toward the highest registers of Arabic also prevailed, but indirectly. Writers of high-register Persian, which became freighted with an increasing load of Arabic vocabulary, must have felt, unconsciously, a brake being applied to their efforts toward innovation.

Bureaucratic inertia was another drag on any desire to innovate. This idea hardly needs much expansion except to say that as time went on and Persian empires increased in size and complexity, the bureaucracy also grew. We have seen examples of the attitude of respect that secretaries had toward their professional forebears and their ways of working. If something such as a style, a format, and expression, an image, a procedure, worked efficiently, why change it? One of tradition's failings is that it can lead to inertia and resistance to change, and this inertia, too, I believe contributed to the stability of the chancellery language.

The rise of lexicography, I submit, had a secondary and conservative purpose beyond defining words and codifying the lexicon of written Persian. As more non-native speakers of Persian entered the chancelleries and became secretaries, especially Hindus in the courts of the subcontinent, the more the native-speaking Persian literati must have worried about the foreign words that began to seep into the written language. Dictionary writers began to state clearly that one of their aims was to keep Persian pure by enshrining it in their dictionaries. An unexpected result of this was the "dictionary wars" of the Mughal period. In Baevskii's chronological (not exhaustive) list of a hundred Persian dictionaries written between 800 and 1800, twenty-six were written before 1510 and seventy-four were written between 1510 and 1800, most of the later in India.[72] In any case, the desire to keep Persian free of (mostly Indian) borrowings, to maintain a fixed and codified lexicon as manifested in the growth of dictionary-writing was another conservative force that worked toward stability of the written language.

Finally, the fact that the medieval Persian literati were not burdened with the compulsions of modernity is of crucial importance. The modernist's need for incessant innovation, the disregard for past precedents and tradition, the perceived necessity of self-realization, and the demonstration of the individual's uniqueness, the social isolation resulting from the notion of the

individual and the Other, would surely have made the medieval Persian literati scratch their heads. Many medieval social institutions operated with an
entirely different ideology. One such institution that was deeply implicated
in literary (and social) stability is the *madrasa,* both in its traditional form and
in its revitalized character as a *nizāmiyya.* Education was carried out in these
establishments largely by memorization and repetition. The basic effort of
memorization was to learn the Qur'an by heart. Whether or not the student
achieved this, he memorized much else and the more that he could recite
by heart, the better he could fare in the disputations that were an important
part of higher education. What could be a stronger conservative force than
education based on memorization? Respect for tradition was strong and it
was always possible to find an example of past practice to counter an effort
to do or say things in a new way. Since a very large number (but not all) of
the medieval literati were educated in this way, its effect would have been felt
in the chancelleries as it was felt in other areas of society.

★ ★ ★

I have tried to show in this chapter that the formal, written language
of the Persian courts, at least up to the 13th or early 14th century, was created and developed as a result of the dynamic interaction of the work of
the secretaries and the poets, with an increasingly important contribution
from the lexicographers. On the one hand, poets and secretaries interacted
with each other in their work and in their social life, and with other *adibs*
in the intellectual and artistic circles of the courts. Many secretaries wrote
divans of poetry in Persian and Arabic in addition to their official prose, and
at least one, Rashid al-Din Vatvāt, became better known as a poet than as
the secretary that he was. Poets, on the other hand, knew the epistolary terminology and wrote letters in verse, even saying that they were letters. In
their ease with, and mastery of, the written language, poets and secretaries
borrowed devices of language and meaning freely from each other or from
the common pool. They also shared a literary form, the tripartite structure
of many *qasida*s. We see this form more often in the panegyric *qasida* than
elsewhere but it also crops up in the prose *qasida* and even Muhammad
`Awfi's (himself a secretary and in charge of the chancellery, *divan-i inshā',*
of Qılıj Arslān Khāqān of Samarqand in 1200–1 or shortly after) prose introduction to his *Lubāb al-albāb.* The early Persian courts provided the setting
or the matrix from which emerged a written language that became standard throughout the Persianate world, which later included the Ottoman

court, many Central Asian courts, and the Mughal courts of the Indian subcontinent.

NOTES

1. For the sake of consistency, I will use "secretary" for *munshi, dabir* or *kātib* throughout. All three Persian terms were in use and were generally interchangeable during the period of time covered by the chapter.
2. "Tamām shod ketābat-i in majmu'a bar dast-e munshi-yi vey Muhammad b. Mahmud b. Mohmmad Zangi al-Bukhāri." See his *Zangi nāma,* 120.
3. See Zilli, "Development of *Inshā* Literature," 309–49, esp. 309.
4. See the introduction to his translation and commentary in `Abd-Allāh Marvārid's *Sharaf Nāma,* 1–26.
5. Abu al-Fazl Bayhaqi, *Tārikh-i Beyhaqi,* 7.
6. Cf. H.R. Roemer's observation concerning the Timurid period: "Es ist bezeichnend für die wertschätzung der *inšā*-Kunst, daß eine Reihe bedeutender Vertreter der Literatur jener Epoche auch als Verfasser von *inšā*-Werken hervorgetreten ist." Marvārid, *SharafNamä,* 21.
7. Unpublished paper by J.R. Perry which, inter alia, discusses the *Frahang-i Pahlavig,* which contains two chapters on the art of the scribe and chancellery usage.
8. R.C. Zaehner, "Nāmak-nipesishnih." See also Tafazzoli, *Tārikh-e adabiyāt.*
9. For a survey of Sasanian practice, see H. Khatibi, *Fann-e nathr dar adab-e Pārsi,* 1:283ff. For the Islamic period, see *Encyclopaedia Iranica,* s.v. "correspondence."
10. See M. Morony, *Iraq after the Muslim Conquest* (Princeton: Princeton University Press, 1984), pp. 64–66, and V. Danner, "Arabic Literature in Iran," in *Cambridge History of Iran* 4 (Cambridge: Cambridge University Press, 1968), pp. 566–94.
11. Muhammad b. Hendushāh Nakhjavāni, *Dastur al-kātib,* 2:65–66.
12. Keykāvus b. Vashmgir. *Qābus nāma,* 207–13.
13. Nezāmi `Aruzi Samarqandi, *Chahār maqāla,* 19–21.
14. Nakhjavāni, *Dastur,* 1:98–122.
15. M. Taqi Bahār, *Tārikh-e Sistān,* 209–10.
16. E.G. Browne, *Literary History,* 1:378. For a discussion of the chapter on *ketāba* and a translation of the technical terms, see C.E. Bosworth, "Secretary's Art."
17. Bosworth, "Administrative Literature," 155–67.
18. Bayhaqi, *Tārikh,* 383.
19. Ibid., 207, 667, and Muhammad `Awfi, *Javāma' al-hekāyāt,* 1:64–65.
20. Abu Sharaf Nāseh b. Zafar Jurfādaqāni, *Tarjoma-yi Tārikh-e Yamini,* 21–28.
21. Dhabih-Allāh Safā, *Tārikh-e adabiyāt dar Irān,* 2:905.
22. Cf. Bosworth's remark: "Every vizier had a secretarial training behind him, all the manuals of secretaryship have relevance [to the vizierate] too"; "Administrative Literature," esp. 164.
23. `Awfi, *Lobāb al-albāb,* 1.
24. Nakhjavāni, *Dastur,* 2:viii–ix.
25. Ibid., 2:365–66.
26. See C.H. Fleischer, "Between the Lines," 45–61, esp. 60–61.
27. Hasan b. `Abd al-Mo'men al-Khui, *Ghunyat al-kāteb,* 2.
28. Ibid., 1.
29. A five-member *ezāfa* phrase that, ironically, is considered poor literary style.

30. Nakhjavāni, *Dastur*, 1:28–54.

31. Ibid., 1:92.

32. Ibid., 2:57–62.

33. Muntajab al-Din Badi` Atābeg Jovayni, *'Atabat al-katabat*, 2–5.

34. Ibid., page *h* of introduction.

35. `Awfi, *Lobāb*, 1:78–80.

36. Muhammad Taqi Bahār, *Sabk-shenāsi*, 2:377–78.

37. `Ayn al-Din `Ayn al-Mulk b. `Abd-Allāh Māhru, *Inshā'*, 64–68.

38. See Marwārid, *Sharaf Nāma*.

39. Muhammad b. `Omar Rāduyāni, *Tarjomān al-balāgha*.

40. See Muhammad Taqi Bahār, *Sabk-shenāsi*, 2:400–404.

41. Shams al-Din Muhammad b. Qays al-Razi. *Al-mo'jam fi ma'ayer ash'ar al-'ajam*, 328.

42. Rāduyāni, *Tarjomān*, 2–3.

43. R. Vatvāt, *Latā'ef al-amthāl*, 55–56.

44. Abu al-Ma`ali Nasr-Allāh Munshi, *Tarjoma-yi Kalila va Demna*, 23, 25.

45. Shams-e Qeys, *al-Mo'jam*, 24. Shams-e Qeys errs in citing Rashid al-Din's *Hadā'eq* as the source of this statement: it is from his *Latā'ef al-amthāl va tarā'ef al-aqwāl*.

46. Ahmad b. Ahmad Domānisi, *Mojmal al-aqwāl*, fols. 4r–5r.

47. V.V. Barthold, *Turkestan Down to the Mongol Invasion*, 14.

48. Māhru, *Inshā'*, 148–49.

49. Sharaf al-Din Rāmi, *Anis al-'oshshāq*, 153, 156–62.

50. Kamāl al-Din Hosayn Kāshifi, *Badāye' al-afkār*, 6–7.

51. Kāshefi, *Anvār-e Suhayli*, 6–7.

52. C. van Ruymbeke, "Kashifi's Forgotten Masterpiece," 571–88.

53. Samarqandi, *Chahār maqāla*, 18–19.

54. Bahār, *Sabk shenāsi*, 2:377; 3:15.

55. Nasr-Allāh Munshi, *Kalila va Demna*, h–t.

56. Māhru, *Inshā'*, 228.

57. Muntajab al-Din Badi, *'Atabat al-Kataba*, 1.

58. See Solomon I. Baevskii, *Early Persian Lexicography*, "Appendix."

59. Ibid., 30.

60. Ibid., 134–41.

61. Ibid., 142–47.

62. Nāser Khusrow, *Safar nāma*, 9. English trans.: *Naser-e Khosraw's Book of Travels*, 6.

63. For further discussion and a partial translation of this poem, see Browne, *Literary History*, 2:386–89.

64. Anna Livia F.A. Beelaert, *Cure for the Grieving*, 35–36.

65. Mas`ud-e Sa`d-e Salmān, *Divān*, 354–56.

66. Ibid., 427–31.

67. Zayn al-Din Mahmud Vāsifi, *Badāya' al-vaqāya'*, 1:345–47.

68. Najm al-Din Abu Bakr Muhammad Rāvandi, *Rāhat al-sodur va āyat al-sorur*, 20–26.

69. Husayn Khatibi, *Fann-i nathr dar adab-i fārsi*, 270–71.

70. Ibn Khaldun, *Muqaddimah*, 442–43. I am grateful to my colleague Dr. Aslam Syed for this reference.

71. Quoted from G.J. Kanazi, *Studies in the Kitāb as-Sinā'atayn of Abu Hilāl al-'Askari* (Leiden: E.J. Brill, 1989, pp. 140–41) in Julie S. Meisami, *Persian Historiography*, 293–94.

72. See Baevskii, *Lexicography*, 211–19.

REFERENCES: *MUNSHIS*, POETS AND THE LITERARY LANGUAGE

'Abd-Allāh, Sayyid. 1371/1992. *Adabiyāt-i fārsi dar miyān-i hindovān,* trans. Muhammad Islām Khān. Tehran.

Abu al-Fazl b. Mubārak. 187?. *Inshā'.* n.p.

Alam, Muzaffar. 1962/1341.'Ali b. Muhammad. Tāj al-halāvi. *Daqāyiq al-shi'r,* ed. M. Kāzim Imām. Tehran.

—— 1998. The Pursuit of Persian: Language in Mughal Politics. *Modern Asian Studies* 32:317–49.

—— 2003. The Culture and Politics of Persian in Precolonial Hindustan. In *Literary Cultures in History: Reconstructions from South Asia,* ed. Sheldon Pollock, pp. 131–98. Berkeley: University of California Press.

—— 2004. The Making of a Munshi. *Comparative Studies of South Asia, Africa and the Middle East* 24:61–72.

Amir Khusrow Dihlavi. 1876. *I'jāz-i khusravi.* 2 vols. in 1. Lucknow.

—— 1950. *Nuh sipihr,* ed. M.W. Mirza. London: Oxford University Press.

Āmuli, Shams al-Din. 1377/1957–58. *Nafā'is al-funun fi 'arā'is al-'uyun,* ed. Abu al-Hasan Sha'rāni. Tehran.

Anooshahr, Ali. 2005. 'Utbi and the Ghaznavids at the Foot of the Mountain. *Iranian Studies* 38:271–91.

Anvari. 1338/1959. *Divān,* ed. M.T. Mudarris-Razavi. 2 vols. Tehran.

Askari, S.H. 1953. Mahmud Gāwān and His Book Manāzir-ul-Inshā. *Indo-Iranica* 6:28–36.

'Awfi, Muhammad. 1903, 1906. *Lubāb al-albāb,* ed. E.G. Browne and M. Qazvini. 2 vols. London.

'Awfi, Muhammad. 1370/1991. *Javāmi' al-hikāyāt va lavāmi' al-rivāyāt,* ed. J. Shi'ār. Tehran.

Baevskii, Solomon I. 2007. *Early Persian Lexicography: Farhangs of the 11th to the 15th Centuries,* trans. N. Killian, rev. John R. Perry. Folkestone, Kent: Global Oriental.

Bahā' al-Din Baghdādi. 1315/1936. *Al-Tavassul ilā al-tarassul,* ed. A. Bahmanyār. Tehran.

Bahār, Muhammad Taqi. 1337/1958. *Sabk shināsi.* 3 vols. Tehran.

Bahār, Muhammad Taqi, ed. 1314/1935. *Tārikh-i Sistān.* Tehran.

Bārilavi, Nithār 'Ali Bukhāri. 1278/1861. *Inshā-yi dilgushā.* Cawnpore.

Barthold, W. 1968. *Turkestan Down to the Mongol Invasion.* 3rd ed. London: Luzac.

Bayhaqi, Abu al-Fazl. 1371/1992. *Tārikh-i Bayhaqi,* ed. 'A.A. Fayyāz. Tehran.

Beelaert, Anna Livia F.A. 2000. *A Cure for the Grieving.* Leiden: Nederlands Instituut voor het Nabije Oosten.

Bosworth, C.E. 1968. The Political and Dynastic History of the Iranian World (A.D. 1000–1217). In *Cambridge History of Iran* 5:1–202.

—— 1969. `Abdallāh al-Khwārazmi on the Technical Terms of the Secretary's Art. *Journal of the Economic and Social History of the Orient* 12(2): 113–64.

—— 1990. Administrative Literature. In *Religion, Learning and Science in the Abbasid Period,* ed. M.J.L.K. Young, J.D. Latham, and R.B. Serjeant, pp. 155–67. Cambridge: Cambridge University Press.

Browne, Edward G. 1902–24. *A Literary History of Persia.* 4 vols. Cambridge: Cambridge University Press.

Busse, Heribert. 1959. *Untersuchungen zum islamischen Kanzleiwesen, an Hand turkmenischer und safawidischer Urkunden.* Cairo.

Cambridge History of Iran 4. 1975. Cambridge University Press.

Christensen, Arthur. 1944. *L'Iran sous les Sassanides.* 2nd ed. Copenhagen.

Dale, Stephen F. 2003. A Safavid Poet in the Heart of Darkness: The Indian Poems of Ashraf Mazandarani. *Iranian Studies* 36:197–212.

—— 2004. *The Garden of the Eight Paradises: Bābur and the Culture of Empire in Central Asia, Afghanistan and India (1483–1530).* Leiden.

Darling, Linda. 2004. Persianate Sources on Anatolia and the Early History of the Ottomans. In *Studies on Persianate Societies* 2:126–44.

Das, Sisir Kumar. 1978. *Sahibs and Munshis: An Account of the College of Fort William.* New Delhi: Orion.

Dumānisi, Ahmad b. Ahmad. 1381/2002. *Mujmal al-aqvāl fi al-hikam wa al-amthāl,* ed. M. Omidsalar and I. Afshār. Tehran.

Dawlatshāh Samarqandi. 1337/1958. *Tazkira al-shu`arā,* ed. M. `Abbāsi. Tehran.

Encyclopaedia Iranica. 1982– . s.v. Correspondence ii-iv, Dabir.

Encyclopaedia of Islam. 1960–2005. 2nd ed. s.v. Hilāl al-Sābi, Inshā. Leiden: E.J. Brill.

Jamāl al-Din Husayn Inju Shirāzi. 1351/1972. *Farhang-i Jahāngiri,* ed. R. `Afifi. 2 vols. Meshed.

Muhammad Fā`iq. 1291/1874. *Inshā'-yi fā`iq [yā] dastur al-inshā'.* Madras.

Fārooqui, Muhammad `Abdul Hamid. 1967. *Chandra Bhān Brahman: Life and Works.* Ahmedābād.

Farrell, Joseph. 2001. *Latin Language and Latin Culture, from Ancient to Modern Times.* Cambridge: Cambridge University Press.

Farrukhi Sistāni. 1335/1956. *Divān,* ed. M. Dabir-Siyāqi. Tehran.

Fekete, Lajos. 1977. *Einführung in die persische Paläographie.* Budapest.

Fisher, Michael H. 1991. *Indirect Rule in India: Residents and the Residency System 1764–1858.* Delhi: Oxford University Press.

Fleischer, Cornell H. 1994. Between the Lines: Realities of Scribal Life in the Sixteenth Century. In *Studies in Ottoman History in Honour of Professor V.L. Ménage,* ed. Colin Heywood and Colin Imber, pp. 45–61. Istanbul: Isis.

Forbes, William. 1829. *A Grammar of the Goojratee Language.* Bombay.

Fowler, A. 1982. *Kinds of Literature: An Introduction to the Theory of Genres and Modes.* Oxford: Clarendon.

Fragner, Bert G. 1999. *Die "Persophonie": Regionalität, Identität und Sprachkontakt in der Geschichte Asiens.* ANOR No. 5. Berlin: Das Arabische Buch.

Gardizi, Abu Sa`id `Abd al-Hayy. 1347/1968. *Zayn al-akhbār*, ed. `A. Habibi. Tehran.

Ghazzāli, Muhammad. 1351/1972. *Nasihat al-muluk*, ed. J. Humā'i. Tehran.

Gorekar, N.S. 1970. *Indo-Iran Relations: Cultural Aspects.* Bombay: Sinhu Publications.

Gurgāni, Fakhr al-Din. 1349/1970. *Vis u Rāmin*, ed. M. Todua, A. Gwakharia, and K. Aini. Tehran. Eng. trans. by D. Davis [New York, 2009].

Harikarana Multani. 1781. *Inshā-yi Herkeren. The Forms of Herheren, Corrected... and Translated into English...by Francis Balfour.* Calcutta.

Hasan b. `Abd al-Mu'min al-Khui. 1963. *Ghunyat al-kātib va munyat al-tālib; Rosum al-Rasā'il va nujum al-fazā'il*, ed. Adnan Sadik Erzi. Ankara.

Haywood, John A. 1960. *Arabic Lexicography.* Leiden: E.J. Brill.

Hilāl al-Sābi'. 1977. *Rusûm Dār al-Khilāfah*, trans. Elie A. Salem. Beirut.

Husain, Iqbāl. 1937. *The Early Persian Poets of India (A.H. 421–670).* Patna.

Ibn Funduq. 1968. *Tārikh-i Bayhaq*, ed. K. Husayni. Hyderābād (Deccan).

Ibn Khaldun. 1969. *The Muqaddimah: An Introduction to History*, trans. F. Rosenthal. 3 vols. Princeton: Princeton University Press.

Jakobi, Jürgen. 1992. Agriculture Between Literary Tradition and Firsthand Experience: The Irshād al-Zirā'a of Qasim b. Yusuf Abu Nasri Haravi. In *Timurid Art and Culture*, ed. L. Golombek and M. Subtelny, pp. 201–8. Leiden: E.J. Brill.

Jāmi, `Abd al-Rahmān. 1364/1944–45. *Nāmahā-yi dastnivis*, ed. `A. Uronbayef and M. Heravi. Kabul.

Jurfādaqāni, Abu Sharaf Nasih b. Zafar. 1345/1966. *Tarjuma-yi Tārikh-i Yamini*, ed. J. Shi`ār. Tehran.

Juvayni, Muntajab al-Din Badi` Atābeg. 1329/1950. *`Atabat al-katabat*, ed. M. Qazvini and `A. Iqbāl. Tehran.

Kāshifi, Kamāl al-Din Husayn. 1977. *Badāya` al-afkār fi sanāya` al-ashār*, ed. R. Moselmānkolof. Moscow.

—— 1362/1983–84. *Anvār-i Suhayli.* Tehran.

Kaykāvus b. Vashmgir. 1345/1967. *Qābus nāma*, ed. Gh.-H. Yûsufi. Tehran. Eng. trans.: *A Mirror for Princes*, trans. R. Levy [New York: Cresset Press, 1951].

Khalil, `Ali Ibrāhim Khān. 1978. *Suhûf-i ibrāhim.* Patna.

Khatibi, Husayn. 1366/1987. *Fann-i nathr dar adab-i fārsi.* Tehran.

Khwārazmi, Abu `Abd-Allāh Muhammad Kātib. 1347/1968. *Mafātih al-`ulûm*, ed. G. van Vloten. Leiden, 1900. Pers. trans. by H. Khadiv-Jam. Tehran.

Kraemer, Joel. 1984. Humanism in the Renaissance of Islam: A Preliminary Study. *Journal of the American Oriental Society* 104:135–64.

Kremer, Alfred, Freiherr von. 1888. *Über das Einnahmebudget des Abbasiden-Reiches vom Jahre 306 H. (918–919)*, pp. 283–362. Denkschriften der kaiserlichen Akademie der Wissen-schaften, Phil.-Hist. Classe. Vienna.

Lane, George. 2003. *Early Mongol Rule in Thirteenth-Century Iran.* London: RoutledgeCurzon.

Law, N.N. 1916. *Promotion of Learning in India during Muhammadan Rule.* London.

Lazard, Gilbert. 1964. *Les premiers poètes persans, IXe–Xe siècles.* 2 vols. Paris: Librairie d'Amérique et d'Orient.

Māhru, Ayn al-Din `Ayn al-Mulk b. `Abd-Allāh. 1965. *Inshā',* ed. Sh. `Abd al-Rashid and M. Bashir Hosayn. Lahore.

Marvārid, `Abd-Allāh. 1951–52. *Sharaf Nāma,* ed. and trans., with an introduction by H.R. Roemer. Wiesbaden.

Mas`ûd-i Sa`d-i Salmān. 1339/1960. *Divān,* ed. R. Yāsimi. Tehran.

Mayhani, Muhammad b. `Abd al-Khāliq. 1962. *Dastur-i dabiri,* ed. Adnan Sadik Erzi. Ankara.

McChesney, R. 1996. "Barrier of Heterodoxy"?: Rethinking the Ties between Iran and Central Asia in the 17th Century. In *Safavid Persia,* ed. C. Melville, pp. 231–67. London: I.B. Tauris.

Meisami, Julie S. 1999. *Persian Historiography to the End of the Twelfth Century.* Edinburgh: Edinburgh University Press.

Mitchell, Colin P. 2003. To Preserve and Protect: Husayn Va'iz-i Kashifi and Perso-Islamic Chancellery Culture. *Iranian Studies* 36:485–507.

Mohiuddin, Momin. 1971. *The Chancellery and Persian Epistolography under the Mughals.* Calcutta: Iran Society.

Muhammad al-Husayni. 1286/1869–70. *Makhzan al-inshā'.* Tehran.

Muhammad Hādi Māzandarāni. 1375/1996. *Anvār al-balāga,* ed. M. `A. Ghulāmi-nizhād. Tehran.

Müminov, Ashirbek, Francis Richard, and Maria Szuppe. 1999. *Patrimoine manuscrit et vie intellectuelle de l'Asie Centrale islamique.* Cahiers d'Asie Centrale, 7. Tashkent: Institut français d'études sur l'Asie centrale.

Mutribi al-Asamm al-Samarqandi. 1998. *Conversations with Emperor Jahangir.* Trans., with an introduction by R.C. Foltz. Costa Mesa, CA: Mazda.

Nakhjavāni, Muhammad b. Hindushāh. 1964–76. *Dastur al-kātib fi ta'yin al-marātib,* ed. `A. `Ali-zāda. 2 vols. Moscow.

Nāsir Khusrow. 1354/1975. *Safar-nāma,* ed. M. Dabir-siyāqi. Tehran: Anjuman-i Āthār-i Milli. English trans. *Naser-i Khosraw's Book of Travels (Safarnama)* (New York: Bibliotheca Persica, 1986).

Nasr-Allāh Munshi, Abu al-Ma`āli. 1343/1964. *Tarjuma-yi Kalila va Dimna,* ed. Mujtabā Minuvi. Tehran.

Navā'i, `Abd al-Husayn. 1363/1984. *Asnād va mokātabāt-i siyāsi-yi irān az sāl-i 1105 tā 1135 h.q.* Tehran.

Nissen, Hans J., Peter Damerow, and Robert K. Englund. 1993. *Archaic Bookkeeping: Early Writing and Techniques of Economic Administration in the Ancient Near East,* trans. Paul Larsen. Chicago: University of Chicago Press.

Nizāmi, Nizām al-Din `Abd al-Vāsi`. 1357/1978. *Manshā al-inshā,* ed. R. Humāyunfarrukh. Tehran.

Nizāmi `Aruzi Samarqandi. 1333/1954. *Chahār maqāla,* ed. M. Qazvini and M. Mu`in. Tehran.

Nurul Hasan, S. 1952. Nigar Nama-i-Munshi (A Valuable Collection of Documents of Aurangzeb's Reign). *Proceedings of the Indian History Congress* 15:258–63.

Pihan, A.P. 1856. *Notice sur les divers genres d'écriture ancienne et moderne des Arabes, des Persans et des Turcs*. Paris.

—— 1860. *Exposé des signes de numération usités chez les peuples orientaux anciens et modernes*. Paris.

Qā'im-Maqāmi, Jahāngir. 1350/1971. *Muqaddima-i bar shinākht-i asnād-i tārikhi*. Tehran.

Qavvās, Fakr al-Din Mubārakshāh. 1353/1974. *Farhang-i qavvās*, ed. Nādir `Ali. Tehran.

Rāduyāni, Muhammad b. `Umar. 1949. *Tarjumān al-balāgha*, ed. Ahmed Ateş. Istanbul.

Rāmi, Sharaf al-Din. 1341/1962. *Haqā'iq al-hadā'iq*, ed. M. K. Imāmi. Tehran.

—— 1376/1997. *Anis al-`ushshāq*, ed. M. Kiyāni. Tehran.

—— 1376/1997. Risāla-yi badāya` al-sanāya`. In his *Anis al-`ussāq*, ed. M. Kiyāni, pp. 151–62. Tehran.

Rāvandi, Najm al-Din Abu Bakr Muhammad. 1921. *Rāhat al-sudûr va āyat al-surûr*, ed. `A. Iqbāl. London.

Roemer, H.R., ed. and trans. 1952. *Staatsschreiben der Timuridenzeit*. See `Abd-Allāh Marvārid, *Sharaf nāma*.

Ruymbeke, Christine van. 2003. Kashifi's Forgotten Masterpiece: Why Rediscover the Anvār-e Suhaylī? *Iranian Studies* 36:571–88.

Sābitiān, D. 1343/1964. *Asnād va nāma-hā-yi tārikhi-yi dawra-yi safavi*. Tehran.

Safā, Zabih-Allāh. 1956–84. *Tārikh-i adabiyāt dar irān*. 5 vols. Tehran.

Salar Jung Museum and Library (Hyderābād). 1966. *A Concise Descriptive Catalogue of the Persian Manuscripts* III, comp. by M. Ashraf. Hyderābād (Deccan).

Shahshahāni, `Abd al-Vahhāb. 1899. *Bahr al-javāhir fi `ilm al-dafātir*. Tehran.

Shamisā, Sirus. 1370/1992. *Anvā`-i adabi*. Tehran.

Shams al-Din Muhammad b. Qays al-Rāzi. 1338/1959. *Al-mu`jam fi ma`āyir ash`ār al-`ajam*, ed. M. Qazvini and M. Razavi. Tehran.

Simidchieva, Marta. 2003. Imitation and Innovation in Timurid Poetics. *Iranian Studies* 36:509–30.

Subtelny, Maria E. 1984. Scenes from the Literary Life of Timurid Herat. In *Logos Islamikos: Studia Islamica in Honorem Georgii Michaelis Wickens*, ed. R.M. Savory and D.A. Agius, pp. 137–55. Toronto: Pontifical Institute of Mediaeval Studies.

—— 1991. A Timurid Educational and Charitable Foundation. *Journal of the American Oriental Society* 111:38–61.

—— 2002. *Le Monde est un jardin; aspects de l'histoire culturelle de l'Iran médiéval*. Paris.

Subtelny, Maria E., and Anas B. Khalidov. 1995. The Curriculum of Islamic Higher Learning in Timurid Iran in the Light of the Sunni Revival under Shāh-Rukh. *Journal of the American Oriental Society* 115:210–36.

Tafazzuli, Ahmad. 1377/1998. *Tārikh-i adabiyāt-i irān pish az islām*. Tehran.

Tauer, Felix. 1968. Persian Learned Literature from Its Beginnings up to the End of the 18th Century, III: Philology. In *History of Iranian Literature*, J. Rypka, pp. 429–37. Dordrecht: D. Reidel.

Tuisirkāni, Qāsim. 1342/1963. *Bahs dar bāra-yi kitāb-i Hadā'iq al-sihr fi daqā'iq al-shi'r*. Tehran.

'Unsuri. 1341/1962. *Divān*, ed. Yahyā Gharib. Tehran.

Vāsifi, Zayn al-Din Mahmud. 1349–50/1970–71. *Badāya' al-vaqāya'*, ed. A. Boldyrev. 2 vols. Tehran.

Vatvāt, Rashid al-Din. 1339/1960. *Hadā'iq al-sihr fi daqā'iq al-shi'r, ed.* 'A. Iqbāl. In his *Divān*, ed. S. Nafisi, 621–707. Tehran.

—— 1358/1979–80. *Latā'if al-amthāl va tarā'if al-aqvāl*, ed. M.B. Sabzavāri. Tehran.

Waldman, Marilyn R. 1980. *Toward a Theory of Historical Narrative: A Case Study in Perso-Islamicate Historiography*. Columbus, OH: Ohio State University Press.

Yahyā b. Mehmed el-Kātib. 1971. *Menāhicü'l–Enşā, The Earliest Ottoman Chancery Manual*, intro. by Shinasi Tekin. Roxbury, MA: Orient Press.

Yārshāter, Ihsān 1334/1955. *Shi'r-i fārsi dar 'ahd-i shāhrukh*. Tehran. Reprint [Tehran, 1383/2004].

Yusûfi, Gh.-H.. 1341/1962. *Farrukhi Sistāni*. Tehran.

Zaehner, R.C. 1937–1939. Nāmak-nipeshnih. *Bulletin of the School of Oriental and African Studies* 9:93–109.

Zafari, Vali-Allāh. 1364/1985. *Habsiya dar adab-i fārsi*. Tehran.

Zangi Bukhāri, Muhammad b. Mahmud b. Muhammad. 1372/1993. *Zangi nāma*, ed. I. Afshār. Tehran.

Zilli, Ishtiyaq Ahmad. 2000. Development of Inshā Literature to the End of Akbar's Reign. In *The Making of Indo-Persian Culture: Indian and French Studies,* ed. Muzaffar Alam, Françoise Nalini Delvoye, and Marc Gaborieau, pp. 309–49. New Delhi: Manohar.

3

The Transmission of Persian Texts Compared to the Case of Classical Latin

A. H. MORTON

The remarks presented here are a by-product of research on the textual transmission of certain Persian prose texts of the medieval period. This in turn stems from an interest in Classical Persian literature which has benefited from the attention to detail encouraged by the experience of reading texts with students. During the last two centuries Iranian and Western scholars have devoted much effort to the editing of works in Persian. Great progress has been made, but the methods used to make it have received little attention in their own right. In the absence of satisfactory guides to the textual criticism of Persian and Arabic texts as such, I have found a useful substitute in those provided for the Greek and Latin Classics, which have long been the object of intense study. Though I have no serious expertise in the Classics, early education provided an initial acquaintance with the methods used in editing Latin and Greek, and makes it possible to use the Classical guides in the applied textual criticism in which I am engaged, that is, in editing texts. Naturally, among scholars of the Classics, as well as those concerned with other languages and periods, agreement is not complete: the usual methods of establishing a text elaborated in the 19th century are sometimes questioned.[1] They have been accepted and defended by others, among them the authors of the works I have found of most practical use.[2] M.L. West puts the positive case firmly: "The canons of textual criticism have long been established, and fashion can only bring aberrations or alternative formulations."[3] As for the Persian aspect of the subject, the great bulk and complexity of even the medieval literary corpus makes any attempt at an overall picture a task well beyond my power. What follows is sketchy and based on a limited quantity of evidence: it does, however, in its way, address the theme of comparative diplomatics that underlies this volume, and may also serve to encourage clearer perception of the problems and possibilities presented by the textual traditions of New Persian literature.

The texts I have been investigating are prose of a mainly secular or belle-lettristic nature dating from the early period up to about AD 1200, in which a number of exceptionally interesting and attractive works in this category were produced. My edition of Zahir al-Din's history of the Saljuqs, dating from the late 12th century, appeared in 2004[4] and I am currently working mainly on the text of the *Safarnāma* of Nāsir Khusraw, which was written in the middle of the 11th. Both these works, to differing extents, show the value of what has been called stemmatic method. To explain this term briefly, it is sometimes possible to show that a group of manuscripts all derive by direct descent, but by more than one line of transmission, from one particular manuscript. The relationships can be illustrated in the form of a branching diagram rather similar to that of a genealogy, which is called a stemma, and, if the "parent" manuscript does not survive, where the text offered by the different branches of the stemma agrees it can be accepted that they represent its text. The case of the *Safarnāma* is a particularly straightforward example of a tradition which depends on such a lost archetype. Numerous common errors demonstrate that all the available manuscripts derive from the same archetype. For instance, there is a series of obvious corruptions in the text of Nāsir's description of the entrances to the *haram* at Mecca.[5] Elsewhere the tradition agrees on the word *kankāj* (consultation), which makes sense in the context but is of Mongolian origin.[6] It was used in Persian in the Mongol period and later but could not have been known to Nāsir Khusraw. It can only have been introduced by a copyist working in the 13th century or later, and the archetype itself can be no earlier. The stemmatic approach is attractive not, as is sometimes suggested, because it allows the editor to force his own views, consciously or subconsciously, on the text but principally because if the existing manuscripts do derive by different routes from a single (lost) archetype the text of the archetype is to a great extent not in question and only where this is not the case is it necessary to choose between variants, to emend or, failing all else, to mark corruption so far as is possible. (Since the existence of the archetype is proved by the common errors of its descendants its own text is *a priori* incorrect in places.)

There has been a tendency among scholars working on Arabic and Persian to misrepresent the use of the stemmatic approach by classicists. It has been said, for instance that "One basic rule on which textual criticism [of Greek, Latin and medieval European texts] rested was the existence of a fairly uncontaminated textual tradition, in which relationships between manuscripts must be visible through common mistakes. A genesis other than that from a single 'lost original' (*Urtext*) was excluded: one archetype had to be established by the editor with, if necessary, hyparchetypes."[7] Others have made similar observations: "the result of [Classical] textual criticism is a stemma,"[8] and "Classical text criticism tends to produce a stemma which leads back to a single source with a single author."[9] Such misrepresentations are probably facilitated by the fact that in some of the best known introductions to Classical textual criticism the technique of dealing with a stemmatic tradition is given prominence and sometimes overemphasized.[10] But the Classical approach does not necessarily reveal a stemma leading back to an archetype.[11] The initial stage is that of recension (*recensio*), the assembly of the evidence for a work, principally manuscripts but also secondary witnesses such as quotations in other works, and the establishing, so far as is possible, of the relationships between the witnesses.[12] The main evidence for the relationships is the presence of common errors, and it may happen that the pattern that emerges will reveal that all the witnesses derive from a single source, an archetype. Any manuscript that can be shown to descend directly from any other existing manuscript has no value as an independent witness to the original work since it cannot add any information about the archetype which is not in the exemplar from which it derived (*eliminatio codicum descriptorum*). If one surviving manuscript proves to be the ancestor of all others, a stemma can be constructed, but for the establishment of the text all the others can be eliminated, since they can add nothing of independent origin to the text given by the (surviving) archetype. Variants in them can only be errors or emendations.

Of course, it cannot be assumed that the pattern of transmission will always be so simple. For instance, one problem is that manuscripts do not always derive solely by a particular line of descent; what is called contamination or horizontal transmission can have occurred, meaning that readings of more than one branch of the tradition appear in a particular manuscript or manuscripts. This indicates editorial selection at some stage and makes the establishment of the lines of descent of the manuscripts more difficult or impossible.[13] The more popular a work has been the less likely is it that it will be possible to construct a stemma leading back to an archetype. No stemma can be found for Ferdowsi's *Shāhnāma*,[14] any more than for the *Iliad* or the *Odyssey*. In fact, a perfect stemma must start from a single manuscript of a work and that means that at some stage the work in question was close to being lost for ever. (This would in fact be the situation with any text at the moment of completion, but in practice editors of works of literature are usually dealing with ones that have been more or less widely published.) The stemmatic approach has occasionally been applied to Persian texts with success. A remarkable example is Heidi Zirke's edition of part of the 14th-century *Safwat al-Safā*.[15] Muhammad Qazwini's edition of the 12th-century *Chahār Maqāla* can also be mentioned: although the editor does not make the point, an archetype can be postulated.[16] However, even if it cannot be established that there was a single archetype, which is certainly the case with many, probably the great majority, of Persian works, stemmatic considerations will often make it possible to eliminate manuscripts which derive from other surviving manuscripts, and this can greatly reduce the body of evidence that needs to be taken into consideration.[17]

Before the adoption of printing, which for Persian only became widespread in the course of 19th century, the mechanical aspects of the transmission of Classical Latin texts and medieval Persian ones were much the same. In the West parchment succeeded papyrus in antiquity as the material on which texts were written and paper came to replace parchment in the later medieval period. By the time New Persian came into existence paper was widely available in the Middle East and had already displaced parchment as the usual material for books. In most of western Europe the quill pen came to replace the classical reed which remained in normal use in Iran until recently, and is still employed for calligraphic work. The social circumstances may have been in some respects different. Many of the copyists in the medieval West may have been monks and humanist scholars. In the Iranian world the ateliers of kings, princes, and their ministers were important; Sufi circles also played a part; and there is some evidence for the regular production of illustrated manuscripts for eventual sale, as at Shiraz in the 15th and 16th centuries.[18] On the other hand, Chardin informs us that the numerous copyists in the cities of Persia in the mid-17th century generally worked on a casual basis, manuscripts being commissioned when needed by private agreement between copyist and customer.[19] Many books

must have been supplied in the same way in earlier and later periods. Whatever differences existed, the process of copying was similar and from the
point of view of a critical editor, the Latin and Persian traditions have much
in common. In any manuscript tradition the same types of commonplace
errors are going to occur, and one may note the correspondence between
Latin and Persian in this respect: Persian manuscripts duly display lacunae
caused by haplography, dittographies, intrusive glosses and marginal comments, corrupted numerals,[20] and so on.

One point of difference that surprised me when I noticed it concerns the
dating of manuscripts. The Latin manuscripts are nearly all undated, while
a considerable proportion of the Persian ones have colophons giving the
date when they were copied. To give some examples, a list of manuscripts
regarded as of value for the text of Horace consists of twelve, ascribed to
the 9th, 10th and 11th centuries. None are dated. For the works of Caesar,
eleven are given (9th–12th centuries), once again all undated.[21] The five available manuscripts of value for the *Safarnāma* of Nāsir Khusraw are all dated.
These are relatively recent: the earliest belongs to the late 17th century, the
remainder to the 19th and three of these were produced under European patronage. However, the dating of manuscripts was common much earlier. In
Darke's list of manuscripts of the *Siyar al-Muluk* or *Siyāsatnāma* the earliest
four manuscripts, of the 13th and 14th centuries, are all dated. Of the sixteen
later ones, ten are dated, six are not.[22] For Nasrullāh Munshi's version of the
Kalila wa Dimna, Minovi was able to list twelve manuscripts from the 12th
to 14th centuries, of which eight are dated.[23] Muhammad Isa Waley of the
British Library has said that, in his experience, just over half of all Persian
manuscripts have dated colophons.[24] In itself the relative frequency of dates
may not seem very important, but there are consequences for editing. In
the process of recension it is desirable, as has been said, to establish how the
manuscripts are related and, obviously, an older manuscript cannot derive
from a younger one. For Persian the fact that manuscripts are often dated
means that much of the time there is no doubt which of two manuscripts is
the older. But for the editors of Latin texts in the Early Modern Period the
dating of manuscripts was difficult. Manuscripts existed in a variety of rather
different scripts, which are now known to have been in use at different periods and places. The sequence is regarded as having first been put on a secure
footing by the *De Re Diplomatica,* based mainly on documents rather than
literary manuscripts, published by the Benedictine Jean Mabillon in 1681.[25]

In both the areas being compared there was an evolution of script. The early Latin manuscripts are in various kinds of majuscule, square or rustic capitals with large letters standing separately, and, emerging slightly later and remaining in use for centuries, the more cursive uncials. The minuscule half-uncial came to be used quite widely and led to a development of various minuscule regional scripts—Caroline, insular, Beneventan, and others.[26] It is the consequence of this variety that is of interest in this context. Miscopyings of letters can easily occur in any circumstances and when faced with a manuscript in an unfamiliar script, which would often be the case with an older one, the copyist was even more liable to misinterpret what was before him. The textual critic has to be aware of the likely confusions, which vary according to the scripts concerned. The classicists have given much attention to classifying the patterns of errors that arise. Such errors, and the similar misunderstandings of abbreviations discussed below, can make it possible to perceive and date the various stages through which a text has passed before any manuscripts survive, as, famously, with the *De Rerum Natura* of Lucretius.

With Persian and the Arabic script there is also development. Recent studies have called into question the terms used for the varieties of Arabic script and demonstrated that ones such as Kufic and *naskh* are extremely vague.[27] Nevertheless, alternative classifications have still to be settled and the usual terminology seems adequate for the present purpose. The Persian literary manuscripts of the earliest period would have been in book Kufic or *naskh,* as is shown by the few specimens that have reached us. Kufic appears to have fallen out of use in the 12th century; *naskh* was still employed to a considerable extent up to the end of the manuscript period. Even today most Persian printing is done in *naskh,* which was relatively easy to accommodate to movable type. However, a rival to *naskh,* in the form of *nasta'liq,* had developed in the 14th and 15th centuries and from then on a high proportion of manuscripts, both poetry and prose, are in *nasta'liq.* Normal modern Persian hands are developments of *nasta'liq,* varieties of its more cursive descendant *shikasta-nasta'liq. Shikasta* and other convoluted scripts were employed for books but tended rather to be used more for correspondence and bureaucratic purposes. A great variety of more or less casual private hands are found in documents, which can be almost impenetrable for anyone unfamiliar with the particular context.[28] However, books were for the most part written in the more easily legible hands. No doubt the transference of a Persian text from one script to another tended to lead to particular errors in the same way as in Latin. For instance, some false readings in late manuscripts of the *Safarnāma* can be explained as caused by the ambiguities of an exemplar written in some form of *shikasta*. It may be possible in future to make more use of the information such systematic errors might provide. However, the differences between the scripts commonly used for Persian books are probably not great enough to cause as much difficulty as exists for Latin.

In the capital scripts used for Latin in the earlier period, words were not written separately. At best, and exceptionally, discreet dots were placed between words. The subject of the separation of words in Latin has recently been studied in detail by Paul Saenger, who draws attention to the effect the lack of separation would have had in hindering rapid reading and comprehension.[29] This would also have tended to make copying slower and less accurate. For the Arabic script separation is guaranteed for the majority of words by the fact that most letters have a distinct final form which marks the end of a word. The letters without final forms can occasionally lead to false word divisions, but scribes often took care to leave some space between words, as was indeed recommended by Muhammad b. `Abd al-Khāliq Mayhani in the 12th century.[30] In some hands words are written in a slight descending slope, with the word-ending overlapping the beginning of the next word at a slightly lower level. Here the difference of level helps to indicate word-ending.

Another feature causing difficulty for the copyist of Latin was the use of abbreviations and shorthand symbols for words or parts of words. Scantily employed in literary manuscripts at first they became very common in many scripts of the later medieval period. Various different systems of abbreviation were employed. Once again abbreviations and the misreadings they could lead to have been collected and classified and an editor needs to be aware of the possibilities. Abbreviations were used in the Islamic world to a limited extent, but for the most part only in dealing with certain technical subjects which were normally treated in Arabic rather than Persian, in particular the study of hadith.[31] In manuscripts of Persian literary works abbreviations are used to mark corrections and glosses, and occasionally as punctuation, but they do not pose a great problem.

One very obvious peculiarity making the Arabic script liable to cause confusion is the fact that diacritical marks are needed to distinguish groups

of letters of identical ductus, that is, shape. The earliest Islamic Kufic inscriptions, for instance the legends on coins, were, with rare exceptions,
completely unpointed, and it is left to the reader (if any) to solve the ambiguities. However, in Arabic books from the earliest period diacritical marks
were normal and by the time New Persian began to be written the system
of diacritical dots or points that is still employed was already in use. However, it was not always used accurately or thoroughly. The absence or inac-
curacy of pointing is a frequent cause of error, though many such mistakes
can easily be corrected. Another, less common but also less obvious source
of error is the system of additional diacritical marks occasionally used on
carefully written manuscripts to distinguish the letters we normally think
of as undotted (*muhmal*).[32] Darke noted that some errors in the best manuscript of the *Siyar al-Muluk* can be explained as misunderstandings of marks
of this kind which must have stood in some earlier copy.[33] It is probable that
errors were occasionally caused by the other system of additional symbols
that used to mark vocalisation. Vocalisation is non-existent or sparse in the
majority of Persian manuscripts. However, Persian manuscripts with extensive vocalisation do exist[34] and the system was familiar to every Muslim
scribe from its employment in copies of the Qur'an.

The orthography of New Persian has been remarkably stable considering that the language has been used for well over a millennium. The regular-
ity of spelling over many centuries almost equals that of modern European
usage. An important factor here is the influence of Arabic, the orthography of which has been even more stable than that of Persian and over a
longer period. In the case of Arabic, stability was encouraged in particular
by the attention paid to the interpretation of the text of the Qur'an and
religious concerns in general. This inspired the study of grammar and the
development of a sophisticated system of grammatical analysis, providing
a prescriptive model for the language. The many Arabic words adopted in
Persian nearly always retain the correct Arabic form. The assimilation in
Persian of sounds represented by different letters in Arabic script might have
been expected to cause confusion, but this does not seem to occur to any
great extent. In poetry those sets of letters pronounced differently in Arabic
but identically in Persian have always been, and to traditionalist poets still
are, regarded as different for the purposes of rhyme. No doubt the attention
paid to the Qur'an and Islamic practices in early education, and later life,
helped sustain correct orthography for Arabic words. (On the other hand, it

is true that scribes can sometimes be seen to have been uneasy transcribing the pieces of Arabic found in many Persian works.) For the Iranian element of the language, as Lazard has shown, in the period up to AD 1200 the texts display some dialectal variation. The literary language of later times was "remarkably uniform and stable,"[35] and this applies to the spelling of individual words as well as to matters belonging to the field of syntax. In respect of orthography, Persian and Latin have both been fairly consistent, far more so than such medieval vernaculars as French and English.

No autograph of any of the Latin Classics survives nor is any known for a Persian work from before the Mongol period. However, in other respects the situations differ. For Latin, the manuscript evidence, with a few fragmentary exceptions, always comes from long after the original date of composition. Very little survives from the time when papyrus was in use. Manuscripts from earlier than the 6th century are only occasionally available, for example, for Virgil and Terence.[36] More commonly none survive from as early as the 8th century or even later. For Persian, the interval between original work and earliest manuscript can vary greatly. In some cases it is very long. Nāsir Khusraw's *Safārnama* was written in the middle of the 11th century; the earliest available manuscript is dated AH 1102/AD 1691. The text of the surviving fragment of the *History* of Bayhaqi, composed at about the same time, depends on manuscripts of which none is earlier than the 16th century. In other cases the interval is less, but still to be counted in centuries. The oldest manuscript of the late 11th century *Siyar al-Muluk* is dated 673/1274. For the *Chahār Maqāla,* from the mid-12th century, the earliest is dated 835/1431–2. On the other hand, for some works there is early evidence. The oldest manuscript of Nasrullāh Munshi's *Kalila wa Dimna* was written in 551/1156–7, when the author was still alive and only a dozen years after the date of composition. Rāwandi's *Rāhat al-sudur* was finished in about 1209. The unique manuscript is dated 635/1238.[37]

At many periods war and insecurity affected Iran and the other areas where the Persian language was important. However, Persian literature was never subject to the wholesale neglect which severely constricted the textual traditions of the Latin Classics during the darkest age, c. 550–750.[38] It is not surprising, then, that a number of early Persian works have come to us in diverging traditions deriving from variant authorial or at any rate very early recensions.[39] Thus Minovi distinguishes three early versions of *Kalila wa Dimna,* all of which he regards as the work of Nasrullāh Munshi himself.[40] Nizām al-Mulk was murdered before he could present his final text of *Siyar al-Muluk* to Malikshāh, but the variant prefaces and some other discrepancies found in the manuscripts are most probably early and suggest that the librarian to whom he entrusted it published it in two different editions. For the *Saljuqnāma* two textual traditions are attested from not long after the book was written and I have maintained that both most probably go back to the author.[41]

For the purposes of comparison it has been convenient to consider the Classical Latin and Persian traditions as if they were phenomena existing largely in isolation, but this is not really so. In the West the evidence for the works produced in the pagan world comes almost entirely from the period when Christianity was the established religion. Manuscripts of the Latin Classics were few compared with those, also for centuries written in Latin, concerned with the Christian religion and other post-classical matters. In later medieval Europe, while Latin may not have been anybody's mother tongue, it was far from a dead language, but the European vernaculars began the long process of displacing it as the favored written medium. I am unqualified to pursue the European situation in any detail but the Persian tradition is in any case the main interest here. In all the areas where it was important Persian was accompanied by Arabic. If Persian came to be widely used for administrative purposes, religious education could only be pursued to an advanced level in the medium of Arabic, and Arabic was necessary for the serious study of other subjects, for instance, medicine, astronomy, and mathematics. Particularly relevant to the topic of textual transmission is the exceptional position of the Qur'an. Familiarity with the Sacred Word was an indication of Muslim piety and it appears that the early stages of the acquisition of literacy in the sphere of influence of written Persian placed considerable emphasis on the rote learning of passages from the Qur'an. The exceptional status of the Qur'an demanded that exceptional care should be taken over its reproduction in written form. It was repeatedly copied throughout the Islamic world, including of course the areas where written Persian was important. Copies of the Qur'an from most countries are distinguished not only by the high quality of the materials used, the calligraphy, and the decoration but also by the accuracy of the text and, from a quite early period, the meticulous employment of diacriticals upon letters, vocalisation, and punctuation. Some of the scribes who copied works in Persian no doubt copied Arabic too, and were capable of producing a fine

Qur'an. But even those who did not rise to such heights, like the poorly paid and slovenly copyists described by Chardin,[42] would have been acquainted with the Qur'an and presumably could appreciate it as, among other things, a model of accurate transmission.

Islamic law and tradition gave preference to orally transmitted rather than written evidence and this affected the transmission of texts in Arabic. It is known from literary references and colophons that Arabic works were often dictated by their authors, or by those authorised to transmit them, and that copies of texts were read out to the author or transmitter in order to check them. Ideally oral transmission was regarded as necessary before a student could be given an *ijāza* or permit to transmit or teach from a text. This was particularly important in the areas of religion and law but not exclusive to them.[43] There is some doubt as to what extent the ideal was ever achieved for Arabic texts and it received diminishing emphasis after the medieval period. I am aware of nothing that suggests that it was ever considered necessary or desirable for Persian ones. There is evidence for the collation of manuscripts, but this would most commonly have been merely a check of the newly made copy with the exemplar from which it was copied. Occasionally, collation with other manuscripts may have occurred,[44] but this cannot be compared to the emphasis on oral transmission found for Arabic. It is evident that the difference in status between the two languages in the Islamic world meant that there was a difference in the way texts in those languages were regarded. Since Persian lacked the religious and scholarly prestige of Arabic it could be treated with, as it were, less deference. The situation has some similarity with that prevailing with native speakers of English who normally have little need of a conscious knowledge of the peculiarities of English grammar and, until recently, acquired whatever notions of grammar they had to a great extent from exposure to Latin. In the ancient English universities, where the Greek and Latin Classics were highly valued, English Literature was not accepted as a subject worth teaching until the beginning of the 20th century.[45] With regard to Persian there is the story, perhaps of 19th- or 20th-century origin, of the *mullā* who maintained that Persian had no grammar: grammar, in his view, was something peculiar to Arabic. Much earlier the well-known Indo-Persian poet Amir Khusraw (1253–1325), in discussing the languages in use in India, notes that Persian had not been provided with a set of rules,[46] in which respect it differed from Arabic and Sanskrit. Khusraw is thinking in terms of codified grammar, for he claims that if he wished he could sort the matter out for Persian. However, since people had no difficulty with Persian it would be pointless for him to do so.[47] A symptom of the casual approach to Persian can be seen in the fact that in the majority of manuscripts the scribe does not bother to employ the diacritical marks available to distinguish the letters representing the sounds found in Persian but not in Arabic (ch, p, zh, g). That an offhand attitude was appropriate in some contexts is also illustrated by Mayhani's recommendation that in correspondence diacriticals and vocalisation should not normally be used: to do so would be to imply that the recipient was ignorant.[48] This comes from the 12th century; an Iranian friend has informed me that it is still regarded as good advice today.

The reasons for the long floruit of written New Persian are complex, but it had at its disposal a system of recording and transmission that, if not without drawbacks, was comparatively efficient. The lack of complete vocalisation does cause difficulty, but has some compensatory benefits: writing takes less time and dialectal differences in the pronunciation of short vowels are to some extent accommodated by ignoring them.[49] Its advantages and disadvantages vis-à-vis Latin have been alluded to above. The Pahlavi script which can be regarded as its predecessor is notoriously difficult. Like the Arabic it represents different sounds by letters of identical form, but apparently it never developed a means of distinguishing them by diacritical marks. As with Arabic, its representation of vowels was incomplete and in addition many words were not written phonetically but as ideograms in the form of Aramaic equivalents of the Persian words.[50] The transfer to Arabic script would have made literacy considerably more accessible. Compared with Latin, the Persian language has the advantage of making little use of inflection, approaching English in this respect. The possibilities of confusion in the course of copying are therefore somewhat less than with Latin, in which many inflections vary only by a letter or two from others with different implications. The availability of paper, a more convenient and less expensive substitute for papyrus and parchment and a relatively recent innovation in the Middle East, would also have favored the greater use of writing for all purposes, including the copying of works of literature of all kinds. And once a substantial amount of written literature was in existence, it provided a corpus of reference, which, in conjunction with that provided by Islam and the scholarly and literary tradition of Arabic, helped maintain the continuity of Persian scribal practice within Iran and far beyond it.

NOTES

1. See, for instance, Sebastiano Timpanaro, *Genesis of Lachmann's Method,* and for one response, M.D. Reeve, "Stemmatic Method," 57–69.
2. Principally, F.W. Hall, Companion to Classical Texts; P. Maas, Textual Criticism; M.L. West, Textual Criticism and Editorial Technique; L.D. Reynolds and N.G. Wilson, *Scribes and Scholars,* esp. Ch. 6.
3. West, Textual Criticism, 5.
4. Zahir al-Din Nishāpuri, *Saljuqnāma.*
5. *Safarnāma,* ed. Muhammad Dabirsiyāqi, Tehran printing of 1363, pp. 126–29.
6. Ibid., 148.
7. Barbara Flemming, "From Archetype to Oral Tradition," 3:7.
8. Jan Just Witkam, "Establishing the Stemma," 98.
9. Robert Irwin, *Arabian Nights,* 59, cf. p. 52.
10. Maas, on whom see Reynolds and Wilson, *Scribes and Scholars,* 288–89, and note 13 below; Reynolds and Wilson, 207–8.
11. Curiously, the Classical scholar Timpanaro (op. cit., p. 113) remarks "I suppose it was the huge number of texts in which all the manuscripts agree in errors and lacunae that gradually convinced Classical philologists that there had been an archetype in all cases," but this was never the conviction of Classicists in general.
12. Works preserved in a single manuscript are a special category, in which recension usually plays little or no part. Medieval Persian examples are the *Tarjumān al-Balāgha,* the *Tārikh-i Barāmika,* and the *Rāhat al-Sudur.* The *Saljuqnāma,* of which there is only one ms, is an exceptional case. So much of its content was transmitted in later works that the relationships of several lost manuscripts can be established.
13. Maas's decision not to deal with contaminated traditions in detail was unfortunate, given the influence of his work, but he was well aware of their significance and briefly alludes to it more than once, as on p. 9 where he mentions "the numerous instances where contamination makes it impossible to hope for a clear-cut solution."
14. So J. Khāliqi-Mutlaq in his edition of the *Shāhnāma,* 1:21.
15. Heidi Zirke, Hagiographisches Zeugnis.
16. Nizāmi 'Arudi, *Chahār Maqāla.* See pp. 84, 255 for a lacuna common to all mss.
17. For a thorough and fruitful investigation of the transmission of a text see Bo Utas, *Tariq ut-tahqiq.* In this a stemma is proposed (p. 113), but the actual existence of an archetype does not seem to be established.
18. B.W. Robinson, *Persian Miniature Painting,* 91; Oleg F. Akimushkin and Anatol A. Ivanov, "Art of Illumination," 50.
19. Chardin, *Voyages,* 4:281–82.
20. E.g., *Safarnāma,* 2, where the mss. agree on giving the Yazdigirdi year as 410, which is a slip for 414.
21. L.D. Reynolds, *Text and Transmission,*183, 35–36.
22. Nizām al-Mulk, *Siyar al-Muluk,* ed. and trans. Hubert Darke (Tehran, 1976), 2535 ShāhinShāhi, pp. v–ix, 11–18.
23. Abu 'l-Ma'āli Nasrallāh Munshi, *Tarjuma, yā, tā kāf.*
24. "Problems and Possibilities in Dating Persian Manuscripts," in François Déroche, *Manuscrits du Moyen-Orient,* 7. The suggestion made on p. 10 that Western manuscripts were usually dated does not hold for Latin and Greek ones.
25. Reynolds and Wilson, *Scribes and Scholars,* 189.

26. For this subject see, for instance, Sir Edward Maunde Thompson, *Introduction to Greek and Latin Palaeography;* and B. Bischoff, *Latin Palaeography.*

27. Cf. François Déroche, *Manuel de codicologie des manuscrits en écriture arabe,* 222, 234.

28. See the discussion and specimens in William L. Hanaway and Brian Spooner, *Reading Nasta'liq.*

29. Paul Saenger, *Space between Words.* I am grateful to John Perry for telling me about this book.

30. Muhammad b. 'Abd al-Khāliq al-Mayhani, *Dastur-i Dabiri,* 4.

31. Fr. Rosenthal, *Technique and Approach of Muslim Scholarship,* 35–37.

32. See the description of such marks in W. Wright, *Grammar of the Arabic Language,* 1:4. Examples of early Persian manuscripts making use of these marks are those of Abu Mansur Hirawi's *Kitāb al-Abniya 'an Haqā'iq al-Adwiya,* dated 447/1056 (facsimile ed., Tehran, 1334), and Rādhuyāni's *Tarjumān al-Balāgha,* dated 507/1114 (Istanbul: İbrahim Horoz basımevi, 1949).

33. Nizām al-Mulk, *Siyar al-Muluk,* vi. Mayhani (p. 5) disapproves of the use of these marks in correspondence.

34. An example with fairly thorough vocalisation is the ms of part of the *Tā'rikh-i Shaikh Uwais,* probably of the 15th century, published in facsimile by J.B. Van Loon, 1954.

35. See Lazard, *Langue des plus anciens monuments,* 18 and passim.

36. The replacement of papyrus by parchment as the normal material for books lessened the chances of survival for the clumsier and less durable papyrus roll. Only a few fragments of early Latin papyri are known. See Reynolds and Wilson, *Scribes and Scholars,* 34–35.

37. Rāwandi, Muhammad b. 'Ali b. Sulaymān, *Rāhat al-Sudur wa Āyat al-Surur,* and, for the date of composition, Zāhir al-Din Nishāpuri's *Saljuqnāma,* Introduction, 20.

38. Reynolds and Wilson, *Scribes and Scholars,* 85.

39. Of course the existence of such variant recensions is known in the Classics, for instance in the case of Martial. See Reynolds, *Text and Transmission,* 243.

40. Minovi's edition, *yā alif.*

41. For a discussion of possible reasons for the existence of variant authorial recensions, see *Saljuqnāma,* Introduction, 39.

42. See note 18 above.

43. On this see Johannes Pedersen, *Arabic Book,* 20–36.

44. For an example see G. Lazard, *Langue des plus anciens monuments,* 49.

45. The story goes that at the time when the neglect of English was coming into question it was stated in defense of the status quo, "There are some books a gentleman is expected to have read before coming up to University."

46. The term used is *dābita,* meaning general rule or regulation.

47. Amir Khusraw, *Nuh Sipihr,* 172–81, in particular 173–74, 180. A translation of this difficult passage is offered in R. Nath and Faiyaz Gwaliari, *India as Seen by Amir Khusrau,* 69–78. Cf. É.M. Jeremiás, "Grammar and Linguistic Consciousness in Persian," 2:19–20.

48. Dastur-i Dabiri, 4–5.

49. Jalāl Matini has noted that in modern Iran speakers of local dialects adjust their pronunciation when dealing with standard written Persian, *lafz-i qalam.* 'Tahawwul-i talaffuz-i Fārsi dar dawra-yi Islami', *Majalla-yi Dānishkada-yi Adabiyyāt-i Mashhad,* 7, 254.

50. See D.N. MacKenzie, *Concise Pahlavi Dictionary,* (London: Oxford University Press, 1986), x–xiv, xviii.

REFERENCES

Akimushkin, Oleg F., and Anatol A. Ivanov. 1979. The Art of Illumination. In *The Arts of the Book in Central Asia, 14th–16th Centuries*, ed. Basil Gray, pp. 35–57. Boulder, CO: Shambhala Publications.

Bischoff, B. 1990. *Latin Palaeography: Antiquity and the Middle Ages*, trans. D.O. Dáibhí ó Cróinin and David Ganz. Cambridge: Cambridge University Press.

Chardin, Jean. 1811. *Voyages*, ed. L. Langlès. Paris.

Déroche, François, ed. 2000. *Manuel de codicologie des manuscrits en écriture Arabe*. Paris: Bibliothèque Nationale de France.

Flemming, Barbara. 1988. From Archetype to Oral Tradition: Editing Persian and Turkish Literary Texts. In *Manuscripts of the Middle East*, 3:7–15.

Hall, F.W. 1913. *A Companion to Classical Texts*. Oxford: Clarendon.

Hanaway, William L., and Brian Spooner. 2007. *Reading Nasta`liq. Persian and Urdu Hands from 1500 to the Present*. 2nd rev. ed. Costa Mesa, CA: Mazda Publications.

Irwin, Robert. 1994. *The Arabian Nights. A Companion*. London: Allen Lane.

Jeremiás, É.M. 1999. Grammar and Linguistic Consciousness in Persian. *Proceedings of the Third European Conference of Iranian Studies* 2, ed. Charles Melville, pp. 19–30. Wiesbaden: Reichert.

Khāliqi-Mutlaq, Jalāl, ed. 1988. *Abu'l-Qasim Firdausi: Shāhnāma*. Persian Text Series. New York: Bibliotheca Persica, Persian Heritage Foundation.

Lazard, G. 1963. *La langue des plus anciens monuments de la prose persane*. Paris: C. Klincksieck.

Maas, P. 1958. *Textual Criticism*, trans. Barbara Flower. Oxford: Clarendon.

Matini, Jalāl. 1350 A.H.S./1972. Tahawwul-i talaffuz-i Fārsi dar dawra-yi Islāmi. In *Majalla-yi Dānishkada-yi Adabiyyāt-i Mashhad*, vol. 7, pp. 249–83. Mashhad.

Nasrullāh Munshi, Abu 'l-Ma`āli. 1343 A.H.S. /1964. *Tarjuma-yi Kalila wa Dimna*, ed. Mujtabā Minovi. Tehrān.

Nizāmi `Aruzi. 1910. *Chahār Maqāla*, ed. Muhammad Qazwini. London: Luzac.

Pedersen, Johannes. 1984. *The Arabic Book*, trans. Geoffrey French. Princeton: Princeton University Press.

Rāvandi, Muhammad b. `Ali b. Sulaymān. 1921. *Rāhat al-Sudur wa Āyat al-Surur*, ed. M. Iqbāl. London: Luzac.

Reeve, M.D. 1986. Stemmatic Method: *"Qualcosa che non funziona"?* In *The Role of the Book in Medieval Culture*, ed. P. Ganz, pp. 57–69. Bibliologia 3-4. Turnhout, Belgium: Brepols.

Reynolds, L.D., and N.G. Wilson. 1991. *Scribes and Scholars*. 3rd ed. Oxford: Clarendon.

———, ed. 1983. *Text and Transmission. A Survey of the Latin Classics*. Oxford: Clarendon.

Robinson, B.W. 1967. *Persian Miniature Painting*. London: H.M.S.O.

Rosenthal, Fr. 1947. *The Technique and Approach of Muslim Scholarship.* Rome: Pontificium Institutum Biblicum.

Saenger, Paul. 2000. *Space between Words.* Stanford: Stanford University Press.

Thompson, Sir Edward Maunde. 1912. *An Introduction to Greek and Latin Palaeography.* Oxford: Clarendon.

Timpanaro, Sebastiano. 2005. *The Genesis of Lachmann's Method,* trans. Glenn W. Most. Chicago: University of Chicago Press.

Utas, Bo. 1973. *Tariq ut-tahqiq. A Critical Edition with a History of the Text and a Commentary.* Scandinavian Institute of Asian Studies monograph series, no. 13. Lund.

Waley, Muhammad Isa. 1898. Problems and Possibilities in Dating Persian Manuscripts. In *Les manuscrits du Moyen-Orient,* ed. François Déroche. Istanbul: Institut français d'études anatoliennes et Bibliothèque Nationale.

West, M.L. 1973. *Textual Criticism and Editorial Technique.* Stuttgart: B.G. Teubner.

Witkam, Jan Just. 1988. Establishing the Stemma: Fact or Fiction? *Manuscripts of the Middle East* 3:88–101.

Wright, W. 1933. *A Grammar of the Arabic Language.* 3rd ed. Cambridge: Cambridge University Press.

Zahir al-Din Nishāpuri. 2004. *The Saljuqnāma.* Warminster: E.J.W. Gibb Memorial Trust.

Zirke, Heidi. 1987. *Ein hagiographisches Zeugnis zur persischen Geschichte aus der Mitte des 14. Jahrhunderts. Das achte Kapitel des Safwat al-Safa in kritische Bearbeitung.* Berlin: Klaus Schwarz.

Part Two: Spread

4

Persian as a Lingua Franca in the Mongol Empire

DAVID MORGAN

It could be argued that the most celebrated European Persian-speaker of the Mongol period was the one such person of whom everyone has heard: the Venetian traveler Marco Polo. But is such an assertion credible? In 1995, Dr. Frances Wood published her skeptical take on Marco's travels, *Did Marco Polo Go to China?*[1] Her conclusion was that in all probability the great traveler, though he did travel, probably went no nearer to China than the Black Sea. Her argument was based on a range of what she believed to be evidence, notably a series of omissions—matters that, she asserted, one would have expected Marco to have mentioned if he had indeed been to China, such as tea, foot-binding, the Chinese script, and the Great Wall. These omissions need not detain us. They were all speedily shown by reviewers[2] to be much more plausibly explicable on grounds other than that of Marco's non-appearance in China: most conspicuously of all, we might well have suspected Marco's bona fides if he had in fact mentioned the Great Wall of China, since it was not there at the time of his visit.[3]

More to the point of this chapter is a rather different objection to Marco Polo's veracity, which Dr. Wood makes a great deal of. That is the fact that he tends to produce Chinese words and names in a recognizably Persian form.[4] For her, this was evidence that he had extracted his material from some, now lost, Persian written source, and having passed it off as deriving from his own experience, had now at long last been caught out by his own linguistic ineptitude.

There was and is, however, an alternative explanation which is a great deal more plausible and for which, unlike the non-existent 13th century

Lonely Planet Guide to China in Persian, evidence actually exists in abundant quantities. This is that Persian was actually spoken and written very widely in China (and elsewhere in the Mongol Empire), in the circles in which Marco Polo moved. Those circles were of two, no doubt overlapping, kinds: official and commercial. Marco tells us that he was regularly employed in an official capacity by the Mongol Great Khan Qubilai, though there is a good deal of dark suspicion—probably justified—that he may well have exaggerated his importance in that respect. What there is no doubt of, however, is that the Polos—Marco, his father, and his uncle, all of whom spent many years in China—were originally Venetian merchants.

Marco tells us that (in the Yule/Cordier translation) "he came in brief space to know several languages, and four sundry written characters."[5] He does not say what these four written languages were. What they may have been has generated a great deal of, I fear inconclusive, discussion; and in any case such discussion is predicated on the assumption that Marco, or his amanuensis, was telling us the literal truth about his linguistic capacities—an assumption the validity of which is by no means self-evident. In their note to the sentence quoted above, Yule and Cordier review the possibilities.[6] Almost everyone agrees that Chinese was not among them—and indeed, few have read Marco Polo's book and come away with any doubt that he was totally ignorant of Chinese[7]: which in itself tells us a good deal about the circles in which he must have moved. The strong contenders are Mongol, some form of Turkic, perhaps Uighur, and, most prominently of all, Persian. The fourth might have been Arabic. I should add, however, that Cordier, in his *Ser Marco Polo. Notes and Addenda,* published in 1920 as a supplement to a reissue of Yule/Cordier, seemed to have moved very sharply away from accepting Marco's linguistic pretensions; he writes of "Persian, the only oriental language probably known to Marco Polo."[8]

Be that as it may, we may note that, whatever else might be in dispute, Persian remains. No one has any doubt that Marco Polo must have known Persian. As mentioned above, his book is full of names and terms in a Persian form—often mangled Persian versions of Chinese words which are remarkably similar to the forms to be found in the works of Rashid al-Din. Cordier[9] cites the great Paul Pelliot as his source for two especially cloquent examples of "Persianization." One is that Marco uses as his term for South China the word *manzi,* which is what Rashid al-Din calls it but is not the Mongolian word, which is *nangias*—of which there is no trace in Marco Polo. Of no less interest is the fact that manzi is a term which, it seems, first begins to appear in the Mongol period; that it is distinctly vernacular (as is revealed by the presence of the nominative suffix zi); and that it is pejorative.[10] The other example, a particularly telling piece of evidence, is that when he is discussing the Chinese/Mongolian twelve-year animal cycle, he gives "lion" in place of the correct "tiger." Here he cannot be translating from Turkic or Mongolian, in which the two animals are clearly distinguished. The obvious solution is that he is translating the Persian word *shir,* which, notoriously, can mean either "lion" or "tiger" (it can also, of course, mean "milk" or "water-tap," but those possibilities can safely be discounted in this context).[11]

What one has to conclude from this is that the essential language for the Polos as they traveled across Mongol-ruled Asia and lived for many years in Mongol China was Persian. The Mongols must, therefore, presumably have favored it. Why? This is the period in which the retreat of Arabic in Iran, except in matters of law and theology, became definitive. One can see that there was no reason why the Mongols should have granted any special status to Arabic, at least in the early decades of their rule, before many of them were converted to Islam. Perhaps, in any case, they found Persian easier to learn? I recall that when, in the late 1960s, I was considering taking up the study of Persian history of the Mongol period, I went to Manchester to consult Professor John Boyle as a possible Ph.D. supervisor. He assured me that Persian was a very easy language, which I could without difficulty, and without formal training, pick up in a couple of years or so. This reminds me of a comment of Ivan Morris about Arthur Waley. In the introduction to his *Japanese Poetry* of 1919, Waley writes of Japanese that "since the classical language has an easy grammar and limited vocabulary, a few months should suffice for the mastering of it." Morris observes that "[u]nfortunately students of classical Japanese will find that this statement applies exclusively to its author."[12] Well, I did not in fact, in the long run, find Persian to be an easy language, and I doubt that the Mongols did either.

No, the reason must surely lie, essentially, in how commercial networks operated across the length and breadth of the Mongol Empire. The Mongols have an unsavory reputation for massacre and destruction which, insofar as it relates to their initial campaigns of world-conquest, is by no means unjustified. But if, at the start of their imperial enterprise, they experienced some difficulty in seeing the point of cities and settled agriculture, they were always very clear about the importance of trade and its encouragement.

In this respect the Mongols were far from being unusual among nomadic powers.[13] One of the many lessons to be learned from Thomas Allsen's great book *Culture and Conquest in Mongol Eurasia*[14] is that the Mongols were not simply passive supporters (or merely taxers) of commerce and the traffic of goods around their empire, but that they were intimately and actively involved in such processes. Indeed, Isenbike Togan ascribes to merchants a highly significant part in the formation of the Mongol Empire.[15] She writes that "a careful examination of the circumstances leading to the formation of the empire reveals that merchants, especially Muslim merchants, played a crucial role"; "the expansion of the empire followed the trade routes between the east and the west. In the setting of the changes from the 12th to the 13th century, the one underlying all local solutions seems to have been those related to trade and trade routes." She concludes that Chinggis Khan "fully cooperated with the Muslim merchants in putting his new order at their disposal."[16] Other scholars agree. Peter Jackson writes that "[t]he relationship between the Mongol leadership and foreign merchants was ... an intimate one," and he draws attention to the interesting fact that "[a]s early as c. 1203 two Muslim traders are found among the few close adherents of the future Chinggis Khan."[17] The fullest discussion of the relationship between the Mongol ruling class and foreign, mostly Muslim merchants which is known to me is Allsen's article "Mongolian Princes and Their Merchant Partners 1200–1260."[18] It is worth quoting his summary of the reasons, beyond commercial activities, why this relationship was of such importance: "As a group, professional merchants were literate, spoke foreign languages, knew how to keep accounts and manage finances, possessed geographical and economic information, and often viewed their new masters as benefactors. Such talents and knowledge were readily transferable to the administrative sphere, and merchants served the empire in great numbers and in many capacities. They functioned as commercial agents ..., diplomatic envoys, spies, tax-collectors, and civil officials."[19]

These Muslim merchants were no doubt of very varied ethnicity (if such a remark has any meaning in 13th-century circumstances). At least they will have spoken a wide variety of languages, and Persian, according to Leonardo Olschki, will have figured very prominently among them. Regarding the period when the elder Polos (Marco's father and uncle) stayed in Bukhara in the early 1260s, he comments that "[t]he trading idiom of the region was the Persian language, and it must have been here that the two Venetians learned this tongue with which Marco became so familiar and which he mainly spoke in China, where foreign merchants and officials commonly used it for purposes of business and trade."[20] But so far as Central Asia and the lands of the Golden Horde were concerned, Turkic of one kind or another will also have been widely used. Bearing in mind the crucial role played by the Uighurs in helping the Mongols organize the administration of their newly constructed empire—not to mention their provision of a script for the previously unwritten Mongol language—it seems certain that, at least during the early Mongol period, Uighur Turkish was the predominant variety. This is confirmed by a well-known grumble from the great Persian historian Juvayni, at the beginning of his *Ta'rikh-i Jahān Gushā,* in which he bemoans how standards have slipped since the Good Old Days. Now, he says, those who are prominent in affairs, particularly in Khurāsān, "regard lying and deception as exhortation and admonishment and all profligacy and slander bravery and courage…They consider the Uighur language and script to be the height of knowledge and learning. Every market lounger in the garb of iniquity has become an emir; every hireling has become a minister, every knave a vizier and every unfortunate a secretary…," and so on.[21]

That was written c. 1260, while the Mongol Empire was still expanding, at least in the east. It does not seem likely that Uighur Turkish, if it seemed pre-eminent in those early decades, retained any kind of supremacy over Persian permanently. Even earlier, there is interesting evidence of the significance of Persian in diplomatic exchanges. In the 1240s, when the West was becoming aware of the Mongol menace in the wake of their campaigns in Russia and eastern Europe, various diplomatic missions were dispatched east in an effort to make contact with these alarming newcomers, as well as to find out about them and how they might best be resisted. Of these the most celebrated, because of the accounts of his journey that survive, is that of the Franciscan John of Plano Carpini, commissioned by Pope Innocent IV at the Council of Lyons in 1245. Carpini brought back with him a letter to the Pope from the newly elected Great Khan Güyük. His account of discussions regarding what language it should be written in is extremely interesting: "[W]e were asked if there were any people with the Lord Pope who understood the writing of the Russians or Saracens or even of the Tartars. We gave answer that we used neither the Ruthenian nor Saracen writing; there were however Saracens in the country but they were a long way from the Lord Pope; but we said that it seemed to us that the most expedient course would be for them to write in Tartar and translate it for us, and we would write it down carefully in our own script and we would take both the letter and the translation to the Lord Pope." The secretaries "came to us and translated the letter for us word by word. When we had written it in Latin, they had it translated so that they might hear a phrase at a time, for they wanted to know if we had made a mistake in any word." More readings followed. Ultimately "they wrote the letter once again in Saracenic, in case anyone should be found in those parts who could read it, if the Lord Pope so wished."[22] This matches neatly what Juvayni tells us, regarding the next decade, about the officials of the Great Khan Möngke (r. 1251–59), that "[t]hey are attended by scribes of every kind for Persian, Uighur, Khitayan, Tibetan, Tangut, etc., so that to whatever place a decree has to be written it may be issued in the language and script of that people."[23]

The letter does indeed exist in Latin versions,[24] but the question inevitably arises, what did Carpini mean by "Saracenic"? On the face of it that might mean Arabic. But in fact it did not: it meant, at least in this instance, Persian. We know this for the best of possible reasons, namely that the Persian original—no other original survives—still exists in the Vatican archives, complete with the Great Khan's Mongolian seal stamp[25] (might this indicate that the Persian was the "official" version?—but we cannot know whether there were also seal stamps on the originals of the copies in other languages). According to Carpini's account, this was itself a translation from a "Tartar" original, which presumably means either Mongolian or Turkish, probably Uighur. Many years ago my Persian teacher, the late Tourkhan Gandjei, who was at much at home in Turkish as he was in Persian, told me that he thought he could detect signs, in the Persian text of the letter, that the original had been in Turkish. Such linguistic subtleties are, I fear, beyond me. Still, it is interesting and significant that the oldest diplomatic document from the Mongol Empire of which we possess an original copy should be written in Persian; and in Mongolia, nowhere near Iran or even, by however generous a definition, the conventionally conceived Persian cultural area.

In that connection it is worth mentioning an observation of William of Rubruck, like Carpini a Franciscan friar, who traveled to Mongolia a decade after him, in the mid-1250s. He records that during his journey "we came across a fine town called Equius, inhabited by Saracens who spoke Persian, though they were a very long way from Persia"[26]—useful confirmation of our conclusion above about the meaning of "Saracenic": it could indeed mean "Persian." Where was "Equius"? The identification is not certain, but Rubruck's editors (Jackson and Morgan), following Paul Pelliot as it is generally wise to do in such circumstances, concluded that it was likely to be "Quyas, one of the principal residences of Chaghatai's ulus."[27] That is to say, there were people for whom Persian was their first language who at this time lived well inside what is now Chinese Central Asia.

What has so far been said establishes, I think, that in Mongol imperial times Persian was a very important and widespread language both in commercial intercourse and in diplomatic exchanges. However, as my citations have shown, other languages, notably Mongolian and Uighur Turkish, were also of much more than local significance. It is however possible to go a good deal further than this, and to assert that the position of Persian was in fact unique. In the words of Igor de Rachewiltz, not a scholar much given to hyperbole, so far as China was concerned "[t]he dominant foreign language, not only a lingua franca but actually the 'official' foreign language until the Ming period, was Persian."[28] The basis on which it is possible to say this is the material marshaled in a remarkable article by Huang Shijian, published in 1986.[29]

He begins with the Chinese word *huihui*, which during Mongol times was a somewhat vague term used for Turks, Persians, and Arabs from Central or Western Asia, who were Muslims—though it could also be used for Jews. The equivalent word in Mongolian is *sarta'ul*. When used to describe a language, it can mean either Arabic or Persian, since they used almost the same scripts, and Chinese who did not know the actual, of course very different, languages found it difficult to distinguish between them. But, Huang argues, during the Yüan period the word means "Persian" in the overwhelming majority of instances.

Two references in the *Yüan-shih*, the official Chinese history of the Mongol dynasty, mention the establishment of a Huihui National University in 1289 (Morris Rossabi calls this "the Muslim National College with Erudites for Teaching the Arabic Script"[30]), renamed a Directorate of Education in 1314, which was charged with teaching the Istifi language and training translators. Istifi is an equivalent of huihui; and elsewhere we encounter an official, a Manager of Governmental Affairs, called Maij al-Din, who is recorded as promoting the idea of teaching Istifi. We learn further that this person has translated many books and written many "in the Pusalman script."[31] Since he was the only Huihui translator at the imperial court at that time, we may take it, Huang argues, that Pusalman=Istifi=Huihui. So the word Pusalman may tell us what the language was. The Chinese used various ways of transcribing "Muslim." In T'ang dynasty times, it was usually Musilam, fairly obviously from the Arabic "Muslim"—and at that period most of the Muslims encountered by the Chinese were indeed Arabs, or at any rate Arabic-speakers. But in Mongol times, and indeed to some extent under the immediately preceding Sung dynasty, the words used tended to be Pusaman, Musuluman or Pusalman. This must represent Musalman, a distinctively Persian adaptation, which according to Huang indicates that this was the language mostly used by the Muslims with whom the Chinese came into contact. He adds that "[a]lmost all of the Islamic terms transcribed into Chinese were Persian words, as we know from documents of the Yuan dynasty"[32]; and he gives a number of examples.

Huang goes on to document the facts that two out of ten known (in 1986) surviving *paizas*, official Mongol "tablets of authority," include lines of Persian; and that there are also copper weights containing inscriptions in four scripts: Chinese, Mongolian in the Uighur script, Persian, and Mongolian in the Phagspa script (invented on the Great Khan Qubilai's instructions so as to represent Mongolian more accurately than the Uighur script did). He concludes that "[t]he Persian inscriptions on these weights offer further evidence that Persian was used by officials in the Yuan dynasty since, according to the code of the Yuan, the authority to cast weights rested with the government."[33]

These pieces of evidence may be scattered, but so is evidence for anything in the Asia of the 13th and 14th centuries. And they do seem to be quite unambiguous. They need, perhaps, to be put into a wider cultural and political context. It should be remembered that neither the establishment of the Ilkhanate as a dynastic kingdom nor its founder Hülegü's elder brother Qubilai's accession as Great Khan went unchallenged in the Mongol world. From 1260, the four Mongol khanates were at odds: neither the Chaghatai Khanate in Central Asia nor the Golden Horde recognized Qubilai's legitimacy. But relations between Yüan China and Ilkhanid Persia were close, despite the geographical distance between them. The Ilkhans accepted a degree of at least theoretical subordination to the Great Khan, always insisting that the accession of a new Ilkhan had to be officially confirmed by Qubilai (who outlasted several of his relatives who successively occupied the Persian throne). A celebrated instance of the relationship is Marco Polo's account of the reason for his return from China, by sea, to Venice via Persia:

he was escorting a Yüan Mongol princess who was to marry the reigning Ilkhan. (In the film *The Adventures of Marco Polo* of 1938, Marco, played by Gary Cooper, has a romance with the princess, but self-sacrificingly gives her up for the greater good.) Incidentally, Marco's story is confirmed in its essentials by both Persian and Chinese sources—a sad blow to those who would like to believe that he made it all up.[34]

It is not, therefore, especially surprising that it should be in China that we find the most evidence of contact with Persia, the Persians, and the Persian language. Rossabi quotes several other instances: the presence of at least one Persian astronomer, whose work provided models for his Chinese colleagues; the importation of thirty-six volumes on Persian medicine and the establishment of an Office of Muslim Medicine; possibly even "so quintessentially Chinese a dish as *jiaozi* (dumplings)."[35] Nevertheless, the spread of Persian—as we have seen, predominantly merchant-generated in the first instance—long predated the later political troubles of the mature Mongol Empire. And in China, the widespread use of Persian proved to be enduring. Olschki points out that according to Friar John of Monte Corvino, in a letter of 1306, "the inscriptions which decorated the first Catholic cathedral at Peking, erected at the end of the [13th] century..., were written... in Latin, Turkish (probably Uigur), and Persian"[36] (not Chinese, we may note). Official Persian even survived the collapse of the rule of the Mongols; as Huang points out, their Ming successors trained translators in twenty languages, and one of those was Persian.[37]

NOTES

1. London: Secker and Warburg, 1995.
2. Most notably, I. de Rachewiltz, "Marco Polo Went to China," 34–92; more briefly, e.g., D.O. Morgan, "Marco Polo in China—or Not," 221–25.
3. See A.N. Waldron, *Great Wall of China*.
4. Stephen G. Haw argues persuasively that "[m]ost of (these names) could just as easily have been transliterated directly from the original Chinese... Marco's transcriptions of place-names, however garbled by copyists, seem to derive from standard Chinese pronunciations, not from dialect forms" (*Marco Polo's China. A Venetian in the Realm of Khubilai Khan*, London: Routledge, 2006, p. 62; see, in more detail, his chapters 6–8).
5. H. Yule and H. Cordier, *Book of Ser Marco Polo,* 1:28.
6. Ibid., 28–30, n1.
7. An exception is Haw, who suggests that "Marco had at least an imperfect knowledge of the Chinese language," though he doubts that he could read or write it (op. cit., p. 63).
8. H. Cordier, *Ser Marco Polo. Notes,* 74.
9. Loc. cit.

10. I owe these points to Professor Victor Mair.
11. Haw, op. cit., p. 61, argues that this confusion occurred "because neither Marco nor Rustichello knew an Italian or French word for 'tiger'." I am not persuaded.
12. I. Morris, *Madly Singing in the Mountains,* 70.
13. See T.T. Allsen, "Mongolian Princes," 83–84.
14. Cambridge: Cambridge University Press, 2001.
15. I. Togan, *Flexibility and Limitation in Steppe Formations,* Epilogue, 151–62.
16. Ibid., 152, 156.
17. P. Jackson, *Mongols and the West,* 291. The source for the two Muslim merchants is the *Secret History of the Mongols,* para. 182.
18. Art. cit.
19. Ibid., 124.
20. L. Olschki, *Marco Polo's Asia,* 86.
21. Juvayni, *Tā'rikh-i Jahān Gushā,* 1:4; trans. J.A. Boyle, 7.
22. C. Dawson, *Mongol Mission,* 67.
23. Juvayni, ed. Qazvini, 3 (1937), 90; trans. Boyle, 607.
24. See K.-E. Lupprian, *Beziehungen der Päpste,* 184–87, who reproduces four Latin versions.
25. The Persian text is in P. Pelliot, "Mongols et la papauté," 15–16 of the separatum reprint. The best English translation, by J.A. Boyle, is in I. de Rachewiltz, *Papal Envoys to the Great Khans,* 213–14.
26. P. Jackson, with D.O. Morgan, *Mission of Friar William of Rubruck,* 147.
27. Loc. cit., n1.
28. de Rachewiltz, "Marco Polo Went to China," 55.
29. Huang Shijian, "Persian Language in China," 84–95.
30. M. Rossabi, "Mongols and Their Legacy," 26–27.
31. Huang Shijian, "Persian Language in China," 89.
32. Ibid., 90–91.
33. Ibid., 94.
34. See F.W. Cleaves, "Chinese Source Bearing upon Marco Polo's Departure from China," 181–203.
35. Op. cit., 26.
36. Op. cit., 86, n100.
37. Op. cit., 94–95.

REFERENCES

Allsen, Thomas. 1989. Mongolian Princes and Their Merchant Partners 1200–1260. *Asia Major,* ser. 3, 2(2): 83–126.

Allsen, Thomas. 2001. *Culture and Conquest in Mongol Eurasia.* Cambridge: Cambridge University Press.

Boyle, J.A., ed. and trans. 1997 [1958]. *Juvaini, The History of the World-Conqueror.* Cambridge: Harvard University Press.

Cleaves, F.W. 1976. A Chinese Source Bearing Upon Marco Polo's Departure from China and a Persian Source on His Arrival in Persia. *Harvard Journal of Asiatic Studies* 36:181–203.

Cordier, H. 1920. *Ser Marco Polo. Notes and Addenda.* London: John Murray.

Dawson, C. 1955. *The Mongol Mission.* London: Sheed and Ward.

de Rachewiltz, I. 1971. *Papal Envoys to the Great Khans.* London: Faber.

—— 1997. Marco Polo Went to China. *Zentralasiatische Studien* 27:34–92.

Haw, Stephen G. 2006. *Marco Polo's China. A Venetian in the Realm of Khubilai Khan.* London: Routledge.

Jackson, P. 2005. *The Mongols and the West 1221–1410.* Harlow: Pearson Longman.

Jackson, P., with D.O. Morgan, eds. 1990. *The Mission of Friar William of Rubruck. His Journey to the Court of the Great Khan Möngke 1253–1255,* trans. P. Jackson. London: Hakluyt Society.

Juvayni, ʿAlāʾuʾl-Din. 1912–37. *Taʾrikh-i Jahān Gushā,* 3 vols., ed. M. Qazvini. Leiden: E.J. Brill, and London: Luzac; trans. J.A. Boyle, *Juvaini. The History of the World-Conqueror* (Manchester: Manchester University Press, 1958).

Lupprian, K.-E., ed. 1981. *Die Beziehungen der Päpste zu islamischen und mongolischen Herrschern im 13. Jahrhundert anhand ihres Briefwechsels.* Vatican City: Biblioteca Apostolica Vaticana.

Morgan, D.O. 1996. Marco Polo in China—or Not. *Journal of the Royal Asiatic Society,* 3rd ser. 6:221–25.

Morris, I., ed. 1970. *Madly Singing in the Mountains. An Appreciation and Anthology of Arthur Waley.* London: George Allen and Unwin.

Olschki, L. 1960. *Marco Polo's Asia.* Berkeley: University of California Press.

Pelliot, P. 1922–32. Les Mongols et la papauté. *Revue de l'Orient Chrétien* 23 (1922–23): 3–30; 24 (1924): 225–335; 28 (1932): 3–84.

Rossabi, M. 2002. The Mongols and Their Legacy. In *The Legacy of Genghis Khan. Courtly Art and Culture in Western Asia, 1256–1353,* ed. L. Komaroff and S. Carboni, pp. 12–35. New York: Metropolitan Museum of Art, and New Haven: Yale University Press.

Shijian, Huang. 1986. The Persian Language in China during the Yuan Dynasty. *Papers in Far Eastern History* 34:83–95.

Togan, I. 1998. *Flexibility and Limitation in Steppe Formations. The Kerait Khanate and Chinggis Khan.* Leiden: E.J. Brill.

Waldron, A.N. 1990. *The Great Wall of China: From History to Myth.* Cambridge: Cambridge University Press.

Wood, Frances. 1995. *Did Marco Polo Go to China?* London: Secker and Warburg.

Yule, H., and H. Cordier. 1903. *The Book of Ser Marco Polo the Venetian.* 3rd ed. 2 vols. London: John Murray.

5

Ottoman Turkish: Written Language and Scribal Practice, 13th to 20th Centuries

LINDA T. DARLING

The written Persian language is remarkable for its stability over a millennium of time. In contrast, the interesting thing about Ottoman written culture is that although Ottoman Turkish was intimately linked with Persian throughout its existence, although Ottoman scribes based their organization and culture on that of Persian scribes, and although Persian literature and documents formed the most important models for those of the Ottomans, the Ottoman written language was not at all stable or unchanging.[1] To an Ottomanist, it seems odd even to think about an unchanging language, because Ottoman Turkish was constantly changing and the changes were one of its most notable features. Ottoman was similar to Persian, however, in that it was a written lingua franca for the governing elite of an empire whose people spoke a variety of different languages and dialects, whether other varieties of Turkish or other languages entirely, such as Greek, Serbian, or Arabic. It therefore shared many of Persian's characteristics as an elite administrative and literary vehicle. The culture of the scribal cadre who were the producers and upholders of written Turkish was, as far as we know, similar to that of the Persian scribes, as described by Hanaway in chapter 2. But there are striking differences in the outcome. If in Persia the scribes were the guardians of the stability of the written language, in the Ottoman Empire the scribal class was responsible for its transformations. In addition, the Ottoman elite was multilingual; its members wrote in Arabic and Persian as well as Turkish and probably spoke several other languages—Mehmed II, for example, knew Greek well.

In making Turkish their written language, the Ottomans followed the example of the Karamanids, who as part of their rebellion against the Persian-writing administrations of Anatolia, the Seljuk Turks and the Mongol Ilkhanids, began writing their government documents in Turkish. The Ottomans actually employed four traditions of writing Turkish. Some scholars call them all "Ottoman Turkish" (a 20th-century term usually meaning all Turkish written in Arabic script), while others reserve that term for the highest and most complex tradition used by the only true "Ottomans," the people of the court. The first of the four, the use of written Eastern Turkic, indicated Anatolia's cultural indebtedness to the Turks of Central Asia, but it died out after the 14th century. The second, sometimes called "Anatolian Turkish" or "old Turkish," was the written representation of Turkish speech. This form of writing was used for popular literature and some Sufi poetry before and during the life of the empire and was the language of court literature in the early period of the empire's history. Although it had already been heavily influenced by Persian in its core vocabulary before the Turks ever left the steppe, later writers found it inadequate for translating Persian texts or for conveying the subtleties of Sufi poetry or theology, and with the invention of the high style it dropped out of favor among the Ottomans of the court.[2] The written representation of ordinary Turkish speech, however, continued as a literary counterculture throughout the empire's existence and motivated the language reform movement of the 19th and early 20th centuries (after which the language reform departed from common speech to create the new artificial elite language of modern "pure Turkish").

The third of these linguistic traditions is what might be called "administrative Turkish," the language that began to be used for government documents in the 14th century. This language was not pure Turkish either, since it contained a great deal of administrative Persian and numerous Arabic root words and grammatical forms, but it was intended to be clear and straightforward. Besides government documents, it was used in prose literature not only by members of the court but also by people outside court circles educated in the *medrese* (cf. Arabic/Persian *madrasa*), some of whom also wrote in Arabic. The fourth tradition, often the only one understood by the term "Ottoman Turkish," is the ornate language of the court, developed at the beginning of the 16th century to bear the weight of the Ottomans' status as a world power. It was laden with vocabulary and grammatical devices derived from Persian and Arabic that were intended to adorn and beautify its messages and to challenge and uplift its audiences. It was used mainly in what is called "dīvān poetry," in royal correspondence, and in the dedicatory introductions of prose works and chancery documents.

This chapter provides an overview of the third and fourth of these traditions and an introduction to the literature about them. For the most part, those who produced these two forms of written Turkish were the same people, or at least belonged to the same elite group: professional scribes, professional poets, and amateurs from the ruling class. They wrote in Arabic and Persian, but they also added massive amounts of these languages' vocabulary and numerous stylistic and grammatical elements to their Turkish, giving it a flexibility and a polish that enabled it to carry considerable cultural weight. As poets too, they imported Arabic and Persian vocabulary that would make Turkish fit into the quantitative poetic meters adopted from Arabic and Persian prosody.[3] They retained Arabic as the language of religion and philosophy and Persian for its poetry and for Sufi literature, but their enhanced Turkish became the medium for the cultural activities— poetry, historiography, administration—that created the Ottomans' identity and distinguished them from the other great Muslim peoples.

WRITTEN TURKISH IN ANATOLIA

Ottoman chronicles and modern Turkish nationalist historiography represent the early Ottomans as pure Turkish nomads, fleeing from before the Mongols and involved in Seljuk border warfare, but dependent for the arts of civilization on Persian-writing scribes from the Seljuk and Ilkhanid realms. This was an ideological exaggeration; the contemporary Persian chroniclers of 14th-century Anatolia—Aksarayi and the anonymous chronicler of Konya—depict Turkish refugee tribes (they do not specifically mention the Ottomans) as closely involved in the politics of the Mongols and the subjugated Anatolian Seljuks, as having capitals and courts and scribes to serve them, and by the beginning of the 14th century as sedentarizing and developing their own trade, architecture, coinage, and documentary forms.[4] A study of surviving 14th-century documents (or their copies) shows that the Ottomans were familiar from the start with standard Persianate documentary practices and institutions but on an elementary level, and that in the early decades these practices were used infrequently.[5] By 1360 the Ottomans had grown more comfortable with the governing Persianate heritage of governance; from that year on their documents became markedly more complex, as did the institutions that they recorded, and simultaneously a translation movement was putting Arabic and Persian literary classics into Turkish. In 1390 the Ottomans conquered Kütahya, then the cultural capital of western Anatolia, and took its poets and authors into Ottoman service, and no doubt its scribes as well. The system of revenue surveys that governed the Ottoman Empire's fiscal and military organization throughout its classical age, the tımar system, also began in the 1390s. That decade saw geographical expansion, a large amount of architectural construction, and the beginnings of original literary composition: all in all, a great development of sophistication at all levels.

The Turkish language had been written for centuries prior to the Ottomans and in a variety of different alphabets; there was no standard form for written Turkish and no standardized spelling until the 20th century. The Orkhon inscriptions of the 8th century were in runes (unrelated to the runic writing used in pre-Roman Germanic languages), and the medieval Turks used the Uighur alphabet. Literary works in the Turkish language but in the Arabic script and in Persian literary genres appeared in Karakhanid Central Asia in the 11th and 12th centuries; they included both courtly works of advice to kings and Sufi poetry for a popular audience.[6] At the same time (ca.1077) a Turkic-Arabic dictionary was produced.[7] In the 13th and 14th centuries, a Turkish literature flourished in Anatolia including both translations or adaptations of classical works from Arabic and Persian and also original works, largely mystical texts and love poetry.[8] The decline of Seljuk patronage in the late 13th century moved the center of Anatolian cultural production from the Seljuk capital of Konya to the border cities, such as Kastamonu under the Çobanids and Candarids and Kütahya under the Germiyanids, and at the end of the 14th century the poetic hub moved to the court of the Ottoman prince Süleyman Çelebi in Edirne. Thirteenth- and 14th-century Anatolian texts were still strongly influenced by the old Turkish dialect and the writing styles of Central Asia, but 15th-century Ottoman writers employed the western Turkish (Oğuz) dialect and a greater amount of Arabic- and Persian-derived vocabulary.[9]

Written Turkish at that time had neither the prestige nor the flexibility of Arabic and Persian, which had been elite languages for centuries. During the 15th century, however, not only in the Ottoman Empire but in the Timurid and Mamluk empires as well, the employment of Turkish in formal writing expanded greatly (at the expense of Persian, although Ottoman scribes continued to use Persian at times for poetry and histories), and Turkish began to develop as a literary vehicle.[10] The Ottoman court avidly collected Timurid literary works in Chagatai Turkish as well as in Persian, and Timurid literature was being translated as quickly as two years after its composition.[11] At the same time, Turkish poets—both indigenous and foreign—flourished at the Timurid court, where Ottoman poetry was well received.[12] Timurid inshā in the 15th century increasingly incorporated Turkish vocabulary and stylistic traits without giving up its Persian base, but some literary works began to be written entirely in Turkish, and Timur himself encouraged the writing of a history of his conquests that could be understood by the common people.[13]

The mere creation of Turkish works by Timurid authors, who had already written great literature in Persian, suggests the rapidly rising prestige of the Turkish language across Islamdom in the late 15th century, a change perhaps not unrelated to Ottoman imperial expansion. Mehmed II wrote poetry in Turkish as well as Persian, and Bayezid II even tried to learn Uighur.[14] Persian and Arabic remained more prestigious, but the Ottomans were proud of their Turkish tribal heritage and anxious to proclaim their distinctiveness from the other powers of the region. Two-thirds of the Ottoman sultans were poets: Murad I wrote quatrains in Turkish in the style of Omar Khayyam, while Selim I wrote his poetry in Persian; Süleyman Kanuni was an accomplished and prolific Turkish poet. In the Persian context the Safavid Shāh Ismaʿil used Turkish, as did Sultan-Husayn Bayqara, Mengli Giray Han, Shaybani Khan, Babur, and Qansuh al-Ghawri. There were also famous women poets in Turkish, such as Zaynab and Mihri, both from Amasya.[15] Both Mehmed II and Bayezid II sought to lure Persian-speaking poets and intellectuals from the Akkoyunlu and Timurid realms to the Ottoman court, but it was the fall of those two realms, the Ottoman capture of Tabriz, and the forcible conversion of Iran by the Safavids that finally brought a significant number of Persians to Istanbul to influence Ottoman arts and letters.[16] By that time, Turkish was well enough entrenched as a literary language that Persian literature could provide a standard of excellence for Ottoman writers, but not a model to be slavishly copied. Scholars used to criticize Ottoman poetry for being a pale copy of the Persian, but Persian-based vocabulary took on a life of its own once it was assimilated into Turkish (from whence it was sometimes borrowed back into Persian), and Ottoman poets had their own agendas. As in the visual arts, so in poetry the genres were the same but what the artists from each society did with them was quite different.[17]

Persian was also used in the oldest surviving Ottoman documents (vakfiye deeds for pious bequests), the earliest of which was written in Persian in 1324.[18] Later vakfiyes, from the 1350s on, exist only in copies or translations, but the originals appear to have been in Arabic, showing the employment of scribes educated in the Islamic tradition.[19] The Ottoman and other Anatolian principalities, however, had already begun using Turkish as their administrative language in the 14th century, setting themselves off from the Seljuks and Ilkhanids, and by the 15th century the Turkish of the Ottoman documents was well established. Early sultanic decrees appear in the inshā collection of Feridun Bey, but they are thought to have been altered or completely invented in the 16th century.[20] In contrast, the 14th-century Turkish decrees found by Paul Wittek in Ottoman registers and document collections seem authentic in their simplicity.[21] No original finance documents survive from the 14th century; the earliest we have are from the 1430s.[22] The language and organization of the finance documents seem to be based on the (lost) Persian registers of the Ilkhanids, as described in three Ilkhanid finance manuals from the 14th century found in Turkish libraries.[23] In the translation from Persian into Turkish a great deal of Persian documentary vocabulary was retained, but by the 15th century the language and format of the Ottoman finance documents had developed beyond the examples in the Ilkhanid registers, exhibiting the standard form seen in most of the later Ottoman registers.[24]

THE DEVELOPMENT OF OTTOMAN INSHĀ

The Ottoman scribes did not write finance manuals like those of the Ilkhanids. They did, however, write inshā works on the science of document composition, following the pattern of the Seljuks.[25] Some of these manuals covered the concrete side of the scribal art—ink, paper, scripts, formats, document coverings—or the proper vocabulary and titles of address; others were collections of model letters, often borrowed and reworked or completely fabricated by the author. These manuals usually concentrated on government correspondence with high officials and foreign powers, where the simultaneous demands for precision and magnificence were equally strong.

The 12th-century Persian inshā manual of al-Baghdādi of Khwārazm, al-Tavassul ilā al-Tarassul, was known in Seljuk Anatolia in the 13th century, as indicated by the composition in 1279 in Anatolia of a secretarial handbook with the imitative title al-Teressül ila al-Tevessül.[26] This work, by the Anatolian Badr al-Din al-Rumi, and the handbooks of Abu Bckr b. Zeki (Konya, 1279) and Hasan b. `Abdi'l-Mu'min el-Hoyi (Kastamonu, 1285, recopied 1309), were part of the Anatolian scribes' late 13th-century output of Persian literature.[27]

The first scribe known to write inshā in Turkish was Ahmed-i Dā'i, whose Teressül appeared before 1417; only four pages of it survive.[28] Its author explicitly stated that he was creating a Turkish inshā that should stand alongside those in Arabic and Persian, which his readers should also know well. He appears to have been writing a general correspondence manual rather than a manual of state correspondence, and one perhaps based on the old Turkish of the century before; the loss of his text suggests that his "Turkish inshā" was superseded by later works. Even at that time, Turkish was not the only language used in the Ottoman chancery. Over the years the Ottomans employed scribcs who wrote in Latin, Greek, Italian, Uighur, Persian, Arabic, Serbian, Hungarian, and other languages. The ability to move between languages was an essential requirement of the bureaucracy and played its part in diplomatic dealings from the foundation of the empire to the end. While the Persians lived in the center of a Persian-writing zone, the Ottomans lived in a borderland shared with many other linguistic groups. No manuals of translation have appeared, but the inshā manuals may give us clues to the process by which the Ottomans transferred ideas expressed in one language into another.

Changes in the elite language and in the empire's importance by the end of the 15th century necessitated the composition of several new inshā manuals in those years. The first, written before 1479, was the imperial secretary Yahya b. Mehmed's Menahicü'l-İnşa.[29] Like Ahmed-i Dā'i, Yahya provided instructions for addressing correspondence to various recipients, but while Ahmed's work may have been meant for people who might address letters to padiShāhs and beys or simply to their own relatives and friends, Yahya was clearly writing for state secretaries; he included terms of address for all government personnel and copies of appointment documents and official letters as well as private correspondence. In 1487–88 Hüsamzade Mustafa Efendi compiled a collection of letters called Mecmu`a-i İnşa.[30] Tācizade

Sa`di Çelebi, a court poet and brother of a high official, collected a Münşeat Mecmuası including texts of official correspondence in Turkish and Persian dated from 1469 to 1500, followed by a list of important dates.[31] An anonymous Münşeat Mecmuası compiled after 1490 may have been put together by the poet's father, Taci Bey; it collected royal and vizierial letters from the period of Mehmed II together with some edicts and proclamations.[32] The Karamanid scribe Niğdeli Pir Mehmed wrote both an inshā collection and a Persian-Turkish dictionary; the inshā collection, containing documents dated from 1394 to 1476, also included a copy of el-Hoyi's 13th-century scribal handbook and another Teressül by Kırımlu Hafız Hüsam describing how to write various kinds of documents, in which the latest document comes from 1422.[33] In the early 16th century Mahmud b. Edhem Amasyavi also wrote both a Persian-Turkish dictionary, Miftahü'l-Lûğa, and an inshā manual, Gülşen-i İnşa.[34]

The classic manual of Ottoman inshā, the Münşeatü's-Selātin, was produced in 1574–75 by Feridun Bey. This work currently exists in two recensions, both of which have been published.[35] In it Feridun Bey put both genuine letters and letters he invented based on those in al-Baghdādi's Tavassul but rewritten by him as examples of early Ottoman correspondence.[36] So complete was Feridun Bey's success in setting an epistolary standard for the empire that later inshā manuals tended to be compiled only for more specific purposes. Mustafa `Ali's Menşe'ü'l-İnşa of ca.1586 was a self-promoting work containing only his own correspondence.[37] The former reisülküttab (head scribe) Sarı Abdullah produced a Münşeat-i Fārsi in 1629, toward the end of a long series of wars with Iran, that was filled with exemplary Persian correspondence of earlier sultans with various Iranian rulers.[38] Okçuzade's Münşeatü'l-İnşa contained mostly private correspondence, testifying to the dissemination of court standards of language and composition throughout polite society; a study of this work also lists several 17th-century inshā compilers not connected with the court.[39] A number of anonymous letter collections in Istanbul's Süleymaniye Library come from the same period and appear to have been compiled for individual use.[40]

Throughout this period, Ottoman writers continued to develop the poetic and administrative language, adding more Persian- and Arabic-derived vocabulary and expanding its grammatical and syntactical complexity.[41] The extension of the inshā tradition into the 18th and 19th centuries has not yet been studied. Also not well studied is the Ottoman inshā itself, the changes in literary standards and recommendations over time.[42] Rhetoric, as taught in Ottoman *medrese*s or outside them, seems to have been an abstract subject without much relevance to actual Turkish composition, being based on Arabic models.[43] While Feridun Bey's manual remained the ostensible gold standard of Ottoman inshā, no studies have been made of the extent to which the correspondence of subsequent generations adhered to that standard. Given only the observable changes in scribal practice in the following half-century, however, it is probable that adherence was not very close and that the language of administration, as well as that of poetry, continued to change after the production of Feridun Bey's masterpiece.

The 18th century Tulip Era poets gave the language of poetry a new delicacy and naturalism, and poetry itself a new originality.[44] Nineteenth-century secretaries, however, began to use the divan language more extensively in government documents for a few decades just prior to the language reform. The resulting complication of the previously straightforward administrative language is thought to have given rise to modern Western and Turkish stereotypes about the impenetrability of all Ottoman writing.[45] Stereotypes about an unbridgeable gap between the languages of the elites and the common people do not reflect actual Ottoman practice. While the most complex tradition of Ottoman Turkish language was doubtless not fully understood by everyone, there was—contrary to the nationalist narrative—a gradation of usage rather than a sharp break between court language and the language of popular literature. "Bureaucrats, soldiers, tradespeople, servants, craftsmen, merchants, and even villagers" might be present at the parties, coffeehouses, and Sufi ceremonies where poetry was sung, recited, and enjoyed.[46] Moreover, the clear and straightforward administrative register, which had been and was still used for most practical prose writing, was intended to be widely understood.

ADMINISTRATIVE TURKISH,
THE STABLE LANGUAGE

The stable language tradition in Turkish was not the tradition of court poetry and prose but that of administration and government documents. The scribes did not write inshā manuals to guide the production of these documents; instead, they modeled them on existing documents, in all their varied types and scripts. Different script styles and document formats, and even sizes, were employed for different genres of writing: divāni for copies of outgoing orders and other extended prose, for example, and the special stylized script called siyākat for finance documents, both numbers and letters. The siyakat script changed slowly over the centuries, becoming more stylized as time went by, but the formulas and vocabulary of the documents remained the same, except for changes due to altered subject matter. While the language of the documents was meant to be clear and unambiguous, especially when read aloud, the script was not; it was intended to make the documents hard to falsify and hard for outsiders to understand or imitate. Scribes writing official Turkish used many Persian and Arabic technical terms, but they repeated these terms for centuries, making them standard Ottoman terms. Their sentences were relatively short and unadorned, and they did not disturb the normal word order. What makes the documents difficult for Westerners (besides the script) is a regular feature of the Turkish language, the omission of whatever can be omitted, such as repetitive verb endings. This linguistic economy did not create a barrier to comprehension among native speakers.

A literature did develop that analyzed official documents and their language and format, but it was not written by Ottomans. Rather, this explanatory literature was produced by European translators and scholars struggling to understand the formal characteristics and meanings of the documents and treaties they were negotiating with the Ottoman Empire. Ottoman documents were first published in Europe in the 17th century, largely in guides to the Turkish language written by official translators (dragomans); they were analyzed using the Latin terminology and concepts already developed in the medieval period for European documents. The earliest documents analyzed in this fashion were the agreements Europeans made with the Ottomans and the edicts of the sultan, but in the 19th century documents on other topics, acquired largely through the capture of campaign archives, were also studied. The 20th-century opening of the Ottoman archives in Istanbul gave scholars access to the whole range of state documents and made possible the modern field of Ottoman history as an archivally based discipline. To mine these riches, historians created handbooks on various aspects of the documents in the archives. This included their location; many articles describe the Ottoman documents in various European and Middle Easstern archives or locate documents on particular subjects. This work was necessitated by the large number of uncatalogued documents in both the Ottoman and other archives. The earliest catalogues of the voluminous Prime Minister's Archives (Başbakanlık or Başvekalet Arşivi, Istanbul) were produced by individual archivists and covered only a small percentage of the millions of documents housed there; more recently, however, the government hired large numbers of archivists to catalogue the remaining documents, publish the catalogues, and digitize and publish the most sought-after documents. The Topkapı Palace Archive catalogue is being published serially, together with some of its documents. The Süleymaniye Library has long been catalogued, and the catalogues of it and its daughter collections have also begun to be published. The registers of the sharia courts have been listed and brought together. Documents in smaller or provincial archives and libraries, however, remain less accessible or have perished altogether due to war and ethnic cleansing.[47]

Modern handbooks on Ottoman-Turkish diplomatics appeared in the 1920s, drawing on the earlier centuries of work on these documents. Friedrich Kraelitz transcribed, translated, and analyzed a series of 15th-century edicts or *fermans*, and Lajos Fekete did the same for a variety of 16th-century documents, discussing their paleography and diplomatics at some length.[48] In the next generation Guboglu and Nedkov wrote similar manuals in Romanian and Bulgarian for the analysis of Ottoman documents held by the new nation-states of Eastern Europe.[49] Additional years of experience and an international bibliography of document studies enriched two later handbooks: the Polish Ottomanist Jan Reychman's explication of document structure and production, with a lengthy bibliography of published documents, and Mübahat Kütükoğlu's monumental collection of documentary protocols and phraseology.[50] Heyd and Biegman each made detailed studies of the *ferman* from orders addressed to a specific region in a specific time period.[51] More recently, Stojanow compiled a history and bibliography of Ottoman diplomatics, completing and expanding upon earlier summaries of the literature by Horniker and Gökbilgin.[52] Finance documents were slower to be examined, but a guide and catalog have appeared in Turkish.[53]

Specific features of the documents have been elucidated in more specialized studies. The different kinds of markings on Ottoman documents have been deciphered by a number of scholars: the *tuğra* (the sultan's signature) by Ali, Uzunçarşılı, Babinger, and Umur[54]; the *pençe* (the signature of officials other than the sultan) by Kraelitz and Velkov[55]; seals by Uzunçarşılı[56]; and watermarks by Nikolaev, Velkov, and Andreev.[57] Ottoman paleography and scripts have been clarified by Uzunçarşılı, Yazır, Fekete, and Baltacı.[58] Particularly useful for finance documents are the studies of siyakat script by Ünver, Yazır, Elker, Fekete, Popov, and Günday.[59] Ayverdi discussed early calligraphy in general.[60] Another group of studies by Uzunçarşılı, Velkov, and İnalcık deciphered the notations placed on documents in the course of processing them through the Ottoman bureaucracy.[61]

This last group of studies points the way to the topic of scribal work and organization. In their textbooks on Ottoman history, İnalcık and Shaw provided good introductions to the Ottoman central administration and scribal service.[62] Fleischer examined the scribal service in its early days and Findley in its last years.[63] Fleischer, Shinder, Woodhead, and Darling wrote about aspects of scribal life and work in the 16th and 17th centuries.[64] Studies have also been made of the impact of document use; some examples are by İnalcık, Murphey, and Darling.[65] This work permits a few generalizations about the Ottoman scribal career.

OTTOMAN SCRIBES

Ottoman scribes have been broadly divided into two main groups, chancery scribes and finance scribes, but this does not exhaust the possible scribal careers. There were also scribes who worked on the timar (land grant) registers, or on provincial registers, or in the naval arsenal. Every military company, every tax farm, almost every organized group had a secretary to keep its books. Chancery work demanded more education, a larger vocabulary, and greater creativity than finance department work. The finance bureaus required greater diligence and accuracy but offered opportunities for travel with the army and other outside appointments. Ordinary scribes advanced gradually from apprenticeship to full scribal status, and there was some opportunity for horizontal movement between bureaus, although that opportunity lessened over the life of the empire. High officials and bureau heads, at least from the 16th century on, were political appointments rather than coming from the ranks, and after a certain point they rotated in office so that all candidates could have a chance to serve. Lower-level scribes did not rotate. Fleischer has written that until the mid-16th century Ottoman scribes came from the retinues of the holders of the chief bureaucratic offices of nişancı (an Ottoman official who inscribed the Sultan's *tuğra* on official documents and edited the laws) and defterdār (Minister of Finance), that is, from a *medrese* background.[66] This conclusion may be of limited application, however; according to the scribal salary registers, even in the second quarter of the 16th century scribal recruits of identifiably religious background or training were very few in the finance department. The registers show that the largest number of ordinary finance scribes was recruited from among the sons of scribes and palace officials, and then from the military services.[67] Still, the scribal career in the Ottoman Empire was not notably hereditary; sons of scribes formed less than half the corps until very late, in the 18th century. Scribes from the conquered peoples were also employed, but not normally in the central bureaucracy.

Through the 15th century, the best higher education had been found in Mamluk Cairo, and most of the Ottomans' top intellectuals and religio-political personnel had received their training there. The 16th-century Ottoman conquest of the Arab lands and the construction of the Fatih and Süleymaniye *medrese*s shifted the center of higher education to Istanbul. The Ottomans, however, had begun founding lower-level *medrese*s as early as the 1320s. These *medrese*s provided a basic education in the Islamic sciences and could have begun the preparation of individuals for scribal positions. The scribal salary registers of the early 16th century, however, show the junior scribes as apprentices of the more experienced personnel; if they had received a *medrese* education, it did not include the details of scribal work.[68]

In the early 17th century the scribal corps expanded greatly, and the largest number of new recruits came from backgrounds that were either unknown or not worth mentioning.[69] It is clear from their work that they had not had a *medrese* education. The archival documents of the period show that, whether through poor training or for some other reason, these scribes began spelling words as they were pronounced in Turkish rather than according to their Arabic or Persian derivation. There may have been other changes in the language as well. While Mustafa `Ali and a few others with *medrese* educations wrote history as well as poetry in an enriched divan style, writings by scribes and court figures with perhaps less elevated backgrounds continued to display a straightforward Turkish style relatively devoid of Persian and Arabic accretions.[70] With the exception of dedicatory prefaces, often in divān Turkish, the texts of the histories and works of political advice produced by such men were usually written in the plain administrative style. In terms of script, the transition from Ottoman to modern Turkish was quite abrupt; it was enacted by law in 1928. In terms of language, however, Atatürk's reforms continued a tradition of Turkification and linguistic accessibility that had begun centuries earlier.

Ottoman scribes were not only poets but historians. The language of historiography has begun to be studied, but more as a political issue than a linguistic one. There are two recent studies of the narratives of the deposition and killing of Sultan Osman II in 1622 and of differences in the way that story was related by different chroniclers.[71] In addition, the study of the earliest histories of the Ottomans has been reopened, though again with more attention to the politicized construction of the narratives than to the language in which they were told.[72] The politics of history-writing is not a new topic,[73] but since most Ottoman chroniclers were also scribes, it could yield insight into issues such as scribal origins, training, and factional divisions. Some study has been made of scribal career paths in the Ottoman Empire, a topic that could be made to reveal the impact of inshā upon Ottoman writing.[74] The career of one scribe, for instance, who moved from a series of strictly secretarial posts to the position of court historian (şehnāmeci), "demonstrates how, by encouraging the study of Islamic literature and the perfection of an elegant style in prose writing, the system of education and training within the dīvān was largely responsible for establishing strong links between the 'secretarial service' and the literary world."[75]

Scribal culture certainly had an impact on the way scribes wrote documents, and its changes should illuminate the ebbs and flows of Persian influence on Ottoman scribal practice.[76] What may in time come to have a still greater bearing on our understanding of scribal practice is the investigation of scribal consciousness. This investigation is being carried on through the literature of advice to kings; even more than history, the writing of advice literature should reveal the mentality of the scribes and their relationship to the empire and its rulers.[77] For this we await studies of the advice works in their literary, social, and historical contexts. One aspect of that culture is the scribes' understanding of their own language. Informal observations suggest that the Arabic and Persian vocabulary imported into the language in the 16th century was domesticated in the 17th, when Arabic words began to be spelled phonetically in Turkish. Turkish historical linguistics, however, has few practitioners, and fewer still who work with the language of Ottoman documents. As these fields develop, we can expect to learn much more about the Ottoman written language and scribal practice and its relationship with Persian.

NOTES

1. I am grateful to Walter G. Andrews, who kindly read this paper and saved me from a number of errors, adding his wish for more studies of the relationship between Persian and Turkish (Turkic) from both sides.
2. Mecdut Mansuroğlu, "Rise and Development of Written Turkish," 252.
3. Talat Sait Halman, "Ancient and Ottoman Legacy," 45–46.
4. Linda T. Darling, "Persianate Sources on Anatolia."
5. Darling, "Development of Ottoman Governmental Institutions."
6. Yusuf Khass Hājib, *Wisdom of Royal Glory;* Ahmed Yesevi, *Divan-i Hikmet.*
7. Mahmud al-Kāshġarī, *Compendium of the Turkic Dialects.*
8. Mansuroğlu, "Written Turkish in Anatolia," 253–54; Najib Ullah, *Islamic Literature,* 376–77.
9. Mansuroğlu, "Written Turkish," 255–62; Ullah, *Islamic Literature, 376.*
10. Was such a development absent among the Akkoyunlu? Does its presence indicate a certain level of imperial confidence and cultural assurance?
11. Gottfried Hagen, "Translations and Translators," 101. Ottoman and Chagatai Turkish works were also copied for the Mamluk sultans.
12. Walter G. Andrews, pers. comm., June 10, 2007.
13. Ishtiyaq Ahmad Zilli, "Development of Inshā Literature," 328, 331.
14. Ullah, *Islamic Literature, 379;* M. Fuad Köprülü, *Türk Edebiyatı Tarihi,* reprint, 374–76; Eleazar Birnbaum, "Ottomans and Chagatay Literature," 165–67 and n27.
15. P. Horn, "Der Dichter Sultan Selim I"; V. Minorsky, "Poetry of Shāh Ismaʿīl I"; Ullah, *Islamic Literature, 380, 382.*
16. Hanna Sohrweide, "Dichter und Gelehrte aus dem Osten im osmanischen Reich"; Darling, "Renaissance and the Middle East," 61–62.
17. Walter Andrews, "Speaking of Power," 282, 285; Darling, "Renaissance," 62 and nn20–21.
18. Irène Beldiceanu-Steinherr, *Recherches sur les actes des règnes des sultans,* 85; İsmail Hakkı Uzunçarşılı, "Gazi Orhan Bey Vakfiyesi." The 1326 vakfiye of the emir of Sivas was written in Arabic and Uighur; Ahmet Temir, "Die arabisch-uigurische Vakf-Urkunde von 1326."
19. Beldiceanu-Steinherr, *Recherches,* 111, 127; Uzunçarşılı, "Çandarlı Zāde Ali Paşa Vakfiyesi"; M. Tayyib Gökbilgin, "Murad I. Tesisleri ve Bursa İmareti Vakfiyesi," 218.
20. Beldiceanu-Steinherr, *Recherches,* 59, 75, 90, 100, et passim.
21. Paul Wittek, "Zu einingen frühosmanischen Urkunden (I)."
22. The earliest complete register has been published: Halil İnalcık, *Hicri 835 Tarihli Suret-i Defter-i Sancak-ı Arvanid.*
23. Mirkamal Nabipour, *Die beiden persischen Leitfäden des Falak ʿAlā-ye Tabrizi;* Nejat Göyünç, "Das sogenannte Ġameʿoʾl-Hesāb das ʿİmād as-Sarāwī"; Walther Hinz, *Risāla-yi Falakiyya.* On these manuals see Philip Remler, "New Light on Economic History from Ilkhanid Accounting Manuals," 162–63; Oktay Güvemli, *Türk Devletleri Muhasebe Tarihi,* 1. Similar works are known to have been written under the Jalayirid and Timurid regimes, but they have been lost; Ahmet Zeki Validi Togan, "Mogollar Devrinde Anadolu'nun İktisadi Vaziyeti," 14; trans., Gary Leiser, "Economic Conditions in Anatolia in the Mongol Period," 216.
24. Only a beginning has been made in investigating the development of Ottoman docu-

ments: Nejat Göyunç, "Osmanlı Maliyesinde Ilhanlı Tesirleri"; Abdulkadir Yuvalı, "L'influence des Ilkhanat."

25. For an overview of Ottoman *inshā* production, see Josef Matuz, "Über die Epistolographie und Inša'-Literatur der Osmanen."

26. Bahā al-Dīn Muhammad al-Baghdādi, *Al-Tavassul ilā al-Tarassul;* Mehmed Fuad Köprülü, *Seljuks of Anatolia,* 34.

27. Abu Bakr b. al-Zaki, *Ravzat al-Kuttāb va Hadikat al-Albāb;* see Ali Sevim, "Anadolu Selçuklularına ait bir Eser"; Osman Turan, *Türkiye Selçukluları Hakkında Resmi Vesikalar,* 147, 172–73; Hasan b. `Abdi'l-Mu'min el-Hoyi, *Günyetü'l-Kātib ve Münyetü't-Tālib;* see Uzunçarşılı, *Anadolu Beylikleri ve Akkoyunlu,* 209–12.

28. Ertaylan, *Ahmed-i Dā'i: Hayatı ve Eserleri,* 3–28, 157–60, 129; Björkman, "Die Anfänge der türkischen Briefsammlungen"; İ. Çetin Derdiyok, "Eski Türk Edebiyatı'nda Mektup"; Şinasi Tekin, "Fatih Sultan Mehmed Devrine āit bir İnşā Mecmuası," 282–90. Nearly contemporary is a copy of the Persian finance manual *Sa`adetname,* copied in Bursa in 1412; the act of copying indicates that the Ottomans at that time had an older copy that no longer exists.

29. Yahyā bin Mehmed el-Kātib, *Menāhicü'l-İnşā;* see Björkman, "Türkische Briefsammlung."

30 Yahyā bin Mehmed el-Kātib, *Menāhicü'l-İnşā,* 11.

31. Tāci-zāde Sa'di Çelebi, *Tāci-zāde Sa'di Çelebi Münşeātı.*

32. Lugal and Erzi, *Fātih Devrine āit Münşeāt Mecmuası.*

33. Tekin, "Fatih Sultan Mehmed," 267, 271, 273, 285, 288.

34. Yahyā bin Mehmed el-Kātib, *Menāhicü'l-İnşā,* 12–13.

35. Ahmed Feridun Bey, *Mecmu'a-i Münşe'āt-i Selātin,* 2 vols. Neither published version apparently represents the entire original manuscript, which was eleven volumes long.

36. Mükrimin Halil, "Feridun Bey Münşeatı," 63–77; *Türk Tarihi Encümeni Mecmuası* 1.78 (1921–22); 2.79 (1921–22); 4.81 (1921–22); Beldiceanu-Steinherr, *Recherches,* passim. For another of Feridun Bey's sources, see Hikmet İlaydın and Adnan Sadık Erzi, "XVI. Asra āit bir Münşeāt Mecmuası."

37. Cornell H. Fleischer, *Bureaucrat and Intellectual,* 129.

38. Adnan S. Erzi, "Sarı Abdullah Efendi Münşeatının Tavsifi."

39. Christine Woodhead, "Ottoman İnşa and the Art of Letter-Writing." Josef Matuz, "Über die Epistolographie und Inša'," 578, provides a long list of *inshā* collections, most unpublished.

40. Snjezana Buzov, "World of Ottoman *Mecmuas.*"

41. Walter G. Andrews, *Poetry's Voice, Society's Song,* esp. 36–61; Victoria Rowe Holbrook, *Unreadable Shores of Love.*

42. For further information on inshā see the works on Persian inshā: Zilli, "Development of Inshā Literature," and Colin Mitchell, "Safavid Imperial Tarassul."

43. Christopher Ferrard, "Development of an Ottoman Rhetoric," 3:171; 4:19–20.

44. Ullah, *Islamic Literature,* 389; Holbrook, *Unreadable Shores,* 56–57.

45. Fahir İz, "Ottoman and Turkish," 120.

46. İz, "Ottoman and Turkish," 119; Halman, "Ancient and Ottoman Legacy," 42, 44; Andrews, *Poetry's Voice,* 16–17, 176–79, quotation on 177. For an example of the shared tradition of poetry parties, see the following site suggested by Walter G. Andrews: http://www.kalfat.com/index.php?option=com_content&task=view&id=98&Itemid=86.

47. Necati Aktaş, *Başbakanlık Osmanlı Arşivi Rehberi;* Uzunçarşılı, Baybura, and Altındağ, *Topkapı Sarayı Müzesi;* İsmet Parmaksızoılu and Sabih Acun, *Türkiye Yazmaları Toplu Kataloğu;* Ahmet Akgündüz and Türk Dünyası Araştırmaları Vakfı and İlim Hey'eti, *Şeriyye Sicilleri: Mahiyeti, Toplu Kataloğu ve Seçme Hükümler;* Meral Alpay and Safiye Özkan, *İstanbul Kütüphaneleri.*

48. Friedrich Kraelitz[-Griefenhorst], *Osmanische Urkunden in türkischer Sprache;* Lajos Fekete, *Einführung in die osmanisch-türkische Diplomatik.*

49. Mikhail Guboglu, *Paleografia ši diplomatica turco-osmana;* Boris K. Nedkov, *Osmanoturska Diplomatika i Paleografija.*

50. Jan Reychman, Ananiasz Zajaczkowski, and Andrew S. Ehrenkreutz, *Handbook of Ottoman-Turkish Diplomatics;* see pp. 14–23 for a fuller history of the European study of Ottoman documents, especially in eastern Europe; Mübahat S. Kutukoğlu, *Osmanlı Belgelerinin Dili (Diplomatik).*

51. Uriel Heyd, *Ottoman Documents on Palestine;* Nicolaas H. Biegman, *Turco-Ragusan Relationship,* Introduction; Biegman, "Some Peculiarities of Firmans."

52. Valery Stojanow, *Entstehung und Entwicklung;* cf. A.L. Horniker, "Ottoman-Turkish Diplomatics"; M. Tayyib Gökbilgin, *Osmanlı İmparatorluğu Medeniyet Tarihi Çerçevesinde.*

53. Bilgin Aydın and Rıfat Günalan, *Osmanlı Maliesi ve Defter Sistemi.*

54. Ali, "Tuğra-yı Hümāyun," 43:53–58 and 44:109–25; Uzunçarşılı, "Tuğra ve Pençeler ile Ferman"; Franz Babinger, *Grossherrliche Tughra;* Suha Umur, *Osmanlı Padişah Tuğraları.*

55. Friedrich von Kraelitz-Griefenhorst, "Studien zur osmanischen Urkundenlehre, I"; Asparouch T. Velkov, "Başdefterdar ottomans."

56. Uzunçarşılı, "Osmanlı Devleti Zamanında Kullanılmış"; Uzunçarşılı, *Topkapı Sarayı Müzesi Mühürler Seksiyonu Rehberi.*

57. V. Nikolaev, *Watermarks of the Ottoman Empire;* Asparukh Velkov and Stefan Andreev, *Vodni znatsi v. osmanoturkite dokumenti,* 1.

58. Uzunçarşılı, "Türk Yazılarının Tetkikına Medhal"; Mahmud Yazır, *Eski Yazıları Okuma Anahtarı;* Fekete, "Arbeiten der grusinischen Orientalistik"; Cahit Baltacı, *İslam Paleografyası.*

59. Ahmet Süheyl Ünver, "Siyakat Yazısı ve Quyudu Atika"; Yazır, *Siyakat Yazısı;* Salâhaddin Elker, *Divan Rakamları;* Fekete, *Siyāqat-Schrift;* Nikola Popov, *Paleografski osobenosti;* Dündar Günday, *Arşiv Belgelerinde Siyakat Yazısı Özellikleri ve Divan Rakamları.*

60. Ekrem Hakkı Ayverdi, *Fatih Devri Hattatları.*

61. Uzunçarşılı, "Buyruldı"; Velkov, "Notes complémentaires"; İnalcık, "Osmanlı Bürokrasisinde Aklām ve Muāmelāt."

62. İnalcık, *Classical Age,* 89–104; Stanford J. Shaw and Ezel Kural Shaw, *History of the Ottoman Empire,* 1:118–34.

63. Fleischer, "Preliminaries"; Carter Vaughn Findley, "Tradition to Reform"; Findley, *Ottoman Civil Officialdom.*

64. Fleischer, "Between the Lines"; Joel Shinder, "Ottoman Bureaucracy"; Christine Woodhead, "From Scribe to Litterateur"; Woodhead, "Ottoman Scribal Service"; Darling, "Ottoman Salary Registers."

65. İnalcık, "Adāletnāmeler"; İnalcık, "Appointment Procedure of a Guild Warden"; Rhoads Murphey, "Ottoman Census Methods"; Darling, *Revenue-Raising and Legitimacy.*

66. Fleischer, "Scribal Training," 27.

67. Darling, "Ottoman Salary Registers," 26.
68. Darling, *Revenue-Raising and Legitimacy,* 57.
69. Darling, "Ottoman Salary Registers," 26.
70. İz, "Ottoman and Turkish," 128–38.
71. Gabriel Piterberg, *Ottoman Tragedy;* Baki Tezcan, "Searching for Osman."
72. Dimitris Kastritsis, "History-Writing in the Court of Mehmed I"; Murat Cem Menguç, "Creativity and Pluralism."
73. See İnalcık, "Rise of Ottoman Historiography"; İnalcık, "How to Read `Ashık Pasha-zāde's History"; rpt. in İnalcık, *Essays in Ottoman History,* 31–50; V.L. Ménage, "Beginnings of Ottoman Historiography"; Shinder, "Early Ottoman Administration"; Murphey, "Ottoman Historical Writing."
74. For a list of these studies, which focus mainly on the upper reaches of the bureaucracy, see Darling, *Revenue-Raising and Legitimacy,* 49–50 and nn3, 4.
75. Woodhead, "From Scribe to Litterateur," 70.
76. Darling, "Treatise on Accounting Methods"; Woodhead, "Ottoman Scribal Service."
77. See Fleischer, *Bureaucrat and Intellectual;* Douglas A. Howard, "Genre and Myth in the Ottoman Advice for Kings Literature."

REFERENCES

Abu Bakr b. al-Zaki. 1972. *Ravzat al-Kuttāb va Hadikat al-Albāb,* ed. Ali Sevim. Ankara: Türk Tarih Kurumu Basımevi.

Ali Tuğra-yı Hümāyun. 1333/1914–15; 1334/1915–16. *Tarih-i Osmani Encümeni Mecmuası* 43:53–58; and 44:109–25.

Ahmet Akgündüz and Türk Dünyası Araştırmaları Vakfı İlim Hey'eti. 1980. *Şeriyye Sicilleri: Mahiyeti, Toplu Kataloğu ve Seçme Hükümler.* 2 vols. Istanbul: Türk Dünyası Araştırmaları Vakfı.

Aktaş, Necati. 2000. *Başbakanlık Osmanlı Arşivi Rehberi.* Istanbul: Devlet Arşivleri Genel Müdürlüğü.

Alpay, Meral, and Safiye Özkan. 1982. *İstanbul Kütüphaneleri.* Istanbul: Ünal.

Andrews, Walter G. 1985. *Poetry's Voice, Society's Song: Ottoman Lyric Poetry.* Seattle: University of Washington Press.

—— 1996. Speaking of Power: The "Ottoman Kaside." In *Qasida Poetry in Islamic Asia and Africa.* Vol. 1, *Classical Traditions and Modern Meanings,* ed. Stefan Sperl and Christopher Shackle, pp. 281–300. Leiden: E.J. Brill.

Aydın, Bilgin, and Rıfat Günalan. 2008. *XV–XVI. Yüzyıllarda Osmanlı Maliyesi ve Defter Sistemi.* Istanbul: Yeditepe Yayınevi.

Ayverdi, Ekrem Hakkı. 1953. *Fatih Devri Hattatları ve Hat Sanatı.* Istanbul: İstanbul Matbaası.

Babinger, Franz. 1966. Die grossherrliche Tughra: Ein Beitrag zur Geschichte des osmanischen Urkundenwesens. *Abhandlungen zur Geschichte Südosteuropas und Levante* 2:99–109. Munich: Rudolf Trofenik.

Al-Baghdādī, Bahā al-Din Muhammad. 1937. *Al-Tavassul ilā al-Tarassul,* ed. Ahmad Bahmanyār and Muhammad Qazvini. Tehran: Shirkat al-Sahami.

Baltacı, Cahit. 1989. *İslam Paleografyası (Diplomatik—Arşivcilik).* Istanbul: Marmara Üniversitesi İlâhiyat Fakültesi Vakfı Yayınları.

Beldiceanu-Steinherr, Irène. 1967. *Recherches sur les actes des règnes des sultans Osman, Orkhan et Murad I.* Societas Academic Dacoromana, Acta Historica, 7. Monachii: Societatea Academica Romana.

Biegman, Nicolaas H. 1967. Introduction. In *The Turco-Ragusan Relationship According to the Firmāns of Murad III (1575–1596) Extant in the State Archives of Dubrovnik.* The Hague: Mouton.

—— 1969. Some Peculiarities of Firmans Issued by the Ottoman Treasury in the 16th Century. *Archivum Ottomanicum* 1:9–13.

Birnbaum, Eleazar. 1976. The Ottomans and Chagatay Literature. *Central Asiatic Journal* 20:157–90.

Björkman, Walther. 1952. Eine türkische Briefsammlung aus dem 15 Jahrhundert. In *Documenta Islamica Inedita,* ed. Johann Fück, pp. 189–96. Berlin: Akademie-Verlag.

—— 1956. Die Anfänge der türkischen Briefsammlungen. *Orientalia Suecana* 5:20–29.

Buzov, Snjezana. 2007. The World of Ottoman Mecmuas. Paper given at Great Lakes Ottoman Workshop, Ann Arbor, April 21–22.

Darling, Linda T. 1989. A Treatise on Accounting Methods by an Official of the Ottoman Financial Administration in the 16th Century. In *Third International Congress on the Economic and Social History of Turkey, Proceedings,* ed. Heath W. Lowry and Ralph M. Hattox, pp. 123–26. Istanbul: Isis Press.

—— 1990. Ottoman Salary Registers as a Source for Economic and Social History. *Turkish Studies Association Bulletin* 14:13–33.

—— 1996. *Revenue-Raising and Legitimacy: Tax Collection and Finance Administration in the Ottoman Empire, 1560–1660.* Leiden: E.J. Brill.

—— 2002. The Renaissance and the Middle East. In *A Companion to the Worlds of the Renaissance,* ed. Guido Ruggiero, pp. 55–69. Oxford: Blackwell.

—— 2004. Persianate Sources on Anatolia and the Early History of the Ottomans. *Studies on Persianate Societies* 2:126–44.

—— 2008. The Development of Ottoman Governmental Institutions in the 14th Century: A Reconstruction. In *Living in the Ottoman Ecumenical Community: Essays in Honour of Suraiya Faroqhi,* ed. Vera Costantini and Markus Koller, pp. 17–34. Leiden: E.J. Brill.

Derdiyok, İ. Çetin. 1994. Eski Türk Edebiyatı'nda Mektup Yazma Kuralları Hakkında Bilgi Veren En Eski Eser: Ahmed Dā'i'nin Teressül'ü. *Toplumsal Tarih* 1(6): 56–59.

Elker, Salâhaddin. 1953. *Divan Rakamları.* Ankara: Türk Tarih Kurumu Basımevi.

Ertaylan, İsmail Hikmet. 1952. *Ahmed-i Dā'i: Hayatı ve Eserleri.* Istanbul: İstanbul Üniversitesi Edebiyat Fakültesi.

Erzi, Adnan S. 1950. Sarı Abdullah Efendi Münşeatının Tavsifi. *Belleten* 14:631–47.

Fekete, Lajos. 1926. *Einführung in die osmanisch-türkische Diplomatik der türkischen Botmässigkeit in Ungarn*. Budapest: Königliche Ungarische Universitätsdruckerei.

—— 1955. *Die Siyāqat-Schrift in der türkischen Finanzverwaltung*. 2 vols. Budapest: Akademiai Kiádo.

—— 1957. Arbeiten der grusinischen Orientalistik auf dem Gebeite der türkischen und persischen Paläographie und die Frage der Formel Sözümüz. *Acta Orientalia Academiae Scientiarum Hungaricae* 7:1–20.

Feridun Bey, Ahmed. 1848–49. *Mecmu`a-i Münşe`āt-i Selātin*. 2 vols. Istanbul: n.p.

—— 1858. *Mecmu`a-i Münşe`āt-i Selātin*. Second recension, 2 vols. Istanbul: Dār et-Tibā`a el-`Amire.

Ferrard, Christopher. 1982, 1984. The Development of an Ottoman Rhetoric up to 1882. *Osmanlı Araştırmaları* 3:165–88; 4:19–34.

Findley, Carter Vaughn. 1970. The Legacy of Tradition to Reform: Origins of the Ottoman Foreign Ministry. *International Journal of Middle East Studies* 1:334–57.

—— 1988. *Ottoman Civil Officialdom: A Social History*. Princeton: Princeton University Press.

Fleischer, Cornell H. 1984. Scribal Training and Medrese Education in the 16th-Century Ottoman Empire. *Turkish Studies Association Bulletin* 8(1): 27–29.

—— 1986a. *Bureaucrat and Intellectual in the Ottoman Empire: The Historian Mustafa `Ali (1541–1600)*. Princeton: Princeton University Press.

—— 1986b. Preliminaries to the Study of the Ottoman Bureaucracy. *Journal of Turkish Studies* 10:135–42.

—— 1994. Between the Lines: Realities of Scribal Life in the 16th Century. In *Studies in Ottoman History in Honour of Professor V. L. Ménage,* ed. Colin Heywood and Colin Imber, pp. 45–61. Istanbul: İsis Press.

Gökbilgin, M. Tayyib. 1951–53. Murad I. Tesisleri ve Bursa İmareti Vakfiyesi. *Türkiyat Mecmuası* 10:217–34.

—— 1979. *Osmanlı İmparatorluğu Medeniyet Tarihi Çerçevesinde Osmanlı Paleografya ve Diplomatik İlmi*. Istanbul: İstanbul Üniversitesi Edebiyat Fakültesi Yayınları.

Göyünç, Nejat. 1962. Das sogenannte Ġāme`o'l-Hesāb das `İmād as-Sarāwi. Ph.D. diss., Georg-August-Universität.

—— 1994. Osmanlı Maliyesinde İlhanlı Tesirleri. In *Aspects of Ottoman History: Papers from CIEPO IX, Jerusalem,* ed. Amy Singer and Amnon Cohen, pp. 162–66. Scripta Hierosolymitana, 35. Jerusalem: Magnes Press.

Guboglu, Mikhail. 1958. *Paleografia ši diplomatica turco-osmana: Studiu ši album*. Bucharest: Editura Academiei Republicii Populare Romîne.

Günday, Dündar. 1974. *Arşiv Belgelerinde Siyakat Yazısı Özellikleri ve Divan Rakamları*. Ankara: Türk Tarih Kurumu Basımevi.

Güvemli, Oktay. 1995. *Türk Devletleri Muhasebe Tarihi: Osmanlı İmparatorluğu'na*

Kadar. Muhasebe Öğretim Üyeleri Bilim ve Dayanışma Vakfı, Vol. 1. Istanbul.

Hagen, Gottfried. 2003. Translations and Translators in a Multilingual Society: A Case Study of Persian-Ottoman Translations, Late 15th to Early 17th Century. *Eurasian Studies* 2:95–134.

Halil, Mükrimin. Feridun Bey Münşeatı. *Tarih-i Osmani Encümeni Mecmuası* 63–77 (1918–21): 161–68; *Türk Tarihi Encümeni Mecmuası* 1.78 (1921–22): 37–46; 2.79 (1921–22): 95–104; 4.81 (1921–22): 216–26.

Halman, Talat Sait. 1973. The Ancient and Ottoman Legacy. *Review of National Literatures* 4(1): 27–52.

Heyd, Uriel. 1960. *Ottoman Documents on Palestine, 1552–1615: A Study of the Firman According to the Mühimme Defteri.* Oxford: Clarendon Press.

Hinz, Walther. 1952. *Risāla-yi Falakiyya der 'Ilm-i Siyāqat, ta'lif Abd 'Allāh b. Muhammad b. Kiyā al-Māzandarānī.* Wiesbaden: Franz Steiner.

Holbrook, Victoria Rowe. 1994. *The Unreadable Shores of Love: Turkish Modernity and Mystic Romance.* Austin: University of Texas Press.

Horn, P. 1906. Der Dichter Sultan Selim I. *Zeitschrift der Deutschen Morgenländischen Gesellschaft* 60:97–111.

Horniker, A.L. 1966. Ottoman-Turkish Diplomatics: A Guide to the Literature. *Balkan Studies* 7:135–54.

Howard, Douglas A. 2007. Genre and Myth in the Ottoman Advice for Kings Literature. In *The Early Modern Ottomans: Remapping the Empire,* ed. Virginia H. Aksan and Daniel Goffman, pp. 137–66. Cambridge: Cambridge University Press.

el-Hoyi, Hasan b. `Abdi'l-Mu'min. 1963. *Günyetü'l-Kātib ve Münyetü't-Tālib, Rüsumu'r-Resā'il ve Nücumu'l-Fazā'il,* ed. Adnan Sadık Erzi. Ankara: Türk Tarih Kurumu Basımevi.

İlaydın, Hikmet, and Adnan Sadık Erzi. 1957. XVI. Asra āit bir Münşeāt Mecmuası. *Belleten* 21:221–52.

İnalcık, Halil. 1954. *Hicrī 835 Tarihli Suret-i Defter-i Sancak-ı Arvanid.* Türk Tarih Kurumu Yayınları, ser. 14, no. 1. Ankara: Türk Tarih Kurumu Basımevi.

—— 1962. The Rise of Ottoman Historiography. In *Historians of the Middle East,* ed. B. Lewis and P.M. Holt, pp. 152–67. Historical Writing on the Peoples of Asia, 4. Oxford: Oxford University Press.

—— 1965. Adāletnāmeler. *Belgeler* 2(3-4): 49–145.

—— 1973. *The Ottoman Empire: The Classical Age, 1300–1600,* trans. Norman Itzkowitz and Colin Imber. London: Weidenfeld and Nicolson.

—— 1980. Osmanlı Bürokrasisinde Aklām ve Muāmelāt. *Osmanlı Araştırmaları* 1:1–14.

—— 1986. The Appointment Procedure of a Guild Warden (Ketkhudā). *Wiener Zeitschrift für die Kunde des Morgenlandes* 76:135–42.

—— 1994. How to Read `Ashık Pasha-zāde's History. In *Studies in Ottoman History in Honour of Professor V. L. Ménage,* ed. Colin Heywood and Colin Imber, pp. 139–56. Istanbul: İsis Press. Rpt. in Halil İnalcık, Essays in Ottoman History (Istanbul: Eren Yayıncılık, 1998), pp. 31–50.

İz, Fahir. 1976. Ottoman and Turkish. In *Essays on Islamic Civilization: Presented to Niyazi Berkes,* ed. Donald P. Little, pp. 118–39. Leiden: E.J. Brill.

Al-Kâshǵarî, Mahmud. 1982. *Compendium of the Turkic Dialects (Dīwān Lugat at-Turk),* ed. and trans. Robert Dankoff with James Kelly. Sources of Oriental Languages and Literatures, 7. Cambridge, MA: Harvard University Printing Office.

Kastritsis, Dimitris. 2006. History-Writing in the Court of Mehmed I and the Representation of Relations between Ottoman Princes of the Interregnum. Paper presented at the Middle East Studies Association Convention, Boston, November 18–21.

Köprülü, Mehmed Fuad. 1926[1984]. *Türk Edebiyatı Tarihi.* Reprint. Istanbul: Ötüken.

—— 1992. *The Seljuks of Anatolia: Their History and Culture According to Local Muslim Sources,* trans. Gary Leiser. Salt Lake City: University of Utah Press.

Kraelitz[-Griefenhorst], Friedrich. 1921. *Osmanische Urkunden in türkischer Sprache aus der zweiten Hälfte des 15. Jahrhunderts: Ein Beitrag zur osmanischen Diplomatik.* Sitzungsberichte der Akademie der Wissenschaftern, Philosophische-Historische Klasse 197, III. Vienna: Akademie der Wissenschaften.

Kraelitz-Griefenhorst, Friedrich von. 1925. Studien zur osmanischen Urkundenlehre, I: Die Handfeste (Pençe) der osmanisch Wezire (Mit drei Tafeln). *Mitteilungen zur osmanischen Geschichte* 2:257–68.

Kutukoğlu, Mübahat S. 1998. *Osmanlı Belgelerinin Dili (Diplomatik).* Istanbul: Kubbealtı Akademisi Kültür ve San'at Vakfı.

Lugal, Necâti, and Adnan Erzi, eds. 1956. *Fâtih Devrine âit Münşeât Mecmuası.* İstanbul Enstitüsü Yayınları (İstanbul: İstanbul Matbaası).

Mansuroğlu, Mecdut. 1954. The Rise and Development of Written Turkish in Anatolia. *Oriens* 7:250–64.

Matuz, Josef. 1970. Über die Epistolographie und Inša'-Literatur der Osmanen. Deutscher Orientalistentag, 1968. *Zeitschrift der Deutschen Morgenländischen Gesellschaft,* Supplementa I, 2:574–94.

Ménage, V.L. 1962. The Beginnings of Ottoman Historiography. In *Historians of the Middle East,* ed. Bernard Lewis and P.M. Holt, pp. 168–79. Historical Writing on the Peoples of Asia, 4. Oxford: Oxford University Press.

Mengüç, Murat Cem. 2006. Creativity and Pluralism in 15th-Century Ottoman Historiography. Paper presented at the Middle East Studies Association Convention, Boston, Nov. 18–21.

Minorsky, V. 1942. The Poetry of Shāh Ismā'īl I. *Bulletin of the School of Oriental and African Studies* 19:1006a–53a.

Mitchell, Colin. 1997. Safavid Imperial Tarassul and the Persian Inshā' Tradition. *Studia Iranica* 26:173–209.

Murphey, Rhoads. 1990. Ottoman Census Methods in the Mid-16th Century: Three Case Histories. *Studia Islamica* 71:115–26.

—— 1993–94. Ottoman Historical Writing in the 17th-Century: A Survey of the General Development of the Genre after the Reign of Sultan Ahmed I (1603–1617). *Archivum Ottomanicum* 13:277–311.

Nabipour, Mirkamal. 1973. *Die beiden persischen Leitfäden des Falak `Alā-ye Tabrīzī über das staatliche Rechnungswesen im 14. Jahrhundert.* Göttingen: Georg-August-Universität.

Najib Ullah. 1963. *Islamic Literature: An Introductory History with Selections.* New York: Washington Square Press.

Nedkov, Boris K. 1966. *Osmanoturska Diplomatika i Paleografija, I.* Sofya: Nauka i Izkustvo.

Nikolaev, V. 1954. *Watermarks of the Ottoman Empire.* Sofia: Bulgarian Academy of Sciences.

Parmaksızoılu, İsmet, and Sabih Acun, eds. 1979– . *Türkiye Yazmaları Toplu Kataloğu.* Ankara: T.C. Kültür Bakanlığı, Kütüphaneler Genel Müdürlüğü.

Piterberg, Gabriel. 2003. *An Ottoman Tragedy: History and Historiography at Play.* Berkeley: University of California Press.

Popov, Nikola. 1955. *Paleografski osobenosti na cislitelnite imena v. pismoto siyakat.* Sofia: Bulgarska Akademiia na Naukite.

Remler, Philip. 1980. New Light on Economic History from Ilkhanid Accounting Manuals. *Iranian Studies* 13:157–77.

Reychman, Jan, Ananiasz Zajaczkowski, and Andrew S. Ehrenkreutz. 1968. *Handbook of Ottoman-Turkish Diplomatics.* The Hague: Mouton.

Sevim, Ali. 1961. Anadolu Selçuklularına ait bir Eser: Ravzatü'l-Küttab ve Hadikatü'l-Elbāb. *Tarih Vesikaları* 13:388–418.

Shaw, Stanford J., and Ezel Kural Shaw. 1976. *The History of the Ottoman Empire and Modern Turkey.* 2 vols. Cambridge: Cambridge University Press.

Shinder, Joel. 1971. Ottoman Bureaucracy in the Second Half of the 17th Century: The Central and Naval Administrations. Ph.D. diss., Princeton University.

—— 1978. Early Ottoman Administration in the Wilderness. *International Journal of Middle East Studies* 9:497–517.

Sohrweide, Hanna. 1950. Dichter und Gelehrte aus dem Osten im osmanischen Reich (1453–1600): Ein Beitrag zur türkisch-persischen Kulturgeschichte. *Der Islam* 46:263–302.

Stojanow, Valery. 1983. *Die Entstehung und Entwicklung der osmanisch-türkischen Paläographie und Diplomatik, mit einer Bibliographie, Islamkundliche Untersuchungen.* Berlin: Klaus Schwarz Verlag.

Tāci-zāde Sa'di Çelebi. 1956. *Tāci-zāde Sa'dī Çelebi Münşeātı,* ed. Necāti Lugal and Adnan Erzi. İstanbul Enstitüsü Yayınları. Istanbul: İstanbul Matbaası.

Tekin, Şinasi. 1996. Fatih Sultan Mehmed Devrine āit bir İnşā Mecmuası. *Journal of Turkish Studies* 20:267–315.

Temir, Ahmet. 1960. Die arabisch-uigurische Vakf-Urkunde von 1326 des Emirs Šeref el-Din Ahmed b. Çakırca von Sivas. *Wiener Zeitschrift für die Kunde des*

Morgenländes 56:232–40.

Tezcan, Baki. 2001. Searching for Osman: A Reassessment of the Deposition of the Ottoman Sultan Osman II (1618–1622). Ph.D. diss., Princeton University.

Togan, Ahmet Zeki Validi. 1931. Mogollar Devrinde Anadolu'nun İktisadî Vaziyeti. *Türk Hukuk ve İktisadi Tarihi Mecmuası* 1:1–42. Trans. by Gary Leiser, Economic Conditions in Anatolia in the Mongol Period. *Annales Islamologiques* 25 (1991): 203–40.

Turan, Osman. 1958. *Türkiye Selçukluları Hakkında Resmi Vesikalar.* Ankara: Türk Tarih Kurumu Basımevi.

Umur, Suha. 1980. *Osmanlı Padişah Tuğraları.* Istanbul: Cem Yayınevi.

Ünver, Ahmet Süheyl. 1931. Siyakat Yazısı ve Quyudu Atika. *İstanbul Belediye Mecmuası* 87:88–95.

Uzunçarşılı, İsmail Hakkı. 1926. Türk Yazılarının Tetkikına Medhal. *İstanbul Üniversitesi İlahiyat Fakültesi Mecmuası* 2(5-6): 111–36.

—— 1937. *Anadolu Beylikleri ve Akkoyunlu, Karakoyunlu Devletleri.* Ankara: Türk Tarih Kurumu Basımevi.

—— 1940. Osmanlı Devleti Zamanında Kullanılmış Olan Bazı Mühürler Hakkında bir Tetkik. *Belleten* 4:495–544 and pls. 86–108.

—— 1941a. Buyruldı. *Belleten* 5:289–318 and pls. 88–107.

—— 1941b. Çandarlı Zâde Ali Paşa Vakfiyesi, 808 H./1405–1406 M. *Belleten* 5:549–76.

—— 1941c. Gazi Orhan Bey Vakfiyesi. *Belleten* 5:277–88 and pls. 86–87.

—— 1941d. Tuğra ve Pençeler ile Ferman ve Buyuruldulara Dair. *Belleten* 5:101–57 and pls. 24–60.

—— 1959. *Topkapı Sarayı Müzesi Mühürler Seksiyonu Rehberi.* Istanbul: Şehir Matbaası.

Uzunçarşılı, İsmail Hakkı, İbrahim Kemāl Baybura, and Ülkü Altındağ, eds. 1985– . *Topkapı Sarayı Müzesi Osmanlı Saray Arşivi Kataloğu.* Ankara: Türk Tarih Kurumu Basımevi.

Velkov, Asparouch T. 1979. Les notes complémentaires dans les documents financiers ottomans des XVIe–XVIIIe siècles: Étude diplomatique et paléographique. *Turcica* 11:37–77.

—— 1985. Les Başdefterdar ottomans et leurs "signatures à queue" (XVIe–XVIIIe s.). *Turcica* 16:173–210.

Velkov, Asparukh, and Stefan Andreev. 1983. *Vodni znatsi v. osmanoturkite dokumenti, 1. Tri luni.* Sofia: Bozhidar Raikov.

Wittek, Paul. 1957. Zu einingen frühosmanischen Urkunden (I). *Wiener Zeitschrift für die Kunde des Morgenlandes* 53:300–313.

Woodhead, Christine. 1982. From Scribe to Litterateur: The Career of a 16th-Century Ottoman Katib. *Bulletin of the British Society for Middle Eastern Studies* 9:55–74.

—— 1988. Ottoman İnşa and the Art of Letter-Writing: Influences upon the Career of the Nişancı and Prose Stylist Okçuzade (d. 1630). *Osmanlı Araştırmaları* 7-8:143–59.

—— 1992. Research on the Ottoman Scribal Service, c. 1574–1630. In *Festgabe an Josef Matuz: Osmanistik—Turkologie—Diplomatik,* ed. Christa Fragner and Klaus Schwarz, pp. 311–28. Berlin: Klaus Schwarz Verlag.

Yahyā bin Mehmed el-Kātib. 1971. *Menāhicü'l-İnşā.* Edited by Şinasi Tckin. Sources of Oriental Languages and Literatures, 2. Roxbury, MA: Orient Press.

Yazır, Mahmud. 1941. *Siyakat Yazısı.* Istanbul: Vakıflar Umum Müdürlüğü Neşriyatı.

—— 1942. *Eski Yazıları Okuma Anahtarı.* Istanbul: Cumhuriyet Matbaası.

Yesevi, Ahmed. 1993. *Divan-i Hikmet.* Ankara: Türkiye Diyanet Vakfı.

Yusuf Khass Hājib. 1983. *Wisdom of Royal Glory (Kutadgu Bilig): A Turko-Islamic Mirror for Princes,* trans. Robert Dankoff. Chicago: University of Chicago Press.

Yuvalı, Abdulkadir. 1995. L'influence des Ilkhanat sur les institutions de l'empire ottoman. In *Histoire économique et sociale de l'empire ottoman et de la Turquie (1326–1960),* ed. Daniel Panzac, pp. 751–54. Paris: Peeters.

Zilli, Ishtiyaq Ahmad. 2000. Development of Inshā Literature to the End of Akbar's Reign. In *The Making of Indo-Persian Culture: Indian and French Studies,* ed. Muzaffar Alam, Francoise Nalini Delvoye, and Marc Gaborieau, pp. 309–49. New Delhi: Manohar.

6

Persian Rhetoric in the Safavid Context: A 16th Century Nurbakhshiyya Treatise on Inshā

COLIN P. MITCHELL

INTRODUCTION: THE *INSHĀ* TRAJECTORY

The emergence and spread of New Persian across greater Iran, Central Asia, and beyond to Anatolia, the Caucasus, and South Asia was undoubtedly one of the most profound developments in terms of literary and administrative dynamics in the medieval Islamic world. By the 16th century, it was common for Ottoman scribes in Istanbul and Uzbek litterateurs in Samarqand to produce Persian prose and poetry, while administrators and literati across the Indo-Gangetic plain, from Lahore to Dacca, functioned consistently in Persian. While Arabic was the domain of religious scholars and pedantic jurists, and Turkish was spoken primarily among sultans and the tribesmen who made up their military, medieval Persian was often the language of aesthetic choice for poets, literati, administrators, and proponents of courtly culture (*adab*) across the central Islamic world for the medieval and early modern periods.

Literary and cultural articulation in the central Islamic lands had been dominated by the Arabic language since the 7th and 8th centuries, but indigenous Iranian languages such as Soghdian, Bactrian, Khwārazmian, and Pahlavi Persian had managed initially to continue at a vernacular level, and indeed played a crucial role in the preservation of many pre-Islamic oral traditions and epic narratives. With the 9th-century emergence of the

Sāmānid dynasty (818–919) in Bukhara and their governance of Central Asia on behalf of the ʿAbbāsids, we see a local Persian-speaking polity consciously reviving the legacy of the Sasanians. As libraries and workshops proliferated in Bukhara, a new and stylized Persian reemerged, now using the Arabic script that fused older vocabulary and pre-Islamic concepts with the energetic and robust stylistic motifs and imagery found in the Qur'ān, the traditions of the Prophets, hagiographies of Companions, and the popular poetic Bedouin tradition. With this New Persian "renaissance," seminal Arabic texts such as al-Tabari's *History of the Prophets and Kings* were translated, as were numerous other works on exegesis, doctrine, theology, grammar, and poetry. However, the most recognizable manifestation of this enduring renaissance was the gradual emergence of a Perso-Islamic poetic canon comprising the work of Firdausi, Daqiqi, Rudaki, Nizāmi, Anvari, Khāqāni, among others. This literary canon played a role in reenergizing and codifying the Persian language, and in tandem New Persian became the preeminent language of historical chronicles, geographies, ethics manuals, political philosophy, and belles-lettres in the central Islamic lands for the next seven hundred years.

While New Persian was adopted nominally as the official language of administration by newly arrived Turkish dynasties such as the Ghaznavids (997–1186) and the Khwārazmshāhs (1077–1231), it is nonetheless more accurate to talk about "Arabo-Persian" when discussing medieval Islamic administrative texts. Indeed, from the perspective of a standard medieval Islamic chancellery, such hybridity has discrete historical roots. In the 7th and 8th centuries, Persian scribes, secretaries, and literati had been among the first co-opted groups to work closely with Arab tribal commanders and the establishment of provisional municipal and provincial governments. When the Abbasids subsequently established their new imperial capital of Baghdad in the former heart of the Sasanian empire, the Sawād region of the Tigris-Euphrates complex, the pre-Islamic Persian legacy became clear as Arabized Persians such as ʿAbd Allāh ibn al-Muqaffaʿ endeavored to rearticulate older Pahlavi administrative traditions. Moreover, it was polyglot Persians who sparked the shuʿubiyya literary movement of the 8th and 9th centuries to articulate their frustrations (in Arabic) with the ethnic chauvinism of the Arab tribes. By the 11th century, New Persian had become sufficiently popular to spread westwards from Central Asia under the auspices of the Saljuqs, who in turn employed and patronized Persian bureaucrats and administrators to run their empire. As a result, medieval administrations and chancelleries in Anatolia, Iran, and Central Asia entered into a new phase of administrative discourse which was effectively a hybridization between the flair and vividness of Persian prose and the exactitude and sanctity enshrined in Arabic grammar and lexicography. The fulcrum of this discourse was the *inshā* tradition.

From a general, contemporary perspective the term inshā denotes prose composition and essay writing, but it entailed much more in the classical and medieval milieus. On the one hand, inshā was a general operative rubric for any administrative and diplomatic material produced by scribes (*kātibs*) in a chancellery (*divān*). Thus, a collection of inshā could include formal correspondence among sovereigns, princes, viziers, judges, and courtiers as well as mundane appointments, royal decrees, and diplomas of investiture. On the other hand, by the 15th century *inshā* had grown beyond such exclusive bureaucratic orientations and emerged as the dominant means of sophisticated prose articulation among literati, poets, and scholar-bureaucrats. This sense of *inshā* as a formal discursive practice saw chancellery stylists adopting and adapting various rhetorical tools and poetic devices to produce epistles and epistolary essays which abounded in rhymed prose (*saj'*). *Inshā* is inherently connected with formal poetry in the Perso-Islamic traditions, and it is no surprise that many of the literary leviathans of the medieval period—Afzal al-Din Khāqāni, Rashid al-Din Vatvāt, `Abd al-Rahmān Jāmi, Husain Vā`iz Kāshifi—produced their own collections of inshā writing.[1] Put another way, *inshā* and the writing of *munsha'āt* (letters) by *munshis* (those who practice *inshā*) was yet another means of articulating urban, civilized *adab* culture. In most instances, *inshā* works by medieval *munshis* were more or less compilations of the best epistolary prose-writing of the day. However, there exist some singular didactic treatises which not only educate scribes on the mechanics of epistolography but also pause and deliberate on the intricate relationship between epistemology, rhetoric, poetry, and the art of *inshā*. While the Khwārazmshāh, Atabeg, and Mongol periods were important in this regard, the zenith for Perso-Islamic *inshā* was undoubtedly the Timurid empire of 15th-century Khorasan. Thanks in part to the benefaction of Sultān-Husain Baiqara and the Chaghata'id Turkish magnate Mir `Ali Shir Navā'i, numerous *inshā* collections and manuals were sponsored and produced by administrative and literary luminaries of the day.[2]

THE *INSHĀ-YI ʿĀLAM-ĀRĀ* AND THE
SAFAVID CONTEXT

The topic of this present inquiry is a treatise entitled *Inshā-yi ʿĀlam-ārā* (World-Adorning Inshā) produced in mid-16th-century Isfahan during the reign of the Safavid ruler Shāh Tahmāsp (r. 1524–76).[3] The author of this work is Muhammad al-Husaini ibn Nāsir al-Haqq Nurbakhshi, who informs the reader in his *dibācha* (preface) that this manual was completed in 956/1549–50 in the city of Isfahan. Other than a brief notice by Muhammad Taqi Dānishpazhuh in his seminal 1973 article "Dabiri va Navisandagi (Secretary-ship and Writing)," to the best of my knowledge nothing has been produced about the three extant manuscripts of this work which exist currently in the Āstāna-yi Quds Library in Meshed, the University of Tehran Library, and the National Parliament Library (Kitābkhāna-yi Majlis-i shurā-yi Islāmi) in Tehran.[4]

The *Inshā-yi ʿĀlam-ārā* is worthy of discussion and analysis for a number of reasons. Most importantly, there is a dearth of *inshā* manuals from the reign of Shāh Tahmāsp, and indeed for the entirety of the 16th century. Anonymous "exemplary" *inshā* manuals (i.e., *Majmuʿas, jongs*) are available, but there are a limited number of works that we can identify confidently with authors and dates. For the 16th century, we have an anonymous *inshā* work entitled *Tarassul* which was written in Rajab 931/April 1525 in the city of Astarābād, while Mullā Mir Qāri Gilāni produced his *Sahāʾif al-akhbār* in 974/1566 and one Shaikh Muhammad ibn Shams al-Din compiled an *inshā* work on behalf of Mirzā ʿAli Khān in the late 1580s.[5] A collection of *munshaʾāt* by Mir Mansur ibn Muhammad ibn ʿAli Munshi Shirāzi entitled *Shams al-siyāqat* boasts a small number of letters from the reign of Shāh Tahmāsp, but Dānishpazhuh dates this work into the later 17th century.[6] The famous historian Ghiyāth al-Din Khwāndamir (d. 1534) produced his own *inshā* manual in the early 1520s, the *Nāma-yi nāmi,* but the bulk of the contents are exclusively Timurid, and there is relatively little from the Safavid chancellery itself.[7] For the 16th century, our only contemporaneous inshā works which include extensive Safavid letters are in fact produced outside of Iran, and here I am thinking principally of the *Munshaʾāt al-salātin* by the Ottoman secretary Faridun Beg and the *Inshā-yi Shāh Tāhir* of the former Safavid scholar and teacher who fled to the Deccan in 1520 and worked actively under the patronage of the Nizāmshāh dynasty.[8] The 17th century, specifically the first half, is better represented with respect to well-established *inshā* works. In addition to the *Munsha'āt al-Tusi* by `Abd al-Husain al-Nasir al-Tusi,[9] who was the *munshi al-mamālik* (chief chancellery official) of Shāh `Abbās, we also have the *Nuskha-yi jāmi`a-yi al-murāsalāt-i ulul albāb* of Abu al-Qāsim Haidar Beg Khwughli, which was also compiled in the early to mid-17th century.[10] Lastly, we have the *Munsha'āt-i Tāhir Vahid,* assembled by the *munshi al-mamālik* Muhammad Tāhir Vahid Qazvini on behalf of `Abbās II towards the second half of the 17th century, of which copies abound.[11] Despite these compilations, we are still faced with a lacuna of considerable proportions in our understanding of epistolography in the first half of the 16th century.

Juxtaposed with the largesse and sophistication of the Timurid period, Safavid *inshā* of the 16th and 17th centuries has historically been categorized, like much of later medieval Persian literature, as hyperbolic and embellished, and as such has been disregarded consistently by both historians and literary specialists.[12] The *Inshā-yi `Ālam-ārā,* however, is in many ways more evocative of standardized Perso-Islamic texts on prosody and rhetoric which were produced during the classical period, namely Muhammad ibn `Umar Rāduyāni's *Tarjumān al-balāghat,* Rashid al-Din Vatvāt's *Hadā'iq al-sihr fi daqā'iq al-shi`r,* and Shams-i Qais's *Al-Mu`jam fi ma`āyir ash`ār al-`ajam.*[13] As Marta Simidchieva has pointed out, the Timurid period followed many of the impulses that were established earlier by these works, and their representation in a diluted form during the Safavid period should not be altogether surprising.[14] There was also a lesser-known work devoted exclusively to Persian rhetorical embellishments (*badi`*), the *Badāyi` al-sanāyi`* which was produced in the early 16th century by `Atā Allāh Husaini (d. 1513).[15] However, despite this sense of continuity in the field of Persian rhetoric and its representation in the *Inshā-yi `Ālam-ārā,* the infusion of Shi`ite and Sufi motifs and tropes by Nāsir al-Haqq Nurbakhshi is unprecedented, and we cannot help but see this as a *sui generis* text for understanding late medieval shifts in conceptions of epistolography and prose.

The *Inshā-yi `Ālam-ārā* is also important in that it allows us to explore a more nuanced understanding of the Safavid empire during a crucial stage of its formation. By the mid-16th century, the Safavids had established themselves as the rulers of a nominal Shi`ite empire which comprised the Caucasus, Iraq, the Iranian Plateau, and parts of Central Asia. Unlike their Sunni neighbors—the Ottomans, Uzbeks, and Mughals—the Safavids had fairly heterodox roots as an Azerbaijan-based Sufi *tariqa* (way, rite) which had become increasingly radicalized and militarized during the 15th century. The transition from *ghuluvv* (exaggeration, heterodoxy)-inspired *tariqa* to formal imperial entity began in 1501 when Shāh Ismaʿil captured the city of Tabriz from the Āq Qoyunlus and had himself enthroned as *shāhanshāh* ("king of kings"). Despite such formal pronouncements Ismaʿil Safavi's state was still very much defined by his rank-and-file supporters: thousands of Turkmen tribesmen who collectively referred to themselves as Qizilbāsh ("Red Heads") on account of their distinctive red headgear. To counter such decentralizing elements Ismaʿil decreed that Twelver Shiʿite doctrine was henceforth to regulate all public and private religious activity, and networks of Persian sayyids from Shiʿite strongholds such as Qom, Meshed, and Astarābād worked with newly arrived, Arabic-speaking juridical scholars to establish a new Shiʿite empire in Iran. Ismāʿil strove to negotiate these divergent orthodox and heterodox elements, and employed the martial millenarianism of his Sufi Qizilbāsh *ghāzis* (warriors for the faith) to successfully conquer the Iranian Plateau and Khorasan while patronizing and appointing educated Shiʿite scholars, bureaucrats, and literati to positions of courtly and administrative power.[16] While Ismāʿil's commitment to Twelver Shiʿism is a matter of debate, his son and successor, Shāh Tahmāsp, was well-known for his familiarity and devotion to the Twelver Shiʿite doctrine. His reign saw continued sponsorship of hierocratic elements such as the Arab al-Karaki family from Jabal ʿāmil and the Persian Marʿashi sayyids from Mazandaran, Tabriz, Isfahan, and Qazvin. The confessional ambiguity of the 15th century appears to have been effaced slowly during this period, as scholars look to a number of large-scale wars between the Safavids and their Sunni neighbors and the flight of a number of high-profile religious personalities, poets, painters, and literati from Safavid dominions to Anatolia, Central Asia, and South Asia.[17]

The historiographical emphasis on the surgical binary of Sunni/ Shiʿite is nonetheless unhelpful and reductionist,[18] and one cannot help but wonder how prominent and powerful Sufi brotherhoods such as the Niʿmatullāhiyya, the Naqshbandiyya, and the Hurufiyya influenced the religious terrain of Safavid Iran in the first half of the 16th century. With respect to the Safavid state, any input or collaboration by such peripheral groups after 1501 has been subsumed, or drowned out, by the increased volume of official Safavid sources and Twelver Shiʿite scholarship which emerged sharply and authoritatively in the second half of the 16th century. Indeed, some of the more compelling studies of late have been those that have endeavored to open up the dominant Safavid political and religious narrative, and in doing so, attempt to locate and reposition the various Sufi dynamics of the 16th and 17th centuries.[19] Compounding the difficulty of understanding the official role of such mystical elements is an entrenched scholarly culture of seeing Sufi brotherhoods as loose congregations of ascetic antinomians who eschewed the contamination of collaborating with temporal authorities. As some have suggested, Sufis and Sufi *tariqa*s cannot be easily distinguished from the markets, *madrasa*s, law courts, and imperial palaces of mainstream medieval and early modern Islamic society.[20] While the Bektāshis and Qalandaris were certainly self-marginalized, networks of elite Sufi brotherhoods were integral to the urban and courtly networks of the Timurid empire, and there is good evidence to suggest that these dynamics were in play during Safavid transitions in the first half of the 16th century.[21] Returning to the *Inshā-yi ʿĀlam-ārā,* we discover an intriguing contemporary text which sheds valuable light on the degree to which literate, urbane Sufi elements were able to participate in the ongoing Safavid imperial project. More importantly, we learn that Safavid bureaucrats such as the author of our source, Nāsir al-Haqq Nurbakhshi, could produce administrative-literary texts which reflected clear theosophical inclinations, and in this way the *Inshā-yi ʿĀlam-ārā* gives us an opportunity to reevaluate the degree to which alternate approaches to rhetoric and epistemology were encouraged within the Safavid milieu.

EXPLORING THE WORLD-ADORNING *INSHĀ*

The Majlis copy of the *Inshā-yi ʿĀlam-ārā* consists of roughly 144 folios, which measure roughly 15 x 20 centimeters, with ten to eleven lines of *nastaʿliq* script per folio; many folios have extensive loss of marginalia, including poetry, blessings, and commentaries. The text is concluded with two folios that are replete with verses from various poets, including the Sufi luminary Shāh Niʿmat-Allāh Vali, Shaukat Bukhārāʾi, and Imām ʿAli b. Abu Tālib.[22] By and large, the main text is written in black ink, but rubrics, section headings, as well as Qurʾanic and Hadith quotes are written in red and gold ink.[23] The text is consistently in Persian prose, but there are numerous invocations of Persian poetic couplets (usually introduced as *nazm*s) and Arabic blessings; by and large Persian verses appear to be the author's own poetry or that of contemporaries but Nurbakhshi does appear fond of quoting (in the first twenty or so folios) Hāfiz, Anvari, Khayyām, Rumi, Nizāmi, and on occasion the Timurid poet Jāmi. Interesting supratextual marginalia include a magic square (*wafq al-a`dād*) on f. 29a, and what appear to be numerological talismans for popular medicine entitled *lauh-i hayāt* (tablet of life) and *lauh-i maitāt* (tablet of death) on fol. 31a. On f. 68b, we find a diagram of how two distichs can be squared (*murabba`*) in order to demonstrate an ongoing point about the opening and closing hemistichs of a *rubā`i*.[24] On f. 63a, there is a distinctive break in the text and two lines of illegible Arabic in a *thuluth* script, but a scribe has written 953 (i.e., AD 1546) numerically; moreover, this is followed by a standard introductory invocation of God (*bism Allāh al-rahmān al-rahim*), suggesting the possibility that Nurbakhshi completed this work in stages.[25] For unclear reasons, the section introducing discussions of "letters of highly ranked lords" (*dar mukātibāt-i arbāb-i marātib*) on f. 138a has a clear, perpendicular notation in the top reading "death of āqā Muhammad in Qazvin in the month of Jumāda I 1242 (December 1826)." The colophon reads how the *Inshā-yi `Ālam-ārā* was finished on Monday, the 26th of Shawwāl 1126 by one `Imād ibn `Abd al-samad al-Danyāli.[26] In terms of organization, Nurbakhshi informs us in his *fihrist* (list, table of contents) on f. 24a that there is one *fātiha* (introductory section), three main sections (*sih lam`a*), and a *khātima* (conclusion), but the *fātiha*—a lengthy, tautological discourse on the rules, customs, and ontology of this genre—is the bulk of the *Inshā-yi `Ālam-ārā,* while the first *lam`a* is hastily introduced and concluded between ff. 138a and 142b. The remaining two *lam`as* and *khātima* are absent, but it is entirely possible that these might be addressed in another of Nurbakhshi's works, *Dastur-i inshā,* which Dānishpazhuh describes intriguingly as having "three sections."[27]

After identifying himself on f. 10a, Nurbakhshi explains how he produced this treatise in 956 A.H. in the city of Isfahan on behalf of the city's vizier, whom Dānishpazhuh identifies as Mirzā Fazl-Allāh Mir Mirān.[28] While Iskander Beg Munshi makes brief mention of this vizier and the importance of him and his brother (Mir Abu al-Futuh) to the administration of Shāh Tahmāsp,[29] information about Nurbakhshi himself is negligible. The language, imagery, and thematic interests of this work identifies the author clearly as a Sufi, and it is reasonable to conclude on the basis of his *nisba* (that part of an Islamic name that indicates a person's relationship to a person, place, tribe, order, occupation, etc.) that he enjoyed some kind of proximity to the Nurbakhshiyya Order. The Nurbakhshiyya had emerged as a successful *tariqa* in the late 15th century, and they continued to prosper in the early, transitional years of Shāh Ismā`il. Two sayyid brothers, Sayyid Ja`far and Shāh Qāsim Nurbakhsh, had been prominent personalities in the Nurbakhshiyya Order and eminent administrators in Damghan under Sultān-Husain Baiqara,[30] but were appointed to serve as Safavid bureaucrats after the conquest of Khorasan by Shāh Ismā`il in 1509–10.[31] By the 1530s the Nurbakhshiyya appear to have become effectively marginalized in Iran.[32] However, as will be seen, the nature of Nurbakhshi's writings in the *Inshā-yi `Ālam-ārā* provides sufficient evidence to reevaluate the position of the Nurbakhshiyya during the reign of Shāh Tahmāsp.

The *Inshā-yi `Ālam-ārā* begins with a lengthy dedication to God and the twelve Imams, which is interspersed with poetry, hadiths, and Qur'anic verses which invoke images and motifs dealing with text and writing (e.g. 29: 48: "and you were not able to receipt a book before this one, nor are you able to transcribe it with your right hand").[33] We quickly appreciate the Shi`ite tenor of this work with numerous poetic elegies and Prophetic traditions about `Ali and his family. Nurbakhshi is particularly attracted to the number twelve, beginning with the hadith of "There are twelve successors from among my family. O God! Send them my understanding and wisdom."[34] He also connects the calendar year with twelve by quoting 9:36 "The number of months in the sight of God is twelve, so ordained by him" which is followed by a *bait* (verse) : "There are twelve kings on the throne of religion / And in one year there are twelve months."[35] Of course, the Persian term for month (*māh*) is a homonym for moon, which Nurbakhshi deftly alludes to by invoking the Arabic hadith "I am like the sun, and `Ali is like the moon" (*anā al-shams wa `Ali ka al-qamar*).[36] Nurbakhshi continues at length in his praise for `Ali, and in doing so intensifies the focus on writing, accounting, and registries as metaphors. After quoting the Arabic hadith "if the gardens were pens, the ocean was ink, the jinns were accountants, and all of mankind was a book, they would not be able to count the virtues of `Ali,"[37] Nurbakhshi fleshes out at length each of these conditional metaphors (which are based largely on Qur'anic imagery), and asks for instance how "if every tree was a pen which was set ablaze on account of praising `Ali, who could raise the great banners of his qualities?" This theme is continued in prose, and is supplemented at length with a number of verses ("if every tree was a pen, every ocean was ink, the world was a page, and humankind was a secretary / would there be places where creatures could write about even one particle of ['Ali's] knowledge?"[38] In another section of praise for 'Ali, Nurbakhshi describes how "if every atom of my being was committed to speech (*nutq*) and expression (*bayān*), I would be an orator (*khwānam sanā*) of your glory until the end of time."[39] On f. 5b, Nurbakhshi introduces the dedicatee of this work, Shāh Tahmāsp, and again we find a discernible chancellery theme which invokes exemplars of the pre-Islamic age: "with the letters *kāf* and *nun*—as in "Be! Behold, it is" (6:73)—and the raqam of "by the Pen, and the (record) which men write" (68:1), the obeyed decrees of grandeur and worldliness and the *farmāns* (orders, commands) of forever-obeyed dominion and conquest have been adorned on the tablets of the age (*bar alwāh-i zamān*) and the pages of the present age (*awrāq-i sahā'if-i dowrān*). These qualities have been joined with kingship of Solomon and the just dominion of Anushirvan."[40]

Nurbakhshi is profuse in his praise of Tahmāsp, and here we see good evidence of the degree to which contemporaries embraced the Safavid propaganda that championed Tahmāsp's sovereignty as part of the pre-eternal program established by God for the Shi'ite Imamate. The Safavid Shāh is linked in personality traits with every one of the twelve Imams,[41] and Nurbakhshi also quotes specific Qur'anic verses which are long-held in the Shi'ite exegetical tradition as proof of the pre-eternal mandate of the Imams, and by extension, the sovereignty of Shāh Tahmāsp.[42] In addition to being "the Just Sultan, the shadow of God" (*al-sultān al-'ādil zill allāh*), Tahmāsp looms large as the "sultan of sultans of the age" (*sultān-i salātin-i zamān*), "the regent of God" (*khalifat rabb al-'ālamin*), and "deputy to the Imams" (*nā'ib a'immat al-ma'sumin*).[43] The auspiciousness of Shāh Tahmāsp's reign is underscored by the circumstances of the date of his birth, and Nurbakhshi includes prose and verse chronograms which signify 919 using the *abjad* system.[44] The month of Tahmāsp's birth—Zu al-Hijja—is cited by the author as the same month in which the Prophet Muhammad is believed to have narrated the two key Prophetic reports of the *hadith-i Harun* and the *hadith-i Ghadir Khumm*: "You are to me like Aaron was to Moses" and "Whosoever considers me his master will also consider 'Ali and his family as his master."[45] Indeed, the Qur'anic verse 17:68–"Truth has arrived and falsehood has vanished"–acquires new meaning with the arrival of Shāh Tahmāsp, who is "the plenipotentiary of the Mahdi, Lord of the Age" (*vakil-i mahdi sāhib al-zamān*). The pre-eternal implications of Tahmāsp's reign are reiterated when Nurbakhshi writes how his accession occurred in the same month that Muhammad allegedly declared "I was a Prophet when Adam was still between clay and water," and that the Qur'anic verse (33:40)–"Muhammad is not a father of any men among you, but a messenger of God and the seal of the prophets"[46] was revealed in Medina.

The scope and purpose of the *Inshā-yi ʿĀlam-ārā* are presented when Nurbakhshi describes how he had been commissioned by Mir Fazl-Allāh Mir Mirān,[47] who wanted "an all-inclusive treatise which gathers together the finer sentences of phrases and provides an intelligent and useful text on the customs, crafts, and beautiful features of this art of rhetoric."[48] Nurbakhshi narrates how this commission from Fazl-Allāh was "from the most honorable of ministers" (*az jānib-i khuddām-i zu'l-ihtirām*) who is "the most sublime paragon of sayyidship, the most regal epitome of the vizierate (*siyādat-panāh-i rafiʿ va vizārat-i dastgāh-i shahryāri*). The ontological purpose of this work and its sponsorship by Mir Fazl-Allāh are expanded to a general discussion of the fundamental importance of administrative prose writing in the establishment and preservation of security and justice in an Islamic state. Here Nurbakhshi invokes the age-old Perso-Islamic tradition of exalting the office of the vizārat, and several folios ensue with prose and poetic commendations for Mir Fazl-Allāh specifically, and bureaucrats and administrators in general. Particularly noteworthy is the author's reliance on the Nahj al-balāghat, a collection of ʿAli's reputed sermons and letters, to demonstrate themes of justice, equity, and societal egalitarianism. In praising Mir Fazl-Allāh's responsible government in Isfahan, Nurbakhshi notes how it complied consistently with ʿAli's admonition: "behave justly with the people, and act in accordance with their needs, because you are treasurers of the people, representatives of the community, and ambassadors of the Imam."[49] Likewise, he quotes other ʿAlid maxims such as "justice puts things in their places" and "the worst minister for you is he who has been a minister for mischievous persons before you because they are abettors of sinners and brothers of the oppressors."[50] The notion of "evil ministers" might very well allude to Mir Fazl-Allāh's predecessor since Nurbakhshi also quotes a Prophetic hadith whereby ʿāisha reported how the Prophet said "when God has a good purpose for a ruler, he appoints for him a sincere minister who reminds him if he forgets and helps him if he remembers; but when Allāh has a different purpose from that for him, he appoints for him an evil minister who does not remind him if he forgets and does not help him if he remembers."[51]

Against this backdrop of good governance, Nurbakhshi's *dibācha* turns to the importance of *inshā,* and the various needs which are fulfilled by epistolary and documentary sciences. The ability to articulate ideas coherently is touted by the author as a sanctified quality, and he buttresses his point with the Arabic maxim of *anā al-afsah* (I am the most eloquent), referring to the Prophet Muhammad's popular description as *afsah al-'arab* (the most eloquent of the Arabs).[52] The first application (*sunuf*) of *inshā* is to ensure petitions (*'arza dāsht*) which consist of claims (*mudda'iyāt*) and requests (*multamisāt*) of those broken-hearted, poor people (*faqirān-i shikasta-bāl*) and ruined folks (*parishān-ahvāl*), which are subsequently brought to the attention of chief ministers and courtiers of the royal courts (*sadr-nishinān-i majālis-i iqbāl va masnad-ārāyān-i mahāfil-i afzāl*).[53] Another application is seen with those missives (*bazzaz*

'*āt*) and letters (*mukātibāt*) which highly ranked nobility (*sā'ir-i arbāb-i darajāt-i 'alā*) write to one another. Nurbakhshi endorses the earthly mandate of the Imamate by insisting that decrees (*amsala*) and orders (*ahkām*) from the Imams are ranked equally with the administrations of sultans, governors, assemblies of great ministers, religious judges, amirs, and viziers (*divān-i salātin va hukkām va majālis-i sudur-i 'uzzām va quzāt-i Islām va umarā va vuzarā*). The writing of the sacred and profane decrees (*ahkām-i shar'iya va 'urfiya*) is the responsibility of eloquent *munshis* who have demonstrated their skill in composition and orthography (*inshā va imlā*).[54] Other types of documents include legal contracts (*qabālāt-i shari'a*), bonds (*tamassukāt*), contracts of purchase (*mubāya'āt*), transactions (*mu'āmalāt*), legal transcripts (*sijillāt*), witness testimonials (*surat-shahādat*), and dispositions (*mazhar-hā*).[55] Nurbakhshi concedes that more mundane genres such as histories (*tavārikh*), narratives (*hikāyāt*), epics (*qissa*), and conferences (*muhāvarāt*) are produced on account of *inshā,* but he is particularly drawn to how discursive writing allows the production of books, panegyrics, and treatises by Sufis ('*ārifān-i muhaqqiq*), which allows them to reveal and unveil (*zuhur va ifshā āvarand*) from the darkness of hidden mystery (*az sawād-i khafā*).[56] Finally, inshā allows the production of genealogies (*nasab nāma-hā*) which, in turn, are critical to sustaining the status and charisma of sayyids (*sādāt*), Shi'ite overseers (*nuqabā*), shrine custodians (*mutawwaliyān*), and shaikhs (*mashāyikh*).[57] In his subsequent general division of the three broad types of *inshā* (*aqsām-i inshā*) discussed in ff. 20a–21b, we learn that the first (*qism-i avval*) deals simply with simple exposition that makes use of abridged metaphors and simple thoughts.[58] This is by and large the domain of those lowly functionaries who busy themselves with matters and issues of state on behalf of the ruler. The second category (*qism-i duvvum*) deals with the writing of letters which make more consistent use of extensive and more complex metaphors and literary devices.[59] The third and last *qism* is for *munshis* and masters of eloquence who are expected to write decrees (*ruqaʿāt*) and letters (*murāsalāt*) with the most rhetorical literary devices (*ablagh-i ʿibārāt*) and the most eloquent metaphors (*afsah-i istaʿārāt*).[60]

The bulk of the remainder of the Inshā-yi ʿĀlam-ārā (ff. 22a–138a) comprises a detailed and nuanced exploration of inshā from a variety of theoretical, methodological, technical, rhetorical, and linguistic perspectives, of which only a few can be addressed with any substance in this present discussion. This notion of rationale was an important one in the *inshā* genre, and most *munshis* and scribes were content to offer their own ontological and epistemological insights in a brief *dibācha* at the beginning of the manuscript; however, in this particular instance, this imperative to understand the provenance and use of scribal writing was of paramount importance. Some of Nurbakhshi's arguments are clearly derived from the impulses found in these *dibāchas*, such as his rationale for writing on the basis that it allows prophets, scholars, historians, and poets to record the revelations, deeds, and events of the time; very similar sentiments can be found in inshā manuals such as Nakhjavani's *Dastur al-kātib*, Khwāndamir's *Nāma-yi nāmi,* and ʿAbd al-Vāsiʿ's *Manshā al-inshā*.[61] The first section by Nurbakhshi on the history of *inshā,* which is styled with a deliberate paronomasia (play on words) in Sufi terms as "the path of *inshā*" (*tariq-i inshā*), begins with discussing the collection and gathering of the different kinds of writing by secretaries in the past. At that time, Nurbakhshi writes, attempts to explain *inshā* (*irād-i inshā*) and expand on its objectives (*bayān-i maqsud*) was such a "rising torrent mixed with different contents" that it brought to mind the mixture of the "water which flows over the rosy-cheeked ones" and "the dust which falls from the cheek mole of the lover."[62] Nurbakhshi explains how the pens of imagination and miraculousness (*kilk-i khiyāl va khāma-yi badāyiʿ*) began writing on the pages of comprehension (*sahifa-yi tafakkur*), and with the ink of purity (*midād-i tabʿ-i safi*), the perfect speech (*nutq-i kāfi-yi vāfi*) was revealed and made clear with the jewels of eloquent allusions (*javāhir-i zavāhir-i ʿibārāt-i fasihiyya)* and the pearls of charming metaphors (*durar-i ghurar-i isti ʿārāt-i malihiyya).*[63]

Returning to the provenance of the inshā tradition, Nurbakhshi talks about those past masters of *inshā* (*qudamā-yi arbāb-i inshā*) who established "the customs of this art of eloquence" (*ādāb-i in fann-i fasāhat*) with pure remnants of Arabic and other foreign languages; with every passing era, contemporary masters had recorded the language of the day for posterity's sake in the form of *munsha'āt* and *tarassulāt* (letters), but they used contemporary metaphors, similes, and other rhetorical devices which reflected their immediate cultural context.[64] In Nurbakhshi's estimation, not one of these "esteemed books" (*musannafāt-i multafāt*) has succeeded in explaining the craft and miracle of this "art of rhetoric" (*fann-i balāghat*). It is at this juncture in the manuscript that the tone and technique of exposition becomes explicitly theosophical, and we sense Nurbakhshi's fascination with a genre that promises so much in the way of hidden truth and esoteric knowledge. When this *mubda'i* (young disciple, i.e., Nurbakhshi) became aware of these antecedent works and began focusing on these issues with respect to perception and knowledge (*ittilā ʿ barin muhtamimāt-i basirat va wuqufi*)—which in itself is an indication of a mystical understanding of this art (*bi-ma'rafat-i in fann*)—he became preoccupied with mastering it. In this sense, Nurbakhshi promises that this treatise will act as a "revealer" (*kāshif*) wherein every one of the customs, features, crafts, and miracles will be described and understood, and thus accomplish what others could not.[65] The Inshā-yi ʿĀlam-ārā endorses inshā as a vehicle of social justice, and argues that it will provide a path for every student and eager apprentice (*tālib, juyanda*) in order that they can illuminate and dazzle the pages of "those [peasants] who are broken-hearted, hopeless, and in a state of ruin." Having outlined his rationale, he succinctly provides his table of contents (*fihrist*) within a clear mystical milieu: the sections are "flashes" (*lam'a*), while the introduction (*fātiha*) will comprise of a "revealing of inshā" (*ifshā-yi inshā*).[66] The three sections (only the first is included in this manuscript) deal with (a) letters of highly ranked individuals; (b) the use of Qur'anic quotes and moral aphorisms in letters; and (c) a general explanation of decrees, letters, orders, *sijjilas*, and *vaqf-nāmas* which had been compiled earlier by masters but are now being properly organized and presented.[67]

For Nurbakhshi, the art of *inshā* and the skill of the *munshi* are metaphors for God's ability to create light and meaning in the universe. With respect to language, *inshā* is synonymous with creation (*khalq*), production (*ijād*), and origination (*āfaridan*), as in 36:79: "He who has created you the first time, He has knowledge of every creation." In this way, the *munshi* must be understood as an inventor (*maujid*), originator (*mubdiʿ*), and a creator (*khāliq*).[68] In fact, it is in the "bridal-hall of thoughts" that the *munshi* adorns the exquisite brides of sublime realities with the jewels of eloquent metaphors and pearls of ornate tropes. In Nurbakhshi's estimation, it is the *munshiyān-i divān* (the stylists of the chancellery)—in the spirit of the Qur'anic admonition *"kun fa-yakun"* ("Be and they were")—who in the darkness of the night sky employ the pen of craftsmanship to adorn the pages of light with the sun-like golden lines of the hidden Truth.[69] This is followed by the Qur'anic quote from 2:257: "From the depths of darkness, we will lead those who have faith to the light." The mystical allegory of the creation of the world as orthography has a rich history in the mystical Perso-Islamic traditions; as al-Suhravardi put it in reference to the letter ba which opens up the Qur'an (*in bism Allāh*): "O Master of the Supreme Circle from which issue all circles, with which terminate all lines, and from which is manifested the First Point which is Thine Exalted World cast upon Thy Universal Form."[70]

In an ensuing subsection, entitled the "Customs of Inshā" (*ādāb-i inshā*), Nurbakhshi expands on his chancellery doctrine of creation *ex nihilo* and discusses approaches to epistemology and text and their function in human history. In a somewhat ecumenical spirit, the author relates how the issue of conveying meaning and intention has no temporal and spatial limits (*har zamān va har makān*). People at all times and in all places communicate in societies through idioms and common language (*mustallih va mutaʿārif*), and it is thanks to eloquent writing that cities of (mystical) truth and knowledge (*madā'in-i haqā'iq va ʿirfān*) are able to exist. In this indulgent spirit, Nurbakhshi observes how in every group of humans (*har guruhi az ādamiyān bani*) there are celestial texts (*kutub-i samavi*) which contain ineffable decrees and commandments which are bestowed on them in their own language (*bi-zabān-i ishān bar ishān nāzil kardānida*), as commanded in 14:4: "We sent not an apostle except [to teach] in the language of his [own] people, in order to make things clear."[71] It is the duty of the *munshis* and orators to make these texts clear by using metaphors, similes, and other tools so that the message is readily understood by elite and plebeians alike (*jumhur-i khwāss va ʿavāmm*); true to his Perso-Islamic orientation, Nurbakhshi points out that many of these terms which were used in the past are "Persian, Arabic and Old Persian" (*fārsi va ʿarabi va fārsi-yi qadim*).[72]

However, it is those who are with gnostic knowledge (*ʿārifān*) who work best in the milieu of *inshā,* and it is the *ʿārifān* who—through the use of metaphors and other literary devices—are able to provide the keys to unlock the doors of truth (*abvāb-i tahqiq*) that would remain otherwise closed for the ages. According to Nurbakhshi, one notable key who had opened such treasuries of secrets (*khazā'in-i asrār*) was Maulānā Amir Husain Nishāpuri Muʿammā'i (d. 1498), a well-known poet and specialist in literary riddles and acrostics from late 15th-century Herat.[73] Nurbakhshi provides a short description of Muʿammā'i and his contribution to the epistolary sciences; we know that Amir Husain Muʿammā'i was in many ways responsible for the popularizing of *muʿammās* (things made obscure, hidden, riddles) during the late Timurid period whereby verses were in fact elaborate constructions of chronograms and formal names.[74] It is no surprise that a scribe chose this location in the manuscript to map out later a prominent magic square (*wafq al-aʿdād*) in the margins of the opposing folio (29a) wherein the columns—with various letters which consist of numerical values based on the *abjad* system—add up to 114, the total number of verses in the Qur'an. The square itself is bordered by the names of the four Archangels: Mikhā'il, Isrāfil, Izrā'il and Jibrā'il, and a *fā'ida* (explanation) appears in Arabic below it. Such squares, also known as *buduh,* are well-known features of Sufi texts since their numerical constancy and symmetry was seen as reflections of God's ordered cosmos. The earliest known square is thought to have appeared in the 10th-century *Rasā'il al-ikhwān al-safā,* while al-Ghazali was sufficiently attracted to the phenomenon that he discussed them extensively in his *Munqiz min al-dalāl.*[75] Its appearance here only underscores the degree to which the *Inshā-yi ʿĀlam-ārā* was circulating among the theosophically inclined *munshis* and scribes in subsequent decades and centuries.

To highlight the rhetorical acrobatics involved in decoding a *muʿammā,* Nurbakhshi provides a quatrain which contains a buried reference to "Amir" which in turn makes clever arrangements with the term *shaid* (meaning "love," or "plaster") and *ganj-i divār* (treasure hidden in a wall). Nurbakhshi explains that, literally and metaphorically, *shaidā'i* ("plaster, love") is the foundation (*tabaqa-yi tavval*) in the construction of a many-layered wall (*tabaqāt-i divār-i gilin*).[76] Nurbakhshi poses the question: how do we explain this *mu'amma* to people who live in places where they use terms such as *muhra* and *china*—rather than *shaid*—to describe the first layer of a wall? The answer is simple: if someone does not understand the particular idiom of *shaid,* this present *mu'amma* is impenetrable. Nurbakhshi extrapolates from this relatively esoteric point to more mundane matters regarding state governance and bureaucracy, and the need for customs and idiomatic expressions to be organized in registries of administrators (*dafātir-i dīvāniyān*) through the collection of state decrees and orders of the time. For example, he describes how original land taxes are called *jāmi'* in the province of Fārs while they are referred to as *bunicha* in Yazd and *kunj* in Isfahan; taxes on bazar merchants in Iraq are called *isnāf* while their equivalents in Azarbaijan were known as *muhtarifa*.[77] Likewise, a standardized tract of property in Yazd is called a *qafiz* while the people of Isfahan and Shiraz use the terms *jarib* and *bayman* respectively.[78] Nurbakhshi argues that it is only the *mun-shis* and *kātibs*—through their dissemination of decrees, commands, and orders—who understand these regional idioms (*istilāhāt*) and local terms. It is the current absence of literary *adab* across all levels of society (*tark-i adab*) which necessitates more than ever the dissemination of this craft of *inshā;* however, decrees, tax assessments, and other documents cannot be produced *ex nihilo* since it is commendable to follow "the writing of the pens and the bases of exposition of the lords of knowledge and wise sayings from past ages" (*zabān-i qalam va bunān-i bayān-i arbāb-i 'ilm va hikam dar savābiq-i azmān*).[79] Nurbakhshi's allusion to a crisis in a prevalent absence of *adab* might indeed be a garden-variety jeremiad, but it also might allude to the cultural disquiet that characterized the Safavid empire since the mid-1530s when Shāh Tahmāsp reversed a policy of healthy patronage for artists, musicians and poets and instead followed the lead of the Shi'ite hierocrats toward promoting an environment of abstemiousness, austerity, and orthopraxy.[80]

After a lengthy narrative (*hikāyat*) about a king's relationship with a poet-cum-administrator—possibly Nizāmi Ganjavi[81]—Nurbakhshi provides a short discussion of the properties of a *munshi* (*sifat-i munshi*). Most importantly, a *munshi* must have a detailed knowledge of Arabic, and here we can sense the endurance of the *'ilm al-balāghat* (science of rhetoric) that had been established by earlier grammarians and rhetoricians of Arabic such as al-Jurjāni and al-Sakkāki. The *munshi* must be familiar with the idiomatic language of all pertinent classes: religious scholars (*ulamā*), accountants (*muhāsibān*), engineers (*muhandisān*), sages (*hukamā*) astrologers (*munajjimān*), poets (*shu'arā*), scribes (*navisandagān*), doctors (*attibā'*), and general notables (*sā'ir-i asnāf-i baraya*).[82] In the event that a *munshi* is not cognizant of the rules and customs of law officials (*arbāb-i shar'*), he cannot comprehend the legal stipulations (*shurut-i shar'i*) and accounting rules (*quyud-i hisābi*) which are the cornerstones in the production of orders, decrees, and other state documents. In the same vein, if a *munshi* is not intimately familiar with linguistics (*'ilm-i lughat*) and the art of Arabic (*fann-i 'arabi*), he will be unable to open up the various meanings of Qur'anic *āyas* (verses).[83] More importantly for Nurbakhshi, a scribe who does not know idioms and expressions used by artistic and scholarly people (*arbāb-i funun va 'ulum*) cannot appreciate the preparation and assembly of the different rhetorical devices which is "what defines this miraculous art."[84] There are three broad types of *munshis* (*sih sinf-i munshi-and*): a) those who command the sources (*sāhib-i bunān*), namely those who write with "exhilarating metaphors" and "world-adorning tropes"; b) those who are good with exposition (*sāhib-bayān*), and who mix stories with clever speech and fine rhetoric; and c) those who can perform both (*sāhib-i bunan va bayān*), and it is this class of *munshi* that excels as both administrators and litterateurs.[85]

What follows is a meandering rhetorical tour of the different literary devices that are employed consistently by poets and prose stylists. As we move through the text, we see increasingly intricate discussions that appear to have little to do with the mundane mechanics of writing petitions, royal decrees, and court correspondence, but in fact refer to an impressive corpus of literary devices that have enjoyed considerable popularity since the advent of New Persian. These are introduced with short expositions (*irād*) which are invariably supplemented by examples (*masal*) in both prose and verse form. The *Inshā-yi 'Ālam-ārā* begins with discussions of rhymed prose (*tasji'*), and its arrangement using the device of *tarsi'* into parallel phrases with respect to sound patterns.[86] He discusses shortly *barā'at-i istihlāl* (arrangement of numerous synonymous words in one sentence), and *iqtibās* (unattributed partial Qur'anic quotations) before focusing on the use of metaphor (*ista'āra*) and metonymy (*kināyat*).[87] These are followed by *ta'kid al-madh bi-ma yushbihu al-zamm* (asteism, praise by apparent vilification, or pseudo-criticism[88]), *tansiq al-sifāt* ("poetic/prose arrangement of contradictory qualities"), *ihām* ("amphibology") and *laff va nashr* ("a form of chiasmus whereby individual elements in one line of poetry are rearranged

in a subsequent line but kept within the same syntactic frame").[89] A very
large section (ff. 48b–62b) is dedicated to *murā`āt-i munāsabāt* which could
be translated as "[rhetorical] observances for particular conditions." There
is a panoply of conditions which are brought up by Nurbakhshi as being appropriate for certain rhetorical phrases and stylings; notable themes include
those dealing with temporal issues such as seasons and festivals (spring,
summer, Nauruz, `id),[90] those dealing with spatial topics (mosques, shrines,
gardens),[91] and as well as certain social parameters (namely rulers, administrators, poets, sages, religious scholars, petitions, taxes, mints, etc.).[92]

After sections on ellipsis (*izmār*), palindromes (*maqlub-i mustavā*) and
rhetorical etymology (*ishtiqāq*), Nurbakhshi describes the phenomenon of
iltizām,[93] and points out how most *qasidas* have in fact been assembled from
baits and lines of verse from earlier poets. The original master of this art,
according to Nurbakhshi, was Jamāl al-Din Salmān Sāvaji of the 13th century but this practice had been revived by a near-contemporary, the Timurid
poet, Maulānā Ahli Shirāzi, who died in 1536.[94] The *Inshā-yi `Ālam-ārā* then
provides a thorough treatment of the practice of *tajnis-i alfāz-i tāmm*, or the
ability to manipulate words and rhyming patters to provide perfect puns and
plays on words in poetry and prose. Nurbakhshi makes reference to a number
of past poets who excelled at *tajnis,* including Salmān Sāvaji, Maulānā Ahli
Shirāzi, and the much earlier Mongol poet, Sayyid Zain al-Din Qudsi. Tell-
ingly, he also mentions his colleague Shāh Qāsim, son of the prominent
Nurbakhshiyya shaikh Qavām al-Din Husain Nurbakhsh, as a master of this
particular skill.[95] Nurbakhshi is deliberate in his discussion of how *munshis*
can combine words which are made up of many of the same letters in the
same order but containing prefixes, suffixes or vowel changes, such as *shān
va nishān, jalāl va ijlāl, raziya va marziya;* likewise, he suggests letters which
can be combined into words on the basis of similar sounding patterns: *jamāl
va kamāl, fusul va usul, ayvān va kayvān, bustān va dustān,* and so on.[96]

Understandably, he makes a distinction among paronomasias (*tajnisiyyāt*),
between oral (*tajnis-i lafzi*) and written (*tajnis-i khatti*), but he does add that
there are some incidences where the two are conjoined (*ijtimā`*) whereby
the written pun is exactly the same as it is pronounced. However, most cases
of *tajnis* are separated (*iftirāq*) and in this situation these are verbal and not
written (*lafzi ast va khatti nist*).[97] He lists good examples of those cases where
the paronomasia is based on their written meaning (*takht/taht* and *bayān/
banān*) while there are those puns which operate better orally (*shabistān/*

shabist). He adds there are many examples of "a general deficient style of tajnis" (*tajnisiyyāt-i nāqis-i a'amm*), whereby poets rearrange letters freely to provide some semblance (*sahifa-i dirafshān/safiha-i darafshān, tavāli'-i fazā'il/matāli'-i favāzil, shaqā'iq-i hadā'iq-ash/shavāriq-i haqā'iq, 'ain-i 'ayān-i sādiqān/ 'ayun-i a'yān-i sādiqān*).[98] To provide some of the best examples of *tajnis*, Nurbakhshi looks to the exemplary poetry (*divan-i iqān*) of Salmān Sāvaji, to make his point and quotes: "The clear purity of your face has the qualities of a rose garden/The paradisical air of your avenue has the [spirit] of eternal life."[99] Nurbakhshi explains that the point of this *tajnis* is that the main words of the first hemistich—*safā'i, sifvat,* and *sifat*—are all *mutamāsil,* or coequals, in that they are made up of the same letters: *vāv, sad, fa'*.[100] Nurbakhshi then provides an extremely lengthy list of words which share the same appearance (*ham-surat*) depending on the location of orthographic dots and which can be used in *tajnis: sikh* and *shih, sanad* and *sayyid, jalil* and *khalil, sang* and *beg,* to mention a few.[101] True to his own admonition that we must look to past models, he mentions the ability of recent poets to approach *tajnis* through the amalgamation of *qasidas* and *masnavis* by past masters.[102] Here, he mentions Sadr al-Din Ismā'il as well as the Ni'matullahi shaikh-cum-vakil, 'Abd al-Bāqi, while later extolling the work of near-contemporaries such as Nizām al-Din Mahmud—mentioned in Sām Mirzā's Tuhfa-yi Sāmi as a master of *mu'ammā* and *balāghat*[103]—and Qavām al-Din Muhammad, whose son worked in Isfahan as an administrator in the mid-16th century.[104] Nurbakhshi is also fond of analyzing the rhetorical complexity of famous verses and blessings from one Khwāja Abu al-Barakat, who had been "one of the most well-known poets of the age of ... Mir 'Ali Shir" (*az mashāhir-i shu'arā'i-yi zamān...Mir 'Ali Shir*).[105] Indeed, this appears to be one Khwāja Abu al-Barakat Qandahāri who had been a prominent poet in the court of Sultān-Husain Baiqara.[106] Nurbakhshi moves from *tajnis* to the issue of hidden, secret meanings in names and phrases, and details how various names of God, Muhammad, 'Ali, the Imams, and the Mahdi can be deconstructed on the basis of these rhetorical tools, as well as *abjad,* or the science of ascribing numerical values to letters. He also discusses a number of Qur'anic texts, hadiths and formulaic blessings which are likewise considered to be epistemologically and numerologically significant.[107]

Between ff. 103a and 138a, Nurbakhshi presents an intense and exclusive analysis of *mu'ammās* which had clearly grown in popularity among litterateurs by the 16th century since it is given fairly short shrift as a major literary technique by Rāduyāni and Shams-i Qais in their own work.[108] *Mu'ammā*s were usually found in distichs or pairs of distichs, in which the object was to unveil hidden references to various letters; upon reading a bait of *mu'ammā*, a reader could conceivably assemble a formal name.[109] We know that this was an especially popular literary device in the 15th and 16th centuries, and Nurbakhshi's emphasis here is not at all surprising.[110] We know that al-Qalqashandi's great Arabic *inshā* manual of the early 15th century includes a lengthy section on *mu'ammā*s and *rumuz* ("things hinted at"), and such devices were often included within the domain of *inshā*.[111] The Chaghata'id poet and statesman under the Timurid ruler Sultān-Husain Baiqara, Mir 'Ali Shir Navā'i, discusses this specific literary phenomenon and identifies several masters: Hāfiz Sa'd, Hājji Abu al-Hasan, Qāzi 'Abd al-Vahhāb Mashhadi, Khwāja Fazl-Allāh Abu al-Laisi, the historian Sharaf al-Din Yazdi, Maulānā 'Alā Shāshi, Maulānā Mir Arghun, and Maulānā Ni'matābādi.[112] The much later 17th-century literary source, the *Tazkira-yi Nasrābādi* confirms this trend in its lengthy presentation of the different *mu'ammā*s penned by major literary figures since the 15th century.[113] Nurbakhshi acknowledges the superlative work of aforementioned Amir Husain Nishāpuri (Mu'ammā'i) in this regard and in fact quotes how a particular verse of Amir Husain could be disassembled and partly rebuilt to form the name of Habib.[114] Despite his enthusiasm for Amir Husain Mu'ammā'i, I had the opportunity to consult a copy of Amir Husain's *Risāla fi al-muammā* in the Bodleian Library and found no evidence that Nurbakhshi borrowed *mu'ammā*s from this text[115]; similarly, no poetic acrostics were copied from the popular ones listed by Nasrābādi.[116] He does, however, admit to replicating a *mu'ammā* for the name 'Aqil which had been first written by Qāzi Amir Husain Yazdi.[117] The list of names, their *mu'ammā*s, and individual analysis is impressive: Habib, Vāsi', Rahib, Adham, Jalāl, Shams, 'Ali, Ahmad, Muhsin, Lāla, Shihāb, Hasan, Bulbul, Masih, Shāh, Amir, Ayub, Zain, Nasr, Nuh, Afriyāb, Qubād, Bāqir, Sa'd, 'Aziz, Tāj, Vais, Nasir, Rashid, Manuchihr, Imān, Abu Sa'id, Shāh Tāhir, Husain, Bābur, Hisām, among others.[118] This lengthy section on the *mu'ammā* concludes with a deconstruction and reassembly of poetic elements to form the name of Shāh Tahmāsp, and his son Sām Mirzā, author of the *Tuhfa-yi Sāmi* and well-known patron of poetry and the arts.[119] Interestingly, the only section where we see a discernible discussion of missives and letters from a chancellery perspective is appended hurriedly and haphazardly to the end of the *Inshā-yi 'Ālam-ārā* in the last

10 folios. This is more consistent with didactic manuals on epistolography, and the emphasis here is noting social stratification and distinction, and how different modes of communication and articulation are needed to address each class. While we sense that sultans are in a different ranking from scribes, who are in turn ranked differently from religious scholars, and so on, Nurbakhshi provides no substantive information here, and it is clear that he is much more enamoured of deciphering the rhetorical arts.

CONCLUSION

In many ways, Nurbakhshi's exposition is singular. First and foremost, this is a treatise that fuses unflinchingly the epistolary art of *inshā* with the intimidating edifice of rhetorical devices and embellishments (*badi'*) associated with the genre of Persian prosody. The *Inshā-yi 'Ālam-ārā* is similar in general structure to seminal works such as the *Tarjumān al-balāghat* and *al-Mu'jam fi ma'āyir ash'ār al-'ajam,* but it does not actively imitate Rāduyāni, Vatvāt or Shams-i Qais in the same manner as Kāshifi demonstrated in his own 15th-century contribution, the *Badāyi' al-afkār.*[120] With respect to the medieval Perso-Islamic *inshā* genre, Nurbakhshi is innovative in that he provides substantially more discussion of theories and examples of Persian rhetoric and embellishments than other didactic *inshā* manuals which operate similarly, such as 'Imād al-Din Mahmud Gāvān's 15th-century *Manāzir al-inshā.*[121] In his perambulatory rationale, Nurbakhshi seems chiefly concerned with identifying and revealing what he sees as an arcane part of literary culture; there is no mistaking that he intended for this treatise to be an explicit analysis of letters and petitions so that justice and addressing of grievances could be assured and guaranteed. Nonetheless, more than ninety percent of this text is concerned with revealing (*ifshā*) the esoteric nature of language and its articulation via rhetorical devices and embellishments, and this gives us good reason to believe that his three main sections (lam'as) were continued in another work or never completed at all. With respect to his analysis of prosody, certain rhetorical topics are ignored or overlooked: for example, nothing is said about popular devices such as *radif,*[122] *talmih* (allusions), and *ijāz* (principles of concision) while Nurbakhshi does provide fairly nuanced and substantive analyses of embellishments such as *tajnis* and *mu'ammās.* Why this is the case is difficult to determine, but almost certainly the proclivity for *mu'ammās* here is rooted in the popularity of this style of poetic riddling in the Timurid period.[123] Nonetheless, this is not exclusively derivative, and the overwhelming bulk of the *mu'ammās* that he provides (over 60) are not borrowed from any of the well-known poets who produced *mu'ammās* in the 15th and 16th centuries.[124]

The *Inshā-yi 'Ālam-ārā* also stands as a distinctive text on rhetoric because Nurbakhshi moves beyond simple discussions of certain literary devices such as *tazmin* (insertions of lines of poetry as well as religious and ethical literature), *tamsil* (use of proverbs), and *iqtibās*. Rather, the *Inshā-yi 'Ālam-ārā* pursues—at least intermittently—a hermeneutical agenda by using these very tools to analyze a number of textual quotes and tropes from the Twelver Shi'ite tradition. Moreover, the use of specific motifs and imagery by Nurbakhshi in his discussion of the provenance of *inshā* (*tariq-i inshā*) and its esoteric rationale (*ifshā-yi inshā*) suggest strong Sufi inclinations, and needless to say such theosophical threads are not found in normative accounts of rhetoric and epistolography. His own name, textual references to the most well-known Nurbakhshiyya personality of the day (Shaikh Qavām al-Din Husain Nurbakhsh) as well as repeated instances of theosophic concepts, terms, and imagery,[125] all combine to suggest that this was indeed a bureaucratic manual produced by a Nurbakhshiyya scholar-bureaucrat. In many ways, such a heterogeneous text is not surprising, given the hybridized nature of the Nurbakhshiyya Order itself in the late 15th and early 16th centuries. Terms and descriptions of Muhammad Nurbakhsh's messianic agenda were more or less directly based on Twelver Shi'ite doctrines, and we can see that a Nurbakhshiyya such as Nāsir al-Haqq was familiar with Shi'ite doctrines on this and other matters. However, as Bashir has pointed out, "Nurbakhsh's messianic discourse was a system that grafted Shi'i traditions onto Sufi cosmology,"[126] and there is much in the *Inshā-yi 'Ālam-ārā* to support the argument that Nāsir al-Haqq Nurbakhshi's Weltanschauung was a bricolage of Sufi impulses and Twelver Shi'ite credo and dogma. As a result, this fascinating source pushes us to reevaluate our conceptions and views of such Sufi Orders in the early Safavid empire. The lively dedication to Shāh Tahmāsp, the proximity of Nurbakhshi and the Isfahani vizier Mirzā Fazl-Allāh Mir Mirān, the spirited defense of the need for government and responsible taxation, plus an enthusiasm for the role of *munshi*s and *inshā* all combine to suggest that the elements of the Nurbakhshiyya continued to comport themselves in the arena of politics and administration with some sense of confidence after the execution of the Order's master

Shaikh Qavām al-Din Husain Nurbakhsh in 1537. Nurbakhshi discusses neither the history nor explicit doctrine of the Nurbakhshiyya, but his staunch
profiling of mystical proclivities might well have functioned as a beacon
for other Nurbakhshiyya to seek patronage and employment in the Safavid
administration.

While the ostensible audience of the *Inshā-yi ʿĀlam-ārā* was Shāh
Tahmāsp and the vizier of Isfahan Mirzā Fazl-Allāh Mir Mirān, it is clear
that Nurbakhshi was writing to a particular constituency of administrators
and bureaucrats who would have been at least sympathetic to his own mystical emphases. At the time of the writing of this manuscript (e.g. the late
1540s), the Safavid administration was firmly controlled by one of the most
important bureaucrats of the 16th century, namely Qāzi-yi Jahān, who was
a moderate Persian vazir who ushered in an era of centralized bureaucracy
that had been conspicuously absent since 1524. Qāzi-yi Jahān, whose full
name was Mir Sharaf al-Din Muhammad, was the scion of a well-established family of sayyids based in the city of Qazvin. Born in Muharram
888 / February 1483, he later became a student of the great philosopher Jalāl
al-Din al-Davvāni at the Madrasa-yi Mansuriyya, and received extensive instruction in philosophy, logic, astronomy, calligraphy, and inshā.[127] Indeed,
this *madrasa,* which was founded in 1477 by the great philosopher Sadr
al-Din Muhammad Dashtaki, would be a lodestar of philosophy and gnostic thought for the next two centuries.[128] Qāzi-yi Jahān was an active patron
and supporter of Persian administrators and men of letters throughout the
remainder of his career. To some extent, this patronage was motivated by
his proximity to al-Davvāni and the Shirazi tradition; his ecumenical stance,
which some have signaled as evidence of crypto-Sunnism, permitted the
incorporation of cosmopolitan scholar-bureaucrats who did not necessarily
share the vision of staunch clerical elements who had dominated the Safavid court since the 1530s. Qāzi-yi Jahān's catholic worldview is perhaps best
seen in the tradition whereby he prevented the public immolation of Jāmi's
divān and the reconstruction of his shrine at Herat.[129] Likewise, during the
Mughal ruler Humāyun's exile in the Safavid court, he successfully moder-
ated a tense dispute in which Shāh Tahmāsp had wanted to publicly ex-
ecute the Mughal for refusing to convert to Twelver Shiʿism. There is good
evidence to suggest that, concomitant with Qāzi-yi Jahān's appointment to
the office of vazir, subtle changes took place in the chancellery and the
divān-i aʿlā. In 942 / 1536, there is a reference to the death of Khwāja Mirak

b. Sharaf al-Din Kirmāni, who had worked for years writing inshā in the divān-i a'lā; this position was then apparently given to Muhammad Beg, the nephew of Mir Zakariyyā Kujaji.[130] Budaq Munshi discusses how Muhammad (or Muhammadi) Beg had had an active career as a *munshi* prior to this appointment as he had served as Prince Bahrām Mirzā's private secretary for a number of years.[131] Another prominent staff member included in Qāzi-yi Jahān's circle was Sharaf al-Din Husaini Qumi (called Mir Munshi), the father of the celebrated historian and calligrapher, Qāzi Ahmad. Mir Munshi was a product of the Shirazi philosophical school, having studied with Ghiyās al-Din Mansur Dashtaki, who then went on to serve as a ranking *munshi* within Tahmāsp's chancellery.[132]

However, from another perspective, many scholars and historians have interpreted Iran's emerging identity as a Shi'ite land as a result of the direct import of Shi'ite Arab jurists and scholars by the Safavid kings and their rise to power in the 1530s and 1540s; in this vein, they look to the profusion of technical and juridical texts, exclusively in Arabic, by scions of the great scholarly Shi'ite families of the al-Karakis and the al-āmilis, proof of an Arab-imposed Shi'ism.[133] Others, however, have pointed out the lively indigenous Shi'ism which had existed for centuries among sayyid networks such as the Mar'ashis in Astarābād, Qazvin and Tabriz.[134] In the case of the *Inshā-yi 'Ālam-ārā*, it is clear that Nurbakhshi's religious orientation suffuses the text at every level, and as such stands as a remarkable departure for a genre which normally eschewed stark confessional identification. With respect to the overarching trends of the New Persian language in the medieval and early modern setting, it is tempting to see the *Inshā-yi 'Ālam-ārā* as being indicative of the increased communalization that characterized so much of 16th-century discourse in the central Islamic lands. Formative Persian texts on prosody like those of Vatvāt and Shams-i Qais were occupied primarily with establishing the fundamentals of Persian prose and poetry within the overarching structure of Arabic literary sciences, and had little or nothing to say about confessional polemics between Shi'ism and Sunnism. Likewise, there is a dearth of explicitly Sunni or Shi'ite language, themes and imagery in the didactic Persian inshā tradition until this period.

With respect to the Sufi Nurbakhshiyya text, we sense a complex overlapping of these issues of language, religion and identity whereby a Sufi-inspired text on epistolography and prosody rationalizes the application of Persian literary devices and rhetorical embellishments within an exclusively

Shi'ite milieu. In this sense, the *Inshā-yi 'Ālam-ārā* might very well have operated as an intermediary discourse between Qāzi-yi Jahān and his Sufi-inspired coterie, and those staunch Shi'ite juridical elements which had come to the courtly fore in Safavid Iran since the 1530s. There is no mistaking that Nurbakhshi's text is sui generis in the Persian genre of epistolography, and none of the later authoritative Safavid inshā manuals, such as the *Munsha'āt al-Tusi* by 'Abd al-Husain al-Nasir al-Tusi and the *Nuskha-yi jāmi'a-i al-murāsalāt-i ulul albāb* by Abu al-Qāsim Haidar Beg Khvughli demonstrate any interest in profiling larger hermeneutical or mystical mandates. While Nurbakhshi might not have redefined the greater scholarly discourse regarding how to articulate and analyze epistolary prose, he was part of a bureaucratic continuum that privileged intellectual and philosophical Sufism, and there are Safavid state letters produced in the 1550s and 1560s that subtly reflect these dynamics. Probably, the best example is the unparalleled *tahniyya nāma* (congratulatory letter) which was written and sent to Salim II following the death of his father and his own accession to the Ottoman throne in 974/1566. This letter, included by Qāzi Ahmad al-Qumi in his *Khulāsat al-tavārikh* and numbering some seventy printed pages, is an epistolary leviathan. After hearing of Sulaiman's death, Tahmāsp ordered that "all Tajik functionaries, confidants, eloquent ones, and poets" be brought together for eight months to recite their verse and prose to the Shāh for possible inclusion into this monumental epistle.[135] It is no surprise that Qāzi Ahmad decided to include the entirety of the letter since it was he who assembled the text which included excerpts from a model *inshā* text (*nuskha*) produced by his father, Mir Munshi Qumi.[136] There is little doubt that this letter bears the imprint of individuals whose training and education was defined by an enduring notion of Perso-Islamic classicism tinged with a respect for mysticism; the staggering number of *masnavi*s, *qasida*s, and *ghazal*s from a wide spectrum of classical poets (Hāfiz, Sa'di, Jāmi, Nizāmi)—as well as contemporary, anonymous Safavid poets—celebrating kingship, imperium, and statehood easily overwhelm the paucity of poetic elegies in honour of 'Ali, Husain and the twelve Imams.

Religious heterogeneity was a constant in medieval Islamic Iran, and the Safavid chancellery was no exception. Nurbakhshi and the *Inshā-yi 'Ālam-ārā* were representatives of a distinct constituency among bureaucrats and religious scholars who were capable of operating in the overlapping spheres of Shi'ism and Sufism. These elements reached their most manifest success in the early halcyon days of Shāh Ismā`il's reign, wherein elements from Sufi orders such as the Naqshbandiyya, Ni`matullāhiyya, the Khwāndiyya, Hurufiyya and Nurbakhshiyya were able to interact with the Safavid state at various administrative, bureaucratic, and judicial levels. This success was short-lived as Ismā`il embarked on a campaign of intimidation against rival Sufi groups, but the greatest threat came about during the reign of Shāh Tahmāsp with the emergence of the formal Twelver Shi`ite juridical and theological class. Some theosophical elements such as Nāsir al-Haqq Nurbakhshi found refuge in the Safavid chancellery, and there is little doubt that letters produced in the reigns of Shāh Khudābanda (r. 1578–1588) and Shāh `Abbās (1589–1629) point to the continued existence of such Sufi-inclined litterateurs and stylists.[137]

NOTES

1. Jürgen Paul, "Ensa'," 457.
2. `Abd al-Rahmān Ahmad Jāmi, *Nāma-hā va munsha'āt-i Jāmi;* Husain Vā`iz Kāshifi, "Makhzan al-inshā" ms. We also have the work of `Abd-Allāh Marvārid—see Hans Robert Roemer, *Staatsschreiben der Timuridenzeit.* Also worthy of consultation are Mu`in al-Din Muhammad Zamchi Isfizāri, "Risāla-yi qavānin" ms., and Nizām al-Din `Abd al-Vāsi`, *Manshā al-inshā.*
3. Muhammad al-Husaini ibn Nāsir al-Haqq Nurbakhshi, "Inshā-yi `Ālam-ārā" ms.
4. Dānishpazhuh mentions the two extant copies in the Āstāna-yi Quds and University of Tehran libraries, but interestingly makes no reference to the Majlis copy. Muhammad Taqi Dānishpazhuh, *"Navisandagi va dabiri,"* 172. I have relied exclusively on the Majlis copy for the present analysis.
5. Dānishpazhuh, *"Navisandagi va dabiri,"* 171–72.
6. Ibid., 172.
7. Two good manuscripts are available of Khwāndamir`s *"Nāma-yi nāmi."* See Bibliothèque nationale, Paris, Supplement Persan, no. 1842, and British Library, London, I.O. Islamic, no. 2711. The only scholarly treatment of this source is Gottfried Hermann, "Historische Gehalt des Nama."
8. Faridun Beg, *Munsha'āt al-salātin;* Shāh Tāhir al-Husaini, *"Inshā-yi Shāh Tāhir"* ms., London, British Library, Harl. 499A.
9. `Abd al-Husain al-Nasir al-Tusi, *"Munsha'āt al-Tusi"* ms., Bibliothèque nationale, Paris, Supplement Persan, no. 1838. Another copy of this source exists in the Andra Pradesh Governmental Oriental Manuscripts Library in Hyderābād.
10. Abu al-Qāsim Haidar Beg Hvughli, *"Nuskha-yi jāmi`a-i al-murāsalāt-i ulul albāb"* ms., British Library, London, B.M. Add. 7688.
11. In addition to Muhammad Tāhir Vahid Qazvini, *"Munsha'āt-i Tāhir Vahid"* ms., Cambridge University Library ms. Or. 1070, several later 18th and 19th century copies of this work exist in manuscript collections in Patna, Aligarh, Calcutta, and Rampur.
12. Ihsan Yarshater has spoken about this trend in "Persian Literature of the Safavid Period," 217–70; see also Paul Losensky, Welcoming Fighani, 1–5.

13. Muhammad ibn `Umar Rāduyāni, Tarjumān al-balāghat; Shams al-Din Muhammad ibn Qais al-Rāzi (Shams-i Qais), Al-Mu`jam fi ma`āyir ash`ār al-`ajam; Rashid al-Din Vatvāt, Hadā'iq al-sihr fi daqā'iq al-shi`r.

14. Marta Simidchieva, "Imitation and Innovation in Timurid Poetics."

15. Natalia Chalisova, "Hyperbole."

16. For an excellent historiographical review of Ismā`il's possible motives, see David Morgan, "Rethinking Safavid Shi`ism," 19–27.

17. B. Scarcia-Amoretti, "Religion in the Timurid and Safavid Periods," 610–55; Adel Allouche, *Origins and Development of the Ottoman-Safavid Conflict;* Rosemary Stanfield-Johnson, "Sunni Survival in Safavid Iran"; Anthony Welch, *Artists for the Shāh,* 5–10; Aziz Ahmad, "Safawid Poets and India"; J.R. Walsh, *Historiography of Ottoman-Safavid Relations;* and Andrew Hess, "Ottoman Conquest of Egypt." More general texts on Islamic history reinforce such trends, such as Carl Brockelmann, *History of the Islamic Peoples,* 288–91; Albert Hourani, *History of the Arab Peoples,* 221; and Ira Lapidus, *History of Islamic Societies,* 253–56.

18. For a more nuanced approach to early modern sectarianism, see Robert McChesney, "Barrier of Heterodoxy?" See also Sanjay Subrahmanyam, "Iranians Abroad."

19. Jean Aubin's "Avènement des Safavides reconsidéré," 1–130; Shahzad Bashir's "Shāh Isma`il and the Qizilbash"; Katherine Babayan's *Mystics, Monarchs, and Messiahs;* Jean Calmard's "Rituels shiites et le pouvoir," 109–50; A.H. Morton's "*chub-i tariq* and Qizilbash Ritual in Safavid Persia," 225–45; Farhad Daftary's "Isma`ili-Sufi Relations," 275–89; Leonard Lewisohn's "Sufism and the School of Isfahan."

20. Margaret Malamud, "Sufi Organizations and Structures of Authority," and Omid Safi, "Bargaining with Baraka," 259–87.

21. An excellent study of antinomian Sufism is available in Ahmet Karamustafa, *God's Unruly Friends,* while Jo-Ann Gross and Asom Urunbaev examine aspects of Timurid high Naqshbandi Sufism with *Letters of Khwaja `Ubayd Allāh Ahrar and His Associates.* For transplanted Naqshbandi networks, see Dina Le Gall, *Culture of Sufism.*

22. Fihrist-i nuskha-hâ-yi khatti-yi Kitâbkhâna-yiMajlis-i Shurâ-yi Islâmi 2:292.

23. Sadly, the colored inks were not reproduced very well in the copy that I ordered, making certain sections largely unreadable. This is compounded by water damage and reverse folio impressions.

24. Murabba`s are also known as chār-suyas, diagrammatic riddles using a quatrain in a circle or square format. Mir Jalāl al-Din Kazzāzi, *Badi`: Zibā-shināsi-yi sukhan-i pārsi* 3, 174–76.

25. This break in the text does not appear to disrupt Nurbakhshi's ongoing discussion of the literary device of *izmār* (ellipsis).

26. Nurbakhshi, *Inshā-yi `Alam-ārā,* f. 141a.

27. This manuscript is in the Sipah-sālar Library No. 7i94/2. See Dānishpazhuh, *Navisandagi va dabiri,* 172.

28. Dānishpazhuh, *Navisandagi va dabiri,* 172.

29. Ibid., 164.

30. There is, in fact, a letter from Sultan-Husain Baiqara to Shāh Qāsim Nurbakhsh in `Abd al-Husain Navā'i's *Asnād va mukātabāt-i tārikhi-yi irān az Timur tā Shāh Ismā`il,* 403–4.

31. Al-Husaini mentions Sayyid Ja`far and Shāh Qalandar (possibly Shāh Qāsim?) as a`yān-i shahr-i Dāmghān. Khurshāh ibn Qubād al-Husaini, *Tārikh-i ilchi-yi Nizāmshāh,*

M.R. Nasiri and K. Haneda, 48.

32. Shahzad Bashir, *Messianic Hopes and Mystical Visions*, 186–95; Andrew Newman, Safa-vid Iran, 33

33. Nurbakhshi, *Inshā-yi ʿĀlam-ārā*, f. 1b.

34. Ithnā ʿashar khalifatun min ahl al-baiti aʿt...hum Allāh taʿālā afhami wa hikmati. Nur-bakhshi, Inshā-yi ʿĀlam-ārā, f. 2a.

35. bar masnad-i din davāzdah shāh / dar sāl-i bāqa davāzdah māh. Ibid., ff. 2a-b.

36. Ibid., f. 2b.

37. Lau inna al-riyāz aqlamun waʾl-bahr madadun waʾl-jinn hisābun waʾl-ins kitābun maʿahu fazāʾil-in ʿAli ibn Abi Tālib. Ibid., f. 2b.

38. Ibid., ff. 3a-3b.

39. Ibid., f. 5a.

40. Ibid., f. 5b.

41. Tahmāsp is presented as having the essence of ʿAli (zāt-i ʿAli), the qualities of Hasan (*sifāt-i hasan*), the countenance of Husain (*surat-i husain*), the temperament of Zain al-ʿābidin (*sirat-i ʿābidin*), the piety of al-Bāqir (*ʿibādat-i bāqiri*), the pedigree of Jaʿfar (*hasab-i jaʿfari*), the right conduct of Musā (*mazhab-i musavi*), the familial stock of Rizā (*nasab-i rizavi*), the acquiescence of Muhammad al-Taqi (*rizā-yi taqavi*), the piety of Ali al-Naqi (*taqavi-yi naqi*), the beauty of ʿAskar (*simā-yi ʿaskari*), and lastly he who holds the banner of the Mahdi (*rāyat-i mahdi*). Ibid., ff. 6a-b.

42. For instance, we see the partial quote of *wa hal ata* (from "was there not a time in the life of a man when he was not even a mentionable thing?"), as well as God's admoni-tion to emulate the prophets of the past: "Say: There is no reward for what I ask of you" (Qurʾan 6: 90).

43. Nurbakhshi, *Inshā-yi ʿĀlam-ārā*, f. 6b.

44. For instance, one line—Shāh Tahmāsp ibn Ismāʿil Haidari—gives 919 using the *abjad* system. Ibid., f. 8a.

45. Ibid., f. 7b.

46. Ibid., f. 8b.

47. Although not explicitly named, he is alluded to with 5:54 and 4:133: "such is the favour of God (fazl allāh) which He bestows on whomever He wills" and "Great have the blessings of God (fazl allāh) been on you."

48. Risāla-yi jāmiʿ-i muntavi bar fiqrat-i munshaʾāt va maqāla-yi nāfiʿa-i mutabbini bar adab va sanāyiʿ va muhsanāt-i in fann-i balāghat (Nurbakhshi, Inshā-yi ʿalam-ārā, f. 12b).

49. Ibid., f. 14b. See also Muhammad Dashti, *al-Muʿjam al-mufahras li alfāz Nahj al-balāgha*, 171.

50. Nurbakhshi, *Inshā-yi ʿĀlam-ārā*, f. 15a-b; Dashti, *al-Muʿjam al-mufahras li alfāz Nahj al-balāgha*, 226, 173.

51. Nurbakhshi, *Inshā-yi ʿĀlam-ārā*, f. 16a. See section *"Kitāb al-kharāj waʾl-imāra"* (Book 13) of Abu Dawud, *Sunan 2*, ed. Ahmad Hasan, Lahore, 1984, p. 828.

52. Nurbakhshi, *Inshā-yi ʿĀlam-ara*, f. 18a. The historian Khwāndamir cites this tradition in his own advice manual which includes discussions of knowledge, poetry, and *inshā*. See Ghiyāth al-Din Khwāndamir, *Makārim al-akhlāq*, 139.

53. Nurbakhshi, *Inshā-yi ʿĀlam-ārā*, ff. 18a-b.

54. Ibid., f. 18b.

55. Ibid., ff. 18b-19a.

56. Ibid., f. 19b.
57. Ibid., f. 19b.
58. Ibid., f. 20b.
59. Ibid., f. 21a.
60. Ibid., f. 21b.
61. Khwāndamir, *Nāma-yi nāmi*, ff. 2b-4a; Nizām al-Din ʿAbd al-Vāsiʿ Nizāmi, *Manshā al-inshā*, 3–4; Muhammad ibn Hindushāh Nakhjavāni, *Dastur al-kātib fi ʾl taʿyin al-marātib*, 6–8.
62. Nurbakhshi, *Inshā-yi ʿĀlam-ārā*, ff. 21b-22a.
63. Ibid., f. 22b.
64. Ibid., ff. 22b-23a.
65. Ibid., f. 23b.
66. Ibid., f. 24a.
67. Ibid., ff. 25a-25b.
68. Ibid., f. 26a.
69. Ibid., f. 26b.
70. Quoted in Seyyed Hossein Nasr, *Islamic Art and Spirituality*, 18.
71. Nurbakhshi, *Inshā-yi ʿĀlam-ārā*, ff. 27b-28a.
72. Ibid., f. 28a.
73. Ibid., f. 28b.
74. Indeed, his impact was such that a collection of commentaries of his work called the *Sharh-i dastur-i muʿammā-yi Nishāpuri* was produced in the early 16th century. Maria Subtelny, "Taste for the Intricate," 76–77; Francis Richard, "Quelques traits d'énigmes (moʿamma) en persan," 241.
75. H. Henry Spoer, "Arabic Magic Medicinal Bowls," 244–48; Schuyler Cammann, "Islamic and Indian Magic Squares I," 199. See also Jacques Sesiano, "Carrés magiques dans les pays Islamiques."
76. Nurbakhshi, *Inshā-yi ʿĀlam-ārā*, ff. 28b-29a.
77. Ibid., f. 29a.
78. Ibid., f. 29a.
79. Ibid., f. 29b.
80. Babayan, *Mystics, Monarchs, and Messiahs*, 319–21.
81. In this story, Nurbakhshi makes several allusions to nazmi, ganjiya, and makhzan al-asrār (Nurbakhshi, *Inshā-yi ʿĀlam-ārā*, f. 29b-30a).
82. Ibid., f. 33a.
83. Ibid., f. 33b.
84. Ibid., f. 34a.
85. Ibid., ff. 34a-b.
86. Ibid., ff. 34b-36a.
87. Ibid., ff. 36a-42b.
88. E.G. Browne, *Literary History*, 2:53.
89. Nurbakhshi, *Inshā-yi ʿĀlam-ārā*, ff. 43b-46b.
90. Ibid., ff. 48b-53a.
91. Ibid., ff. 53a-56b
92. Ibid., ff. 56b-62b.
93. In Arabic and Persian prosody, *iltizām* involved the insertion of one or more invariable consonants before the rhyme consonant itself (*rawiyya*) in existing *masnavis* and

qasidas. See S.A. Bonebakker, *"Luzum ma la yalzam."*

94. Nurbakhshi, *Inshā-yi 'Ālam-ārā,* f. 70b.

95. Ibid., ff. 76a-77b.

96. Ibid., f. 75b.

97. Ibid., f. 78b.

98. Ibid., f. 78b.

99. Ibid., f. 79b.

100. This particular example by Nurbakhshi appears to have been borrowed from Mir 'Ali Shir Navā'i's, *Muhākamat al-lughatain.* See Maria Subtelny, "Taste for the Intricate," 73.

101. Nurbakhshi, *Inshā-yi 'Ālam-ārā,* ff. 80b-81a.

102. Ibid., ff. 81b-82a.

103. Sām Mirzā, Tazkira-yi tuhfa-yi Sāmi, 171.

104. Ibid., 98.

105. Nurbakhshi, *Inshā-yi 'Ālam-ārā,* f. 83b.

106. Ghiyās al-Din ibn Humām al-Din Khwāndamir, *Habib al-siyar,* 287; Muhammad Tāhir Nasrābādi, *Tazkira-yi Nasrābādi,* 789.

107. Nurbakhshi, *Inshā-yi 'Ālam-āra,* ff. 83b-103a.

108. Rāduyāni, *Tarjumān al-balāghat,* 155–57; Shams-i Qais, *Al-Mu'jam fi ma 'āyir ash 'ār al-'ajam,* 426–35.

109. Losensky gives a nice overview of Timurid and Safavid *mu'ammā*s. See Losensky, *Welcoming Fighani,* 154–64.

110. Richard, "Quelques traits d'énigmes (*mo'ammā*) en persan," 233–34. For an excellent review of all *mu'ammā* sources produced in the medieval and early modern period, see Shams Anwāri-Alhosseini, *Logaz und mo'amma: eine Quellenstudie zur Kunstform des persische Rätsels.*

111. C.E. Bosworth, "Section on Codes."

112. Mir 'Ali Shir Navā'i, *Majālis al-nafā'* is quoted in Ihsan Yarshater, *Shi'r-i fārsi dar 'ahd-i shāh rukh,* 239.

113. Nasrābādi, *Tazkira-yi Nasrābādi,* 759–817.

114. Nurbakhshi, *Inshā-yi 'Ālam-ārā,* f. 103a.

115. Amir Husain Nishapuri (Mu'ammā'i), *"Risāla fi al-mu'ammā"* ms. Oxford, Bodleian Library, Ouseley no. 143.

116. Nasrābādi, *Tazkira-yi Nasrābādi,* 759–817.

117. Nurbakhshi, *Inshā-yi 'Ālam-ārā,* f. 113b.

118. Ibid., ff. 103a-129b.

119. Ibid., ff. 127b-130a.

120. Simidchieva, "Imitation and Innovation in Timurid Poetics," 516–17.

121. 'Imād al-Din Mahmud Gāvān, *Manāzir al-inshā.*

122. In Persian prosody, this refers to the word or word phrase that follows the rhyme letter (raviyy) and appears in every line of the poem in question. See W.P. Heinrichs, "Radif."

123. Losensky, *Welcoming Fighani,* 154–56; Subtelny, "Taste for the Intricate," 75–76; Anwāri-Alhosseyni, *Logaz und Mu'ammā,* 184–88.

124. In addition to Nishāpuri and Nasrābādi, I consulted the relevant sections in the poetic works of Muhtasham Kāshāni, Vahshi Bāfqi, and 'Abd al-Rahmān Jāmi and found no evidence of replication.

125. Bashir notes the exceptional emphasis by Muhammad Nurbakhsh on light and brilliance in understanding Nurbakhshiyya sensibilities. This dynamic is perhaps seen in the *Inshā-yi ʿĀlam-ārā* and its division of sections and subsections into flashes (*lamʿa*) and sparks (*zuʾ*).
126. Bashir, *Messianic Hopes and Mystical Visions*, 77.
127. Mir Fazaluddin Ali Khan, *Life and Works of Mirza Sharaf Jahan Qazwini*, 42–46.
128. An original document from 893/1488 discussing the foundation and funding of this *madrasa* is profiled in Vladimir Minorsky, " 'Soyurghal' of Qasim b. Jahangir Aqqoyunlu (903/1498)," 953.
129. Emboldened by the Arab jurist al-Karaki, and informed that Jāmi had been anti-ʿAlid, the Shāh had ordered the demolition of the great Timurid's shrine at Herat. Tahmāsp was about to order the public immolation of all copies of Jāmi's Divān but was dissuaded by Qāzi-yi Jahān. Qāzi-yi Jahān, in turn, revealed a number of *qasidas* in honor of ʿAli and the Imamate and successfully used one of them as an augury. Jāmi's tomb was subsequently rebuilt and revered thereafter by the Safavid family.
130. Ahmad ibn Sharaf al-Din al-Husain al-Husaini al-Qummi, *Khulāsat al-tavārikh* 1, 263.
131. Budaq Munshi Qazvini, *Javāhir al-akhbār*, 185.
132. Muhammad Yusuf Valih Isfahāni, *Khuld-i barin*, 641, 976.
133. Rula Abisaab, *Converting Persia: Religion and Power in the Safavid Empire*.
134. Andrew Newman, *Safavid Iran: Rebirth of a Persian Empire*.
135. Qāzi Ahmad, *Khulāsat al-tavārikh* 1, 477–78.
136. Ibid., 478.
137. See my "Out of Sight, Out of Mind."

REFERENCES

ʿAbd al-Husain al-Nasir al-Tusi. Ca. 1630. *Munshaʾāt al-Tusi*, ms. Bibliotheque Nationale, supplément persan, no. 1838. Paris.

Abisaab, Rula Jurdi. 2004. *Converting Persia: Religion and Power in the Safavid Empire*. London: I.B. Tauris.

Ahmad, Aziz. 1976. Safawid Poets and India. *Iran* 14:117–32.

Ahmad ibn Sharaf al-Din al-Husain al-Husaini al-Qummi. 2004. *Khulāsat al-tavārikh*, ed. I. Ishrāqi. Tehran: Dānishgāh-i Tehrān.

Allouche, Adel. 1983. *The Origins and Development of the Ottoman-Safavid Conflict 906–962/1500–1555*. Berlin: K. Schwarz Verlag.

Amir Husain Nishāpuri Muʿammāʾi. Ca. late 15th century. *Risāla fi al-muʿammā*, ms. Bodleian Library, Ouseley no. 143. Oxford.

Anwari-Alhosseini, Shams. 1986. *Logaz und moʿamma: eine Quellenstudie zur Kunstform des persische Rätsels*. Berlin: Schwarz.

Aubin, Jean. 1988. L'Avènement des Safavides reconsidéré. *Moyen Orient et océan Indien* 5:1–130.

Babayan, Kathryn. 2002. *Mystics, Monarchs, and Messiahs: Cultural Landscapes of Early Modern Iran*. Cambridge, MA: Harvard University Press.

Bashir, Shahzad. 2006. Shāh Ismaʿil and the Qizilbash: Cannibalism in the Religious History of Early Safavid Iran. *History of Religions* 45:234–56.

Bashir, Shahzad. 2003. *Messianic Hopes and Mystical Visions: The Nurbakhshiyya between Medieval and Modern Islam.* Columbia: University of South Carolina Press.

Bonebakker, S.A. 2010. *Luzum ma la yalzam. Encyclopedia of Islam,* 2nd ed., vol. 5, ed. P. Bearman, Th. Bianquis, C.E. Bosworth, E. van Donzel, and W.P. Heinrichs. Brill, Brill Online.

Bosworth, Clifford E. 1963. The Section on Codes and Their Decipherment in Qalqashandi's Subh al-a`sha. *Journal of Semitic Studies* 8:17–33.

Brockelmann, Carl. 1949. *History of the Islamic Peoples.* London: Routledge and Kegan Paul (1979).

Browne, E.G. 1929. *A Literary History of Persia.* 4 vols. Cambridge: Cambridge University Press.

Budaq, Munshi Qazvini. 2000. *Javāhir al-akhbār,* ed. M. Bahrāmnizhād. Tehrān: Mirās-i Maktub.

Calmard, Jean. 1993. Les rituals shiites et le pouvoir: l'imposition du shiisme safavide: eulogies et malédictions canoniques. In *Études Safavides,* ed. J. Calmard, pp. 109–50. Paris: Institut français de recherche en Iran.

Cammann, Schuyler. 1969. Islamic and Indian Magic Squares. Part I. *History of Religions* 8(3): 181–209.

Chalisova, Natalia. 2004. Hyperbole. In *Encyclopaedia Iranica,* vol. 12. http://iranica.com/articles/search/keywords:hyperbole.

Daftary, Farhad. 1999. Isma`ili-Sufi Relations in Early Post-Alamut and Safavid Persia. In *The Heritage of Sufism,* Vol. 3: *Late Classical Persianate Sufism (1501–1750),* ed. L. Lewisohn and D. Morgan, pp. 275–89. Boston, MA: Oneworld.

Dānishpazhuh, Muhammad Taqi. 2002. *Navisandagi va dabiri.* In *Hadis-i `eshq,* ed. N. Mottalebi-Kāshāni and S. Mohammad-Hossein Mar`ashi. Tehrān: Kitābkhāna-i Mauzih va Markaz-i Asnād-i Majālis-i Shurā-yi Islāmi.

Dashti, Muhammad, ed. 1974. *al-Mu`jam al-mufahras li alfāz Nahj al-balāgha.* Qum: Majmu`a-i Āshnā'i bā Nahj al-Balāgha.

Faridun Beg. 1858. *Munsha'āt al-salātin.* Istanbul.

`Imād al-Din Mahmud Gāvān. 2002. *Manāzir al-inshā,* ed. Ma`suma Ma`dan-Kan. Tehran: Nashr-i āsār-i Farhangistan-i Zabān va Adab-i Fārsi.

Gross, Jo-Ann, and Asom Urunbaev. 2002. *Letters of Khwāja `Ubayd Allāh Ahrār and His Associates.* Leiden: E.J. Brill.

Heinrichs, W.P. 2010. Radif. In *Encyclopedia of Islam,* 2nd ed., vol. 8, p. 368.

Herrmann, Gottfried. 1968. Das historische Gehalt des Nāma-ye nāmi von Hāndamir. Ph.D. diss., Göttingen.

Hess, Andrew. 1973. The Ottoman Conquest of Egypt (1517) and the Beginning of the Sixteenth-Century World War. *International Journal of Middle East Studies* 4:55–76.

Hourani, Albert. 1991. *A History of the Arab Peoples.* Cambridge, MA: Harvard University Press.

Abu al-Qāsim Haidar Beg Hvughli. *Nuskha-yi jāmiʿa-i al-murāsalāt-i ulul albāb,* ms. British Library, B.M. Add. 7688. London.

Muʿin al-Din Muhammad Zamchi Isfizāri. *Risāla-yi qavānin,* ms. Lahore: Punjab University Library, Pe II Li 2324/231.

ʿAbd al-Rahmān Jāmi. 2002. *Nāma-hā va munsha'āt-i Jāmi,* ed. ʿIsam al-Din Urunbayif and Asrar Rahmanof. Tehran: Markaz-i Nashr-i Mirās-i Maktub.

Karamustafa, Ahmet. 1994. *God's Unruly Friends: Dervish Groups in the Islamic Later Middle Period, 1200–1550.* Salt Lake City: University of Utah Press.

Kashifi, Husain Vaʿiz. *Makhzan al-inshā,* ms. Bibliotheque Nationale, supplément fonds persan, no. 73. Paris.

Mir Jalāl al-Din Kazzāzi. 1993[2002]. *Zibā-shināsi-yi sukhan-i pārsi.* Tehran: Nashr-i Markaz.

Khurshāh ibn Qubād al-Husaini. 2000. *Tārikh-i ilchi-yi Nizāmshāh,* ed. M.R. Nasiri and K. Haneda. Tehran.

Khwāndamir, Ghiyās al-Din. 1983. *Tārikh-i Habib al-siyar fi akhbār-i afrād-i bashar,* ed. Muhammad Dabir Siyāqi. Tehran: Kitābfurushi-i Khayyām.

Khurshāh ibn Qubād al-Husaini. 2000. *Tārikh-i ilchi-yi Nizāmshāh,* eds. M.R. Nasiri and K. Haneda. Tehran: Miras Maktub.

Ghiyās al-Din Khwāndamir. Ca. 1522. *Nāma-yi nāmi,* ms. British Library, I.O. Islamic, no. 2711. London.

Lapidus, Ira. 2002. *A History of Islamic Societies.* 2nd ed. Cambridge: Cambridge University Press.

Le Gall, Dina. 2005. *A Culture of Sufism: Naqshbandis in the Ottoman World, 1450–1700.* Albany: State University of New York Press.

Lewisohn, Leonard. 1999. Sufism and the School of Isfahan: Tasawwuf and ʿIrfan in Late Safavid Iran (ʿAbd al-Razzāq Lahiji and Fayz-i Kāshāni on the Relation of Tasawwuf, Hikmat and ʿIrfan). In *The Heritage of Sufism,* Vol. 3: *Late Classical Persianate Sufism (1501–1750),* ed. L. Lewisohn and D. Morgan, pp. 63–134. Oxford: Oneworld.

Lewisohn, L., and D. Morgan, eds. 1999. *The Heritage of Sufism,* vol. 3: *Late Classical Persianate Sufism (1501–1750).* Oxford: Oneworld.

Losensky, Paul. 1998. *Welcoming Fighani: Imitation and Poetic Individuality in the Safavid-Mughal Ghazal.* Costa Mesa, CA: Mazda Publications.

Malamud, Margaret. 1994. Sufi Organizations and Structures of Authority in Medieval Nishapur. In *International Journal of Middle East Studies* 26:427–42.

McChesney, Robert. 1996. Barrier of Heterodoxy? Rethinking the Ties Between Iran and Central Asia in the Seventeenth Century. In *Safavid Persia: The History and Politics of an Islamic Society,* ed. Charles Melville, pp. 231–68. London: I.B. Tauris.

Melville, Charles, ed. 1996. *Safavid Persia: The History and Politics of an Islamic Society.* London: I.B. Tauris.

Minorsky, V. 1939. A "Soyurghal" of Qasim b. Jahangir Aq-qoyunlu (903/1498). *Bulletin of the School of African and Oriental Studies* 9:927–60.

Mir Fazaluddin Ali Khan. 1995. *Life and Works of Mirzā Sharaf Jahān Qazwini: A Poet of Shāh Tahmāsp Safawi's Regime.* Hyderābād: M.F. Ali Khan.

Mitchell, Colin P. 2005. Out of Sight, Out of Mind: Shāh Mohammad Khodabanda and the *Safavid Dar al-ensha.* In *Studies on Persianate Societies* 3:65–98.

Morgan, David. 1999. Rethinking Safavid Shi`ism. In *The Heritage of Sufism,* Vol. 3: *Late Classical Persianate Sufism (1501–1750),* ed. L. Lewisohn and D. Morgan, pp. 19–27. Oxford: Oneworld.

Morton, A.H. 1993. The chub-i tariq and Qizilbāsh Ritual in Safavid Persia. In *Études Safavides,* ed. J. Calmard, pp. 225–45. Paris: Institut français de recherche en Iran.

Muhammad Tāhir Vahid Qazvini. *Munsha`āt-i Tāhir Vahid,* ms. Cambridge University Library ms. Or. 1070. Cambridge.

Muhammad ibn Hindushāh Nakhjavāni. 1964. *Dastur al-kātib fi`l ta`yin al-marātib,* 3 vols., ed. `Abd al-Karim `Ali-oglu `Ali-zāda. Moscow.

Nasr, Seyyed Hossein. 1987. *Islamic Art and Spirituality.* Albany: State University of New York Press.

Nasrābādi, Muhammad Tāhir. 1999. *Tazkira-yi Nasrābādi,* ed. Ahmad Mudaqqiq Yazdi. Tehrān: Dānishgāh-i Yazd.

Navā`i, `Abd al-Husain. 1963. *Asnād va mukātabāt-i tārikhi-yi Irān az Timur tā Shāh Ismā`il.* Tehran: Shirkat-i Intishārāt-i `Ilmi va Farhangi.

Newman, Andrew. 2006. *Safavid Iran: Rebirth of a Persian Empire.* London: Tauris.

Nizām al-Din `Abd al-Vāsi` Nizāmi. 1978. *Manshā al-inshā,* ed. Rukn al-Din Humāyun Farrukh. Tehrān: Dānishgāh-i Milli-i Irān.

Nurbakhshi, Muhammad al-Husaini ibn Nāsir al-Haqq. *Inshā-yi `Ālam-ārā,* ms. Tehrān, Kitābkhāna-yi Majlis-i shurā-yi Islāmi, no. 13757.

Paul, Jürgen. 1998. Enşa. In *Encyclopedia Iranica,* vol. 8. http://iranica.com/articles/ensa.

Rāduyāni, Muhammad ibn `Umar. 1960. *Tarjumān al-balāgha,* ed. `Ali Qavim. Tehrān: Chāpkhānah-yi Muhammad `Alī Fardīn.

Richard, Francis. 1995. Quelques traits d'énigmes (mo`amma) en persan des XVe et XVIe siècles. In *Pand o Sokhan: Mélanges offerts à Charles-Henri de Fouchecour,* ed. C. Balay, C. Kappler, and Z. Vesel. Tehran: Institut Français de Recherche en Iran.

Roemer, Hans Robert, ed. and trans. 1952. *Staatsschreiben der Timuridenzeit: das Sharaf Namä des `Abdullah Marwarid im kritischer Auswertung.* Weisbaden: Franz Steiner Verlag.

Safi, Omid. 2000. Bargaining with Baraka: Persian Sufism, 'Mysticism,' and Pre-Modern Politics. *Muslim World* 90:259–87.

Sām Mirzā. 1936. *Tazkira-yi tuhfa-yi Sāmi,* ed. Rukn al-Din Humāyun Farrukh. Tehran: Asātīr (2005/2006).

Scarcia Amoretti, B. 1986. Religion in the Timurid and Safavid Periods. In *The Cambridge History of Iran,* Vol. 6: *The Timurid and Safavid Periods,* pp. 610–55.

Cambridge: Cambridge University Press.

Sesiano, Jacques. 2004. *Les carrés magiques dans les pays Islamiques.* Lausanne: Presses polytechniques et universitaires romandes.

Shāh Tāhir al-Husaini. *Inshā-yi Shāh Tāhir,* ms. British Library, London, Harl. 499A.

Shams al-Din Muhammad ibn Qais al-Rāzi (Shams-i Qais). 1959. *Al-Mu`jam fi Ma`āyir ash`ār al-`ajam,* ed. Muhammad Qazvini. Tehran: Tabmiz Ketābforushi Tehrān.

Simidchieva, Marta. 2003. Imitation and Innovation in Timurid Poetics: Kāshifi's Badāyi` al-afkār, and Its Predecessors, al-Mu`jam and Hadā'iq al-sihr. *Iranian Studies* 36:509–30.

Spoer, H. Henry. 1935. Arabic Magic Medicinal Bowls. *Journal of the American Oriental Society* 55(3): 237–56.

Stanfield-Johnson, Rosemary. 1994. Sunni Survival in Safavid Iran: Anti-Sunni Activities during the Reign of Shāh Tahmasp. *Iranian Studies* 27:123–33.

Subrahmanyam, Sanjay. 1992. Iranians Abroad: Intra-Asian Elite Migration and Early Modern State Formation. *Journal of Asian Studies* 51:340–63.

Subtelny, Maria. 1986. A Taste for the Intricate: The Persian Poetry of the Late Timurid Period. *Zeitschrift der Deutschen Morgenländischen Gesellschaft (ZDMG)* 136:73, 76–77.

Vālih Isfahāni, Muhammad Yusuf. 1993. *Khuld-i barin,* ed. Mir Hāshim Muhaddis. Tehran: Intišārāt-i Bunyād-i Mauqufāt-i Duktur Mahmūd Afšār Yazdī.

Vatvāt, Rashid al-Din. 1945. *Hadā' iq al-sihr fi daqā'iq al-shi`r,* ed. Ibrāhim Amin al-Shurabi. Cairo.

Walsh, J.R. 1961. The Historiography of Ottoman-Safavid Relations in the Sixteenth and Seventeenth Centuries. In *Historians of the Middle East,* vol. 4, ed. B. Lewis and P.M. Holt, pp. 197–211. London: Oxford University Press.

Welch, Anthony. 1976. *Artists for the Shāh: Late Sixteenth-Century Painting at the Imperial Court of Iran.* New Haven: Yale University Press.

Yarshater, Ihsan. 1955. *Shi`r-i fārsi dar `ahd-i Shāh Rukh.* Tehran: Chāpkhāna-yi Dānishgāh.

—— 1974. Persian Literature of the Safavid Period: Progress or Decline? *Iranian Studies* 7:217–70.

Part Three: Vernacularization and Nationalism

7

Historiography in the Sadduzai Era: Language and Narration

SENZIL NAWID

In this chapter I examine two genres of premodern Persian historiography by reviewing two chronicles written during the period of the Sadduzai dynasty (1747–1842) in Afghanistan. One conforms to the literary style of chancery protocol and the other is a popular history written by an independent chronicler. My purpose is not to analyze these works as historical texts. It is rather to examine the difference in their style of writing and mode of expression. First, it will be useful to review briefly the development and characteristics of premodern Persian historiography.

Historiography and Chancery Prose

Persian historiography developed in the 4th/10th century with the emergence of literary *Dari* Persian. The region of Khurasan, in the far eastern fringes of the Abbasid Empire, assumed a distinctive literary culture with the establishment of independent sultanates, beginning with the Ṭāhirid dynasty in 821 in Nishapur and eastern Khurasan, which is now partly northern Afghanistan. In the mid-8th century Ibn Muqaffaʿ wrote that *Dari* was the vernacular of Khurasan and was different from Fārsi, the dialect of Fars, and Pahlavi, the vernacular spoken in Media and Azerbaijan.[1] *Dari* was written in the Arabic script by court scribes and developed as a literary court language under the patronage of the Sāmānids, the dynasty that supplanted the Ṭāhirids. Marv (modern Mary), Balkh, Herat, Bādghis, Soghdiana, Tus, Ghazni, and Gorgān were the centers from which this literary language then spread westward to present-day Iran and came to be known as *Dari* Persian (*fārsi-ye dari*). *Dari* replaced Arabic as the language of administration only later during the rule of the Ghaznavids in the 11th century.

Under the Sāmānids the bureaucratic system of government was fully developed and was organized into several departments (*divān*). The most important of these was the office of Chief Minister (*'amid al-mulk*), which handled the official and diplomatic correspondence of the state. This department continued to exist during the rule of the later dynasties—the Ghaznavids (975–1187), the Seljuks (1037–1157), and the Khwārazmshāhs (1098–1231)—under different names: department of correspondence (*divān-i rasā'il*), private office (*divān-i khāss*), and the office of writing (*dāru'l-inshā*). It was in this office that chancery-style prose (*inshā-i munshiāna*) began to develop among the scribal elite. Persian prose assimilated some of the characteristics of Arabic prose. The three characteristic modes of Arabic were "simple or unornate" (*'ari*), "cadenced" (*murajjaz*), which has meter without rhyme; and rhymed (*musajja'*), which has rhyme without meter.[2] Of these three modes, *musajja'*, the rhymed prose, which gives the text a rhythmic quality, was favored by all Muslim prose writers, including Persian writers.[3]

Regional historiography developed under court patronage along with classical prose writing during the time of the Ghaznavids. Persian chroniclers by and large belonged to the royal chancery and wrote at the command of kings. Two examples of historical works produced during this early period are *Tārikh-i Zain al-Akhbār*, written in about 440/1009 by 'Abd al-Haiy Gardizi at the court of the Ghaznavid ruler 'Abd al-Rashid, and *Tārikh-i Bayhaqi*, a celebrated work written by 'Abu al-Fazl Muhammad ibn Husain Bayhaqi (d. 1077) on the rule of Sultan Mas'ud of Ghazni. Court historians were expected to be well-versed in religious scriptures—the Qur'an, the traditions of the Prophet (*hadith*), and jurisprudence (*fiqh*)—in order to be able to quote from them to defend or justify actions of their patron. As panegyrists, their principal objective was to glorify the might of their patron in the eyes of rival rulers and petty princes and advance the legitimacy of his rule by recording his achievements in promoting justice and defending Islam. As a result, numerous chronicles written by court historians are rhetorical, i.e., "history designed to be persuasive rather than simply to convey facts."[4]

The art of *inshā* became more complicated during the time of the Seljuks and the KhwārazmShāhs with the development of an artificial ornamental style. Rhetorical embellishments and sets of panegyric phrases, formulated by a handful of scribes and poets in the court, became the dominant features of the writing of history. Consequently, style and message came to be inseparable parts of rhetorical history.[5] The secretary-historians strove to excel in the art of literary rhetoric—so much so that, as von Grunebaum has pointed out, "the substance of what the author had set out to convey almost evaporated in the fireworks of rhetoric."[6]

Interest in history writing grew stronger after the Mongol invasion and the establishment of the rule of the Ilkhanid Mongols (1256–1335). Muhammad Taqi Bahār cites two reasons for the advance of historiography during this period: first, the Mongols' appreciation of the importance of history and their traditional interest in immortalizing their deeds by leaving behind records of their accomplishments; and secondly, the significance of their vast military conquests, which included the occupation of Baghdad.[7]

Mongol rulers initially disfavored the use of appellations and honorifics with their names and preferred simple writing. Juvayni writes that Chingiz Khan forbade the use of epithets with names and decreed that the successors to the throne of the khanate add only one word, *khān* or *qa'an,* to their first name.[8]

و از آنچ یاسای چنگیزخانست که همه طوایف را یکی شناسد و بر یکدیگر فرق ننهند عدول...
نجویند, و از عادات گزیده آنست که چنانک شیوه مقبلان و سنّت صاحب دولتان باشد ابواب
تکلف و تنوّق القاب و شدّت امتناع و احجاب بسته گردانیده اند هرکس که بر تخت خانی
نشیند یک اسم در افزایند خان یا قاآن و بس زیادت از آن ننویسند...

...and according to Chengiz Khan's Yasa ("mandate"), they [Chengiz Khan's descendents] should consider all religions as one and make no distinction among them and not deviate from the mandate. Among the praiseworthy customs, as have been the preferred practice among our predecessors and the tradition among statesmen, are the closing of the doors of complication and cleverness in titles and the excessive withdrawal and remoteness [of the ruler], and whoever occupies the throne as Khān has one word and only one added to his name, Khān or Qa'an, and no more than that is appended... (Juvayni, Tārikh-i Jahāngushā, pp. 18–19; Eng. trans. I, p. 26)

Notwithstanding Chingiz Khān's recommendation, panegyrics became a predominant feature of history writing under the later Mongols. The complicated style of writing that had begun earlier under the Seljuks and the KhwārazmShāhs had an impact on the Mongol chancellery. In fact, the trend toward complication in prose became even more pronounced in the post-Mongol period. Turbidity (*ta`qid*), affectations (*takalluf*), and verbosity (*atnāb*) turned out to be the dominant features of history writing. According to Ja`far Shahidi, the reason for the development of this style was to gratify the patrician taste of the nobility in the court, who admired ornamental prose and considered simple language the vernacular of common people. Hence, a grandiloquent style (*sabk-i tajammuli*), overabundant in figures of speech, developed in response to the taste of·the elite.[9] Inasmuch as some of the prominent court *munshi*s, such as Juvayni and Vassāf, were excellent scholars of Arabic, the influence of Arabic attained its peak during this time. As a result of these influences, the graceful style of early Persian prose began to vanish.[10] In addition to Arabic many Mongolian administrative terms and words entered the language. Similes, metaphors, Persian and Arabic verses, proverbs and epigrams, and long quotations suggestively drawn from the Qur'an and the Hadith became prominent features of history writing. Also, the number of grandiose titles and epithets (*alqāb va `anāvin*) increased as panegyrics (*mudāhina va madāhi*) became a dominant theme of history writing.[11]

The literary pedigree of this genre of historiography goes back to the *History of the World Conqueror* (*Tārikh-i Jahāngushā*), written in 1297 by `Ata-Malik Juvayni. However, the preeminent example of turbid writing (*nasr-i mukhallaf*) of the Mongol period is *Tārikh-i Vassāf,* written in about 1328. Reportedly, when Sharaf al-Din Vassāf read his work aloud, it was unintelligible to his patron, Uljaitu, until Rashid al-Din Fazl Allāh and other courtiers explained the embellishments to him. Despite the need to explain his writing, Vassāf was rewarded with a robe of honor and the title of *Vassāf al-Hazrat,* meaning "His Majesty's Panegyrist."[12] Bahār, an admirer of Vassāf's writing style, admits that the author's excessive use of technical embellishments (*sanāye`i muzayyin*) and Arabic phraseology makes his work difficult and tedious reading, even for those who appreciate ornamental prose. Although *Tārikh-i Vassāf* includes important historical information, more recent scholars simply regard it as the prototype of high literary Persian prose rather than as a useful historical text.[13] Rypka contends "… with his excessive tendency to arabizing, his monstrous bombast, unbearable floridness and dallying, Vassāf did tremendous harm to Persian prose."[14] Browne has also labeled *Tārikh-i-Vassāf* as a work that had "an enduring evil influence" on later historians.[15] Vassāf's turbid and excessively ornamental prose style was widely emulated by Persian chroniclers many years after the fall of the

Ilkhanid Mongols in 736/1335. Court *munshi*s, who produced the bulk of historical writings, preserved and assimilated the ornate style.[16] According to Faridun Ādamiyat, Persian historiography declined from the 14th to the 19th centuries as a result of exaggeration (*ighrāq-gui*), ambiguity (*mughallaq nivisi*), verbosity (*pur harfi*), and the parading of the author's learning.[17]

Under the Timurids (871–906/1370–1507) a new school of historiography developed which had its centers in Samarqand and Herat. According to John Woods, it was this school that affected the historiographers of the later periods.[18] The prose style of the Timurid era is characterized by Bahar as intermediate (*nasr-i miyāna*) "because it has neither the fluency of the earlier prose writers nor the turbidity of Vassāf's style of writing."[19] The historians of this period did not totally abandon Juvayni and Vassāf's ornamental style but conveyed the historical content in less complicated language. Literary embellishments appeared predominantly in the opening chapter and sometimes at the beginning of the chapters that followed or in the depiction of new seasons, feasts, hunting scenes, and the description of gallantry on the battle field, etc. A prominent example of this genre is the *Zubdat al-tavārikh* (Cream of Histories) by `Abd al-Rashid Bahā al-dini, better known as Hāfiz Abru (d. 833/1430). Abru, a famous historian of the Timurid era, devotes the opening chapter of *Zubdat al-tavārikh* in praise of Timur and his son, Shāhrukh Mirzā, with a long list of grandiose epithets and kingly attributes that covers several folios. The essential content, however, is void of intense literary embellishment and is written in lucid language, such as the following passage.[20]

و بعد از آن خبر رسید که پسر سیفل قندهاری و ملک محمد که بموجب حکم و فرمان
بندگی آنحضرت هر یک بر طرفی از آن نواحی حاکم بودند, با یکدیگر نزاع میکنند و
رعایای آن نواحی بدین سبب در زحمت و تشویش اند. بندگی حضرت را معاش ناپسندیده
ایشان معلوم شد. امیر اعظم اعدل امیر حسن صوفی ترخان را مقرر فرمود که بدان
طرف رود و آن دیار را ضبط نماید ....چون بدانجا رسید و احوال انطرف معلوم
گردانید, پسر سلطان
.....تواجی شاه ویس غزنین را محاصره کرده بود

And after that, news arrived that the son of Seyfal of Qandahar and Malek Muhammad who, according to the order and command of His Majesty's servant [i.e., minister], were in charge of a portion of those districts, had quarreled with each other and for this reason the people of those areas were suffering hardship and disorder. The minister learned of the unfortunate state of their lives. The greatest, most just commander [i.e., the ruler], ordered Amir Hasan

Sufi Tarkhān to go there and seize that territory. When he had arrived there and become aware of the situation, the Sultan Tuwaji's son had surrounded the commander of Shāh Veys of Ghazna.

Despite the panegyrics, Abru understood the importance of recording history accurately and objectively. He argues that history is based on truth. Its purpose is to record the good and the bad, justice and injustice, good deeds and bad deeds, as well as the virtues and the vices of the past generation in order to make the next generation aware of the advantages and detriments of good and bad statesmanship and help them follow the good examples and refrain from malevolence. He also stresses that a historian must avoid partiality (*meyl*) and prejudice (*ta'assub*).[21]

بباید دانست که بنای علم تاریخ صدق است ...در علم تواریخ نقل خیر و شر و عدل و ظلم و استحقاق و غیر استحقاق و محاسن و مقابح و اطاعت و معاصی و فضائل و رذائل سلف است تا خوانندگان خلف از آن اعتبار گیرند و منافع و مضار جهانداری و نیکوکاری و بدکرداری دریابند تا نیکوکاری را اتباع نمایند و از بدکاری بپرهیزند...[مورخ] باید آنچه مینویسد بی میل و تعصب نویسد....

One must know that the foundation of the science of history is truth ... The science of history embraces relating the good and the bad, justice and oppression, entitlement and the opposite, praiseworthy and offensive actions, loyalty and rebellion, and the virtues and vices of our ancestors, so that readers in the future may profit by this and learn of the benefits and harm of rule, and come to know benevolence and malevolence so that they will adhere to benevolence and avoid malevolence...The historian must write his works without partiality and prejudice ...

The historiography of the Safavid period (1502–1737) displayed most of the characteristics of the school of Herat, but the chroniclers of this period, according to Woods, also relied on histories written under the Aqquyunlus (White Sheep Turkmen, 1378–1508) in western Iran.[22] Contemporary Iranian literary critics characterize the Safavid era as a period of literary stagnation. Bahār, for example, regards the prose writings of the period to be hollow and tasteless.[23] The only historian of high literary standard, according to Bahār, was Mirzā Mehdi Khān Astarābādi, the author of *Tārikh-i Nādiri*, also known as *Tārikh-i Jahāngushā-yi Nādiri* (History of Nādir Shāh's Conquests), who was trained during the Safavid era. Bahār considers Astarābādi's work, from a literary point of view, to be the masterpiece of prose writing of the late Safavid era and compares its elegant and innovative style to *Tārikh-i Vassāf.*[24] Astarābādi's work, as will be seen later, served as a model for the author of *Tārikh-i Ahmad Shāhi* (The History of Ahmad Shāh), one of the two texts discussed in this chapter.

Unofficial and Popular Historiography

Although court historians produced the most important historical literature in Persian, they were not the only writers of history. In addition to the official chroniclers, who wrote at the command of kings and nobles, there were literati who wrote on their own initiative and recorded whatever they deemed interesting and important—significant contemporary events, stories, romances, folk wisdom, etc. These unofficial historians had more latitude than court historians, who were often compromised when it came to recording sensitive issues. Consequently, their works appear more objective. This is not to say, however, that they were unbiased. Racial, ethnic, and religious slurs, exaggerated phrases of praise or censure, obscenity, and satire are common in their work. Despite the inclusion of these elements, they contain important social history not usually found in official rhetorical histories. Two examples of this type of historical work are *Badāye' al-vaqāye'* (Remarkable Tales) by Zain al-Din Mahmud Vāsifi (b. 890/1484 in Herāt) and *Rustam al-tavārikh* (Champion of Histories) by Muhammad Hāshim Rustam al-Hukamā, written in 1209/1797.

HISTORY WRITING IN THE SADDUZAI DYNASTY IN AFGHANISTAN

In the following pages I will examine these two types of history writing by comparing two historical documents of the Sadduzai period in Afghanistan: *Tārikh-i Ahmad Shāhi* (The History of Ahmad Shāh), written in 1186/1773 by Munshi Mahmud al-Husaini, and *Navā-i Ma'ārik* (The Sound of Battles), written by Mirzā Atā Muhammad Shikārpuri in 1272/1855. The earlier work was written during the formative period of the Sadduzai era, which was a time of conquest and empire building. It was written by a court *munshi* of high rank, who was trained in the tradition of the chancery. The second work was written by a lower-ranking *munshi,* who was in the service of several important officials and noblemen. In this capacity, he was an eyewitness to many of the important happenings described in his work. He wrote on his own initiative in a time of political instability when the chancellery had lost its grandeur and epistolography was released from the constraints of the royal court.

Establishment of the Sadduzai Dynasty

The Sadduzai dynasty began with Ahmad Khān of the Pashtun Abdāli tribe. He was proclaimed Shāh in 1747 by the chieftains of the Abdāli and Ghilzai tribes in a grand inter-tribal council (*loya-jirga*), in Qandahar.[25] Originally a Pashtun tribal institution, the *loya-jirga* has since the time of Ahmad Shāh been convened in Afghanistan to address issues of national importance. After his accession to the throne Ahmad Khān assumed the title of Ahmad Shāh Durr-i Durrāni (Pearl of Pearls).[26] Henceforth, the Abdāli tribe, of which the Sadduzais were a branch, became known as the Durrānis. He also established the rule of the Durrāni Pashtuns, who founded the state of Afghanistan and continued to control it until 1978.

Ahmad Shāh's twenty-six year reign was a period of military conquest and territorial expansion. After his accession to the throne, he took advantage of the unsettled situation following Nādir Shāh's assassination and the dwindling power of the Mughals in India to extend the frontiers of his authority into northern India, the eastern parts of Iran, and Central Asia. He succeeded in building a vast empire that extended from Nishapur and Mashhad in the west to Kashmir in the east and from Transoxiana in the north to the Arabian Sea in the south.

Dār al-Inshā-i Ahmad Shāhi

Ahmad Shāh's government consisted of many departments under the direction of the *Divān Begi* or *Ashraf al-Vuzarā* (prime minister), with the literati and the Durrāni Pashtun nobles occupying the most important positions in the bureaucracy. Although Ahmad Shāh was a native speaker of Pashto, he continued to use Persian as the official language of administration. As mentioned earlier, *Dari* Persian developed in Transoxiana and northern Afghanistan and became the language of literature and administration in the region from the time of the Ghaznavids. Ahmad Shāh and his successors were all conversant with the Persian language and its literature and wrote with great facility in Persian as well as in Pashto. Timur Shāh (1772–93), Ahmad Shāh's successor, was an accomplished poet. So was

Shāh Shujā' (1806–9, 1839–41), Timur Shāh's son, who like his father produced a divan of Persian poetry in addition to an autobiography (*Ruznāma-i Shujā'*). According to Mountstuart Elphinstone, Zamān Shāh (l793–1802) was skilled in Persian prose.[27] He and his brother, Shāh Shujā', and Prince Qaisar, Zamān Shāh's son, wrote some of the royal mandates and diplomas themselves.[28] The same was true of members of the Durrāni administrative elite, such as Shāh Vali Khān Fāfulzai, Ahmad Shāh's prime minister, and his nephew, 'Abd-Allāh Khān, who held the same position under Timur Shāh.[29]

One of the most important divisions of Ahmad Shāh's administration was the royal chancery (*dār al-inshā-i huzur,* also known as *daftar-i rasā'il*).[30] With the expansion of the empire and commensurate increase in administrative correspondence, the *dār al-inshā* became an even more important division of the government. It was in this office that all letters and documents were produced, copied, and archived. Individuals of superior wit and learning were recruited from diverse regions of the empire to serve as secretaries in the imperial chancellery. Fāfulzai mentions the following individuals among the famous *munshi*s of this early period: Mirzā Sayyid Mahmud Husaini of Herat (the author of *Tārikh-i Ahmad Shāhi*); Shāh Pasand Ishāqzai; Mirzā Ahmad Durrāni; Mirzā Darvish 'Ali (a Hazāra); Mirzā Ja'far Shāmlu (from Herat); Mirzā 'Aziz-Allāh (from Lahore), and Mirzā Muhammad Kāzim Barnābādi (from Ghur).[31] Some of the prominent *munshi*s of the early Sadduzai period came from Isfahān, Sabzevār, Tabriz, Mashhad, and Kashmir. The head of the chancellery in the time of Ahmad Shāh and Timur Shāh was Mir 'Abd al-Hādi Lāri, belonging to the Musavi Safavids of Isfahan, who according to Fāfulzai, entered the service of Ahmad Shāh in Iran and later converted into Hanafism, the School of Islamic Law that was official in the Durrani state.[32]

The *munshi*s of the Sadduzai era followed the conventions of Central Asian and Turkic epistolography. A highly qualified *munshi* was one who distinguished himself in profound scholarship and learning. Such a *munshi* would have a sound knowledge of the techniques of prose (*zavābit-i sanāyi'-i inshā*), would have developed a style ornate with artistic embellishments (*chehra-nāma-yi badāyi'-i sanāyi'*), would be keenly aware of the unique characteristics of proper writing and orthography (*qā'ida-dān-i qavā'id-i nādira-i imlā*), be conversant in accounting (*siyāq*), and skilled in the art of calligraphy.[33] The *munshi*s of this period were all accomplished calligraphers of the *nasta'liq* and *shikasta* scripts, which were considered formal and stately.

The chancery was headed by the *munshi-bāshi,* the chief secretary, who was closely associated with the person of the Shāh. He was responsible for drafts of royal orders (*farmān*s), diplomatic and political correspondence, and for the supervision of the secretaries who worked under him. Significant ranks among the *munshi*s were the king's private secretary (*munshi-i huzur*), newswriter or political correspondent (*vāqi`a-nivis*), military scribe (*lashkar-nivis*), and history scribe (*munshi-i tārikh,* also known as *majlis-nivis*).[34] The secretary historian held a high position in the court and had to have, in addition to what was expected of other secretaries, qualifications expected of a diplomatic stylist: a sound knowledge of the Qur'an and Hadith, complete familiarity with the theory of the state, and a command of prosody and poetics.

The person who held the position of secretary historian in Ahmad Shāh's chancellery was Munshi Mahmud al-Husaini, the author of *Tārikh-i Ahmad Shāhi.* As a chancery scribe, his duties also included composing letters, documents, and diplomatic messages.[35] Al-Husaini's place and date of birth are unknown. In his book he introduces himself as Mahmud al-Husaini al-Munshi ibn Ibrahim al-Jāmi. The addition of Jāmi as a *nisba* at the end of his name suggests that he was from Jām—most likely the same Jām in the province of Herat where the famous poet `Abd al-Rahmān Jāmi came from. It is also possible that he belonged to the highly literary Al-Husaini family of Herat. A prominent member of this family, Mir `Abd al-Qāsim Khān Namakin, was the author of *Munsha'āt al-Namakin* and a famous *munshi* in the court of two Mughal emperors, Akbar and Jahangir.[36] A family of the same name is still highly regarded in Herat for producing several generations of accomplished literary members.

TĀRIKH-I AHMAD SHĀHI (HISTORY OF AHMAD SHĀH)

Al-Husaini's *Tārikh-i Ahmad Shāhi* is a significant source of history. As Moradov points out, it is a history written in Afghanistan about its founder "by an eye-witness to and participant in many important events of the epoch."[37] The manuscript was obtained by the Asiatic Museum of St. Petersburg in 1900 along with 46 other manuscripts from Bukhara and was later deposited in the Institute of Oriental Studies in Leningrad.[38] An incomplete copy of *Tārikh-i Ahmad Shāhi* is also held in the Bombay University Library.[39] The work was unknown to scholars until it was made available as a photographic facsimile in Moscow in 1974.[40] In 2000, *Tārikh-i Ahmad Shāhi* was printed from a photocopied version in Peshawar, Pakistan, with marginal notations and an introduction by Sarvar Homāyun. (All references in this chapter refer to the original facsimile version.)

Framework

The chronicle is written in a fine and legible *nasta'liq* hand. It consists of two volumes and is divided into twenty-six chapters that correspond to Ahmad Shāh's twenty-six year reign. There are subdivisions of various lengths that create 166 sections altogether. Following the pattern of historiography of the earlier periods, Al-Husaini begins his work with the usual invocation followed by a long list of epithets attributed to the king to whom he dedicates the work. Following the traditional convention, Al-Husaini then introduces himself and explains his reason for writing the chronicle. He reports that Ahmad Shāh wished to find an accomplished *munshi* capable of recording accurately his deeds and accomplishments in a simple and clear style (*'āmm fahm*), similar to the style of *Tārikh-i Nādiri* written by Astarābādi. Muhammad Taqi Khān Shirāzi, who was commissioned to find such a person, discovered Al-Husaini in the vicinity of Mashhad during Ahmad Shāh's occupation of that city. Al-Husaini claims that Taqi Khān introduced him to Ahmad Shāh as a highly qualified *majlis nivis* who was skilled in the art of panegyrics (*mādih sigāli*), was a long associate of Mirza Mehdi Khān Astarābādi, the author of *Tārikh-i Nādiri*, had learned from him the art of judicious writing and the adornment of style, but wrote even better and in a livelier style than Astarābādi, and had a magical hand (*yad-i beyzā*) in conveying the purpose of a message.[41]

روزگاری با میرزا مهدی خان مصنف تاریخ نادری بسر برده است و مدت های مدید با او
طریق مرافقت سپرده و طرز نکته پردازی و عبارت آرائی از او فراگرفته و حتی مطالب را از
او بهتر و رنگین تر میسراید و در مدعا نویسی ید بیضا مینماید

He [i.e., al-Husaini] had spent some time with Mirzā Mahdi Khān [Astarābādi], author of Tārikh-i Nādiri, *and they had been friends for a long time and he had learned from him the ways of subtle expression and elegant prose, and even expressed things better and more colorfully than he [Astarābādi] did and was a wizard at crafting arguments.*

Notwithstanding this audacious claim of superior credentials, Al-Husaini humbles himself as was customary among the writers, by stating that although he had not practiced his profession for years and did not feel qualified to take up the grave responsibility of serving as royal panegyrist (*vassāf*), he was obliged to accept the position, because disobeying the sovereign was considered morally reprehensible by the literati (*ahl-i adab*) and would result in his losing the respect of peers in the profession.[42]

He follows the conventional practice of beginning his work with an account of the king's genealogy (*ansāb*) and the history of his tribe, the Abdālis, who ruled in Herat before Nādir Shāh's conquest of that city. He then recounts several prophesies to the effect that it was God's will for Ahmad Shāh to ascend the throne. Prophesy and divine intervention were means by which the historians legitimized the rule of the founder of a new dynasty. Even Juvayni, who had a hard time finding words to rationalize Chingiz Khān's rise to power, cites prophesy by an ascetic to confirm that Chingiz Khān's rule was ordained by God.[43]

در آن سرمای سخت که در آن حدود باشد برهنه چند روز بیابان و کوه رفتی و باز آمدی...
گفتی خدای با من سخن گفت و فرمود که تمامت روی زمین بتمرجین و فرزندان او دادم و اورا
نام چنگیز نهاد...

I heard from Mongols of reputation that at this time someone appeared and that in the severe cold that prevailed in that area he went about naked for several days in the deserts and mountains and returned and said that God had spoken to him and had said "I have given everything on the face of the earth to Temorjin (i.e., Chengiz Khān] and his descendants, and I have named him Chengiz Khān." (Juvayni, Jahāngushā, p. 28; Eng. trans., p. 39)

Astarābādi relates that before Nādir Shāh rose to power, he had a dream about having captured a swan and a large white fish. When he told this dream to his companions, one of them predicted that he would certainly become king one day and recited the following verse.[44]

اگر در خواب بینی مرغ و ماهی   نمیری تا رسی بر پادشاهی

If you dream of a bird and a fish / you will not die until you have become king.

Al-Husaini reports that a wise and holy dervish by the name of Sāber had predicted, long before Ahmad Shāh ascended the throne, that he would become king after the collapse of Nādir Shāh's reign. Then Sāber showed up in Qandahar during the debate over kingship, when the young and unassuming Ahmad Khān appeared reluctant to accept the throne at the people's request; he placed a wreath in the form of a crown on Ahmad Shāh's hat and with this gesture sanctioned his right to the throne[45]:

در اثنای استدعا و التماس مردم , و ابا و استنکاف خدیو جهان ستان گیاه سبزی به دست... گرفته به جالی جیغه بر گوشهء کلاه آنحضرت استوارساخته ...در همان ساعت فاتحه فتح و فیروزیو دوام سلطنت و بهروزی به اسم والقاب نامی آن حضرت در مجمع عام بگوش هوش کافهء انام رسانید...

In the midst of the prayers and supplications of the people, and the reluctance and re-jection of the World-Conquering Leader, he [i.e., Sāber] took a green sprig in his hand and stuck it on the shining ornament on the side of His Honor's turban … At the same moment the prayer for triumph and victory and the endurance of the rule and good fortune of the name and celebrated titles of His Majesty were conveyed to the keen ears of everyone in the crowd.

He also writes that Ahmad Shāh's decision to choose the title Durr-i Durrān was based on a dream.[46]

As in *Tārikh-i ʿĀlam Ārā-yi ʿAbbāsi* (The World-adorning History of ʿAbbas) and some other works of the Safavid era, Al-Husaini identifies chronology by the year of accession of the ruler (*julus*) in the Turkic animal year, followed by the lunar Islamic date (*hijri qamari*) in the title of the main chapters. Each chapter title is then followed by details of the vernal equinox and a poetic description of spring. The following are examples from *Tārikh-i ʿĀlam Ārā-yi ʿAbbāsi* by Iskandar Begi, *Tārikh-i Nādiri* by Astarābādi, and *Tārikh-i Ahmad Shāhi* by Al-Husaini:

Example #1 (*Tārikh-i ʿĀlam Ārā-yi ʿAbbāsi*)

وقایع سال میمون و ایام سعادت مقرون توشقان ئیل ترکی مطابق الف هجری سال پنجم جلوس همایون

The events of the auspicious year and joyous days of the Turkish year Tushqan'il, corresponding to the year one thousand Hijri, the fifth year of [His Majesty's] august reign…[47]

چون فصل شتا به نهایت انجامید و باد بهاری صلای نزهت و خرمی داده عشرت سرای باغ و بوستان از گل ریحان آرایش یافت.

ز اعتدال هوا و ز دور چرخ اثیر   و عهد شاه جهان تازه گشت عالم پیر

When the winter season drew to a close and the spring breeze brought the

warmth of pleasure and happiness, the pleasure gardens and orchards were adorned with the flowers of sweet basil.

From the equinox, the air, and from the turning of the heavens / and the reign of Shāh Jahān (or of the King of the World), the old world became new.

اعنی نوروز جهان افروز بخرمی و فیروزی در روز چهارشنبه بیست و پنجم شهر جمادی الاول وقوع یافته خسرو چهار بالش سپهر در شرفخانهٴ حمل قرار گرفته گیتی آرای گشت.

That is to say, the world-warming New Year occurred with joy and triumph on Wednesday, the twenty-fifth of the month of Jumādi al-avval, and as the King of the heavens' throne settled into the noble house of Aries (hamal), the world became decked out.

Example #2 (*Tārikh-i-Nādiri*)

در ذکر وقایع قوی ئیل مطابق سال همایون فال 1139 هجری

Concerning the events of [the Turkish year] Qui'il, corresponding to the auspicious year 1139 Hijri.[48]

روز بیست و ششم شهر رجب المرجب خسرو سیارگان بشهرستان حمل کشید شاهد گل پیرهن بهار در شبستان چمن و دامن جویبار آغاز جلوه گری کرد عروس دلارای لاله و ریحان در حجلهٴ گلشن بنشو و نما برخواست....

On the twenty-sixth day of the month of Rajab al-murajjab, the ruler of the planets moved his entourage to the city of Aries (hamal). The blossom-bloused beauty, spring, began to reveal her loveliness in the bed-chamber of the meadows and beside the brooks. The tulip (a heart-cheering bride), and the sweet basil began to grow in the bridal chamber of the flower beds.

Example #3 (*Tārikh-i-Ahmad Shāhi*)

وقایع سال فرخنده فال قوی ئیل ترکی مطابق سنهٴ یک هزار و یک صد و هفتاد و هفت هجری موافق سال هفدهم جلوس میمنت میمنت مأنوس

The events of the auspicious Turkish year Qui'il, corresponding to the year 1177 Hijri, and the seventeenth year of his felicitous reign.[49]

ادراین نوروز عالم افروز که آغاز سال هفدهم لشکرکشی این خدیو موید کفر «سوز است پادشاه فارم چارم و خسرو انجم زرین کلاه به تاریخ سیم ماه رمضان سنهٴ 1177هجری مطابق سنهٴ میموننهٴ قوی ئیل ترکی به میمنت وفرخندگی متوجه دارالسلطنه حمل کشته ... و طلیعهٴ صبح نوروزی از افق بهروزی و فیروزی نمایان گشت. صیت آمد آمد موکب بهار در شش جهت روزگار پیچید و نسیم شگفتگی و خرمی به ساحت باغ و بستان وزید...

On this world-warming New Year, which is the seventeenth year of the military attack of this victorious, infidel-burning king, the king of the fourth firmament and the golden crowned king of the stars [i.e., the sun], on the thirtieth of the month of Ramazān in the year 1177 Hijri, corresponding to the auspicious Turkish year Qui'il, marched toward the kingdom of Aries (hamal) with fortune and happiness...and the dawn of the morning of the New Year became apparent on the horizon of good fortune. The clamor of the marching troops of spring echoed throughout the six directions of the world and the zephyr of wonder and happiness wafted through the gardens and orchards.

Imitating other historians' writing was actually quite permissible. Rather than being considered plagiarism, as Quinn points out it was seen as the acknowledgment of a predecessor's work.[50]

Writing Style and Narrative Mode

Inasmuch as Al-Husaini considered himself better qualified than Astarābādi, it is not surprising to find that his style of writing differs in some ways from the writing style of *Tārikh-i Nādiri*, Ahmad Shāh's ideal history model. Al-Husaini's style falls between the writing styles of *Tārikh-i ʿĀlam Ārā-i ʿAbbāsi* of Iskandar Beg and *Tārikh-i Nādiri* of Astarābādi, as it is more ornate than the former and less complicated than the latter, in which respect it resembles the style of the historians of the Timurid era. In the introductory chapter Al-Husaini indulges in the use of artful devices, figurative speech, and balanced rhymed phrases (*saj*ʿ), reminiscent of the work of Hafiz Abru's *Zubdat al-Tavārikh*. Al-Husaini dedicates his book to "the King of Kings, the Protector of Islam, whose wholesome nature is the embodiment of Divine compassion, endowed with the four elements of virtue: water of serenity, soil of humility, wind of kindness, and fire of bravery."

این کتاب مستطاب احوال شاهنشاه اسلام پناهی است که طینت پاکش مظهر رحمت الهی است بآب حلم و خاک تواضع و باد لطف و آتش شجاعت ترتیب یافته

This distinguished book is an account of the King of Kings, protector of the faith, whose pure nature reveals God's mercy and is composed of the water of clemency, the earth of humility, the air of benevolence and the fire of bravery.

Prolixity (*atnāb*)— the use of similes and metaphors—and parallel rhyming sentences are particularly noticeable in the two-page description of the attributes he ascribes to Ahmad Shāh. The following are a few examples:

فرازنده لوای کشورکشایی برازنده اریکه فرمانفرمائی اختر فلک خلافت و ظل الهی گوهر
صدف سلطنت و جهان پناهی

The hoister of the standard of conquest, the grace of the throne of sovereignty, the star of the firmament of rule, the Shadow of God, the pearl of the crest of kingship.

جوهر صمصام فتح و ظفر میعار امتحان فضل و هنر

The essence of the sword of conquest, the standard for the assessment of knowledge and art…

مروج دین بیضای احمدی حامی شرع والای محمدی نظریافت عین عنایات ربانی موید
بتائیدات و پیغامات سبحانی السلطان اعظم و الخاقان اکرم سلطان احمدشاه در دران خلدالله ملکه
و افاض علی العالمین بره و عدله و احسانه..

The expounder of the resplendent Ahmadi religion, the protector of the glorious Muhammadan law, the beneficiary of God's benevolence, the upholder of Divine messages and injunctions, the great sultan and the generous khāqān, *Sultan Ahmad Shāh Durr-i Durrān. May God eternalize his kingdom and pour upon him His bounty, justice, and grace in both worlds…*

Parallel rhyming, as the following passage demonstrates, appears occasionally in the texts:

سپاهیان نصرت نشان و غازیان ظفر اقتران را فنون دشمن افگنی و شئون لشکر کشی تعلیم
مینمودند و نوادر تدابیر ملک کشائی و بدایع منصوبه های عالم آرائی که دستور العمل سلاطین
اقالیم گیر و سرمشق ملوک عالم تسخیر باشد به مقتضای مراحم جبلی دلنشین ملازمان فرمان
پذیر و بندگان دار النظیر میفرمودند.

They taught the victorious soldiers and triumphant fighters for the faith the arts of overthrowing the enemy and the ways of attacking, and they imparted the fine points of planning the conquest of kingdoms and the details of strategies for adorning the world, which are the operating manuals for world-conquering sultans and the models for world-seizing kings, in accordance with the innate, heart-warming kindness of obedient attendants and worldly slaves.

In addition to Arabic words and phrases, the author uses words of Turkic and Mongolian origin, mostly administrative and military terms that had gained currency in the post-Mongol era. In addition, every now and then Al-Husaini uses Turkic and Mongolian words, in vogue in earlier periods, instead of their Persian equivalents, perhaps to show his mastery of the style of his predecessors. Here are a few examples: *chilanchi* (cook), *yurt* (house or residence), *ilghār* (attack), *yurqa māl* (hostage), *dastāq* (hostage), *bāshqul* (messenger), *yasaq* (expedition), *tughali* (sheep), *turgi* (successor to throne).

به وصول این خبر شهد زندگانی به کام جان تلخ تر از زهر گشت و دانست که شیلانچی...
.قضا نمکدان قسمت او را از نعمای دنیا خالی ساخته بر زمین شکست دست از طعام باز کشید

Receiving this news, the sweetness of life became even more bitter than poison to him. He understood that the cook of fate has emptied his dish of the joy of the world; he broke down and stopped eating...[51]

شاه ولیخان وزیر [را] که مقرب پایهء سریر خلافت مصیر بود مربی خود نموده و بوساطت
.او رو بیورت قدیم آورد

He sought the support of Vazir Shāh Vali Khān, who was closely associated with the royal court and through his intervention returned to the old quarters.[52]

نشاندن عمادالدین عالمگیر را بر تخت سلطنت هندوستا ن و دستاق ساختن او...
پسر محمدشاه پادشاه را بزندان

The installation of `Imād al-Din `Ālamgir on the throne of India and the detention of Muhammad Shāh's son as a hostage.[53]

در این حال باشقول که به جهت استخبار احوال پیشقراولان نصرت شعار رفته بود آمده
...عرض نمود

At this point, the messenger, who had gone to collect information about the gallant front guards, came back and said...[54]

...در این اثنا تغلی از رمه یی که به دامن صحرا در چرا بود پیدا شد...

At this time, a sheep that belonged to the herd that was grazing in the pasture appeared.[55]

و به این اندیشه که مبادا کسی از مخالفان دولتش شاهزاده را به تورگی برداشته مصدر...
...هنگامه آرائی شود آن کوکب برج سروری را از خانه بیرون نمیگذاشت

...fearing that one of his opponents might make trouble for him and position the prince [Shāhrukh Mirzā] as the successor to the throne, he prevented that star

of royal lineage from leaving the house…[56]

As in the case of chroniclers of the earlier period, Al-Husaini uses Arabic plural forms with Persian and other non-Arabic words: *basātin* for *bustan*, *dakākin* for *dukkān*, *sarādiq* for *sarā parda*, *akrād* for *kurd*, *atrāk* for *turk*.

شاه سلیمان خان محمد حسن خان قاجار و سرداران اکراد و اتراک را رخصت رفتن اوطان .
حسب الخواهش ایشان بخشید.

Shāh Sulaymān gave permission to Muhammad Hasan Khān Qājār and the leaders of the Kurds and Turks to return to their home towns, as they wished.[57]

Following the writers of the Safavid period, Al-Husaini frequently uses the Arabic relative suffix, *-iya*, instead of the Persian suffix with ethnic and tribal names:

آدینه بیگ خان و سیف الدین خان را با قشون قزلباشیه و هندیه به طرف دست راست و سید جمیل الدین
خان و خواجه میرزا خان را با قشون اوزبکیه و راجپوتیه سمت دست چپ ...در عرصهء جدال انداخت.

He positioned Ādina Beg and Saif al-Din Khān with the Qizilbāsh and Hindu troops to the right side of the battlefield and Sayyid Jamil al-Din Khan and Khwāja Mirzā Khān with the Uzbek and Rajput troops to the left.[58]

هزار کس از قشون ترکیه جمع کرده در شهرکلات برآمد

He collected one thousand Turkish troops and proceeded to the city of Kalāt.[59]

A few Pashto words, such as *nanawat* (the Pashtun practice of honoring a woman's appeal for peace), appear occasionally in the text:

صلاح کار در آن و بهبود خود در آن دید که مادر خود را به طریق نانوات به اتفاق ملا محمد...
...و جمع دیگر از سرکردگان نامی بلوچ برای استیمان و استعفا روانهء درگاه والا سازد

He deemed it advisable and to his advantage to send his mother in a gesture of nanawat to His Majesty's court along with Mulla Muhammad and a group of important Balochi dignitaries to plea for forgiveness.[60]

The general tone of *Tārikh-i Ahmad Shāhi* is bombastic and laudatory. The author's main objective is to enhance the reputation of his patron as the champion of Islam. A skillful diplomatist, well acquainted with the protocol of the chancery, he selected passages from the Qur'an to glorify the ruler as the custodian of justice, peace, and stability. Al-Husaini stresses that royal authority is needed to preserve Islamic order and public security. He compares the role of the king in his country to that of a gardener. Just as a garden will perish and be plundered without the care and watchful eye of a gardener, a country will be destroyed and its people will become victims of vicious acts of evil-doers and plunderers without a king. Al-Husaini further exalts the kings as the adornments of the world, epitomizing human dignity.[61]

نباشد اگر باغبان در سراغ   شـــود میـــوهٔ باغ تـاراج زاغ

نباشد اگر در میانه شهـی   بهر گوشه شیری کند روبهی

شهان زیب و زینت عالمند   شهان فخر نـوع بنـی آدمند

If the gardener is in pursuit / The crow will not plunder the garden's fruit
If a king is present / The fox will not emulate the lion
Kings are the adornment and embellishment of the world / Kings are the pride of mankind

Victory over aggressors and the royal defense of the weak and helpless are two major themes of the chronicle. Al-Husaini's depiction of Ahmad Shāh is that of a king endowed with virtues that surpass those of all his predecessors. Several stories illustrate Ahmad Shāh's generosity to his subjects and his kindness toward rulers in conquered lands. He draws attention to events that are usually occasions for praising the king, not only as a great conqueror but also as a generous emperor and bestower of the crown. One such instance is Ahmad Shāh's munificent act of bestowing the kingship of Iran a second time to Shāhrukh Mirzā, Nādir Shāh's grandson, after conquering the region and then suppressing an uprising led by Suleimān Shāh in Mashhad.[62]

شاه رخ میرزا که از اول مشمول عواطف کبری و منظور نظر عاطفت پیراست در بن زمان میمنت اقران چنان پرتو انداز رای عالم آرا شد که پادشاهی ولایت ایران باو مفوض فرموده پایهٔ قدر و منزلتش بعطای تاج سلطنت افزوده...

بگفتش که این ملک آبای تست   به بیگانگان چون دهم جای تست

طمع نیست مارا بمک شهان   بجز تاج بخشی و سیر جهان

Shāhrukh Mirzā, who has been a beneficiary of royal favor from the very beginning, at this propitious moment became the recipient of his kindness for a second

time, when [the king] bestowed upon him the kingship of Iran, increasing his power and prestige with a royal coronation.

He said to him "This is the kingdom of your fathers / How could I give your [rightful] place to foreigners?"

I have no desire for the realm of a king / [I want only] to make kings and travel the world.

Another example of Ahmad Shāh's extraordinary bravery and generosity, of which Al-Husaini writes in detail, is his victory over the Maharata Hindus, a formidable emerging force in India.[63] Al-Husaini provides a detailed account of Ahmad Shāh's "holy war" against the Maharata Hindus and his victory in the battle of Panipat, the highpoint of Ahmad Shāh's military achievements. The main reason for this war, he explains, was Ahmad Shāh's determination to defend the Muslims of India against the Hindus, whose hostility toward Muslims had reached a point where Muslims in many parts of India had been forced to abandon daily prayers and live in isolation for fear of the treacherous infidels.[64]

کار بجائی رسیده بود که در اکثر ممالک وسیع الفضای هندوستان مسلمانان از خوف کفار نابکار دست از آذان و صلوات برداشته به کنج عزلت بسر میبردند.

Matters had reached the point where in most of the extensive kingdoms of Hindustan, out of fear of the wicked infidels, the Muslims had given up the call to prayer and praying itself and had taken refuge in out-of-the-way corners.

Al-Husaini then gives a flowery description of Ahmad Shāh's meeting with `Ālamgir the Second in the Shalimar Gardens in the city of Shāhjahānābād (Delhi), where Ahmad Shāh bestows a dazzling jeweled crown upon `Ālamgir and reinstates him, to the latter's great surprise, as the king of India.[65]

در همان مجلس تاج مرصعی که افسر مکلل خورشید از غیرتش در تب و تاب و اکلیل زرین گل در برابر آب و تابش بی آب بود از جواهر خانهء خاص طلبیده والاجاه را به نوید بخشش سلطنت مملکت وسیع الفسحت هندوستان سر افراز و ارجمند به عطای تاجداری آن ولایت مفتخر وسربلند فرمودند..

In the same meeting he called for a jewel-studded crown from his private treasury, at which the jeweled crown of the sun was twisting and turning from jealousy and a chaplet of golden flowers looked flat and dull beside its splendor, and rendered His Majesty pleased and proud with the news that he was giving him the rule of the broad and extensive land of Hindustan, and the gift of the crown of that land made him happy and delighted.

Al-Husaini then praises Ahmad Shāh and writes that no other king has ever performed so great an act of generosity. He states that the world and its people may be sacrificed to such a king, who brings happiness with magnificent gifts to those in despair.[66]

جان عالم و عالمیان فدای چنین خسرو گرامی که دل از دست رفتگان بینوا را به چنین عطایای
جلیله مسرور میفرماید

May the life of the world and its people be sacrificed to such a generous king who gladdens the hearts of the despairing with such splendid gifts.

Notwithstanding the preponderance of accounts of military engagements and the author's use of figurative language, *Tārikh-i Ahmad Shāhi* is not dull or difficult to read. The entire work is written in an elegant prose style. It is apparent that Al-Husaini was well versed in literature and like his patron Ahmad Shāh was a man inclined to poetry. The text is interspersed with verses, mostly the author's own compositions, sometimes filling one or two folios. The meter (*mutaqārib*) corresponds to that found in the *Shāhnāma* of Ferdowsi, which, as Pandit points out, "...had set the trend for future poet-historians in the choice of meter for recording popular events and legends of heroism and valor."[67]

تهمتن توانان کشور کشای	به فرمان فرمانروای زمان
گشادند بازوی روئین تنی	به دشمن گدازی و خصم افگنی
چو گردید بر دشمنان فتح یاب	خدیو فلک قدر مالک رقاب
همی کرد با خیل و لشکر عبور	زدریا به تأئید رب غفور

At the command of the commander of the age / Rostam [sent] the world-conquering warriors
Out to melt and defeat the enemy / they opened their bronze-bodied arms
The king of celestial might, commander of men / when he had defeated the enemy "Crossed the river with his troops and army / with the assistance of the forgiving Lord"

Al-Husaini also demonstrates his artistic literary skill and poetic imagination in describing the advent of new seasons. His chronicle also includes colorful accounts of royal hunting trips and feasts. One such example is the description of the wedding of Timur Shāh, the crown prince, to the daughter of `Ālamgir the Second in Shāhjahānābād (Delhi).[68]

The last chapters of *Tārikh-i Ahmad Shāhi* deal with Ahmad Shāh's illness and death, and the succession of his son Timur Shāh to the throne. The ultimate lament is the unfaithfulness of the world in which no one is allowed to stay.[69]

دبیر قضا از طریق ممـات   نداده کسـی را بـرات نجات

نبـاشد همیشه ثبات و قرار   در این عالـم فانی بیـمدار,گ

یـل شکفد گر بباغ جهان   به گلبـن نمـاند ز باد خزان

The penman of fate gives nobody / exemption from the path of death
Stability and permanence do not exist / in this transitory and frightening world
If a flower blooms in the world's garden / it will not stand against the wind
of autumn

The final pages of the chronicle are devoted to the remembrance of Ahmad Shāh as a world conqueror, describing him as a monarch great in wisdom, prudent in counsel, vigorous in military action, outstanding for generosity, and most of all a devout and law-abiding Muslim.

For some unknown reason, Al-Husaini did not finish the last chapter of the chronicle himself. The final pages of *Tārikh-i Ahmad Shāhi* were written by his son, Muhammad Ismā`il. The book ends with an elegy about the passing of Ahmad Shāh with two chronograms which give the date of Ahmad Shāh's death.[70] The combination of letters in each of the following phrases, *"jān-i afghān"* (the soul of the Afghan) and *"ze izad shāhi-i firdows yāft"* (received from God the kingship of heaven), when added together, add up to the number 1186, which is the year of Ahmad Shāh's death.

Al-Husaini expressed a desire toward the end of the work to embark on a new history, *Tārikh-i Timur-Shāhi,* to commemorate the accomplishments of the new ruler, but there is no evidence to show that such a work was actually started. The fact that the final chapter of *Tārikh-i Ahmad Shāhi* was written by Muhammad Ismā`il may suggest that Al-Husaini wished to delegate this task to his son, or that he had fallen ill or died. As with many other chroniclers, the last year of Al-Husaini's life remains obscure. Fāfulzai claims to have seen the seals of Al-Husaini's son, Muhammad Ismā`il Al-Husaini, and of his grandson, Qāsim Al-Husaini, on the documents of the later Sadduzai period, which would indicate the continuance of Al-Husaini's line in scribal positions in the Sadduzai chancery.[71]

TĀZA NAVĀ-I MA`ĀRIK

The second text of inquiry, *Navā-i Ma`ārik* (The Sound of Battles) or *Tāza Navā-i Ma`ārik* (The Fresh Sound of Battles) was written by Atā Muhammad Shikārpuri. The original manuscript was housed in the Kabul Museum. It was published, unedited, in 1341/1962 by the Afghan Historical Society with an introduction by the Afghan historian `Ali Ahmad Kohzād. An edited version of the manuscript with a different introduction, several appendices, and corrections by `Abd al-Haiy Habibi was printed earlier in 1959 by Gulshan-i Adab in Karachi. In the edited version Habibi attempted to clarify vague phrases by comparing the original manuscript with three other copies found in Pakistan. However, some ambiguities remain. (The Persian quotations I use in this article are from the edited version by Habibi unless noted otherwise.)

Navā-i Ma`ārik covers the final decades of Sadduzai rule, at a time when the central chancery founded by Ahmad Shāh was greatly diminished as a result of the fragmentation of the Sadduzai authority and the endless competing claims to the throne. By the time of the establishment of the Muhammadzai dynasty (1823–1973), another branch of the Durrani Pashtuns, the boundaries of Durrani territory were reduced more or less to the areas forming present-day Afghanistan. About eighty years elapsed between the completion of *Tārikh-i Ahmad Shāhi* and the *Tāza Navā-i Ma`ārik*. However, during this period many important events transpired. *Navā-i Ma`ārik* was written by an "independent" chronicler, who was not obligated to use elaborately flattering language. The chronicle was not intended for the elite only but was rather to reach a wide audience. It covers the beginning of the second reign of Shāh Mahmud in 1809 through the end of the first Anglo-Afghan War (1839–1842) and the establishment of a new dynasty.

Ahmad Shāh died in 1772 and was succeeded by his son, Timur Shāh, who spent much of his twenty-one year reign (1772–1793) quelling rebellions. Timur Shāh was however able, at least nominally, to hold on to the territories conquered by his father. George Forster, who traveled to the Durrani state at that time, describes Timur Shāh's reign as a period of relative peace and prosperity.[72] Zamān Shāh (1793–1801), Timur Shāh's son and first successor, faced immediate internal and external challenges. His nine-year reign was plagued by strife with his half brother, Mahmud, and threats from the Sikhs in Punjab and the Qajars in Iran. Zaman Shāh was overthrown by Mahmud in 1801, but power struggles continued between Shāh Mahmud and Shāh Shujā`, Zaman Shāh's full brother. Shāh Mahmud was then overthrown by his half brother, Shujā` al-Mulk, in 1803. Six years later in 1809 Shāh Mahmud regained power with the help of Fateh Khān Bārakzai, the Ashraf al-Vuzarā, who became Shāh Mahmud's capable and powerful prime minister. As a result of power struggles among Timur Shāh's sons the Durrani Empire began to disintegrate. The Sadduzais lost the western regions of the empire to the Qajars of Iran and the province of Punjab to the Sikhs. Shāh Shujā` fled to Lahore and then settled in Sind, where Ata Muhammad Shikārpuri, the author of *Navā-i-Ma`ārik,* became his private secretary.

Conflict started anew in 1818 with the blinding of the Ashraf al-Vuzarā Fateh Khan Barakzai in Herat by Kāmrān Mirzā, Shāh Mahmud's son, who became jealous of the Ashraf al-Vuzarā's growing influence and popularity. This incident happened after the latter's courageous defense of Herat against the Qajars. Shikārpuri, who accompanied Fateh Khān to Herat during this campaign, gives a detailed account of the way in which Kāmrān tricked Fateh Khān into attending unarmed a banquet in his honor and the cruel way in which Kāmrān's henchmen blinded him. The blinding and subsequent execution of Ashraf al-Vuzarā Fateh Khān in 1818 triggered eight years of bloodshed. From 1818 to the time that Fateh Khān's younger brother, Dust Muhammad Khān Bārakzai, seized power in 1826, chaos reigned in Afghanistan as the Bārakzai brothers and the Sadduzai princes struggled for supremacy.

The establishment of British colonial power in India and the ensuing rivalry between Great Britain and Russia resulted in years of regional conflict that involved Afghanistan. The origin of British involvement in Afghanistan can be traced back to Russian expansion into Central Asia and northwest Iran in the 1820s. In 1937, Muhammad Shāh, the Qājār ruler of Iran, was encouraged by the Russians to seize Herat, which was at the time under the rule of the Sadduzai prince Kāmrān. The ensuing attack on Herat was met with strong resistance by Yār Muhammad Khān Alikozai, Kāmrān's powerful vizier, and by Herati citizens who feared being ruled by the Shi`a Iranians.[73]

Sustained resistance by Herati forces resulted in a stand-off that lasted for ten months. The British became alarmed by Russian intrigue in the siege because Herat was important as a strategic passage to India. By occupying Khārg, an Iranian island in the Persian Gulf, the British created a diversion that forced Muhammad Shāh to lift the siege and relinquish claims on Herat.[74]

In the same year Russian overtures to establish contact with Amir Dust Muhammad, the ruler of Afghanistan, prompted the British to extend their power northward. In an effort to preempt further Russian advances, Lord Auckland, the British governor general of India, entered into negotiations with Shāh Shujā`, the former Sadduzai ruler of Afghanistan (1803–1809), then in exile in India, and Maharaja Ranjit Singh, the ruler of Punjab, to enlist their cooperation in a joint military operation against Dust Muhammad Khān. A treaty signed in 1838 promised Shāh Shujā` the throne of Afghanistan on the condition that he accept the stationing of permanent British troops in Kabul. Parts of Afghanistan, including areas that later came to be known as the North-West Frontier of British India, were promised to Ranjit Singh. In 1839, the combined forces, known as the Army of the Indus, advanced toward Kabul. On August 7, 1839, they installed Shāh Shujā` as the ruler of Afghanistan with little resistance. Dust Muhammad Khān was forced to flee to Bukhara. He later returned from Bukhara and submitted to the British, who transferred him to India as a hostage.

The situation remained calm until 1841 when William Macnaghten, the British commissioner in Kabul, took charge of government affairs, and it became clear that Shāh Shujā` was a British puppet. An uprising against the British presence in Kabul resulted in the deaths of Macnaghten and his assistant Alexander Burnes, and the surrender of the British garrison in early 1842. Several thousand departing British troops were massacred before reaching the British garrison in Jalālābād. In retaliation, the British invaded again the next year with a large Indian army under Lord Ellenborough and General Pollack but quickly evacuated after exacting harsh penalties. They took from Ghazni the doors of the Somānat Temple that had been brought from India by Sultān Mahmud, the Ghaznavid ruler, and burned Chahār Sath, the central covered bazaar in Kabul. In the negotiations that followed, the British agreed to release Dust Muhammad Khān from detention in India and recognize him as the independent ruler of Afghanistan. The Afghan hero of the First Anglo-Afghan War was Vizier Akbar Khān, Dust Muhammad's son, whose bravery is highly praised by Shikārpuri.

Shikārpuri covers these events in detail. He refers to the Sadduzai territory as Khurasan, a region extending from Herat in the west to Peshawar
in the east, with Herat, Qandahar, Balkh, Kabul, Ghazni, and Peshawar as
its main provinces, and Sind, Baluchistan, and Kashmir as dependent territories. This territorial depiction contrasts with Al-Husaini's discussion of
the imperial state under Ahmad Shāh, which consisted of various *dār al-
saltana*s (realms), such as the realms of Kabul, Herat, the Punjab, Mashhad,
etc., under the *dār al-khalāfa* (central authority) in Ahmadshāhi (Qandahar).
Comparing the two reveals a considerable reduction in the size of the Sadduzai territory by the time that *Navā-i Ma'ārik* was written and suggests a
shift in the concept of statehood from multi-national to territorial, where
the inhabitants of the latter were referred to as Khurasanis.

Atā Muhammad Shikārpuri

Mirzā Atā Muhammad Shikārpuri, who sometimes refers to himself as
Atā, or Atāi, as a pen name, was originally from Shikarpur in Sind. According
to his own account, he was trained as a traveling secretary (*munshi-i sayyār*)
in Shikarpur, which at the time was a part of Sadduzai domain.[75] He began
his career in his hometown, where he worked for the local government.

روزی چند در میخانهء خدمت و ملازمان مخموران صهبای ریاست و حکمرانی بسر آورده
خصوصا در ملک شکارپور در ایام بهارستان جوانی در اکتساب هنر انشاء پردازی
سیار [پرداختم] و هر حاکمی که سر شار رحیق حکومت و کامرانی میگردید این درد آشام
قدح خاکساری از می تقرب و ملازمی هر یکی از آنها جرعه نوش بادهء منشی گری شدم.

*In the springtime of my youth I spent some time in the wine shop of service and
attendance on some who had hangovers from the wine of leadership, especially in
the town of Shikarpur, in the vain pursuit of acquiring training as a traveling secretary. With every governor who became full of the wine of rule and success, this
dreg-drinker of the cup of abject humility drank a draft of the wine of propin-
quity and attendance, and downed a gulp of the wine of secretaryship to each.*[76]

From his description of minute details of events, it appears that he traveled extensively in the company of his employers and was an eyewitness to
important events of the time. He went to Kabul with his uncle, Shir Muhammad, a representative of the Mirs of Sind, shortly after Shāh Mahmud's
ascendance to the throne in 1809.[77] In Kabul, he became acquainted with

high-echelon officials, including Shāh Mahmud's famous Prime Minister, Ashraf al-Vuzarā Fateh Khān Bārakzai. Shikārpuri's comments about Ashraf al-Vuzarā's character and the portrayal of incidents in his personal life suggest that he was closely associated with him and that he accompanied him as a staff member on his travels to Peshawar, Sind, and Herat. After Fateh Khān was blinded in Herat and then executed, Shikārpuri worked for Fateh Khān's brother, Shirdil Khān Bārakzai, in Qandahar. He recounts fondly his years of service to Shirdil Khān, during which time he became acquainted with every important dignitary in Khurasan.[78]

و با هرکسی مردم اعزّهء خراسان راه معرفت پیدا نمودم

And to every person of importance in Khurasan I found the path of acquaintance.

Unlike Al-Husaini, Shikārpuri wrote on his own initiative with encouragement from William Eastwick, a British financial official in Shikarpur whom he greatly admired. Shikārpuri uses grandiose epithets and laudatory phrases usually reserved for great scholars in referring to Eastwick: *'unvān-i risāla-i dānishvari* (the title page of the discourse of scholarship); *dibācha-i divān-i balāghat* ('the preface to the book of eloquence); and *nādira-i al-ayām* (the rarity of the age).[79] Shikārpuri's intention in writing *Navā-i Ma'ārik,* as he explains in his introduction, was to amuse himself and entertain his readers. He humbly begs the pardon of his readers for the inadequacy of his work and refers to himself as "the drinker of the wine of imperfection" (*jur'a-nush-i bāda-i bi-kamāli*).

According to his own account, Shikārpuri's chronicle is based on random notes he wrote as an eyewitness to events during the course of his employment and travels in Herat, Qandahar, Kabul, and Peshawar, and when he was in the service of the deposed Shāh Shujā' in exile.

بحسب قسمت آبخورد ...سیّار تسافر ولایات خراسان. هرات خلد آیات و قندهار و کابل و پشاور گردیده , بعضی تسویدات از وقوعات خراسان و مقدمات شاه شجاع الملک ...که از مملکت سلطنت آواره شده بود , و غیره وقوعات که بچشم خود دیده بودم هر آینه نگاشتهء کلک خیال گردیده بود...

As was determined by fate, I traveled around Khurasan: the heavenly Herat, Qandahar, Kabul and Peshawar. I wrote up some notes about events in Khurasan and concerning King Shujā' al-moIk, who was exiled from his kingdom, and about other things, events to which I was an eye witness and which were indeed recorded in my mind.

Navā-i Ma`ārik is an authentic and important source of historical information about the social and political history of this period with details not found in any other source. It is, in fact, as Habibi points out, "a mirror reflecting the era in which the author lived."[80]

Framework

Shikārpuri begins his work with the usual elaborate doxology used by his predecessors in praising God, and the benediction on the Prophet and his family. Casual comments about the house of the Sadduzai in the introduction suggest an indifferent attitude toward the dynasty. His brief summarization of the Sadduzai period in his introduction appears to be a routine formality.

The chronicle consists of a chain of episodes connected by narrative in a storytelling mode. Every chapter begins with a poetic gesture of the pen, embellished with similes and metaphors, to signal the beginning of a new story. For example, in the following phrases that open different chapters, the pen takes the form of a nightingale, an arrow, a river, a candle, and a steed, illustrating the author's finesse with his pen:

بلبل قلم خوش رقم در بوستان این داستان چنین خوش الحان میشود

The nightingale of the silver-tongued pen sings in the rose garden of this story as follows…

دریای قلم صاف رقم در تحریر این مدعا چنین گوید.

The river of the clear-inscribing pen flows on explaining this issue…

تیر قلم راست رقم از کمان مدعای چنین نشانه بر هدف بیان میزند

The arrow of the smooth-writing pen aims from the bow to explain the matter this way…

شمع قلم روشن رقم درمجلس افروزی این مدعای چنط شعله افروز بیان میگردد

The candle of the clear-writing pen brightens the festivity with its light this way…

خنگ قلم تیز رقم در عرصهء این مدعا چنین جولان بیان میکند

The steed of the swift-writing pen rides thus in the arena to explain this matter.

The similes and metaphors in these introductory lines often correspond with the topic discussed in the chapter. For example, the chapter describing the story of the arrival of Alexander Burnes, the British agent, in Kabul begins with a phrase in which the pen is compared to Alexander the Great, the possessor of seven realms, who drinks from the black ink of the fountain of life in Khurasan, alluding to Burnes' death in Kabul:

اسکندر قلم که مالک هفت قلم سخنوریست, از چشمهء حیوان مداد سیه فام چنین بر ولایت
خراسان بیان نگارش میدهد

The Alexander-like pen, possessor of seven styles of eloquence, draws blackish ink from the fountain of life and writes thus in describing Khurasan…

Similar sentences were occasionally used by the historians of earlier periods to demonstrate their command as "master of the pen" (*sāhib-i qalam*), an appellation used for those who have achieved great proficiency in writing. For example, the following phrases in *Tārikh-i ʿĀlam Ārā-i ʿAbbāsi*:

طوطی شیرین مفال قلم در شکرستان قصه پردازی شرح آمدن جلالیان را بدین ترانه ادا
مینماید...

In the sugar field of storytelling, the sweet-spoken parrot of the pen sings the following song on describing the arrival of Jalālian.[81]

Shikārpuri, in contrast to Iskander Beg, indulges in the use of these types of similes and metaphors at the beginning of each chapter.

Writing Style and Mode of Narration

Like Al-Husaini, he uses the artful devices of the *munshis*. The text is interspersed with Persian verses and proverbs, verses of the Qur'an, and proverbs in Arabic. The quotation of Arabic proverbs and Persian poems attests to his knowledge of Arabic and Persian poetry. It is difficult, however, to ascertain whether any of these verses was composed by the author himself.

The similarities in the works of these two authors are, however, minimal compared to differences in their writing and narrative style. A glaring dissimilarity is the absence of phrases of praise and tributes to a king or a patron in Shikārpuri's work. Shikārpuri avoided using pompous titles and epithets in his work. He did however use polite appellations in referring to the political actors. For instance, he mentions Shāh Shuja's name with the appellations *ashraf-i sarkār* (the noble superior) and *awliya-i dowlat* (the sovereign) even when recording his brutal deeds. Also, notwithstanding his sharp criticism of the actions of the British, he refers to individual British officers politely as *sāhib* (Mr. or Sir), or *sāhib-i mamduh* (commendable sir), along with the epithet *bahādur* (valiant).[82]

The author sometimes indulges in the use of embellishments and complex sentences. His style of writing is oblique and often replete with odd metaphors and similes. In the words of Habibi, "it seems as if he puts food in his mouth from an angle rather than eating it straight from his hand." For example, instead of saying that so-and-so was dismissed from his post, he writes that he was pain stricken by the wine-goblet of dismissal.[83]

نایب ممدوح درد آشام قدح عزل گردید

The deputy of the patron drank the dregs of the cup of dismissal.

Another characteristic of Shikārpuri's work is the use of excessively long phrases. There are also some visible syntactic irregularities, such as the omission of the object maker (*rā*) and frequent absence of verbs in sentences. Habibi attributes these aberrations in Shikārpuri's writing to the general decline of literary Persian in the region at the time.[84] Ahmad ʻAli Kohzād, on the other hand, claims to have seen other examples of Shikārpuri's writings which attest to his high literary competence. He attributes these deficiencies to the inferior training of the copyist, Muhammad Hasan, the author's son.[85]

Unlike the unvarying, immaculate, formal writing style that appears in *Tārikh-i Ahmad Shāhi,* the mode of narration in *Navā-i Maʻārik* is inconsistent. The author of the latter switches every now and then from an ornamental literary style to an idiomatic mode. He quotes pithy sayings and expressions current in the spoken *Dari* of Afghanistan, perhaps to appeal to a wider group of readers and not just to sophisticated intellectuals. His descriptions are colorful and lively, sometimes with conversations in direct speech, which give his work a fictional quality. Such variations in the prose style within the same work were not unusual in popular histories. Another dissimilarity is the absence of Turkic and Mongolian administrative terms and the Turkic calendar in *Navā-i Ma'ārik*. Frequent use of the Christian calendar along with Islamic calendar in the final chapters of *Navā-i Ma'ārik* indicates the growing Western influence in the region.[86]

A notable characteristic of Ata Muhammad's writing is the abundant use of words of foreign origin, mostly Sindhi, revealing the influence of his native language. Some of these words had by then become a part of the *Dari* vernacular in Afghanistan. For example: *jutha* (fake), *cha* (military camp), *muri* (underground passage for water), *ganjini* (harlot), *nāch* (dance), *pahra* (guard), *panchāyat* (commercial council) and *sahukār* (money lender).

The occasional use of Pashto words such as *dira* (residence), *chawki* or *sawki* (guard), *bus* (hay), *ispist* (alfalfa), and *palwa* (from one's side) indicates that Shikārpuri had at least some knowledge of Pashto or that these words were commonly used in the Persian vernacular of this time and region. For example:

صاحب ممدوح یک دیر ئکلان درباغ متصل بنگلهء خود به جهت آرام و استراحت امیر بر پا"
"... کندانیده

The exalted Sahib [Macnaghten] built a large residence on a plot next to his house for the Amir's [Dust Muhammad] comfort...

"حاجی فیروزالدین شاه بر در وازه های قلعه هرات چوکی مقرر نموده بود ."

Hajji Firuz Shāh had stationed guards at the gates of the citadel of Herat.

کاه فروشان از فروش بوس و رشقه و اسپست جوالهای زر از سکهء کمپنی بهادر مالامال"
"نمودند

The straw dealers filled gold sacks with the coins of the esteemed [East India] Company from the sale of hay and alfalfa.

"ازپلو خود قلیی سپاه را جدا کرده پیش بفرستیم"

We must separate a small section of the army from our side and send it forward.

The text is occasionally punctuated with a direct quotation of a conversational phrase in Sindhi:

هی هی "جوان هو, جنکجو پهلوان هو..." هی هی

Alas, he was young, a hero fighter...

Or in Pashto:

"اوس وقت د مرانی وی, همت وکانی, تول فرنگیان ژوندی ونیسی."

It is now the time to be courageous. Be brave. Capture the Europeans all alive.

The use of English words such as "regiment," "orders," "court," "troop," "company," "general," "commander," "chief," "collector," which appear frequently in the formal chapters, signals divergence from the traditional style of history writing.

Another interesting feature of his writing is the use of peculiar verb forms, such as: *fahmāyish* (understanding), *kunādidan* (to do) as a verbalizer, *dādani kardan* (to pay), *fawtidan* (to die, or death), which had come into vogue in the Safavid period:

"...به صاحبان انگریز که در جلال آباد بودند فهمایش نمود..."

...he impressed upon the English, who were then in Jalālābād...

"... هرگاه محاربان در فهمایش آمدند"

if the fighters would come to an understanding...

"چندین قسم طعام از طباخان ولایتی تیار کنادیدند."

they prepared several dishes of provincial cuisine.

مبلغ چهارلک نقد عوض اخراجات و پانصد نفر شتر بجهت باربرداری در سرکار اشرف
دادنی کردند."

They paid four hundred thousand cash in property tax and five hundred camels for the transport of goods to the Eminent Chief [Shāh Shujā']...

"در بیان فوتیدن مسمات بها گل منکوحهء اشرف الوزراء"

On recounting the death of the wife of Ashraf al-Vuzarā, named Bahā Gul

فوج سرکار انگلیسیه بتاریخ دوازدهم نومبر سنه یک هزار و هشت صدو چهل عیسوی مطابق...
سنه1256 هجری از کابل تشریف فرمای جلال آباد از جلال آباد داخل درهء خیبر شدند

The English army left Kabul for Jalālābād in 1840 of the Christian era, corresponding to Hejri 1256; from there they proceeded to Khyber valley.[87]

Rather than focus on the accomplishments of one ruler only, Shikārpuri recounts political and personal rivalries, feasts and pleasure trips, love stories, and the rise and fall of numerous men of power that reflect the unsettled and turbulent era in which he lived. The major themes of the chronicle are the uncertainty of life, the inevitability of fate, and the consequences of one's good or bad deeds. These themes play out in Shikārpuri's observations about the rulers and ministers, religious personalities, local governors, heroes and villains that he encounters in his travels and about their good and evil traits and their rise and fall.

In a manner similar to other writers of popular history, Shikārpuri is candid in his criticism of some of the personalities he writes about. In describing events and people, he writes with a greater degree of objectivity than his predecessor. He recognizes that "telling the truth is sometimes distasteful" (*haqiqat talkh ast*) and apologizes for passages in his book that might be offensive to some people. For example, he describes the heart-wrenching blinding of the Ashraf al-Vuzarā Sardār Fateh Khān by Kāmrān in Herat.

Despite Shikārpuri's frequent statements of admiration for Fateh Khān's bravery and statesmanship and his expression of sadness about the incident, he writes that the Ashraf al-Vuzarā reaped the consequence of his own treachery. He then adds that "the world is the abode of justice" (*dunyā dār al-mukāfāt ast*), an epigram that affirms that a person will eventually receive punishment for bad deeds and reward for good deeds. He writes about Yār Muhammad Khān's astute leadership during the siege of Herat, but also reports his deviousness in dealing with Eldred Pottinger, the British officer who had come to Herat to assist Kāmrān in defending that city against the Qajars. He explains how in the end Pottinger was able to free himself from the snare of the shrewd vizier and return to England.[88]

بالاخره به تجویزی طایر جان خود از دام وزیر کشیده چون شاهین تیز پرواز بال افشان فضای انگلستان...
...گردید

...finally, through a scheme, he freed the bird of his life from the snare of the vizier and like a fast-flying hawk, found himself flying in the skies of England.

He also gives a detailed account of Shāh-Shujā's atrocities, particularly his assaults on women in Shikārpur, where the author served temporarily as the Shāh's private secretary, and curses him for these acts.

بماند بر او لعنت پایدار   نماند ستمکار بد روزگار

The evil tyrant will not last / eternal curses will remain with him

He then ends this account with an Arabic phrase: *la 'natu'llāh 'alā al-zālimin* ("May the curse of God be upon oppressors.")[89]

Another example of Shikārpuri's candor is illustrated in his expression of great admiration for William Eastwick and his simultaneous condemnation of the British for playing one leader against the other in Sind, and cruel acts, such as the burning of the covered bazaar of Kabul in retaliation for William Macnaghten's death:

فوج انگریز ... بهزار خواری و هزارهای کشتخون داخل کابل شده دوچندان خرج عمارات منهدمه بمالکان داده بعد به تخریب عمارات وچهار سطح بازار کابل پرده کار خود نموده و ابواب سومنات هندوستان از غزنین برداشته عازم هنوستان شدند

The English army entered Kabul with many difficulties and lots of bloodshed. They destroyed the Chahār Sath Bāzār of Kabul and many houses, after paying twice their value to the owners, took the doors of the Somanat [taken by Sultān Mahmud from the great Hindu temple in India] from Ghazni to cover up [their great losses], and left for India.

Shikārpuri gives a detailed account of the First Anglo-Afghan War and the defeat of the British. He then relates a rather long story about "crows" (*zāghān*) taking over an island, previously inhabited by "falcons" (*bāzān*). As the falcons return to the island, it becomes clear that the crows' occupation brought them nothing but destruction.[90] The story is an allegory about the British invasion, their defeat in Afghanistan, and the return of Amir Dust Muhammad Khān to his homeland following his captivity in India. Shikārpuri then draws the following conclusion:

هرگاه صاحبان انگلیسهء بهادرهوس تسخیر خراسان نمی کردند هر آینه این همه خزاین و دفاین و گدام و اتواب و دواب از قسم اسبان و شتران و غیره که تعداد آن از حساب بیرون است و هزارها سپاه سیاه و سفید از هندوستان و انگستان مانند زاغان سرپنجهء اقتدار غازیان شهبازان خراسان نمیشدند

Had the esteemed British officials not desired the occupation of Khurasan, all these funds, treasures, reserves, cannons, countless camels and horses and thousands of black and white soldiers from India and England would

not have become prey like crows in the claws of the eagle-like fighters of Khurasan ...

از آنجا که سلطنت خراسان آسان نیست. نادرشاه پادشاه با وجود حشم و چندین خزاین و دفاین
و اسباب رزم نتوانست که تمام خراسان[را] در قبضهٔ اقتدار خود آورد. اگر یک کوهستان
میگرفت, دیگر کوهستان یاغی و باغی میبود و چندین سالهای سال جنگها کرد, هرگز بملک
خراسان قادر نشد. چه جای صاحبان انگریزان باین لشکر هندوستان که صورت زاغان بودند که
در عرصهٔ ده پانزده ماه تصرف خراسان نمایند.

*Clearly, it is not easy to rule Khurasan. Nādir Shāh, despite his might, abun-
dant funds, and military weapons, was not able to control all of Khurasan.
Whenever he captured one mountainous region, insurgence would break out in
another. He [Nādir Shāh] fought for many years, but was never able to establish
control over the land of Khurasan. So how could British officers, with crow-
faced Indian soldiers, gain control of Khurasan in fifteen months?*[91]

At the end of this account, Shikārpuri asserts that Khurasan is the home of
falcons and India the abode of crows. Falcons cannot become friends with
crows.[92]

خراسان محل بازان و ملک هندوستان محل زاغان است که بازان را با زاغان آشنائی نیاید

*Khurasan is the land of falcons and the kingdom of Hindustan is the land of
crows; falcons cannot become friends with crows.*

In another place Shikārpuri comments

والاصاحبان انگریز ولایت خراسان را بجان خریدار بودند که خیال هوس در سر داشتند که در
آنجا محکمه خود گرفته سد راه روس شوند. لیکن چه فایده که هم جانها دادند و هم زر
افشاندند بجزخرابی و هزیمت نتیجه دیگری نیافتند و داغ حسرت بدل گذاشتند.

*The highly revered English would have given their lives to possess Khurasan, as
they dreamt of establishing their rule there in order to create a barrier against
Russian advances. They profited nothing. Instead they suffered great loss of life
and money, destruction, retreat, and disappointment.*

He then refers satirically to the evacuation of the British army with a popular idiom:

خانه نشینی بی بی از بیچادری است نه از مستوری .

Her ladyship remains in the house not in piety, but because she has no veil with which to cover herself to go out.

Idiomatic expressions such as the above appear throughout the chronicle, which adds to its popular appeal and distinguishes its narrative mode from the formal tone of *Tārikh-i Ahmad Shāhi*.

Official chroniclers in general avoided writing about women, except in rare instances, when they wrote about politically arranged marriages or when women were involved in some important political event, or were the mother, wife, daughter, or sister of some important political figure. Even then they sometimes refrained from mentioning the name of the woman in question. There are several references, for instance, in Al-Husaini's work to Ahmad Shāh's mother, who had great influence over her son and who accompanied him on some of his campaigns. Al-Husaini writes about the plea of the mother of one of the chiefs of Baluchistan to Ahmad Shāh and about the marriage of the daughter of Ālamgir II to Timur Shāh. In no instance are the names of the women mentioned. It was considered improper for a diplomatic historian to call a woman by her first name or to disclose her identity beyond being the mother, wife, sister, or daughter of an important man.

In contrast, Shikārpuri talks openly about the dancing girls of Kashmir and tells interesting stories about the infatuation of some eminent notables with these girls. One such instance is the account of a romantic affair be-tween a chieftain by the name of Mir Ismā`il Shāh and a Kashmiri dancing girl named Latifi. Shikārpuri relates Ismā`il Shāh's burning love for the girl and includes a letter that he wrote for Ismā`il Shāh to Latifi and Latifi's re-sponse. He also describes his role in fueling the fire of love between them. He adds that Ismā`il Shāh, being a learned man himself, was overjoyed with the letters and praised him and gave him a handsome reward for his services.[93]

از آنجا که میر اسمعیل شاه بلباس رنگین حسن دانش و کمال آراستگی تمام داشت بعد از
مطالعهء جواب مذکور نهایت حظی برد و سرخوش بادهء تعشق گردیده و این کمترین را بزبان
تحسین آفرین خوانی نمود و هم صلهء عطای نمود...

Since Mir Ismā`il Shāh was fully adorned with the colorful garb of learning and perfection, after reading the above-mentioned reply he was extremely happy *and became drunk with the wine of love and praised me highly and even gave me a gift.*

Shikārpuri also writes about the Ashraf al-Vuzarā's enchantment with the dancing beauties of Kashmir and about the death of his beloved wife, Baha Gul, who belonged to the Kashmiri entertaining class (*ahl-i tarāb-i kash-mir*), and about his love for another woman of the same class in Peshawar. Shikārpuri also mentions that Ismā`il Shāh and his uncle went to congratulate the Ashraf al-Vuzarā on his union with his newly found beauty and received robes of honor for their courteous gesture.[94]

He talks about the fascination of British officers with certain Kabuli women and recounts in detail the seduction of a slave girl from the household of Abdullāh Khān Āchekzai, a nobleman of Kabul, by Alexander Burnes. He describes how the incident became an excuse for the "gallant fighters" to rise up against the British and kill Alexander Burnes and William Macnaghten, who were by this time resident agents in Kabul.

در آن وقت برنس صاحب در حرمسرای با معشوقهء خود در حمام بحوض عشرت نشسته دیگ
مهر و محبت از آتش خوشوقتی بجوش آورده گرما بصحبت از اختلاط رنگین ساخته ... در این
اثنا غازیان نصرت توامان از روی دلیری در سرای صاحب ممدوح جلوه ریز گردیده کنیزک
مذکور و دومیم صاحبهء که معشوقهء صاحب ممدوح بودند معهء صاحب بهادر از حمام بیرون
کشیده در جامه کن جامهء زندگانی آنها [را] از برش[ان] بضرب شمشیر های کشیدند...

His Excellency Burns was at the time in his harem taking a bath with his mistress and was overjoyed with the warmth of the fire of love and sweet conversation..., when the gallant fighters attacked his residence, grabbed the slave girl and two mem sahebs [a distorted form of the English appellation "Madam" used in India to refer to English women], who were also mistresses of His Excellency, dragged them all into the dressing room and killed them, along with His Excellency.[95]

Other writers of popular history have also covered romances and incidents of sexual transgression. Shikārpuri's accounts of Shāh Shujā` and Fateh Khān's pleasure-seeking way of life are analogous to Asif's description of Shāh Husain Safavi's intemperate lifestyle in *Rustam al-Tavārikh*. In a manner similar to other writers of non-official and popular history, Shikārpuri occasionally ignores the protocol of polite writing and uses obscene language. He is however less explicit in his description of details than Asif.

Like Āsef and Zain al-Din Mahmud Vāsifi, the author of *Badāye` al-*

Vaqāye', Shikārpuri's intention in recording these stories is to enthrall his readers. In doing so he gives rare glimpses of the indulgent lifestyle of court members and notables.

The Last Chapters of Navā-i Ma`ārik

We know very little about Shikārpuri's private life, because he does not give accounts of what happened to him personally except that at such-and-such a happening he was present and a witness. It appears however that he spent the last years of his life in Shikarpur, where he completed *Navā-i Ma`ārik*. By that time, Sindh was under British control. We can assume from events he recounted that he lived at least through the middle of the 19th century.

In the last chapters of the chronicle, Shikārpuri shifts his attention to events in Sindh. He depicts events at the end of an epoch and expresses despair about the coming of new actors and new institutions and the collapse of the old political, social, and moral order. He also expresses displeasure with changes brought by the British, as the loosening of restrictions regarding the seclusion and veiling of women (*bi pardagi-i masturāt az khāss va `āmm*) and the freeing of slave girls from the households of the nobility (*mutlaq al-`inān sākhtan-i jariya az khāndān-i `uzzām*).

Similar to *Tārikh-i-Ahmad Shāhi*, the theme of the final chapter of *Navā-i Ma`ārik* includes platitudes and ruminations about the uncertainty of life in a world where nothing lasts. The chronicle ends with an account of the rivalry between two religious leaders in Sindh, who competed with each other to assist the British in exchange for material gain. Shikārpuri points out that both men died, ironically, before receiving the reward they competed for.

چقدر کوشیدند و در تنور حرص و آز جوشیدند و عمامه های افترا بستد و در خدمت صاحبان...
انگریز دویدند و بر کرسیها نشستند, آخر نتیجه ندیدند و در طرفه العین بی یکدیگر مردند و
حسرتها بردند....

...they tried hard, baked in the oven of greed, and put the turban of shame on their head by serving the English in appointed positions, but in the end they gained nothing. Each died suddenly and separately in envy and grief...

In the end, Shikārpuri expresses the hope that those who have reached high levels of enlightenment and literary eloquence will look upon his work with approval, appreciate it and not find fault out of haughtiness with the shortcomings of which he is well aware.[96]

امید از آهنگ نوازان ساز بلند فطرتان عالی همت, و روشن طبعان اهلیت و فصاحت آن دارم
که بمقتضای پاکی نظر و حسن خلق, اگر فقط بعظم تحسین و آفرین, متاع هیزم را بخرند عین
عطائی بر عطا است و گرنه بزبان عیبجوئی و نخوت نام عطا به خطا نبرند, معاف دارند , که
.من از کساد متاعی و بی هنری خود معترفم

*I have great hopes that if the players on the lute of high-mindedness and the
enlightened and eloquent experts, by virtue of the purity of their vision and the
decency of their nature would buy my firewood with only the greatest praise
and admiration it would be a gift (`atāi) to me (`Atā), and otherwise that they
will not mention my name with haughty criticism, for I am aware of the unsale-
ableness of my material and my own lack of talent.*

CONCLUSION

The rule of the Sadduzai dynasty was too short and unstable to allow
the development of a particular type of historiography. The two historical works that have survived from this period represent two diverse genres
of Persian historiography, each of which had its root in the styles of earlier periods. *Tārikh-i Ahmad Shāhi,* the first history written in the Sadduzai
period, displays patterns consistent with the figurative rhetorical chancery
style, which developed in the 14th and 15th centuries and continued with
traditional chancery practices. The writing style and mode of narration are
reminiscent of the style and mode in works written by historiographers of
the Timurid and Safavid periods. As a court historian attached to a royal
chancery, Al-Husaini wrote at the behest of the king. His work recounts the
deeds and accomplishments of his patron, whose prowess, fame, and dedication to Islam he extols. His style of writing is ornate and full of verbosity appropriate to the status of his employer. Formal and panegyric modes
dictate the manner in which he relates historical events.

The second work, *Navā-i Ma`ārik,* includes many characteristics of the
ornamented writing style of earlier chronicles—rhymed phrases, couplets,
poems, proverbs, and quotations from the Qur'an. However, its mode of
narration differs greatly from the laudatory and bombastic mode that characterizes *Tārikh-i Ahmad Shāhi.* In sharp contrast to the rhetorical and panegyric style of *Tārikh-i Ahmad Shāhi,* the tone of narration of *Navā-i Ma`ārik*
is emotive and good-humored, and has often the flavor of oral narration.

Differences in the style of these two chronicles reflect the different purposes of the authors in writing history and the different political milieus in which they lived. The chroniclers used contrasting modes of narration in response to the different audiences each intended to reach. In *Tārikh-i Ahmad Shāhi* Al-Husaini, like other official historians, used rhetoric and panegyrics to please his patron and impress the literary elite. In contrast, Shikārpuri's motivation seems to have been a personal need to record events he had witnessed and, in turn, to entertain his readers. Not having to vie with other scribes to flatter his patron, he wrote freely and more objectively.

Comparing the two chronicles reveals changes in the literary language between the time of the establishment of the Sadduzai dynasty by Ahmad Shāh and its fall nearly a century later. The frequent use of words from other languages in Shikārpuri's work corresponds to the rapid expansion of Ahmad Shāh's empire and the commingling of people of different linguistic backgrounds. These modifications occurred over the period of the careers of the two authors (approximately eighty years) and resulted from influences from without.

Although Shikārpuri's history exhibits some of the features of popular histories written in earlier periods, its language and writing style are quite different from those of earlier popular histories. Complex Persian prose had begun to wane about the time of the completion of *Navā-i Ma'ārik* with the advent of a new literary movement referred to as "the literary return." Shikārpuri, however, does not seem to have been much influenced by this movement, because his work displays many characteristics of the figurative writing style of the earlier historiographers. What distinguishes his work from the works of the earlier periods is not just his freewheeling approach but also his liberal use of foreign words and phrases of diverse linguistic origin. Shikārpuri's frequent use of English terms and dates from the Christian calendar and the French word *monsieur* in the last chapters reveal the beginning of contact with the West and the particular influence of the British. Unfortunately, the number of historical documents from the late Sadduzai period is too scant to allow us determine with certainty whether these peculiarities in Shikārpuri's work are unique to his own style of writing or reflect the characteristics of the prose writing of the region at the time. In the absence of other contemporary historical documents, it is also difficult to determine to what extent the ethnic origin of the author affected his rather unusual writing style.

NOTES

1. Fihrist, ed. Flugel, 13, 1–10, cited by Jan Rypka, *History of Iranian Literature,* 72.
2. E.G. Browne, *Literary History,* 2:20–21.
3. Ibid.
4. Julie Scott Meisami, *Persian Historiography to the End of the Twelfth Century,* 289.
5. Meisami, *Persian Historiography,* 12.
6. von Grunebaum, *Medieval Islam,* 227, cited by Meisami, ibid.
7. Muhammad Taqi Bahār, *Sabk Shināsi,* 3:168–69.
8. Juvayni, *Tārikh-i Jahāngushā,* 1:18–19.
9. Ja'far Shahidi, "Introduction" to Mehdi Khān Astarābādi's *Durra-i Nādiri,* quoted by S.K. Jawadi, *Zubdat al-Tavārikh,* 56.
10. Zabih-Allāh Safā, *Tārikhi-i-Adabiyāt dar Irān,* 4:468.
11. Bahār, *Sabk Shināsi,* 96–99.
12. C. Rieu, *Catalogue of the Persian Manuscripts in the British Museum,* 1:162, cited by Kenan Inan. Rashid al-Din Fazl-Allāh was the famous vizier in the court of the IlKhānid Mongol rulers. He is the author of *Jāmi' al-Tavārikh,* another important historical work of the period.
13. Bahār, *Sabk Shināsi,* 101
14. J. Rypka, *History of Iranian Literature,* 314.
15. Browne, *Literary History,* 4:443.
16. Safā, *Tārikh-i Adabiyāt,* 4:468.
17. Faridun Ādamiyat, *Enhetāt-i tārikh-negāri dar Irān,* 29.
18. John E. Woods, "Rise of Timurid Historiography," 82.
19. Bahār, *Sabk Shināsi,* 198.
20. Hāfiz Abru, *Zubdat al-Tavārikh,* 667.
21. Hāfiz Abru, *Joghrāfiyā-i Tārikhi,* 8, cited by S. Kamāl Jawādi, in the "Introduction" of *Zubdat al-Tavārikh,* 36–37.
22. Woods, *Aqquyunlu: Clan, Confederation, Empire,* 221–23, cited by Sholeh A. Quinn, *History Writing During the Reign of Shāh 'Abbās,* 23.
23. Bahār, *Sabk Shināsi,* 300–301.
24. Ibid., 311.
25. Ghobār claims that the *loya-jirga* in Qandahar was also attended by Uzbek, Tajik, Hazara, and Balochi chieftains; M.G. Muhammad Ghobār, *Āfghānistān dar Masir-i Tārikhi,* 354.
26. Ahmad Shāh inaugurated his reign by introducing a royal seal (*muhr-i shāhi*) bearing the inscription: *al-hukm Allāh yā hu yā Fattāh Ahmad Shāh Durr-i Durrāni.*
27. Mountstuart Elphinstone, *Account of the Kingdom of Caubul,* 261; Fāfulzai, *Timur Shāh Durrāni,* 2:449–61, 471–73, 489.
28. Fāfulzai, ibid., 376; Faiz Muhammad Kātib, *Serāj al-Tavārikh,* 1:68.
29. Fāfulzai, *Timur Shāh Durrāni,* 376.
30. Ibid., 375–78.
31. Ibid., 706–18.
32. Ibid., 701.
33. Ibid., 377.
34. Ibid., 316–317.
35. Herawi and Fāfulzai claim to have seen the seal of Husaini on several *farmāns* issued at

that time, which suggests that Husaini may have served, at least on occasion, as Ahmad Shāh's private secretary, as well. Mayil Herawi, *Āryānā*, 22, cited by Dustmorad S. Moradov, "Introduction" to *Tārikh-i Ahmad Shāhi*, 1:79; Fāfulzai, *Ahmad Shāh*, preface.

36. Mohiuddin Momin, *Chancellery and Epistolography*, 173.
37. See summary of Moradov's introduction in English. *Tārikh-i Ahmad Shāhi*, 1:83–84.
38. Ibid., 83.
39. Ganda Singh, *Ahmad Shāh Durrāni*, 437.
40. Fāfulzai, who has quoted Al-Husaini extensively in his history of Ahmad Shāh, writes that although he knew about Al-Husaini's work and had noticed the seal of the author on the back of documents belonging to Ahmad Shāh's era, he had not seen the manuscript until it was made available to readers in Afghanistan of Fāfulzai, *Ahmad Shāh*, preface.
41. *Tārikh-i Ahmad Shāhi*, 22–23.
42. Ibid., 24–25.
43. *Tārikh-i Jahāngushā*, 28.
44. *Tārikh-i Nādiri*, 70.
45. Joseph Ferrier does not mention Saber's prediction but gives a detailed account of a long debate in Qandahar over the issue of leadership, during which time Ahmad Khān, the youngest of all the chieftains, who led a relatively small clan, remained quiet. When the tribal chieftains failed to reach an agreement, Saber Shāh, who was impressed by Ahmad Khān's demeanor during the debate, rose and announced that Ahmad Khān was the only person among them who deserved to be king. According to Ferrier, Saber then placed a wreath on Ahmad Khān's head and declared him king. The declaration by Sāber Shāh, a holy man who was highly revered in Qandahar, was accepted by other contenders, including Hājji Jamāl, the influential leader of the Muhammadzai clan. Ferrier, *History of the Afghans*, 69. The wreath was adopted as the royal insignia, as well as the national emblem of Afghanistan, in the 1920s.
46. *Tārikh-i Ahmad Shāhi*, 31.
47. *Tārikh-i ʿĀlam Ārā-i ʿAbbāsi*, 1:439.
48. *Tārikh-i Nādiri*, 70.
49. *Tārikh-i Ahmad Shāhi* (Peshawar edition), 441.
50. Quinn, *History Writing*, 142.
51. Ibid., 173.
52. Ibid., 1080.
53. Ibid., 394.
54. Ibid., 834.
55. Ibid., 554.
56. Ibid., 162–63.
57. Ibid., 195.
58. Ibid., 323.
59. Ibid., 338.
60. Ibid., 787.
61. Ibid., 482.
62. Ibid., 507–10.
63. Ahmad Shāh waged war against the Maharata Hindus in India on three different occasions. The Battle of Panipat (January 1761), the last battle, resulted in Ahmad Shāh's decisive victory.

64. *Tārikh-i Ahmad Shāhi,* 672.

65. Ibid., 661.

66. Ibid., 664.

67. K.N. Pandit, *Bahāristan-i Shāhi.*

68. *Tārikh-i Ahmad Shāhi,* 681–88.

69. Ibid., 1274.

70. Ibid., 1292. The chronograms were deciphered by Moradov in his introduction to the *Tārikh-i Ahmad Shāhi,* 1:82.

71. Fāfulzai, *Ahmad Shāh,* introductory chapter.

72. George Forster, *Journey from Bengal to England,* 1:88–89. Forster's view is shared by Afghan historians. See, for example, Ghobār, *Āfghānistān dar Masir-i Tārikhi,* 377.

73. Ferrier, *History of the Afghans,* 235–36; Kātib, *Serāj al-Tavārikh,* 135; Fāfulzai, *Durrat al-Zamān,* 116; Ghobar, *Āfghānistān,* 406.

74. The Qajar government officially renounced its claims on Herat in a treaty signed in Paris in 1858.

75. *Munshi-i sayyār* (or *munshi-i rekābi*) was a term most likely used in reference to secretaries who accompanied their employers on their travels.

76. ʿAbdul Haiy Habibi, "Introduction," *Tāza Navā-i Maʿārik,* 6.

77. *Navā-i-Maʿārik,* 55.

78. William Joseph Eastwick assisted Sir Henry Pottinger in Sindh. In 1841, Eastwick participated in the First Anglo-Afghan War in the company of General William Nott in Qandahar. He returned to England in the same year and in 1846 became the general director, and then in 1858, the vice president of the East India Company. Ata Muhammad became a friend of Eastwick's in Shikarpur, when Eastwick worked in that city as a financial official assisting Pottinger. (Habibi, *Tāza Navā-i Maʿārik,* Appendix 1, 749.)

79. Habibi, "Introduction," *Tāza Navā-i Maʿārik,* 12.

80. *Tārikh-i ʿĀlam Ārā-i ʿAbbāsi,* 2, part 2:772.

81. According to F. Steingass the term *sāhib* was used in India as a title of courtesy. The term *bahādur* (brave) was a title of honor conferred by the Great Mughal rulers and other Eastern potentates on military men, and bore some resemblance to the European title of military knighthood. Steingass, *Persian-English Dictionary,* 209.

82. *Tāza Navā-i Maʿārik* (Karachi edition), "Introduction" by Habib, 12.

83. Ibid., 1.

84. *Navā-i Maʿārik* (Kabul edition), "Introduction" by ʿAli Ahmad Kohzād.

85. *Tāza Navā-i Maʿārik,* 516.

86. *Navā-i Maʿārik* (Kabul edition), 145.

87. Ibid., 190.

88. Ibid., 125.

89. *Tāza Navā-i Maʿārik,* "Naql-i-Bāzān va Zāghān" (The story of falcons and crows), 582–89.

90. Ibid., 536.

91. Ibid., 563.

92. Ibid., 45–51.

93. Ibid., chapter 5.

94. *Navā-i Maʿārik,* 152.

95. *Tāza Navā-i Maʿārik,* 744–45.

96. Ibid., 745–46.

REFERENCES

Faridun Ādamiyat. 1346/1967. Inhitāt-i tārikh-negāri dar irān (Decline of Historiography in Iran), in *Sokhan* 17(1): 18–29.

Munshi Mahmud ibn Ibrahim al-Jāmi Al-Husaini. 1974 [c. 1773]. *Tārikh-i Ahmad Shāhi.* 2 vols. Photographed copy with introduction by Dustmorad S. Moradov. Moscow: U.S.S.R. Academy of Sciences.

—— 2001. *Tārikh-i Ahmad-Shāhi,* ed. Homāyun Sarvar. Peshawar: Danesh Tolena.

Mehdi Khān Asterābādi. n.d. *Tārikh-i Nādiri.* Copied manuscript.

Muhammad Taqi Bahār. 1369/1990. *Sabk Shināsi.* Tehran: Mu'assisa-i Intishārāt-i Kabir.

Browne, Edward G. 1977. *A Literary History of Persia.* 6th ed. Cambridge: Cambridge University Press.

Elphinstone, Mountstuart. 1972. *An Account of the Kingdom of Caubul.* 5th ed. Karachi: Oxford University Press.

`Aziz al-Din Wakili Fāfulzai. 1959. *Durrat al-Zamān fi Tārikh-i Shāh Zamān.* Kabul: Historical Society.

—— 1346/1967. *Timur Shāh Durrāni.* Kabul: Historical Society.

—— 1359/1980. *Ahmad Shāh.* Kabul: Ministry of Information and Culture.

Hāfiz Farmān-Farmāiyān. 1345/1966. Nokāt-i chand dar bāra-i mushkilāt-i tārikh-nivisi dar Irān (A Few Comments Regarding the Difficulties of History Writing in Iran). *Bar-rasihā-i Tārikhi,* 1(5/6).

Ferrier, J.P. 1858. *History of the Afghans.* London: John Murray.

Forster, George. 1808. *A Journey from Bengal to England Through the Northern Parts of India, Kashmir, Afghanistan and Persia.* London: R. Faulder & Son.

M.G. Muhammad Ghobār. 1346/1967. *Āfghānistān dar Masir-i Tārikh.* Kabul: Mo'assissa-i-Chap-i-Kotob.

Habibi, `Abd al-Haiy. 1959. Introduction and Editions of Atā Muhammad Shikārpuri. *Tāza Navā-i Ma`ārik.* Karachi: Gulshan-e Adab.

Hafiz Abru. 1380/2001. *Zubdat al-Tāvarikh,* ed. Kamāl Jawādi. Tehran: Sāzmāni-Chāp va Intishārāt, Vizārat-i Farhang.

Inan, Kenan. 1993. The Effects of Ornamental Prose Style on Ottoman Historiography: *Tarih-i Ebu'I-Feth* [History of the Father of Conquest] by Tursun Bey, in A Summary and Analysis of the Tarih-i Ebü`l-Feth (History of the Conqueror) of Tursun Bey (1488). Ph.D. diss., University of Manchester.

Iskandar Beg Turkman. 1350/1961. *Tārikh-i `Ālam Ārā-i `Abbāsi.* Tehran: Chap-i Golshan.

`Ala al-Din Ata Malik Juveyni. 1912. *Tārikh-i Jahān-Gushā.* Leyden: E.J. Brill.

Faiz Muhammad Kātib. 1331/1952. *Serāj al-Tavārikh.* Kabul.

Meisami, Julie Scott. 1999. *Persian Historiography to the End of the Twelfth Century.* Edinburgh: Edinburgh University Press.

Momin, Mohiuddin. 1971. *The Chancellery and Epistolography under the Mughals.*

Calcutta: Iran Society.

Pandit, K.N. 1991. *Bahāristān-i Shāhi: A Chronicle of Medieval Kashmir.* Calcutta: Firma KLM.

Quinn, Sholeh A. 2000. *Historical Writing During the Reign of Shāh `Abbās: Ideology, Imitation and Legitimacy in Safavid Chronicles.* Salt Lake City: University of Utah Press.

Rieu, C. 1879. *Catalogue of the Persian Manuscripts in the British Museum.* London.

Rypka, Jan. 1956. *History of Iranian Literature.* Dordrecht, Holland: D. Reidel.

Safā, Zabih-Allāh. 1341/1962. *Navā-i Ma`ārik* (introduction by `Ali Ahmad Kohzād). Kabul: Afghan Historical Society.

—— 1362/1983. *Tārikhi-i Adabiyāt dar Irān.* 2nd ed. Tehran: Intishārāt-i Firdowsi.

Singh, Ganda. 1977. *Ahmad Shāh Durrani: Father of Modern Afghanistan.* Quetta: Gusha-e-Adab.

Spuler, Bertold. 1962. The Evolution of Persian Historiography. In *Historians of the Middle East,* ed. Bernard Lewis and P.M. Holt, pp. 126–32. London: Oxford University Press.

Steingass, F. 1977. *Persian-English Dictionary.* 6th ed. London: Routledge and Kegan Paul.

von Grunebaum, Gustav. 1962. *Medieval Islam.* 2nd ed. Chicago: Phoenix Books.

Woods, John E. 1987. The Rise of Timurid Historiography. *Journal of Near Eastern Studies* 46:81–107.

8

How Could Urdu Be the Envy of Persian (rashk–i–Fārsi)!

The Role of Persian in South Asian Culture and Literature

MUHAMMAD ASLAM SYED

L anguage permeates every aspect of cultural life from lullabies to fu-
neral rites. What happens when such fundamental rhythms of life are
overtaken by a foreign language? The new language brings new cultural
paradigms. The influence on the speakers depends to a large extent on the
circumstances. This chapter deals with the introduction of Persian in South
Asia as the language of administration and literature. It inquires, first, to
what extent Persianate culture pervaded the lives of ordinary people, and
how it remained stable and uniform for almost eight centuries. Did it face
challenges? If so, what countered them? Second, in what ways did the interests of readers and audiences in the assemblies of poets (*mushāʿira*) influence the practice of writers in general? The first questions are answered
with a brief historical narrative that introduces a discussion of the last,
which is addressed through the ideas of two prominent writers and poets:
Ghālib (1797–1869) and Iqbāl (1873–1938).

EMERGENCE OF PERSIAN AS THE LANGUAGE
OF EASTERN ISLAM

Before we address the question of the pervasiveness of Persian language
and culture in South Asia, it would be appropriate to see how Persian language had emerged as the language of eastern Islam during the Umayyad
and Abbasid periods. Long before Persian was introduced in South Asia, it

had achieved distinction as the language of administration, bookkeeping, revenue records, and for expressing subtle and philosophical ideas in the Islamic world. It seems appropriate to emphasize this point as that would explain the longevity and stability of Persian not only as the language of administration but also of religion, philosophy, mysticism, and poetry. Most of us know the name and the status of Salmān the Persian (568–656), one of the distinguished Companions of the Prophet whose strategy saved Medina in the battle of the Trench (khandaq) in 627. Shortly after the conquest of Iran, the Caliph Umar was confronted with the question of how to manage the income and the expenditure. Al-Fakhri[1] has reported an incident which would be relevant to our discussion:

> Now there was in Medina a certain Persian *marzubān,* who seeing Umar's bewilderment, said to him, "O Commander of the Faithful! Verily the Kings of Persia had an institution which they called the *diwān,* where was recorded all their income and expenditure, nothing being excepted therefrom; and there such as were entitled to pensions were arranged in grades so that no error might creep in." And Umar's attention was aroused, and he said, "Describe it to me." So the *marzubān* described it, and Umar understood, and instituted the *diwāns*...[2]

The institution of *diwān* required people skilled in the art of writing and accounting. In the early period of Islam, very few Arabs knew how to write and those who did often concealed it as it was considered disgraceful.[3] Therefore, many Persians were employed in different offices especially in the revenue and finance departments. It was not just the Persian system that was adopted in these institutions but the figures were also written in the Persian language. When the governor of Kufah, Hajjāj bin Yusuf (about 700 CE), ordered the scribes to write the accounts in Arabic only, the chief scribe is reported to have said: "May God cut off thy stock from the world even as thou hast cut the roots of the Persian tongue."[4] The orders were only partially obeyed and only for a short period.[5]

Persian language and culture remained so pervasive during the Umayyad period that the officers of the Caliph ʿAbdul-Malik (r. 658–705) complained to Ibrahim ibn Ashtar that "from the time they entered his lines until they reached his presence they had scarcely heard a word of Arabic." Ashtar told them that "there is no people endowed with greater discernment wherewith to combat them than these whom thou seest with me, who are none other than the children of the knights and satraps of the Persians." Similarly, when some Arabs complained to Amir Mukhtar that he had ignored them and had put trust in the foreigners, they were reprimanded: "I honoured you, and you turned up your noses, I gave you authority, and you destroyed the revenues; but these Persians are more obedient to me than you, and more faithful and swift in the performance of my desire."[6]

The real blossoming of Persian language and culture, however, started with the Abbasids' rise to power in 749. It was after all because of the efforts of Abu Muslim of Khurasan that the house of Abbas had assumed the leadership of the Muslim world whom al-Biruni called "a Khurasani and Eastern dynasty."[7] It was not just a political revolution but a real Islamization of Iran. The contemporary accounts tell us that almost all Persian *dihqāns* (land owners) embraced Islam. Some Arab poets complained that clients (*mawāli*) of yesterday who were humble and servile had suddenly become haughty and arrogant.[8] From the middle of the 8th century to the time of the Caliph al-Mutawakkil (r. 847–861), the most distinguished advisors, ministers, and writers at the Abbasid courts were Persians, mostly from Khurasan, including the famous Barmakids who hailed from Balkh. The Persian ascendancy reached its peak during the reign of al-Ma'mun whose mother and wife were both Persians. Baghdad looked like a Persian metropolis. Old Persian festivals like Nauruz, Mihrgan, and Ram were celebrated. The Caliphs adopted Persian dress, and the *qalānis* (conical Persian hat) was declared the official headgear in 770.[9] Garments decorated with gold inscriptions were introduced but remained an exclusive privilege of the Caliph to bestow upon whosoever pleased him. One caliph is reported to have said that "the Persians ruled for a thousand years and did not need us Arabs even for a day. We have been ruling them for one or two centuries and cannot do without them for one hour."[10]

While the Arab Caliphate in its administration, court manners, and revenue system was Persianized, the Persian language experienced a transformation through Arabic that made it the international idiom of eastern Islam. We have already seen how Persian scribes used to write the accounts in their own language. The language indeed was Persian but it was written in the Arabic script. It is difficult to give the exact date of this important moment in the life of this language; however, the process of change to the new script was gradual. Some scholars have pointed out that the new script was adopted shortly after the conquest of Iran, others insist, on the basis of the existence of Persian poetry in the new script, that it began in the 8th century. The new script was adopted but the Arabic emphatic consonants were retained. Commenting on this development, Jan Rypka says that the "Arabic script has the advantage of an almost stenographic terseness, and is moreover extremely ornamental...Artists soon became aware of its aesthetic importance and raised fine penmanship to one of the highest ranks of Iranian art."[11]

We have scattered evidence of the existence of modern Persian poetry in the 8th and 9th centuries in different sources. Tabari, for example, has cited four verses which the inhabitants of Balkh sang when the Umayyad army under Asad bin Abdullah was defeated in 737. We also know that the famous poet of Merv, Abbas (d. 816), greeted al-Ma'mun with a Persian poem (*qasida*) in 809.[12] But these verses were in excessively Arabized form. The same was the case under the Tāhirids (821–873) and the Saffārids (861–1003). With the advent of the Sāmānids (864–1005) who hailed from Balkh, the situation changed. In addition to *qasida,* the *mathnavi* and *ghazal* genres appeared, containing themes of nature and love. The prominent poets of this period are Rudaki, Daqiqi, and Kisā'i. During the Buyid period (945–1055), while Ray, Isfahan, and Shiraz were still largely under the spell of Arabic language, the area of Khurasan witnessed some Persian literary movements.

Many prominent writers of this period wrote both in Arabic and Persian. Ibn Sina wrote his famous 'Book of Knowledge' in Persian.[13] Similarly, al-Beruni's (972–1051) book on astrology appeared in Persian. Tabari's history was translated into Persian. That shows that by this time, many readers either preferred to read in Persian or they did not know Arabic. For example, when Yaqub bin al-Laith's victory over the Khārijites in 865 was celebrated by a *qasida* in Arabic, "Why," he asked, "do you compose verses which I do not understand?" One of his secretaries, Muhammad bin Vāsif, had the same translated into Persian.[14] In the year 963, the Samanid ruler Abu Sālih Mansur bin Nuh received the forty volumes of Tabari's *Commentary on the Quran* in Arabic. After realizing that the book was too difficult to be understood, he sought the opinion of the *ulamā* (scholars) regarding its translation into Persian. The ulama gave the permission and the book was translated into Persian.[15] The oldest extant copy of the Qur'an in Persian written in Mashhad in the 10th century also demonstrates that Persian had indeed emerged as "worthy of Islam."[16]

While Arabic changed the script of Persian and introduced many new words, this relationship was not unilateral; Arabic literature also experienced the impact of those Persians who wrote in Arabic. The old Bedouin poetry lost its relevance in the towns where the economic and social conditions were different from those of the tribal past. Arabic literature did retain some of its previous traits but new themes were introduced that appealed to the town dwellers, aristocrats, and the ruling classes. These themes were mostly inspired by the idea of *razm u bazm* (fighting and feasting). The task of the poets was to "greet their feudal lords with songs of praise on the occasions of public audiences and on Muslim as well as national feast-days, to offer congratulations on important family events, to bewail the dead, to scoff at and scorn the enemy, to accompany their masters on campaigns of war and to the hunt, to enliven drinking parties with song and play, etc. Both sides had equally strong interests—the princes in the propaganda, notably the extension and establishment of their power, the poets in acquiring fame and pecuniary award, above all the latter."[17] This pattern would continue not only in the Arab world especially under the Abbasids but also in the Muslim empires in the east.

In summation, it would be fair to say that while Arabic retained its status as the language of religion, Persian received new strength not only as the language of culture and poetry but also as the language of Islam at least for those who did not know Arabic. The political embrace of the Arabs and Persians was violent, but in literature it was warm and (to paraphrase Ḥāfiz in this context) the warmth of this embrace between a young religion and an old civilization infused such a youthful vigor in its veins that it awoke from its slumber to an almost everlasting youth.[18] This process was facilitated by political factors. We need not repeat here what we have discussed earlier. However, the emergence of semi-independent rulers of Persian origin and the gradual decline of the political power of Baghdad indeed contributed to this development. The Persian feudal lords and their satellites needed local support and had to turn to the vernacular of the people who in many parts of the east had not known Arabic except as a language for saying prayers and reciting some verses from the Qur'an. Before its transmission to India, Persian indeed had become a language of Islam or at least as Browne has suggested a "Musulman Persian."[19]

THE ADVENT OF PERSIAN IN SOUTH ASIA

Gabrieli has rightly observed that "Three ethnic groups underwent the religious and cultural influence of Islam through Persia as intermediary: the

Hindus, Mongols and Turks."[20] In Hindustan, the advent of Persian influence began when Sindh came under the suzerainty of the Saffarids in the third quarter of the 9th century. But a "more formal relationship between this language (Persian) and the subcontinent was established ... in the wake of the founding of Ghaznavid power in Punjab in the 11th century."[21]

Mahmud tried to build Ghazni on the model of Samanid Bukhara as the cultural center of his empire. He invited poets and writers of repute to settle in Ghazni. Luminaries like Firdowsi and al-Beruni were part of this constellation. He even tried to persuade Avicenna (Ibn Sina) to settle in Ghazni but did not succeed. One of his enduring cultural innovations was the institution of poet laureate (*malik al-shu'arā*), which was adopted later by the Timurid court in Herat and became a position of distinction during the Mughal period. Mahmud appointed 'Unsari in this position. These cultural and literary activities earned him "a reputation for being the greatest Maecenas ever known in the literature of Persia."[22] During this period, Punjab had the distinction of being a "great centre of Iranian culture."[23]

Lahore emerged as one of the important centers of Persian literature and culture in the 11th century when as the eastern outpost of Ghaznavid power, it attracted Persian scholars from Khurasan, Iran, and Central Asia.[24] With the advent of Muslim rule in this western part of India, Persian influence did not remain confined to literature only; a process of giving Persian names to various products, offices, and even towns and introducing new idioms of Persian also began which continued during the next three centuries under the Delhi Sultans (1206–1526).[25] Persian culture became so pervasive that Hafiz of Shiraz (d. 1369) said his famous lines: "All the Indian parrots will turn to crunching sugar with this Persian candy all the way to Bengal." Commenting on the influence of Persian culture during this period, Gavin Hambly notes that the Sultanate period provided "a unique opportunity for the continual transmission to India of a broad range of cultural manifestations emanating from the Persian plateau: language and literature, customs and manners, concepts of kingship and government, religious organization, music and architecture."[26] In addition to the political dynamics of the Sultanate period, the Mongol invasions and large-scale destructions of the cities in Persia and Khwārizm forced many Persian-speaking mystics, nobles, artists, and theologians to seek refuge in India.

Bābur (d. 1530), the founder of the Mughal Empire, was a Turk who wrote his memoirs and poetry in Chaghatai Turkish, but his political fortunes owed a great deal to the help he received from the Persians in his battle against the Uzbeks in 1511. By the time he consolidated his hold on India, the Safavids (also Turks) had emerged as the supreme power and conducted their administration in Persian from Mesopotamia to Central Asia. Babur's son and successor, Humāyun (d. 1556), lost his empire to the Afghans but regained it with the help of Safavid troops. Muzaffar Alam argues that Persian "did not occupy such a position of dominance in the court of early Mughals...even after Humayun's return from Iran."[27] Muhammad Abdul Ghani, however, gives evidence from the poetry and letters of Humayun that the latter "seemed to have little liking for Turki, and employed it on few occasions only. The rapidly dwindling influence of Turki at his court is clearly noticeable. While Babur had tried all his life to raise the status of Turki, Humayun, in inverse ratio, neglected it from deference to the feelings of the Persians at his court, as well as his own liking for Persian."[28] The influence of the Persian language was so pervasive at this stage that Humayun, according to Ghani, used Turkish "rarely" and even then with his attendant or to "keep the prestige of the Khan [Tardi Beg] in the eyes of those present intact...merely with the object that his other courtiers might not under-stand him."[29]

Humayun's fascination with Persian language and literature attracted many poets and scholars from different parts of Iran, Turkistan, Bukhara, and Samarqand. Many entered his retinue in Kabul while others followed him to India. Some of the names mentioned in *Tārikh-i-Humāyun* (History of Humayun) are Abdul Baqi Sadr Turkistani, Mir Abdul Hayi Bukhari, Khwaja Hijri Jami, Maulana Bazmi, Mulla Muhammad Salih, and Mulla Jan Muhammad. The popular poets like Jahi Yatmian of Bukhara and Hairati of Transoxania received his favors at Kabul and continued their journey to India, while still others like Khwaja Ayyub from Transoxania, Maulana Nādiri from Samarqand, and Maulana Janubi from Badakhshan migrated to the Mughal capital and received grants and *mansab*s (a Mughal military rank).[30]

During Akbar's reign (1556–1605), the influence of Persian culture on India further accelerated. He had no formal education but that did not prevent him from acquiring knowledge. The important books that were read to him were mostly in Persian. Akbar had a special fascination with all things Persian; a contemporary document reveals his admiration:

Love of the people of Iran has been deeply ingrained in his (Akbar's) heart from the very beginning; it is his desire that this exalted community should come close to him spiritually as well as materially, and thereby prosper materially and spiritually, and the high and low (that is, all classes) of that community should partake of imperial favor.[31]

Akbar sent his emissaries with generous offers to Iran to recruit writers, artists, philosophers, poets, and administrators to work for him. He asked his revenue minister to change the system of government accounts and regulations on the pattern of Persian *zavābit* (secular state regulations).[32] In order to train scribes and functionaries for different levels of administration, he invited teachers from Fars and Shiraz. These teachers attracted students from all classes and creeds. Those who could not come to these institutions learned through correspondence. Many Hindus earned distinction as excellent *muharrirs* ("secretaries") and *munshis*.[33] He instituted the position of poet laureate at his court that continued until the period of Shāh Jahan (1628–1658). Those who occupied this prestigious position during these years were all from Iran with the sole exception of Faizi (1547–1595). His celebrated minister, Abul Fazal, informs us that only nine out of the fifty-nine "rated in Akbar's court as the best among the thousand poets in Persian who had completed a *diwān* or written a *masnawi* were identified as non-Iranians."[34]

The Mughal nobility also actively followed this pattern of surrounding themselves with poets and writers. Abul Rahim Khān-i-Khānān indeed achieved a distinction in attracting Persian poets and scholars to his establishment. It is estimated that over a hundred poets and thirty-one scholars enjoyed his patronage. The famous poet of Isfahan, Shakibi, came to Agra to join his court and expressed his gratitude in the following verses:

Come, o cup-bearer, give me that water of nectar,
Give me from the stream of the Khān-i-Khānān;
Alexander sought it but did not get it,
For it was in that India that was the region of darkness.[35]

There were many others who were attracted to India and sought the patronage of nobles like Khān-i-Khānān. The court poet of Shāh Abbās, Kausari, who had extolled the achievements of the Safavid ruler in his *Farhād wa Shirin,* was not happy with the situation in Iran and wrote a long poem entitled "Complaint for the inattention of the people of Iran towards the possessors of the real meanings" (Arbāb-i-Ma'āni). We quote here some parts of that poem:

> In this domain there is no purchaser of speech,
> No one is eagerly busy in the market of speech;
> To speech value and weight remained not,
> Nor for meaning any customer remained;
> From the greatest to the humblest, there is not,
> Anyone whose heart is inclined to verse; …
> In Persia the palate of my soul has become bitter,
> Now, go I ought towards Hindustan;
> All the sugar-eating parrots,
> Have for this reason made their abode in India;
> Kausari, I am now determined that my verses,
> Which are signs descended from the ninth heaven;
> Like a drop towards the ocean I should send,
> I should send my commodity to India;
> That there is not among the learned of the age,
> A customer of speech except the Khān-i-Khānān[36]

Many scholars of Persian literature postulate that the reason behind this frustration of Persian poets in Iran was the religious policy of the Safavids who thought that the real recipients of the praise were not the rulers but the Shi'ite Imams. History does not support this contention. Almost every Safavid ruler patronized and encouraged the panegyrists. However, as a poet of the reign of Shāh Tahmasp has pointed out, perhaps more patronage was extended to calligraphy, painting, and riding than poetry:

> Without trouble they have made good progress,
> The scribe, the painter, the Qazvini, and the ass.[37]

Moreover, if we compare the rewards that Persian poets and writers received in India with those that were given at the Safavid court, we will understand the reason behind this influx of these notables to India. Except for Shani Taklu who was once weighed in gold by Shāh Abbas for his wonderful poetry, the usual payment never exceeded more than thirty tumāns. On the contrary, we have a long list of Persian poets and scholars who received enormous amounts of money, property, and glory in Hindustan.[38] Commenting on this warmth and appreciation of Persian poets and scholars in India, Ghani writes:

> This is the age when the liberalities of the Deccan and the Mughal kings in jealous rivalry with each other were attracting, more than they did ever before, the Persian poets and scholars from the remote corners of Persia, and the Western and Central Asia. Not only the Mughal kings but their *'umarā* too, extended an equal patronage to these literate emigrants, who in their turn sang praises of their benefactors in their beautiful poems which resounded in Persia and served as an impetus to others who yet lagged behind. This is one of main reasons why the literary activities at the Indian courts in the field of Persian literature outweigh those of the Persians in Persia.[39]

By the end of the 17th century, the Persian presence was visible at all levels from the royal court to the minor government offices all over the country. In one of his *Farmans* ("imperial orders"), Aurangzeb (d. 1707) writes:

> No nation is better than the Persians for acting as clerks. And in war, too, from the age of Emperor Humayun to the present time, none of this nation has turned his face away from the field, and their firm feet have never been shaken. Moreover, they have not once been guilty of disobedience and treachery to their masters. But, as they insist on being treated with great honour, it is very difficult to get on well with them. You have anyway to pacify them, and should employ subterfuges.[40]

The influence of Persian was not restricted to the state institutions only. It was visible in almost every field such as literature in local languages, music, architecture, festivals, cuisine, medicine, etiquette, and dress. To begin with, the state institutions were modeled after the Persians'. The Arabic words for rulers like amir or caliph were hardly used by any Muslim ruler in India. They were called *pādshāh* or *shāhinshāh* and were largely perceived as the shadow of God on earth. Secondly, as we have seen earlier, the system of administration was shaped by those who were either from

Iran or were Persianized Turks. Thirdly, most of the manuals containing instructions for the rulers were not only in Persian but also reflected the Persian legacy of governance with justice; and finally, "All Mughal government papers, from imperial orders *(farmān)* to bonds and acceptance letters *(muchalka, tamassuk-i qabuliyat)* that a village intermediary *(chaudhuri)* wrote, were in Persian."[41]

The Sufis wrote their books *malfuzāt* ("conversations") in Persian and introduced Persian poetry in their music assemblies. This led to the development of *qawwāli,* a performance that is still practiced not only at the shrines of saints but also in social gatherings in South Asia. The popularity of this music is not confined to Muslims but has become an important part of general South Asian culture. Moreover, these mystics, especially of the Chishtiyya, Suharwārdiyya, and Qādariyya orders, transformed God and the Prophet into the objects of ultimate love where they appear as the Leader and the Guiding Light respectively in the assembly of poets and devotees.[42] The influence of Persian language was no longer confined to the restricted and formal environment of the court. The Sufis extended its horizons to musicians, mystical poets, and a large number of their respective followers hailing mostly from small towns and rural areas. Persianate thinking became so pervasive that even those Sufis who composed their thoughts in local languages like Sindhi, Saraiki, and Punjabi borrowed heavily from Persian literature. The `urs (death anniversary commemorations) at Sufi shrines were held like country fairs and provided yet another space for the common folk to bring home a few couplets, some idioms, and thoughts that they had heard from the *qawwāls* and other singers. These frequent encounters with the Persian language were destined to play an important part in the development of local culture and literature.

Education in general and school curriculum in particular equally demonstrate the Persian influence. *Khulāsatu'l-Makātib,* written in 1688, provides the curriculum of Persian during Aurangzeb's times. It was divided into five sections: Prose Composition, Poetry, Fiction, History, and Ethics. Required readings for each section were:

I. Prose Composition:
    1. *Badi'ul-Inshā,* also called *Inshā-i Yusufi;*
    2. Prose works of Mulla Jāmi and Mulla Munir;
    3. Letters of Abu'l Fazl;

4. Handbook of Shaikh Inayātullah, secretary of Shāh Jahan;

5. *Bahār-i Sukhan* by Shaikh Muhammad Salih;

6. Letters of Mullā Munir;

7. Epistles of Shaida and Mulla Tughrā;

8. Story of Lāl Chand;

9. *Lilavati* (Persian translation by Faizi).

II. Poetry:

1. Mulla Jāmi's *Yusuf Zulaikhā, Tuhfatu'l-Ahrār, and Nuzhatu'l Abrār;*

2. Nizāmi's *Sikandar Nāma, Makhzanu'l Asrār, Haft Paikar, Shirin Khusraw,* and *Lailā va Majnun;*

3. Amir Khusraw's *Qirānu's Sa'dain, Matla'u'l-Anwar,* and *Ijāz-i-Khusravi;*

4. Diwans of Shams-i-Tabriz, Zahir-i-Fāryābi, Sa'di, Hāfiz, and Sā'ib;

5. *Qasā'id* of Badr-i-Chāh, Anwari, Khāqāni, Urfi, and Faizi.

III. Fiction:

1. *Tuti Nāma* of Nakhshabi;

2. *Anwar-i-Suhaili* of Husain Wā'iz Kāshifi;

3. *'Iyār-i-Dānish* of Abu'l Fazl;

4. *Bahār-i-Danish* of Shaikh Inayatullah.

IV. History:

1. *Zafar Nāma* of Sharafu'd-Din 'Ali Yazdi;

2. *Akbar Nāma* of Abu'l Fazl;

3. *Iqbāl Nāma-i-Jahāngiri;*

4. *Razm Nāma* (Persian translation of *Mahabhārata*);

5. Barni's *Tārikh-i-Firuz Shāhi;*

6. Firdowsi's *Shāh Nāma.*

V. Ethics:

1. *Akhlāq-i-Nasiri;*

2. *Akhlāq-i-Jalāli;*

3. Works of Sharafu'd-Din Maniri;

4. *Nuzahatu'l-Arwāh;*

5. *Masnavi* of Jalāl al-Din Rumi;

6. *Hadiqat al-haqiqat* of Sanā'i.[43]

While most of these works on poetry, fiction, history, and ethics provided a general framework of vocabulary, general knowledge, and treasures of Persian verses that students could use or quote in their writings, the first section of the curriculum provided models of composition and the art of letter writing. Maulanā Hakim Yusufi's *Badi'ul-Inshā* (Wonders of Composition), a treatise on epistolography, introduced the future *munshis* and scribes to some of the best examples in the art of composition. Nur al-Din Abul Rahmān Jāmi's prose works and letters were not only reflective of his deep knowledge of mysticism and history but also demonstrated his mastery of Persian lexicography. Abu'l Fazl's prose writing in general and letters in particular are ranked very high in the art of conveying thoughts on difficult and controversial subjects without annoying the reader. Many royal secretaries and *munshis* followed his style for more than three hundred years. Similarly, Mullā Tughrā Mashhadi (d. 1665), in his *Munsha'āt-i Tughrā,* included some of the best specimens of inshā. Akbar's poet laureate Faizi had translated *Lilavati,* a 12th century Sanskrit work on mathematics; in today's terminology, it would be like Mathematics Made Easy. This was included as required reading to train the future writers in the art of computation as well as composition on subjects like mathematics.

More significantly, Persian gained the status of a sacred language for Muslims. The prayers were said in Arabic but books on religion were mostly composed in Persian. Moreover, both Sufis and Mullas delivered their lessons and sermons in Persian with the result that many Persian terms, such as *Khudā* (God), *Paighambar* (Prophet), *namāz* (prayer), *ruza* (fasting), *bihisht* (paradise), and *duzakh* (hell), replaced even the religious terminology of Arabic for the main pillars of Islam and are still in use in South Asia, Central Asia, and Turkey. Mosques were decorated with Persian verses and calligraphy. *Ruz-i-Mahshar ki Jān gudāz buvad/ Avallin pursish namāz buvad* could be seen on the entrance of almost every mosque. 'Urfi and Sa'di provided relevant couplets to the shopkeepers, physicians, teachers, writers, and general public to welcome their customers, pupils, readers, and guests respectively. Women in distress would seek guidance from *Diwān-i-Hāfiz* after opening it with their eyes closed and then reading the first, fifth, or seventh line to see what the *Lisān-al-Ghaib* ("the voice of the Unseen") says. Maulana Rumi's *Masnavi* was declared "the Qur'an in Persian."[44] It was not just metaphorical; its recitation was held with as much esteem as that of the Holy Book. Maulana composed two verses in Arabic after he saw the Prophet in a dream holding his Masnavi:

Inni absarto fi naumi al-Rasul,
Fi yadih-i masnavi wa huwa yaqul:
Sannaft o kutab kathir ma'navi,
laisa fihā kal-kitāb al-ma'navi.[45]

(Once, during my sleep, I saw the Prophet holding my *masnavi* in his hands. He said: "many books have been composed on the real meanings [of the Truth], but there is none like this one.")

One verse declared that the Maulana was not a Prophet yet he gave a book.[46] Still another verse encouraged the believer to "recite the Masnavi every morning and every evening so that the fire of hell would not harm him and he would attain the status of a perfect '*arif* [one who knows the Truth], and on the Day of Judgment his affairs would be judged along with those of the prophets."[47] Many Sufis, particularly in Sindh, read only three books for spiritual nourishment: the Qur'an, the Masnavi, and the divan of Hafiz, which left permanent imprints of Persian on Sindhi mystical literature.[48]

INDIA UNDER THE SPELL OF PERSIAN

When Babur came to India, he noted in his Memoirs many things that surprised him. One note that is relevant to our discussion is about "the fixed state" of professions. He says that there was always a "set ready and a fixed group of workmen of every profession and trade, for any employment, to whom vocation descends as a family heirloom." The art of writing (*kitābat*), accounting (*siyāq*), secretaryship (*inshā*), and revenue (*divān*) assumed family traditions. Fathers passed on the skill to their sons. By the 18th century, a large number of positions in the departments of accountancy, secretaryship, and revenue were filled mostly by specialists with a long family tradition. They used old manuals prepared by the masters (in many instances, their ancestors) as the standard texts.[49] These skills ensured employment, and since fluency in high Persian was essential for higher administrative positions, they also qualified the bearer for a career of distinction. Mirza Muhammad Bakhsh Āshob, a distinguished poet and writer of the later Mughal period, believed that those nobles who could not communicate in good Persian failed in carrying out their administrative responsibilities.[50]

How did Persian attain this status and how did it hold for so long, especially when not a single family of the ruling class, especially in North India,
had come from Iran for several centuries, and there was no political or intellectual center that could have regulated Persian usage? Is it possible that
the absence of all the usual factors that normally sustain the life and power
of other languages actually contributed to the stability and the spell of the
Persian language?

The Persian koine faced three challenges: one was Turkish, the language
of different dynasties that ruled over India; the second was the evolution of
an Indian dialect of Persian; and the third was the emergence of Urdu. Se-
buktagin, the founder of the Ghaznavid Sultanate in Ghazni and North India
(977–1186) was a pagan Turkish slave from Kirghizia. His successors, as we
have seen, were more enthusiastic about Persian than perhaps many rulers of
Persia. The Ghurids, whose successors were mostly Persianized slaves, came
from Balkh. Aibak (r. 1206–1210) was bought in Turkistan and then trained in
Nishapur. His successor and son-in-law, Iltutmish, was bought from the Ilbari
Turkish tribe. Balban was reportedly a descendant of Afrasiyab of Turan.
The Khaljis were originally from Khalj but had settled in Garmsir area between Ghazni and Sistan, and the Tughlaqs were from Khotan. With such
diverse backgrounds, it is difficult to imagine that they had any other option
but to sustain the Persian koine. These political changes on the top did not
displace the system that was already working. Moreover, their rise to power
had much to do with the skills of *jahāndāri* ("governing") that they had
learned in Persian-medium schools of Bukhara, where slaves were educated
and trained in almost every skill so that they would fetch a good price. Therefore, it would be fair to say that even though many of them spoke Turkish with their family members or close friends, Turkish never really posed a
big challenge to Persian as the language of administration and culture. Even
when the Ottomans established their empire in the west, they invited many
Persian scholars, writers, and scribes to Istanbul. Sultan Muhammad, the
Conqueror of Constantinople, is reported to have recruited many Iranians
to work for him in different departments of the administration and to teach
their skills in diplomatic correspondence, calligraphy, and poetry to Turks.

During the Sultanate period Persian was written according to the standard of Samarqand, Transoxiana, and Turkistan, which Amir Khusraw
called the Turāni idiom. For many pre-Mughal authors, the Persian of
Shiraz and other places in Persia were simply dialects of the Turani Persian.

Rashid-ud-Din Vatvāt and Bahā-ud-Din of Khwārazm inspired the Indian writers. Their writings were widely read and their style was imitated. Introduced by the writers who came from Herat, these traits spread in the Indian environment, becoming what Bausani called "even more baroque." Some of these poets and writers introduced "the terminology of the bazaar and other popular expressions into their verses."[51] According to Rypka: "In substance and form the verses are true labyrinths, riddles that often make the impression of being soluble only with the aid of geomancy and astrolabe. Niceties of style become strained, thus excluding the expression of emotion. The Indian elements owe their effect to their novelty and result in an alienation of the poets from the old established masters."[52] This pebble that was thrown into the waters of Persian created many ripples which reached many parts of Persia, Transoxania, and "especially to the Tajik people."[53]

With the passage of time, many Indian words also started to appear in Persian prose and poetry. The Mughals were not happy with these developments and they decided to purify Persian of Indian words. Although Nasir Ali Sirhindi (d. 1696) could still boast that "the Iranian nightingale did not possess the grandeur of the Indian peacock," the movement to reform Persian continued. We will see later how the poet Ghālib was involved in this controversy. The Mughals were nonetheless successful in purifying Persian of foreign elements and putting Persian on the pedestal of Shiraz and Fars. Akbar asked Jamāl-ud-Din Husain to prepare a standard lexicon for writers that excluded non-Persian words and phrases. His *Farhang-i-Jahāngiri* became a standard work. In the middle of the 17th century, Mulla Abdu'l-Rashid compiled a new dictionary which pointed out that the previous works had included many Arabic and Turkish words as Persian and that some of them had been wrongly pronounced.[54]

This fascination with the classics written by the masters is evident from a letter written by a *munshi* to his son in the middle of the 17th century in which he advises his son to be discreet and virtuous.[55] He is asked to start with Sa`di's Gulistan and Bustan and the letters of Jami. Then it is absolutely necessary for him to read books such as *Habib-u'l-Siyār, Rauzat'ul-Safā, Rauzatu'l-Salātin, Tārikh-i-Guzida, Tārikh-i-Tabari, Zafar Nāma,* and *Akbar Nāma.* "The benefit of these will be to render your language elegant, also to provide you knowledge of the world and its inhabitants. These will be of use when you are in the assemblies of the learned. Of the master poets, here are some whose collections I read in my youth ... When you have some leisure, read them, and they will give you both pleasure and relief, increase your abilities, and improve your language."[56] The list of names includes Sanā`i, Rumi, `Attār, Hāfez, Sa`di, Jāmi, Firdowsi, Khāqāni, Anvari, Amir Khusraw, and many others. He stresses the importance of learning *adab* (norms of behavior): "It is appropriate to listen always to the advice of elders and act accordingly… the main thing is to be able to draft in a coherent manner, but at the same time good calligraphy possesses its own virtue and it earns you a place in the assembly of those of high stature… And along with this, if you manage to learn accountancy (*siyāq*) and the skills of a scribe, that would be even better. A scribe who knows how to write good prose as well as accountancy is like a brighter light among lights."[57]

The second half of the 18th century witnessed a similar movement in Iran. Indian style was rejected and a literary movement of return to the classics, called the *bāz-gashti adabi,* started from Isfahan after the Afghan massacres of 1722. Many poets and writers escaped to India and Afghanistan. Hazin (d. 1767) arrived in India with his *bāz-gasht* doctrine and voiced his concerns about the prevalent style in many pamphlets, sometimes disparaging the Persian poets of India as "crows." Similarly, Shihāb (d. 1800) sought refuge in the court of Herat. He also criticized the Indian style and followed the old masters, especially Anvari. In India, many Indian writers tried to update their Persian in the light of usages current in Iran. The major philological works like *Sirāj-ul-Lughat* of Khān-I Ārzu, *Mirātu'l-Istilāh* of Anand Ram "Mukhlis," *Mustalahātu'l-Shu`arā* of Siyalkoti Mal "Wārasta," and *Bahār-i `Ajam* of Munshi Tek Chand "Bahār" provide good examples of this trend.[58] What is noteworthy in such undertakings is that they were not driven by any political pressure from Iran. These writers were led to the process of self-correction by the conviction that Indian Persian received no approval from the masters of Shiraz and Isfahan.

PERSIAN AND THE EMERGENCE OF URDU

Urdu is a creole that developed as a successor to Persian in India as part of the larger process of vernacularization that has also led to the replacement of Persian in some other parts of the Persianate world. Except for its grammar and some vocabulary, it owes almost everything to Persian—so much so that even the history of early Urdu poets is available in Persian anthologies such as *Nikātu'sh Shu`arā* (1752) by Mir Taqi Mir, *Makhzan-i*

Nikāt (1754) by Hakim Abu al-Qāsim, *Gulzār-i Ibrāhim* (1783) by Ibrāhim Khān Khalil, *Tazkira-i Hasan* (1776) by Mir Hasan, and *Tazkira-i Shuʿarā-yi Hind* (1794) by Mushāfi. While the text in these works is in Persian, selected verses of various poets are in Urdu. The objective was to introduce Urdu poetry to the Persian-reading public and to show its closeness to Persian.[59]

The word Urdu itself is Turkish and means a military camp.[60] Apparently, the language developed in camps where soldiers from different ethnic and linguistic backgrounds needed to communicate with one another. It has also been known in literary history by different names such as Hindavi, Hindustani, and Rekhta. We can see that except for Urdu, the other names owe their origin to Persian. The word Rekhta means poured, spilled, thrown, or injured. Amir Khusraw, however, used this word in musical terms meaning "a harmonizing of Hindi words with Persian melodies."[61] Dr. Gilchrist is usually credited with coining the word Hindustani for Urdu but according to Saksena, this word was used for the first time in 1616.[62] The Mughal Emperor Shāh Jahān called this language Urdu-yi muʿallā (elevated Urdu).[63] However, it took a long time for this language to be identified by its present name. Around 1838, the poets and writers of Lucknow gave up the word Rekhta and used Urdu. In Delhi, the word Rekhta, in addition to Urdu, remained in use until the late 19th century.[64]

The origins and development of Urdu as a medium of literary expression has been the subject of controversy. Scholars have debated whether it developed in Punjab, Delhi, or the Deccan. The Punjab presumably felt the impact of Persian before any other part of India, starting in the Ghaznavid period. Bailey believes that "the formation of Urdu began as soon as the Ghaznavi forces settled in Lahore in 1027."[65] He is not sure as to "what time they gave up Persian and took to speaking Panjabi-Urdu alone." However, he thinks that it happened within a few years of the Ghaznavi and Ghuri troops' entry into Delhi: "In a short time Urdu was probably their usual language of conversation. We must, therefore, distinguish two stages: (1) beginning in 1027, Lahore-Urdu, consisting of old Panjabi overlaid by Persian; (2) beginning in 1193, Lahore-Urdu, overlaid by old Khari [spoken around Delhi], not very different then from old Panjabi, and further influenced by Persian, the whole becoming Delhi-Urdu."[66] The influence of Khari was confined only to conversation because it was "considered unfit for poetry, was not used for serious literary purposes." Hence Persian dominated both the diction as well as the composition of Urdu.[67]

While Urdu reached Delhi from Lahore as the language of troops, it moved on southward to the Deccan with the constant flow of sufis traveling from the Punjab via Gujarat and Malwa as a local medium to reach the masses. Early Urdu poetry in this part of India contains many words of Punjabi and Saraiki. The Chishti saints of Bijapur wrote both in Persian and Deccani Urdu. Shāh Miranji's (d. 1499) poetry substantiates this point.[68] Another wave of Urdu also reached the Deccan from the north in the time of Muhammad Tughlaq, when he changed his capital from Delhi to Daulatābād in 1326. After two decades, `Alā'u'd-Din Bahmani revolted against Delhi and became the first ruler of the Bahmani dynasty in the south. Many of his soldiers spoke Urdu. The local population of Marathi, Telugu, and Kanarese inhabitants also spoke Urdu.[69] It was perhaps because of these reasons that the Sultans of Golconda and Bijapur not only patronized Urdu some of them also used it to write poetry.[70] The Deccan thus emerged as the champion of Urdu. Wali Dakkhani (1667–1744), a well-known poet of Urdu, visited Delhi around 1700 and is believed to have set the diction of Urdu in Delhi after he recited his poems in a *mushā'ira*. He remembered the appreciation and warmth of the people of Delhi in a couplet.[71]

Deccani Urdu was written in a very simple style and as Bailey points out, in conversational style: "the author wrote the language as he spoke it."[72] We have no evidence of any prose work in Urdu at this stage. As indicated earlier, even the anthologies of Urdu poetry were written in Persian. The first Urdu anthology appeared after more than a hundred years after Wali's visit to Delhi.[73] Gradually, cultural paradigms changed and a class of poets and writers emerged which had adopted a synthesis of Persian and Indian culture in dress, mannerism, and cuisine. By the late 18th century, Urdu had blossomed as a court language in some independent states, mainly as a language of poetry. There were many reasons for this development.

The writers in Persia had called the Indian Persian *sabk-i hindi* ("Indian style") which gave an impression that Indian Persian was different and could not be considered equal to the Persian of Iran. It could be illustrated from a dialogue between the Persian-born `Urfi and the Indian-born Abu'l Fazl who was one of the most outstanding figures at the court of the Mughal Emperor Akbar and known for his mastery of Persian. Abu'l Fazl told Urfi that he had studied Persian so thoroughly that he attained perfection in this language. "Well," said Urfi, "but I have one advantage that you cannot match; ever since I was old enough to understand, my ears have heard the

Persian spoken by the old men and women of my house." Abu'l fazl replied, "So you learnt Persian from the old women, while I learnt it from the great masters of Persian, Anvari and Khaqani." "Yes," said Urfi, "and they learnt it from the old women."[74] While such episodes could be considered as exceptional interludes in the relationship between Indian Persian and the Persian of Shiraz, it is a fact that Persian writers in India remained under the spell of Iranian poets and writers. They always looked to Persia for approval and acceptance of what they wrote in Persian.

It is difficult to be sure just when Indian writers generally started to write in Urdu in preference to Persian but we can see this trend in the changing circumstances of the relationship between Iran and India during the second half of the 18th century. Nādir Shāh attacked India and sacked Delhi in 1739. The Iranian troops under his command plundered and humiliated Delhi. It is perhaps not a coincidence that after that Khān-i Ārzu, a respected teacher and guide in Persian poetry and an uncle of the famous Mir Taqi Mir (1722–1810), asked one of his pupils, who wanted his guidance in composing Persian poetry, to start writing in Urdu. It would be relevant to quote this pupil:

> On account of my training and temperament, I was inclined to write poetry in Persian. I used to go for corrections to Siraj al-Din Ali Khān Ārzu. One day, Khān-i Ārzu said to me: "The stature of Persian poetry is very high indeed… Even if people from Hind have raised Persian to a great level, even so, before the Iranians and poets from the past whose language this was, our efforts are like showing a mere lamp to the sun."[75]

This could also be a polite way of saying that since Persian poetry demanded higher standards, it was better for those who could not reach that level to write something in their own language. Still another reason was the emergence of a new class which the contemporary chronicles called *umarā-i jadid* (the new nobility) which consisted of merchants and shopkeepers. In his editorial comments to an 18th century anthology of Urdu poets, Hafiz Mahmud Shirani says that after the invasions of Nādir Shāh and Ahmad Shāh Abdāli, Delhi "is devastated but from the nobility to the common folks, almost everybody is under the spell of poetry. Men, women, Muslims, Hindus, and even the British have developed a taste for Urdu poetry." He identifies this new breed of poets with their professions, such as blacksmiths, masons, cloth merchants, tailors, barbers, water-carriers, and sweepers.[76] In cultural and social norms, it was not possible in a status-conscious community to accept them as part of the Persian nobility. Commenting on their reaction, Muzaffar Alam says "this class was not so comfortable with Persian, and preferred to see the elegance of elite Persian integrated into the spoken language that they considered their own…They responded to the abuse thrown at them by the erstwhile elites (that their culture was 'rustic' and their language 'ignorant') with an attempt to show that, on the contrary, their literary idiom was equally capable of elegance and sophistication. They buttressed this position by encouraging active appropriations of Persian vocabulary, metaphors and allusions into an increasingly refined register of Hindavi (Urdu)."[77]

We can also attribute this change to the political situation in India especially when the Mughal governors in some areas revolted against Delhi and established their independent states. The rulers of Awadh, for example, faced the hostility of the old Mughal nobility. In order to get rid of them, they brought in the local groups who were not Persianized. Nawāb Shujā`-ul-Daula was not happy at the performance of the old nobility during the battle of Buxar in 1764. He recruited a large number of Shaikhzadas, Telingana Rajputs, and Gosain mercenaries, the so-called low-born to replace the Mughal nobility.[78] These new social groups were more inclined to patronize Urdu than Persian.

With the advent of the Qajars in Iran in 1779, Persian literature and poetry received patronage at home. Therefore, fewer Iranians were eager to settle in India. This should not mean that Persian language and literature in India was dependent on Iranian immigrants. Nonetheless, this contact reinvigorated Indian enthusiasm for Persian and those writers and poets who had the privilege of learning from someone from Iran always boasted that their excellence in Persian was because of the fact they had learned it from the source.[79] The *bāzgasht* (return) literary movement made many writers realize that they could not possibly excel in this language and receive appreciation from those who knew its high standards. More importantly, the new political groups in the late 18th and early 19th centuries were not Persianized, but spoke a local dialect of Urdu. Even the Mughal court came under their influence and the Mughal Emperor, Shāh `Ālam II, composed poetry in Urdu.[80]

In 1835 the East India Company replaced Persian with English as the official language, and with Urdu as the language of the law courts in 1837. Could Urdu replace Persian not only as a language of fine poetry and prose but also as a princely court language in some states? Viqār-al-Mulk, a North Indian Muslim who later joined the Aligarh movement, was a minister at the Nizām's court at Hyderābād, and he raised this question. He suggested to the Prime Minister, Sālār Jang I (Mir Turāb Ali Khān 1829–1883), that Persian should be replaced with Urdu as the state language. Salar Jung's reaction to this suggestion is noteworthy:

> You Hindustani (North Indian) people have little practice in Persian speech and writing. Persian language is the symbol of the victory of the Muslims…Having destroyed this symbol in your own country (North India); you people now want darkness here too. Persian shall remain here and flourish so long as I am alive.[81]

Persian remained the state language of Hyderābād as long as Salar Jang was alive. His son, Sālār Jang II (Mir Lāiq Ali Khān), however, replaced it with Urdu within one year of his father's death, perhaps under pressure from those state functionaries who preferred Urdu over Persian (see next chapter). Moreover, the Urdu-Hindi controversy over the Persian and deva-nagari scripts had indeed raised the status of Urdu as "the Muslim lan-guage." Nonetheless, Salar Jung I was not alone in defending Persian. Many other nobles, writers, and poets, even in North India and the Punjab, also felt that Urdu could not possibly offer that vast medium in expressing sub-lime thoughts as Persian did. It is generally believed that the supremacy of Persian depended on the state patronage. We cannot deny that the Turks and the Mughals were, indeed, instrumental in generating its popularity and prestige. But the fact that it continued to hold a commanding position even after the demise of the Mughal Empire in 1857, at least in literary circles, testifies to its effectiveness in expressing cultural accomplishments as revealed in the writings of Ghālib and Iqbāl.

Jo yeh kahay keh 'rekhta kiyun keh ho rashk-i-Fārsi'
Gufta-i-Ghālib ek bar parh kay usay suna kih 'yun'.

If someone says "how could Urdu be the envy of Persian?"
Read him some verses of Ghālib and say "This is how!"

These verses would appear to assure the reader that Urdu indeed had attained the same status as Persian, but this was Ghālib's way of saying that if anyone could come up to that level, it was he! Indeed he is considered not just the greatest poet of Urdu but one of the greatest poets of all times. But his first love was always Persian. On many other occasions, he took pride in his Persian poetry. In a rejoinder to the court poet and tutor of the last Mughal Emperor, he says, "The poetry, for which you are so proud [Urdu], is a matter of shame for me" (*Unchi dar guftar fakhr-i-tust, an nang-i-man ast*). About his Persian poetry, Ghālib says that "if you want to see all the colors of life, read my Persian poetry, my Urdu diwān does not have all those colors. Persian is the mirror (of life) and Urdu is just like rust on that mirror (with which you start but when it is clean, it is Persian)."[82] In his correspondence, he was aware of the status of his addressees. While he wrote informal letters to his friends and students in Urdu, his letters to the nobility and the ruling class were written in Persian.

Ghālib had learned the diction and intricacies of Persian from a Persian scholar, Mulla Abdu'l-Samad, who stayed with him for two years (1811–1813) and assured Ghālib that he had a "natural inclination" towards Persian. Ghālib believed that Persians alone could be considered the true custodians of the Persian language. "Don't imitate the local writers," he wrote to a disciple, "follow the masters of this art" who wrote and lived in Iran.[83] Ghālib rejected those critics who judged his verses in the light of the style of Indian Persian. He not only ridiculed their Persian diction but also wrote a critique of a well-known Persian dictionary, *Qāti`-i Burhān*, compiled by Muhammad Hussain Dakkhani who, according to Ghālib, had made many mistakes. When he published his findings under the title of Burhān-i Qāti`, many followers of Dakkhani were furious. The matter went so far that Ghālib had to go to the court.[84] While this debate continued in many literary circles, a new literary movement challenged both the content and style of Persian poetry that had influenced the Urdu writers.

This new literary movement was initiated by Colonel Holroyd who was director of Public Instruction in Punjab. He employed the services of two prominent Urdu writers, Maulvi Muhammad Hussain Āzād (1830–1910) and Altāf Hussain Hāli (1837–1914), and laid the foundation of a new school of literature under the auspices of Ajuman-i-Panjab in Lahore. In his *Muqaddima-yi shi`r o shā`iri,* Hāli asked the poets to write on social issues and to come out of the imaginary world that did not exist. In the opening session of the first *mushā`ira* held under the auspices of this Anjuman in Lahore in 1874, Azad appealed to the poets to "come out of the grooves of responses conditioned by Persian culture and root their thoughts in the ethos of the land." These efforts proved ephemeral and after a few sessions, no more *mushā'iras* were held because the poets and writers continued writing on those themes that their audience in the *mushā'iras* wanted to hear and their readers wanted to read. Before we discuss Iqbāl, it seems appropriate to introduce this unique cultural institution, the *mushā'ira,* in more detail.

It is difficult to give an exact date or the names of the poets who were invited to present their verses in a particular assembly. We know from pre-Islamic Arab customs that poets were not only honored by tribal leaders but that they were also considered almost indispensable in social gatherings and on battlefields. This practice continued during the early Islamic period and as we have already seen, many poets wrote *qasidas* for rulers and conquerors. However, we can assume that when the office of the poet laureate was instituted by Mahmud of Ghazna, the foundations of this institution were already in place. Shibli Nu'māni's *Shi'r u'l-'Ajam* provides the earliest reference to this assembly in the 16th century when Fighāni (d. 1519), the court poet, held "a competition of poets."[85] By the second half of the 18th century, it had become a familiar event with most of its current features. The *mushā'ira* was held in the court usually presided over by the ruler or a prince, or in the house of a nobleman. Invitations were sent to all notable poets and on some occasions new poets were also asked to participate. The organizers made sure to have the consent of all the invitees; any absence especially of a well-known poet was considered a blemish on the reputation of the host. Each poet was requested to compose a *ghazal* on the pattern of a given specimen of meter and rhyme, usually half a line of a famous verse (*misrā'-i tarah*). The poets were expected to show their skill and grasp of the language within these limits. The appreciation of the participants for the whole poem or even one verse determined who had conquered the hearts and minds of the listeners. If during the recitation, someone pointed out that a certain phrase or construction of words (*bandish*) was not proper, the poet would immediately recite some verses of the well-known masters in which they had used the same words and the critic would be silenced.

What really mattered for the poet was not just appreciation from anybody, but from those who really understood the meanings and the context of the verses. "Appreciation of the ignorant of the art of poetry and silence of the one who knows its intricacies and sophistication are two things that would ruin the value of a beautiful verse."[86] Sometimes, if a poet like Mir Taqi Mir or Ghālib would ask a poet to recite his verse again, even that would be considered an honor for the writer who would proudly write in his divan that the verse in question was repeated in the *mushā'ira* at the request of Mir or Ghālib.

Mirzā Farhāt-ullāh Beg (1883–1947) has written about an imaginary *mushā'ira* with real poets and actual ceremonies held in Delhi before the formal end of the Mughal dynasty in 1857. A descendant of a noble family, Abdul Karim, plans to hold a *mushā'ira*. He visits the elite of Delhi and asks for their help. After visiting the known aristocrats, he is presented before the last Mughal ruler, Bahādur Shāh Zafar, who is known for patronizing poets and also writes beautiful poems. The king promises to send his poem and a prince to preside over the session. After seeking the approval of the king, Karim goes to the houses of all the poets and succeeds in getting their consent to participate in this unique event. An aristocrat offers his help in preparing his house for the occasion. On the eve of the *mushā'ira,* he is pleasantly surprised that his residence has been so lavishly decorated that it is difficult for him to recognize whether this is the same place or through some magic it has been transformed into a palace. Chandeliers and lights of different colors are so tastefully placed that it seems like a fairy land. The courtyard where the mushā'ira is going to take place is adorned with flowers, candles, carpets, and cushions, with all the amenities like nuts, betel leaves, and smoking pipes placed at proper places. The seating arrangement is done in accordance with the status and reputation of the participants. The event begins with recitation of the first chapter of the Holy Qur'an (*fātiha*). The order of introducing poets begins with lesser known poets after the king's poem is recited by his representative in an ascending order ending with the recitation of the king's poetry teacher. A lighted candle is placed before the poet who is to recite his poem and then moves to the next. The recitation is done either as *tahtu'l-lafz* (the spoken words with emphasis on rhyme and rhythm) or with *tarannum* (singing like a chant with a two-line tune). It continues all night and ends with a *fātiha* just at the time when the call for morning prayer is heard from a nearby mosque. Each participant receives proper protocol and thanks.[87]

While the above-mentioned *mushā'ira* was restricted only to the elite, in the beginning of the last century it gradually became public and lacked much of its ceremonial character. The candle disappeared and in many cases the requirement of a specimen of meter and rhyme was also not followed. Sometimes a *mushā'ira* can be a huge affair where thousands of people come to listen to famous poets. The listeners respond immediately with shouts of *mukarrar* (again) to the verses that they like. This institution plays a very important role in inspiring many listeners to become poets. Commenting on this aspect of *mushā'ira,* Marion Molteno says: "I once asked a friend what made him start composing poetry. Well, he said, as a young man I loved going to the *mushā'iras,* and each time I went someone would say, Come on, it's your turn to recite, show us what you have composed. It got to the point where I had to avoid this embarrassment. I had to either give up the pleasure of going to *mushā'iras* or start composing poetry!"[88] Quoting couplets as a comment on some aspect of daily life, as a political slogan, and in serious articles and columns in magazines and newspapers is indeed a very visible part of South Asian culture. Even illiterate and barely educated people would surprise their listeners by inserting famous verses from masters of Urdu, Persian, or Punjabi poetry. Couplets from known or even unknown poets are painted on buses, trucks, and rickshaws in Pakistan. *Mushā'iras* are also broadcast from radio and television which indeed provide some verse to the listeners to be used in daily life.

Dr. Muhammad Iqbāl recited his poetry in *mushā'iras* held by Anjuman-i Himāyat-i Islam. He wrote on current political and social themes and attracted a huge number of listeners. He started writing in Urdu but his father insisted that he should write in Persian. During his Cambridge years, he came under the spell of Persian philosophers and poets. His doctoral dissertation, "The Development of Metaphysics in Persia," reveals his admiration for the Persian contribution to Islam. He wrote that "the conquest of Persia meant not the conversion of Persia to Islam, but the conversion of Islam to Persianism."[89] One of his closest friends of these years, Atiya Begum, tells us: "I discovered that Iqbāl was a great admirer of Hafez. 'When I am in the mood for Hafiz', he said, 'his spirit enters into my soul, and my personality merges into the poet and I myself become Hafiz.'"[90] But soon Iqbāl realized that Hafez could not help him in the message that he wanted to convey to his readers. When he published his *Asrār-i Khudi* (the Secrets of Self) in 1915, he remembered Hafez in disparaging terms. He wrote that the poetry of Hafez had the effect of an opiate on the minds of its readers and he warned his readers against yielding to his magic. However, in the second edition of this work, Iqbāl deleted these remarks.[91]

Like Ghālib, Iqbāl's Urdu poetry is also considered of high merit. But he knew that Urdu still has to go through many refinements (*gasu-i Urdu abhi mannat pazir-i shāna hai*).[92] Therefore, he composed most of his verses in Persian. In fact the poetry that earned him a knighthood and elevated his status as the "Poet-Philosopher of Islam" was written in Persian. Books like *Ramuz-i Bekhudi* (The Mysteries of Selflessness), *Zabur-i `Ajam* (The Persian Psalms), *Zarb-i Kalim* (The Stroke of Moses), and *Jāved Nāma* were all written in Persian with numerous insertions of couplets from the masters of Persian literature. His last work, *Jāved Nāma*, was inspired by Dante's *Divina Commedia* except that, instead of Beatrice, Rumi leads Iqbāl through the celestial spheres and enlightens him on different mystical and philosophical questions. Even in his Urdu poetry, we often come across translations of Persian poetry. Commenting on his switch over from Urdu to Persian, Muhammad Sadiq says: "To the students of psychology this switch over to Persian is symptomatic of an unconsciously waning interest in India and things Indian, and a growing absorption of Islam. He must have come to feel that Persian was somehow nearer to the heart of Islam than Urdu."[93]

South Asian culture in general shows clear influences of Persian culture in almost every field. In literature, however, its influence is so pervasive that "it would be hard to find any branch of science or art, any form of Persian poetry, didactic, lyrical, romantic, mystical or otherwise, or any Persian meter which has not in the course of history been adopted by the Indians, Moslems as well as Hindus. It might indeed be difficult to point out a comparable example in the history of world literature of a language being adopted, and to find another country having mastered a foreign language to such a degree as was the case with Persian in India."[94]

During the struggle for independence, Urdu did emerge as "the language of Muslims" so much so that even celebrated Hindu writers of Urdu like Munshi Prem Chand, a great supporter of Urdu language, were accused by some Hindu nationalists of siding with the Muslims. The culture of Urdu-speaking populations in India and Pakistan shows the impact of Persian culture in mannerism, etiquette, and speech. But over time, this culture has been influenced by local practice and is invariably identified not so much with Persian as with the culture of cities where it flourished such as Lukhnow, Delhi, and Hyderābād or in the case of Pakistan, Lahore and Karachi.

Urdu writers have indeed produced many masterpieces in literature, but their most popular poems, especially their *ghazals*, continue to be composed in those themes and metaphors that were introduced by the Persian poets. Hafeez Jalandhary (d. 1983) wrote a long poem on Muslim history with the title *Shāhnāma-i Islām* on the pattern of Firdowsi's classic. He also wrote Pakistan's national anthem in Urdu— but it was all Persian except the one word ka.[95] The most popular poet of Urdu after Iqbāl is Faiz Ahmad Faiz (1911–1984), who followed the style of Hafez in his love poetry. With titles such as *Zindān Nāma, Dast Tah-i Sang, Shām-i Shahr-i Yārān,* and *Sar-i Wādi-i Sinā,* his books reveal the stamp of Persian influence. Therefore, we can say that even though Persian language and culture do not enjoy the pervasiveness that they once had, still the best and most popular pieces of literature continue to echo the voices of Persian nightingales.

NOTES

1. Shams al-Din Muhammad bin Fakhr al-Din Saʿid Isfahāni, a philologist of the 14th century, author of the *Miʿyār-i Jamāli va-miftā-i Bu Ishāqi.*
2. Quoted in Edward G. Browne, *Literary History of Persia,* 1:205.
3. Al-Jāhiz, *Kitābu'l-Bayān wa'l-Tabyin,* quoted ibid., 1:260.
4. Ibid.
5. Shibli Nuʿmāni, *Shiʿr-ul ʿAjam,* 5:16.
6. Dinawari, quoted in Browne, *Literary History,* 238.
7. Al-Beruni, *Chronology of Ancient Nations,* Sachau's translation quoted in Browne, *Literary History,* 247.
8. Ibid., 247.
9. *Qalānis,* plural form of *qalānsuwa,* was in use even during the time of the Prophet and the early caliphs. Sometimes this headgear was also called *al-ʿamāʾim ʿalā al-qalānis* (turbans on caps). Ibn al-Kalbi, *Jamharat al-nasab,* quoted in Michael Lecker, "King Ibn Ubayy," 62–64.
10. Quoted in Bertold Spuler, *Muslim World,* 1:29.
11. Jan Rypka, *Iranische Literaturgeschichte,* 75.
12. Some scholars doubt the authenticity of these verses for reasons that explain more the stability of Persian than any sound historical grounds. Gilbert Lazard, for example, says that it is apocryphal "because the command of classical rhetoric in them is unlikely to be achieved in a first attempt." See his "Rise of the New Persian Language," 595.
13. *Dānish-nāma-i-ʿAlā'i.*
14. G. Lazard, "New Persian Language," 595.
15. A.J. Arberry, *Classical Persian Literature,* 40.
16. Ali Rawaqi, Qur'ān-i quds, Kuhnatarin bargandān-i Qur'ān ba fārsi, quoted in Bert Fragner, *Die "Persophonie": Regionalität, Identität und Sprachkontakt in der Geschichte Asiens,* 28.
17. Rypka, *Iranische Literaturgeschichte,* 142.
18. *Garche piram to shabi tang dar āghosham gir, ta sahar gāh ze kināre to jawān bar khezam.*
19. Browne, *Literary History,* 1:82.

20. F. Gabrieli, quoted by Ehsan Yarshater, in Richard Hovannisian and Georges Sabagh, *Persian Presence*, 87n.

21. Muzaffar Alam, *Languages of Political Islam: India 1200–1800*, 116.

22. Rypka, *Iranische Literaturgeschichte*, 173.

23. Mumtāz Hasan, "Foreword" to Khwāja Abdul Rashid, *Tazkira-i Shuʿarā-i Punjāb*.

24. For details, see Sayyad Muhammad Latif, *Lahore: Its History, Architectural Remains and Antiquities*.

25. Muhammad Hussain Āzād provides some examples; see his *Sakhundān-i-Paras*, 20.

26. Gavin Hambly, *Encyclopaedia of Islam*, 7:242.

27. Alam, *Languages*, 123.

28. Muhammad Abdul Ghani, *Persian Language and Literature*, 5.

29. Ibid., 6–8.

30. Bā Yazid, *Tārikh-i-Humāyun*, quoted in Ghani, ibid., 149.

31. Akbar's letter to Amir Ahmad Kāshi, quoted in Alam, "Pursuit of Persian: Language in Mughal Politics," 322.

32. For details, see Ghulam Hussain Tabātabāʾi, *Siyār al-Mutakhirin*, 1:200.

33. Syed Muhammad Abdullāh, *Adabiyāt-i-Fārsi men Hinduon ka Hissa*, 240–43.

34. Abul Fazl, *Āʾin-i Akbari*, quoted in Alam, *Languages*, 127.

35. Ghani, *Persian Language and Literature*, 166.

36. Quoted in Ghani, ibid., 169–71.

37. *Be takalluf khush taraqqi karda and, kātib o naqqāsh o Qazvini o khar* (quoted in Ghani, ibid., 167.

38. Hayāti Kāshi was weighed in gold by Jahāngir; Abu Talib Kalim, Saida-i Gilāni, and Bāfiya were weighed in gold by Shāh Jahan; Maulvi Abdul Hakim Siālkoti was weighed twice in gold; Abdul Hamid Lāhori was weighed in gold and received a large sum in cash; Zahuri received several elephants loaded with gold and silver and other valuable presents from Burhān Nizām Shāh of Ahmadnagar; Urfi received 100,00 coins from Khān-i-Khānān; Naziri received from Khān-i-Khānān 100,000 coins in addition to 30,000 gold *mohars* from Jahāngir; and Qudsi had his mouth filled with precious jewels twice by Shāh Jahan. For details, see Ghani, ibid., 150–51.

39. Ibid., 151–52.

40. Hamid-ud-Din, *Ahkām-i-ʿĀlamgiri*, quoted in Alam, "Pursuit of Persian," 325.

41. Alam, *Languages*, 132.

42. Amir Khusraw's still very popular *ghazal* ends with this verse: *Khudā khud mir-i majlis bud under lā-makān Khusro, Muhammad shamiʿ mehfil bud shab jā ay kih man budam.*

43. Quoted in G.M.D. Sufi, *Al-Minhāj*, 77–78.

44. *Masnavi-i maulavi-i maʿnavi, hast qurān dar zabān-i-pahlavi*, quoted in Maulana Qazi Sajjad Husain, *Masnavi-i-Maulavi-i-maʿnavi*, Publisher's Note, 1.

45. It is interesting to note that the Maulana wrote these verses in Arabic perhaps to convey the message in the Prophet's tongue. Ibid., 3.

46. *man chi guyam vasf-i ān ʿāli janāb, nist payghambar vali dārad kitāb.* Ibid.

47. *masnavi-ra har ki khwānad subh o shām/ātish-i duzakh bar u gardad harām sirri-i hikmat pesh–i u roshan shavad, sāhib-i sukr fanā-i tan shavad az balliyāt-i jahān yā ba dāman, ʿārif-i kāmil shavad andar zamān dar qiyāmat hashr-i u ba anbiyā, mai shavad az himmat-i ān pishvā.* Ibid.

48. Ghulam Mustafa Qasimi, "Hashimiya Library" in *Mihran ja Moti*, (Karachi, 1959), p. 309.

49. Syed Abdullah, *Adabiyāt-i-Fārsi men Hinduon ka Hissa*, 241–43.
50. Quoted in Alam, "Pursuit of Persian," 330.
51. Bausani, quoted in Rypka, *Iranische Literaturgeschichte*, 303n12.
52. Ibid., 295.
53. Ibid.
54. Husaini, *Indo-Persian Literature*, quoted in Alam, *Languages*, 145.
55. For details, see Muhammad Abdul Hamid Faruqui, *Chandra Bhan Brahman*.
56. Abdullah, *Adabiyāt-i-Fārsi men Hinduon ka Hissa*, 242.
57. Ibid., 241.
58. H. Blochmann, *Contributions to Persian Lexicography*, quoted in Alam, *Languages*, 147.
59. For details, see T. Grahame Bailey, *History of Urdu Literature*, 1–5.
60. It is believed that the English word "horde" is derived from Urdu; see ibid., 5.
61. Quoted ibid., 5.
62. Ram Babu Saksena, *History of Urdu Literature*, 7.
63. Ibid.
64. Bailey, *Urdu Literature*, 3.
65. Ibid., 7.
66. Ibid.
67. Ibid., 9.
68. Maulavi Abdul Haq, *Urdu ki Ibtadā'i Nashvonumā men Sufia-i Karam ka Kām*, 76.
69. Bailey, *Urdu Literature*, 7–8.
70. Maulavi Abdul Haq, *Urdu ki Ibtadā'i Nashvonumā men Sufia-i Karam ka Kām*, 76.
71. *Dil Wali ka lay liya Dilli na Chin, Ja kaho koi Muhammad Shāh sun* (Will someone go and tell Muhammad Shāh [the Mughal Emperor] that Delhi has captured the heart of Wali), in Ishrat Haque, *Mughal Society*, 20.
72. Bailey, *Urdu Literature*, 10.
73. Ali Lutfi's *Gulshan-i-Hind*.
74. Quoted in Ralph Russell, *Pursuit of Urdu Literature*, 23.
75. Āshiqi Azimābādi, quoted in Alam, *Languages*, 180–81.
76. Hāfiz Mahmud Sherāni, *Majmu'a-i Naghaz*, passim. See also Muhammad Hasan, *Dehli men Urdu Shā'iri ka Tehzibi aur Fikri Pas manzar*, 94–95.
77. Alam, *Languages*, 182.
78. Najmul Ghani, *Tārikh-i Awadh*, 157–58.
79. Ghālib used to say that he learned Persian from Mulla Abdul Samad, an Iranian who stayed with his family for a few years. See Maulana Ghulam Rasul Mehr, *Diwān-i Ghālib*, 8.
80. Ishrat Haque, *Mughal Society*, 46.
81. S.M. Kamal, *Hyderābād men Urdu ka Irtiqā*, quoted in Alam, "Pursuit of Persian," 331.
82. Z. Ansari, *Ghālib Shanāsi*, 68–69.
83. Letter to Bilgrami, quoted in Ansari, ibid., 23.
84. *Qāti'-i burhān* was published in March 1862, then a second, augmented edition was published in 1865 as *Dirafsh-i Kāwiāni* (Ralph Russell and Khurshidul Islām, *Ghālib: 1797–1869, Life and Letters*, 1:357–59).
85. *Shibli Nu'māni, Shi'r ul-'Ajam*, 3:17.
86. Saib's famous lines: *Saib, do chiz mi shikand qadr-i shi'r rā, tahsin-i nā shanās wa sakut-i sukhan shanās.*
87. Mirzā Farhāt-ullāh Beg, *Dilli Ka ek Yādgār Mushā'ira*, passim.
88. Marion Molteno, "Approaching Urdu Poetry," in Russell, *Urdu Literature*, 6.

89. Quoted in Latif Ahmad Sherwani, *Speeches, Writings and Statements of Iqbāl*, 22.
90. Atiya Begum, *Iqbāl*, 15.
91. Sir Abdul Qadir, "Persian Poetry of Iqbāl," in Masud-ul-Hasan, *Life of Iqbāl*, 2:3–15.
92. Literally "tress of Urdu still needs a comb." See his poem, "Mirzā Ghālib," in *Kulliyāt-i Iqbāl* (reprint), 26–27.
93. Muhammad Sadiq, *History of Urdu Literature*, 450.
94. Jan Marek, "Persian Literature in India," in Karl Jahn, *History of Iranian Literature*, 732–33.
95. Instead of saying "sar zamin-i pāk ra nizām," he wrote "pāk sar zamin ka nizām." See Mazhar ul Islam, *Adabiyāt-i Pākistān*, 37.

REFERENCES

Muhammad Abdu'l Ghani. 1983. *A History of Persian Language and Literature at the Mughal Court.* Karachi: Indus Publications.

Maulavi Abdu'l Haq. 1968. *Urdu ki Ibtidāi Nashvonumā men Sufia-i Karam ka Kām.* Aligharh: Anjuman-i Taraqqiye Urdu.

Khwaja Abdu'l Rashid. 1967. *Tazkira-i Shu`arā-i Punjāb.* Karachi: Iqbāl Academy.

Syed Muhammad Abdullah. 1967. *Adabiyāt-i Fārsi men Hinduon ka Hissa.* Lahore: Majlis-i Taraqqi-i Adab.

Alam, Muzaffar. 1998. The Pursuit of Persian: Language in Mughal Politics. *Modern Asian Studies* 32(2): 317–49.

—— 2004. *The Languages of Political Islam: India 1200–1800.* London: Hurst & Company.

Ansari, Z. 1965. *Ghālib Shanāsi.* Bombay: International Adab Trust.

Arberry, A.J. 1958. *Classical Persian Literature.* London: Allen & Unwin.

Muhammad Hussain Azad. 1898. *Sakhundān-i-Paras.* Lahore: Dar-al-Isha'at.

Bailey, T. Grahame. 1932. *A History of Urdu Literature.* London: Oxford University Press.

Mirza Farhat-ullah Beg. 2003. *Dilli Ka ek Yādgār Mushā`ira.* Lahore: Sang-i-Meel.

Atiya Begum. 1947. *Iqbāl.* Lahore: Āina-i-Adab.

Browne, Edward G. 1928. *A Literary History of Persia.* Cambridge: Cambridge University Press.

Muhammad Abdul Hamid Faruqui. 1966. *Chandra Bhan Brahman: Life and Works with a Critical Edition of His Diwan.* Ahmedābād: Khalid Shahin Faruqi.

Fragner, Bert G. 1999. *Die "Persophonie": Regionalität, Identität und Sprachkontakt in der Geschichte Asiens.* ANOR No. 5. Berlin: Das Arabische Buch.

Frye, R.N., ed. 1975. *The Cambridge History of Iran,* vol. 4. Cambridge: Cambridge University Press.

Najmu'l Ghani. 1919. *Tārikh-i Awadh.* Lucknow.

Haque, Ishrat. 1992. *Glimpses of Mughal Society and Culture.* New Delhi: Concept Publishing Company.

Masudu'l-Hasan. 1978. *Life of Iqbāl.* 2 vols. Lahore: Ferozsons.

Muhammad Hasan. 1983. *Dehli men Urdu Shā`eri ka Tehzibi aur Fikri Pas manzar.* Delhi: Idārah-yi Tasnīf.

Hovannisian, Richard G., and Georges Sabagh, eds. 1998. *The Persian Presence in the Islamic World.* Cambridge: Cambridge University Press.

Maulana Qazi Sajjad Husain. 1974. *Masnavi-i Maulavi-i Ma`navi.* Lahore: Hamid and Co.

Mazharu'l-Islam, ed. 1995. *Adabiyāt-i Pakistan.* Islamābād: Pakistan Academy of Literature.

Jahn, Karl, ed. 1968. *History of Iranian Literature.* Dordrecht, Holland: Reidel.

Latif, Sayyad Muhammad. 1981. *Lahore: Its History, Architectural Remains and Antiquities.* Lahore: Oriental Publishers and Booksellers.

Lazard, Gilbert. 1975. The Rise of the New Persian Language. In *Cambridge History of Iran,* vol. 4, ed. R.N. Frye, pp. 595–632. Cambridge: Cambridge University Press.

Lecker, Michael. 2003. King Ibn Ubayy and the Qussas. In *Method and Theory in the Study of Islamic Origins,* ed. Herbert Berg, pp. 29–71 Leiden: E.J. Brill.

Maulana Ghulam Rasul Mehr. 1967. *Diwān-i Ghālib.* Lahore: Sheikh Ghulam Ali.

Shibli Nu`mani. 1945. *Shi`r ul-`Ajam.* Azamgarh: Dara al-Musannifin.

Russell, Ralph. 1992. *The Pursuit of Urdu Literature: A Select History.* London: Zed Books.

Russell, Ralph, and Khurshidu'l-Islam. 1969. *Ghālib: 1797–1869, Life and Letters.* London: George Allen and Unwin.

Rypka, Jan. 1959. *Iranische Literaturgeschichte.* Leipzig: Harrassowitz.

Sadiq, Muhammad. 1984. *A History of Urdu Literature.* London: Oxford University Press.

Saksena, Ram Babu. 1927. *A History of Urdu Literature.* Allāhābād: Ram Narain Lal.

Hafiz Mahmood Sherani, ed. 1933. *Majmu`a-i Naghaz.* Lahore: Punjab University.

Sherwani, Latif Ahmad, ed. 1977. *Speeches, Writings, and Statements of Iqbāl.* Lahore: Iqbāl Academy.

Spuler, Bertold. 1960. *The Muslim World.* Leiden: E.J. Brill.

G.M.D. Sufi. 1941. *Al-Minhāj.* Delhi: Idāra-i-Adabiyāt.

Ghulam Husain Tabatabai. 1876. *Siyar al-Mutakhirin.* Lucknow.

9

Urdu Inshā: The Hyderābād Experiment, 1860–1948

ANWAR MOAZZAM

The Nizām's State of Haidarābād (to use the standard system of Romanization), officially known as Mamālik-i Mahrusa-i Sarkār-i `Āli, ruled by the Āsaf Jāh dynasty (1724–1948), the largest princely state of India, never hesitated in taking risks of experimentation with political, administrative, economic, cultural, and educational restructuring for the peoples of the State as well as ensuring its own stability. With only a 13 percent Muslim population the Muslim monarchy continued to rule over an 87 percent non-Muslim population, mainly Hindu, for more than two hundred years of what today would be described as secular public policy and administration, almost free of religious tensions. It was quite an unusual situation compared with British India in general and other Hindu states that were undergoing recurrent religious and communal convulsions rationalized and encouraged in terms of theories of Indian nationalism, leading, ultimately, to the partition of the country in 1947 into two independent states. Some of Haidarābād's major government departments were put under the supervision of Hindu nobles and, later, were strengthened by able and visionary administrator-academicians (such as Muhsinu'l-mulk, Vaqāru'l-mulk and `Imādu'l-mulk) from North India, appointed in consultation with the ever-present British residents in the State, and on the recommendations of distinguished reformers like Sir Sayyid Ahmad Khān of the Madrasatu'l-`ulum, Aligarh. Haidarābād was the first of India's princely states to take steps for a comprehensive program of reformation of all departments of the State—legislative, executive, and judiciary, including education, transport, and communications.

Like all areas of medieval India where Persian served as the language of administration, the Nizām's State also inherited from the Mughal Empire, of which it was a province until 1724, the institution of Dāru'l-inshā, which involved a particular Persianate conception of administration. Starting in the 1860s Urdu began to replace Persian as the official language of the State. This process was completed in 1884. Attainment of official status by Urdu was facilitated by two historical factors: (1) about four hundred years of creative and scholarly traditions built up in Dakkhani Urdu from the Bahmanis onwards, enriched by both Persian and Hindavi vocabularies, idioms, and literary norms and styles highly capable of expressing complex themes, both social and Sufistic, and, (2) by the end of the 18th century, Urdu had already become a full-fledged language of literature and scholarship, alongside Persian, in all the regions of India except southern India. In several parts of North India, it was also already being used as a court language.

PERSIAN INSHĀ IN INDIA

Persian language entered South Asia through two streams—as a vehicle of Persianate Central-Asian culture and as the administrative language of the Turko-Mongol chieftains who established their rule in the sub-Himalayan regions, starting with the Ghaznavids in the 11th century. Persian was not the native language of these empire-builders; it was the language of their administration and of the culture of the vast expanse of western Asia stretching from the Persian Gulf in the south to the Oxus in the north of the territory now divided among Afghanistan, Iran, Pakistan, and the Central Asian republics. Under royal patronage, Persian also became the language of literary and scholarly contributions, attracting a large number of poets and scholars from Iran and Central Asia to the courts of the rulers and the nobility. In the North, during the Sultanate and the Mughal periods, these Muslim rulers of Central Asian origin set the precedent of establishing the same Persian-based administration in a country where Persian was the language neither of the elite nor of the general population. Still, the use of it by the government ensured the continuity of an administrative, political and cultural tradition that had served the overall interests of those ruling classes of western and Central Asia for a long time.

Besides administration, Persian had always been the chief vehicle of artistic, literary, and scholarly expression in those regions and it acquired the same status in India as well. More importantly, there was a silent acceptance by the common people of certain values of culture as defined by the Turko-Mongol administrators, particularly by the Mughal Rajput nobility and ruling elite. These values included love of learning (*'ilm-dosti*), patronage of poets, writers, and scholars, and deep respect for Sufis and the Sufi institutions (*khānqāh*s, *dargāh*s) which enjoyed an extensive following among both the Muslim and non-Muslim populations. This value-oriented politico-cultural style of governance was very effective in eliciting spontaneous support from the common people for whom these values provided a sense of social security. This tradition was maintained by the Muslim kingdoms of the Bahmanis of Gulbarga (1346–1494) and by its successor five dynasties, the Barid Shāhis of Bidar (1503–1619), Qutb Shāhis of Golkonda (1495–1685), 'Ādil Shāhis of Bijapur (1489–1685), Nizām Shāhis of Ahmad Nagar (1436–1496), and 'Imād Shāhis of Barar (1480–1514), with certain significant changes through linguistic and cultural inputs from respective regional environments. A fact that seems to underlie the continuity and maintenance of high literary values, protocol, and the official etiquette in Persian *insha* during the Sultanate and Mughal periods is that it helped in maintaining the hierarchical system of the court and the nobility which had become an integral part of their statecraft. However, the role of Persian was limited: it was an institution of administrative communication as well as the medium of literary and scholarly expression of a minority of the ruling elite and the nobility—both Muslims and Hindus—while the vast majority of common people of both urban and rural India continued to speak and write in their own Indian languages. As such, all the post-Mughal Muslim states, north and south, followed a bilingual policy of administration—using local languages for official purposes at the village and district levels and Persian for higher levels, translating where necessary. Thus, the framework and functioning of Persianate administration, working through its government office, the Daru'l-inshā, remained intact throughout the Sultanate and the Mughal periods and their successor Muslim princely states.

The main features of this Persianate model of administration, as implemented under the Nizām until 1884, were as follows:

I.   Departments (*dafātir*),[1] including:

Daftar-i Divāni (Office of Civil and Military Administration)

Daftar-i Istifā (Department of Auditing and Review)

Daftar-i Manāsib va Khitābat (Office of Ranks and Titles)

Daftar-i Mavāhir (Office of Seals)

Daftar-i Māl (Office of Administration of Haidarābād and Bidar)

Daftar-i Mulki (Land Office)

Daftar-i Bakhshigari (Office of Military Accounts)

Daftar-i Dāru'l-inshā (Office of the Private Secretary)

Daftar-i Munshikhāna

Daftar-i Peshkāri

Daftar-i Khazāna-i `umarā

Sadāratu'l-`āliya, etc.

The working language (*nazm va nasq*) was Persian, calligraphed, generally, in the *shikasta* style of the script.

II.   Types of communications[2]:

   i)   Incoming mail:

Letters: *khatt, ma`ruza, suvāl*

Treaties: Tahnāma, Iqrārnāma, *`ahd va paimān, qaul va qarār*

Newsletters: *akhbār, vāqa`i, kaifiyat, ruznāma*

Miscellaneous: *ishtihārnāma, qabuliatnāma, ta`ahhudnāma, mu`āfi-nāma, muchalka, qabz, rasid*

   ii)   Interdepartmental papers:

Official letters and notes: *vājibu'l-`arz, iltimās, darkhwāst, yaddāsht, tafviz-i alqābnāma, jantri, gushvāra, fihrist*

   iii) Outgoing mail:

Letters: *`arzdāsht, kharita, `ināyatnāma, ruq`a*

Orders: *ahkām, ta'kid, dastak, parvānagi*

Miscellaneous: *dasturu'l-`amal, nirkhnāma, citthi, rasid*, etc.

III. Officials of Dāru'l-inshā[3]:

Mir Munshi: the head of Dāru'l-inshā and, as such, the most important official after the monarch, was responsible for the correct writing of the monarch's orders

Muhr-bardār: keeper of the royal seal, closely associated with the Mir Munshi

Qalamdān-bardār: one who carried the pen-holder

Muharrir: clerk, scribe, writer, a section-head in the Dāru'l-inshā

Mutasaddi: clerks trained in *nastaʿliq* and *shikasta* styles of drafting routine documents

Khushnavis: a calligrapher trained in all styles of calligraphy, who prepared copies of dispatches, including farmans and personal letters of the Nizām

Mama: "It was a peculiar feature of the administration under the Asaf Jahs that maid-servants would carry oral orders or messages from the Nizām (while he was in harem) to the administration, who took formal written action based on them. They became so important and influential that even the nobles respected them."[4]

IV.   Alqāb and protocol[5]:

There was a hierarchy of authorities, with the Nizām at the top, followed by the members of the royal dynasty, the nobles (*umarā*), the governors of provinces (*subedār*), the ministers, and a host of officials staffing different wings of the empire—military, administration, the executive, and the judiciary, religious leaders, and dignitaries of other Indian states including the British ruling class. All these personages were assigned various titles (*alqāb*, sing. *laqab*) by, or with the approval of, the Sultān/Bādshāh/Shāhinshāh.

This pattern of hierarchy and assignment of titles continued in the Āsaf Jāhi period, and was continued from 1884 onwards from Persian into Urdu. The titles were purely ceremonial and decorative, normally related either to the nature of their qualifications, the work they had been assigned, or to the services they had rendered to the monarchy. There was a separate department, Tajviz-i Alqāb, within the Dāru'l-inshā that coined and recommended titles for the honored persons with due approval of the King, and maintained a register (*alqāb-nāma*) for this purpose. The titles were issued by the Dāru'l-Inshā. Each laqab was specific to a certain noble or official and was used as the initial part of the letter. After the alqāb, the letter started with certain phrases in accordance with the status of the addressee, like *hadd-i dāb, umrat darāz bād, ziyāda che navishta shavad*.[6] Some examples of such titles are given below[7]:

The Emperor:

Hazrat-i zill-i subhāni, bādshāh-i jām-jāh anjum-sipāh, falak-bargāh,
  maliku'l-riqāb-i zamān, āya-i rahmat-i hazrat rabbu'l-ʿālamin
  khalada'llāhu mulkahu

Raja Maharao, Kotvala:

> *Ināyat-i khāqāni qarin-i hāl farkhund-ahmāl, hashmat va shaukat manzilat*

Maharana Partab Singh:

> *Jalā'il-i `ināyat-i khāqāni va jazā'il-i tafazzulāt-i zill-i subhāni*

Fatima Begum (sister of an *amir*, Zu'l-fiqāru'd-daula):

> *Mukhaddar-asrā`-i izzat va iffat va ismat-manzilat, mashmul-i altāf-i*
> *bādshāhi*

Shāh Nizāmuddin (a Sufi):

> *`Ārif-i ma`ārif-i haqiqat va tariqat, jamāl-i marātib-i afnun-i mulk va millat,*
> *zubdat-i arbāb-i safvat va'l-safā*

Wives of Humayun Jah:

> *Iffat martabat, iffat-panāhi*

SOUTH INDIA: PRE-ĀSAF JĀHI PERIOD

In the south (Gujarat, Deccan), however, the situation was different. Muslim rule reached Gujarat by the end of the 13th century and by 1310 a large area of the Deccan was conquered by the Khiljis. Amirān-i Sāda, the governors of various regions in the Gujarat and the Deccan, gradually became independent of Delhi. In 1347, as a result of a revolt against the Tughlaq king in Delhi, the independent state of the Bahmanis was established in the Deccan. The linguistic map of south India was different from North India: North India under the Persian administration was largely the area of (Indo-European) Khari Boli and Brij Bhasha, two of the main sources of Urdu (the others being Arabic, Persian, and Turkish), while the south Indian region was a land of robust and popular languages like Marathi and the Dravidian Tamil, Malayalam, Kanada, and Telugu, each with their own literary traditions which, as we shall see later, posed serious challenges to the continuity and functionality of the Persianate administration. It is to be noted that Urdu in its earliest form was not introduced in south India along with the arrival of Muslim armies in those areas; it was carried there even before the Khilji armies by certain Sufis who had traveled to south India with the message of love as the teaching of Islam.[8] After `Alāu'l-din Khilji more Sufis belonging to different *silsilas* (orders), particularly the Chishtis, made the Deccan their home.[9]

The Bahmani Sultanate consisted of three linguistic regions: Kanada, Marathi, and Telugu. Persian was the official language, but it was soon realized that it could not serve as a means of mass communication in the three linguistic regions of the Sultanate. Besides these three, there was also a fourth language, Dakkhani (as the early south Indian form of Urdu was called), which had a large component of Persian vocabulary, its own grammar, and a literature that was an extension of the Persian tradition of prose and poetry. It had created a wide space for itself as a means of communication among different linguistic groups as a result of the humanitarian activities of the Sufis, who used Dakkhani Urdu for reaching out to the common people. Dakkhani Urdu was gradually adopted by the ruling class also, since it was very close to both Persian and the Hindavi languages (that is, the non-Persian Indian languages spoken in these areas) and was understood by all sections of society. Although Persian maintained intact its position as the language of administration, it was losing its position as the language of the nobility and the elite. One reason for this could be the process of gradual disconnection of Bahmani society with the culture of the north and its natural growth as a south Indian cultural area. This same process appears to have been operating in all the successor states to the Mughal Empire. The Bahmani period may be considered as the era of inauguration of the trend of dual operation of Persian and Urdu writing in the Deccan. Dakkhani Urdu had emerged as the language of the Sufis and the poets and prose-writers during the era of the Bahmanis and its five successor states.[10]

THE QUTB SHĀHI PERIOD (1518–1686)

Like their predecessors, the Qutb Shāhi kings were deeply involved in literature and were great patrons of poets and scholars, who were invited to their courts. Due to their Shi`i faith they had established very close cultural relations with Iran. They invited poets and scholars and administrators from Iran to serve in the court and in various high positions. For instance, Mulla Muhammad Sharif Vuqu`i was the poet laureate of the court of the second ruler, Jamshed Quli. In the court of Muhammad Quli Qutb Shāh, Mir Muhammad Mu'min Astarābādi and Mirzā Muhammad Amin were the Vakil-i Saltanat and Mir Jumla, respectively. With the court of `Abdullāh Qutb Shāh were associated Shamsu'l-din Muhammad Allāma Ibn Khātun, Mullā Jamālu'l-din, Mullā Fathullāh Simnāni, and Mullā Nizāmu'l-din Ahmad. The earlier dual linguistic pattern continued. Persian remained the official language, with all its cultural conventions, while the other trend of emergence of local languages gained more vitality and the enlargement of its area of acceptance across all classes of society. It was furthered strengthened during the Qutb Shāhs. Several Dakkhani Urdu poets and prose writers produced literature reflecting various aspects of the social and cultural pluralism of the region. The best example of Qutb Shāhi Urdu literature is the poetic composition of the ruler Muhammad Quli Qutb Shāh (1580–1610), who is also known as *Urdu ka pahla sāhib-i divān shā'ir* (first Urdu poet who has a properly compiled collection of his poetic compositions).[11] During an interregnum of 37 years of the rule of Nizāmu'l-mulk Āsaf Jāh as a Mughal governor in the Deccan before he declared independence in 1723, the poets Vali Aurangābādi (d. 1707) and Siraj Aurangābādi (d. 1763) heralded the beginning of a new era in the art of the Urdu *ghazal,* which paved the way for the development of Urdu poetry and expression for the North Indian world in the 18th and 19th centuries.

ĀSAF JĀHI PERIOD (1723–1948): THE DĀRU'L-INSHĀ

The Āsaf Jāhi dynasty succeeded the Qutb Shāhis in 1788. While the people's culture was reflected in the literature of local languages and dialects, the folk arts, and music of the region, the Dakkhani Urdu inshā shaped by the nobility and the administrative class continued to observe all protocols and cultural conventions embedded in the Mughal Persian *inshā,* that is, alqab and all the details of etiquette (*adab*) in communications to different officials, ministers, and external dignitaries. The ruling class was not given any reason to revise or change the tradition of Persian usage that had been serving them successfully for several centuries. In other words, inshā conventions for Dakkhani Urdu were set by the King and the ruling nobility and the managers of the administrative class who belonged to the Deccan, socially and culturally, and spoke and wrote Dakkhani Urdu. Up to the middle of the 19th century, the dual operation of Urdu and Persian continued at the literary and official levels. However, with the British colonial institution making its intentions clear of introducing English at all upper levels of administration in British India and the status of English as the source-language of Western sciences, the princely states of India found that they had to take a second look at their administrative and educational policies.

THE 19TH CENTURY: NORTH INDIA

The 19th century heralded an era of revolutionary change in the form of Westernization and modernization in West, South and Southeast Asia through the presence of the British and the other European colonial powers. In India, the British with their complete hold over almost the whole peninsula, were able gradually to overhaul the administration, transport, communications, and educational systems, generating a debate among the Indian elite on the validity of traditional values, social behavior, and knowledge that were being challenged by the new Western values. This debate led to the emergence of reform movements questioning these values. Among Muslims, the main concern was in the sphere of culture and education, with special attention to traditional religious norms. The cultural and educational movement started by Sayyid Ahmad Khān, also known as the Aligarh Movement, set in motion a powerful trend of social and cultural reform along the lines of Western education. This movement also had an impact on Urdu literature and was successful in liberating it from the world of imagination and fancy and focusing it on the world of social realities. The social role of Urdu was, for the first time, highlighted by this movement and was carried forward, later, by the Progressive Movement of the 1930s and 1940s. Interestingly, the social reform considerations excluded Urdu, like all other Indian languages, as a language of modern education. Sayyid Ahmad Khān himself ruled out Urdu as a medium of education for the Urdu-speaking Muslims and strongly advocated that education in English was the only way for social and economic rehabilitation. However, as we will see, the Asaf Jahi administration in South India rejected Sayyid Ahmad Khān's assumptions and inaugurated a firm movement for adopting Urdu as the official language and the medium of education from the primary to the higher levels of education.

During the second half of the 19th century big changes appeared in the outlook of academicians, administrators, and the ruling classes regarding political, social, economic, and cultural life. Along with Urdu, learning English as the means for accessing Western knowledge and culture began to increase. In this connection, the contribution of Shamsu'l-umarā is very significant. Navāb Fakhru'l-din Khan Amir Kabir Shamsu'l-umarā Sāni (1780–1872) developed a keen interest in the Western sciences which, in his view, were essential for progress. Steps were taken to make government

departments more efficient, and for this purpose, able persons from North
India were recruited. The shift, after 1886, in Urdu *inshā* from its Dakkhani
version to the version which had become the standard academic and literary Urdu in North India from the beginning of the 19th century could be to
a certain extent due to the influence of these North Indian scholar-administrators.[12] The process took place in two phases.[13]

PHASE 1: 1860s–1884

It was Bashiru'l-daula, Sir Āsmān Jāh, Muhammad Mazharu'd-din Khān
Bahādur, the Sadru'l-maham, `Adālat-i `Āliya (Minister of Justice), who in
the late 1860s realized for the first time the futility of carrying on the dual
linguistic policy in running the administration of the state in the context of
the changing social and intellectual scenario of the country and the administrative changes that were being introduced in the Westernization policy
of British colonial rule. Adoption of Urdu as the official language was the
initial step in making the administration more efficient and responsive to
the needs of the common people. An account of the steps taken by policy-
makers and administrators from the middle of the 19th century onwards
with regard to the introduction of Urdu in place of Persian as the official
language will be helpful for understanding the social and cultural factors
that operated in determining the twin functions of Persian as a representative of literature and culture and as a language of administration.

In 1871 Bashiru'l-daula issued a circular (*gashti*)[14] in which he referred
to the administrative confusion resulting from the inadequate linguistic administrative policy of the courts (particularly at the district level). For instance, Telugu was being used for official purposes in non-Telugu areas because the officials happened to know Telugu. In the courts, statements and
representations (*izhārāt*) by the litigants were made in their own languages
(Telugu, Marathi, Kanada, Urdu) and then they were translated into Persian
and forwarded to higher courts. This procedure, he commented, was full
of defects, as in the lower courts a correct translation and representation of
the izhārāt in Persian could not be assured and the cause of justice and the
legitimate rights of the litigants cannot be protected. Besides, except for the
recording of representations in Persian, all other discussions at the lower
and the higher levels of the justice department were conducted in Urdu. He
therefore ordered that as a first step in eliminating this difficulty the izharat

were to be recorded in Urdu, a language that was easy to learn and known to all language communities.

In 1293 A.H. (1876), Bashiru'l-daula submitted to the King a proposal for making Urdu the language of the State judiciary. The proposal argued that Haidarābād was a multi-lingual state; the district offices were working in three local languages—Telugu (42 percent), Marathi (31 percent), Kanada (12 percent)—and Urdu (10 percent). While Telugu, Marathi, and Kannada were spoken and understood in their respective regions only, Urdu was spoken and understood by both the literate and illiterate peoples of all other linguistic groups. The current practice was creating great difficulties in the work of the courts. He therefore proposed that in order to make official work easier and more efficient, Urdu was the most obvious choice to be used as the language of the law courts. In 1295 A.H. (1878) through another official circular he instructed all officials and the staff of the state to learn Urdu, at least to the extent of being able to carry out routine work. Urdu could be adopted as the official language in stages and, wherever necessary, Persian translations of Urdu documents could be prepared without difficulty.[15] A circular issued in 1298 (1880) and published in the *Jarida-i Ghair Ma'muli,* dated 27 Rabi'u'l-sāni, 1301 (1883), gives full details of the rationale behind the move of adopting Urdu as the court language and the steps that were taken in 1867, 1876, and 1878 in this regard.

PHASE 2: FROM 1884 ONWARDS[16]

In 1884 a circular entitled *"Āinda jumla 'adālati daftaron men Urdu ke zariye khatt va kitābat hogi"* (henceforth all correspondence in the offices of the courts would be in Urdu) was issued[17] from the office of Madāru'l-mahām (Prime Minister) Sālārjang II. Mir Lā'iq 'Ali Khān stated that a comprehensive view of the issue related to the language policy in force in the judicial courts showed that no uniform procedure was being followed for maintaining official records in different departments at the district and higher courts. They were kept in both Persian and Urdu. It was noted that there was not a single case or even judgment where a single language, Urdu or Persian, was used. Sometimes, a judgment started in Urdu and ended in Persian, it was noticed. In other words every official was free to use any of the two languages at his will. This dichotomy had to be removed, particularly in departments dealing with judicial problems of common people. The circular, therefore, declared that from then onwards Urdu would be the official language of the courts.

The *Madāru'l-mahām* then made an insightful comment: if they continued to maintain a language (Persian) as an official language that was neither an ancient nor a modern language of the country, nor of the ruler or the ruled, spoken neither in offices nor in private, it would amount to nullifying all our precious efforts of the past 12 or 13 years to prevent such an eventuality, and would recreate all those obstacles from which we had gradually extricated ourselves. Keeping Persian as the official court language would also continue the sufferings of litigants and miss a great opportunity for reducing expenditure. Sounding a realistic note, the Madāru'l-mahām agreed that Persian was a sweet and chaste language and full advantage would be taken of such a historically rich language by teaching it in the schools and maktabs. However, to implicate Persian in the official proceedings of litigants was not advisable. The ordinance was approved by the ruler, Mir Mahbub ʿAli Khān, and came into effect immediately. It was also explained that non-Urdu speakers could record their izharat (representations) in their own languages which could be rendered into Urdu for further action. It was observed that it was not difficult for the officials who were accustomed to write in Persian to switch over to Urdu.

This circular reflects the general thinking of policy makers in the Nizām's State and of local Urdu speakers: that, in the middle of the 19th century, Urdu was in a position to take the place of Persian as the administrative language, while Persian would be retained for continuation of the literary and scholarly heritage. This shift may also be understood as representing the general feeling outside the State, in northern India, and in the princely states of Rampur and Bhopal. Accordingly, in a gradual way Urdu was introduced for official purposes in different offices starting with the courts of law.

It is to be noted here that by this time the state had passed through several phases of modernization and many new institutions dealing with administration, railways, judiciary, education, finance, and law and order had been established. Modernization on such a broad scale called for highly qualified managers who would need to be recruited from outside the State. Hence, the services of intelligent, experienced, and highly educated persons were obtained from North India in consultation with the British Indian officials and distinguished figures like Sir Sayyid Ahmad Khān.[18] Language standardization facilitated this process.

The policy statements mentioned above show that the logic of administrative practice had been oriented purely to monarchical interests, and had to give way to the pressures of regional, cultural, and political realities of the modern period. The roles were reversed——the needs of the society, and not the monarchical feudal interests, dictated policies of the media and modes of administration. The bilingual policy continued, but with a major difference. While Urdu displaced Persian as the official language, the records at the district and village levels continued to be maintained in local languages.

FEATURES OF THE URDU INSHĀ

Dafātir (departments): The Dafatir of the Urdu Daru'l-inshā were the same as in the Persian Dāru'l-inshā, but later were reorganized by the reformer Prime Minister, Sālār Jang I (appointed in 1859).

Vocabulary: The volume of the vocabulary was small, limited to the routine requirements of different offices; language was simple and easy to understand by the officers concerned, who were not always well-versed in Persian.

New terms: Most of the terms and phrases were retained but several new terms were added. The new terms were mostly taken from the local languages—Marathi, Telugu, and Kanada. Some new legal terms were coined for certain specific circumstances, cases like *mudākhalat-i bejā bar khāna* (theft in a house), *mahrumi va mutazarrari–i shadid* (rape), *muttahim kardan ba badkāri va ba-digar chunin af āl* (defamation), etc. Some English words were also used as terms like "office" and "unclaimed khutut."

Etiquette and protocol: Practices peculiar to the Persian *insha* were kept intact. However, the language of documents and communications from one level to another higher level became simple and brief. Farmans on all issues selected by the king were frequently issued in simple style with a Dakkhani flavor, but with Persian terms and style (which was considered as reflecting high literary merit). A large number of farmans on literary and some issues of social, cultural, and political interest were regularly published in one or two Urdu dailies, with all the importance a royal opinion can carry. Urdu was used extensively for official purposes, with all Persian and other terms from the local regional languages dealing with revenue and other rural issues that had become part of the terminology of the administration unchanged. In certain cases records were kept in the regional as well as in their Urdu translations. Again, this was in line with conventions followed since the Bahmanis. The real change appeared in the style of correspondence in view of the fundamental changes of institutional modernization initiated in India under the British. Until the 1860s all decisions of the State were taken by the king and some officials or nobles close to him. That is, the authority descended from the top to the lower levels. It was changed. The recommendations regarding an issue were made at the lower levels and passed through the concerned higher offices up to the king, who normally approved them, though sometimes they were amended or rejected. Second, the customary terms and phrases were simplified, made briefer and less ceremonial. During the first phase, old-style prose was continued for recording and correspondence, but with liberal use of local and popular idioms and modes of expressions that were part of the spoken language. One may say that the spoken Dakkhani Urdu set the style of administrative practice in this phase. In fact, the Dakkhani Urdu phase prepared the ground for the usage of the second phase starting in 1886.

Some more factors may be discerned underlying these changes, as follows:

1. The people's issues being dealt with by the government had become more complex under the influence of the fast pace of institutional modernization initiated in British India. It is to be noted that the aristocracy led by two reformist Prime Ministers, Salar Jang I and II, was persuaded to restructure the medieval style and approach of the administration serving the vested interests of the ruling aristocracy and classes and to reorient it to the issues related to the peoples of the State. This, of course, did not involve any dilution of the supreme authority of the monarchical system.

2. Three factors seem to have helped in the adoption of Urdu as the official language: (i) Urdu had developed from a spoken language into a written language equipped with the style, vocabulary, and terminology required for expressing literary and scholarly themes; (ii) it was the language of the ruling class; and (iii) it was a language that was understood in all three linguistic regions of the State.

3. There appears to have emerged, by the middle of the 19th century, a section of the educated people in the State which considered learning Western sciences essential for progress. Introductory tracts on scientific subjects were either translated or were written for general readers and students.

The above factors led gradually to the build-up of an energetic convergence of popular and official support in favor of Urdu as the vehicle of progress of the State as a whole. Urdu was made the medium of education in several schools, alongside the schools imparting education in other local languages. These factors and developments led in 1918 to the historic decision to establish Osmania University, with Urdu as the medium of instruction.

A study of the twin roles that Persian played in South Asiaas the language of administration and as the powerful transporter of Persian literature and Persianate, Central Asian cultural values poses the question whether there is a necessary relationship between the two roles, or if they operate in separate areas without necessarily influencing each other. It is very difficult to answer this question. It involves a vast area of enquiry covering the political and cultural history of the different societies of the whole of western and Central Asia of the last two thousand plus years of the pre- and post-Islamic eras. There is always the temptation to generalize. However, a few observations would not be out of place. A state rules through various departments of administration—political, financial, economic, religious, judicial, educational, etc. Changes of regimes do not necessarily imply changing such administrative wings of governance. During the whole medieval period, the Persian administrative system, originally evolved out of the Persianate cultural ethos, continued to function without any disturbance, since it was able to meet the requirements of governance—with self-survival or military expansion as the only two main objectives—of different monarchical regimes in different eras. The culture, language, and the economy of the peoples were irrelevant to its monarchical interests. It would be interesting to study the connection between the cultural values of the original Persianate administrative institution and the cultural ambiance of the Central Asian and South Asian Muslim-ruled societies during the later medieval era.

The original Persianate *Dāru'l-inshā* model might have been generated by the culture of the Sasanid-Safavid combination of royalty and aristocracy with a feudal upper class. However, it is not convincing to assume that this original Persianate culture remained the same during the succeeding generations of ruling classes of different regimes, countries, societies, and linguistic areas of Central and South Asia. What appears to have happened is that the *Daru'l-insha* in the course of a few centuries was converted from a culture into a sort of convention or tradition of administrative documentation having no reference to the culture of the area where the administration functioned. The traditional alqab, protocols, and other expressions continued in use as mere ceremonial phrases, just as today we continue to use phrases like "Dear Sir", "Sincerely yours," or "Yours faithfully" as expressions of mere custom or convention.

NOTES

1. Zaib Haidar, *Dār-ul-Inshā*, 15–20. The purpose here is to show the sophisticated complexity of the administrative system. Since the names of the offices are not sufficient to explain their function, most are left untranslated.
2. Ibid., 33–34.
3. Ibid., 34–38.
4. Ibid., 38.
5. Ibid., 176ff.
6. Ibid., chap. 6
7. Ibid., 178–80.
8. Jamil Jalibi, *Tārikh-i Adab-i Urdu*, 1: chap. 3. These Sufis included Hajji Rumi (d. 1160), Sayyid Shāh Mumin (d. 1200), Shāh Jalāluddin Ganj-i Ravān (d. 1246), Sayyid Ahmad Kabir Hayāt Qalandar (d. 1260), Bābā Sharafuddin (d. 1288), and Bābā Shihābuddin (d. 1291).
9. Ibid. They included Shāh Muntakhabuddin Zarzari Zar Bakhsh (d. 1309), Sayyid Yusuf Shāh Raju Qattal, father of Hazrat Gesudarāz (d. 1335), and Shāh Burhānuddin Gharib (d. 1337).
10. Jamil Jalibi, *Adab-i Urdu*, 1:379–517.
11. Ibid., 145–517. Some of the literary personalities whose contributions have now become a part of the history of Dakkhani Urdu are:
    Bahmani period: Fakhruddin Nizāmi (*masnavi, Kadam Rao Padam Rao*), Ashraf Biyabani (*masnavi, Nausar Har*), Miranji Shamsu'l-ushshāq
    `Ādil Shāhi period: Mulla Zahuri (*Seh Nasr-i Zuhuri*), Muhammad Qāsim Farishta (*Tārikh-i Firishta*), Ali `Ādil Shāh Jagat Guru (*Kitāb-i Nauras*), Shāh Burhānuddin Janam, Shāh Aminuddin Alā, Mirzā Muhammad Muqim (*masnavi, Chandr badan Mahyār*)
    Qutb Shāhi period: Some of the prominent poets are Ghavvasi, Ibn Nish`ati, Junaidi, Taba`i, Miranji Hasan Khudā Numā, Mirān Yaqub, Sayyid Bulāqi.
12. See Sayyid Mustafā Kamāl, *Haidarābād men Urdu Ki Taraqqi Ta`limi aur Sarkāri Zabān Ki Haisiyat Se*, 213–26, for a detailed description of the measures taken by Shamsu'l-umarā for the empowerment of the Urdu language through the translation of scientific terminology and scientific literature from European languages into Urdu and Persian, the opening of schools imparting education in European sciences, and establishing a printing press in 1865.
13. Ibid., 91–180; Dā'ud Ashraf, "Enforcement of Urdu," 117–26; Ghulām Jilāni, "Urdu Sarkāri Dafātir," 45–80.
14. Kamāl, *Haidarābād men Urdu*, 91–124.
15. Ibid., 100–102.
16. Ibid., 125–38.
17. For the full text of the circular, vide Ahsan Marahravi, *Namuna-yi Mansurāt*, 419–27.

18. For details on these personalities, see Dā'ud Ashraf, *Beruni Arbāb-i Kamāl*, 69–82; Kamāl, *Hyderābād men Urdu*, 151–55.

REFERENCES

Ashraf, Syed Dawood. 2005. *Beruni Arbāb-i Kamāl*. Hyderābād: Shagūfah Pablikeshanz.

—— 2006. Enforcement of Urdu as the Official Language during the Āsaf Jāhi Period. In *Archival Glimpses of the Dakan* [Deccan], 117–26 Hyderābād: Moazzam Husain Foundation.

Haidar, Zaib. 2002. *Dār-ul-Inshā, the Nizām's Personal Secretariat, 1762–1803*. London: Discovery Publishers.

Jamil Jalibi. 1975– . *Tārīkh-i Adab-i Urdu*. 2 vols. Lahore: Majlis-i Taraqqī-yi Adab.

Ghulam Jilani. 2002. *Urdu Sarkāri Dafātir, Adliyah aur Intizāmiyah ki Zabān*. In H.E.H. the Nizām's Trust, Hyderābād, Mamlukat-i Āsafiya Men Urdu Zabān Ki Tarvij va Taraqqi, Hyderābād.

Sayyid Mustafā Kamāl. 1990. *Hyderābād men Urdu Ki Taraqqi: Ta'limi aur Sarkāri Zabān Ki Haisiyat Se*. Hyderābād: Shigūfah Pablīkeshanz.

Ahsan Marahravi. 1986. *Tārīkh-i nasr-i Urdū: Namuna-i Mansurāt*. Reprint. Islamābād: Muqtadirah-yi Qaumī Zabān.

10

Teaching Persian as an Imperial Language in India and in England during the Late 18th and Early 19th Centuries[1]

MICHAEL H. FISHER

PERSIAN AS AN IMPERIAL LANGUAGE IN INDIA AND ENGLAND

Persian served as the imperial language in India for 300 years, from the time of the Mughal Empire through the early British Empire. During the late 18th and early 19th centuries in both India and England, Persian teaching became highly contested by rival representatives of these conflicting imperial cultures. Indian scholar-officials, who for generations had served the Mughal Empire or one of its successor states, sought to perpetuate the types of Persian-based learning that they embodied. In both India and England, they and also Persians worked to instruct the British in Persian language, literature, and high culture generally. British authorities, however, gradually reduced the standing of these Persians and Indians both as teachers of Persian and as imperial officials. Thus, the official uses and cultural meanings of Persian shifted fundamentally during the transition from the Mughal to the British empires.

From the late 18th century onward, as the British rapidly extended their conquests across India, they sought mastery of Persian as the prime language of command and means of rule over India. While the East India Company (established 1600) invested in Persian education, it did so largely to provide its British civil officials and military officers with this technology of governance. In the early 19th century, the English East India Company established advanced training institutions in India, most notably Fort William College in Calcutta (1800), and also at Haileybury (1806) and Addiscombe (1809) colleges in England. In all of these East India Company establishments (as well as in long-established British universities), British professors asserted their presumed superiority over Indian teachers of Persian and also over the content of officially sponsored education in Persian language and literature.[2] While some Britons certainly studied and savored Persian language and literature, few personally identified themselves with Persian or composed their own poetry or literary prose in it. Rather, many of the most knowledgeable among these British scholars analyzed Persian through their British-style grammars, dictionaries, and other educational tools, or translated the works of Indian or Persian authors into English. Further, especially after 1837, British advocates of Anglicization displaced Indian teachers in England and replaced Persian with English as the official language of imperial rule in India.[3]

Yet, some scholars are currently coming to recognize the problematic role that Indians themselves played in resisting but also collaborating with the British appropriation of Indo-Persian administrative technologies and cultures.[4] In India, especially in regions or courts outside of direct British control, Indians continued throughout the 19th century to produce Persian literature as a means to perpetuate and advance their self-identified culture. But, as these regions and courts fell to British annexations, such sources of patronage for this Persianate culture diminished in number and, in some cases, in resources. Instead, to secure employment as teachers or officials under the British, Indians had largely to accept British formulations and uses of Persian. Indian employees of Fort William College in Calcutta were commonly hired to become tutors of their British students, while those at Haileybury or Addiscombe colleges in England could at best be only assistants to British professors. Thus, while employed on the basis of their mastery over Persian at levels beyond those achieved by any Briton, their status nonetheless became dependent on their British superiors and became degraded with the decline of the prestige of Persianate culture itself.

This chapter explores the dynamics of Persian language teaching in both India and England during the transitional period of the late 18th and early 19th centuries. It traces the changing personnel and curriculum of educational institutions that taught Persian in each location. It also examines the contests and collaborations between British and Indian professors of Persian in these institutions. It concludes with consideration of the long-term effects of these struggles over Persian, and the consequences of its replacement by English-medium elite education in India.

PERSIAN AS THE MUGHAL IMPERIAL LANGUAGE

When the Mughals founded their empire in India in 1526, they found that the appreciation of Persian language and culture was well-established there, especially in certain elite Muslim circles.[5] Unevenly from the 13th century onward, various Indian Muslim royal courts, especially those of the Delhi and the central Indian sultanates, had come to value and patronize (often in a localized form) Persian-derived arts including prose, poetry, painting, manuscript illustration, architecture, and music.[6] Among the most prominent Indians who composed works of literature in Persian was Amir Khusraw (1253–1325).[7] Further, Sufism became an important medium for the expansion of aspects of Persian culture deeper into Indian society.

Under the influence and patronage of the imperial Mughals, Persian language and Indo-Persian culture rose further in prominence and extent across northern and central India. Although the Mughals (or the Chaghatai Timurids as they thought of themselves) originally spoke Turkish, Emperor Akbar (r. 1556–1605) determined that Persian should be their language of rule. The Mughals favored the variety of Persian which they considered the purer style of Fars, rather than that of their original Central Asia.[8] Persian styles also merged with traditional Indian ones to produce the distinctively Indo-Persian forms favored by many in the Mughal imperial court and in the provincial courts of its governors and other subordinates. In addition, the Mughals modeled much of their administration on that of the Safavids.

Substantial numbers of Persian men and women emigrated to India where their identity provided them with great prestige and advancement in service to the Mughals.[9] Indeed many Persians were specifically recruited by Mughal imperial envoys bearing lucrative offers of patronage. They formed the core of one of the leading factions among imperial officials and courtiers, which Mughal emperors used to counterbalance the Turani, Afghan, Rajput Hindu, Muslim Indian, and other parties vying for power. The largely non-sectarian character of the Mughal court further made it particularly attractive to those Persians who did not find congenial the strongly Shi`ite character of Safavid rule. The culture and religious attitudes these Persians brought with them further resonated with the more inclusive models of Islam supported by the Mughal court (at least until the mid-17th century).

Strengthened by the Mughal imperial court and administration, Persian language and culture diffused further into the general society of India's cities, towns, and even villages. All official documents, including landholding and revenue records, were in the Persian language and script. Hence, not just Muslims but Hindu scribal communities or castes also studied Persian, often at *madrasas* with teachers from Fars. Eventually, many Hindus used Persian in their daily as well as official activities, appreciated and contributed to its literature, and displayed the associated Indo-Persian etiquette and deportment.[10] Even Hindu religious texts were occasionally composed in or translated into Persian.

While this strongly shared high Indo-Persian court culture provided a powerful bond for imperial officials, it also proved a limitation on Mughal expansion. One major cause of the fragmentation of the empire from the late 17th century onward was its failure to assimilate non-Persian speaking peoples and power-brokers. Many of the groups most resistant to the Mughals, including the Marathas in west and central India and the Sikhs in the Punjab, identified strongly with a regional language and culture.[11]

Yet, even after the Mughal empire fragmented during the early 18th century, many regional successor states sought to revive and perpetuate Mughal traditions. Rulers and scholar-officials in these states valued Persian as their court, administrative, and high-cultural language, even if they also spoke and wrote in Urdu (or its forms as Deccani, Hindavi, Hindustani, or Hindi) or a regional language. Most prominent among these later littérateurs was Mirza Asadullah Ghālib (1797–1869), who valued his compositions in Persian above those in Urdu. Sharif Husain Qasemi argues that the early 19th century saw an unprecedented volume of Persian literary production, as the surviving Mughal successor courts sought to establish their cultural and political credentials through lavish (if anxious) patronage of Persian-language arts, especially history-writing about their dynasties and states, that referenced early Mughal glory.[12] Further, these rulers and scholar-officials strongly supported these arts in order to resist the cultural as well as political and military assertions of the British.

PERSIAN AS THE LANGUAGE OF INDIAN CULTURAL RESISTANCE AND BRITISH COLONIAL RULE

Especially during the late 18th century, a number of the Persian-language trained Indian scholar-officials whose families had traditionally served the Mughal Empire or its regional successor states shifted to working for the English East India Company. They often made this adjustment reluctantly but saw no viable alternative. Over the century from 1757 to 1857, the British annexed two-thirds of India (roughly a million square miles) and established indirect rule over the remaining Indian princely states. British rule and British culture appeared increasingly as the wave of the future while Persianate culture evoked a fading ancient regime, nonetheless a culture with which many of this service elite continued to identify closely.

As these traditional service elite-Indians perforce accepted employment under the British, however, many still sought to instruct the British in the established Indo-Persian modes of high cultural etiquette and its related administrative techniques and technologies of rule. Inherent in their efforts was their conviction that Britons who accepted the high culture of the collapsing Mughal empire would better understand, appreciate, and govern Indians. These scholar-officials therefore taught Persian to Britons in both India and Britain.

In contrast, many Britons had long believed that gaining access to Persian empowered them to master and control Indian peoples and polities. As Bernard Cohn puts it:

> The British realized that in 17th-century India, Persian was the crucial language for them to learn. They approached Persian as a kind of functional language, a pragmatic vehicle of communication with Indian officials and rulers through which, in a denotative fashion, they could express their requests, queries, and thoughts, and through which they could get things done. To use Persian well required highly specialized forms of knowledge.[13]

By the late 18th century, the English East India Company successfully began the program of appropriating Indian languages to serve as a crucial component in their construction of a system of rule. Thus, the British largely recognized the value of Persian as the "language of command," although they were often more reluctant to accept the virtues, manners, and morality of the old regime which they were displacing. Those who adopted Persianate culture, men whom William Dalrymple terms "White Mughals," declined in number and social prestige over time.[14]

The new British colonial regime established state-supported institutions where Indians taught (among other subjects) Persian language and literature. The Calcutta Madrasa (established 1781) perpetuated many of the established traditions of Persian-based education. However, reflecting growing British cultural assertions, at Fort William College (established 1800 in Calcutta for recently arrived British civil servants and military officers), British professors took charge with Indians in subordinate roles as assistants and tutors (*munshis*). Even the young British students asserted their pride of place, treating their Indian instructors as hirelings. Thus, "the teacher-taught relation with which the Indian teachers were familiar did not exist in the College of Fort William. It was a new relationship, that of Sahibs and Munshis, that of European officers and their servants."[15] Such policies at Fort William and the other presidency colleges degraded Indian scholars, but they at least preserved Persian as a major subject, albeit under British control. These policies, however, themselves gradually gave way to even more powerful British cultural assertions of Anglicization.

Gaining strength over the early decades of the 19th century, many Britons asserted that English language and culture, including the morality of the Protestant Church of England, stood superior to anything Asian or Islamic.[16] Such policies of Anglicizing English-medium education and degradation of Persianate culture (and of India generally) reflected growing colonial-based British racial policies. The famous 1835 "Minute on Education" by Thomas Babington Macaulay (1800–59) institutionalized this shift. Indeed, Macaulay explicitly regarded Persian as a competitor for government funds with English: "To teach Persian, would be to set up a rival, and as I apprehended, a very unworthy rival, to the English language."[17] From that point until today in India, Pakistan, and Bangladesh, English-medium education has remained highly prestigious while Persianate education has tended to be marginalized, even within many Muslim communities.[18]

During early colonial rule, however, Indian scholar-officials who embodied Persianate culture continued to resist such Anglicizing pressures. Some traveled to England to establish Persian language training, and positions for themselves as expert teachers. Living there, they found somewhat different conditions from what prevailed in colonial India, including, in different ways, the curriculum they taught and their social lives.

EARLY PERSIAN TEACHING IN ENGLAND

The study of Persian language and literature in England grew significantly as a result of international trade and diplomacy, especially spurred by British colonialism, rather than as a purely academic subject. Prior to the mid-18th century, there were very few British scholars of Persian in established British universities. The most notable among them was Thomas Hyde, Laudian Professor of Arabic (1691–1703) at Oxford University, a man who had a largely self-taught knowledge of Persian.[19] Yet, he had virtually no serious students. Many of the manuscripts from which he worked came both from European merchants returning from the East, and from the small but growing Indian and Persian presence in England.

From the early 17th century, many Persian-speaking visitors, travelers, and royal diplomatic and commercial missions from Persia and India, together with their servants, lived for considerable periods in London, some marrying Britons. One of the first women to come from India was Mariam, daughter of Mubārak Khān, who moved from her home at the Mughal imperial court in Agra to London (1613–17) with her English husbands.[20] In 1625, a delegation of Persians reached London, led by Naqd Ali Beg, Ambassador from Shāh Abbas, and Shāh Khwaja Muhammed Shāhsuwar Beg, a silk merchant buying and selling goods in that Emperor's service. The Ambassador (whose portrait hangs in the British Library) took an Englishwoman as his mistress. The merchant's son, Mahomet, married an English chambermaid.[21] Both did at least some informal teaching of Persian. Substantial numbers of Indian scholars, diplomats, merchants, servants, seamen, and others (totaling several thousand by the end of the 18th century), some of whom spoke Persian, began sailing directly to London at this time as well.[22] Many of these Indians also married or formed liaisons with Britons, presumably teaching them, and perhaps others, Persian and other Asian languages. Further, increasing numbers of Levant Company (established 1581) and East India Company European employees returned home with a knowledge of Persian and its literature.

With the growth of British trade and political exchanges in India, increasing numbers of Britons demanded Persian language training, not from an abstract academic interest but rather to empower themselves in India. But, at universities such as Oxford, interest in Persian remained limited until much later. Consequently, most teaching, as well as other cultural and social interaction, went on outside of formal institutions; many Britons turned to private instruction in Persian under the direction of Indian and Persian teachers who had traveled to Britain.

As British colonialism began and expanded in India, various Indian scholars ventured to Britain as part of their larger effort to educate Britons in the superior moral and literary values, as well as forms and technologies of rule, inherent in Indo-Persian culture. Among these men, Mirza Sayid I'tisām al-Din of Bengal went to Britain (1766–68) as an expert in Persian diplomacy, representing the Mughal Emperor; while there he also taught Persian privately. Various other Indian teachers of Persian published advertisements in London newspapers for British pupils to whom they could teach, for a fee, "the true Court Persian Tongue, as also the Arabic and Hindostannee Languages, as Pronounced in the Country," skills a cultured Englishman going to India should desire.[23] By stressing their accurate pronunciation, unattainable by an Englishman, these Indians highlighted their superiority as teachers.

Most, but not all, of such scholar-administrators going to England were Muslim. A Bengali Hindu by birth, Goneshamdass served as Persian translator to a Colonel Graham in India. He also traveled to England and testified in English before Parliament in 1773 as an expert on Islamic and Hindu legal practices as they related to British colonial courts.[24]

The most famous of these scholars-officials, Mirzā Abu Tālib Khān Isfahāni (1752–1806), ventured from Calcutta to England (1799–1802). Already renowned in North India as an accomplished author of books in Persian of history, poetry, and other literary forms, he prided himself in his mastery of Persian culture, although his parents had immigrated from Persia to India before his birth. In England, he intended to establish a government-sponsored Persian-language training institute (*madrasa*) under his own direction at London or Oxford. He wished thus to establish a firm foundation in England for the knowledge of Persian and for his own fame. He also began to teach Persian and Hindustani privately; he asserted that thereby the desire to study Persian would spread through the country "as one candle lights a hundred."[25] Despite Abu Talib's reasoned advocacy of his plan, it met with delay due to distractions such as the Napoleonic wars.

Lord Pelham, British Secretary of State for the Foreign Department, requested that Abu Talib remain in London for an additional 16 months to
give the British Government more time to consider his proposal for an institute. Just before Abu Talib finally left England in June 1802, the British
government indeed proposed that he head such an institute with an annual
salary of £600 (equivalent to £21,231 today) plus expenses.[26]

In England, these Indian teachers offered what they presented as accurate and authentic Persian language and cultural training directly to Eng-
lishmen. Perhaps out of professional rivalry, they derided their rival British
"false teachers [*ustādān-i jāhil*]," who were outrageously charging a guinea
and a half for each useless ninety-minute lesson.[27] For example, Abu Talib
wrote his opinion about the works of Sir William Jones and other putatively
inexpert British teachers:

> Whenever I was applied to by any [British] person for instruction in the
> Persian language who had previously studied [Jones'] grammar, I found
> it much more difficult to correct the bad pronunciation he had acquired,
> and the errors he had adopted, than it was to instruct a person who had
> never before seen the Persian alphabet. Such books are now so numer-
> ous in London, that, in a short time, it will be difficult to discriminate or
> separate them from works of real value.[28]
>
> Nevertheless, Abu Talib graciously excused Jones personally for
> his immature efforts, continuing: "Far be it from me to depreciate the
> transcendent abilities and angelic character of Sir William Jones; but
> his Persian Grammar, having been written when he was a young man,
> and previous to his having acquired any experience in Hindoostan, is, in
> many places, very defective; and it is much to be regretted that his public
> avocations, and other studies, did not permit him to revise it, after he
> had been some years in India."

In particular, Abu Talib recalled how he had saved one eager pupil from the
errors of ill-informed British teachers:

> an amiable young man, Mr. [George] Swinton; and I agreed, that, if he
> would attend me at *eight* o'clock in the morning, I would instruct him.
> As he was full of ardour, and delighted with the subject, he frequently
> forsook his breakfast, to come to my house in time. Thanks be to God,

that my efforts were crowned with success! and that he having escaped the instructions of *self-taught* masters, has acquired such a knowledge of the principles of the language, as so correct an idea of its idiom and pronunciation, that I have no doubt, after a few years' residence in India, he will attain to such a degree of excellence as has not yet been acquired by any other Englishman![29]

Thus, in Abu Talib's judgment, Europeans who presumed inappropriately to claim expertise in Persian needed to be humbled.

Expressing their mastery of the Persian language, four of these Indian teachers composed books in it about their direct experiences of, and moral judgments about, Britain for the edification of other Indians. Among them, Abu Talib's published articles and books had especially wide audiences in both India and Europe.[30] In these books, the authors generally recorded their sense of their own Persianate and Islamic cultural superiority, which exposure to growing British military, political, and technological assertions especially about India, clearly threatened. They appreciated in the English a respectful emulation of their culture, but not the appropriation of it by the unworthy. Indians visiting English libraries were impressed by the vast, and growing, collections of books and manuscripts showcased there; for example, Abu Talib was astonished, as well as proud, that Oxford held some "ten thousand" books in Persian and Arabic about Islamic sciences [*ʿulum-i Islāmi*].[31] They also criticized Britain for its religious practices and the overly free treatment and behavior of British women. Therefore, many such Indian visitors to Britain used a knowledge of Persian culture and language as one measure of the quality of British society and used their own expertise in it to prove their deservedly high status in Britain.

INDIAN AND PERSIAN PROFESSORS OF PERSIAN AT THE EAST INDIA COMPANY'S COLLEGES

Reflecting the colonial rather than purely scholarly British interest in Persian, the East India Company, rather than a British university, first established an extensive teaching program of Persian in Britain. As part of its training of its new civil officials and military cadets respectively, the East India Company created colleges at Haileybury (established 1806 near Hertford) and Addiscombe (established 1809 in Croydon, south of London).

Four Indians and one Persian held faculty appointments in them teaching Persian over four decades, 1806–1844, where they provided formative training to thousands of young Britons bound for colonial rule over India.

In these colleges at Haileybury and Addiscombe, the East India Company's Directors in London (especially the Christian evangelist and long-time Chairman of the Court of Directors, Charles Grant, 1746–1823) asserted an alternative model of education different from either the Calcutta Madrasa or Fort William College in Calcutta. The Directors believed that young British civil servants and cadets should first receive what they needed above all: moral training in British Christian values, fully available only in Britain.[32] Yet, so that these students should not be, or at least appear to be, ignorant of Indian languages on their arrival in India, they should simultaneously study Persian (as well as Arabic, Bengali, Hindustani, and/or Sanskrit) in England.[33] The Directors simultaneously ordered Fort William College, which had proven quite expensive, to be reduced in size and cost, and most of its language training shifted to England.[34] In 1830, they largely closed Fort William College except as an examination center.

The careers and curricula of the five Indian and Persian teachers at Haileybury and Addiscombe illustrate the complexity of their roles in British imperial constructions of knowledge about India. Three of these men traveled to England and volunteered themselves from London for these faculties, while two responded to offers from the East India Company to leave India and journey to England. Continuing faculty, experts in Persian and other languages and literatures, they taught about their own cultures. They also wrote and translated texts on "oriental" subjects, generating British-style grammars and other teaching aids. Four took European wives or long-time mistresses (generally of lower social status than themselves), several had children there, thus demonstrating how their male gender and professional class standing overcame their difference by "race" in English metropolitan society at the time.

Nevertheless, both Haileybury and Addiscombe placed them under the administrative authority of British faculty who defined and then gradually marginalized their expertise. By the mid-19th century, college policy rejected employing Indians as faculty members in future. Further, their former pupils, once in India, largely reversed the social examples demonstrated in the metropolitan society by their Indian professors: in India these colonial officials and officers "feminized" men of their teachers' social class, and tried to enforce firm racial barriers against Indian men's intercourse with European women.[35]

From the beginning, the staffing of the Oriental languages departments of these two colleges in England proved contested. British scholars, many of whom were veterans of the East India Company's service in India, argued that they had the moral right to be handsomely employed to teach these languages.[36] Yet, even they recognized that only native-language teachers could provide "that idiomatical accuracy (which never can be attained by any foreigner) so essential to such works."[37] In consequence, Haileybury and Addiscombe accepted the superior linguistic accomplishments of Indians.

On their part, these Indian faculty regarded themselves as bestowing a service on their British students by teaching them the Persian language and culture appropriate to administrators in India. They generally enjoyed far superior salaries to what they would have received teaching languages in India, took positions of authority over their British students, and also held the status of scholar, professional, and gentleman in the surrounding English society. Yet, they taught in institutions designed and run by Britons, using British codifications and pedagogy, to British students who were preparing to administer and militarily expand a colonial state ruling large parts of India.

The first Indian to join the faculty at Haileybury College, Sheth Ghulam Hyder (1776–1823), had journeyed independently to London, seeking employment teaching Persian. Hearing of the newly opened college, he applied directly in August 1806 "as Persian Writing Master to the College... on such terms as the Hon'ble Court of Directors may dictate."[38] To demonstrate his abilities, he enclosed with his unsolicited application a sample of his handwriting, using some Persian verses as his text. Although the College deemed his English barely adequate for the position, he was appointed within days at a modest annual salary of £200 (worth £8,522 today).[39] This was equivalent to salaries of British junior faculty at Haileybury. It was also within, but toward the top of, the scale paid to *munshis* working at Fort William College, which ranged from £36 to £240 annually (but far less than the £1,800 to £3,200 paid British Professors of Persian, Hindustani, or Arabic there).[40] Ghulam Hyder served under Captain Charles Stewart, just appointed Professor of Persian Language at £500 annual salary in what was called "the Muhammadan Division" (which also included Hindustani and Arabic), as opposed to the "Hindoo Division" (Sanskrit and Bengali) which remained exclusively in British hands.[41]

In his pedagogy, Ghulam Hyder served much as a *munshi* would in Fort William College (or as a "native drill-master" would at Western university in the 21st century); indeed, Ghulam Hyder was occasionally titled in official documents as "the Munshi." Under his direction, the students at Haileybury copied "Select passages" in Persian and Arabic characters, which had been "engraved upon several copper plates of the same size, so that they may be used separately, or bound up together..."[42] He also drilled and corrected them on their pronunciation. In addition, the East India Company authorities asked Hyder "at such periods as would not interfere with his Duties at the College" to teach "Persian Writing" to the pupils in the preparatory school associated with Haileybury.[43] At the same time that Ghulam Hyder joined the faculty, the East India Company's Directors were seeking to recruit additional Persian language teachers directly from India.

First, the Directors sent an invitation in May 1806 to Abu Talib, proposing that he return to England and take up his plan, as he had advanced it a few years earlier.[44] Unfortunately, Abu Talib died in December 1806, a few days before the message could reach him.[45] Lacking him, the East India Company's Directors entrusted Fort William College to recruit (at the lowest possible salaries acceptable, they insisted) two more teachers; they simultaneously ordered Fort William College to cut drastically back on its own staff and costs in deference to the new college in England.

Even with these cutbacks among the Indian staff at Fort William College, attracting a learned man to leave his family and teach in England for three years or more proved difficult. Abu Talib's autobiography, and therefore his proposed salary and plans for an institute under his control, were known to his peers in India.[46] After much effort, the East India Company finally found two qualified men, Maulvi Mir Abdul Ali and Maulvi Mirza Khalil, willing to accept these appointments, but only by offering exactly the same substantial annual salary that Abu Talib had proposed for himself: £600, plus expenses (including free passage to and from England). This was more than double the highest salary paid a Munshi at Fort William College. Indeed, the salary offered to these two appointees exceeded by £100, or 20 percent, the annual salary of the highest paid British Professors at Haileybury (including Thomas Malthus); this would be a source of tension thereafter.[47] The Directors ordered these high salaries charged to the Government (and hence the taxpayers) of India.[48]

One of these two men, Maulvi Mir Abdul Ali of Varanasi, had already worked for the East India Company's College at Calcutta as a *munshi* in the Persian Department since about 1801. The other, Maulvi Mirza Khalil of Lucknow, was qualified to teach Persian, Urdu, and Arabic.[49] These two men came separately to England in 1807 and 1808 respectively, each attended by a Muslim personal servant.[50]

On their arrival, they received appointments as Assistant Professors, higher in status than "writing master" Ghulam Hyder (as well as over three times his salary). These two Indian faculty taught the rudiments of Persian, Hindustani, and Arabic to sizable numbers of students each year.[51] They, along with the British professors in each department, read out, glossed, and parsed selections in these languages from works of literature, which the students would memorize, as well as occasionally translate easy passages into and out of English. Thus, Abdul Ali and Mirza Khalil were comparable to the highest British faculty at the College, rather than *munshis*, in duties and in salary, if not in rank or administrative responsibilities.

While they socialized with each other, these three men also entered deeply (albeit to different degrees) into the local English society. While they apparently accepted British models for teaching their languages at the College, they also assumed English social roles for themselves as middle-class professionals. Both Abdul Ali and Ghulam Hyder converted (at least nominally) to the Church of England, married English women, and established themselves and their children in local English society. Both were buried in Anglican parish churchyards.[52] Thus, their social position in England and their personal relations there contrast strikingly with those they had had in India.

The other Assistant Professor, Mirza Khalil, in contrast to his two Indian colleagues at Haileybury, apparently remained the most orthodox of these three Muslims. He never married in England. After eleven years of employment at the College, he was forced to resign suddenly in the middle of the term, after what he called an "unfortunate event."[53] The college authorities suppressed the details in the official records, but it seems to have involved a conflict with Charles Stewart, his direct supervisor, and quondam landlord.[54] After negotiations with the East India Company, Mirza Khalil agreed to a pension of £360 annually, plus his expenses for his equipment and passage for a two- or three-year journey via the Islamic holy lands, back to India.[55]

The language training imparted to Haileybury students by these three men, and by their British supervisors, tended to be limited. Until 1814, the students did not even need to take a test in these languages, which militated against their taking their training in them very seriously. Thereafter, the required test administered by an outside British "Visitor" apparently helped draw the students' attention to those languages. This test required students to "write the character in a fair and legible hand, thorough acquaintance with terms of grammar [and] reading, translating, and parsing an easy passage."[56] Yet, while some students individually sought out and learned much from their instructors, the language training in general tended to be relatively impractical and was less emphasized as a subject.[57] Overall, language training at Haileybury, as at Fort William College, differed significantly from the ways these languages were traditionally taught in India. The Indian faculty perforce followed the British model of pedagogy.

In 1809, a few years after the East India Company established Haileybury to train its civil officials, it opened for its army cadets a Military Seminary at Addiscombe.[58] Mir Hasan Ali of Lucknow, a scholar and former administrator for the East India Company and the Nawab of Awadh, had come on his own to England in September 1809 seeking employment as a teacher of Persian, Arabic, Hindustani, and/or Bengali.[59] He applied first for an appointment to Haileybury but, since the three Indian faculty discussed above were already in place, no positions were available there. Then he turned to the newly opened Addiscombe, where, in May 1810, he accepted appointment on the faculty at £400 annually as Assistant to the Professor of Oriental Literature, John Shakespear.[60] His duties were "teaching the Cadets to write, and the proper pronunciation of the Hindostani and Persian Languages," their pronunciation being something Shakespear had little knowledge about.[61] He also taught cadets orthography in Perso-Arabic and Devanagari characters. On occasion he was referred to by the college authorities by his official title, "Assistant to the Professor of Oriental Languages," yet elsewhere, including in the same document, he holds the more "native" title of "the Persian Moonshee," like Ghulam Hyder.[62]

Mir Hasan Ali sought advancement of himself and his students through creating learning aids, using his status as a native speaker to assert the superiority of his pedagogy over that of British teachers. In 1812, Mir Hasan Ali completed his 150-page *Grammar of the Hindoostanie Language,* which he described as:

being the first work of the kind ever attempted by a Native of India, which contains also many useful additions, I have also corrected several material Errors that are to be found in works of a similar kind in English, I humbly beg leave to solicit your patronage towards the publication of this my work, referring (if need be) its merits to be tried by any of the Oriental Scholars at your Civil College, or by Dr. Gilchrist, an eminent Writer on the Subject. The book consists of 3 parts; 1st containing the Hindoustanie as taught in India by the Natives; the 2nd, that Grammar reduced to the English scale, and accompanied as far as possible to the Rules of Grammar received in this Country; and the 3rd containing a selection of Vocables, Dialogues, and Exercises very useful to Hindoustanie Scholars when beginning to read or write the Language.[63]

Even before it was completed, the College Committee recommended that Hasan Ali be granted "an advance of £100 towards enabling him to defray the expense of printing and publishing" this Grammar, "as a mark of the Committee's approbation of his endeavours."[64] They also sent his grammar to British scholars for their assessment of its merits.

In general, language teachers at Addiscombe and Haileybury, including Hasan Ali's supervisor, Shakespear, greatly enhanced their incomes by publishing textbooks and requiring their students to purchase them. Indeed, Shakespear had just published a very similar grammar.[65] Mir Hasan Ali also received a £50 reward for translating the Gospel of St. Matthew into Hindustani.[66] Thus, working under the standards set by the higher-ranking British faculty, Mir Hasan Ali was not rewarded for his original Persian literary or poetic compositions but rather for his teaching aids and service to Christianity.

Following the death of Mir Abdul Ali in 1812, Mir Hasan Ali applied for the vacant position of Assistant Professor of Oriental Literature at Haileybury.[67] To bolster his application, Mir Hasan Ali unsuccessfully argued that these languages, due to their difficulty, require "to be taught by a duly qualified Native."[68] He further cited his years of satisfactory service at Addiscombe. He obtained warm testimonials from the Indian faculty currently at Haileybury, his friends Mirza Khalil and Ghulam Hyder. They both testified not only to his abilities, but to his high birth and accomplishments: "descended from a Noble Family...the Grandson of the Nawaub Birem Khan (peace be unto him)...proficient in the Arabic, Persian, and Hindoostanee

Languages, and in his Style of writing has not his equal in this Kingdom."[69] Should his request for appointment not be approved, Mir Hasan Ali threatened to resign from Addiscombe and return to India "by the first Fleet."[70] Nevertheless, he did not get the desired appointment nor did he resign until four years later.

During his six years at Addiscombe, Mir Hasan Ali established a place for himself in local English society. Although relatively isolated as the only Asian on the Addiscombe faculty, he and the Indian faculty at Haileybury met occasionally, forming something of a support group. We know that he attended Ghulam Hyder's wedding, for example.[71] Mir Hasan Ali finally resigned from Addiscombe in 1816, on the grounds of ill-health (asthma). He received an annual pension from the East India Company of £120 plus a one time gift of £205 for his sea passage, and an order on the Bengal Government for his transportation via Calcutta to his North Indian home in Awadh.[72] Just before his departure, Mir Hasan Ali married by Anglican rites an Englishwoman, Miss Biddy Tims, in March 1817, and they went back to India together.[73]

With the death of two and the resignation of two other of these Indian faculty, exclusive British control over Persian language teaching in these two institutions triumphed for a time. The positions of these Indian faculty either went vacant, or they were replaced by a British teacher. The College authorities had decided that the linguistic advantages of having a "native speaker" teach British students was outweighed by the alleged disruption these Muslim Indian men had on the students' moral education. As Stewart put it in 1816: "such is the prejudice of Young Men against the Tuition of a Native of India, that only the few steady ones derive any benefit from his Lectures."[74] While increases in the number of students at Haileybury led the College administration to make new appointments in Oriental language departments, for the next three years they appointed only Europeans to these posts.

Yet, the British faculty at Haileybury futilely attempted to sustain the Persian language program on their own. When Stewart wished to show his students model letters in idiomatic Persian and accurate and elegant orthography, he published some of the correspondence he had received from Haileybury's former Indian teachers.[75] Such indirect access to the expertise of Indian Persian speakers, however, was not enough. By 1826, the Haileybury administration recognized the "attachment of some learned Asiatics to the College is not only conducive to the credit and respectability of the institution, but also essential to the accomplishment of one of its declared objects, the attainment of a high degree of proficiency in a few of the languages of the East."[76] As evidence, they acknowledged the evident decline "both of pronunciation and classical attainment between the earlier Students at the College, and those of a more recent period." A compromise solution to their dilemma came in the form of Mirza Muhammed Ibrahim, a Persian, therefore a native speaker of that language, but without many of the associations inherent in British minds about Indians.

Initially, Mirza Ibrahim had come to England in 1826 to teach at a proposed Christian religious college. The Reverend Mr. Wolfe had recruited him in Persia and sent him on to England, but Wolfe's colleagues had failed to come through with the establishment of this college, leaving Mirza Ibrahim stranded. While living in London, Mirza Ibrahim impressed Sir Gore Ousely (the former British ambassador to Persia) with his morals, his knowledge of Persian, and his moral suitability for the Haileybury faculty. British scholars who examined him on behalf of Haileybury wrote: "He is a man of excellent character and first respectability, received a College education in Persia, and is an Arabic as well as a Persian and Turkish Scholar."[77]

The College recognized that a Persian like Mirza Ibrahim, however, still presented significant problems. He might know Arabic and the Persian of Persia well, but knew nothing of Hindustani or other Indian languages. Further, as the College appointment committee explained:

the [Iranian] Persian, which he must be supposed to write and to speak with the utmost purity and correctness, is nevertheless by no means either the written or colloquial Persian of men of business or even of education and science in India, and is further unquestionably different, both in idiom and pronunciation, from that at present taught in the College; so that the students, alternately engaged with their English and Persian instructors, might receive lessons from each counteracting the efforts of the other and thus in the end be deprived of any permanent advantage from either... The apparent improvement in Persian pronunciation which might be derived from the labors of a Native Persian in the College, would probably fail to render the English Students more intelligible by the Natives of India on his first arrival in that Country, than he may become under his present [British] Instructors.[78]

Nevertheless, they continued, given the alternative of no native speakers on the faculty, he would be better than nothing and his knowledge of Persian was "unquestionably superior...to the Person formerly employed in the College (a Native of Bengal) [Mirza Khalil]." Since, they admitted, Haileybury's students did not require much Persian training anyway: "all that can be expected during the short term of residence at the College is merely an elementary knowledge."

These College officials went on to say that, to further recommend Mirza Ibrahim personally, he had made good progress in Anglicizing himself. His new supervisors at Haileybury reported, "[He] has adopted the European Costume for the avowed purpose of acquiring knowledge, and rendering himself useful in this Country without attracting public observation which might interfere with those objects [and has]...commenced and made some progress in the study of the English language." Additionally, "he would not object to [eating in] Commons with the English Professors and Teachers, an objection which was always made by the Mussulman Natives of India, and attended probably with inconvenience and additional expense." Finally, he appeared a "young man of agreeable manners, correct demeanor, and studious habits." Thus, the College offered and he accepted an appointment (at £400) as Assistant to the Professor of Arabic and Persian, Professor Reverend H.G. Keene.[79] Mirza Ibrahim proved so successful that he was tenured and promoted early.[80]

As did the British faculty, Mirza Ibrahim wrote books that demonstrated his expertise in Persian and also enhanced his income. He began by assisting the work of other faculty at Haileybury by marking the vowel-points in a collection of Persian fables designed as a teaching aid. Subsequently, he himself wrote a Persian Grammar (later translated into German). He co-translated liturgies, Anglican Common Prayers, and sections of the Bible into Persian.[81] The East India Company's Court of Directors demonstrated their trust in his confidentiality and linguistic expertise by commissioning him to translate diplomatic documents between Persian and English.[82] He also met and socialized with visiting Indian and Persian dignitaries who came to England.[83]

In addition, Mirza Ibrahim established himself in local society. He rented a cottage on Hertford Heath, "Rose Cottage."[84] Here he installed trained singing nightingales (allegedly to remind him of Isfahan). He also took an English mistress, with whom he had a son.[85] In local society, he was remembered as "a perfect Englishman in manners, language, and feeling."[86]

Eventually, after eighteen years on the faculty, his health failed and he retired in 1844; he received a gift of £700 plus a pension of £350 per annum.[87] He married a European woman (reportedly Dutch) and returned to Persia with her. There, living under the diplomatic protection of the British consul, he educated Persians in British customs and manners until his death in 1857.[88]

He was remembered fondly in Hertford for his Anglicized manners, his religious faith and yet openness to Christianity:

> Few foreigners ever mastered the idiom and accent of the English language so completely as Mirza Ibrahim. If his foreign origin could be detected at all, it was by his physiognomy, not by his speech. He had accurately studied many of our standard authors, and few English scholars could discourse more critically or more luminously than himself on the beauties or difficulties of Shakespeare. Although, as a very young man, he left his own country in consequence of some suspicion the Mollahs entertained of his orthodoxy, yet he never abandoned his creed, but, during his sojourn in England, uniformly professed that Mohammad was his prophet. Nevertheless, we have heard one of the most distinguished Oriental linguists of the day assert that the translation of Isaiah into Persian, made by the Mirza for one of the religious societies, was the most faithful and spirited version of any portion of Scripture to be found in a modern language.[89]

None of his Indian faculty predecessors proved able to combine these qualities as attractively to English society as he had.[90] After Mirza Ibrahim's retirement, no further Asians were appointed to Haileybury. Indeed, there were complaints that "too much time and attention are devoted to oriental study" by the students.[91]

Even after the termination of Indian and Persian faculty at Haileybury and Addiscombe, various other types of Persian teaching continued in Britain. British professors taught this language at these two colleges until they closed in the 1850s. Other colleges and universities in Britain also offered Persian occasionally, sometimes from Indian instructors, although the demand was not heavy. Most notable among these institutions was University College, London, which had been established in 1826 as a more inclusive alternative to Oxford and Cambridge. University College had a Chair in Arabic and Persian (filled by Britons) from 1834.[92] It also had eight Asian faculty teaching Asian languages there during the late 19th century.[93] Further, across Britain, there was some informal Persian teaching, as Asians and British men offered tuitions on a private basis.[94] Overall, however, British cultural assertions remained central to British imperialism and to the teaching of Persian in Britain and India until the end of the British Empire.

PERSIAN TEACHING IN INDIA AND IN BRITAIN

This chapter has explored the role of Persian as an imperial language, both before and during early British colonialism, both in India and in Britain. In particular, it considered the perspectives and purposes of those Indians and Persians who established themselves as expert professional faculty in the East India Company's colleges in India and England in order to educate future British colonial rulers directly about Persianate culture. In the complex process of the creation of British colonial knowledge about India and its cultures and languages, Europeans gradually established during the 19th century a cultural dominance, but not a hegemonic monopoly. Even at the height of British imperial expansion across India, British officials recognized the superior abilities of Indian and Persian "native speakers" in aspects of Persian language training. Yet, these British authorities increasingly discounted the importance of those abilities and rather asserted the superiority of British moral training over linguistic competence.

Overlapping interest in and knowledge of Persian culture brought early visiting Indians and native British scholars together in England, with implications for their relative status. Even among the leading British authorities, few composed original works in Persian, largely confining themselves instead to translation from Persian into English, or to compiling dictionaries and grammars as teaching aids for Anglophone students. Yet they did seek to codify Persian into European epistemologies and pedagogies. In contrast, throughout this period, Indians in India and Britain composed new books in Persian, often using their own cultural forms of organizing knowledge. Visiting Indians perforce recognized their own culture's less advanced status in the physical sciences and technology, including the military sciences and publishing. In traditional Persian learning and literature, however, visiting Indians felt more empowered. Therefore the cultural stakes were more contested for them in these areas. Even, however, when Indians wrote Persian texts within traditional norms, British scholars often assumed the editorial reshaping and publication of this knowledge. In the end, British colonial authorities and scholars thus transformed this traditional information into colonial forms of knowledge that advanced European imperialism.

Mohamad Tavakoli-Targhi sees early Persian-language travel writers in Europe as part of the "heterotopic experiences of crisscrossing peoples and cultures [which] provided multiple scenarios of modernity and self-refashioning."[95] Only with the shifts of military, political, and economic power inherent in colonialism could Europeans suppress memory of their formative exchanges with Indian and Persian scholars. He calls this as an act of "genesis amnesia" since it denied the role of non-Europeans in the development of European study of the East. Thus, problematizing the conventional Western narrative of modernity as solely the product of the European Enlightenment, Tavakoli-Targhi also demonstrates the complex ways that these explorers and their narratives contested with "counter-modernities" within their homeland. The result has been making "homeless" these early Indian and Persian scholars and their works, suppressed in British historical narratives about Persian language study and teaching and also in those of their Asian homelands as well.

Yet, British society proved by no means uniformly exclusive of these Indians and Persians who chose to settle within it. Despite the growing British stress on biological race as determining social identity in the metropole, as it had been established earlier in the colonies, the gender and class status enjoyed in British society by these Indian and Persian men elevated them over their British wives or mistresses. Their positions within these educational institutions placed them above their British pupils, not as hired servants like *munshis* in India, but as faculty with titular and pedagogic authority over them.

Nonetheless, in Britain, as in India, the advocates of Anglicist policy largely won out by the 1830s–40s. This conflict was marked by the official degradation of Indians as teachers of their own languages and the consolidation of that education in British hands. Each of the Indian faculty at the East India Company's colleges struggled, often unsuccessfully, to sustain their professional and social status in Britain. Their topics of instruction were never central to the educational mission of these institutions. Two of these Indian faculty died deeply in debt, apparently having exceeded their often generous salaries, in an effort to sustain their social standing in Britain. The other two resigned prematurely after career frustrations and/or setbacks. Later Indian applicants for their positions met only with rejection based on their Indian identity and on British assertions of monopoly over positions in the East India Company's colleges.

Yet, the private market for "oriental" language teaching, from which some Indians could find employment, persisted in Britain. For a number of Indians and Persians in Britain, establishing for themselves an institutionalized position of authority as teachers of their languages and cultures appeared an attractive and lucrative vocation. While the East India Company's colleges and Britain's oldest academic universities eschewed appointing Asians, some other British educational institutions came to appreciate the abilities of native speakers, and the need for their skills. This meant employment for Indian instructors of their languages, even in the metropole. Thus, we see the complex and changing historical process of making Persian a part of colonial knowledge about India, as it took place in Britain, as well as in the colonies.

In South Asia, language has remained a highly political subject. Especially from the late 19th century onward, Persian and Urdu became identified as "Muslim" languages. Hindu nationalists, particularly those in North India, stressed the development of an ever more Sanskritized Hindi in Devanagari, not Perso-Arabic, script.[96] For people in non-Hindi speaking regions, this Hindi appeared as the new imperialist language imposed by North Indians on them. Pakistani nationalists argued for Urdu as their national language, using Persian vocabulary and Perso-Arabic script. Much of the regional resistance that created Bangladesh in 1971 grew out of a Bengali language movement that opposed West Pakistani imposition of this Urdu on East Pakistan, now Bangladesh. In all this, Persian primarily evoked the ancient imperial regime of the Mughals, something that the "modern" British Empire and later the new nations of South Asia would seek to leave behind.

NOTES

1. I thank the American Council of Learned Societies, the American Institute of Indian Studies, and Oberlin College for their generous financial support for the research for this chapter.
2. Edward Said has labeled the larger process of such European appropriations of Asian cultures as "Orientalism."
3. Government of India Act 29 of 1837. See also Gauri Viswanathan, *Masks of Conquest*.
4. See Kumkum Chatterjee, "History as Self-Representation," 912–48; Juan R.I. Cole,

"Invisible Occidentalism," 3–16; Gulfishan Khān, *Indian Muslim Perceptions.*

5. See Muhammad `Abdu'l Ghani, *Pre-Mughal Persian;* Muzaffar Alam, *Languages;* Alam, "Pursuit of Persian"; and Mohammad Ishāq Khān, "Persian Influences," 1–9; Alam, Delvoye, and Gaborieau, *Indo-Persian Culture.*

6. For Persian historiography, see Rao, Shulman, and Subrahmanyam, *Textures of Time,* especially pp. 181–226, and Alam, "Politics of Persian," 131–98; Francis Richard, "Deccani Persian Manuscripts," 239–49; Som Prakash Verma, *Mughal Painters;* Milo Beach, *Mughal and Rajput Painting.*

7. Mohammad Habib, *Hazrat Amir Khusrau of Delhi.* For praise of other Indian poets of Persian, including Abu'l Faraj Runi (d. 1091), Ziā-ud Nakhshabi, Mas`ud Sa`d Salmān (d. 1131), and Hasan Sijzi, see Alam, "Pursuit of Persian," 318, and Alam, Delvoye, and Gaborieau, *Indo-Persian Culture.*

8. Alam, "Pursuit," 317–49. See also Ghani, *History of Persian Language,* and N.S. Gorekar, "India as a Second Home," 223–36.

9. Anil Kumar, "Persian Immigration"; J.F. Richards, *Mughal Empire;* M. Athar Ali, *Apparatus of Empire;* Satish Chandra, *Parties and Politics;* Momin Mohiuddin, *Chancellery and Persian Epistolography;* Douglas E. Streusand, *Mughal Empire;* Richard C. Foltz, *Mughal India;* Sanjay Subrahmanyam, "Iranians Abroad."

10. N.S Gorekar, "Persian Impact."

11. See Symposium: Decline of the Mughal Empire, special issue of *Journal of Asian Studies* 35, 2 (February 1976), and Pollock and Alam, "Forms of Knowledge.

12. Sharif Husain Qādemi, "Persian Chronicles in the Nineteenth Century," in Alam, Delvoye, and Gaborieau, *Indo-Persian Culture,* 407–16.

13. Bernard S. Cohn, *Colonialism,* 18.

14. William Dalrymple, *White Mughals,* and *Last Mughal.*

15. Sisir Kumar Das, *Sahibs and Munshis,* 108. See also David Kopf, *British Orientalism,* and Cohn, *Colonialism,* 49ff.

16. Lynn Zastoupil and Martin Moir, *Great Indian Education Debate.*

17. Cited in Alam, "Politics of Persian," 189.

18. For contrasting views, see Viswanathan, *Masks,* Shamsur Rahman Faruqi, "Unprivileged Power," and S.A.H. Abidi, "Relevance of Persian."

19. P.J. Marshall, "Oriental Studies."

20. Her first husband, William Hawkins, died on the passage to England; she married her second husband, Gabriel Towerson, in London. See Michael H. Fisher, *Counterflows,* Chapter 1.

21. The merchant died in London, while the rest returned to Surat, India, in 1627 but the Ambassador and Mahomet died there. Many other Persian diplomatic and commercial missions followed. See W. Noel Sainsbury, *Calendar of State Papers,* and *Calendar of Court Minutes,* 225–34; William Foster, *English Factories,* xxiii; see also 87, 183.

22. See Fisher, *Counterflows,* Chapter 1.

23. E.g., *Public Advertiser* (5 November 1777); *European Magazine* 39 (January-June 1801): 7–8; *Home Political Consultation* no. 50 (15 May 1797); *Home Miscellaneous,* vol. 559, ff. 297–301, 405, National Archives of India.

24. Sheila Lambert, ed., *House of Commons, Sessional Papers,* 147 vols. (1975), vol. 135, pp. 546–49; vol. 138, p. 124; Elijah B. Impey, *Memoirs,* 237.

25. Mīrzā Abu Tālib Khān, *Masir Tālibi fi Bilād Afranji,* Persian reprint of British Library [hereinafter BL] Add 8145–47 [my pagination hereinafter is from the Persian reprint

edited and published by Hosein Khadive-Jam, Tehran, 1983], pp. 107–8, 175.

26. Minutes of the Court of Directors, 10 February 1801, f. 1015, BL; Abu Talib to Pelham, Persian letter with translation, 28 August 1803, Add 33112 Pelham Papers, ff. 138–39, BL; John J. McCusker, "Purchasing Power."

27. Morning Chronicle (29 March 1800): 4a; *European Magazine and London Review*, 43 (January-June 1803): 3.

28. Abu Tāleb Khān, *Travels of Mirzā Abu Tāleb Khān*, 173–74.

29. Khān, *Travels*, 101; see also 92.

30. Mir Muhammad Husain, *Risālah-i Ahwāl-i Mulk-i Farang*, MS. R.IV-51, K.R. Cama Oriental Research Library, Bombay and Maulana Azad Library, Aligarh; Munshi Isma'il, Tārikh-i Jadid, in Simon Digby's private collection, discussed by him in "An Eighteenth Century Narrative of a Journey from Bengal to England: Munshi Ismail's New History" in Christopher Shackle, *Urdu and Muslim South Asia*, 49–65; Mirzā I'tisām al-din, *Shigarf Nāma-i Walāyat*, translated into English and Urdu and published by James Edward Alexander and Munshi Shamsher Khān, London, 1827. See also Mohamad Tavokoli-Targhi, *Refashioning Iran: Orientalism, Occidentalism and Historiography* (New York: Palgrave, 2001) and Michael Fisher, "Representing 'His' Women."

31. Abu Talib, *Masir*, 116.

32. Report Plan for the College 26 October 1804, J/2/1 Minutes and Reports of Committee of College 1805–15, BL.

33. The choice of languages was not well suited to the career needs of its students. The Directors intended "the elements of one or two Eastern Languages of general use," but chose more classical languages mainly used in high literature (in the case of Sanskrit) or that and official records (in the case of Persian) or in popular use only in certain parts of the subcontinent (like Hindustani), rather than regional vernaculars like Tamil or Telugu. Report Plan for the College 26 October 1804, J/2/1 Minutes and Reports of Committee of College, BL.

34. Yet, in 1812, the East India Company opened Fort St. George College, in Madras, for training Britons in south Indian languages and also in law.

35. Mrinalini Sinha, *Colonial Masculinity.*

36. Jonathan Scott, *Observations on the Oriental Department.*

37. Scott, ibid., 10.

38. Munshi Ghulam Hyder, letter of 15 August 1806, Haileybury Records, J/1/21, ff. 456–57, BL.

39. McCusker, "Purchasing Power."

40. Bengal Public Consultation 4 September 1808 No. 29; Letter from Bengal 8 February 1808 para 71, 79. Das, *Sahibs*, p. 12 citing Gilchrist letter 15 June 1803.

41. See Thomas Trautmann, *Aryans and British India.*

42. Order, 1 October 1806 in J/2/1 Minutes and Reports of Committee of College 1805–15, BL.

43. This school, established in 1805, was run largely autonomously by its Head Master, Rev. H. M. Luscombe, but was designed to feed students into the College. Minute 9 March 1808, J/2/1 Minutes and Reports of Committee of College 1805–15, BL.

44. Public letter to Bengal 31 May 1806 in Boards Collections F/4/212/4732, para 15, BL.

45. Political Consultations 1 January 1807 no. 99, National Archives of India. See also Extract of Political Letter from Bengal 26 February 1807 in Boards Collections F/4/212/4732, BL.

46. In addition to Abu Talib circulating his manuscript among his peers, the *Calcutta Gazette* serialized a selective translation in its Supplement (September 1807–February 1808). Later, the East India Company commissioned his son to edit and publish the Persian text at Fort William College: Mirza Husain Ali and Mir Qudrat Ali, *Masir-i Talibi*. See Extract Public Letter from Bengal 9 May 1812, F/4/384/9741, BL.

47. Memorandum on the present state of the Oriental Department at the College, Extract Public Letter to Bengal 7 September 1808, J/1/35, f. 267, BL.

48. Court of Directors orders of 23 February 1810 para 10, BL.

49. Public Letter from Bengal 8 February 1808 para 71 in F/4/259/5665, BL.

50. L/MAR/B/117 H; L/MAR/B/296 D. F/4/259/5665, BL; Extract Letters from Bengal 14[24]/7/1807, 25 September 1807, BL; Letter to Bengal 21/5/1806 para 13ff. J/1/35, BL.

51. In a typical year, the Persian class had 71 students, Hindustani 55, Arabic 10, for a total 136; Sanskrit had 16, Bengali 34 for a total of 50. Stewart to College Committee 13 March 1817 J/1/32 1817, ff. 233–35, BL.

52. For the details of their lives, see Fisher, *Counterflows*, Chapter 3.

53. Mirza Khalil to Court from London 20 October 1819, J/1/35 ff. 271–72, BL.

54. Letter of Charles Stewart to College Committee 31 July 1823, J/1/38 ff. 571–72, BL.

55. Mirza Khalil to Court from London 20 October 1819, J/1/35 ff. 271–72, BL; Letter from Mirza Khalil 17 April 1820, J/1/35 ff. 304–5, BL; College Committee Consultation 19 April 1820, BL; Court Consultation 14 June 1820, J/1/35, ff. 304–5, BL; Letter from Mirza Khalil 17 April 1820, College Committee Consultation 19 April 1820, BL; Court Consultation 14 June 1820, BL; Petition of Mirza Khuleel 3 May 1826, Minutes of Court 4 April 1826, B/179, BL.

56. Committee of College 15 February 1814 J/2/2 fol. 127, BL.

57. Resistance to Hindustani continued, see Parliamentary Papers (Lords) 1852–53 (41) XXX, 5738.

58. The East India Company only allowed Britons to attend as students, despite a request from an Indian aristocrat to do so. Secretary to Meersa Jaafar 29 May 1817 Misc. Letters from Court 1817 E/1/253 No. 662, BL.

59. Minutes of the Court 13 September 1809, B/149, BL; Log of Dorsetshire L/MAR/B/13, BL.

60. Scott, *Observations*, ii, 7. Memorial of Meer Hasan Ali J/1/27 ff. 218–19, BL; College Committee Consultation 6 November 1812, 21 October 1813, BL.

61. Lutfullah wrote that on 30 May 1844 he met "John Shakespear, the author of the Hindustani Dictionary... I addressed to him a very complimentary long sentence in my own language. But, alas! I found that he could not understand me, nor could he utter a word in that language in which he had composed several very useful books." Lutfullah, *Autobiography of Lutfullah*, ed. S.A.I. Tirmizi (New Delhi: International Writers' Emporium, 1985, reprint of 1857), 412.

62. Committee of the College, Minutes 24 September 1813 no. 146, BL.

63. Stewart and Hamilton Letter November 1813, College Committee References J/1/27, ff. 374–76, BL.

64. College Committee Minutes 26/11/1813, BL.

65. John Shakespear, *Grammar of the Hindustani Language*.

66. Letter of Charles Stewart and A. Hamilton November 1813, J/1/27 ff. 374–76, BL; Committee of the College, Minutes, 26 November 1813, BL; Meer Hasun Ali, trans.,

The Gospel of St. Matthew [crossed out] and Morning Prayer translated into Hindoostanee I.O.ISL 3063, BL; Colonel H.M. Vibart, *Addiscombe: Its Heroes and Men of Note,* 42.

67. Letter of Foster Maynard to Sir Hugh Ingles 23 October 1812, J/1/27 ff. 220–29; J/1/25 ff. 447–48, BL.

68. Petition of Meer Hasun Ali College Committee 14 January 1814, J/1/27, ff. 186–88, BL.

69. Petition of Mirza Khaleel 17 October 1812, J/1/27 ff. 214–15; Memorial of Moonshe Gholam Hyder, J/1/27 ff. 216–17, BL.

70. Petition from Mir Hasan Ali to College Council 27 November 1812, College Council 2 December 1812, J/1/27 241–42, BL.

71. See their wedding license, Guildhall Library.

72. Committee of the College, Minutes, J/1/35 ff. 273–76, BL.

73. He and his British wife lived in North India for a dozen years, employed by the East India Company. Following his English wife's separation from him and return to England, she published an epistolary account of her life as a Christian wife in a leading Muslim family, *Observations on the Mussulmauns of India,* 2 vols. (London: Parbury, Allen, and Co., 1832). Mir Hasan Ali subsequently married women of his own class and had descendants who continued to work for the East India Company. Bishop of London, Marriage Allegations 22 March 1817, Diocese of London, Marriage Bond 22 March 1817, Westminster Archives; St. James Parish, Westminster (Piccadilly) 27 March 1817 Guildhall Library.

74. Stewart to J. Taylor 7 April 1816, J/1/31 1816, f. 213, BL; Memorandum of N. B. Edmonstone and J. Baillie to College Committee, 19 July 1836, J/2/5, ff. 279–85, BL; Wilkins, "Report on the Oriental Department," J/1/19 ff. 464–65, BL.

75. Charles Stewart, *Original Persian Letters, and Other Documents, with Facsimiles.*

76. Memorandum of N.B. Edmonstone and J. Baillie to College Committee 19 July 1826, J/2/5, ff. 279–85, BL.

77. Gore Ousely to Committee 26 May 1826, J/2/5, f. 254, BL.

78. Memorandum of N.B. Edmonstone and J. Baillie to College Committee, 19 July 1836, J /2/5 ff. 279–85, BL.

79. Memorandum of N.B. Edmonstone and J. Baillie to College Committee 31 July 1826, Minutes and Reports of Committee of College 1826, J/2/5: fols. 286–89, 308–9, BL.

80. Minutes of Court 2 August 1826 B/179 and 1 August 1827, B/180, BL.

81. James Michael, *Persian Fables;* Meerza Mohammad Ibraheem, *Grammar of the Persian Language;* H.L. Fleischer, *Gramatik der lebenden Persische;* Ishaia al Nabi (Bible), trans. into Persian by Mirza Ibrahim, ed. Francis Johnson (1834); Liturgiae Ecclesiae Anglicanae Partes Praecipuae: et Preces Matutinae et Vespertinae, Ordo Administrandi Coenam Domini et Ordo Baptismi Publici: In Lunguam Persicam Traductae, Opera Samuel Lee and Mirza Ibrahim Persae (1828); Minutes of Court, 14 October 1840, BL.

82. Minutes of Court, 14 November 1838, 21 November 1838, BL.

83. Dyce Sombre against Troup, Solaroli (Intervening) and Prinsep and the Hon. East India Company (also Intervening) in the Goods of David Octerlony Dyce Sombre, Esq., Deceased, In the Perogative Court of Canterbury (London: Henry Hansard, n.d.), 867; James Baillie Fraser, *Residence of the Persian Princes,* 1:93ff, 109, 303–4.

84. Pigot's Directory Hertfordshire for 1839, 1840.

85. Frederick Charles Danvers, et al., *Memorials of Old Haileybury College,* 186–88.

86. *Hertford Mercury* (7 November 1857).

87. His health may have been damaged by a nearly fatal accident when a railroad train startled his horse. *Chronicle* (8 March 1844), 27–28.
88. Court Minutes 5, 12 July 1843, 13 September 1843, 7 August 1844, BL; Finance and Home Papers, Z/L/F/2/13, BL; Danvers, *Memorials,* 186–88.
89. *Hertford Mercury* (7 November 1857).
90. Danvers, *Memorials,* 73–74.
91. Memorandum on Haileybury Studies: Oriental Department c. 1844, MSS EUR F 303/445, BL.
92. This Chair was held by Forbes Falconer (1805–1853) from 1834 to 1846 when he resigned. Falconer was a scholar rather than colonial veteran. He had studied Persian at Marischal College, Aberdeen, and then in Paris and Germany, but never traveled to either Iran or India. After a decade-long hiatus, this Chair was filled by William Wright (1830–1899), a specialist in Arabic, from 1855 to 1856, and then by Charles Rieu (1820–1902) from 1856 to 1895. H. Hale Bellot, University College London, 1826–1926 (1929), p. 264 and Chart 2.
93. Bellot, University College, Chart 2.
94. Testimonials of J.A. Emerson, Hanwell College, 5 May 1853, and W. Keiser, 4 May 1853, L/P&J1/64 References Revenue, Judicial and Legislative Committee 1853, L/P&J1/64, f. 235a, BL; Rozina Visram, *Ayahs, Lascars and Princes,* 63; Rakhal Das Halder, *English Diary,* 32, 23; Syed Ameer Ali, *Memoirs and Writings of Syed Ameer Ali,* 24; Joseph Salter, *East in the West,* 118–19.
95. Mohamad Tavakoli-Targhi, "Modernity, Heterotopia, and Homeless Texts," 3. See also his *Refashioning Iran* (see note 30, above). He thus contradicts Cole, who argues that these same Indo-Persian authors criticized the West but largely modeled their depictions on Western categories. Juan R.I. Cole, "Invisible Occidentalism: Eighteenth-Century Indo-Persian Constructions of the West."
96. Vasudha Dalmia, *Hindu Traditions.*

REFERENCES

`Abdu'l Ghani, Muhammad. 1929–30. *A History of Persian Language and Literature at the Mughal Court, with a Brief Survey of the Growth of Urdu Language (Babur to Akbar).* Allāhābād: Indian Press.

——— 1941. *Pre-Mughal Persian in Hindustan: A Critical Survey of the Growth of Persian Language and Literature in India from the Earliest Times to the Advent of the Mughal Rule.* Allāhābād: Allāhābād Law Journal Press.

Abidi, S.A.H. 1994. Relevance of Persian in Modern India. *Indo-Iranica* 47(1-4): 31–39.

Alam, Muzaffar. 1998. The Pursuit of Persian: Language in Mughal Politics. *Modern Asian Studies* 32(2): 317–49.

——— 2003. The Culture and Politics of Persian in Precolonial Hindustan. In *Literary Cultures in History: Reconstructions from South Asia,* ed. Sheldon Pollock, pp. 131–98. Berkeley: University of California Press.

——— 2004. *The Languages of Political Islam in India, c. 1200–1800.* Delhi: Permanent Black.

Alam, Muzaffar, Françoise Nalini Delvoye, and Marc Gaborieau, eds. 2000. *The Making of Indo-Persian Culture.* New Delhi: Manohar.

Ameer Ali, Syed. 1968. *Memoirs and Writings of Syed Ameer Ali.* Lahore: People's Publishing House.

Athar Ali, M. 1985. *The Apparatus of Empire: Awards of Ranks, Offices, and Titles to the Mughal Nobility, 1574–1658.* New Delhi: Oxford University Press.

Mirza Husain Ali and Mir Qudrat Ali, eds. 1812. *Masir-i Talibi.* Calcutta: Fort William College.

Beach, Milo. 1991. *Mughal and Rajput Painting.* Cambridge: Cambridge University Press.

Chandra, Satish. 2002. *Parties and Politics in the Mughal Court, 1707–1740.* New Delhi: Oxford University Press.

Chatterjee, Kumkum. 1998. History as Self-Representation: The Recasting of a Political Tradition in Late Eighteenth-Century Eastern India. *Modern Asian Studies* 32(4): 912–48.

Cohn, Bernard S. 1996. *Colonialism and Its Forms of Knowledge.* Princeton: Princeton University Press.

Cole, Juan R.I. 1992. Invisible Occidentalism: Eighteenth-Century Indo-Persian Constructions of the West. *Iranian Studies* 25(3-4): 3–16.

Dalmia, Vasudha. 1997. *The Nationalization of Hindu Traditions: Bharatendu Harischandra and Nineteenth-Century Banaras.* Delhi: Oxford University Press.

Dalrymple, William. 2002. *White Mughals: Love and Betrayal in Eighteenth-Century India.* London: Harper Collins.

—— 2007. *The Last Mughal: The Eclipse of a Civilisation, 1857.* Delhi: Random House. [Also published as *The Last Mughal. The Fall of a Dynasty: Delhi, 1857.*]

Danvers, Frederick Charles, M. Monier-Williams, Steuart Colvin Bayley, Percy Wigram, Brand Sapte, et al. 1894. *Memorials of Old Haileybury College.* Westminster: A. Constable and Company.

Das, Sisir Kumar. 1978. *Sahibs and Munshis.* Calcutta: Orion.

Digby, Simon. 1989. An Eighteenth Century Narrative of a Journey from Bengal to England: Munshi Ismail's New History. In *Urdu and Muslim South Asia: Studies in Honour of Ralph Russell,* ed. Christopher Shackle, pp. 49–65. London: SOAS.

Faruqi, Shamsur Rahman. 1998. Unprivileged Power: The Strange Case of Persian (and Urdu) in Nineteenth Century India. *Annual of Urdu Studies* 13:3–30.

Fisher, Michael H. 2000. Representing "His" Women: Mirzā Abu Tālib Khān's 1801 "Vindication of the Liberties of Asiatic Women." *Indian Economic and Social History Review* 37(2): 215–37.

—— 2004. *Counterflows to Colonialism.* Delhi: Permanent Black.

Fleischer, H.L., trans. 1875 [1847]. *Gramatik der lebenden Persische Sprache nach Mirza Mohammed Ibrahim's Grammar of the Persian Language.* Reprint. Leipzig: F.A. Brockhaus.

Foltz, Richard C. 1998. *Mughal India and Central Asia*. New York: Oxford University Press.

Foster, William. 1908. *The English Factories in India 1622–1623. A Calendar of Documents in the India Office, British Museum and Public Record Office*. Oxford: Clarendon Press.

Fraser, James Baillie. 1838. *Narrative of the Residence of the Persian Princes in London, in 1835 and 1836*. 2 vols. London: Richard Bentley.

Gorekar, N.S. 1990. India as a Second Home of Persian Studies during the Medieval Period. *Islam and the Modern Age* 21(4): 223–36.

—— 1995. Persian Impact on Indian Life. *Journal of the Asiatic Society of Bombay* 70:59–70.

Habib, Mohammad. 1927. *Hazrat Amir Khusrau of Delhi*. Bombay: Taraporevala Sons.

Halder, Rakhal Das. 1903. *English Diary of an Indian Student*. Dacca: Asutosh Library.

Ibraheem, Meerza Mohammad. 1841. *A Grammar of the Persian Language*. London: W.H. Allen.

Impey, Elijah B. 1846. *Memoirs of Sir Elijah Impey*. London: Simpkin, Marshall.

Khan, Abu Taleb. 1814. *Travels of Mirza Abu Taleb Khan in Asia, Africa, and Europe during the Years 1799, 1800, 1801, 1802, and 1803*, trans. Charles Stewart. 3 vols. 2nd ed. London: Longman, Hurst, Rees, Orme, and Brown.

Khan, Gulfishan. 1998. *Indian Muslim Perceptions of the West during the Eighteenth Century*. Karachi: Oxford University Press.

Khan, Mohammad Ishaq. 1977. Persian Influences in Kashmir in the Sultanate Period 1320–1586. *Islamic Culture* 51(1): 1–9.

Kopf, David. 1969. *British Orientalism and the Bengal Renaissance*. Berkeley: University of California Press.

Kumar, Anil. 1984. Persian Immigration to India during the Mughal Period. *Prabuddha Bharata* 4:191–98.

Marshall, P.J. 1986. Oriental Studies. In *The History of the University of Oxford*, vol. 8, ed. L.S. Sutherland and L.G. Mitchell, pp. 551–63. Oxford: Clarendon.

McCusker, John J. 2001. Comparing the Purchasing Power of Money in Great Britain from 1264 to Any Other Year Including the Present. Economic History Services, URL: http://www.eh.net/hmit/ppowerbp/.

Michael, James. 1827. *Persian Fables from the Anwari Sooheyly of Hussein Vaiz Kashify, with a Vocabulary*. London: the author.

Mohiuddin, Momin. 1971. *The Chancellery and Persian Epistolography under the Mughals, from Babur to Shāh Jahan, 1526–1658*. Calcutta: Iran Society.

Pollock, Sheldon, and Muzaffar Alam, eds. 2004. Forms of Knowledge in Early-Modern South Asia. Special issue of *Comparative Studies of South Asia, Africa, and the Middle East* 24(2).

Rao, Velcheru Narayana, David Shulman, and Sanjay Subrahmanyam. 2001. *Textures of Time*. Delhi: Permanent Black.

Richard, Francis. 2000. Sixteenth-Century Deccani Persian Manuscripts. In *The Making of Indo-Persian Culture: Indian and French Studies,* ed. Muzaffar Alam, Françoise Nalini Delvoye, and M. Gaborieau, pp. 239–49. New Delhi: Manohar.

Richards, John F. 1993. *The Mughal Empire. The New Cambridge History of India,* Part 1, Vol. 5. Cambridge: Cambridge University Press.

Sainsbury, Noel. 1884. *Calendar of State Papers, Colonial Series, East Indies, China, and Persia, 1625–29.* London: Her Majesty's Stationery Office.

—— 1907. *Calendar of the Court Minutes of the East India Company 1635–1640.* Oxford: Clarendon Press.

Salter, Joseph. 1896. *East in the West.* London: S.W. Partridge.

Scott, Jonathan. 1806. *Observations on the Oriental Department of the Hon. Company's East India College, at Hertford.* Hertford: the author.

Shakespear, John. 1813. *Grammar of the Hindustani Language.* London: Cox and Baylis.

Sinha, Mrinalini. 1995. *Colonial Masculinity: The "Manly Englishman" and the "Effeminate Bengali" in the Late Nineteenth Century.* Manchester: Manchester University Press.

Stewart, Charles. 1825. *Original Persian Letters, and Other Documents, with Facsimiles.* London: the author.

Streusand, Douglas E. 1989. *The Formation of the Mughal Empire.* New York: Oxford University Press.

Subrahmanyam, Sanjay. 1992. Iranians Abroad: Intra-Asian Elite Migration and Early Modern State Formation. *Journal of Asian Studies* 51(2): 340–63.

Tavakoli-Targhi, Mohamad. 1998. Modernity, Heterotopia, and Homeless Texts. *Comparative Studies of South Asia, Africa, and the Middle East* 18(2): 2–13.

Trautmann, Thomas. 1997. *Aryans and British India.* Berkeley: University of California Press.

Verma, Som Prakash. 1994. *Mughal Painters and Their Work: A Biographical Survey.* New Delhi: Oxford University Press.

Vibart, Colonel Henry Meredith. 1894. *Addiscombe: Its Heroes and Men of Note.* Westminster: Archibald Constable.

Visram, Rozina. 1984. *Ayahs, Lascars and Princes: Indians in Britain, 1700–1947.* London: Pluto.

Viswanathan, Gauri. 1989. *Masks of Conquest.* New York: Columbia University Press.

Zastoupil, Lynn, and Martin Moir, eds. 1999. *The Great Indian Education Debate: Documents Relating to the Orientalist-Anglicist Controversy, 1781–1843.* London: Curzon.

Part Four: The Larger Context

11

The Latinate Tradition as a Point of Reference

JOSEPH FARRELL

INTRODUCTION

The history of Persian as an imperial language, as a vehicle of cultural continuities, and as a focus of communal identity, whether of an ethnic, religious, aesthetic, or intellectual nature, is one of the great sagas of civilization. As such, it demands comparison with similar stories if we are to understand the processes at work, both in their general similarities and in their specific differences. In this essay I will consider the cultural empire of Latin in comparison to that of Persian in an effort to determine to what extent these two remarkable traditions are able to illuminate one another and to state as clearly as possible those aspects that resist explanation.

GENERAL COMPARISON

Let me begin by stating the obvious points of similarity and difference between these objects of inquiry. Both the Romans and the Achaemenians of Persia controlled important empires during antiquity. Both of these empires were later "revived" as the Carolingian and Sasanian Empires. The former quickly broke apart through dynastic squabbling; the latter lasted longer, but was then absorbed by the more powerful imperial force of Islam. In both cases, however, even in the absence of a single political center, Latin and Persian continued to exert enormous influence over the cultural life of Europe and the Islamic Caliphate during the late medieval and early modern periods. To this extent, the histories of Latin and Persian as imperial languages have been remarkably parallel.

There are, of course, limits to this parallelism as well as some very pointed differences. In particular, the specific trajectories followed by the two languages differ considerably; for, if we divide the histories of Latin and Persian each into two broadly-defined periods, "antiquity" and "afterwards," we find that these histories move almost in opposite directions.

History of Latinity

Early Period (Antiquity), ca. 750 BC–AD 426

Throughout antiquity, Latin is the language of a very powerful and long-lived political empire. The Roman state experienced an extended and virtually uninterrupted period of expansion and consolidation of power that began perhaps with the foundation of the city in the mid-8th century BC, or at any rate with the foundation of the Roman Republic in about 500 BC. By the late 3rd or certainly the mid-2nd century BC, this republic had developed into a de facto empire, although official reorganization of the state on the basis of this reality did not occur until more than another century had passed. The territory encompassed by this empire remained relatively stable until the end of the Severan dynasty in AD 235. Its fortunes waxed and mainly waned for another couple of centuries until the last Western emperor, Romulus Augustulus, was executed in 476, after which time the Western empire ceased to exist. The eastern empire of course survived as the Byzantine state, but for many reasons it makes sense to consider this a distinct entity.

Latin was the native language of the Romans, and it became the administrative language of the Roman Empire. In the course of Rome's expansion to imperial proportions, the language, too, took on an imperial character. That is to say, it came to be more widely used not only in administration but for many purposes, from the most humble, quotidian exchanges to the most elevated forms of literary expression. In Italy and in most of the western provinces as well as in Dacia (Romania) in the east, it permanently replaced all the indigenous languages. It did not take hold to the same extent in Britain or in some areas of north-central Europe, but it did so in north Africa, where it held sway until the Arab conquest. Only in the eastern provinces did Greek and other languages, such as Aramaic, continue to be used for non-administrative purposes.[1] At its height, the Roman Empire covered an area of almost two million square miles and claimed, on a conservative estimate, about fifty-six million subjects.[2] The east, however, was more populous than the west, so Latin was probably the primary language of no more than twenty-two million.[3]

Later Period (Medieval and Modern), AD 426–present

By the end of antiquity, Rome's empire had given way to incursions by alien forces that held localized political power in different regions across a disunified Europe—a situation that persists (the European Union notwithstanding) down to the present day. But throughout the former Western empire, Latin for centuries continued to hold sway as the language of the people and even to be adopted as the court language of some successor states.

Throughout late antiquity and even during the middle ages, the Latin of the elite remained remarkably stable, even as Latin underwent a series of significant changes that ultimately brought about the rise of the various Romance languages. At the same time, though, the institutional support of the Catholic Church and the reform efforts of educators like the Carolingian courtier Alcuin ensured that the ancient language maintained much of its integrity and remained in use as a language of learning, administration, and diplomacy.[4] As a result, it is probably safe to say that most of the Latin that has ever been written should have been quite intelligible to anyone who had received a grammatical education in any period from the 3rd century BC to the present day.

History of Persian

Early Period (Antiquity), ca. 750 BC–AD 637

Politically, we must speak (as was suggested above) not of one Persian Empire, but at least two—the Achaemenian (550–330 BC) and Sasanian (226–651) empires—as well as periods of domination by foreign powers, primarily Alexander the Great and his Hellenistic successors (330–250 BC) and the Parthians (250 BC–AD 226). As political power changed hands, use of the Persian language ebbed and flowed, and the language itself underwent significant changes. Under the Achaemenians, for instance, an archaic form of the language known to linguists as Old Persian came to be written for the first time. How long this language had been spoken, and whether it was in fact still used outside of the inscriptions that begin to appear only in about 650 BC, we do not know.[5] We do know that already by the end of the Achaemenian period a simpler form of the language, Middle Persian, was coming into use; we also know that for administrative purposes the Achaemenians adopted the language and bureaucratic structures of the Elamites, their predecessors in the region. So, it is in fact somewhat misleading to say that Old Persian was the language of the Achaemenian Empire. Under Alexander, his successors, and the Parthians, Middle Persian continued to be used for various purposes, along with other Iranian languages; but it did not gain the status of an imperial language until the Sasanians came to power, claiming to revive the ancient Persian Empire of the Achaemenians and promoting the Persian language along with other cultural institutions.

The achievements of the Sasanians themselves were undeniably important; but, for our purposes, their greatest contribution was to create the conditions under which Persian would achieve its most notable success, after the Sasanian empire came under Arab rule. Nevertheless, even if the greatest glories of Persian were still in the future, througout the history of ancient Iran a succession of languages—Elamite, Greek, Aramaic, and others—came and went, each serving for a time as the dominant lingua franca or koine, while Persian, in one form or other, endured.[6]

Later Period (Medieval and Modern), AD 637–present

It was with Arab contact that Persian underwent its most decisive change and, as New Persian, became an imperial language under Islam. To an equal or greater extent than Latin in the West, Persian became a language not only of administration, but of literature, of the other arts and sciences, of business, and of everyday exchange. This was true not only within the traditional borders of ancient Iran. Persian was the language of literacy and administration par excellence throughout the early Ottoman Empire and extended its reach eastwards to western China and south into peninsular India. Most remarkably, as Morgan and Aslam explain in this volume, it was used as a lingua franca among traders in Mongol China and it enjoyed official status as the administrative language of at least one important state, the Mughal Empire (1526–1857), that was situated largely outside the territory of any previous Persian empire and entirely outside the Iranian plateau.

Like all living languages, New Persian has continued to develop over its fourteen centuries of existence; but it continues to be the mother tongue of some sixty million modern Iranians, and at least ten million Afghans, Tajiks, and Uzbeks, who would recognize the New Persian of the 9th century AD (but not Middle or, still less, Old Persian) as a form of their own language, much as a modern English speaker would recognize Shakespeare's language (but not the language of Beowulf) as an early form of his own.

Comparison

Through this comparison, it is clear that the history of Latin is inverted with respect to that of Persian. Latin derives its power mainly from developments in antiquity, above all from the fact that it was the administrative language of the Roman Empire. Its significance steadily lessened througout the medieval and modern periods, so that its current position is largely vestigial; it has no native speakers and so is widely regarded as a "dead language." This is perhaps the expected trajectory for a language that achieved imperial status over two thousand years ago: a robust, creative early period followed by centuries of living largely on prestige accumulated in the distant past.

Viewed against this paradigm, the experience of Persian is all the more remarkable. Beginning in antiquity as the language of a polyglot empire controlled by one in a series of dynastic groups that governed ancient Iran, centuries later it experienced a resurgence under rulers who drew upon the prestige of Achaemenian achievements to establish and exploit the idea of a connection with ancient Persia. Only with the conquest of the Sasanians by the Arabs, however, were the conditions created that allowed Persian to become a truly imperial language, not only in Iran but in other parts of the Islamic world. Of course, the imperial status of Persian largely evaporated with the colonization of the Islamic world by Western powers; but New Persian continues to be widely spoken, and the political importance of modern Iran is hardly negligible. In a way that is simply not true of Latin, the imperial history of Persian remains an open book.

IMPACT OF OTHER IMPERIAL LANGUAGES
(GREEK AND ARABIC)

The respective histories of Latin and Persian are thus rather different from one another. But these histories do share at least one other remarkable feature. The most significant periods in the development of Latin and Persian as imperial languages were inaugurated and in large measure caused by contact with other imperial languages. In the case of Latin that language was Greek, and in that of Persian, it was Arabic. About this aspect of Persian I will say little beyond referring to the excellent account of Perry in this volume. I will try to bring out some of the parallel aspects concerning Latin and Greek.

Greek influence on the Romans goes back a long way, but it seems clear that during the 3rd and 2nd centuries BC, the quantity and especially the quality of this influence increased significantly. The Romans themselves saw things this way: to quote the poet Horace, after the Roman conquest of Greece in the 2nd century BC, "conquered Greece made her uncouth conqueror her captive."[7] Greek influence at this time takes a number of forms. One of the most notable is the energy with which the Romans set about acquiring a national literature specifically fashioned along Greek lines, involving the translation and creative adaptation of canonical texts, chiefly dramatic extending to epic and other genres as well. This is such a familiar story that it is important to understand how strange it is. One student of the phenomenon has recently proposed the following, hypothetical analogy: An English schoolmaster is shipwrecked on the West African coast. Carried inland by slave traders, he makes himself useful to the most powerful chief of Ife. There his old skills as scholar and teacher come to the fore, and, almost by accident, he launches one of the world's great literatures when he translates *Paradise Lost* into Yoruba and adapts the plays of Dryden for a local festival.[8]

This sounds, and is, comically far-fetched, but it was in just such terms that the Romans imagined the founding of Latin literature by Livius Andronicus, a prisoner of war who allegedly launched Latin literature by translating the *Odyssey* from Greek into Latin and by adapting Greek New Comedy for the Roman stage. The truth of course has to be more complex; but our near total lack of literary material antedating Livius makes it very difficult to say more than that; and the ubiquitous presence of specific Greek models behind almost every work of Latin literature over the next several centuries makes the importance of Greek impossible to deny.

What set Greek apart from other foreign languages, however, was its immense cultural prestige. Even those rough-and-ready Roman generals of the 3rd century BC, who (we are told) took no interest whatsoever in art, literature, or anything except war and politics, had to acknowledge that Greek was the language not only of international culture but also of international relations. Over time, the Roman elite became familiar with Greek both from this point of view and from the study of Greek literature, philosophy, and the other arts. The process of "hellenization" was occasionally controversial at Rome, and some strain of resistance to this process must have been crucial to the long-term development of Latin culture. In fact, it remains an unanswered question why the Romans—uniquely, so far as we know, in the Hellenistic world—decided to create a national literature in Latin on the Greek model, rather than simply adopting Greek literary culture entirely, language and all. In fact, this almost happened. When members of the Roman elite in the 3rd century BC began to write, they adopted not only the conventions of established Greek genres, such as history; they even wrote in Greek.[9] But within a generation of two, a new and more lasting trend began. From the late 3rd century onwards, Latin literature took the form of translations and adaptations of Greek models, gradually gaining more independence but never quite losing a specifically Greek point of reference. In all periods, Roman intellectuals are explicit about this fact and endorse the necessity for serious writers to look to Greek models of excellence.[10]

This is just one of the ways in which Greek had a decisive influence on Latin (and we shall consider some others as well), and one of the reasons that we can say that Greek had as important an impact on Latin as Arabic did upon Persian. If we press this comparison a bit harder, though, we quickly find that it, too, has limits. If one were to ask, Is Latin to Greek as Persian is to Arabic?, then the answer from several points of view would be, No; rather, Arabic, the language of the conqueror, is the proper correlative of Latin in this analogy, as Greek is that of Persian. Consider: the Romans' decisive encounter with Greek was at the time when their own imperial expansion put them in conflict with the remnants of Alexander's empire, a Greek-speaking super-state that had broken up into a number of smaller kingdoms of still significant size that were still Hellenistic in their cultural and linguistic character. These states, while in certain ways culturally more advanced than Rome, became politically subservient, while Rome adopted many Greek ways and made Greek culture more familiar than it had been in the western Mediterranean. It would be going too far to say that "the same thing happened" in the Islamic conquest of the Sasanian Empire; but similarities do exist. The Arab caliphate took political power over the former Sasanian state, but Arabic language and culture also absorbed a great deal from Persian (as it did from Greek, Aramaic, and the other traditions with which it came into contact) and exported much of what it absorbed throughout the Islamic world. Thus Persian became the second language of the Islamic world. This situation has something in common with the one that obtained in the Roman provinces of northern Africa in the 2nd or 3rd century AD, when an educated person's proudest boast was to be *utriusque linguae peritus,* "thoroughly educated in both languages," where "both languages" means Latin and Greek—regardless of the individual's native language (which might be Punic, Berber, or anything else). Indeed, under the Roman empire we witness such phenomena as the rhetor Favorinus (ca. AD 80–150), who was born in Arlate (Arles), the first Roman town built in Gaul after Julius Caesar's victory over Gnaeus Pompeius in the civil war, and who under the Emperor Hadrian became one of the world's greatest experts not in Latin but in Greek rhetoric.

CLASSICAL AND VULGAR DIALECTS

John Perry raises the question of homoglossia as a factor in the stability and longevity of Persian, holding that the literary language evolved along with the everyday idiom in such a way as to insure that they remained in close contact. The history of the relationship between literary and spoken Latin may be instructive here.

Literary Latin, as I have noted, is a relatively stable medium of expression. Some of the earliest prose that survives from about the 3rd century BC differs in style, but hardly at all in grammar and syntax, from much of what was written in the 2nd, 3rd, 4th, or 5th centuries AD. Many medieval writers cultivated a Latin style that differed little from that of the ancient authors, and most Renaissance and Neolatin authors were stricter still in their observance of classical norms. It is easy to get the impression from written sources that the language was inherently quite uniform and resistant to change. But this is only part of the story.

Alongside the classical dialect was another, which is known to scholars as "Vulgar Latin." The name is not primarily pejorative: it denotes the language spoken by "the crowd" (*vulgus*) as opposed to the one best represented by authors who had attained a "high tax-bracket" (*classici*).[11] Of course, our knowledge of this dialect in antiquity stems almost exclusively from traces of it in written sources, so that we cannot confront it in a form uncontaminated, as it were, by the elite dialect. But this very fact shows that the elite and the vulgar dialects existed alongside one another for centuries, not just during the middle ages but in antiquity as well. Further proof of this is the pattern in which "vulgarisms" occur in ancient texts. Such things are relatively common in early authors, such as the comic poet Plautus (3d–2d c. BC), who is concerned to reproduce everyday speech or, at least, to suggest it as much as the metrical conventions of his genre will allow. After Plautus these features then disappear from our texts for generations, never or hardly ever to be found in authors like Cicero, Sallust, Livy, or Tacitus, only to reappear in an inscription or even in the vocabulary or sentence-structure of the Romance languages.

The example of Plautus (and one could cite other authors, like Petronius, who imitate vulgar speech in a literary context) and all other available evidence shows that the two dialects were recognizably distinct. But how far did these differences go? A useful comparison that I have cited before concerns the classical and vulgar Latin equivalents of the English sentence, "I bought a horse."[12] If we work backwards from the Romance languages, where we find the sentences "Io ho comprato un cavallo" (Italian) and "Yo he comprado uno caballo" (Spanish), we would conclude that the Latin equivalent would be "Ego habeo comparatum unum caballum." And so it would be—in the vulgar dialect. But the classical Latin equivalent would be "Equum emi." The syntax of the two sentences is identical, as are some elements of the grammar.[13] Practically everything else, however, differs, from lexicon to word order to aspects of usage and style.[14] The example is thus useful for illustrating how distant the two Latin dialects could be. We should not therefore assume that they were mutually incomprehensible, however; most of our specimens of vulgar Latin are perfectly intelligible, although uneducated speakers of this dialect might well have been challenged to follow the orotundities of a Ciceronian period from one end to the other. The real point is, first, that they were distinct dialects and, second, that the classical dialect was sufficiently regular to ensure that it would be relatively resistant to change; while the vulgar dialect was much less strict and so relatively open to influences of all sorts.

It may be, then, that the situation in Roman antiquity was similar to that in medieval Persia in that the elite and the everyday forms of the language were at all times reasonably close. What is not clear is why they remained close in these periods, when in the case of later Latin and, apparently, earlier Persian as well, the written and spoken dialects were farther apart.[15] We will return to this question below in considering the later history of Latin and the development of Romance.

FACTORS AFFECTING THE DEVELOPMENT OF LATIN AS AN IMPERIAL LANGUAGE IN ANTIQUITY

In this section I will consider some of the institutions that affected the development of Latin as an imperial language in antiquity, some of which help to explain the stability at least of the elite dialect over such a long period of time. Most but not all of these institutions are in some way products of the extensive Hellenization that took place in Rome beginning in the 3rd century BC. In this section I will not try to give detailed accounts of the parallel Persian instituitions, if any, but instead will refer to discussions of these institutions by experts elsewhere in this volume.

Schools

The development of Latin grammar is probably the most significant and efficacious factor in creating a form of the language that could and did remain stable and intelligible to people of different circumstances living far apart in space and in time. The fact that grammar became the basis of elementary education throughout the Roman world made its influence, for all practical purposes, universal, in spite of the fact that advanced literacy probably remained rare, by modern standards, throughout antiquity.[16] All of this was a direct result of Rome's adoption of a Hellenistic literary culture.

During the Hellenistic period, the Greeks developed what they called the *techne grammatike*. Within it, rules were developed to determine what was correct or incorrect in the form of a word, in the structure of a sentence, and so forth. In this system, that which was correct was simply *hellenismos,* or "Greekness." What was not correct was *barbarismos,* i.e., "not Greek." When the Romans began to take a serious interest in understanding and acquiring Greek culture, efforts were made to provide Latin with a grammar on the Greek model, and in this system as well an error was labeled *barbarimus,* while correctness became *latinitas.* The effort to adapt Greek grammar to Latin was greatly facilitated by the fact that both languages are highly inflected and in fact quite similar in structure. In vocabulary they are less similar, but there are enough obvious cognates, such as *patêr*/*pater* and *mêtêr*/*mater,* along with loan words like Latin poeta (< Greek *poietes*), to convince some in antiquity that Latin was not a separate language at all, but rather a dialect of Greek.[17] But quite apart from this theory, it is a fact that ancient students of the Latin language— that is, of classical Latin— modeled their understanding of Latin grammar and syntax as closely as possible on Greek models.

In addition to descriptive elements, the *ars grammatica* was highly prescriptive in matters of correct morphology and syntax, but also of usage and style. It balanced conservatism with a capacity to evolve by basing proper latinity on five elements, which I list here in order of ascending importance: *ratio*, which consisted of *analogia* and *etymologia; vetustas; auctoritas;* and *consuetudo*, otherwise known as *natura*. The first elements assume the existence of an idealized past when language was a rational system that developed analogically and admitted no anomalies. In this ideal past, words possessed their "true meaning" (i.e., their etymology) as well. Of course, the idea that there was such a time suggests the existence of a later period during which anomalies did creep into the system and words started to change their meaning. For this reason, "systems" (i.e., "analogy" and "etymology") are theoretically standards of correctness, but they are relatively weak ones, and in practice grammarians invoke them to explain ancient puzzles more often than to establish meaning in the present, which has drifted away from these archaic standards. *Auctoritas*, "authority," is a more serious matter. In the ancient grammarian's schoolroom, pupils committed to memory choice passages of approved authors, a canon that was fashioned on the model of Hellenistic scholarship.[18] One might for instance approve a particular usage because it was found in Vergil. But it was more likely that a schoolmaster of, say, the 4th century might justify an unfamiliar usage in Vergil on the basis of *vetustas*, "antiquity," noting that a word had changed its meaning since Vergil's time. For this reason, he would advise his students *not* to imitate Vergil's authority, but to write in accordance with contemporary usage. This is what is meant by *consuetudo*, "custom," which was also known, remarkably, as *natura*, "nature." It is this factor, "nature," that is the most effective determinant of proper usage in the present. And what is this nature? In the end, nothing more or less than the grammarian's opinion about the best or most correct way to say any given thing!

In a system like this, in which so much depends on the grammarian's judgment, one might have expected *latinitas* to become fragmented and multiform. But in fact, the conservative elements in the system, and particularly the memorization of canonical authors as stylistic models, seem to have informed *consuetudo* or *natura* to a considerable extent. The result is that the language of the literate, educated classes remained quite stable over long stretches of both time and space, and also that the writings of the great grammarians, such as Donatus, exercised a stabilizing effect on post-antique latinity as well, making possible the periodic revivals of classical latinity that took place during the middle ages and especially in the Renaissance.

Cultural Institutions

In addition to grammar and schooling, the Romans borrowed and adapted from the several Hellenistic kingdoms a number of institutions designed to support their cultural ambitions. These had the direct or indirect effect of fostering the growth of Latin as an imperial language, as they had done with Greek beforehand.

It was the Hellenistic successor-states to Alexander's empire that created these institutions. In the classical period, Greek culture was supported primarily by the institutions of the city state, which tended by their nature to be somewhat limited in size and oriented towards the interests of communities that balanced local and tribal interests against panhellenic ideals. It was a highly philhellenic king of Macedon, Philip II—a man whom traditionalists like Demosthenes could represent as a foreign power and even as a barbarian—who first successfully effected a universal hegemony over Greek political affairs, and then bequeathed to his son Alexander the Great the means for extending this hegemony throughout much of the east. Alexander's empire of course did not outlive him, but it left in its wake a number of powerful superstates that commanded wealth on a scale that no individual polis could match, and that outdid the traditional poleis in willfully asserting their "Greek"—or, as we would say, following Winckelmann, their Hellenistic—cultural identity. It was an overwhelming "will to Greekness" on the part of rulers like the Macedonian general Ptolemy, usurper of the throne of the Pharaohs, that led to the foundation of such institutions as the famous Museum of Alexandria and its library, where the classic works of Greek literature in all fields were collected and where linguistic and philological research on these texts was carried out at a high level.

This process was an important forerunner of and indeed a model for the Romans. In time, Roman leaders mimicked both the ancient centers of culture, such as Athens, and the great Hellenistic rulers in providing institutional support for literary culture. The early period (late 3rd and 2nd centuries BC) is characterized by the institution of state-sponsored dramatic festivals in Rome, at which masterpieces of 5th- and 4th-century Athenian tragedies and comedies were translated and adapted for Roman audiences. Rome of course was not the first state to do something of this sort. Even in the heyday of the Athenian stage, poets such as Aeschylus and Euripides were in demand at the courts of parvenu rulers who wished to enhance their cultural prestige. Later, roving troupes of actors enjoyed something like diplomatic status as they moved about the Hellenistic world, performing classic plays for local audiences.[19] What is unusual about the Romans' experience is that this sort of participation in Greek literary culture was not sufficient to their purposes. They are the only people known to have created a literature in their own language on this Greek model. In this sense, the Romans' adoption of this institution and their adaptation of it into something of their own, seems to have been decisive.

Libraries were another institution imported to Rome from the Hellenistic world. The first of these were imported literally as the spoils of war. These include the library of King Perseus of Macedon, which was brought to Rome by L. Aemilius Paullus in 168, and that of Aristotle, which L. Cornelius Sulla brought from Athens in 82. More peaceful and more spectacular was the library of Pergamum, second only to that of Alexandria in the Hellenistic world, which Attalus III bequeathed to the Romans, along with the rest of his kingdom, upon his death in 133.[20] All of these libraries of course contained books in Greek. The same could be said of some, perhaps most private libraries in the Roman world until the 1st century BC.[21] But even before that time, Latin scholars had applied themselves not only to providing the language itself with a sound grammatical foundation, but also to establishing the authenticity of their most important literary texts, and so to developing a literary canon. The research of earlier scholars informed the definitive work of M. Terentius Varro, a senator who in his leisure found the time to write some three hundred books, including a major treatise *De lingua latina* (25 books) and another establishing the authenticity of the twenty-one plays of Plautus that now form that author's literary corpus.[22] In this activity, Varro was following in the footsteps of Hellenistic scholars in the Alexandrian library. Fittingly, then, Julius Caesar chose Varro to be the head of one of his most symbolic cultural projects, the first public library planned as a new foundation on a grand scale. After Caesar's death the project was completed by one of his associates, C. Asinius Pollio; and soon afterwards Caesar's heir, Augustus, continued Caesar's legacy by founding a number of libraries, setting a pattern followed by many subsequent emperors.

Once again, it is worth mentioning an important linguistic feature of Roman libraries. Greek libraries, to the best of our knowledge, contained only Greek books. At least, we know of no special provisions made for books in other languages. But all Roman libraries that we know of were composed of two main reading and storage areas, one devoted to books in Latin, the other to Greek. This feature is to be seen as a correlative to the Romans' adaptation of Greek into Latin drama. The Greek model or models of a typical Roman play would be known to the audience; indeed, they are not infrequently announced and even discussed in the prologue to a comedy. The bicameral plan of a Roman library instantiates the mimetic relationship between these two literatures in architectural form, and invites comparison between original and copy in the belief that the process of imitation and adaptation has been successful.[23]

At length, imperial patronage extended to something like state-funded professorships. Having begun with Greek slaves and freedmen who tutored their Roman masters in Hellenistic culture, scholarship had become by Caesar and Varro's time to a large extent the province of the aristocracy. But in the early Empire the situation changed, and such pursuits became at once less socially distinguished and more professionalized.[24] It was the Emperor Vespasian (AD 69–79) who began the practice of paying a regular salary of a hundred thousand sesterces to Latin and Greek teachers of rhetoric.[25] According to Jerome's *Chronicle* the first person to occupy one of these positions was Quintilian, the great rhetorician and educational theorist. It is to him that we owe our most complete account of the canon of Greek and Latin authors, genre by genre, which forms book 10 of his *Institutio oratoria*, which begins by advising the parents of future Latin orators to begin educating their children in Greek first, since a knowledge of Greek will be so important to him and Latin will come more naturally, anyway.

Administration

As I have mentioned in passing, all of these cultural institutions had to be run by someone, and together they formed only a small part of the imperial bureaucracy. The role of administration itself in promoting the use of Latin and in maintaining a high standard of correctness is a topic that has not received much attention from classicists, nor has any possible interaction between the bureaucratic and the creative spheres been properly investigated. This is so probably because the grammar schools themselves seem to have been the primary vehicle for spreading and maintaining a high standard of literacy. It is possible, however, that we could learn something about the latinate tradition by looking for connections between the activities of poets and clerks, such as William Hanaway finds in the world of the Persian *munshi*.

One obstacle to such an effort is the comparatively low status that men of letters held in the Roman world. This is one area in which the Romans did not follow the lead of the Greeks. In the classical Greek polis, a gentleman was expected to have considerable knowledge and appreciation of poetry and some ability as well. Really successful poets were held in high esteem, and a few of the most important actually received hero-cult status after their death. This was never true at Rome. Some have posited that in archaic times the Roman aristocracy practiced a musical culture not unlike that of the Greeks; but there is no direct evidence for this, and both the scanty ancient Roman comments about the very distant past and the efforts of some scholars to reconstruct that past are heavily influenced by what we do know about Greece. At any rate, after the point when Latin literature begins to develop in earnest, we find, as was noted above, that virtually all of the important poets are foreigners who lack citizen rights and are in some cases not even free. The situation improves over time, but the position of the poet never becomes in Roman society what it had been in Greece.

One has to admit, then, that the social position of the literatus in Rome was normally less exalted than in medieval Persia. But if the question is, were there Roman writers who made names for themselves in the field of belles-lettres while taking an active role in the imperial bureaucracy, then the answer is yes. To take a famous example, the poet Horace, after fighting on the wrong side of the war between the future Augustus and those who had murdered Augustus' adoptive father, Julius Caesar, somehow obtained a pardon, returned to Rome, and scraped together enough money to purchase a civil service post as *scriba quaestorius*. This amounted to a franchise that gave Horace control over the reproduction of certain official documents and thus provided him with an income that placed him in the equestrian order, the second-highest wealth bracket in Roman society. With the income derived from this monopoly, Horace was able to devote himself mainly to the poetry that eventually won him a close relationship with Augustus himself.

From this relationship came a commission to compose a hymn that was sung during the most important religious celebration held during Augustus' principate, the Secular Games, and an invitation—which Horace declined—to become the Emperor's *a secretis,* his personal secretary.

Horace's example is not unique. Decades later under the Emperor Hadrian, Suetonius, who is known today principally as author of *The Lives of the Twelve Caesars,* held the same post that Augustus had offered Horace, thus combining the literary career of a scholar rather than a poet with the bureaucratic career of an imperial secretary. At a less exalted level, the freedmen Gaius Verrius Flaccus and Gaius Julius Hyginus both composed important scholarly works on various topics while supporting themselves as, respectively, the head of a school located in Augustus' own house, and as the director of the Palatine Library, directly adjacent to Augustus' house. These individual examples, at least, seem to be rather good parallels to Persian practice.

So, careers like those of several *munshi*s can be found at Rome. But did these careers have any influence in the realm of language? According to Hanaway, "the formal, written, court language of the Persian courts...was created and developed as result of the dynamic interaction of the work of the *munshi*s and the poets." Can the same thing be said of Rome? Horace's work as *scriba quaestorius* verges very closely on that of the *munshi.* But if we compare Horace's poetry with the formulaic language of the documents from which he derived his living, it is difficult to see what they might have in common.[26] Still, it may be possible to find among less famous individuals or groups a more convincing parallel than Horace to the case of the *munshi.*

We do know, for instance, that from the late 3rd or early 2nd century BC there existed at Rome a *collegium scribarum et poetarum,* an organization of scribes and poets.[27] What its nature may have been is very unclear. The word *collegium* can denote anything from a club to what we might call a political action committee, a guild or union hall, a mutual assistance organization, and so on. Such organizations enjoyed no special status; in fact, they were occasionally suppressed on account of suspected subversive activity. For that matter, exactly what is meant by "scribe" or "poet" is not clear, either. How did one get to be acknowledged as a member of either profession? We simply do not know. And yet the existence of such an organization suggests that the two professions of "poet" and "scribe" were viewed as broadly comparable—and, for that matter, that they were viewed as professions, rather than utilitarian chores to be performed by members of the household staff or, conversely, as the appropriate occupations of civilized leisure. They were these things as well, of course; but the existence of the *collegium* suggests that they were also acknowledged as professions.

What role did poets and scribes have in creating classical latinity? The poet's expertise is clearly visible to us, of course, in distinction to the efforts of gentlemen amateurs; over time, the Romans came to recognize a canon of authors in each of the major genres, and these authors themselves eventually played an important role in defining latinity. We know less about the scribes, but we can catch a glimpse of their influence as well in some of the few documents that survive from the Republic. Chief among these is a *senatus consultum,* a senatorial decree in response to official consultation by the consuls in 186 BC, concerning the spread of Bacchus worship among cities allied with Rome. The document is in two parts, one formally summarizing the senate's decree and written by professional scribes (who evidently were citizens, since they are named in a fashion that normally denotes such status), and another in which the consuls in their own words address the affected parties. At the point where the change occurs, the most recent commentator on this document makes the following interesting observation:

> So far all has been reasonably plain sailing, but confusion of thought and expression now sets in...Until now the consuls have been quoting from the senatorial decree framed by professional draughtsmen; now they are telling the local officials what they have to do and, being more used to the sword than the pen, do so in an incoherent way.[28]

In his notes on this passage, Edward Courtney shows that the consuls depart in all sorts of ways from the style employed by the scribes, a style that is entirely consonant with the norms of classical Latin as it was to develop during the time of Cicero and into the Empire. To put it simply, the consuls write much more poorly than do the scribes, according to the standards of classical latinity, of which the consul Cicero several generations later was to become the chief exemplar. This is an impressive example of the influence of professional expertise in forming the language of the Roman elite.

For that matter, we know that one particular example of official language was part of the educational system. Cicero tells us that even in his day young students were made to memorize the archaic legal code known as the Laws of the Twelve Tables.[29] Further, it would be easy to demonstrate the stylistic influence of documents such as the *annales maximi,* annual records kept by the state college of pontifices, on such works as Ennius' poetry and Livy's history.[30] Indeed, from this and other evidence one could probably stitch together a plausible, fairly comprehensive picture of the various ways in which bureaucratic and belletristic pursuits came together, sometimes in the same individual, to define a stable elite dialect. The younger Pliny offers a notable opportunity. Nine books of his letters to friends read very much as epideictic exercises in correct Latin style and literary self-fashioning. The tenth book shares in these qualities, but it is unified as the preceding books are not by the fact that it records Pliny's correspondence with the Emperor Trajan during the period when Pliny was governor of Bithynia. Pliny's style remains recognizable as his own, although it veers in the direction of officialese, especially in phrases that refer to standard policy. Trajan's style is more the uniform production of the imperial chancery, although it, too, is not without touches that suggest the Emperor's personal attention. Here one must bear in mind that Pliny, as governor of an important province, was a significant member of the imperial government: he did not bother the Emperor needlessly, and he had reason to expect that his inquiries would be singled out by Trajan's secretaries for the Emperor's personal attention. If we can extrapolate from what we know about the habits of Trajan's predecessors, we even have some idea of how this process worked at the practical level.[31] But Trajan's replies to Pliny form only a small part of an enormous volume of correspondence collectively known as imperial "rescripts," responses to inquiries of all sorts that came to the emperor from virtually anyone in the Empire. It was the business of the imperial chancery to handle this correspondence, and of the Emperor to involve himself in particular issues at his discretion. As I have already suggested, Pliny's letters to his friends, to say nothing of the poetry that we know he wrote for his own and his friends' amusement, had little in common with the chancery style of the rescripts. Nevertheless, Pliny's literary style and the chancery style were both subsets of the classical dialect cultivated by the Roman elite, and as such were distinct from the more malleable vulgate that was spoken by the great majority of imperial subjects—if indeed they spoke Latin at all. So in ways such as this, we can glimpse the broad outlines of a collaborative relationship between creative writers and bureaucrats and a common purpose in maintaining a uniform, imperial Latin style. If we compare the situation to what we know from the Persian sphere, the main differences are perhaps that the Roman scribe is a less distinct figure than the Persian *munshi,* that the connections between the world of the scribes and the world of belles lettres are, with a few outstanding (and perhaps misleading) exceptions, less direct, and above all, that literary pursuits as a career conferred less status per se in Rome than they seem to have done in Persia. But the possibility that both Latin and Persian were fashioned and maintained as imperial languages by the parallel and sometimes conjoined efforts of poets and of bureaucrats seems quite real.

FACTORS AFFECTING THE CONDITION OF LATIN AFTER ANTIQUITY

About the post-antique period, though it is longer, I will be briefer. In this period, Latin remains an imperial language, but in contrast to Persian, the trajectory followed by Latin during this time has been characterized mainly by entropy. While institutional factors, such as the use of Latin by the Roman Catholic Church and by European universities, for a long time helped Latin to maintain an important role, its role as a truly imperial language was behind it by the time that Persian had just begun to come into its own. In this section, I will try to state briefly how the conditions that supported latinity during antiquity changed in the post-antique period, and where possible I will compare or contrast these developments with relevant ones in Persian.

Bilingualism

As I have been saying, one of the main parameters of Latin's development as an imperial language in antiquity was its sustained contact with Greek. With the division of the Roman Empire into eastern (i.e., Byzantine Greek) and western (latinate) halves, a long period of elite Latin-Greek bilingualism came to an end. It was replaced by a period in which literary Latin came to be defined as the only language of the elite. This language remained relatively stable, as it had done in antiquity. The spoken dialect, however, which had always diverged to some extent from the written, as we have seen, developed in ways (such as the loss of certain morphological features and the consequent need to represent syntactic relationships in ways that did not depend so much on morphology) that caused it to diverge more and more from the language of the elite. Some of these features are common to all of the modern Romance languages; but the very fact that these languages are distinct, not only from Latin but from each other, shows clearly that vulgar Latin and proto-Romance were more open to regional variation than the elite dialect. This is because, as I have said, the elite dialect was always susceptible to "correction" by appeal to grammar. But one such effort is instructive about the differences between the Latin of antiquity and that of later times. When the Saxon scholar Alcuin came to Charlemagne's court, he was appalled at the state of latinity that prevailed there. Of course, as a native speaker of a Germanic language, Alcuin learned Latin as a wholly foreign tongue, as the language of a governmental and cultural elite. On the continent, it was possible to distinguish between more or less cultivated latinity, but there was as yet no sharp distinction between Latin and Romance; at any rate, the "elite" Latin spoken at court resembled all too much, to Alcuin's ears, the vulgar Latin or proto-Romance spoken by commoners out on the street. The situation moved Alcuin to "restore" continental Latin on grammatical lines, a move that became influential by virtue of a concommitant reform of Carolingian schooling. This intervention is an important episode in the history of Latin as the imperial language of medieval Europe. But it may be even more important in having finally separated the classical (or classicizing, since Alcuin's standards were not identical with those of antiquity) from the vulgar dialect and allowing the former to remain relatively fixed while the latter went on to develop into a number of wholly different languages.

In tandem with this colossally important development we must reckon with at least three others that altered the character of Latin after antiquity.

Religion

The first of these is religion. In antiquity, Latin was of course used as a religious language by the Romans, just as Greek was used by the Greeks, and so on. But neither language as such was marked as a religious language. Religious utterances had their own style, characterized by specific lexical, syntactic, and rhetorical elements, and above all by an almost pathological conservatism. But Latin itself was not, for the Romans, a religious language any more (or any less) than it was a legal language, a diplomatic language, or what have you.

With the advent of Christianity, this situation changed. In the first place, the Roman Church adopted Latin as its official language. This meant, of course, that when the secular power of the Empire disintegrated, there was still a latinate central whose authority extended throughout Europe. As I have just been saying, however, as the difference between the elite and vulgar dialects increased, the language of the Church, and especially of liturgy, became more and more marked as Latin in contrast to the vernacular that most people spoke. To this was added the fact that the Church regarded Latin, along with Greek and Hebrew, as the *tres linguae sacrae* ("three sacred languages") because of the trilingual inscription "Here is the King of the Jews" that was affixed to Jesus' cross. Greek and Hebrew, of course, were largely unknown in the West, leaving Latin for all practical purposes as the only "sacred language" that anyone ever encountered.

The situation is thus very different from that of Persian in the early centuries of Arab rule. Arabic was, of course, in early Islamic Persia a sacred language par excellence. Persian, at that point anyway, was not. The development of Persian in these early centuries was, therefore, perhaps facilitated by not having to bear this burden. In medieval Europe, by contrast, the language of the elite was marked as a sacred language, enhancing its prestige, perhaps, but also distancing it that much more from the realities of everyday speech.

Vernacular Languages

John Perry states an important corollary to this last point: Early New Persian "stood in much the same relationship (from a linguistic and a socio-religious perspective) as Early Romance to Late Latin in Europe of the same period." In some sense, then, we should perhaps regard Latin as playing something like the same role in Europe between, say, the 9th and the 12th centuries, that Arabic played in Persia between the 7th and the 11th. Both languages dominated the religious sphere, and they were the language of the elite, whether old (as in Europe) or new (as in Persia). One limit to this comparison is that Latin at this time was a language of literature and of the other arts and sciences, while Arabic, as yet, was not. As I have already observed, it was Arabic contact with Persian (and with Greek and other languages, such as Syriac) that helped it become an imperial language in the realm of secular culture, as happened to Latin via contact with Greek in an earlier period. But the fact that Arabic was ill-equipped to overwhelm Persian in the realm of secular culture allowed Persian room to develop and to serve as a catalyst for the development of Arabic in the same field. In

Europe, it took time for a distinctive vernacular elite language—the theme of Dante's *De vulgari eloquentia*—and culture to develop and eventually to surpass that of Latin.

Collective Identities

The role of collective identities in this story is too complex to address in any detail. I have occasionally spoken of "regional variations" or "vernacular traditions" in the development of Latin and Romance. For a long time, the central authority of the Roman Church was able to counterbalance the centrifugal tendencies of local power throughout the continent. Ultimately, this power was broken, and the history of Europe is best understood in terms of the nation state—its roots, its myths of ethnic identity, and the institutions that support these ideas, among which national language takes pride of place. The point is that Latin has been, certainly since the Reformation and arguably since the end of antiquity, still the language of an empire, yes, but one that was doomed over the long run to fighting a rear-guard action, cutting its losses, and shoring fragments against its ruins. Persian might have been seen to be in such a position between the end of the Achaemenian Empire until AD 226, when the Persian nationalist Ardashir I had himself crowned ShāhanShāh at Ctesiphon, much as Charlemagne in 800 was crowned Emperor at Rome. But it was only after the Persian revival of the Sasanians that the language went on, chiefly under foreign rulers, to enjoy true imperial status. After Charlemagne—beginning, in fact, with the quarrels that divided his immediate successors—ethnic forces would play a decisive role in the rise of modern states, to which Latin would become increasingly irrelevant.

Grammar, Education, and Literary Canon

Alcuin's reforms were successful in distinguishing Latin from vernacular speech. In so doing, they may also have cut the language off from an important source of renewal and rendered it less flexible than it needed to be to adapt to a changing world. In this way, Alcuin may have established a pattern followed by most subsequent Latin educators of rejecting any form of the language that could not be justified by direct appeal to ancient practice.

The most extreme form of this attitude is represented by the Humanist quarrel over Ciceronianism. It was, of course, a concern of the Humanists, as it had been of Alcuin, to reform the language. It is an irony that the standard medieval Latin that they scorned in comparison to that of the

ancients was probably created, or at any rate codified, by the reforms that
Alcuin instituted with very similar goals in mind. But with access to many
more ancient texts the Humanists were able to cultivate a more thoroughly
classicizing style. The problem was how far to go. It occurred to some writers, as of course it would, that living in a world different from that of the
Romans, they would occasionally find it necessary to talk about things that
had been unknown to the Romans. How could one do so in a purely classical idiom. The problem has been faced many times in many languages,
but the decision proposed by some Humanists with regard to Latin may be
unique. For Lorenzo Valla and others, the works of Cicero should be the
one and only standard of correct latinity. Valla was opposed by men such
as Angelo Poliziano and others; later Ciceronians were opposed by no less
a figure than Erasmus. And it would be impossible to say that the dispute
was ever universally resolved. But the fact that men like Valla could advocate such a narrow basis for correct latinity shows to what extent, even in
the era of its supposed "rebirth," Latin had advanced towards becoming a
corpus language.

Cultural Institutions

The institutional support for Latin was clearly different in the middle
ages from what it had been in antiquity. Instead of dramatic festivals, imperial libraries, and the like, Latin became the preserve of monasteries and
cathedral schools. These places, together with such institutions as the Vatican chancery, are the principal setting within which the influence of professional administrators is to be sought. Again, in contrast to antiquity, it seems
difficult to credit the medieval formularies, the *ars dictandi* manuals, and so
forth—many of them described as "anything but models of good Latinity;
with the exception of the Letters (*Varae*) of Cassiodorus, and the St. Gall
collection 'Sub Salomone,' they are written in careless or even barbarous
Latin, though it is possible that their wretched 'style' is intentional, so as
to render them intelligible to the multitude"—with making a very positive
contribution to the survival of Latin.[32] With the rise of universities, some
aspects of ancient scholarship were eventually restored; but inevitably the
vernacular languages became media of scholarly communication, to the
extent that the advantages even of an academic lingua franca such as Latin
offered were not outweighed by the necessity of learning several modern
languages in order to stay abreast of current research.

CONCLUSION

In sum, there are clearly many points of similarity between the imperial histories of Latin and Persian. Chief among these, as it seems to me, is the way in which these languages interacted with others in the course of taking on their imperial character. The interaction between belles lettres and administrative language in medieval Persia and in Roman antiquity seems another promising area for further study. On balance, however, the differences between these two histories may be even more intriguing than the similarities. It would be fascinating to raise many of these same questions especially in regard to those languages, Arabic and Greek, that played such in important role in the histories of Persian and Latin, to say nothing of other, less directly related imperial traditions.

NOTES

1. On the spread of Latin and the survival of other languages see R. MacMullen, "Provincial Languages."
2. Estimates vary from about 60 to 120 million, depending largely on whether one means to estimate the size of the citizen population alone or of the entire human population of the Empire.
3. About 60 percent of the population is thought to have lived in the eastern provinces during the age of Constantine and Justinian. Latin will have been the mother tongue of the great majority in the west, but by no means of all. No doubt it was spoken as a second language, with varying degrees of fluency, throughout the Empire. On bilingualism see J.N. Adam, *Bilingualism and the Latin Language.*
4. On Alcuin's role in this story see Roger Wright, *Late Latin.*
5. The prevailing view that Old Persian was used only as a ceremonial language is challenged by a text that was recently discovered in the Persepolis Fortification archive at the Oriental Institute of the University of Chicago. The text is the first and so far the only known administrative document written in Old Persian. As such, it could be "just a quirky experiment" or else "the tip of an iceberg," according to Matthew W. Stolper, head of the Oriental Institute's Persepolis Fortification Archive Project (http://www-news.uchicago.edu/releases/07/070615.oldpersian.shtml).
6. In truth, one might argue that both Greek and Aramaic have endured as well. Greek gradually replaced Latin as the official language of the Byzantine Empire, held that status until the fall of Constantinople in 1453, remained in common use under Ottoman rule, and is of course today the official language of a modern nation state. The estimated number of speakers runs from 15 to 25 million people (R. Browning, *Medieval and Modern Greek*). Varieties of Aramaic remained important throughout the Middle Ages and into the modern period especially for scriptural and liturgical purposes; but the number of native speakers has dwindled to about 500,000, and the fragmentation of spoken dialects is such that many groups of Aramaic speakers can no longer understand one another. On July 31, 2006, the Arameans of Aram-Naharaim

Foundation presented their case to the UNESCO Working Group on the Indigenous Populations that Aramaic must now be considered an endangered language.

7. Epist. 2.2.157.

8. Sander Goldberg, *Constructing Literature*, 1.

9. The earliest known Roman writer of history is Fabius Pictor, who was himself a senator (Polybius 3.9.4). Other Romans of this period who wrote in Greek include L. Cincius Alimentus, C. Acilius, and A. Postumius Albinus. The surviving fragments of their works can be found in F. Peter, *Historicorum Romanorum reliquiae.*

10. For an overview of the situation (one that stresses the influence of Greek in the service of explaining the supposed "decline" of Latin literature in the 1st and 2nd centuries AD), see Gordon Williams, *Roman Literature,* Ch. 3, "The Dominance of Greek Culture," esp. 138–58.

11. Aulus Gellius *NA* 19.8.15.

12. Joseph Farrell, *Latin Language,* 18.

13. Both words for "horse" (*equus* and *caballus*), for instance, exhibit the regular *-um* ending of the second-declension accusative, signalling that the word is the direct object of the main verb. It would be easy to find examples of vulgar Latin, however, in which this ending had been replaced by *-us,* the nominative. In both of these endings, the final consonant was but weakly pronounced, and in Romance both developed into *-u* and, eventually, into *-o* (as Latin *caballus/caballum* became Spanish *caballo/caballo* and Italian *cavallo/cavallo*).

14. The lexical differences, such as *equus* v. *caballus,* are obvious. The usual word-order of classical Latin is SOV (subject-object-verb), while the vulgar dialect (like Romance) is SVO. The classical dialect is spare, using personal pronouns (such as *ego*) mainly for emphasis (since the information they convey is already contained in the ending of the verb), dispensing with the indefinite article *unus,* preferring the simple to the compound form of the perfect tense, etc. On the history and characteristic features of vulgar Latin see József Herman's *Vulgar Latin.*

15. On the situation in regard to Latin see Herman, "Spoken and Written Latin."

16. Estimates of the literacy rate in Greek and Roman antiquity are very controversial. The fullest analysis of the evidence is that of W.V. Harris's *Ancient Literacy,* which argues that the literacy in the Roman Empire never exceeded 10 percent of the total population. But Harris's methods are regarded by many as too conservative: see for instance the responses of Mary Beard et al., "Literacy in the Roman World." For some scholars the question turns on the definition of literacy. It seems clear that there were different degrees or kinds of literacy and that any individual might be proficient in one or more, but not all of them. Thus the number of people who were literate in commercial matters but who could not easily understand a relatively challenging author like Lucan or Juvenal might be much larger than 10 percent of the total population. What seems clear is that literacy rates, especially in cities, were higher and perhaps much higher during the Empire than was typical of most premodern cultures; but it is very difficult to be more specific than that.

17. Dionysius of Halicarnassus states that "The Romans speak a language that is neither entirely foreign (*barbaron*) or quite Greek, but rather a mixture of the two. It is mainly Aeolic [one of the three main dialects of classical Greek], and the only defect, which is the result of their absorbing so many peoples, is that they do not maintain proper pronunciation. Otherwise they preserve the evidence of their Greek ancestry better than

any other colonists" (*Ant. Rom.* 1.90.1). This theory was probably developed by Greek intellectuals whose amour propre was offended by their political subservience to Rome.

18. On classical canon formation see Mario Citroni, "Concept of the Classical and the Canons of Model Authors in Roman Literature," 204–34.

19. On these groups see A. Spawforth, *Oxford Classical Dictionary*, s.v. "Dionysus, artists of," with further references.

20. The bequest was controversial at Rome, and the disposition of the library is uncertain. On Attalus III and the Attalid dynasty in general see Esther V. Hansen, *Attalids of Pergamon.*

21. Probably the best known private library is the one that was found at Herculaneum in the Villa dei Papiri, presumed to be the property of L. Calpurnius Piso Caesoninus, consul in 58 BC and father-in-law of Julius Caesar. Over 1800 books have been found; most are works of Greek philosophy, but several works of Latin poetry are represented as well. The books are in containers and were evidently in the process of being rescued from the impending eruption of Vesuvius in AD 79 when the situation got out of hand and the villa was buried in lava. It is known that additional books remain unrecovered, and it is thought that the number of these may be quite large, but certainty about this and other aspects of this important library awaits further exploration.

22. In antiquity about 130 plays circulated under Plautus' name; on the whole problem see Gellius, *NA* 3.3.

23. Similarly Quintilian's canon is divided into separate lists of Greek (*IO* 10.1.46–84) and Roman (85–131) authors.

24. Andrew Wallace-Hadrill, "*Mutatio morum:* The Idea of a Cultural Revolution," 3–22.

25. Suetonius, *Div. Vesp.* 18.

26. It is true that Thomas Habinek (*Politics of Latin Literature*) has argued against the idea that poets like Horace—or like Ovid, the poet with whom Habinek is chiefly concerned (pp. 151–69)—should be set apart from writers of other kinds because of their superior imagination or craftsmanship. On Habinek's view, which derives from recent studies of writing under the British colonialism in the 19th century, all writing does the work of empire.

27. On this institution see Nicholas Horsfall, "Collegium Poetarum," 79–95.

28. Edward Courtney, *Archaic Latin Prose,* 98.

29. De legibus 2.59.9.

30. On the annales maximi see B.W. Frier, *Libri annales pontificum maximorum;* Elizabeth Rawson, "Prodigy Lists."

31. A.N. Sherwin-White, *Letters of Pliny,* 536–46.

32. A. Boudinhon, *Catholic Encyclopedia,* "formularies."

REFERENCES

Adam, J.N. 2005. *Bilingualism and the Latin Language.* Cambridge: Cambridge University Press.

Beard, Mary, ed. 1991. Literacy in the Roman World. *Journal of Roman Archaeology,* Supplementary series 3. Ann Arbor.

Boudinhon, Auguste. 1909. Formularies (*libri formularum*). In *The Catholic En-*

cyclopedia, Vol. 6. New York: 22 Jun. 2009 <http://www.newadvent.org/cathen/06141a.htm>.

Browning, R. 1983. *Medieval and Modern Greek.* 2d ed. Cambridge: Cambridge University Press.

Citroni, Mario. 2005. The Concept of the Classical and the Canons of Model Authors in Roman Literature. In *Classical Pasts: The Classical Traditions of Greece and Rome,* ed. J. Porter, pp. 204–34. Princeton: Princeton University Press.

Courtney, Edward. 1999. *Archaic Latin Prose.* Atlanta, GA: Scholars Press.

Farrell, Joseph. 2001. *Latin Language and Latin Culture from Ancient to Modern Times.* Cambridge: Cambridge University Press.

Frier, B.W. 1979. *Libri annales pontificum maximorum: The Origins of the Annalistic Tradition.* Papers and Monographs of the American Academy in Rome, vol. 27. Reprint (Ann Arbor: University of Michigan Press, 1999).

Goldberg, Sander. 2005. *Constructing Literature in the Roman Republic.* Cambridge: Cambridge University Press.

Habinek, Thomas. 1998. *The Politics of Latin Literature: Writing, Identity, and Empire in Ancient Rome.* Princeton: Princeton University Press.

Hansen, Esther V. 1971. *The Attalids of Pergamon.* Ithaca: Cornell University Press.

Harris, W.V. 1989. *Ancient Literacy.* Cambridge, MA: Harvard University Press.

Herman, József. 1996. Spoken and Written Latin in the Last Centuries of the Roman Empire. A Contribution to the Linguistic History of the Western Provinces. In *Latin and the Romance Languages in the Early Middle Ages,* ed. Roger Wright, pp. 29–43. University Park, PA: Pennsylvanian State University Press.

—— 2000. *Vulgar Latin,* trans. Roger Wright. University Park, PA: Pennsylvania State University Press.

Horsfall, Nicholas. 1976. The Collegium Poetarum. *Bulletin of the Institute of Classical Studies* 23:79–95.

MacMullen, Ramsay. 1966. Provincial Languages in the Roman Empire. *American Journal of Philology* 87:1–14.

Peter, F. 1914. *Historicorum Romanorum reliquiae.* 2nd ed. Leipzig: Teubner.

Rawson, Elizabeth. 1971. Prodigy Lists and the Use of the Annales Maximi. In *Classical Quarterly* 21:158–69. Republished in *Roman Culture and Society* (Oxford: Oxford University Press, 1991), 1–15.

Sherwin-White, A.N. 1966. *The Letters of Pliny: A Historical and Social Commentary.* Oxford: Oxford University Press.

Spawforth, Antony. 2001. Dionysus, Artists of. In *The Oxford Classical Dictionary,* 3rd ed., ed. Simon Hornblower and Antony Spawforth, pp. 482–83. Oxford: Oxford University Press.

Stolper, Matthew W. 2007. Persepolis Fortification Archive Project, Oriental Institute (http://www-news.uchicago.edu/releases/07/070615.oldpersian.shtml).

Wallace-Hadrill, Andrew. 1998. *Mutatio morum:* The Idea of a Cultural Revolution. In *The Roman Cultural Revolution,* ed. Thomas Habinek and Alessandro Schiesaro, pp. 3–22. Princeton: Princeton University Press.

Williams, Gordon. 1978. *Change and Decline: Roman Literature in the Early Empire.* Berkeley: University of California Press.

Wright, Roger. 1982. *Late Latin and Early Romance in Spain and Carolingian France.* Liverpool: F. Cairns.

12

Persian Scribes (munshi) and Chinese Literati (ru)

The Power and Prestige of Fine Writing (adab/wenzhang)

VICTOR H. MAIR

INTRODUCTION: SCRIPT AND SOCIETY

The Chinese and Persian writing systems both facilitated the maintenance of impressive polities and lasting cultural traditions. In each of these cases, the chief guardians of the scripts were elite, learned scribes: the *munshi*s in Persia and the *ru* ("[Confucian] literati") in China. Although there were many similarities between the two writing systems and the ways in which they were applied—a heavy emphasis on calligraphic excellence, a preference for poetic genres, dense allusiveness, and so forth—fundamental linguistic distinctions and basic esthetic preferences meant that the *modi operandi* and cultural implications of the two scripts in their respective societies were by no means identical. Other authors in this volume collectively provide a rich account of the *munshi* and his role, thus I shall only briefly describe them for China specialists who may be interested in the rudiments of another important Asian scribal tradition. The primary purpose of this essay is to sketch the history and nature of Chinese literati practices in such a fashion that specialists on Persian writing will be readily able to draw useful comparisons and make meaningful contrasts.

ORIGINS OF PERSIAN AND CHINESE SCRIBAL PRACTICES

From my archeological and textual studies of the last thirty-odd years, I have come to the conclusion that the Iranian peoples (i.e., speakers of Iranian languages) were the paramount *Kulturvermittlers* (culture brokers / transmitters) of Eurasia from the Bronze Age through the late medieval period. I believe that one of the main reasons why the Iranian peoples excelled at the transmission of culture and ideas is that they were among the earliest to master the horse and the chariot. The transmission of information across vast expanses requires speed and mobility, and the horse gave both of these to the early Iranians. Once they developed the expertise of rapid transmission of ideas and techniques, it became a sort of specialty for them, and they continued to play this role to which they were so well accustomed even after other groups became adept at riding and driving horses[1] (Anthony 2007).

Let us look briefly and specifically at some of the realities of language and technologies of writing that facilitated the role of the Iranians as transmitters of information throughout much of Asia. I am thinking particularly of the evolution of certain scribal practices that became a characteristic and long-standing tradition, especially among the Achaemenids and Persians. One feature of this tradition that needs to be kept in mind is that spoken and written language were separate and distinct.

It is obvious that, even within the Iranian group, there are many variations among spoken languages that would have acted as a bar to mutual intelligibility. Naturally, when we look outside the Iranian linguistic area, the obstacles to communication would have been far greater. Consequently, the perfection of writing as a tool that could transcend local variations in spoken language was a key factor in the ability of the Iranians to function as communications specialists across large expanses encompassing speakers of many different languages. Within China, we have a similar situation, where the gulf between written language and spoken languages was, and still is, enormous; I shall expand upon this aspect of Sinitic linguistics at greater length below.

In the Iranian cultural area, excellence in the craft of writing is ultimately a legacy of the Achaemenian administrative infrastructure. Aramaic was already the most widespread language during the period of the New Assyrian empire (934–609 BC); starting around the end of the 6th c. BC, it became the official language of the Achaemenian chancellery (Shaked

1987:251). As such, it was an effective device for exercising control over a wide geographical and culturally disparate area.

Aramaic is a Northwest Semitic language that, from ca. 300 BC–AD 650, was a lingua franca for nearly all of Southwest Asia and was the language of everyday speech in Syria, Mesopotamia, and Palestine. (Jesus—as we know, *inter alia,* from Mel Gibson's recent movie—spoke Aramaic.) Aramaic also refers to the script used for the writing of Aramaic from about the 9th c. BC and from which were derived the Armenian, Pahlavi, Old Uyghur, Mongolian, Manchu, and other scripts, probably including also Brahmi in India, which, in turn, was used to write various languages of eastern Central Asia, such as Tocharian. Incidentally, another Northwest Semitic script, Phoenician, which preceded Aramaic, was the foundation for the Greek alphabet, and we know that ultimately evolved into other important scripts, several of which are still used today (Roman/Latin, Cyrillic). Note that the Phoenicians were very much a mercantile people, as were the Aramaeans, and, still later, the Sogdians.

Thus, as we have seen, it was not an accident that the Achaemenids selected Aramaic as their official chancellery language, since already during previous centuries Aramaic had functioned as the *de facto* lingua franca in the Near East as a result of the extensive commercial activities of the Aramaeans. The official status of Aramaic as the basis of written communication under the Assyrians established a precedent for future multi-national bureaucracies. As an official Achaemenian language, and through its ongoing usage for trading purposes and private correspondence, the knowledge of Aramaic writing spread across the eastern Achaemenian domains to areas where writing was hitherto unknown, reaching even Sogdiana and Chorasmia in western Central Asia and the extreme northwestern portion of South Asia. Consequently, Achaemenian chancellery Aramaic became the basis of the craft of writing for many centuries in Iran and had a definite influence on the way writing developed there—namely as the more or less secret profession of a powerful, specialized guild. (One might well think of them as the forerunners of the *munshi.*) Scribes were called *dipibara-,* Mid. Pers. *dibir* (cf. Sogdian *dpyr*), a word ultimately derived from Sumerian DUB, Akkad. *tuppu* ("writing tablet"), probably through the intermediary of older Elamite *tuppi,* later Elamite *tippi* ("inscription"). They received their training at a *dipibarastana-,* Mid. Pers. *dibiristan,* New Persian *dabirestan* (Heinrichs 1997:250; Bailey 1949:127–28; Harmatta 1997:397–98), now meaning a secondary or high school.

In the early Achaemenid period, Aramaic would have been chiefly the preserve of foreign scribes who were already familiar with it. Eventually, however, Iranians themselves must have become conversant with the special craft of scribesmanship. Recently, exciting news has come of the discovery of a cuneiform tablet proving unmistakably that Old Persian was used for administrative purposes and not just for display, already from ca. 500 BC (Stopler and Tavernier 2007). However, while Aramaic continued as the main language of written communication, the populations of the various Iranian satrapies maintained their own languages (e.g., Parthian, Sogdian, and Khwarezmian), instead of adopting Persian, the native language of the Achaemenians.[2]

Of course, there is much more that could be said concerning the evolution of Persian writing, the origin and evolution of the scribal tradition of the *munshis*, the vital role of Persian as an Asian lingua franca during the medieval and early modern period, and the modeling of other scribal traditions upon it. The above account, however, should give a basic idea of the deeper historical background of these practices and provide a platform for comparison with the Chinese scribal tradition.

In contrast to the Iranian/Persian scribal tradition, which arose in a wide-ranging, continental context, the Chinese writing system and literati practices evolved in relative isolation.[3] At the time of the earliest extant evidence for writing in the East Asian Heartland (EAH) around 1200 BC, the script was already fully formed, yet no clear antecedents have been found in East Asia itself. During the initial stage of the script's existence (the late Shang period), around 1200 BC, its use was restricted exclusively to recording divinations on oracle bones (chiefly bovine scapulae) and shells (turtle plastrons). The next stage, the Western Zhou period (1045–771 BC), saw the use of dedicatory inscriptions on bronze vessels and in a somewhat different form of the script. The following stage, that of the Spring and Autumn and Warring States periods (770–476, 475–221) witnessed the proliferation of regional variants, but these were standardized in a "seal" form of the script according to the draconian unifying policies of the First Emperor of the Qin (r. 221–210 BC) and his advisers. Although there subsequently were additional developments of the script ("clerkly," "regular," "grass," "running," etc.), the foundations of the writing system as a powerful instrument of bureaucracy were firmly laid during the Qin (221–207) and Han (206 BC–AD 220) periods (Yee 1973; Tsien 2004). In this concatenation of writing,

authority, and empire, not only were the Persian and Chinese realms un-
cannily similar, the same effects were witnessed in the Latinate realm even
long after the collapse of the Roman *imperium* (Connery 1998; Lewis 1999;
Waquet 2001; but cf. Ostler 2005, who speaks to quite a different aspect of
language as empire-building).

While the sinographic script may not have been as monumental as Egyptian and Hittite hieroglyphic writing nor as architecturally integrated as the
Perso-Arabic script, it was nonetheless prominently displayed in public and
private spaces for its immediate visual effect, apart from any semantic content. Consequently, we may consider the characters to be highly iconic in
nature, and it is this iconicity that accounts for many details in the history of
Chinese writing that will be explored in the following sections.

THE CULT(URE) OF WRITING

The fortunes of all religions in the EAH waxed and waned, with individuals expressing degrees of adherence to Magianism, Shamanism, Buddhism,
Taoism, Manicheism, Mazdaism, Christianity, Islam, Judaism, and so forth,
sometimes subscribing to several faiths simultaneously. By turns, the central government promoted one or another religion, while at other times it
persecuted and proscribed them.[4]

Many of the literati claimed not to profess belief in any *jiao* ("doctrine")
other than their own (*rujiao*, lit., "doctrine of the literati," i.e., Confucianism). One might, then, argue that the leading doctrine of East Asia was not
Buddhism, Taoism, Islam, or any other religion, but the doctrine of the
literati, which we may style—in essence—the cult of writing. Indeed, in
premodern China, it would not be an exaggeration to speak of the sacrality
of the written word. So revered were the characters that individuals were
enjoined not to wrap anything unclean in paper with writing on it nor to
use paper that had been written on to wipe anything filthy. Furthermore,
when it was necessary to dispose of paper that had been written on, one
was expected ideally to burn it in special incinerators to release its potency
to the spirits in heaven (Naquin 2000:652n93). And so numinous was writing held to be that tesserae consisting of complex combinations of graphs
were considered spiritually and even medically efficacious (e.g., affixing a
thunder-quelling character-charm to the abdomen of a pregnant woman
was thought to diminish prenatal pains).

Of course, most of the other jiao besides Confucianism had their own textual traditions, some quite extensive—such as the hundreds of scriptures, treatises, and commentaries in the Buddhist and Taoist canons. But none were so focused on writing for writing's sake as was the doctrine of the ru. We may get a better sense of the nature of the doctrine subscribed to by the literati by reflecting upon this dictum attributed to Confucius: "If Heaven were going to destroy this culture, no one of later date could have managed to take part in this culture"[5] (*Analects* 9.5). The expression translated as "this culture" is *si wen* in the original, where *si* is simply a demonstrative. That leaves us with *wen,* which is of monumental significance in East Asian intellectual history. Wen is both writing and culture,[6] so that one may say writing *is* culture and culture *is* writing. To the East Asian mind, without writing there can be no culture, which speaks volumes about the attitude of those who possessed writing toward those who were without it.

One cannot help but notice a striking parallel between the ethos of si wen as the nucleus of "culture," "civilization," and "literature" on the one hand, and *adab* ("courtesy, civility, etiquette" > "knowledge of poetry, oratory, rhetoric, grammar, and philology" > "belles lettres") as the core of *adabiyāt* (literature) on the other."[7] While the correspondence is not exact, it is evident that, for both the Persian and Chinese traditions, writing (and particularly fine writing, i.e., literature, belles lettres) was the quintessence of culture.

Returning to si wen, however, the successors of Confucius seized upon this formulation as the hallmark of their faith. By the time of the neo-Confucians (flourishing roughly from the 11th century through to the end of the empire a millennium later), they had come to regard themselves as the privileged guardians of this precious essence of all that is good in humanity. Consequently, it is not surprising that Peter Bol felicitously and perceptively renders si wen as "this culture of ours" in his seminal study of this keystone of Confucianism (1992).

A BURGEONING BUREAUCRACY

In general, all young men of means and ability in premodern China aspired to succeed in the civil service examinations, or were commonly considered odd and eccentric if they did not.[8] Those who passed the various levels of the examination system were funneled into the extraordinarily elaborate imperial bureaucracy, which extended its tentacles from the highest organs of central government to the county magistracies spread across the land. The proliferation of ranks, grades, and titles was bewildering, but somehow it all managed to cohere as a more or less smoothly functioning system for over two millennia. Undoubtedly, a key factor in the perpetuation of this stunningly complex and politically pervasive bureaucratic structure was the proficiency in the demanding writing system that typified its members. Indeed, in the EAH, dynasties came and went, and were headed by non-Sinitic peoples as often as not.[9] What persisted was the bureaucracy and the command of the sinographic script that constituted its very essence.[10]

The *ne plus ultra* of literati achievement was attainment of the *jinshi* (Presented Scholar or Metropolitan Graduate) degree. Comparable to an academic doctorate in the modern world,[11] the jinshi certified that the holder possessed mastery of the sinographic script and its application for literary composition. So vital was possession of this advanced degree (attained by only a tiny fraction of those candidates who embarked upon the lengthy, demanding process of preparation and testing at various levels) that often the sole biographical fact known about a poet or official is the year in which he passed the jinshi examination. Passing the jinshi examination was a virtual *sine qua non* for attaining high office.

The jinshi degree, which was current from about the 7th century, had its predecessor in the erudites (*boshi*) of roughly a thousand years earlier. It is curious that, through an extraordinarily roundabout way, this ancient designation came in modern times to be identified with the Ph.D. from the West (Mair 1992). Already from 124 BC, erudites were teaching "scions of the state" (*guozi*) in the National University (*taixue*). Beginning around the 8th century, academies (*shuyuan*) were founded to prepare students for success in the examinations, and from the 11th century on, many of these were privately funded[12] (Walton 1999). In terms of the potential returns that would accrue to the family and friends of anyone who passed the examinations, the establishment of an academy was certainly a good investment. In addition, many of the academies espoused particular politico-philosophical viewpoints that were directly tied to policy struggles at court.

Similarly, calligraphy groups and poetry societies were usually unofficial gatherings of literati and officials, and thus had a semi-political character. The members of such gatherings who were unhappy with current policies often used their calligraphy and poetry to express their displeasure, albeit in an oblique and veiled fashion (Elman 1984). Moreover, calligraphy had a direct bearing on the examinations. It mattered greatly for the local and palace examinations where examiners read the original papers. Calligraphy mattered less for the triennial provincial and metropolitan examinations where the originals were recopied to keep them anonymous. But even there an incorrect form or a careless smudge could disqualify a candidate (Elman 2000). Calligraphy, of course, was valued for its aesthetic properties, but it also had philosophical properties (Billeter 1990) and social functions (Ledderose 1986). For persons who have grown up in cultures where script is valued above all for its intrinsic ability to convey information and less for its artistic and numinous qualities, it is difficult to imagine the overwhelming status of writing per se in Chinese society. For users of primarily pragmatic writing systems, it is perhaps even harder to grasp the ethical and political dimensions of writing in China.[13] Suffice it to say that, for Chinese literati, an individual's calligraphy was a reflection of his moral character.

The importance of fine writing in the operation of the Chinese bureaucratic apparatus cannot be overstressed. Accomplished litterateurs not only served as valued advisers to the court, nearly all of them were also appointed to official positions in the bureaucracy. The supreme exemplars of the fraternity of the highly literate were concentrated in the celebrated Hanlin Yuan (Hanlin Academy) (Bischoff 1963; Liu 1981). This was "a loosely organized group of litterateurs who did drafting and editing work in the preparation of the more ceremonious imperial pronouncements and the compilation of imperially sponsored historical and other works, principally designated Hanlin Academicians (*hanlin xueshi*)."[14]

We may contrast this heavy emphasis on the scribal, bureaucratic tradition in the EAH with India, where writing was actually disparaged by the sacerdotal authorities for centuries after it was available, and hence which lacks formal, written history during the classical period. Indeed, even during the medieval period, much of India's history must be reconstructed from the records of Chinese Buddhist pilgrims such as Faxian (fl. 399–416), Xuanzang (600–664), and Yijing (635–713). This differs sharply from the situation in China, where history writing alone was a grand enterprise with a sophisticated body of historiographical scholarship.[15] It is no accident that the first recognized historian of China, Sima Qian (145–ca. 86 BC), was called *taishigong* (the grand scribe).[16]

Yet history writing was just one sanctioned genre among the literati.[17] Also greatly valued was short, lyrical verse, which afforded an outlet for the personal emotions. Moral essays, epitaphs, ornate parallel prose (*pian[ti] wen*), and other carefully crafted, usually relatively brief, genres were also highly developed. Even official decisions (*pan*) of a purely bureaucratic nature were carefully scrutinized for their style and were considered as potential *wenzhang* (fine writing) (Yang 2007). Not favored among premodern authors emphasizing Classical Chinese were fiction, drama, and long narrative works, whether in verse or prose, or a combination of the two. The epic, for example, was left to be developed in diverse bardic, non-literati domains, particularly among the non-Sinitic peoples of Eastern Central Asia (ECA) and East Asia (e.g., the Tibetan tale of Gesar of Ling).

During the late imperial period, the examinations became stultified and rigidified to such a degree that they were no longer able to identify the most capable talents in the land. To be sure, so highly formalistic were the examinations that they functioned more as a mental straitjacket than as an invitation to creative thought. The epitome of this facet of the latter-day examinations was the notorious "eight-legged essay" (*baguwen*), which was the standard form of answer from the mid-15th century to the demise of the entire system at the beginning of the 20th century.[18] To be successful, a candidate had to develop philosophical themes according to Zhu Xi's (1130–1200) Neo-Confucian commentaries on the classics. The essay (roughly 300–600 characters long) had to follow strict rules of composition requiring grammatical as well as thematic parallelism developed in specific rhetorical segments. Until the abolition of the civil service examinations at the beginning of the last century, skill in the composition of the complicated eight-legged essay remained a prescription for coming out on top of the list of those who passed. It is curious, incidentally, that the rigidly structured formal Persian ode known as the *qasida*, which both appealed to and praised the ruler, also predetermined most of what could be written before an author set pen to paper. Traditionally the Persian *qasida* had a tripartite structure: an opening section with conventional content (e.g., a description of spring, a description of the beloved, etc.); a middle section that is the meat of the poem, its *qasd* or purpose (e.g., congratulations to the patron on the birth of a son, a victory in battle, a carefully worded complaint, praise of the patron's bravery, and the like); and a final section which always concludes with conventional wishes for the well-being and long life of the patron. Not every *qasida* written in Persian had this structure, but the vast majority (perhaps ninety percent or more) did.

LITERARY VERSUS VERNACULAR

By and large accomplished poets and essayists, Chinese literati were not necessarily tied to any particular genre—though they were certainly intimately linked to the general style of writing known as *wenyan(wen)*, usually called Classical Chinese in English, but perhaps more fittingly referred to as Literary Sinitic (henceforth LS). This was an extremely conservative type of writing which, for at least the last two millennia, had come to diverge so radically from all forms of spoken Sinitic (i.e., "Chinese") that it was literally "unsayable." In other words, LS could not be used for unrehearsed, spontaneous conversation and did not function as the form of speech adopted by any segment of society. Instead, individuals (including officials) spoke whatever variety of speech prevailed in the locale where they were born and grew up. These speech forms were termed *fangyan* (lit., "speech [characteristic of a particular] place"), commonly mistranslated as "dialect," but more accurately rendered as "topolect."[19] There were hundreds, if not thousands, of different fangyan, and it is essential to observe that the vast majority were mutually unintelligible.[20]

Here there is a difference with Persian, where even the most elegant and ornate kinds of writing were potentially intelligible to educated auditors—even though they did not represent any particular pattern of daily Persian speech. The disparity is due to the nature of the two writing systems, with Persian employing a phonetic script that essentially transcribed utterances (stilted though they may have been), whereas LS was written with morphosyllabic[21] characters that permitted the proliferation of huge numbers of homograms and starkly dissimilar pronunciations according to the vast range of the multitudinous topolects. In principle, then, a passage of LS would only have been intelligible when read aloud if it had previously been memorized by the auditor and if the auditor's customary topolectal pronunciation of the characters was more or less the same as that of the person reading out the passage. LS was certainly not available for spontaneous conversation, although it is possible that two "speakers" of LS could "converse" with each other on severely limited topics by utilizing a series of quotations, citations, phrases, and expressions that were common "parlance" with both of them. Thus, LS is strictly a book language (i.e., for writing only), one that was neither intended for nor capable of lengthy oral recitation, much less unrehearsed dialog.

The situation with regard to Vernacular Sinitic (VS) is altogether different. In this case, written VS would have been intelligible to listeners, provided they more or less shared the same topolect as the person who read a given text aloud. The contrast with genuine topolectal writing, however, is stark. In fact, aside from Cantonese (particularly Hong Kong Cantonese) and, to a lesser extent, Taiwanese, written forms of the topolects never developed in China. Even written Cantonese and written Taiwanese have extremely limited circulation and application. The chief problem in both cases (and, indeed, for all other topolects) is that many of the basic morphemes of the topolects cannot be represented with the standard character set, enormous though it be.[22] Theoretically, and even practically, it would be easy to write the topolects in a phonetic script, and this has in fact been done with a considerable degree of success for Taiwanese[23] (DeBernardi 1991; Alvin Lin 1999; Christine Lin 1999; Klöter 2005). Nonetheless, cultural proclivities—namely, the identification of the characters as being somehow at the heart of "Chineseness," and the customary desire of topolectal speakers to remain within the Chinese sphere—have precluded the lasting establishment of any form of Sinitic writing aside from LS and VS. All other (besides the relatively uncommon instances of Cantonese and Taiwanese) manifestations of writing in China that claim to be topolectal in nature are either actually VS (very rarely LS) with a mere sprinkling of local lexical elements or tour de force displays of non-standard characters and Romanization (as for Cantonese and Taiwanese) that have not gained widespread acceptance even in their own linguistic communities.[24]

During the Six Dynasties period (220–581), largely under the impact of Buddhism, small bits of vernacular began to creep into certain types of writing, especially translations from Sanskrit (Mair 1994a). By the Tang Dynasty (618–907), a predilection for writing in a semi-vernacular style started to emerge. At first, this new trend was restricted essentially to aficionados of Buddhist popular storytelling (Mair 1983, 1988, 1989). Gradually, however, it came to be adopted by those who wished to record the "sayings" of the Zen (Chan) masters, and eventually was emulated by disciples of several famous Neo-Confucian masters who were desirous of presenting the discourse of the latter as accurately as possible (Hymes 2006). Linguists call the supra-dialectal form of the vernacular that emerged in medieval China a *koine,* and this ultimately led to the establishment of *guanhua* (lit., "officials' talk," i.e., "Mandarin").

The grammar, the syntax, the lexicon—everything about LS was radically unlike even the koine (from which evolved VS writing in China), much less the countless topolects. It is remarkable that New Persian appeared at roughly the same time as the koine did in China. An examination of the causes for the rise of the koine in the Persianate and Sinitic realms is sure to result in valuable insights into the dynamics of cultural systems vis-à-vis historical circumstances.

By the Yuan (1279–1368), Ming (1368–1644), and Qing (1644–1911) periods, a full-blown vernacular literary movement had flowered, but it is crucial to observe that it was limited almost entirely to fiction and drama, precisely those genres that formerly had languished, or remained stillborn, when LS was the only option available for writers. Furthermore, the creators and consumers of this vernacular literature were primarily members of the middle and lower middle classes, such as merchants, entertainers, "failed B.A.'s," local teachers, clerks,[25] and so forth. This type of "vulgar" literature was enjoyed by illiterate women of all classes and even the lowest social strata when read aloud or performed before them by storytellers and entertainers.

In premodern times, VS was never accepted by the literati (the educated body of officialdom and other "proper" intellectuals who commanded LS) as a legitimate form of writing. This all changed radically, however, with the complete collapse of the imperial system in 1911. The end of the imperial bureaucracy also resulted in the cessation (actually already in 1905) of the civil service examinations which functioned as the conduit into officialdom of those who were thoroughly proficient in LS. The final death knell of LS was sounded in 1919 with the outbreak of the May Fourth Movement which included as one of its central tenets the replacement of LS by VS in government, literature, and education (Chow 1960; Schwarcz 1986).

This objective of eliminating LS from the public sphere became official policy under the Republic of China (1912–1949) and was further cemented and expanded under the People's Republic of China (1949–). Today, almost no one can write in exemplary LS, and vulgarization (both haute and basse) continues apace, with English, Japanese, and other lexical and stylistic borrowings flooding both the spoken and the written languages. On the other hand, just as there is a latent consciousness of the need to familiarize Chinese youths with the rudiments of the major thinkers of their nation's past, so is there an awareness on the part of some conservatives of the desirability of reinstituting moderate proficiency in LS. Those who advocate the educational policies of *dujing* ("reading the classics") do so in hopes that a certain amount of classical learning and training in LS will provide a source of stability in a fast-changing world. Likewise, those who call for mandatory training in calligraphy for elementary schoolchildren do so in the belief that it will make them better citizens.

CONCLUSION: THE ENDURING LEGACY

There are numerous indications of the continuing importance in contemporary China of the ancient script and traditional styles of writing. This is evident in the prominent role of calligraphy in public life (Yen 2005; Kraus 1991). Famous calligraphers such as Zhao Puchu (President of the Chinese Buddhist Association from 1980 till his death; 1908–2000) and Qi Gong (a Manchu belonging to the royal clan; 1912–2005), now as in the past, are in great demand to produce plaques, couplets, book titles, and colophons. (Many commentators, however, bemoaned that, with the passing of these two great masters, Chinese calligraphy had come to the end of an era.) Political figures who cannot dash off an appropriate brush-written inscription on the spur of the moment inevitably find themselves in an embarrassing position. Stores that can afford elaborate calligraphic signage are more than willing to hire qualified practitioners of the art. And now, with the advent of digitized photography and advanced printing techniques, illustrated biographies are filled with specimens of handwriting, to a degree that would be unthinkable in the West, particularly since the purpose of including so many letters, memoranda, and notes is not so much for their content as for their capability of displaying the sheer nature of the biographee and his associates as evidenced by their brushwork and penmanship. In short, there are still distinct talismanic and at times transcendental qualities to the entire enterprise of handwriting in China. These attributes are perpetuated through classes in primary school, through special weekend and evening sessions, and through constant inculcation by parents who are concerned that their children will grow up lacking genuine *culture*.

Despite the termination of the civil service examination system, the heritage of elaborate, scribally oriented bureaucracy persisted under the Republic of China and the People's Republic of China. Bureaucratic procedures generating a plethora of written documents are still an essential feature of Chinese officialdom and, indeed, of the daily life of citizens to the extent that it intersects with the world of officials. For instance (and here I speak from the poignant personal experience of Chinese friends and associates), it is absolutely essential to obtain a multitude of written (now generally typed!) documents—all signed with a flourish by the relevant authorities and stamped with the red seals of their bureaus and departments—to accomplish anything that requires government approval (and it seems that most initiatives do require the authorization of a welter of agencies at various levels). Starting a school in Qingdao (home of the famous Germanic beer, Tsingdao) demands a welter of permits and certificates that seem almost impossible to procure. An archeologist from the Xinjiang Uyghur Autonomous Region who wishes to travel to Mongolia for collaborative research needs at least three months lead-time to visit all the offices that must issue the necessary papers for travel outside of the Region. Similar horror tales could be told about virtually all activity involving contact between individuals and the government, and they all boil down to procuring impressive documents. It is noteworthy, however, that most documents nowadays are written in a language that tends more toward the VS end of the stylistic spectrum than to the LS end. Especially at the national level, PRC documents tend to be consciously composed in a largely VS idiom, a mark of commitment to the interests of the proletariat. Still, there is occasional slippage into snippets of LS. Curiously, it is often at the local level that officials tend to wax somewhat more LS in their documents. Perhaps one may conclude that, when it comes to bureaucratic transactions in China, LS still retains residual power and no little pomp.

⋆ ⋆ ⋆

APPENDIX

A NOTE (CHIEFLY BIBLIOGRAPHICAL) ON THE PLACE OF PERSIAN IN CHINESE HISTORY

Some of the bloodiest uprisings in Chinese history have involved Muslims. In certain cases, the retribution was so devastating that it led to tremendous dislocations of the population (e.g., the flight of the Dungans to Kazakhstan and Kirghizstan) and the near extinction of Hui Muslims in regions of the northwest and southwest where they had formerly been dominant (Chu 1966; Forbes 1986; Atwill 2005). Partly for the mutual suspicions that these terrible events engendered, and also partly because of the innate separatist tendencies of Islam vis-à-vis Chinese culture and society, the presence and influence of Muslims from the time of their first appearance in China during the 7th century has generally been understated and undervalued.[26] Despite the fact that there are now more than 20,000,000 Muslims of various sorts (Hui, Uyghur, Kazakh, Dongxiang, Kirghiz, Salar, Tajik, Uzbek, Bonan, and Tatar) in China, having to a degree rebounded from the depopulation of the latter half of the 19th century, they seem to be relatively invisible—except for their *halāl* restaurants (often with Perso-Arabic script in the windows), white skull caps, and scattered mosques. Yet the overall impact of Islam in Chinese history was arguably among the greatest of any foreign religion.[27]

Indeed, it has been alleged that one emperor was so enamored of Islam that he may have converted to this Middle Eastern religion:

> In the second section of the first part of his *La route de la soie,* the late Iranian scholar Aly Mazahéri translates and annotates a Persian text entitled *Khitay-Nāmeh* (A Treatise on China). This text was written by a Bukhara merchant, Ali-Akbèr Khitayi, who was sent by a Samarkand prince on a tributary trade mission to China some time around 1500. His knowledge of and experience in China won him a special nickname, Khitayi, meaning "the Chinese," or "the traveller to China." Probably composed in Tabriz and completed in Constantinople in 1516, the *Khitay-Nāmeh* provides an interesting account through an Iranian looking-glass on the legislature, financial system, economic products, religions, prostitutes, Tibetan travellers, etc. in 16th-century China. Khitayi, who later resided in Constantinople, makes a striking statement in his book that he learned from several traders who had returned from Beijing that the Zhengde emperor (Wuzong, Zhu Houzhao, r. 1506–21) of the Ming Dynasty in China had converted to Islam, thus becoming "le premier empereur chinois à avoir embrassé la vraie Foi." (Mazahéri 1983:160, characters omitted; as quoted in Toh 2000:1, with small adjustments)

Whether the Zhengde emperor actually converted to Islam or not, it is clear from the Chinese sources cited by Toh that he had an "affinity for Islam, or perhaps more precisely, for Persian Sufism" (Toh 2000:3).

Among the more hidden aspects of Islam in China, and in particular of Persianate Islam, is the use of Persian language itself.[28] Persian was undoubtedly present in the EAH from at least the Tang Dynasty onward. Schafer (1963:282b–83b), drawing on work by Nakamura Kushiro and others, refers to Persians and diverse foreigners in Canton and environs who were captured and enslaved on the far southern island of Hainan by the pirate captain Reng Ruofang. He also notices Persian shops in Yangzhou, which lies at the crucial juncture of the Grand Canal and the Yangtze Valley, and fabulously rich Persian merchants in the capital, Chang'an, in the Yellow River Valley—all during the medieval period (Schafer 1951; So 1987–88).

The interfusion of Persian into the Chinese cultural realm described in the preceding paragraph came from the southeastern oceanic route. But Persian had already begun to infiltrate the sphere of Chinese political interest from the northwest through the desert region of ECA. This is attested to by Manichaean and Christian texts in Middle and New Persian in the Turfan collection, a Judaeo-Persian letter from Dandan-Uiliq (one of the earliest New Persian manuscripts of any kind anywhere), and other manuscripts recovered from various sites around the Tarim Basin.[29] The earliest Persian inscription in the EAH is the tombstone of the Zoroastrian Ma (Pahlavi *Mahnus), wife of General Su Liang (Pahlavi Farrokhzad), inscribed both in Pahlavi and Chinese and dated 874 in Xi'an (Huang and Feng 1991:446b–47a).

During the Mongol period (Yuan Dynasty) Persian played a significant role in the far-flung empire that stretched across the whole of Asia and even encroached upon Europe. So important was Persian to the Mongols that they relied on it as a lingua franca and it was taught in special schools (using the *yisitifei [istifa]* script) at the behest of the rulers (Leslie 1981:95; Huang 1986; Morgan 2008).

After the Mongols, the role of Persian continued to be of considerable significance throughout much of the Ming Dynasty, and gained strength during the Manchu period (Qing Dynasty), particularly among Muslim brotherhoods, such as the Naqshbandi (Wang 2001:84; Fletcher 1995). The "Han Kitab," written by Muslim literati and constituting a synthesis of Neo-Confucianism and Islam, was widely distributed during the century and a half between the early 1600s and the late 1700s, and translations from Persian into Chinese were fairly common among Muslims in late imperial China (Ben-Dor Benite 2005). It is particularly intriguing that a Perso-Arabic transcription system called *xiaojin(g)* was devised for Mandarin and other Sinitic languages such as Dungan (the latter normally later written in Cyrillic [Mair 1990]). The *xiaojin(g)* transcription system may be divided into two types, a more demotic style that is mostly straight Sinitic, and a more pretentious style that is laden with somewhat Sinicized Persian and Arabic. This is a hugely important topic with relevance for writing theory and reform, linguistic exchange, and cultural influence that is waiting for an enterprising scholar (or scholars) familiar with Persian and Chinese to tackle.

The place of Persian among Chinese Muslims has also been touched upon by Donald Leslie (1975; 1981; 1986). Sachiko Murata (2000) has carried out fascinating investigations of the Persian sources available to Liu Zhi (ca. 1662–1730), the most important Muslim writer in China, and other Sino-Muslim literati. Barbara Stöcker-Parnian (2003) has studied the intersection of Persian and Chinese learning from the 17th to the 19th centuries. And Françoise Aubin (1998) has made a revealing presentation of the art of writing among Chinese Muslims. Persian continues to be taught in contemporary China (*EI* 5.453a–454a).

By no means is this survey intended to be exhaustive. It is meant purely to give a representative sampling of avenues of research that might be further pursued. Even from this cursory look, however, it is obvious that Persian was an integral part of the Chinese political, economic, and cultural (especially religious) scene from late medieval through late imperial times.

Acknowledgments

I am grateful, first of all, to Brian Spooner and William Hanaway for inviting me to both the conferences (one in Hyderābād, India, and one at the Penn Museum) that resulted in this volume, but also for encouraging me to complete this paper and being patient when I was slow in doing so. In addition, they have continually inspired and instructed me during the past two decades and more through their dedication to the study of all aspects of Persian writing and their erudition concerning the *munshi*s, the quintessential exemplars of the Persian scribal tradition. Appreciation is also due to Joanna Waley Cohen, Jonathan Lipman, Nicholas Sims-Williams, and Oktor Skjærvø for providing valuable references concerning the usage of Persian in Central Asia and East Asia. Likewise, I am indebted to Benjamin Elman, Richard John Lynn, Susan Naquin, Cynthia Brokaw, and Qianshen Bai who kindly offered helpful assistance concerning Chinese scribal practices and calligraphic customs. Thanks are due as well to Jidong Yang, Maiheng Dietrich, and Jiajia Wang for providing me with samples of contemporary bureaucratic documents. John Perry kept me on the straight and narrow concerning possible connections between various early Eurasian postal horse relay systems, and Stephen F. Dale enlightened me about the very different realms of the *munshis* and the *mirzas*. Finally, Ivan Aymat supplied me with detailed information concerning *xiaojin(g)* and Dungan writing.

NOTES

1. It would appear that Iranian peoples were also among the earliest to utilize the camel for transport in arid regions. As masters of these formidable "ships of the desert," the Iranians would have had an advantage over other groups in the development of trading networks (Kuzmina 2007a, 2007b).

2. This account of writing under the Achaemenians draws heavily on Utz (1991), who provides extensive primary and secondary references. See also Frye (1996).

3. I use the word "relative" carefully and judiciously, because I strongly maintain that the East Asian Heartland (EAH) has been part of the Eurasian ecumene since at least the Bronze Age. Nonetheless, situated at the far eastern extremity of the supercontinent, it was less closely tied to seminal events in Central and West Asia than was Persia.

4. Among the numerous general studies of Chinese religion are Yang 1961, Thompson 1969, 1975, Adler 2002, and Overmyer 1986, 1998. Foltz 1999 is especially valuable for understanding the history of the religions that came to EA from the west.

5. The translation given is that of Brooks and Brooks (1998:52), but there are many widely differing interpretations of this passage, especially the second portion, e.g., "If Heaven intends civilization to be destroyed, why was it vested in me?" (Leys 1997:39).

6. Here I shall not enter into the complicated question of the prior evolution of the word *wen* and the character that was used to write it, other than to mention that the earliest meaning of the etymon was "tattoo" (Mair 2003:182b, Mair 2001b:2–3; Karlgren 1972:130–31, no. 475a-g; Schuessler 1987:641b–42a, Schuessler 2007:514). This is utterly ironic in that, from the classical period (post-Confucius) on, tattoo was looked upon as a sure sign of barbarism or criminality. Nonetheless, the actual path of the development of the word *wen* may be schematically represented more or less in the following fashion: tattoo à pattern à writing à culture / civilization. Eventually, various binomial words developed to convey the last four meanings (*wenli, wenzi, wenhua,* and *wenming*), but they were etymologically implicit in the original monosyllabic term *wen*. Of particular interest to readers of this volume are two additional terms closely linked to wen, namely, *wenxue* (literature = *wen* + learning) and *wenxian* (documents = *wen* + respectfully and solemnly offer/present/dedicate/devote). Just as culture (*wenhua*) and literature (*wenxue*) are etymologically linked through wen, the paramount preoccupation of the literati (*ru*), so—as we have seen—are *adab* (etiquette; [literary] culture) and *adabiyāt* (literature) directly related. Furthermore, the primary guardians of *adab* and *adabiyat* in the Persian tradition were the *munshi,* a term which derives from the same Arabic root (*n-sh-ʿ*) as inshāʾ (prose composition, literary writing). Thus, the inherent connection between *adab* and *adabiyāt* is reinforced by the literary predisposition of the *munshi* whose business it is to preserve, practice, and perpetuate them.

7. This elegant formulation ("*adab* as the core of *adabiyāt*") of the relationship between

adab and *adabiyāt* is taken from the editors' introduction to the present volume.

8. The standard works on the examination system in English are Franke 1960, Ho 1962, Menzel [Meskill] 1963, Miyazaki 1976, Elman and Woodside 1994, and Elman 2000. For a succinct, informative introduction to the subject, including a historical sketch that begins in 178 BC, see Dillon 1998:94–96. For additional bibliographical references and annotations, together with a detailed description of degree holders and officials recruited through the examination system, consult Wilkinson 2000:527–29.

9. See Mair 2005, especially the tables on pp. 56–62. It is curious that similarly in the Persianate world, it is difficult to find a dynasty or sultanate after AD 1000 that originated in a community where an Iranian language was spoken at home.

10. The Chinese script, exalted and prestigious though it may have been, reached down into the lives of the illiterate who were affected by it (Hansen 1995; the role of professional scribes is particularly to be noted). Separate treatment would be required to examine adequately the relationship between the Chinese characters and the vast majority of the population who could not read them.

11. The actual term for Ph.D., however, is *boshi,* another exalted official title, for the convoluted story of which see Mair 1992.

12. A comparison of the role of the shuyuan in late medieval, early modern Chinese society and the *madrasa* in Persian society during a comparable period is sure to yield valuable insights into the similarities and differences concerning the educational practices and institutions of the two cultures.

13. For a detailed discussion of the intricate relationship between calligraphy and politics, see McNair 1998.

14. Hucker 1985:223a no. 2154. The designation *hanlin* literally signifies a grove or forest of quills (i.e., writing brushes). Perusal of Hucker's invaluable tome on official titles offers an eye-opening exposure to the labyrinthine intricacies of the imperial Chinese bureaucracy.

15. There are many excellent studies on Chinese historiography, including Gardner 1938, 1961; Han 1955; Leslie, Mackerras, and Wang 1973, 1975; and Twitchett 1992.

16. To use the translation of Nienhauser 1994.

17. See Hightower's important study (1957) on early genre theory, and the introductions to Mair 1994b and 2001a.

18. For an English translation of a typical eight-legged essay, see Qu Qingchun's (d. 1569) "That Which Is Mandated by Heaven Is Called Natur" (Mair 1994b:645–48).

19. Coined by the author, "topolect" has been accepted by the 4th edition of the *American Heritage Dictionary of the English Language,* albeit with a slightly different slant than originally intended (it is expected that the original intention of the coinage will be restored in the 5th edition of the dictionary). Whereas topolect was meant to signify the speech form of any locale, large or small, the editors of the dictionary restricted its usage only to major groupings of Sinitic. Roughly speaking, topolect may be understood as signifying regional languages and local dialects, i.e., speech forms of various places.

20. For this reason, some scholars recommend that the major groups of *fangyan* be referred to as "branches" of Sinitic, which are in turn composed of various "languages," "dialects," and "sub-dialects." This, at least, is how the enormous variety of Sinitic languages should be classified according to strict rules of linguistic taxonomy. It must be noted, however, that—following politico-cultural beliefs—many Chinese maintain that there is a single Han / Sinitic language, and that it differs very little except for pro-

nunciation. How completely out of touch with linguistic reality such a view is may easily be demonstrated by a rudimentary comparison of the vocabulary, grammar, and syntax between, say, Cantonese and Pekingese. For a basic introduction to some of the serious obstacles involved in the scientific classification of Sinitic languages, see Mair 1991. For a sober assessment of the phonological and morphological history of the Sinitic group, see Norman 1988, 2003.

21. Some refer to them as "logographic," which is a less accurate designation. To characterize the characters as "pictographic" or "ideographic" is simply wrong. See De Francis 1984, 1989, and Unger 2004.

22. There are well over 100,000 Chinese characters to contend with, but they cannot account for many of the most common morphemes in Taiwanese. For instance, the particle of subordination, which is far and away the most frequent Taiwanese morpheme, is commonly written with the Roman letter "e" and pronounced somewhat like the English interjection "eh": there is no character with which it may be written. The same is true of innumerable frequent (and not-so-frequent) morphemes in all of the topolects.

23. This is evident from the investigations of Cheung and Bauer 2002, Bauer 1988, Klöter 2005, Cheng 1978, and Groves 2008. See also Mair, "How to Forget Your Mother Tongue and Remember Your National Language," available on the World Wide Web at http://www.pinyin.info/readings/mair/taiwanese.html.

24. After their arrival in the late 16th century, however, Christian missionaries created many romanized writing systems for local Sinitic and non-Sinitic languages. Since the founding of the PRC, all of these have become defunct, though some of the non-Sinitic romanizations persist in modified form.

25. The latter three categories were often filled with men who spent their lives repeatedly failing the civil service examinations.

26. As a matter of fact, much of the shrouded Persian influence on Chinese culture, especially literature, was long ago exposed in an extraordinary work by J.C. Coyajee entitled *Cults & Legends of Ancient Iran & China* (ca. 1936). Unfortunately, Coyajee's work itself is almost as unknown (even to Chinese and Persian specialists) as are the materials he describes. Furthermore, Coyajee's treatise must be used with some caution, since he occasionally overreaches and is insufficiently familiar with Sinological and Iranological niceties. Nonetheless, students of both Chinese literature and Iranian would profit from a close, critical reading of Coyajee.

27. This covert quality of the Iranian peoples and their cultures in the EAH is in sharp contrast to the overt nature of Indian influence in China after the arrival of Buddhism there in the 1st century AD.

28. The first place to turn for gaining an appreciation of the place of Persian in China are the articles in *Encyclopaedia Iranica* by Chen, Huang and Feng, and Skjaervø.

29. Personal communication from Nicholas Sims-Williams (February 23, 2007). See also Foltz 1999:15, 78–79, 99. We know for certain that speakers of other Middle Iranian languages were active as key players in Buddhist cultural politics between the Tarim Basin and the Gansu Corridor (the Khotanese) and as masterful merchants all the way from western Central Asia to the Tang capital at Chang'an (the Sogdians). Indeed, the Sogdo-Turkic general An Lushan (703–757), whose name is a partially abbreviated transcription of Arsacid (a vague Chinese reference to his supposed ultimate Bukharan origins) Rowshan (cf. Roxan), unleashed a rebellion that almost toppled the

Tang Dynasty. The far-ranging activities of the Sogdians are evident from the fact that An Lushan's career was launched in Manchuria (Mallory and Mair 2000, Pulleyblank 1955, Lerner 2005).

Abbreviation

EI = Encyclopaedia Iranica

REFERENCES

Adler, Joseph A. 2002. *Chinese Religions.* London: Routledge. This same book published in America was called *Chinese Religious Traditions* (Upper Saddle River, NJ: Prentice Hall, 2002).

Anthony, David W. 2007. *The Horse, the Wheel, and Language: How Bronze-Age Riders from the Eurasian Steppes Shaped the Modern World.* Princeton: Princeton University Press.

Atwill, David G. 2005. *The Chinese Sultanate: Islam, Ethnicity and the Panthay Rebellion in Southwest China, 1856–1873.* Stanford: Stanford University Press.

Aubin, Françoise. 1998. L'art de l'écriture chez les musulmans de Chine. In *Calligraphies: Hommage à Nja Mahdaoui. Horizons Maghrébins*, nos. 35–36:29–43. Cologne.

Bailey, H.W. 1949. Irano-Indica II. *Bulletin of the School of Oriental and African Studies* 13(1): 121–39.

Bauer, Robert S. 1988. Written Cantonese of Hong Kong. *Cahiers de Linguistique Asie* 17(2): 245–93.

Ben-Dor Benite, Zvi. 2005. *The Dao of Muhammad: A Cultural History of Muslims in Late Imperial China.* Cambridge, MA: Harvard University Asia Center.

Billeter, Jean François. 1990. *The Chinese Art of Writing.* New York: Skira/Rizzoli.

Bischoff, F.A. 1963. *La Forêt des Pinceaux: étude sur l'Académie du Han-lin sous la dynastie des T'ang et traduction du Han lin tche.* Paris: Presses Universitaires de France.

Bol, Peter K. 1992. *"This Culture of Ours": Intellectual Transitions in T'ang and Sung China.* Stanford: Stanford University Press.

Brooks, E. Bruce, and A. Taeko Brooks, trans. and comm. 1998. *The Original Analects: Sayings of Confucius and His Successors.* New York: Columbia University Press.

Chen, Da-sheng. 1991. Persian Settlements in Southeastern China during the T'ang, Sung, and Yuan Dynasties. *EI* 4:443b–46b.

Cheng, Robert L. (Zheng Liangwei). 1978. Taiwanese Morphemes in Search of Chinese Characters. *Journal of Chinese Linguistics* 6(2): 306–14.

Cheung Kwan-hin, and Robert S. Bauer. 2002. *The Representation of Cantonese with Chinese Characters. Journal of Chinese Linguistics* monograph series, 18.

Berkeley: University of Berkeley.

Chow Tse-tsung. 1960. *The May Fourth Movement: Intellectual Revolution in Modern China*. Cambridge, MA: Harvard University Press.

Chu Wen-djang. 1966. *The Moslem Rebellion in North-West China, 1862–1878: A Study of Government Minority Policy*. The Hague: Mouton.

Connery, Christopher Leigh. 1998. *The Empire of the Text: Writing and Authority in Early Imperial China*. Lanham: Rowman and Littlefield.

Coyajee, J.C. ca. 1936. *Cults and Legends of Ancient Iran and China*. Bombay: Jehangir B. Karani's Sons.

DeBernardi, Jean. 1991. *Linguistic Nationalism: The Case of Southern Min*. Sino-Platonic Papers, 25, pp. 1–22, 3 figs. Philadelphia: University of Pennsylvania, Dept. of Asian and Middle Eastern Studies.

De Francis, John. 1984. *The Chinese Language: Fact and Fantasy*. Honolulu: University of Hawai'i Press.

—— 1989. *Visible Speech: The Diverse Oneness of Writing Systems*. Honolulu: University of Hawai'i Press.

Dillon, Michael, ed. 1998. *China: A Historical and Cultural Dictionary*. Durham East Asia Series. Richmond, Surrey: Curzon.

Elman, Benjamin A. 2000. *A Cultural History of Civil Examinations in Late Imperial China*. Berkeley: University of California Press.

—— 1984. *From Philosophy to Philology: Intellectual and Social Aspects of Change in Late Imperial China*. Cambridge, MA: Harvard University, Council on East Asian Studies.

Elman, Benjamin A., and Alexander Woodside, eds. 1994. *Education and Society in Late Imperial China, 1600–1900*. Berkeley: University of California Press.

Fletcher, Joseph. 1995. *Studies on Chinese and Islamic Inner Asia,* ed. Beatrice Forbes Manz. Aldershot: Variorum.

Foltz, Richard C. 1999. *Religions of the Silk Road: Overland Trade and Cultural Exchange from Antiquity to the Fifteenth Century*. New York: St. Martin's.

Forbes, Andrew D.W. 1986. *Warlords and Muslims in Chinese Central Asia: A Political History of Republican Sinkiang 1911–1949*. Cambridge: Cambridge University Press.

Franke, Wolfgang. 1960. *The Reform and Abolition of the Traditional Chinese Examination System*. Cambridge, MA: Harvard University, Center for East Asian Studies.

Frye, Richard N. 1996. *The Heritage of Central Asia: From Antiquity to the Turkish Expansion*. Princeton: Markus Wiener.

Gardner, Charles S. 1938. *Chinese Traditional Historiography*. Cambridge, MA: Harvard University Press. Rev. ed. 1961.

Gharib, B. 1995. *Sogdian Dictionary: Sogdian-Persian-English*. Tehran: Farhangan.

Groves, Julie M. 2008. *Language or Dialect—or Topolect? A Comparison of the Attitudes of Hong Kongers and Mainland Chinese towards the Status of Cantonese*. Sino-Platonic Papers, 179, pp. 1–103. Philadelphia: University of Pennsylvania, Dept. of Asian and Middle Eastern Studies.

Han, Yu-shan. 1955. *Elements of Chinese Historiography*. Hollywood, CA: W.M. Hawley.

Hansen, Valerie. 1995. *Negotiating Daily Life in Traditional China: How Ordinary People Used Contracts, 600–1400*. New Haven: Yale University Press.

Harmatta, J. 1997. Languages and Scripts in Graeco-Bactria and the Saka Kingdoms. In *History of the Civilizations of Central Asia*, Vol. 2, ed. János Harmatta, B.N. Puri, and G.F. Etemdai, pp. 397–416. Paris: UNESCO.

Heinrichs, Wolfhart. 1997. Prosimetrical Genres in Classical Arabic Literature. In *Prosimetrum: Crosscultural Perspectives on Narratives in Prose and Verse*, ed. Joseph Harris and Karl Reichl, pp. 249–75. Cambridge: D.S. Brewer.

Hightower, James R. 1957. The *Wen Hsüan* and Genre Theory. *Harvard Journal of Asiatic Studies* 20(3-4): 512–33.

Ho, Ping-ti. 1962. *The Ladder of Success in Imperial China: Aspects of Social Mobility, 1368–1911*. New York: Columbia University Press.

Huang, Shi-jian. 1986. The Persian Language in China during the Yuan Dynasty. In *Papers on Far Eastern History* 34:83–95.

Huang, Shi-jian, and Ibrahim Feng Jin-yuan. 1991. Persian Language and Literature in China. *EI* 4:446b–49b.

Hucker, Charles O. 1985. *A Dictionary of Official Titles in Imperial China*. Stanford: Stanford University Press.

Hymes, Robert. 2006. Getting the Words Right: Speech, Vernacular Language, and Classical Language in Song Neo-Confucian "Records of Words." *Journal of Song-Yuan Studies* 36:25–55.

Karlgren, Bernhard. 1972. *Grammata Serica Recensa*. Reprint. Stockholm: Museum of Far Eastern Antiquities. (Museum of Far Eastern Antiquities *Bulletin* no. 29 [1957]).

Klöter, Henning. 2005. *Written Taiwanese*. Studia Formosiana (Ruhr University, Bochum), vol. 2. Wiesbaden: Harrassowitz.

Kraus, Richard Curt. 1991. *Brushes with Power: Modern Politics and the Chinese Art of Calligraphy*. Berkeley: University of California Press.

Kuz'mina, Elena E. 2007a. *The Origin of the Indo-Iranians*, ed. J.P. Mallory. Leiden Indo-European Etymological Dictionary Series, 3. Leiden: Brill.

—— 2007b. The Prehistory of the Silk Road. In *Encounters with Asia*, ed. Victor H. Mair. Philadelphia: University of Pennsylvania Press.

Ledderose, Lothar. 1986. Chinese Calligraphy: Its Aesthetic Dimension and Social Function. *Orientations* (Oct.): 35–50.

Lee, Thomas H.C. 1999. *Education in Traditional China: A History*. Leiden: E.J. Brill.

Lerner, Judith A. 2005. *Aspects of Assimilation: The Funerary Practices and Furnishings of Central Asians in China*. Sino-Platonic Papers, 168, pp. 1–51, i–v, 9 plates. Philadelphia: University of Pennsylvania, Dept. of Asian and Middle Eastern Studies.

Leslie, Donald Daniel. 1975. Arabic Sources. In *Essays on the Sources for Chinese History*, ed. Donald D. Leslie, Colin Mackerras, and Wang Gungwu, pp. 147–53. Columbia: University of South Carolina Press.

—— 1981. *Islamic Literature in Chinese, Late Ming and Early Ch'ing: Books, Authors and Associates*. Canberra: Canberra College of Advanced Education.

—— 1986. *Islam in Traditional China: A Short History to 1800*. Canberra: Canberra College of Advanced Education.

—— 2006. *Islam in Traditional China: A Bibliographical Guide*. Monumenta Serica Monograph Series, 54. Sankt Augustin: Monumenta Serica Institute.

Leslie, Donald D., Colin Mackerras, and Wang Gungwu, eds. 1975. *Essays on the Sources for Chinese History*. Columbia, SC: University of South Carolina Press. Originally published in 1973 by Australian National University.

Lewis, Mark Edward. 1999. *Writing and Authority in Early China*. Albany: State University of New York Press.

Leys, Simon, trans. and annot. 1997. *The Analects of Confucius*. New York: W.W. Norton. (© Pierre Ryckmans.)

Lin, Alvin. 1999. *Writing Taiwanese: The Development of Modern Written Taiwanese*. Sino-Platonic Papers, 89, pp. 1–4, 1-41, 1-4. Philadelphia: University of Pennsylvania, Dept. of Asian and Middle Eastern Studies.

Lin, Christine Louise. 1999. *The Presbyterian Church in Taiwan and the Advocacy of Local Autonomy*. Sino-Platonic Papers, 92, pp. i–xiii, 1–136. Philadelphia: University of Pennsylvania, Dept. of Asian and Middle Eastern Studies.

Liu, Adam Yuen-cheng. 1981. *The Hanlin Academy, 1644–1850*. Hamden, CT: Archon, Shoestring.

Mair, Victor H., trans. 1983. *Tun-huang Popular Narratives*. Cambridge: Cambridge University Press.

—— 1988. *Painting and Performance: Chinese Picture Recitation and Its Indian Genesis*. Honolulu: University of Hawai'i Press.

—— 1989. *T'ang Transformation Texts: A Study of the Buddhist Contribution to the Rise of Vernacular Fiction and Drama in China*. Harvard-Yenching Institute Monograph Series, 28. Cambridge, MA: Harvard University Council on East Asian Studies.

—— 1990. *Implications of the Soviet Dungan Script for Chinese Language Reform*. Sino-Platonic Papers, 18, pp. A1–19. Philadelphia: University of Pennsylvania, Dept. of Asian and Middle Eastern Studies.

—— 1991. *What Is a Chinese 'Dialect/Topolect'? Reflections on Some Key Sino-English Linguistic Terms*. Sino-Platonic Papers, 19, pp. 1–31. Philadelphia: University of Pennsylvania, Dept. of Asian and Middle Eastern Studies.

—— 1992. Perso-Turkic Bakshi = Mandarin Po-shih: Learned Doctor. *Journal of Turkish Studies* (Türklük Bilgisi Arastirmalari) 16:117–27.

—— 1994a. Buddhism and the Rise of the Written Vernacular in East Asia: The Making of National Languages. *Journal of the American Oriental Society* 53(3): 707–51.

——, ed. 1994b. *The Columbia Anthology of Traditional Chinese Literature.* New York: Columbia University Press.

—— 1997. The Prosimetric Form in the Chinese Literary Tradition. In *Prosimetrum: Crosscultural Perspectives on Narratives in Prose and Verse,* ed. Joseph Harris and Karl Reichl, pp. 365–85. Cambridge: D.S. Brewer.

——, ed. 2001a. *The Columbia History of Chinese Literature.* New York: Columbia University Press.

—— 2001b. Introduction: The Origins and Impact of Literati Culture. In *The Columbia History of Chinese Literature,* ed. Victor H. Mair, pp. 1–15. New York: Columbia University Press.

—— 2003. The Horse in Late Prehistoric China: Wresting Culture and Control from the "Barbarians." In *Prehistoric Steppe Adaptation and the Horse,* ed. Marsha Levine, Colin Renfrew, and Katie Boyle, pp. 163–87. McDonald Institute Monographs. Cambridge: McDonald Institute for Archaeological Research, University of Cambridge.

—— 2005. The North(west)ern Peoples and the Recurrent Origins of the "Chinese" State. In *The Teleology of the Modern Nation-State: Japan and China,* ed. Joshua A. Fogel, pp. 46–84, 205–17. Philadelphia: University of Pennsylvania Press.

Mallory, J.P., and Victor H. Mair. 2000. *The Tarim Mummies: Ancient China and the Mystery of the Earliest Peoples from the West.* London: Thames and Hudson.

Mazahéri, Aly. 1983. *La route de la soie.* Première partie, 2, *Le traité de la Chine de Sayyid Ali-Akbèr.* Paris: SPAG Papyrus.

McNair, Amy. 1998. *The Upright Brush: Yan Zhenqing's Calligraphy and Song Literati Politics.* Honolulu: University of Hawai'i Press.

Menzel (Meskill), Johanna M., ed. 1963. *The Chinese Civil Service: Career Open to Talent?* Boston: Heath.

Miyazaki, Ichisada. 1976. *China's Examination Hell: The Civil Service Examinations of Imperial China,* trans. Conrad Schirokauer. New York: Weatherhill. Japanese original 1963.

Murata Sachiko. 2000. *Chinese Gleams of Sufi Light: Wang Tai-yü's Great Learning of the Pure and Real and Liu Chih's Displaying the Concealment of the Real Realm, with a New Translation of Jami's* Lawa'ih *from the Persian by William C. Chittick.* Albany: State University of New York Press.

Naquin, Susan. 2000. *Peking: Temples and City Life, 1400–1900.* Berkeley: University of California Press.

Nienhauser, William H., Jr., ed. 1994– . *The Grand Scribe's Records.* Bloomington, IN: Indiana University Press.

Norman, Jerry. 1988. *Chinese.* Cambridge Language Surveys. Cambridge: Cambridge University Press.

—— 2003. The Chinese Dialects: Phonology. In *The Sino-Tibetan Languages,* ed. Graham Thurgood and Randy J. LaPolla, pp. 72–83. London: Routledge.

Ostler, Micholas. 2005. *Empires of the Word.* New York: HarperCollins.

Overmyer, Daniel L. 1986. *Religions of China: The World as a Living System.* San Francisco: Harper & Row. 2nd ed. 1998 (Prospect Heights, IL: Waveland).

Pulleyblank, Edwin G. 1955. *The Background to the Rebellion of An Lu-shan.* London Oriental Series, 4. London: Oxford University Press.

Schafer, Edward H. 1951. Iranian Merchants in T'ang Dynasty Tales. In *Semitic and Oriental Studies. A Volume Presented to William Popper (Professor of Semitic Languages, Emeritus) on the Occasion of His Seventy-Fifth Birthday (October 29, 1949),* ed. Walter J. Fischel, pp. 403–22. Berkeley: University of California Press.

—— 1963. *The Golden Peaches of Samarkand: A Study of T'ang Exotics.* Berkeley: University of California Press.

Schuessler, Axel. 1987. *A Dictionary of Early Zhou Chinese.* Honolulu: University of Hawai'i Press.

—— 2007. *ABC Etymological Dictionary of Old Chinese.* Honolulu: University of Hawai'i Press.

Schwarcz, Vera. 1986. *The Chinese Enlightenment: Intellectuals and the Legacy of the May Fourth Movement of 1919.* Berkeley: University of California Press.

Shaked, Saul. 1987. Aramaic. *EI* 2:250–61.

Skjaervø, P.O. 1991. Iranian Words in Chinese Texts. *EI* 5:449b–52b.

So, Francis K.H. 1987 1988. Middle Easterners in the T'ang Tales. *Tamkang Review* 18(1-4): 259–75.

Stöcker-Parnian, Barbara. 2003. *Jingtang Jiaoyu—die Bücherhallen Erziehung: Entstehung und Entwicklung der islamischen Erziehung in den chinesischen Hui-Gemeinden vom 17.– 19. Jahrhundert.* Europäische Hochschulschriften Reihe 27, Asiatische und Afrikanische Studien, Bd. 88. Frankfurt-am-Main: Peter Lang.

Stolper, Matthew Wolfgang, and Jan Tavernier. 2007. An Old Persian Administrative Tablet from the Persepolis Fortification. Persepolis Fortification Archive Project, 1. *Achaemenid Research on Texts and Archaeology (ARTA* 2007.001). Electronic resource; see http://www.achemenet.com/document/2007.001-Stolper-Tavernier.pdf.

Thompson, Laurence G. 1969. *Chinese Religion: An Introduction.* Belmont, CA: Dickenson. 2nd ed. 1975 (Encino, CA: Dickenson).

Toh, Hoong Teik. 2000. *Shaykh 'Alam: The Emperor of Early Sixteenth-Century China.* Sino-Platonic Papers, 110, pp. 1–20. Philadelphia: University of Pennsylvania, Dept. of Asian and Middle Eastern Studies.

Tsien, Tsuen-Hsuin. 2004. *Written on Bamboo and Silk: The Beginnings of Chinese Books and Inscriptions.* 2nd ed. Chicago: University of Chicago Press.

Twitchett, Denis. 1992. *The Writing of Official History under the T'ang.* Cambridge: Cambridge University Press.

Unger, J. Marshall. 2004. *Ideogram: Chinese Characters and the Myth of Disembodied Meaning.* Honolulu: University of Hawai'i Press.

Utz, David A. 1991. *Language, Writing, and Tradition in Iran.* Sino-Platonic

Papers, 24, pp. 1–24. Philadelphia: University of Pennsylvania, Dept. of Asian and Middle Eastern Studies.

Walton, Linda. 1999. *Academies and Society in Southern Sung China.* Honolulu: University of Hawai'i Press.

Wang, Jianping. 2001. *Glossary of Chinese Islamic Terms.* Richmond, Surrey: Curzon, on behalf of the Nordic Institute of Asian Studies.

Waquet, Françoise. 2001. *Latin or the Empire of a Sign: From the Sixteenth to the Twentieth Centuries,* trans. John Howe. London: Verso. First published in 1998 as *Le Latin ou l'empire d'un signe: XVIᵉ–XXᵉ siècle* (Paris: Éditions Albin Michel).

Wilkinson, Endymion. 2000. *Chinese History: A Manual.* Rev. and enl. Cambridge, MA: Harvard University Asia Center and Harvard-Yenching Institute.

Yang, C.K. 1961. *Religion in Chinese Society: A Study of Contemporary Social Functions of Religion and Some of Their Historical Factors.* Berkeley: University of California Press.

Yang, Jidong. 2007. The Making, Writing, and Testing of Decisions in the Tang Government: A Study of the Role of the Pan in the Literary Bureaucracy of Medieval China. *Chinese Literature: Essays, Articles, Reviews* 29:129–67.

Yee, Chiang. 1973. *Chinese Calligraphy: An Introduction to Its Aesthetic and Technique.* 3rd ed., rev. and enl. Cambridge, MA: Harvard University Press.

Yen, Yuehping. 2005. *Calligraphy and Power in Contemporary Chinese Society.* London: Routledge.

Zi, Étienne. 1894. *Pratique des examens littéraires en Chine.* Variétés sinologiques 5. Chang-hai: Impr. de la Mission Catholique à l'Orphelinat de T'ou-sè-wè. Taipei: Ch'eng-wen, reprinted 1971.

Afterword

We have followed the trajectory of written Persian from its emergence as a new koine well over a millennium ago down to its recent fragmentation and decline, and we have indicated how comparison of Persian with the parallel trajectories of Latin and Chinese can illuminate the role of writing in world history better than the study of a single tradition of literacy. At the beginning of the period covered in this volume, Persianate civilization was at the vanguard of human achievement. At the end it had been overtaken by the Latinate West. Does our explanation of the success of Persian imply a similar explanation of its decline?

We have argued that the remarkable record of Persian was a function of the social models that were expressed in it, the unchanging configuration of society that privileged it, and the way the practice of writing was embedded within it. The process began with the transformation of society that was brought about by the Arab conquest of the Sasanian Empire and the establishment of a new legal system, which broke down the structures of an earlier period and allowed the development of new social forms over a vast area. Persian facilitated this process, because it carried over from the Sasanian period many models that were useful in the development of sultanates that filled the power vacuum left by a declining caliphate in the 9th and 10th centuries. Latinate models similarly facilitated the redevelopment of the cultural and economic life of western Europe after the fall of the Roman Empire. But the Persianate case was different in that the process was encouraged by the openness of the Islamic outlook: the Caliphate evolved into a symbolic center and the civilization as a whole worked for a millennium without any central authority. For most of the millennium the traveler could pass freely from the Atlantic coast to China and south to the Maldive Islands without restriction on trade or residence. Why did this era end? We cannot leave this investigation without acknowledging that the association of Persian with the advance of civilization raises an awkward question about its similar association with its decline, with the failure of western Asia to keep up with developments elsewhere in the world since the 18th century. A full treatment of this question would require another book. But the answer implied by the arguments of this book may be stated briefly as a conclusion.

Why would Persianate civilization fail to change in step with the world around it, when to begin with it had outstripped the world around it? The relationship between writing and social organization suggests an answer to the first clause of this sentence as well as the second. The emergence and spread of Persian was a function of the revolutionary reorganization of society that resulted from the Arabo-Islamic conquest. Persian emerged as a new koine within two hundred years of that conquest, which had over-turned the centralized Sasanian imperial regime in the 7th century. But then for a thousand years nothing happened to bring about a similar transfor-mation. The recurrent warfare throughout the Persianate world and the rise and fall of sultanates did not serve the same purpose. Each new ruler depended on the same social configuration for both legitimacy and funding (cf. Crone 1989). Nothing happened to change that configuration. Nothing happened in Persianate civilization comparable to what happened in the West (in the 16th-century loss of the central authority vested in the Church) that would allow a comparable reorganization of social life at the end of the medieval period—until the arrival of Western imperial authority.

In the West transformational change began with the Black Death in the mid-14th century. As a result of the unprecedented death rate of these years, over such a large area of northwestern Europe, large holes were torn in the social fabric, which opened up opportunities to the survivors. The movement thus generated disturbed the stability of society and led to ques-tioning of the order of the world, which eventually facilitated the Reforma-tion—one of the most comprehensive reorganizations of society in world history. The delegitimization of the Church's authority in the first half of the 16th century led to a complete reevaluation of the legitimacy of all forms of authority and organization.

The removal of the old authority opened the way for the print revolu-tion (cf. Eisenstein 1979). "A culture which the need for memorisation ren-ders static is replaced by a culture liberated by print to put all its powers into original thinking and advance…The new print culture printed everything" (Yates 1979:60). Under the Persian language and its cultural code (*adab*) there was no incentive for change. The writing class controlled not only literacy but also numeracy (see Spooner and Hanaway 2009), and protected its vested interests. Nothing happened to facilitate any social transformation until it was forced by the intrusion of Western interests, in what we now know as the colonial period.

Change was finally generated from outside, by Western imperialism. Colonial administrations killed the dynamism of the Persianate socio-political systems. When they withdrew in the 20th century they left a void which was immediately filled by new ideas and new forms of organization. The change is more obvious in Iran, which actively revolutionized its society in 1979, than in India or Pakistan which sought to build on the imported Western administrative system. But in both these and other Persianate cases the relationship between written language and society has been transformed by complete socio-political reorganization.

Social change has been accelerating noticeably for a generation. There is still much in the present both in western Asia and in the West that cannot be understood except in its historical context, but much that is new. In England, the way you talk to the Queen may not have changed; but the way you talk to your father has. The conservatism of ceremony and ritual maintains an apparent continuity with the past, even while the reality of the present is changing out of recognition. In Iran and Pakistan *adab* still (at least for the time being) provides the code against which day-to-day interaction is evaluated, even though the quality of interaction has changed.

We have come to the end of the age of writing as we knew it. The digital revolution now is comparable to the print revolution of 400 years ago. SMS, icons, and widgets are everywhere, leaving the written text in the dust.

Brian Spooner
William L. Hanaway

REFERENCES

Crone, Patricia. 1989. *Preindustrial Societies.* Oxford: Blackwell.

Eisenstein, Elizabeth L. 1979. *The Printing Press as an Agent of Change.* Cambridge: Cambridge University Press.

Spooner, Brian, and William L. Hanaway. 2009. Siyaq: Persianate Numerical Notation and Numeracy. In *Oxford Handbook of the History of Mathematics,* ed. Eleanor Robson and Jacqueline Stedall, pp. 429–47. Oxford: Oxford University Press.

Yates, Francis. 1979. Print Culture. *Encounter* 52(4): 59–64.

Glossary

Key: AM=Anwar Moazzam; AS=Aslam Syed; D=Darling;
DM=Morgan; F=Fischer; H=Hanaway; JF=Farrell; N=Nawid; M=Mitchell, P=Perry;
S=Spooner; SM=Morton; VM=Mair

Words defined in the text upon first appearance are generally not included here.

Abdāli (N): an Afghan tribe that assumed the name of Durrāni in the 18th
century

abjad (M): the system of numerical notation based on selected letters of the
Arabic alphabet

adab (M): a corpus of linguistic and behaviorial models in Persianate culture

adabiyāt, adabiyyāt (H): literature

adib (H): a littérateur

ahl-i qalam (H): a man (or men) of the pen, a writer, scribe, or secretary

amir (S): military commander

aphesis (P): the dropping of an unaccented initial vowel

`ārif (S): one having gnostic knowledge

`aruz (P): prosody

Ashraf al-vuzarā (S): prime minister

Āstāna-yi Quds (M): the shrine of the eighth Shi`ite Imam, `Ali Rizā, at
Mashhad (Meshed)

Atābeg (M): a noble, vizier, or tutor, esp. to princes

āya(h) (M): a verse or rhetorical unit of a Sura or chapter of the Qur'ān

Bactrian (M): a Middle Iranian language once spoken in what is today northern Afghanistan, surviving only in epigraphic inscriptions

bait, bayt (M): a verse of classical Arabic or Persianate poetry

Bektāshi (M): an order of dervishes founded in eastern Turkey in the 14th
century, still active today

Bey, Beg (D): an Ottoman Turkish provincial governor; a rank or title

buduh (M): a magic square (see *EI* 14:370, s.v. *jafr*)

caliphate. See Khilafat

calque (P): a loan translation, e.g., Fr. *gratte-ciel* for Eng. skyscraper

chancery, chancellery (D): the office of the secretaries in a ruler's court

contact vernacular (P): a well-established language which is also the mother-tongue of some influential group of speakers

creole: a language that has evolved from a pidgin to serve as the native language of a speech community

dabirestān (H): traditionally a school for reading and writing; today, a middle school

Dakkhani (AM): a regional form of Urdu used in the Deccan, southern India

Dār al-Inshā, dārulinshā (N): a chancellery

dār al-Saltana (N): the capital city

defterdar (D): Turkish spelling of Pers. *daftardār,* a keeper of records, Minister of Finance

dehqān (P): a landowner; today, a farmer

dibācha (M): Introduction (to a book)

diglossia (P): a systematic distinction in grammar and lexicon between "high" and "low" stylistic registers of language use in a particular community

dihqān (AS): See *dehqān*

diplomatics (D): the study of the physical qualities of documents, and the spatial organization of writing in them

dittography (SM): unintentional repetition of letters or words by a copyist

divān, diwān (M, AS): (a) collected poems of a poet; (b) government department

ikhvāniyyāt, ekhvāniyat (H): letters between friends or social equals

enshā (D, N). See *inshā*

epideictic (JF): rhetorical category of poetry, generally in praise or blame of something; occasional poetry

etymon (P): word or morpheme from which a later word is derived

farhang (P): dictionary

farmān (M): written order or command; edict

ferman (D, N): Turkish spelling of Pers. *farmān*

fihrist (M): table of contents, catalogue, index; a famous Arabic bibliography by Ibn Nadim (10th cent.)

fiqh (N): Islamic jurisprudence

garmsir (AS): geographical area with warm winters

ghazal (M): monorhyme lyric poem of generally 7–14 lines in Persian, usually meant to be sung

ghāzi (M): Islamic warrior for the faith

ghuluww, ghuluvv (M): certain Shi'a sects displaying extreme or antinomian
forms of practice

hadith (N): accepted record of an utterance or act of the Prophet Muhammad

haplography (SM): unintentional writing of a letter or word, or a series of
letters or words, once, when it should be written twice

haram (SM): the sacred enclosure in the shrine at Mecca

Hindavi (AM): earlier Persian word for Hindi

homoglossia: absence of diglossia

inshā, enshā (AM): written composition; a style of composition cultivated
by chancellery scribes

izhārāt (AM): declarations or statements

jahāndāri (AS): monarchy, rule

jong (M): literary collection or miscellany

Jumāda I (M): fifth month of the Islamic lunar year [also given as Jumādi
al-avval]

kadkhudā, kadkhoda (H): village head-man

kātib (M): scribe or secretary

ketāba (H): writing; an inscription

khān (N): noble, ruler, or governor (Mongol title, assimilated throughout
the Persianate world)

khānate (N): area governed by a *khān*

Khwārazm (P): region that historically included the lower valley of the
Oxus River and extended west to the Caspian Sea and east to Bukhara

Khilāfat, Caliphate (N): the office or domain of the caliph

Khwāndiyya, Khvandiyya (M): Sufi order that flourished during the Safavid
period (16th-18th cent.) in Iran

Kitābkhāna-yi Majlis-i shurā-yi Islāmi: the library of the Iranian *majles* (parliament)

koine (P, AS): standard language, rooted in a heritage of written genres, in
use over a large area irrespective of local variation in spoken language.
It was the term used for Hellenistic Greek, meaning "Common (Language)." The standardization of a koine is a consequence of its being
rooted in the practice of writing, unlike a lingua franca in which usage

varies independently of any written form

Koran (P): anglicized spelling of Arab. Qur'ān

Kufic (SM): early, formal style of the Arabic script

Kulturbund (P): culture area

loya-jirga (N): grand council of elders (in Pashtun cultural tradition)

madrasa (VM): traditional school. Also general term for modern school. See also *medrese*

Mahdi (M): twelfth and last Shi'ite Imam (in the Twelver tradition), who will return at the end of time

majmu'ah (M): collection, compendium, miscellany

malfuzāt (AS): words, sayings; the conversations or "table talk" of renowned Sufi shaikhs

mansab (AS): office or position (Mughal Empire)

marzban (AS): landholder, local ruler; lit. "border lord"

masnavi, mathnavi, masnawi (AS): poem in rhyming couplets

matres lectionis (P): consonant used to indicate a vowel in the Perso-Arabic and other Semitic alphabets (pl. of Latin *mater lectionis,* "mother of reading")

Māwarā un-Nahr (AS): Transoxiana, lands east and north of the Oxus River

medrese: Turkish spelling of Arab./Pers. *madrasa*

mu'ammā, mo'ammā (M): riddle

muchalka (AS): receipt, acceptance letter. See also *tamassuk-e qabuliyat*

muharrir (AS): scribe or secretary

mujtahed (Introduction): Muslim scholar qualified to decide issues of Islamic law (shari'a)

munsha'āt (M): writings, things written

munshi, monshi (H): scribe, secretary

munshi-bāshi (N): chief secretary

mutaqāreb, motaqāreb (N): Persian poetic meter, generally used for narrative poetry

naskh (SM): style of the Arabic script developed in the 9th century and still employed today

nasta'liq (N): style of the Perso-Arabic script developed in the 14th century and widely used in the Persianate world since then

Nauruz (M): Persian New Year, at the vernal equinox

nezāmiya, nizāmiya, nizāmiyya (H): educational institution, begun by the Seljuq vizier Nizām al-Mulk, originally to educate a cadre of government servants *nisba* (M, P): the element of an Arabic personal name that refers to lineage

Nişancı (D): Ottoman official who inscribed the Sultan's *tughra* on official documents

Orkhon, Orhan (D): a river in northern Mongolia, in which region the earliest Turkic inscriptions were found

orthoepy (P): customary pronunciation of a language

pādishāh, pādeshāh (D): Persian title of rulers of kingdoms and empires, often translated "king"

paronomasia (M): word play

pençe (D): signature of officials other than the sultan in Ottoman administration

pidgin: a simplified form of language, with limited vocabulary, that has emerged for purposes of communication between people who do not share a common language

qa'an (N): Mongol royal title

qasida(h) (M, AS): monorhyme poem of a serious nature (usually long), generally intended for declamation in a public setting

qawwāl (AS): traditional South Asian singer of Sufi or religious songs

qawwāli (AS): singing of Sufi or religious songs in South Asia

raqam (M): decree, written order

reisülküttab (D): head scribe, the Ottoman Minister of Foreign Affairs

robā'i, rubā'i (M): quatrain

sāhib (F): owner, master, Mr. A title of respect

saj' (M)`: rhymed prose

sawād (M): blackness; environs, suburbs

Shāh-Nāma, Shāhnāma (SM): Persian national epic, completed by Abu al-Qasim Firdawsi ca. AD 1010

Shāhinshāh, Shāhanshāh (M): a Persian royal title, "Kings of Kings"

shari'a(h) (D): Islamic code of law, based on the Qur'an and records of the acts and sayings of the Prophet Muhammad

Shawwāl (M): tenth month of the Islamic lunar year

shekasta, shikasta, shikasta-nasta'liq (N): ultra-cursive style of the Perso-Arabic script widely used in Persia since the 17th century

şehnāmeci, shenāmeci: a reciter of the *Shāh-Nama* in Turkey

shu'ubiyya (M): anti-Arab movement among Persians, starting in the 9th century asserting the superiority of the Persians

sijjila (M): legal transcript

siyākat (D): special script used for writing Ottoman finance documents

Soltāniyat (H): letters to rulers and high officials

SOV (JF): subject-object-verb, a syntactic word order, distinguishing (e.g.) SOV from SVO English and VSO Arabic

surah (P): verse of the Qur'ān

tajnis (M): homonymy, in Persian and Persianate poetry

tamassuk-i qabuliyat, tamassuk-e qabuliyat (AS): receipt, acceptance letter. See also *muchalka*

tarassulāt, tarassolāt (M): correspondence, letters written in prose

tariqa (M): doctrine or "way" of a Sufi order

tarsiʿ (M): Persian rhetorical device whereby the words of two hemistichs match each other in rhyme and meter

thuluth (M): style of the Arabic script developed in the 9th century and used for formal or inscriptional purposes

topolect (VM): speech form of any locale, large or small

tuğra, tughra (D): stylized signature of a Turkish sultan

Tulip Era (D): period between 1718 and 1730 in Turkey when the fad for raising and displaying tulips reached its height

tuman (AS): ten thousand (Turk.); in medieval Persia a coin worth ten thousand dinars

Turani (F): of or pertaining to Turan, a general term for Central Asia, implying "land of Turks"

Turki (AS): Persian word referring to the Turkic languages in general

Uighur (D): Turkic language spoken in Xinjiang and parts of Central Asia

ulus (DM): people (from Mongolian)

ʿ*ulamā* (AS): scholars, the religious class in Islamic society

umarā (AS): leaders or rulers, pl. of *amir*

vakfiye (D): in Ottoman usage, a document defining a pious bequest

vaqfnāma (D): deed or legal document creating an endowment (*vakf, mawkuf*) by sequestering money or property which is then out of the control of the donor, the income from which is to be used for purposes relating to the general good

vernacular (VM): language of local use

vernacularization (Introduction): process whereby the vernacular (e.g., French or Urdu) gradually supersedes the koine (e.g. Latin or Persian)

vizārat (M): office of vizier; today, a ministry of government

Zu al-Hijja (M): twelfth month of the Islamic lunar year

Index

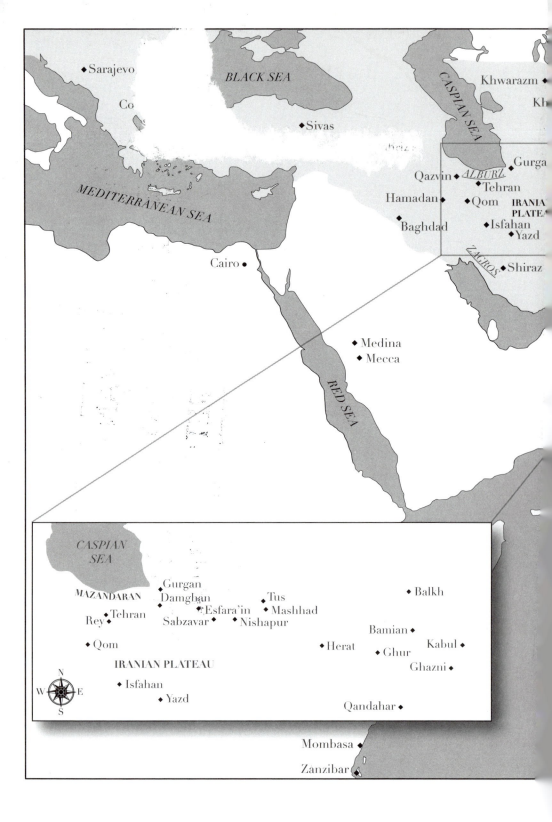